# Coca-Colonization and the Cold War

# Coca-Colonization

## and the Cold War

The Cultural Mission of the

United States in Austria after

the Second World War

REINHOLD WAGNLEITNER

Translated by Diana M. Wolf

The University of North Carolina Press

Chapel Hill & London

The paper in this book meets the guidelines
for permanence and durability of the
Committee on Production Guidelines for
Book Longevity of the Council on Library
Resources.

Publication of this book has been supported
by a generous grant from the L. J. Skaggs
and Mary C. Skaggs Foundation, and its
translation was underwritten by generous
grants from the Stiftungs- und
Förderungsgesellschaft der Paris-Lodron-
Universität Salzburg and the Austrian
Ministry for Science and Research.

Reinhold Wagnleitner is associate professor
of history at the University of Salzburg.

Library of Congress
Cataloging-in-Publication Data
Wagnleitner, Reinhold, 1949–
    [Coca-colonisation und Kalter Krieg.
English]
    Coca-colonization and the Cold War : the
cultural mission of the United States in
Austria after the Second World War / by
Reinhold Wagnleitner ; translated by Diana
M. Wolf.
      p. cm.
    Includes bibliographical references (p.)
and index.
    ISBN 978-0-8078-2149-7 (cloth : alk. paper).
  — ISBN 978-0-8078-4455-7 (pbk.)
    1. Austria—Civilization—American
influence. 2. Austria—Intellectual life—20th
century. 3. United States—Relations—
Austria. 4. Propaganda, American—Austria.
5. Austria—Relations—United States. I. Title.
DB91.2.W3413 1994
303.48'2436073—dc20      93-38431
                                          CIP

12   11   10   09   08      8   7   6   5   4

FOR DIANA

# Contents

# Foreword to the American Edition

We only have to teach German kids how to play baseball—
then they'll understand the meaning of democracy.
—An American general in Berlin, autumn 1945

When I was born in Upper Austria in 1949, Mauerkirchen was a small, sleepy market town—but it was also situated in the American occupation zone of Austria. Although during the period of occupation, 1945–55, the U.S. Army was barely visible in our part of the woods, we children religiously waited for the best action of the year: the annual U.S. Army maneuvers and our rations of chewing gum.

For us, the horrors of the Second World War were in the distant past, but still they were everywhere. Our everyday experience included quite a few mutilated men, and for the nicer ones we picked up cigarette butts from the streets. It seemed absolutely normal that most men and many women looked old and tired—and not only because we were children and they wore dark clothes. But what a contrast when we saw pictures of GIs or, even better, met "the real thing." Somehow, they clashed with our images of soldiers. They looked young and healthy. Contrasted to our poverty, they seemed incredibly rich, and many were generous to us kids. Of course, their casualness and loudness were proverbial—but we admired them precisely for that.

Although most families with a Nazi past repressed and hid this past from the children, the war remained everywhere—and we did not need a war memorial to be reminded of the many ghosts roaming our streets. Unspoken Nazi-past or not, it was clear that most adults objected to those crass boys from across the Atlantic. "We" had indeed lost the war, but look at those uncultured American guys who chewed gum and put their feet on the table. (This, it seemed, was the utmost crime!) How could an army manned by such unmilitaristic, childish, and undisciplined boys (even blacks!) win a war, especially one against Germany! A few of us children, however, secretly suspected that an army advancing to the rhythm of swing music *deserved* to win the war. It did not help our elders to warn us that if we chewed gum we would look like Americans: that was exactly what we wanted to look like!

In my family, I was spared this routine of Austrian cultural superiority versus American cultural inferiority mostly for two reasons. First, my parents and grandparents had not been Nazis, and my mother loved American music, while my father enjoyed American action movies, which had returned to Mauerkirchen's little cinema in the wake of the U.S. Army. Second, a traumatic incident in my father's childhood—he had lost one foot in a car accident at age thirteen—spared him the fate of having to fight in the Second World War. It was rather rare, indeed, to grow up in Austria during the 1950s with parents like that. (Of course, for most of my teenage friends, American pop culture became *the* major vehicle of protest against their parents.)

While our household was uncharacteristically open to what parents of my friends despised as "American trash," I was far from being the vanguard of American popular culture in our family. It is my only brother, Günter, born in 1940, who has to take the main responsibility for my un-Austrian behavior. Günter is extremely musical. He started to take piano lessons at age four and passed the entrance exam to the Vienna Boys Choir at age six—we still possess a 78 shellac recording of Günter's voice, which my father had ordered for this occasion. But in the end, my parents decided against sending him to Vienna. They did not want to hand over their six-year-old boy to a boarding school, especially to a boarding school in Vienna, which was surrounded by the Soviet occupation zone. (After all, we lived in the *Goldenen Westen* of Austria.)

Yet, my parents had no idea that they built the perfect stage for American music for their still-unborn second child. Günter, who had a voracious appetite for any kind of good music, did more than simply improve his playing of Mozart and Beethoven, Bach and Brahms, Schubert and Strauss; he also discovered Frank Sinatra and Ray Charles, Dizzy Gillespie and Miles Davis. And when he discovered rock 'n' roll in the middle of the 1950s, nothing remained the same. While he worked the piano and made our living room rock like a jailhouse, I would work the matchboxes and pretend I was something like a rock 'n' roll drum machine. Many were the sighs of my poor parents—not because we played American music, but because we didn't do *anything else*. And then one day Günter really became the King. A friend of my mother gave him the absolutely most yearned for article of clothing imaginable: the first and only pair of Levi's in Mauerkirchen, which she had received as a present from an American officer.

While my brother was lost for good to any "respectable profession" and became a musician in dance bands, I finished *Gymnasium* (high school), although I had been playing in amateur dance bands since the age of fourteen. After copying my major role model's rock 'n' roll, however, I had my second awakening in 1963 when the British beat bands confronted us—just as they simultaneously confronted white American teenagers, to the annoyance of *their* parents—with the Liverpool, Birmingham, and London version of American blues and rhythm and blues.

So it happened that shortly before entering university, I already had a sort of final graduation: my brother picked me as the bass player for his band. Hardly a weekend passed during my teenage years when our living room was not transformed into a rehearsal room for a band of screaming and strumming kids. Still, I will always be grateful for the proud look on my parents' faces when they saw their sons on stage together for the first time.

Of course, I had no money to buy records, and the Austrian radio stations still pretended that we lived in an age before "Roll Over Beethoven." My major source of musical information about British and American groups consisted of the daily fix of three hours of rock programs that were aired by Radio Free Europe every weekday afternoon. The political messages of Radio Svobodna Evropa (ten minutes of news to fifty minutes of music for three hours) were directed at Czechoslovakian listeners and, as bait, had far and away the best music program of any European station. It really worked like a commercially sponsored program, only here the commercials were the news and the political commentaries. As their reactions showed, the Czechoslovak and other Eastern European governments had not the least inkling of what was really going on. Otherwise they would have jammed the music, not the news.

Contemporary parallels must not be overlooked; the present transformations in Eastern Europe should remind us of the developments in Western Europe after the Second World War. It is of the utmost political significance that practically the whole East German population chose to emigrate to the West every night via television. The effects of such a temporary electronic emigration, the impact of thus becoming quasi-Americans by tuning in to modern mass media, should not be underrated. The Iron Curtain—is not its name already symbolic for an outdated industrial sector, largely connoting the nineteenth century?—in the end was no match for the messages produced by the electronic-consciousness industry in the West, the real heavy industry of the twentieth century (in the apt words of Hans Magnus Enzensberger). Or what does it really mean that during the weekend of February 19–21, 1993, only 6 Russian movies were shown in the cinemas of Moscow compared with 111 American films?

During my student days, I soon learned that there was another side to the United States. Just like many of my peer group on American campuses, I objected to American involvement in Indochina and other foreign policy adventures as well as the repression of minorities in the United States. Yet, we demonstrated in blue jeans and T-shirts and attended sit-ins and teach-ins. What's more, quite a few of us understood what it meant to be able to demonstrate against a war in wartime without being court-martialed. Some of us were also aware that we had learned our peaceful tactics of democratic protest and opposition from the American civil rights movement and the anti-nuclear-armament movement. After all, we did not intone the "Internationale" but instead sang "We Shall Overcome."

What has my personal socialization as a quasi-American to do with this book? I think a lot! There can be no doubt that my generation not only passively experienced the stupendous success of U.S. popular culture in postwar Europe but *actively partook in creating* this success. But was this only a question of economics of scale? Only a result of the quality of the products of U.S. popular culture? Only the victory of the principles of free-market forces and the fair play of the respective players? Or was there an active and decisive role played by the American state in what the (West) German film director Wim Wenders once termed "the colonization of the European subconscious"?

These are some of the basic themes analyzed in my book. It has become commonplace during the last decade in the United States to complain about the preponderance of Japanese cars (and now even motorbikes) on American roads. American readers of this book should keep this jeremiad in mind. Unless American readers can imagine a situation in which 85 percent of *all* movies showing in American cinemas were produced in Austria, or more than half of *all* television programs on American TV channels were of Austrian origin, or 80 to 90 percent of the pop music on *all* American radio stations was of Austrian origin sung *in German*, they will not be able to understand at all that a phenomenon called *American cultural imperialism* actually existed. They will not understand at all that such a concept makes sense practically, if not theoretically, especially when one looks at the United States as a quasi-American, but still *from the outside*.[1]

The concept of American cultural imperialism or cultural hegemony is much too simplistic if it is used only to describe a combination of military, economic, and political pressures and thereby fails to understand aspects of indirect structural dependency, which are probably more important but much harder to quantify. However sophisticated these U.S. pressures may have been applied in some instances, I do not want to join the chorus of those who, for their own reasons, invent a political conspiracy of the United States against the supposedly eternal cultural superiority of the European Occident (*das Abendland*). Too often, the term "Americanization" has been instrumentalized by those who are apt to forget that the United States, however indigenous its cultural developments, is a result of the Europeanization of the world. Too often, the phenomenon of American cultural imperialism has been used simply to promote rather stupid anti-American diatribes. But this phenomenon is much more complex not only because the United States can be perceived as an artifact of European expansion but also because it contains—and substantially so—the *attraction* of many facets of American popular culture as well as the problem of invitation and self-colonization.[2]

Apropos of self-colonization, one example should suffice. On January 12, 1950, the Viennese Communist newspaper *Der Abend* published a negative article entitled "U.S.-Miracle-Drink in a Viennese Café: I Drank Coca-Cola," in which the soft drink was compared to stinking, melted shoe-cream, which the author managed to consume only in defiance of death. Only four days later, an unsolicited letter was sent from Vienna to James A. Farley, chairman of the board of the Coca-Cola Export Corporation, in New York. Its content:

January 16, 1950

Dear Mr. Farley,

The Austrian Communist Party press has recently attacked the sale of Coca Cola, as they did in many other countries.

I am sure the attached clipping [of the article in *Der Abend*] will give you fun as it was the case with us.

As the characteristics of the publication would suffer by a bad translation, I present it as it is.

I avail myself of the occasion to express to you sincere wishes for a happy and prosperous 1950.

With best greetings

Yours truly

Its author: the foreign minister of the Republic of Austria, Karl Gruber.[3]

Any idea of a conspiracy becomes even more absurd when one considers the central irony of the cultural Cold War. The official propagators of American culture wanted to portray the United States as equal if not superior to European "high culture"—which was absolutely not what we wanted! *We created our own image* of the United States to the background of the pictures of Hollywood and to the soundtrack of rock 'n' roll, jazz, the blues, soul, and rhythm and blues. In other words, what we sucked up with every bottle of Coca-Cola were exactly those products of U.S. culture that not only were abhorred by most members of the European cultural elites (on the right *and* the left) but also were deemed un-American by the majority of the contemporary cultural elites *in the United States*.[4] To us pseudo-Americans, the United States signified an amalgam of freedom, fun, modernity, wealth, mobility, and youthful rebellion. We would not touch a German song with a ten-foot pole. We sang in English not only because most of our folk music seemed tainted by the Nazis or because most German pop songs were rather ridiculous; we also sang in English, however badly and naively, as an act of protest against the older generation. When we sang Bob Dylan's "Masters of War," those who understood the lyrics were not reminded of Vietnam but of the Second World War.

Imagining America as paradise or hell, as the haven of freedom and wealth, violence and youthful rebellion, is nothing new; it is probably the essence of the European perception of America since Columbus. In Austria, already during the 1920s, many fashionable Viennese youngsters looked more toward New York than Berlin, Paris, or London; the swing youth and the *Schlurfs* (zoot suits) antagonized the Nazis until 1945; not only Viennese pimps tried to prove their manhood by driving huge phallic American road cruisers through small city streets throughout the 1950s; and Marlon Brando's black leather jacket became the sign of fashionable otherness, together with rock 'n' roll, bebop, and many other originally African-American creations. Still, however misunderstood many products of American pop culture may have been outside the United States (e.g., Elvis as a left-wing working-class hero), at least one thing was understood. After all, young African-Americans had mimicked and mocked the white (and black) establishment with their cultural expressions, and also, however naively, their European copycats have been doing the same until this very moment.

p.s. Can cultural imperialism and cultural hegemony work like a boomerang? While I am writing these lines (March 1993), young German right-wing terrorists have set fire to another home for asylum seekers. As an outward sign of their rebellion against the postwar (West and East) German system(s), many of these *German* nationalists not only have appropriated the style of a group of the British lumpenproletariat but also proudly call themselves Skinheads and fanatically groove to the rhythms of their own right-wing *Glatzen-Rock* bands. To make things even more complicated, German left-wing skinheads (Redskins) have begun to fight their right-wing look-alikes (Boneheads). Many Redskins have already joined SHARP (Skinheads against Racial Prejudice), which was founded—where else?—in the United States in 1988.

It has become fashionable to brand these depressed, desolate, and aggressive youngsters as the children of the Nazis. In German they are not called *Nazi-Kinder* nowadays but *Nazi-Kids* and *Fascho-Kids*. Yet, this is not only a question of the proliferation of "Germlish" but even more so just another easy way out. These simplistic slogans only disguise real social, economic, political, and cultural problems and thereby, once more, prevent their analysis and solution.

Whatever these children may in fact be, they clearly also are the children of the cultural Cold War, which has been a total war of consumption. More than many other things, consumerism has defeated Communism, and it is surely more than a tragic irony that these losers at the end of the Cold War are now waging a new war and beat up their victims—with American baseball bats.

*Salzburg, March 1993*                                    *Reinhold Wagnleitner*

# Acknowledgments

The research in the United States for this book was made possible by the generous support of the American Council of Learned Societies and the Fulbright Commission. The translation was generously supported by the Stiftungs- und Förderungsgesellschaft der Paris-Lodron-Universität Salzburg and the Austrian Ministry for Science and Research.

My research was facilitated by archivists Sally Marks and Kathy O. Nicastro of the National Archives in Washington, D.C.; Fred Pernell of the Washington National Record Center in Suitland, Md.; Martin J. Manning and Kathryn T. Shimabukuro of the U.S. Information Agency Library, Historical Collection, in Washington, D.C.; the librarians of the Library of Congress; Gertrude Weitgruber of the Department of History of the University of Salzburg; and Roswitha Haller of the Amerika Haus Library in Vienna. I also thank Melvyn Dubofsky, Gottfried "Pongo" Hutter, Heidrun Maschl, Barbara and Herbert Peretti, Emily S. Rosenberg, Nicole Slupetzky, and Siegbert Stronegger.

In particular, I extend my gratitude to Diana M. Wolf, who patiently saw the book grow from beginning to end. I am grateful not only for her critical support but especially—and this is most important for this version of my book—for her congenial translation of the text into English as well as the compilation of the index.

Last, but not least, I thank my parents and my brother, Günter. After all, it was my family that made it possible for me to grow up in an environment in which the otherwise defamed musical influences emanating from America were always appreciated. In the Upper Austrian town Mauerkirchen, that was anything but normal in the 1950s and 1960s.

*Salzburg, December 1993*        *Reinhold Wagnleitner*

# Abbreviations

| | |
|---|---|
| AFL/CIO | American Federation of Labor/Congress of Industrial Organizations |
| AND | American News Service (Amerikanischer Nachrichtendienst) |
| AP | Associated Press |
| APA | Austrian Press Association |
| CAD | Civil Affairs Division |
| CIA | Central Intelligence Agency |
| ECA | Economic Coordination Administration |
| ERP | European Recovery Program (Marshall Plan) |
| HUAC | House Un-American Activities Committee |
| ICB | Information Coordinating Board |
| ISB | Information Services Branch |
| KPÖ | Austrian Communist Party (Kommunistische Partei Österreichs) |
| MPEA | Motion Picture Export Association |
| NA | National Archives |
| NS | National Socialists |
| ÖGB | Austrian Trade Union Federation (Österreichischer Gewerkschaftsbund) |
| ORF | Austrian Radio and Television (Österreichischer Rundfunk) |
| ÖVP | Austrian People's Party (Österreichische Volkspartei) |
| OWI | Office of War Information |
| SPÖ | Austrian Socialist Party (Sozialistische Partei Österreichs) |
| UPI | United Press International |
| USFA | United States Forces in Austria |
| USIA | United States Information Agency |
| USIAL/HC | United States Information Agency Library/Historical Collection |
| VdU | Association of Independents (Verband der Unabhängigen) |
| WNRC | Washington National Record Center |

Coca-Colonization and the Cold War

# Introduction

> Black people have always been used as a buffer in this country between
> powers to prevent class war, to prevent other kinds of real conflagrations. . . .
> If there were no black people here in this country, it would have been Balkanized.
> The immigrants would have torn each other's throats out, as they have done
> everywhere else. But in becoming an American, from Europe, what one has in
> common with that other immigrant is contempt for *me*—it's nothing else but color.
> Wherever they were from they would stand together. They could all say, "I am
> not *that*." . . . So in that sense, becoming an American is based on an attitude: an
> exclusion of me.
> —Bobbie Angelo, "Interview with Toni Morrison," *Time*, May 22, 1989

You will probably wonder why I begin a book about the cultural influence of the United States in Austria with this unsettling statement by the African-American author Toni Morrison. I might as well start with the moment of disbelief when I finally realized that the Soviet Union would be a thing of the past. That moment came in late 1989, when the spokesman of former president Michael Gorbachev was asked by journalists how the Soviet government would react if the Baltic States attempted to break away and Gennadi Gerassimov replied, "The days of the Brezhnev Doctrine are over. We now follow the Frank Sinatra Doctrine: I'll do it my way."

Those Europeans who complain about the Americanization of their continent were surely happy to see that the Donald Duck party only won 175 votes in Sweden's parliamentary election in 1982. But what should we say about an Austrian right-wing farmers' demonstration against the agricultural policies of the Socialists in 1986, where banners proclaimed, "More Power to the Bauer"? Was I sitting in a time machine of the global village when I saw the Soviet leadership watch an acrobatic rock 'n' roll parade at the May Day celebrations of May 1, 1989?

Actually, it should not be disputed that in dealing with the global success of U.S. culture, we are talking about one of the most important chapters of history in this century. This development is particularly interesting because we are talking not only about a cultural process in a narrow sense but also about an economic and eminently political phenomenon, namely, the phenomenon of symbolic power, the power over cultural capital. By no means did these products of U.S. culture automatically penetrate foreign countries. To be sure, we must understand the United States as the original version of modernity, whereas

Europe, in keeping with Jean Baudrillard, represents only the dubbed-in version, the version with subtitles.[1] In any event, after two bouts with European self-annihilation and self-imposed cultural ruin, it seemed that the United States alone had a corner on the codes of modernity. Especially the fascination that the myth "America" had for young people must not be underestimated in this context.

This global success story of U.S. culture has yet another dimension, namely, the massive direct and indirect support that the export of this culture received from the government of the United States. This support was so massive particularly because it was not a secondary product of a general political, military, and economic strategy; rather, it was an important, if not *the* most important, means in establishing a Pax Americana.

Any analysis of the staggering amount of information that flows through the one-way channels of U.S. media, the organization of the means of communication and their distribution, the structure of industrial arrangements of the media, the substance of their ideological values, the grammar and idioms of the media, the specific media content—in other words, any analysis of the existing asymmetry in the transfer of culture leads to the conclusion that we are dealing with cultural or media imperialism.[2] It stands without question that we are confronted with the most successful development so far of earlier forms of colonialism and imperialism. For the media industry—as a technological parasite and as the chief ideological apologist of the military-industrial complex—has become the real heavy industry of our epoch.

If we can formally speak of U.S. cultural imperialism, we should nevertheless take the following seven points into consideration, especially with regard to the Austrian situation after 1945. First, U.S. cultural imperialism in many ways acted as a welcomed antidote to the imperialism of National Socialist culture. My life would be so much poorer without Arthur Miller and Marilyn Monroe, Kurt Vonnegut and Philip K. Dick, Ray Charles and Muddy Waters, Miles Davis and Laurie Anderson, blues, jazz, soul, rock 'n' roll, funk—and Donald Duck.

Second, the congruent anti-Communist values shared between the U.S. occupation forces and the majority of the Austrian citizenry allows no other conclusion than that we are dealing with a classic case of *self*-colonization. Even if U.S. denazification politics remained piecemeal because it was sacrificed on the altar of the Cold War, the political culture of Austria was nevertheless decisively influenced, namely, by the Marshall Plan, which in its ideological essence was *the* ideology to end all ideologies. Contrary to historical prejudice, it was especially the Social Democrats who were attracted by the solutions of this internationalized New Deal, which promised to abolish class conflict, not through redistribution, but through economic growth, the solution of social problems through social engineering that was supposedly free of ideology—in other words, the metamorphosis of politics into economy.[3]

Third, to understand the phenomenon of U.S. cultural imperialism in Austria, one must speak more accurately of the metropole United States, the colony Germany, and the subcolony Austria.

Fourth, Umberto Eco is right in pointing out that in the shadow of a continually growing communication network that will soon envelop the whole world, everybody everywhere will become a member of a new information proletariat.[4] If we interpret culture as an information network, then we must also deal with the fact that the most ingenuous information networks with which people have ever been confronted increasingly define all parameters of culture. And the culture of capitalism in which the marketplace is promoted as *the* highest cultural value *in itself* is by definition popular culture, and pop connotes the United States. "Pop goes the culture," *Time* magazine laconically summarizes and at the same time delivers an exemplary definition of our cultural situation that means nothing but "advanced capitalism with a beat you can dance to."[5] As we know, this hegemonic discourse is also buttressed by the power over symbols, dissolving the borders between hardware and software. However, *high tech* does not necessarily mean *high quality*—and by no means *high fidelity*. The new proletariat of the information age, therefore, needs nothing more urgent than a semiological guerrilla.

Fifth, we must not forget that the identity of exported cultural signs is altered exactly at the moment in which they intersect with other cultures. Blue jeans, the pants of the victor, initially promised not only comfort but freedom as well. In addition, they were best suited as symbols of Marshall Plan culture, where the cloth of labor became the emblem of liberation. Most important, the riveted pockets were also sturdy enough to hold the money that, for the first time ever, was available to its young wearers.[6]

Sixth, René-Jean Ravault's thesis that U.S. cultural imperialism turned into a boomerang is at least worth considering. Here I am not referring to the vehement reactions that we are currently experiencing, especially in the Islamic world, but quite simply to the fact that in 1966 a seventeen-year-old Upper Austrian could understand the Rolling Stones when they sang that "the pursuit of happiness just seems a bore."[7] Yet, even if U.S. cultural imperialism is only a paper tiger, or perhaps a celluloid tiger or a plastic tiger and maybe a silicon tiger, it still remains a tiger.[8]

Finally, it is of primary importance that official U.S. cultural imperialism ran on the psychological track of *defending the Occident*. The responsible U.S. experts saw themselves in many ways as the better Europeans and as now having to enlighten their poor cousins that European culture had been well preserved and was blossoming across the Atlantic. This emphasis on the similarities of a *Europe-American* culture meant no more and no less than that there was a conscious exclusion of those areas of U.S. culture that apparently did not count as part of that common heritage, especially the culture of African-Americans and all mixed cultural forms developing therefrom. In other words, we are confronted with the initial European and later Euro-American Christian mentality that—as a variety of cultural racism—is well suited as an ideological justification for imperialism.[9] Anthropologically speaking, the real cultural conflicts never occurred between "white America" and "white Europe" but between the "white" Euro-Americans and the "Indians" and Africans. This is also the decisive reason why the spreading of U.S. culture in Europe was not confronted with insurmountable hurdles with regard to either formal or material acculturation.[10] Should not the harmony of the cultural values of the liberators and the liberated seem somewhat striking? Should it not be thought provoking that the great majority of U.S. cultural officers despised the so-called "nigger culture" just as vehemently as many Europeans did?

How did Ingeborg Bachmann put it in *The Good God from Manhattan*?

> At the green light think
> Be careful of the red and brown
> The black and yellow danger
> What should our murderers think
> You can't do it
> Stop!
> Stop at the red light![11]

Once again, after a dialectical somersault, we are back to Toni Morrison. It cannot be stated clearly enough: that which generally is called American culture in a pejorative sense asserted itself not only against the opposition of many Europeans but also against the angry resistance of the "white" elite in the United States. The containment strategists in the U.S. government were the last ones to imagine rollback as rock 'n' roll back. Not in vain were the U.S. cultural officers in Austria warned from New York: "I fear that some of our hearty Congressmen may prove allergic to the word Cultural. I admit it's frightening."[12] However, the advantages of the Marilyn Monroe Doctrine would become quite clear even to them, and such fears proved unnecessary; rock around the bloc also would in time decay into rock 'n' ruble.

In any event, the positive and negative fascination with the "phenomenon America" is, at the same time, one of our greatest problems in analyzing it scientifically. It becomes even more difficult when we are made aware of the fictitious contents of the European "creation America," the European "simulation America." The America, then, of which we are speaking is for the most part a construction, a simulation. Time and again, America has served only as a justification for European prejudices. Time and again, it has been invoked to serve European goals. Karl May assigned the role of the good Indian to the Apaches, that of the bad cannibal to the Comanches, quite simply because in the French novel upon which May based his writings, the Comanche fought on the side of the French (which is true historically). Therefore Karl, the German, naturally could only side with their archenemy—by fighting on the side of the

Apaches. Not without reason, a character in Alain Resnais's film *My Uncle from America* states: "America—that doesn't exist. I know it because I lived there for a very long time." Is, therefore, all of America a single Oakland? An Oakland, at which Gertrude Stein once scoffed: "There is no there, there."

No, there really is a there, there. It is, however, a different "there" than many Euro-Americans care to admit. Ever since the military conquest of America by Europeans, we have been dealing with mechanisms of repression—not just with the repression of millions of people from America, Africa, *and* Europe, but especially with the sublimation of this repression.[13] The core of this problem already becomes apparent in the colonization through language. The name of the continent America itself is a sign of the European conquest. When dealing with the entire European "enterprise America," does not the misleading expression "Indian" lead us to question whether we are not confronted with a characteristic mistake in the navigation coordinates of European culture? Finally, the term "New World" signifies that the old world of the "Indians" was not even acknowledged as part of human history by the European conquerors. How many American enthusiasts about Europe regret deeply that "America" unfortunately does not have a long history! Is its history really that short? The results of this mental block are well known.

Are we not confronting one of the central contradictions of world history when we consider the actual consequences of the European conquest of America? Does not the Euro-American interpretation of world history count as one of the greatest achievements of mental repression when we celebrate the settlement of America by the "white" conquerors as a decisive prerequisite for the overcoming of political, social, and economic inequality—yes, even more, as the final point of human progress? We should know that this overcoming of inequality for one group was inseparable from the intensification of inequality for others. The wars of independence on the American continent created new states that, in demanding democracy, detached themselves from Europe. However, almost all of these new societies were, in turn, based upon the exploitation of a slave caste—monarchy was followed not by democracy but by ethnocracy. The economic sector resembled a similar paradoxical picture. The unprecedented profits of one part of America were based, at least partially, on the unprecedented exploitation of labor in another part of the continent. Finally, the phenomenal increase in population corresponded with the almost complete annihilation of the "Indians."[14]

If America is marked as the enlargement and extension of Europe on our cognitive maps, as the extrapolation of European history, then we should not forget that America also means the unwilling expansion of Africa by force. Until 1840, the number of abducted Africans that were carried off to America exceeded, by far, the number of European emigrants. Toward the end of the 1820s, not more than approximately two million people from Europe had emigrated to both North and South America, whereas at least eight million

Africans were kidnapped during the same period.[15] This means that until the middle of the nineteenth century, for every European who went to the New World, at least four, more than likely five, Africans were enslaved. This figure corresponds only to those Africans who reached the American continent alive. The number of persons who died as a result of inhumane transportation conditions or sickness as well as those who escaped their fate through suicide is estimated at 20 to 50 percent of all enslaved individuals.[16] It should not escape our attention that even today Brazil has the second largest African population in the world after Nigeria. America is therefore an extrapolation of African history, at least in the area of human grief.

Note that more than half of all slave transports from Africa to America took place in the eighteenth century. The rays of the Enlightenment did not shine equally bright for all men and women. To be sure, it would be more than an anachronism to expect that a character in a Mozart opera should have sung the blues, but "A Slave Trader Am I" would have been most appropriate as a title for an aria of an Enlightenment opera.

In light of the preceding observations, then, I reject the term "Americanization," a term that represses and hides more than it explains. This term attempts to define the development of the modern world with the unsuitable criteria of nationalistic stereotypes, which serves, for the most part, only one task—namely, to conceal the fact that behind the phenomenon "Americanization" lies the actual "Europeanization" of the world. The development of the modern world has much less to do with the propagation of the supposed national characteristics of those people who live in the United States than with the further development of the system of capitalism.

Malcolm Bradbury once described this global process in his unsurpassable fashion as a process of "-ization": centralization, mechanization, rationalization, standardization, nationalization, internationalization, multinationalization—in other words, modernization. This "-ization" is a process of change that happens everywhere where the culture of capitalism takes root. The secret of its success is the promise that we have all waited for this change because we have seemingly had enough of the same old thing for much too long. Bradbury's culture of "-ization" is by definition anational, antitraditional, ahistorical, polyglot, and burlesque. If the heroes in traditional society were the elders, it was because their wisdom was valued. The heroes of consumer society, in contrast, are the young because now innocence, naïvité, and harmlessness are valued—innocent, naive, and harmless people no doubt spend more money. The cycles of this constant transformation occur so quickly that not only last year's car is outdated but also its ideas. Bradbury calls this the ten-minute revolution, which means that the brain is usually empty and the wastebasket is constantly full. A recent cigarette ad noted: "I enjoy, therefore I am." *Consumo, ergo sum*—that is the slogan of "-ization."[17] Credit cards instead of Descartes.

The slogan "Americanization" describes, then, the development of a consumption-oriented social order within capitalist societies—the pursuit of happiness as the pursuit of consumption. The American dream, as the saying goes, means that one stacks up so much money and property until one reaches heaven. But we should be careful: the "American dream" is a Euro-American dream. There are, however, no grounds for malicious joy because in the end the most damage has been inflicted upon others. "Americanization" signifies, therefore, a process of cultural transformation, a process in which the parts of the social memory that refused to identify themselves with the logic of the consumer society—the equation "survival = consumption"—had to be worked over by propaganda and advertisement. Not without reason did "consumption" mean tuberculosis until the seventeenth century, and "to consume" meant to destroy, to use, to waste.[18] Perhaps this process *can* be called "Americanization." It would only mean, though, that the development of the modern consumption-oriented society is inconceivable without the consumption of America by the Europeans; before Europe could become Americanized, *America* had to be Americanized first. In this sense, we are surely all Americans—in other words, strangers in a strange land.[19]

# 1

## The Problem of America as
## Artifact of European Expansion

### European Stereotypes and Clichés, Dreams and Nightmares, Imaginings and (Mis)Perceptions

Europe and America no longer exist; there is only the phase of Western civilization which we call American because it came to birth in a European colony named America. . . . Today Europe is a colony of its colony—and well on the way to becoming a second America.
  —Ludwig Marcuse, *European Anti-Americanism* (1953)

It is wiser to confront American culture as something as alien as that of the Eskimos.
  —E. N. W. Mottram, *American Studies in Europe* (1955)

In the revolutionary year 1849, the Austrian satirist Johann Nestroy posed the penetrating question in his play *Lady und Schneider*: Would Europe become a province of Pennsylvania, or North America a suburb of Frankfurt. Even today, after the apparent victory of the American way of life in Europe, this question cannot be answered easily: while both became the other's counterpart, they also remained each other's *other*. "America, you have got it better," Johann Wolfgang von Goethe exclaimed. Was this the reason why, during the years of writing *Dichtung und Wahrheit*, he still found ample time to advise Karl August of Weimar to speculate with dollars in New York as well as to invest in Mexican silver mines? Or what are we to make of the poet Nikolaus Lenau's famous (and incorrect) lament that a poetic curse must be hanging over the promised land on the other side of the Atlantic because the United States lacked nightingales?

The discovery of the American continent by Europeans not only increased the living space of the Old World by five times—42 million square kilometers were now available in the New World for European colonization and imperialism after 1492, a nice piece of real estate indeed! This discovery also opened unlimited possibilities for European experience and knowledge, hopes and dreams, judgments and misjudgments, actions and misactions. Our difficulties with America already begin with the seemingly magical number 1492, with the heroic phrase of the discovery of the Americas by Christopher Columbus, whose Spanish name, Cristóbal Colón, most appropriately means bearer of God as well as colonizer. Naturally, in the discourse of the European victors, the four-hundred-year war against the "Indians" became divine destiny and a mission pleasing to God, presenting the European "superrace" with the opportunity to establish total hegemony over "primitive and pagan barbarians." The year 1492, to paraphrase Kurt Vonnegut, quite simply marked the beginning of an epoch in which European pirates began to cheat, rob, and murder the peoples of the New World. The City upon a Hill, the New Canaan, the New Jerusalem, could not be built without war and destruction—a tradition, by the way, that was quite in step with its biblical models. The European conquerors disguised their land-grabbing expansion with the more-than-handy fable of America as an unpopulated continent, and "barbarians" as proverbial nonhumans. This unfolding of Europe's *Lebensraum* thereby became the premise for the suffering of the subjugated; Europe's living space turned into the death space for the Americans.

Was America, then, paradise or hell? Or perhaps both? Since the discovery of the New World, that continent preoccupied the fantasies of the Europeans. This preoccupation includes not only those who opted for emigration but also particularly those who remained in the Old World and had, for the most part, access only to inaccurate information. The waves of this America fascination swept over all of Europe, with a certain time-lag from west to east. The increasing emigration and the improved means of transportation and communication brought a growing number of Europeans in direct or indirect contact with America. Until the beginning of the eighteenth century, by the way, the term "America" in Europe mostly signified Central and South America, to be usurped by the United States only after the War of Independence. These changes of meaning and transpositions not only signify the character of "America" as a construct; they also show that to name is to take over.

America became a metaphor for total enthusiasm, but also for total rejection. The mental baggage of many Europeans was filled with images, clichés, prejudices, and stereotypes in which the New World became situated somewhere between El Dorado and barbarian wilderness, paradisiacal deliverance and hell, noble savages and bloodthirsty cannibals—in short, between wishful thinking and nightmares that most likely had been dreamed in the Old World since antiquity. In any case, the phantasmagorias that were provoked by the discovery of the real existence of America definitely show that the *discovery* of the New World was accompanied by a simultaneous *invention* of America.

The importance of this discovery and invention for the European *imago mundi* is reflected in the immeasurable quantity of publications in which authors were forced to adapt to a radically different view of the world. Usually these discourses reflect Europe in a kaleidoscopic image of America. More often than not, America appears to be filtered and broken by the distorting mirror of European inadequacies, European frustrations, and European failures. Very rarely do we find answers to the actual questions posed by the real America. For the most part, we find an America only in the eyes of others, the image of a *Strange New World* as a European vision.[1]

Had the Europeans, as the new Adams (where was the new Eve?) found paradise in America, or was America perhaps even a European mistake? Merely to formulate these questions shows clearly the construct character of America.[2] The absurdity of the counterquestion—whether Africa, Asia, or Australia were Europe's mistakes—proves that in our context of the creation of European *images* of America, we must not construct a cognitive hierarchy between the *reality* of America and the New World as a *symbol*. Quite obviously, we are moving here in a realm in which fact and fiction intermingle: in the realm of *faction*.

The ever-increasing presence of U.S. culture in Europe and other parts of the world is not just an unstoppable phenomenon accompanying the rise of the United States as an imperialist world power since the middle of the nineteenth century. For the products of American culture collide(d) with already-existing powerful European clichés, stereotypes, associations, perceptions and misperceptions, images of foreign people and places—in short, all the reflections and (mis)representations of this *Strange New World* in the cognitive maps of Europeans. This has been especially true for the products of the consciousness industry, which, since the First World War, were particularly pushed by a complex comprising economics, the military, diplomacy, and the media.

The European helplessness vis-à-vis the enigma "America," the *fata morgana* in the West, is further deepened by extremely complex interactions between, and even jamming of, European clichés about America and U.S. prejudices toward Europe.[3] A speech by General George S. Patton, delivered to his troops immediately before the landing in Italy in 1944, may suffice: "Many of you have in your veins German and Italian blood, but remember that those ancestors of yours so loved freedom that they gave up home and country to cross the ocean in search of liberty. The ancestors of the people we shall kill lacked the courage to make such a sacrifice and continued as slaves."[4] I really wonder how those about to be liberated would have reacted?

But we must be careful. To point one's finger blamefully at *the other* all too often leads to the tendency to compare the worst of the foreign with the best at home. Although the impact, influence, and power of these mental pictures have very little to do with "reality," these stereotypes still influence feelings, thoughts, and actions. We know only too well how history has always been distorted in myths, legends, and hagiographies disguised as scholarship, not only producing hero worship and amnesia, but also serving as the apologetic blinders for the powerful. And then, the textbook wisdom of the victors again makes history. Autostereotypes and heterostereotypes are not only exceptionally long lived; they actually exist in a symbiotic relationship, feeding one another in a circuit of utter simplification. All this results in limited perceptions and creates behavioral dispositions.[5] Like self-fulfilling prophecies, then, only information that fits into our preformed patterns of thought and feeling is allowed to pass through the filters of our tunnel vision. In our case of America stereotypes in Europe and Europe stereotypes in the United States, we are rarely dealing with the requirements of necessary simplification that we need to make some sense of the world. Instead, we are mostly confronted with mental defense mechanisms and extrapunitive means of assigning fault to the other.[6]

Comparative image research has shown that the acceptance and continued influence of stereotypes and national prejudices are dependent upon personal factors such as age, gender, class, social status, education, profession, mobility, and political views as well as upon one's psychological disposition (e.g., introversion or extroversion). In addition, general social developments such as the general political situation, the relationship of one's own country to the United States, the reputation of a nation in the international community, and the degree to which an individual has experienced the United States must also be taken into consideration.[7] Clearly, the origin of national stereotypes can be traced to early childhood. Comparative long-term studies indicate that European images of America, never exactly defined and always highly ambiguous, belong to the realm of the *longue-durée*.

Naturally, European stereotypes of America have become modified as a result of an increase in geographic knowledge, colonization, and immigration; the growth of economic, political, and military interdependence; and the apparent conquest of geographic distance through technical developments. However, technical progress in transportation and communication has mostly increased the quantity of information available while doing little to change the substance of stereotypes.[8] Today, El Dorado is encapsulated by *Dallas, Dynasty,* and *Miami Vice.* The part of Hernando Cortés and the robber barons has been usurped by the Ewings and Carringtons; the role of the savage barbarian by Marlon Brando and all his successors. In an ironic twist, the Old Empire seems to have struck back—with Arnold Schwarzenegger.

These stereotypes, "that the United States is a country where . . . ," are socially transmitted. At the same time they function like a hall of mirrors of the superstructure, in which information and experiences are reflected by the distorting mirrors of deeply ingrained prejudices. They develop a self-propelled cognitive dynamism, which has already been proved in the observation of children's views about their own environs and their conceptions of foreign countries.[9]

I do not want to deny that the ever-increasing ties between Europe and America have not promoted both formal and material forms of acculturation.[10] A review of all cultural encounters, cultural clashes, and cultural relationships until now, however, indicates that even the split-second transmission of news will not substantially change geocentric and ethnocentric stereotypes. Furthermore, most bits of information are—consciously or unconsciously—already predigested and prefiltered by the autostereotypical views of their American producers. They are therefore not only reflected through a *camera obscura Americana* but also touch upon already-existing cognitive maps of each recipient.[11]

In 1987, fully 79 percent of all film and television exports worldwide originated in the United States; in 1991, European TV productions accounted for just 20,000 hours out of a total 125,000 hours of air time of all European TV stations. The European-produced contributions will decline even more dramatically with the proliferation of television channels that will provide a projected 300,000 hours air time already by 1995. Because of the lack of local production alone, most of these slots will be filled by American movies and shows.[12] Perhaps we should also consider that about three-quarters of all computer programs in the world store information in the English language. Yet, this explosive increase of signs emanating from the United States does not necessarily facilitate a better understanding per se. As long as we do not improve methods and means to decipher these signs intelligently, the ever-increasing quantity of audiovisual bits of information will only further strengthen already-existing opinions, indifference, passivity, and dependence. Undoubtedly, the communication possibilities between Europe and America have been dramatically improved—from the caravels of Columbus to a network of satellites. It would be much too optimistic, though, to expect the disappearance of our stereotypes, just because technology seems to be offering apparent solutions in overcoming distances in space and time. Our problem does not become any easier when realizing that the understanding and misunderstanding, the production and reproduction of such clichés, occurs not only on a horizontal scale of synchronicity but also on the vertical scale of asynchronicity.

The European images of America seem to have been produced by a time machine, one that transforms and transports European dreams and myths of the past and the future. Whether the questions are ones of science, politics, religion, culture, economics, political and military influence, or technical developments, the European discourse has always interpreted America either as a part of Europe's illusionary past, namely, in the sense of a paradisiacal, precivilization second chance (catchword: the new Adam), or as anticipatory dreams of America as Europe's future, which, more often than not, turn into nightmares.[13]

### The Myth of the West: From the Ideology of a Colonizing Mission to the Practice of Conquest and Exploitation

Particularly important in this context is the myth of "the West," a myth that existed long before the discoveries of Columbus and his contemporaries. "The West," an ambiguous conception of both space and time, had fascinated African, Asian, and European people since antiquity. Long before Columbus set sail, "the West" had already become a fundamentally fixed image. These anticipations of America range from Egyptian mythology to Homer and Pindar, Plato and Aristotle, Virgilius, Plinius and Plutarch, the early fathers, and the legendary travels of the Irish St. Brendan; from the Greek science fiction of Atlantis to the medieval legend of the Golden Epoch. Long before the lost continent of Atlantis seemed to have been rediscovered by crossing the *Atlantic* ocean, long before the missing hemisphere America was incorporated into the European view of the world (America as Europe, Inc.?), Europeans were engrossed by the unknown, mysterious, and therefore extremely attractive, exotic, and already-preconceived terra incognita.

The Pillars of Hercules, accepted as the truly insurmountable western border, did not prevent the New World from casting its shadow, in myths, to exist as magical reality. By no means was this mythical West limited to Elysium, the blissful empire of the dead. It also included Eden, the Island of the Enchanting Women, El Dorado, Ultima Thule, Arcadia, eternal life, total happiness, the millennium, and unmeasurable wealth. Greek and Roman commentators, early fathers, and the ancestors of English colonialism, among them Sir Walter Raleigh and Richard Hakluyt, all agreed that the center of the empire was continually shifting from east to west.[14]

All that was needed was the actual discovery of this imaginary continent by Europeans, and the idea of "the West" finally could be Christianized in missionary crusades. The secularization of these ideas, then, required just one more dialectical turn: the combination of the Christian mission with the continual westward movement of the New Empire. Herein we can already see the contours of the (un)official ideological basis of the United States—Manifest Destiny, or the providential determination and mission for spreading the empire of freedom. Apologists of this Manifest Destiny, like Edward Everett, clearly discerned the continuity of these ideas and the New World's takeover of the Old World's supposed mission: "There are no more continents to be reached; Atlantis hath risen from the ocean."[15]

Already in the primary reasoning behind Columbus's mission—on the one hand, the search for immeasurable wealth to finance the crusade for reconquering the "Holy Land"; on the other, the Christianization of all "pagans"— we can find the leitmotif of European expansion, the Europeanization of the world. The diffusion of ideas is indeed inseparable from expansion. The ideology of Manifest Destiny is European in its roots—expansion disguised as a Christian mission, multiplied by an unshakable belief in progress. The identity of America as a frontier, as a border, as the New Canaan, as the New Jerusalem, is a European creation. The new Atlantis became the new empire. Augustine's City of God became the City upon the Hill, and the profanity of the Old World found its reflection in the holiness of the New. The establishment of these new settlements, supposedly pleasing to God, required, however, the expulsion and extermination of the peoples of America. The colonization of the New Jerusalem could occur only after the "Indians" had been expelled from the land that was holy to *them*. This apparent contradiction between the Christian missionary ideology of bringing salvation and deliverance and the reality of subjugation and annihilation of *the others* not only explains the mendacity of European expansion but also shows that America for many Europeans represented a territorial map rather than a geographic reality.[16]

Reports of the "civilized" about the "savages" thus tell us very little indeed about the people who originally lived in America, but quite a lot about their European observers. The reports about America in the sixteenth century were full of exactly those infamous monsters that had already inhabited the West in the medieval legends. However, these tales could not be upheld for long. In their stead, we see how the once-noble savage was suddenly mutated into the wild beast and the lazy cannibal, whose land could easily be robbed—international law as ideology of conquest. The elimination of *the other*, the expulsion, the forced Christianization, and the genocide of the Moors and Jews in the Spanish *Reconquista*, the year of Columbus's first trip in 1492, surely was not a good omen for *the others* who lived in the New World.[17]

The discovery of America had unexpected consequences for practically every aspect of European life. Most significantly, it meant the triumph of experimentation and direct observation over the traditional way of viewing the world. America was an intellectual challenge of the first order and occasioned revolutions in the sciences, political power, economic relations, the distribution of populations, the arts, and religious life. The scientific advances of Copernicus and Galileo are unthinkable without these discoveries, and ultimately Darwin was to unveil the origin of the species at the Galápagos Islands. Only because of America did geo-*magic* become geo-*graphy*.[18]

The discovery of the New World resulted in a dramatic change in the ratio between the number of people and the amount of arable land available. It transferred the European center of power from the Mediterranean to the Atlantic Coast. The most dramatic repercussions, however, were felt not in Europe but without a doubt in America itself—and in Africa. The brutal consequences of these conquests did not escape some European critics. Already in 1773, J. H. Bernardin de Saint Pierre noted that while the New World was depopulated in order to create the needed space for sugar, tobacco, and coffee plantations, Africa was depopulated to rob the workers necessary to cultivate these plants.[19]

The economic impact in Europe was already apparent in the sixteenth century as the stability of finances seemed to be increasingly dependent upon the secure arrival of the treasure ships from America in Seville. Between 1500 and 1650 alone, at least 181 tons of gold and 16,000 tons of silver were shipped to Spain.[20] I certainly do not want to suggest that the economic effects of the exploitation of America were the only source for the rapid increase in capital accumulation in Europe. However, the transatlantic trade was clearly one of the most important prerequisites for the European price revolution as well as for the rapid growth in manufacturing and industrial production. The treasures from America also created additional cash in hand, which in turn intensified the trade with the Orient, and the large profits from these dealings again increased further capital accumulation. Without question, a large part of the power of Spain and England was financed by the profits from the colonies. We could also ask ourselves if the lavish art of Baroque, with its wasteful use of gold and silver, would have been possible without the exploitation of American mines.

These economic changes also contributed to the intensification of the existing class divisions in Europe. However, by becoming the main attraction for many Europeans who were tired of the Old World, America soon functioned as a safety valve against upcoming social conflicts; first and foremost, America offered mobility, not only for people and wealth, but also for ideas. In America, geographic and social mobility even seemed to become one. America became synonymous with freedom, and the European view of the world became transatlantic.

For this reason, Adam Smith concluded in *The Wealth of Nations* (published in 1776, the year of the American Declaration of Independence) that the discovery of America had not simply brought a considerable increase in the standard of living and economic growth. It could also be counted as one of the most important events in human history.[21] For Friedrich Engels and Karl Marx, these discoveries were instrumental for the decay of the feudal system and the development of capitalism. "Modern industry has established the world market, for which the discovery of America paved the way," proclaims the *Communist Manifesto* of 1848; here America is anticipation *and* motor of capitalism. Engels and Marx also anticipated the essential meaning of this new territory for the up-and-coming middle class, prophesying that the entire world would fall into the hands of the capitalist bourgeoisie, which would create "a world after its own image" with the help of the "immensely facilitated means of communication."[22] Was this an anticipation of Hollywood?

Actually, the economic, social, and moral consequences of the American treasures for the European elites had already been subject to criticism centuries earlier. In 1612, Garcilaso de la Vega developed two clichés that proved to be long-lasting, according to which the influence of America would result in the degeneration and feminization of European culture.[23] The Flemish scientist Joest Lips had anticipated this critique already in 1603: "The New World, which you have conquered, will now conquer you."[24] This statement would shortly prove to be true with respect to the decline of Spanish hegemony. Europe, as the center of world power, would still have a reprieve until the First World War; only then would the center become the periphery. Such terms, however, are probably as meaningless as the pair civilization versus barbarism.[25]

Still, the discovery of America revolutionized more than just European economies and customs. It led—long before Coca-Cola and fast-food culture—to a dietary revolution. The sheer insatiability of European hunger for Asian spices, such as cinnamon, pepper, nutmeg, saffron, and cloves, had been one of the decisive motives for the coincidental discovery of the Americas. And America enriched European cuisines with surprising ingredients: potatoes and tomatoes, corn and cocoa, chocolate and vanilla, sunflowers and avocados. Even American turkeys were soon to be found on the tables of the wealthy. If we try to imagine how the large majority of Europeans would have lived during the last few hundred years without potatoes and corn, then it is hardly exaggerated to say that these food imports belong to the most important events of modern European history (seeds of change, indeed!). What would Vienna be without cafés, Italy without tomatoes, and Russia and Poland without vodka made from potatoes?

Tobacco and, to a lesser extent, cocaine changed European social habits as well as the state of health of smokers and sniffers. The worst scourge proved to be syphilis—in all probability imported from America—which dramatically would influence the sexual manners and health of many generations of Europeans. Even among the large imports of medicinal herbs there was nothing to cure this disease. Still, however harmful syphilis became in Europe, it was much less disastrous than the European export of diseases to America; smallpox, measles, influenza, mumps, diphtheria, and others eradicated entire Indian nations.[26]

## America as Metaphor and Provocation in European Philosophy and Literature

America did more than change European material life. It also represented a massive intellectual challenge, which was taken up first in Spain, Portugal, England, and France. Although in most cases, these discourses reveal only an America created by European wishful thinking, the sheer newness of the New World alone shattered many traditional certainties.[27]

Thomas More's *Utopia* and Francis Bacon's *New Atlantis* initiated the discussion about the ideal Republic, the ideal Commonwealth, as the best of all possible worlds with America as the background, thus influencing all future constitutional debates. Utopia and the new Atlantis reflected the reality America, and I would like to assert that utopia was an "unreal" fantasy before 1492, a fantasy that became "real" thereafter. However, utopia meant not only a good place or an ideal state but, in an ironic inversion, a place that did not even exist, a no-man's-land, a cloud-cuckoo-land. The construct "America" in European imagination all too often denoted something that America never was and never could be—Asia, utopia, paradise on earth with gold lining the streets.

When America failed to fulfill all of these European dreams, the disillusionment became that much more intense. Instead of correcting these illusions, instead of admitting that the European dream of the American dream had always been unreal, the disillusioned "idealists" now accused America of fraud.[28]

The dialectical tension of America as utopia *and* as dystopia runs through all literary discussions about America and was accompanied by parallel developments in material culture. Whereas the potato was still considered an aphrodisiac in Elizabethan times, it was supposed to be the highly poisonous devil's root in the early eighteenth century. The image of the young, innocent, and mythical New World of Shakespeare, Marlowe, and Spenser soon found its counterpart in accusations of barbarism, degeneration, immaturity, soulless materialism, and cultural inferiority—in short, America acted the part of a wasteland of civilization. The publications of Bartholomé de Las Casas, Francisco de Vitoria, and Montaigne with their nostalgia for the Golden Epoch and the lost paradise, the escapist dreams of exotic lands and the ideal state, and their support for the rights of the "Indians"—which, by the way, was an early contribution to the theme of human rights—were countered by the negative attacks of Georges Leclerc Comte de Buffon, Corneille de Pauw, and Guillaume Thomas François de Raynal and their many followers. Their outrageous accusations about the absolute degeneration of all life in America—yes, the absolute inferiority of all people, animals, and plants—remained influential until well into the twentieth century.[29]

The Declaration of Independence of the United States in 1776 and the following revolutions in Latin America—on the one hand, as a result of the European Enlightenment, on the other, because of the increasing weakness of the European metropoles—were of greatest importance for ideological and political developments in the Old World. This is also true for the "Indian" rebellions in Latin America around 1780 and the dissolution of the Jesuit order in Paraguay in 1758, fifteen years earlier than in Europe.[30] Long before Alexis de Tocqueville's vision of the future importance of democratic developments in the United States for the rest of the world was published in *Democracy in America* (1835, 1840), at least no later than the Seven Years' War (French and Indian War, 1756–63)—which actually was the *real* first world war—attentive European observers became aware of worldwide changes of historical proportions that would push Europe out of the center of power, into a second-class, peripheral position, overshadowed by America and Russia. In 1780, the former English governor of Massachusetts, Thomas Pownall, observed that America had become the new major planet that not only would influence the orbit of all others but would also displace the center of gravity in the entire European world system.[31] Joseph Mandrillon, too, argued that "it is the New World, formerly our slave, peopled for the most part by our own emigrants, that will come in turn to enslave us. Its industry, its force, and its power will increase as ours diminish. The old world will be subjugated by the New; and this conquering nation, after having undergone the laws of revolution, will itself perish at the hands of a people it will have been unfortunate enough to discover."[32]

Although the contours of European images of America became more precise after 1776, they still maintained the character of magical reflections fluctuating between total hope and complete rejection. While liberals and republicans, even socialists and Communists, directed many of their hopes toward the land of freedom, virtue, and prosperity, for the representatives of the ancien régime and many conservatives, the United States became the horrific example for the insurrection of the mob and barbaric excesses of democracy, whose influence on the European order must be hindered at all cost.

For the ever-increasing flood of European emigrants who went to America because of economic and political repression, the direction east-west doubtless also marked the direction of paradise. The emigrants were not the only ones to benefit from the rapid improvements in transportation. More and more, information about America could now reach its goal faster, and safer too. This flood of messages about the United States—in the form of travel reports, letters from immigrants, countless literary products, or reports in newspapers and magazines—transformed America, once a topic of conversation for the elites, into a beacon of hope for the lower classes. This phenomenon was caused not only by the mass poverty in Europe. Increasing literacy rates also assisted in the massive spreading of news from America. Especially in areas where the worst nationalist conflicts raged, such as Ireland, Norway, Russia, the Italian peninsula, the states of the German League, the Balkans, and the non-German-speaking territories of the Habsburg monarchy, the United States became the epitome of a freedom that seemed unobtainable in one's own country. Not without reason was the ship on which Lord Byron sailed to Greece called *Bolívar*, and the influence of the North and South American developments on Casimir Pulaski, Thaddeus Kosciusko, Guiseppe Mazzini, and Guiseppe Garibaldi cannot be overestimated.[33]

Even the music world contracted America fever. Between 1733 and 1831 alone, more than a dozen operas dealing with American themes and starring American heroes were produced in Europe. In 1755, a Montezuma opera was produced in Berlin; the music had been composed by Karl Heinrich Graun, the libretto written by Frederick II of Prussia.[34]

The extent to which interest in America had grown can easily be detected in a bibliography of German literature on America compiled by Horst Dippel in which, for the period 1770 to 1800 alone, approximately one thousand titles are listed.[35] The greatest influence can be attributed to the *Letters from an American Farmer* by St. John de Crèvecoeur (1782). This book, which soon appeared in many translations and was particularly well received in the German states, already contained the basic essence of the modern myth of the American dream, which would soon gain tremendous ideological thrust.[36] This modern myth was based on the notions of the United States of America as the synthesis of republican virtue and enlightened government; the land of freedom and of individual self-realization through work; the frontier as wilderness and the land of unlimited possibilities; the new person in a society without class differences; the melting pot and the unstoppable ascent as the future world power. Crèvecoeur's importance as one of the literary founding fathers of the United States and his role in spreading the basic literary themes of the American myth are undisputed.

The most-ridiculed, nonetheless perhaps most important, literary genre was the Western, which spread like wildfire. In the 1820s the heat of the European mania for James Fenimore Cooper made all of the former literary America enthusiasm seem like little flames indeed. The Europeans' enthusiasm for Cooper's books seemed to make the Western the logical successor to the symbolic dramas of the Old World. Between 1843 and 1875 alone, over eighty European Western novels were published. The passion for Cooper's Leatherstocking series, Karl May's Old Shatterhand and Winnetou, and Buffalo Bill's Wild West Show was carried over to the Hollywood and spaghetti Westerns of the twentieth century. In 1960, in West Germany alone, 91 million Western novels were sold.[37]

Enthusiasm for America and criticism of Sturm und Drang and the Romantic period show similar unreal tendencies as the literature of earlier epochs, in spite (or perhaps because?) of the fact that these authors already had access to more and better information. From the Enlightenment to the second half of the nineteenth century, America lay somewhere between Ernst Willkomm's Europe-weariness and Ferdinand Kürnberger's America-weariness. From Voltaire to Jules Verne, from Jean-Jacques Rousseau to Henryk Sienkiewicz—European authors again showed that America represented an ahistorical territory, a place without history. Even in the nineteenth century, most European authors perceived America as a continent untouched by civilization, as natural wilderness. Their pictures of America were ahistorical; the history of the United States was largely ignored; the mental floodgates toward the reality of America remained mostly closed. In short, ancient prejudices reigned supreme, and "the vivid experience of exploration, colonization, and immigration seems to have altered Europe's initial expectations hardly at all."[38]

Yet, disappointment was also apparent in the works of many authors who actually got to know the United States personally. For Charles Dickens, the United States appeared as a monstrous delusion, a Garden of Eden gone wrong, a barbaric wilderness disguised as paradise. He especially complained that U.S. materialism, business culture, and economic shrewdness were just so many synonyms for deception. This criticism could be heard more and more as the economic importance of the United States became more directly felt in Europe. According to Dickens, the citizens of the United States understood freedom not so much as freedom from tyranny but as freedom to tyrannize.[39] The final remarks in Frances Trollope's immense best-seller *Domestic Manners of the Americans* (1839) show what irked European visitors most about the upstart across the Atlantic: "A single word indicative of doubt, that anything, or everything, in that country is not the very best in the world, produces an effect which must be seen and felt to be understood. If the citizens of the United States were indeed the devoted patriots they call themselves, they would surely not thus encrust themselves in the hard, dry, stubborn persuasion, that they are the first and best of the human race, that nothing is to be learnt but what they are able to teach, and that nothing is worth having which they do not possess."[40]

The influential cultural critic Matthew Arnold charged the U.S. democracy with lack of respect, soullessness, lack of feeling, lack of education, the dominating pursuit of comfort, materialism and boosterism, false modesty and false courage.[41] Rudyard Kipling quipped that there was not enough of Romeo in the United States but too much of the balcony. The Swiss historian Jakob Burckhardt completely wrote off the United States and gloomily warned not to copy every latest American folly because life across the Atlantic was totally dominated by business.[42] While Karl Marx did not see the United States as the promised land, he acknowledged that it had the most progressive political system in the world, which, however, was also accompanied by new levels of alienation. In his introduction to *Das Kapital*, he stressed the eminent importance of the developments in the United States for the rest of the world: "One should not deceive oneself. Just as the American War of Independence was the alarm signal for the European middle class in the eighteenth century, so was the American Civil War for the European working class in the nineteenth century."[43] Werner Sombart, in explaining why this was not true for the U.S. working class, quipped that all socialist utopias had been ruined by roast beef and apple pie. This was true not only in America.[44]

Alienation became the major theme of European literature about America of the late nineteenth and twentieth centuries. Many European observers acknowledged that this alienation also influenced their own existence, perhaps at a slower pace, and that the techno-civilization of the United States only anticipated the future of Europe and therefore became a general metaphor for modernity. Nevertheless, most authors concentrated their criticism on the United States, whose citizens they held especially suspect with regard to their outward appearance, tastelessness, pluralistic conformity, superficiality, naive optimism, infantility, and misunderstanding of quantity as quality. The accusation that U.S. culture is uniquely based on a denial of any limitation of human existence is quite absurd, especially when such an accusation is made by the inhabitants of the European continent, whose people had already Europeanized large parts of the world. Quite clearly, the rapid progress of corporate capitalism in the United States developed certain new dynamics and specifically American characteristics. Modern America and the "machine civiliza-tion" did not, however, just fall from the sky. The ardent belief in the benefits of technology was of European origin. It was (and is) by no means an American phenomenon alone.

Still, it was America, European authors implied, that was in essence the original version of modernity. Gerhard Hauptmann's antiemigration novel *Atlantis* (1912) attacked the vulgarity and emptiness of U.S. society. For Rainer Maria Rilke, American mechanization clearly symbolized the main enemy of humanity. Franz Kafka's *Amerika* (1913, 1927) is dominated by themes of cold-ness, anonymity, loneliness, and the inhumanity of modern business. In Ben-jamin Franklin Wedekind's works, the United States is dominated by pred-atory capitalist animals. In Vladimir Majakovsky's *150,000,000* (1919–20), America appears as the futurist projection of nightmares of a streamlined doomsday. Salvador de Madariaga insisted in 1928 that Americans were noth-ing but little boys. In Georges Duhamel's *Scènes de la vie future* (1930), the United States becomes synonymous with the pending destruction of culture. Bert Brecht used the United States as metaphoric stage for the violence and greed of capitalists and fascists in his plays *Aufstieg und Fall der Stadt Ma-hagonny* (1927), *Die heilige Johanna der Schlachthöfe* (1932), and *Der Aufhaltsame Aufstieg des Arturo Ui* (1941). Ultimately, with Evelyn Waugh's *Loved One*, we come back to the point of departure: the European conception of the West as the kingdom of the dead. The Elysian Fields found their real equivalent in the cemetery culture of Southern California. With regard to Los Angeles, Harrison Salisbury noted: "I saw the future—and it does not work."[45]

Without a doubt, many developments in the United States had to lead to astonishment and even provoke criticism. Yet, European accusations against the United States clearly had a different quality than criticism toward similar developments in Europe. They usually revealed two dimensions of unease, a double alienation: they were similar to accusations made by disillusioned lovers who themselves had lost their innocence long ago and simply would not acknowledge that the supposed virginity of their transatlantic mistress had never been anything else but a European fantasy. From that moment on, when Europeans began to dream, "America, you have got it better," the count-less misunderstandings and disappointments were steadfastly programmed.

## *The Periphery Becomes the Center: The Impact of the United States in Europe during the First Half of the Twentieth Century*

In Carlo Levi's novel *Christ Stopped at Eboli* (1945), the poor farmers and agricultural workers in Mezzogiorno were convinced that the streets in the United States were lined with gold. For these degraded people, who could not and would not identify themselves with their own nation, their mythical capital was not Naples or Rome but New York, and *fare l'America* meant, simply, to have success. Since the turn of the century, New York became more than just a mythical capital and guiding light of hope for countless deprived Europeans. It actually developed into a center for the world economy.

Already forty years prior to the journalistic proclamation of "The American Century," the financial power of the United States could no longer be ignored in Europe. In 1901, the year in which Great Britain became the first European nation to receive credit from the United States, W. T. Stead's cautionary book entitled *Americanization of the World; or, The Trend of the Twentieth Century* was published in London.[46] Stead's book was not an isolated case, for around the turn of the century a large number of authors recognized the importance of American economic superiority. Already in 1894, the growing dependence of Great Britain upon the United States was recognized, and publications warning of the threatening dangers coming from the Land of the Dollar were soon to follow. By 1906, even H. G. Wells saw, as he titled his book, *The Future in America.*[47]

Two million U.S. soldiers followed U.S. goods, credits, and investments between 1917 and 1919, and at the end of the First World War, not only the conquered Central Powers but also the victorious Allies were economically dependent upon the United States. The former debtor nation had become the most important creditor for Europe in 1918. The government of the United States was now in the position to force European nations to acknowledge the international gold standard as well as to implement deflationary politics, which caused well-known social repercussions. The United States financed both war debts and reparations and, where applicable, could threaten to withhold aid and credits from unwilling European governments in order to re-establish capitalist economies. All this fell under the official ideology of peaceful trade and the politics of the "open door"—as well as anti-Communism. Law, order, and business constituted the Holy Trinity.

U.S. credits surely served more than the reconstruction of the hard-hit European countries. For those, the conditions were too unfavorable, the burdens and profits too unequal because "the international economic structure was also weakened by American insistence on rebuilding with policies that stacked most burden on the eastern shore of the North Atlantic and most benefits on its own."[48] Between 1913 and 1929, the volume of U.S. foreign trade jumped from $4.5 billion to $10.2 billion. Direct investments in Europe rose from $573 million in 1914 to $1.35 billion in 1929.[49]

During the interwar period, the American dream became for many Europeans a distorted vision of mass democracy, consumer abundance, standardization, mass production, efficiency, technocratic progress, automation, mechanization, Taylorism, Fordism ("Fordizatsia" in the Soviet Union), spontaneity, and—most important—culture with mass appeal. U.S. exports, investments, credits, missionaries (who followed the motto "Anywhere with Jesus, everywhere with Jesus"), tourists, artists, philanthropists, international associations, and particularly the continually increasing domination of mass communication—all guaranteed the United States the establishment of their "Awkward Dominion" (in Frank Costigliola's phrase) in Europe after 1918.

Although official U.S. foreign policy gladly cultivated political isolationism (this, too, is a euphemism for the support of right-wing problem solving abroad), U.S. companies still enjoyed complete support by the respective administrations in their foreign endeavors. The business of the United States was ultimately business, and the interwar governments saw to it that the companies of the United States could cultivate their informal world empire. Especially in the areas of the most modern technical developments, such as with cable communications, radio waves, news agencies, movies, aviation, the automobile and electronics industries, and the food processing and chemical industries, the American lead—only to be shortly interrupted by the Second World War—could be augmented and secured. The list of U.S. companies that profited from this expansion in Europe reads like a Who's Who of American industries: All-American-Cables, Radio Corporation of America, Associated Press, United Press International, Pan-Am, Hollywood companies, International Telephone and Telegraph, Kodak, International Business Machines, National Cash Register, Coca-Cola, Carnation Milk, F. W. Woolworth, J. Walter Thompson, Du Pont, Standard Oil, Ford, General Motors, and General Electric.

Owen D. Young was not only the chairman of the New York expert committee for reparation questions and originator of the Young Plan, but also chairman of the board of General Electric and RCA as well as director of American & Foreign Power and member of the board of AEG. The political weight of the communications industry was fully known to economics experts like Young: "The power of communications is a greater power than that of the combined armies and navies of the world."[50]

Yet, since the end of the First World War, the administrations of the United States could not solve the inherent dilemma of the export of American products and (therewith) the culture of the United States, the conflict between liberal-idealistic-universalistic theory and real power politics. For, "by helping American investments, products and culture reach more people, they claimed to combat injustice, poverty and ignorance. But they often offered ethnocentric solutions disguised as internationalist ones and subjective judgments dignified by the name of rationality and fact. Inspired yet blinded by faith in expertise, most of the new professionals failed to see that foreign policy based on the exportation of American-style liberalism might itself be illiberal."[51] The ideology of liberal-Protestant capitalism of American persuasion, the insisting upon the open door for economic expansion and the national interests of the United States, as well as the belief in the improvement of the standard of life for all people through the introduction of American living and standards of hygiene were interchangeable. This in fact had characterized U.S. foreign policy since the second half of the nineteenth century.

The economic dominance of the United States in Europe after the First World War broadened the traditional image of America as the New Jerusalem. The City on the Hill mutated to become the Factory on the Hill.[52] In Europe—from Great Britain to the Soviet Union, from France to Germany, from Italy to Norway—an exceptionally intense discussion, transcending all ideological borders, addressing desirable or feared developments had been initiated and ran under the slogan "Americanism." The impressive economic power of the United States, the tremendous power of the dollar, the material destruction and spiritual devastation in Europe, and the seemingly unsolvable social and national problems made the United States—at least until the stock market crash and worldwide depression—an extremely emulated goal, but also an object of hatred. The artists of *Neue Sachlichkeit* copied American models, as did the Soviet apostles of modernization, who saw Lenin as the god of political rejuvenation and Henry Ford as the St. Peter of material modernization.[53] More than ever before, the United States was either stylized as the ideal model for the future or the threatening center of a world conspiracy poised to undermine the future of Europe. Although unnoticed by many, the periphery had surpassed the metropole. The remigration of U.S. political and economic power allowed America to appear as the new Rome, which could dictate to the European Greeks the new, unavoidable living standards of modernity.[54]

Again, fascination and disillusionment balanced each other on the scales. The Russian notion of Chicagoism and of Amerikanski speed; the French ideas on the *système américain, américanisme, américanisation, machinisme, système machine, homme-machine, and technicisme*; and the German fears of the quasi-mythical powers of U.S. capital, the Yankee civilization, the flight into consumption, the emancipation of the robot nation into the complicated world of consumer market products, the lowland of American equality, the deep-seated amorality of imperialistic pragmatism, the demo-plutocracy, the smiling soullessness of the U.S. middle class, the choir of eunuchs in the iron chapels of plutocracy, the culture of comfort, softness, feminization, the machine man, trivial literature, the cults of technology and industry, and the feared effeminization of the Occident through sexual bolshevism(!)—all were representations of European confusion, copies of older, now-solidified prejudices.[55]

During the 1920s, not only did Berlin develop into the European capitol of Americanism, it also became *the* center for anti-American reaction. Many intellectuals who had not yet come to terms with the defeat in the First World War and the transition from monarchy to republic saw themselves cornered between the U.S. and Soviet models. Both became the metaphor for the greatest fear of the educated classes and the petty bourgeoisie: the loss of supposed individuality in a threatening mass society. These fears culminated in the most famous anti-American book, written by Adolf Halfeld, *Amerika und der Amerikanismus* (1928). According to Halfeld, the United States, with the energy of a young usurper, attempted to force the Europeans into the barracklike existence of prehistoric man through the Taylorization of private life. Furthermore, the mammonlike machine civilization would inevitably require a machine man. This would be influenced by the dollar cult as the national religion of these people in God's own country, whose money heralded the trust in God and whose salesmen, as true missionaries, personified their businesses in the trusted spirit of continual advertising, of proselytizing and of preaching. These archphilistines, who would turn into zombies from the monotony of life in a water-closet civilization of industrial feudalism, were characterized by a lack of historical depth and constant nervosity, the cowardice of the mass soul, and an avowal of the ideals of the herd; therefore they seek refuge in the democracy of numbers and mob tyranny. This average type formed like an industrial model, this intellectual rubbish from all over the world, subjugates itself to the decay of all intellect through feminization, cornered between philistinelike matrons and girls, those feared greenhouse growths of a mechanized world. In this country of regulated happiness, this parvenu country par excellence, uniform people require uniform menus and desire herdlike feedings—in short, life in the United States corresponded to a national psychosis of the most brutal collectivism. The main responsibility for the worldwide propagation of this "niggerlike" aberration of civilization was, according to Halfeld, especially the fact that the United States controlled 90 percent of worldwide film production by the end of the First World War, and thereby the most influential propaganda medium: "Trade no longer follows the flag, but instead film, as America's leading economic leaders assert. And we can add: not only trade, but also customs and traditions. The irony is, however, that the world contributes to the commercial, which film creates for America, seventy million dollars of pure profits from film exports for the American balance of payments yearly."[56]

In plain view for all to see, evil U.S. trust magnates now were forcing their way into the reservations of the surely more responsible European captains of industry. Fordism, the total rationalization of human society, was interpreted as a purely American phenomenon and not as a general possibility inherent in every capitalist culture. The dichotomy between European culture and U.S. civilization was, in turn, only a result of the inability of bourgeois cultural criticism that, in reality, did not understand that culture is not created outside of social processes. Precisely as a result of these ideological blinders, many Europeans could deceive themselves about the phenomenon "America." Hence, "they did not recognize the 'standardization' of life in the USA as a technique of governing in which contradictions are forcefully repressed, but as a sign of a completely different, bewitched society."[57]

Only a few commentators, such as Antonio Gramsci, Walther Benjamin,

Siegfried Kracauer, and Theodor W. Adorno, acknowledged that Americanism did not necessarily have its roots in the United States, but instead in capitalism as such. Siegfried Kracauer correctly commented that the precision of the Tiller Girls, one of the most-admired U.S. revue groups of the time, represented neither the "girlization" of U.S. civilization nor cultural feminist tendencies of women stepping over men (contra Adolf Halfeld) but "corresponded to the reflex of the aspired rationality of the ruling economic system."[58] Adorno describes the hysteria with which educated classes in Europe reacted to the products of capitalist mass culture as the prevailing fear of the infringement of the capitalist rationalization upon the holy halls of the bourgeoisie. Even Adorno shows, however, that he could not completely remove himself from the thought processes of European cultural critics when he asserts that "American civilization . . . [is] a system which encompasses all aspects of life without even allowing a few loopholes for the unregimented consciousness which, in contrast, European sloppiness has held open until well into the age of large companies."[59]

Many Europeans, especially those who felt that Europe had a monopoly on high, pure, and true culture, were thoroughly convinced that the United States was a cultural wasteland. Nevertheless, a large number of U.S. artists—authors, actors, musicians—and also intellectuals were accepted and imitated by the European elite. In this respect it was certainly also decisive that the artists who were welcomed in Europe were precisely those who had been increasingly labeled as un-American in the United States.

A comparative study of prejudices shows that European pictures of America of the interwar period were in structure exceptionally similar to those existing in the nineteenth century. As it has for many hundreds of years, America represented the continent of hope and dreams, the myth of the West, as well as wildness and barbarity. In European eyes the image of the "noble savage" was attributed, if at all, only to the decimated "Indian." White Americans were increasingly equated with the role of the barbarian, who possessed the following characteristics: rawness, lawlessness, tastelessness, brutal materialism, having emancipated women and sassy children that were demanding and unruly, a primitive system of education, a lack of manners, linguistic primitiveness, a mania for speed and for setting records, superficiality, high rates of crime and divorce, a dazzling advertising world, lynch justice, unethical business methods, corruption, praise of money, prohibition, mafia, Hollywood, and black music.[60] The same Europeans who devoured American sensations accused U.S. media of lacking seriousness. As always, the lack of knowledge of the actual developments within the United States was abundantly evident during the interwar period.

British images of America seemed so misguided and miserable to U.S. ambassador Joseph P. Kennedy, even on the eve of the Second World War, that an intensive cultural enlightenment campaign seemed necessary "so that the people in England would believe that something happens here besides gangster shootings, rapes and kidnappings."[61] A public-opinion survey taken in October 1940 showed that only 27 percent of Britons asked were positively disposed toward the United States. The popularity rating of Americans was ranked behind that of Greeks, Poles, and Jews.[62] Immediately after its entry into war, the United States may have been in the number-one position on the popularity scale, but already the friction that had arisen toward U.S. GIs who were stationed in Britain during the Second World War ("oversexed, overpaid, and over here") indicated the postwar trend. After 1945 the popularity of the United States sank back to the prewar level.

Scandinavian clichés about America included certain positive attitudes, although these were challenged by accusations of decadence.[63] In Spain, in contract, attacks on the United States for its lack of originality, lack of creativity, monotony, vulgarity, megalomania, and intellectual inferiority grew and grew. The prevailing curriculum for Spanish history students between 1939 and 1952 was brief: "The United States of America. The materialist and inferior spirits of American civilization. The lack of fundamental principles and moral unity. Immoral financial practices. Their unjustified aggression against Spain and the Spanish-American states, Nicaragua, Haiti. Moral Superiority of Spanish-America vis-à-vis North America."[64]

The prevailing French prejudices were somewhat more qualified because of a longer and deeper interaction with U.S. themes. Although most results of U.S. capitalism were vehemently rejected, many French intellectuals nevertheless admired the American myth of freedom. Especially French authors introduced the art and literature of America in Europe and had imitated and further developed le style américain long before direct encounters with the authors of the Lost Generation in Parisian cafés.[65]

The situation in Italy was similar to that in France. In spite of the twenty years of fascism, U.S. troops did not encounter simply negative prejudices in 1943, perhaps because of the close family ties of many Italians in the United States. Until the end of the war, both Italy and France functioned as testing grounds for all attempts by U.S. authorities to promote positive pictures of the United States and to test cultural programs that would later be implemented in Germany and Austria.

The problems of the U.S. liberators in Europe are dramatically exemplified by their experience soon after their landing on the small Italian island of Lampedusa, where the U.S. Army published its first newspaper in an occupied territory. The editorials, however, were used not only to persuade the inhabitants of Lampedusa of the blessings of Western democracy. Wholly convinced of the blessings of Western hygiene, the U.S. Army prohibited Lampedusians from defecating in public. As the protests of the liberated bore no fruit with the occupation authorities—Lampedusians could just not understand why their old freedom should be exchanged for another—a large group of men finally gathered on the central piazza, "and with one accord they struck a blow for freedom."[66]

Although the liberal traditions of U.S. political culture strongly influenced Italian liberalism, the *New Deal italiano,* voices on the Italian left and right could be heard insisting that the reestablishment of the Mafia in the South and the introduction of the Christmas tree through the U.S. Army were the only significant contributions of the United States to postwar Italian culture.[67]

National Socialist propaganda against most things American reflects general trends of reactionary xenophobia, intolerance, and ignorance and certainly marked the low point of traditional European lack of understanding toward the United States. The series in the *Völkische Beobachter* "Aus der Unkultur Amerikas" (From the unculture of America), published between July and December 1930, initiated only the first wave of attack,[68] which would be more tightly focused on the following concepts especially after the U.S. entry into war. America was a boundless continent that wanted to usurp world rule under the leadership of Jewish Wall Street, as a part of the Jewish world conspiracy; a world power of trivialities; a standardized homogenous civilization of canned culture; the *Homo Cummunis Hollywoodiensis* as patent-homunculus; Hollywood civilization as the realization of mass mania, whose breeding grounds are the uprooted and racially inferior masses; a streamlined imperialism of Americanism as the absolute poison and death of culture; the final fight of uniformed Puritan barbarism against Europe. Party comrades were not the only ones to criticize the hypocritical Puritanism of prohibition, which would supposedly deny the already sorely afflicted German-Americans of that which was honestly earned: a holy glass of beer.

Anti-American sentiments and propaganda in Europe surely reached their peak during the reign of the National Socialists, but the propagandists of the "Third Reich" hardly had to invent new prejudices. They could easily build upon already deep-seated stereotypes, and these, mixed in with a shot of extreme anti-Semitism, were driven to the height of paranoia. After 1933, the National Socialists sought to reestablish the "Reinheit der deutschen Kultur" (The purity of German culture) through the identification and annihilation of that which was different, supposedly un-German, inferior, abnormal, and degenerate. The "U.S.-American-Jewish-Nigger-Culture" was thereby a main target. It may be rather ironic, still National Socialism and Fascism could be interpreted as the attempt to find another alternative between Henry Ford and Karl Marx.[69]

Even the forced exile and finally the annihilation of the putative other could not prevent NS film production from operating on a formal level that was dictated by the U.S. sound motion picture, or German dance orchestras from simply Germanizing U.S. hits, playing, mostly without swing, a variation of jazz. Apparently, these German bands were not quite the real thing. Joseph Goebbels, the National Socialist chief of culture, had English orchestras flown into Berlin for his film balls.

As Peter von Zahn attempted to summarize the German ideas about America during the interwar period in 1959, he spoke not only for German but also for many of his European contemporaries. He asserted that the United States seemed as simple as did its tourists; they looked just as violent as Al Capone and Dillinger, and they were as generous as the presents from the emigrated uncle and as exciting as jazz and as funny as Buster Keaton. In any event, the United States did not appear any more real than a Hollywood film. In short, it represented a collection of curiosities.[70]

Just how deep-seated these clichés were in almost all European countries still after 1945 would become apparent for U.S. interviewers who asked Czech, Polish, and Hungarian refugees in Linz, Salzburg, Munich, and Nuremberg in 1951 and 1952 about their impressions of the United States. All of those interviewed had just turned their backs toward "real socialism" and wished to emigrate to the United States at any cost. The interviewers were quite aghast as they heard the opinions of these future U.S. citizens, even more so when those interviewed made it clear that their assessments were not based on Soviet anti-American propaganda. Only one-quarter felt that the United States was culturally equal to Europe. A large majority of the refugees found that the United States had a type of pseudoculture at best, in which cultural values could be measured only by quantitative criteria and that the total lack of history had reduced aesthetic judgment to the acknowledging beauty in cars and pin-ups. The cultlike admiration for money would curtail all possibilities to enjoy life. The United States had never made cultural progress but had created only a progressive material civilization. In all, the European mentality was quite simply closer to general human ideals because natural human emotions in the United States were repressed through the drive for uniformity. For this reason, it should not be surprising that truly fine taste could have been developed only in Europe. These opinions did not, by the way, come from "uneducated" people. Questions of cultural significance pertaining to the United States were presented only to so-called intellectuals because initial interviews with individuals possessing limited education showed either complete misunderstanding or even more catastrophic results. An example of a somewhat complimentary statement came from a Hungarian philosopher who felt that Americans were naturally more primitive than the Europeans, but they were at least more progressive.[71]

If we can imagine the exceptional situation in which these individuals found themselves, and if we furthermore understand that these opinions were mentioned not only by refugees from Communist countries who wanted nothing more than to emigrate to the United States, then the following conclusion is unavoidable. The European prejudices toward the United States, characterized by the dialectical tension between total fascination with America and the aggressive-defensive, cultural feeling of superiority, would always have a decisive impact upon the developments of European-U.S. relations.

## Austria and America

### EARLY CONTACTS

The Austrian images of America and also its relationship to the United States developed more slowly and with more reserve than in the Atlantic European nations. This was a consequence of its position in central Europe and the absence of colonial endeavors of the Austrian Habsburg dynasty. The colonial politics of England, France, Portugal, and especially Spain were followed with great interest in Vienna, but the immediate problems of denominational conflicts and the war against the Ottoman Empire and other European powers let the distance from mid- and eastern Europe to America seem that much greater as compared with the distance from the west of the continent. Because of their own lack of interest, the Habsburg rulers disallowed the emigration of their subjects, particularly because large areas of the Habsburg Empire were destroyed after the Turkish wars. Especially the southeastern section of the monarchy itself had become a quasi emigration land.

Austrian Jesuits had participated in the scientific research and proselytization of areas in what is today Canada, New York, Pennsylvania, Maryland, Colorado, Arizona, and California (in 1681 a South Tyrolean priest with the fitting name Eusebio Francisco Kino was appointed the imperial cosmographer of California), but the main interests of the Austrian Jesuit mission did not lie in America.[72] Austrian trade with the British colonies in North America naturally never reached the volume of British trade or that of other European maritime states. But already prior to 1776, a modest export and import business had been developed via the harbors in the Austrian Netherlands and Trieste. Not only did glass and textiles from Bohemia cross the Atlantic, but also playing cards from Vienna found great popularity in the thirteen colonies, and in the 1780s, the British-born George Simpson founded the Austrian-American Company.[73] For the rulers of the monarchy, prerevolutionary America was more a fascinating assembly point for beautiful, interesting, obscure, and exotic flora and fauna than an economic opportunity. After 1776, this fascination was replaced by the fear that the United States could potentially be a contaminating trouble spot.

Between 1783 and 1788, Emperor Joseph II financed a scientific expedition under the leadership of Joseph Maerter that was to research the West Indies. Joseph II was a passionate collector of the exotic, as was his father, Franz Stephan von Lothringen, and his brother Leopold II. This expedition brought the desired scientific results and collection pieces for museums, zoos, and

botanical gardens—including grass seeds from Carolina for the lawn of Schönbrunn Palace. Two members of the expedition—court painter Bernhard Al-
brecht Moll and botany student Matthias Stupitz—jumped ship and settled in
the United States. Not only was Joseph II personally disappointed, but he also
saw this "desertion" as a confirmation of his fears that the sheer existence of
the United States could tempt desperately needed craftsmen in the Habsburg
Empire to emigrate. The emperor thus issued a decree in 1784, according to
which emigration would be granted only in extreme exceptions, with each
case requiring government authorization. Even if Gerard van Swieten admired
Benjamin Franklin (Leopold II incorporated a Franklin stove into his collection) and all of Empress Maria Theresa's children enjoyed Sutton's smallpox
vaccination (which had been imported from America by Dr. Jan Igenhousz),[74]
the rejection of emigration and the fear of a brain drain generally characterized
the position of the Viennese court until the twentieth century.

### THE AUSTRIAN EMIGRATION

In contrast to the practice of Western European states, the Habsburg Empire
resettled its religious dissidents, placing them mainly in the eastern sector of
the territory—at least after the government abandoned the effort to annihilate
them, recognizing their colonial potential. Only small groups, such as the
Bohemian *Herrenhuter* under Augustin Hermann, were able to emigrate to the
British colonies in the sixteenth century. They were followed in 1734 by approximately fifty exiled Lutheran families from Salzburg, who eventually settled in Ebenezer, Georgia. These Salzburg emigrants with Johann Adam Treut-
len not only provided the first elected governor of Georgia but also protested
vehemently against the practice of slavery.[75] The more than one hundred Catholic missionaries of the Leopoldinenstiftung, which had been founded in
Vienna in 1829, could only later be attributed to the phenomenon of religious
emigration—in the sense of the strengthening of U.S. Catholicism.

Official statistics on Austrian emigration to the United States are exceptionally inaccurate. Austrian data were incomplete because of the noninclu-
sion of illegal emigrants, and U.S. records illustrate the difficulty in defining
and determining areas of origin within the Austrian empire. Therefore, we
must settle for estimates. All emigrants from the Habsburg Empire were considered Austrian before 1866. But even after the Austro-Hungarian Compromise, not only were the inhabitants of Cisleithania seen as Austrians, but so
were the Swabian settlers on the Danube in Hungary and the Transylvanian
Saxons. The uncertainty as to who was a U.S. citizen of Austrian descent did
not end even with the establishment of the First Austrian Republic in 1918.
U.S. emigration statistics reflect the complex territorial changes and ethnic
shifts after the collapse of the Danube monarchy. This confusing situation
caused even the best experts on the subject to sigh when in 1920 a German-

speaking Transylvanian was asked to answer accurately the question of his origin: Did he come from Austria, Austria-Hungary, Hungary, Romania, or Transylvania?[76] U.S. data still remained confusing well after the Second World War. While many former Austrians who came to the United States at the beginning of the war had taken up the citizenship of their European host nations and were counted as Britons or French, after the war many German-speaking immigrants from Czechoslovakia, Hungary, Yugoslavia, and Romania were again counted as Austrians. Additional factors of uncertainty are caused by the incompletely counted "Birds of Passage," those European guest workers in the United States who returned to their homelands with their savings and, as "Americans with gold teeth," caused envious bewilderment. In the year 1907 alone, 800,000 individuals returned to Europe.

In 1850, the statistics show that fewer than 1,000 U.S. citizens referred to themselves as Austrians. Only at the turn of the century did emigration from the Habsburg monarchy reach the dimensions of a mass movement. Between 1891 and 1900, there were 597,047 people (15.5 percent of all U.S. immigrants) who emigrated from Austria-Hungary, and between 1902 and 1911, the immigration really reached dramatic proportions: 2,191,734 Austro-Hungarians left their home for the United States, which was the largest group (27.9 percent) of all immigrants during this period. The centers of immigration were mostly situated in the nonindustrial periphery. The greatest number were agricultural workers, with many being poorer artisans; they came from eastern and western Hungary, Galicia, and Bukovina, Slovenia, Croatia, and Transylvania. In 1912, for every 100,000 inhabitants of the monarchy's Polish territories, 711 emigrated; from the contemporary area of Austria, only 182. While especially it was entire families who emigrated during the second half of the nineteenth century, young single men dominated this movement during the period immediately preceding the First World War, 30 percent of whom would return to their homeland. In contrast to the German emigrants, the Austrians mostly settled in U.S. cities.

After the emigration gap caused by the First World War, 24,000 Austrians came to the United States between 1919 and 1924. Seventy percent of these individuals came from the Burgenland alone. As a consequence, the dollar became an attractive second currency in this province. The anti-immigrant quota measures that were passed by Congress in 1924 (785 Austrians per year) and in 1929 (1,412 per year) again significantly reduced emigration. Only the forced exile (and later annihilation) of the Jewish population and political dissidents after the Anschluss through the National Socialists initiated a development that had already been feared by Emperor Joseph II, namely, a tremendous brain drain. Between 1938 and 1941 alone, 21,000 Jewish Austrians emigrated to the United States. Even in poor postwar Austria, the material promise of the United States in particular would lure 40,000 Austrian emigrants until 1960. They included brides of U.S. soldiers, but also a large majority of highly qualified professionals, which had been a prerequisite of U.S. quota measures until 1965. As a result of the small *Wirtschaftswunder* in Austria in the 1960s, the number of emigrants decreased, and by the 1970s only 500 people emigrated per year. These figures, however, do not take into consideration the approximately 18,000 Austrians who have lived in the United States for years but who did not have or did not want U.S. citizenship. In any event, U.S. census figures of 1970 show that 214,014 U.S. citizens declared themselves Austrians and 761,311 people as children of Austrian parents. In this latter group, only 56 percent mentioned German as their mother tongue.[77]

The territory of the Austrian Republic surely does not count as the most important origin of emigrants to the United States. The impact of emigration upon Austria, however, should not be underestimated. The economic importance of the money that flowed back into Austria from Austrian guest workers in the United States and the influence of the modernization of agriculture introduced by those who returned from America, which was particularly envied in the rural areas of the monarchy, stand without question, not only because of the often-ridiculed insistence upon hygiene and the water closet. The term "guest worker," used here outside of its historical context, could perhaps help us to understand the economic discrepancy between the United States and Europe at the time. The losses for Austria resulting from the emigration of artistic and scientific elites in the 1930s and 1940s are perhaps not quantitatively measurable. Those who ridicule the Freudianization of America should remember that the emigration of the most important artists and scientists was carried out with force, whereby highly necessary innovations were either postponed or completely hindered in Austria.[78] Those who lament the "Americanization" of Austria after the Second World War should not forget that it was the supporters of Austro-fascism and National Socialism who were responsible for the human, artistic, and scientific void, which amounted to the further Europeanization of the United States. This, in turn, would create the essential prerequisite for the "Americanization" of Europe after the Second World War.

THE DEVELOPMENT OF DIPLOMATIC, POLITICAL,
AND ECONOMIC RELATIONS BETWEEN THE UNITED STATES
AND AUSTRIA AND ITS REFLECTION IN AUSTRIAN IMAGES
OF AMERICA

The economy of the Habsburg Empire profited during the American War of Independence from the secret weapons trade with the American rebels. The Viennese government did, however, forbid the participation of Austrian mercenaries. Archduke Leopold's Tuscan constitution project clearly showed parallels to the constitutions from Virginia and Pennsylvania. Leopold, nevertheless, refused to offer any financial support to the United States during the War of Independence. This neutral position of the archduke should be less surprising than the fact that the future emperor was suspected of possibly sympathizing with the American revolutionaries and with the request of Philipp Mazzei in 1778.[79]

The posture of the Viennese government toward the newly founded United States at first was officially negative, even though the Viennese court had made an offer to mediate during the latter phase of the war. U.S. ambassador William Lee, in any event, did not even receive an audience with the emperor in 1778. Lee, however, was a main attraction in Viennese salons. The politically interested followed the events on the other side of the Atlantic with keen attention and a curiosity that was not easily stilled. For example, the news of the July 4, 1776, Declaration of Independence was first noted in the Viennese *Diarium* on August 28, 1776. The dependence of the Austrian press upon French and British (increasingly German in the nineteenth century) papers throws an illuminating light upon the quality of Austrian reports on America. This frequently led to the dilemma that the Austrian reader, who could compare information on the American War of Independence originating from London or Paris, could not actually be certain that the same occurrences were being described. In any event, the offer of the Philadelphia Congress in 1777 to allocate free trade rights to the Habsburg monarchy was rejected. Similarly frustrated were the negotiations on the establishment of diplomatic relations and the conclusion of a trade agreement arbitrated by Baron de Beelen-Bertholff in Philadelphia beginning in 1783 and lasting until 1792. This lack of success was not only a result of the overattention to details of protocol by the Viennese court.[80] The fear of the proliferation of democratic and republican thoughts, such as those of the American-French-German Union founded by radicals, Freemasons, and illuminati in Vienna in 1781, made the United States seem like a democratic nightmare especially after the "terror" of the French Revolution and the ascension to the throne of Emperor Francis.[81]

Only in 1820 was an Austrian consulate general established in New York under the direction of Alois Baron von Lederer, who concluded a shipping and trade agreement with the United States in 1829. This agreement remained in force until 1917. One of the primary duties of the first Austrian ambassador, Wenzel Philipp Baron von Mareschal, who served in Washington from 1838 to 1841, documents the ambivalent position of the Viennese government toward the United States. Not only did the Austrian diplomat have the assignment of reporting on the newest political, economic, and cultural developments in the United States, but he was also required to observe and report the activities of the "political criminals" who had fled the monarchy as well as exiled revolutionaries—who at that time could choose between five years imprisonment or deportation to the United States! After 1841, the Austrian mission in Washington was again occupied only by diplomats with the rank of chargé d'affaires; in contrast to the other European great powers, the government in Vienna maintained its distinguished disinterest toward the United States until the late nineteenth century.[82]

Count Metternich surely could rely upon his chargé d'affaires Johann Georg Hülsemann, accredited in 1841. Hülsemann had compiled a study on the history of the United States in 1823 in which he diagnosed all developments in the United States to be based on hostility toward religion, state, and social order, commenting, "The defenders of the ruling European politics are content when our continent is not haunted by that which belongs to America."[83]

The active support of the Catholic church in the United States by the Habsburgs as well as the Metternich system, the deportation of political prisoners, and the repression of the revolution of 1848/49 did not exactly contribute to the improvement of relations between the United States and the Habsburg Empire. Although the U.S. government refused all political and financial support for the Hungarian fight for independence during Ludwig Kossuth's U.S. trip in 1851, the tremendous sympathy for Hungary in America—showing itself in true-to-life Kossuth fashions with Kossuth hats, Kossuth cigars, Kossuth cakes, and even a Kossuth flu that was, of course, treated by the Kossuth pill—clearly demonstrated that the majority of the American citizens detested the Habsburg Empire as a jailer of nations and would welcome its defeat in the future.[84]

The United States certainly played a less significant role in the political-reform discussions in Austria of the Biedermeier period than in the German states. But even the Habsburg Empire experienced romantic enthusiasm for America, which captured many more than Nikolaus Lenau, Anastasius Grün, and Count Stephan Szécheny. In 1821 even Ludwig van Beethoven considered composing an opera to be entitled "The Founding of Pennsylvania; or, The Arrival of Penn in America."[85] The exotic appeal evoked through travel reports and novels with the theme of America could also be enjoyed in the Habsburg monarchy. These publications, which at that time had flooded Europe, routinely conquered the dams of Metternich's censorship. The works of Basil Hall, Frances Trollope, Charles Dickens, Gottfried Duden, Alexis de Tocqueville, Charles Sealsfield, and Friedrich Gerstäcker are only the most well-known examples of the avalanche of such publications on America.[86] In the Hungarian half of the empire alone, eight travel reports were published, including Sándor Bölöni Farkas's very successful *Reise in Nord-Amerika* in 1834.[87]

The United States not only was the projection screen for romantic America-mania and a longing for democracy but also increasingly became an object for the study of technical developments. For example, the Steyrer Association for Manufacturing and Trade sent sixteen technicians to the United States for extended education in 1836, and in 1842 Carl Ghega began a trip to America to study the building of rail and canal systems, steamboats, and grid bridges.

Later to be given an aristocratic title, the railroad pioneer brought his experiences in the United States to his Austrian rail projects, including the building of bridges based on the Howes system. The American William Norris also organized workshops for the building of locomotives and train cars for the Austrian State Railroad in the 1840s.[88]

The inhabitants of the Habsburg Empire were therefore not completely isolated from developments in the United States. The majority of the population, however, had a minimal familiarity with America. The monarchy's press reports never reached the levels of British, French, Italian, or even German journalism. Austrian newspapers reported mostly only American roughness, primitiveness, drunkenness, and criminality, and these were also used by the government in Vienna to fight emigration. Negative reports by Austrian diplomats about the poor treatment and shameless exploitation of emigrants in the United States repeatedly appeared in the newspapers.[89] Even after the laying of the Atlantic telegraph cable, which allowed regular coverage, the quality of America stories hardly improved, and Austrian reports became increasingly dependent upon the German press.

The political and economic relations between the Habsburg monarchy and the United States developed rather slowly compared with other European nations. Yet, they were stable enough by 1860 that they withstood the fatal conclusion of Archduke Maximilian's Mexico adventure. However, Maximilian could not count on the support of his brother Emperor Francis Joseph anyway. The stabilization of relations also was certainly enhanced by the monarchy's strict neutrality during the U.S. Civil War, which hardly reflected any sympathy for the Northern states but rather for its own grain-exporting interests.[90]

After the Civil War these relations gained a new dimension. Trade developed not only to the disadvantage of the monarchy but to that of all Europe. U.S. competition began to shake up the European-dominated world economic system toward the end of the nineteenth century; it became the "sour dough, which fermented and transformed the middle European economy."[91] In 1881, Alexander Peez, member of the Austrian imperial diet, pointed out that Austria-Hungary had exported 165,000 metric tons of fat and bacon to the United States in 1870 but that it imported 150,000 metric tons from the United States in 1874. Already in 1873, northern Bohemian mills ground American wheat. In 1880, the pressed yeast factories around Pilsen purchased 30,000 metric tons of U.S. corn, and even in a city like Reichenberg, American apples belonged to the daily diet. These massive foodstuff imports from the United States initially brought a substitution for poor European harvests. In the long term, however, they meant the loss of important export income for Austria-Hungary. The huge agricultural areas in the United States now revolutionized the relation between world food supply and demand, and modern industrialized agriculture revolutionized the prices. Between 1877 and 1880 alone, the Austro-Hungarian export decreased: oxen by 86 percent, cows by 78 percent, veal by 72 percent, pigs by 46 percent, lambs and goats by 89 percent, flour by 100 percent.[92] The use of huge areas of land in the United States (and Russia) through technological progress fundamentally changed the (rural) economic condition of Europe; attentive observers realized the powerful political consequences of this development.

The situation for the Danube monarchy continually deteriorated until the First World War, by which time, in addition to agricultural products, more and more industrial goods were being imported from the United States. Still, in 1891, the United States was only the sixth largest importer into Austria-Hungary (tied with Switzerland), with 3.8 percent of the total imports. By 1910, the United States, with 8.3 percent of the entire import volume, already exceeded Great Britain and was in second place only to Germany. U.S. imports amounted to 231.1 million crowns; the Austro-Hungarian exports, in contrast, came to only 84.5 million crowns.[93] This period also saw the first U.S. direct investments, such as the Austro-American Magnesit AG, founded in 1908, or the Viennese subsidiary of the United States Machinery Corporation, in 1907. U.S. investments in Austria-Hungary remained relatively limited in contrast to other European nations; they amounted to only 1 percent of all American monies in all of Europe.[94]

The first industrial products from the United States that flooded the European market in the 1820s had been harmless Yankee apple peelers. Locomotives, machines of all types, the Colt revolver, and the "American Wagon" (the *Américaines*, which revolutionized the wagon fashion of the whole continent) were all soon to follow. Agricultural machines in particular became the symbol of U.S. exports. These machines not only created technical progress in the United States but also contributed to the change of the economic and social circumstances in European agriculture through making farm work more efficient.

Already by the middle of the nineteenth century, the United States had developed its typical mixture of patriotism, democratic mission, and belief in progress (i.e., technology as ideology), which, with the help of the advancement of American goods on the world market, attempted simultaneously to deliver the American Way. In 1865 Simon Stern summarized this ideological contract of U.S. technology to liberate repressed people, the Manifest Destiny of U.S. goods: "Is it not a glorious result . . . that with every cut of the McCormick reaper, . . . the shackles of a bondsman of Europe fall clanging to earth?"[95]

This belief in the liberating strength of American products and goods was often a reason for coy condescension in Europe, in particular at the first World Fair in London in 1851. This position, however, provoked the following prophetic poem in the United States in which "Brother Jonathan" wrote of his relatives across the Atlantic, especially his father, "John Bull":

John Bull, you laugh in proud emotion
At our small wares sent o'er the ocean

.   ..    .    .     .    .      .     .

But to my own plain Yankee notion
We're in the right.

You laughed aloud, in high disdain
At our machine that cuts the grain,—
And swallowed down your words again,
Conceited John.

We beat you, John, at all that pays
'Tis idle in these stirring days,
To fool yourself, and only raise,
What's old tomorrow.[96]

Toward the end of the nineteenth century, U.S. industrial goods asserted themselves again and again in Europe. In certain areas, such as in the machine tool trade, in which specialized machines slowly replaced the European all-purpose machines, the superiority was especially clear. U.S. investments in Europe increased around the turn of the century, particularly in the building of factories for office and sewing machines, machines for the leather and textile industry, machines for agriculture and the printing and building trades, and pumps and elevators. Already at this time, European industrialists, bankers, business people, and workers had direct contact with U.S. norms, standardization, use of replaceable parts, and aggressive marketing strategies. The "knock-out method" would not be a foreign term for long.[97]

Forty years prior to the great Americanism debate, Alexander Peez stressed that U.S. competition, this greatest economic revolution of his time, could be countered only through modernization and standardization, only through "the strengthening and condensing of all productive factors." The United States continued to develop into a type of large cooperative, into businesses that served only the purpose of securing their societies with the largest possible portion of earthly goods. England and America, which both embodied this tendency most clearly, could force all other nations to follow because "those who do not wish to remain behind and be destroyed must go along. Peace and romanticism are disappearing all over the world. The old nations of the Continent must acquire a drop of American blood. Popular dreams of thousand-year-old prejudices are no longer feasible. How will the strained survive on this racetrack? And will there still be room for the sport of the nationality discord?"[98] These were surely prophetic words in 1881.

Even in the diplomatic reports sent to Vienna, these developments are clearly reflected. The United States was perhaps still depicted as a conglomerate of the uneducated, naive, and tactless, as an asylum for anarchists and the land of endless contradictions. Yet, Ambassador Baron Ladislaus Hengel-müller von Hengervar also observed that the governments of the most power-ful states in the world were competing for the favor of the United States to help them avoid being bypassed as trading partners.[99] The governments of Austria-Hungary participated only halfheartedly in this diplomatic competition, and the monarchy would in the end be counted among the losers. Although scien-tists and doctors like Adam Politzer, Theodor Escherich, Paul Clairmont, Sig-mund Freud, and Ernst Fuchs had been impressed with the progress in sur-gery and the standards of hygiene during their visits to the United States between 1893 and 1912;[100] and although Buffalo Bill's Wild West Shows and Karl May's novels stirred the enthusiasm of the masses, as did Adolf Loos's modern architecture (e.g., his American Bar in the Kärntnerstrasse passage in Vienna), the United States remained a country that was observed with distrust and completely misunderstood by the ruling elites during the last years of the Danube monarchy.

The reason for these difficulties went beyond the differences in the respec-tive systems and cultures as well as the geographic distance. Even the analyses of the politics of the Wilson administration by Austro-Hungarian diplomats showed, for the most part, a complete lack of knowledge of domestic develop-ments and a misinterpretation of the foreign policy power of the United States. In addition, these reports documented the incurable mental dependence of diplomacy and politics of Austria-Hungary upon the dangerous plan for world power of the German Reich.[101] The Austro-Hungarian propaganda failed from the outbreak of the First World War until 1917, not only as a result of the lack of understanding for America, but also because of its own helpless-ness.[102] The few actions that reached the planning stage were not carried out because of Austria-Hungary's halfheartedness, lack of professionalism, and ignorance of politics and diplomacy.[103] The spirit of aggressive war enthusiasm and certainty of victory hindered serious negotiations until the U.S. entry into war, as did the ignorance on both sides—and speechlessness, in the true sense of the word. Even the potential U.S. negotiation partners—Woodrow Wilson, Robert Lansing, and Colonel Edward M. House—had only sketchy and super-ficial knowledge of the actual problems existing in the Danube monarchy. In addition, they were also confronted with Austro-Hungarian diplomats who were locked into the thinking of nineteenth-century cabinet diplomacy and who continuously misinterpreted the power and politics of the United States; furthermore, they did not even master the English language.[104]

New economic, social, and military-political constellations, which were ignored by the Austro-Hungarian elites, led to the U.S. entry into the First World War in 1917 and to the October Revolution in Russia. Even though many did not see at that time that the classic age of European world leader-ship had become an anachronism, only the self-deceived among the defeated (German-)Austrian republic could not see the influence of the United States upon the defeated Central Powers, the destruction of the Danube monarchy, the peace treaties, and the economic future of the new republic. By the end of the First World War, Europe would bear the loss of ten million dead and twenty million wounded. The brutality and senselessness of the war led many people to wonder whether the repeatedly praised traditions of European high culture had not become obsolete, given the annihilation and mutilation of an entire generation. In addition to this moral crisis, which was also strengthened by the fear of a Communist revolution, the countries of Europe—winners and losers alike—faced the complete destruction of their economies, which could not be rebuilt by European efforts alone.

With Russia shaken by revolution, the civil war, and Polish and Allied interventions, only the United States came out of the First World War more powerful than ever. The United States could now assume the role of the "neutral" arbitrator, whose strongest argument was a not-yet-formulated fifteenth point of Wilson's program: the open door for the dollar. Within the next decade, Europeans repeatedly experienced the phenomenon of their nations' catching pneumonia when Wall Street only coughed.

The principle of national self-determination, which President Wilson had suggested as the solution to Europe's nationality conflicts, was more than ineffective—not only in the Austrian case. This was a result not only of U.S. consideration of Allied interests and the voting trends of hyphenated Americans but also of the complex ethnic situation in the areas that came into question. Anyway, in the areas of the Yugoslavian-Austrian and Austrian-Hungarian borders, the active negotiations and insisting upon plebiscites by the U.S. expert commissions would become more influential than local border clashes, which were stylized as heroic German defensive battles.[105]

Together with Italian, French, British, and Japanese members of the Allied commission, U.S. representatives controlled the disarmament of the Austrian military. The power to meet the great, immediate physical needs, however, could be fulfilled only by the United States. It alone now controlled the accessible world reserves of foodstuffs. Yet, the substantial American foodstuff deliveries served more than just humanitarian purposes. They were also used for stabilizing the political situation as well as for fighting against social revolutions that potentially threatened American economic interests. The American Relief Administration European Children's Fund not only saved countless children from hunger but also organized supplies for the White Army in Russia. Political conformity in the U.S. sense also swayed the Austrian Social Democrats to adopt Wilson's antibolshevist course by using the threat of discontinuing foodstuff deliveries.[106] Under Herbert Hoover's leadership, the American Relief Administration not only insisted upon implementing modern capitalist economic relations but also propagated the American way of life as the patented recipe for solving social, economic, national, and political conflicts. The governments of Czechoslovakia, Poland, Yugoslavia, and Austria actually hired technical advisers from the United States who were officially completely independent, yet unofficially worked closely with Hoover. The role of these advisers for the resuscitation of the capitalist economies in the respective countries was much more significant than their legally unresolved position suggested. Between 1919 and 1923, William B. Causey saw to it that striking workers in Austria understood that the continuation of work conflicts would lead to the immediate cutoff of foodstuff supplies. He not only advised Austrian government and business leaders about questions of industrial modernization but also was officially an *Austrian* delegate in the conferences of Portorose in 1921 and Geneva in 1922. Commissioned by U.S. businesses, Causey naturally collected information on the possibilities of investment, especially in the areas of mineral resources and communication, and was quite actively involved in the acquisition of desperately needed loans. These expensive loans, organized by British and American banks (particularly J. P. Morgan and Company), meant extremely deflationary, antisocial economic policies, layoffs, and reductions in pay. The commissioner of the League of Nations, Alfred Zimmermann, acted in actuality as the governor of banks in order to control the implementation of the stringent measures and asserted himself particularly in the fight against the social measures of Red Vienna.[107]

At the same time, J. P. Morgan, the European Mortgage & Investment Corp. (Boston), and the American, British & Continental Trust purchased major shares of the Allgemeine Österreichische Boden-Credit Anstalt. Similarly, W. A. Harriman, in New York, through the Niederösterreichische Escompte-Gesellschaft und Hallgarten & Co. together with E. F. Hutton & Co., New York, purchased shares of the Wiener Bankverein and the Bank & Wechselstuben-Actien-Gesellschaft "Merkur."[108] In addition, the Anglo-International Bank; the New York International Acceptance Bank; Kuhn, Loeb and Co.; and the Guarantee Trust Company of New York invested in the Credit-Anstalt. The latter two banks alone had purchased 125,000 shares of stock, and of the twenty-two foreigners on Credit-Anstalt's board of directors (fifty-one members in total), one now was an American.[109] They controlled not only important parts of Austrian industries but also factories in Poland, Hungary, Yugoslavia, and Czechoslovakia. Direct U.S. investments in Austria were relatively limited in comparison to those in Germany, Great Britain, and France. Two-thirds of all worldwide foreign investments originated from the United States in the 1920s. But in Austria the portion of the volume of U.S. investments hardly changed and was still only a bit more than 1 percent of total U.S. investments in all of Europe. Nevertheless, the Austrian economy and politics became more dependent upon the United States than at any time previous. Even a small newspaper announcement from the Midwest could disturb Austria's monetary stability. When the *Chicago Tribune* announced on July 22, 1921, that the release of liens on Austrian property would be delayed by Congress for months, the value of the crown to the dollar sank from 841:1 to 958:1 in one day. While the

Austrians streamed into the Kosmos Theater to see Charlie Chaplin and Clara Bow, Mary Pickford and Douglas Fairbanks, and as the first jazz band from America played in the Kaisergarten in Vienna's Prater, the value of the Austrian currency continued to sink. In August 1922, the happy owners of one dollar would receive 83,600 crowns.[110] The new Austrian currency perhaps had a British name model, but the deflationary politics soon turned the schilling into the Alpine dollar. It would, however, still take some time before an Austrian *Bankier* would become a *Banker*.

During the interwar period, the Viennese as well as particularly those Austrians living in tourist areas had direct contact with business people, speculators, and tourists from America who wanted to consume high culture at low prices. Goods and aid from the United States and especially radio and film brought the message of overflowing wealth in the United States. Jazz, the flapper, Rudolph Valentino and Charles Lindbergh, the Charleston and the quickstep, but also Sacco and Vanzetti and Black Friday, were well known even in the most remote areas. The U.S. film industry ruled the Austrian film market to the extent that Austrian filmmakers finally took to the streets for an increase in import quotas in the mid-1920s.

The America images of the Austrian elites were thoroughly ambivalent in the interwar period and reflected—through all shades of the ideological spectrum—the European, and especially German, discussion. Here, the stock market crash of 1929 and the collapse of the Credit Anstalt Bank in 1931 created a certain fatigue with America. While U.S. dynamics and efficiency were still enviously admired, it was precisely the supposedly typical economic competence and the "business chutzpa of the Yankees" which also became exceptional points of attack. According to one's ideological standpoint, the United States seemed like either the central switchboard of the class enemy or the avant-garde of the international den of iniquity that was responsible for the softening and decomposing of traditional morals and values. Even when an Austrian left-wing intellectual such as Ernst Fischer asserted that U.S. capitalism had grown into the realms of the absurd, he still was amazed by the vitality and independence of the creations of the "wonderfully traditionless" U.S. culture and saw himself caught between the spirit of Americanism ("the will of the drunkenness of anarchist life") and the spirit of Communism ("the will of the collective formation of life"). "The electrically illuminated barbarism lets us suppose the possibility of culture," wrote Fischer in the *Arbeiter Zeitung* in 1928, and, "one must read the young Russians and the young Americans in order to see one's own life in the mirror."[111] Ernst Fischer also coined a literary type in 1931 that culminated ten years later in Bertolt Brecht's *Arturo Ui*. Here, in a trial after the Pfriemer coup attempt, Fischer commented on the behavior of a *Heimwehr* leader: "Every inch a Styrian Al Capone or Jack Diamond."[112]

The fascination that organized crime in the United States had upon many Austrians could not obscure the fact that the threats for Austrian democracy and independence in the 1930s did not arise from Al Capone and Jack Diamond. Instead, they originated much more accurately from another type of organized crime that had established itself both to the south and north of Austria and found more and more supporters in Austria. Did not Adolf Hitler solve the problem of unemployment better than Franklin Delano Roosevelt's New Deal? Did not the Germans prove that a mixture of total armament and other infringements upon the peace treaty of Versailles, of aggressive politics and peace rhetoric, could achieve more than the persistence on civilized forms of political behavior? The larger the number of fascism's supporters grew, the stronger the attraction of this supposed synthesis of Joseph Stalin and Henry Ford, this mixture of collective forced labor and power through happiness, of autobahns and dreams of Volkswagens, the more the positive image of the United States faded.

The American dream had lost much of its shine and attractiveness as a result of the world economic crisis and mass unemployment. The seeming weakness of U.S. foreign policy also contributed to this loss of image. All of the politically responsible in Vienna and Berlin knew that the Roosevelt government supported the independence of Austria in theory but would never have the will or be in the position to come to the aid of Austria as a result of a German attack. The actual Anschluss, then, was laconically accepted by Washington. Austria's future played only a secondary role in America's postwar planning. Indeed, the United States virtually had to be forced by the Allies, especially the Soviets, to declare itself willing to participate in the occupation of Austria during the last years of the war.[113] After 1938, and particularly after the French campaign in 1940, the United States offered asylum for ten thousand Austrians who were attempting to escape the political terror of National Socialism through flight and emigration. In Europe the Austrians, now Germans, were confronted with the extremely negative image of America in NS war propaganda until 1945. Only a minority of Austrians risked listening to the propaganda transmissions of the Allies; those who did not consider this information to be completely exaggerated learned more about the course of the war than about domestic developments in the United States.[114]

This war, which had been provoked by the "Third Reich," now brought an increasing number of Austrians in contact with the United States, a contact that had deadly consequences for many soldiers and civilian victims of air attacks. As U.S. troops marched into Austria in May 1945, they found hungry, demoralized, and disillusioned citizens to whom the well-fed, "cool" GIs—particularly the African-American soldiers—seemed like beings from another planet. Many Austrians were thankful for the first material aid and surely hoped for support against the Soviet occupation force in the eastern half of the country. In any event, the presence of U.S. troops led to an unusual reestablishment of the myth of the West: the western provinces occupied by the Western Allies consequently became *the Golden West* of Austria.

As soon as the U.S. occupation authorities presumed to accompany material aid with a cultural reorientation program, they were confronted with incomprehension. Not only former National Socialists and their families, who were the first to be affected by the strict denazification measures, but also many Austrians, who actually did feel that they had been liberated, were still convinced after the end of the Second World War that the United States was culturally inferior and had little to offer. Demoralization here, demoralization there, but all the desired wealth of the GIs—cigarettes, nylons, gasoline, chocolates, white bread—could certainly not hide the fact that these actually rather nice "boys" surely lacked education and manners. If someone were to be culturally reoriented, then it should quite certainly have been these uneducated louts who actually dared to put their feet up on tables. In 1945, many Austrians reacted similarly to Mr. Punch. As the news had spread across the globe that the United States wanted to civilize Japan in 1852, this well-known British cartoon character asked the question whether Brother Jonathan should not be civilized by the Japanese.[115]

Even in the moment of total defeat (or perhaps for this reason?), the majority of Austrians would not relinquish the deceptive impression that depicted the United States as culturally subordinate to Europe in general and—naturally— to Austria in particular. Even in renowned cultural journals, the United States was again depicted as "the nation of greed and success . . . the thundering America, the new world of inexperience."[116] According to Hermann Keyserling, the Zeitgeist of North America—the mechanical age—was already beginning to pale, and now the age of a deeper, European humanism was to be expected.[117] The age-old prejudices were difficult to combat in spite of the direct contacts between the Austrian population and the U.S. occupiers. Too many people agreed with the opinion of the American architect Frank Lloyd Wright, who once had asserted that the United States was the only nation on earth that had directly evolved from barbarism to decadence without ever becoming civilized in between.

The American occupation power, however, was well prepared for this situation. European prejudices against America were all too well known and were recognized as the decisive hindrance for the trouble-free implementation of U.S. interests. To counteract these images, U.S. Army experts and the Department of State developed a comprehensive concept for a cultural offensive that was to fight against the negative image of the United States as a soulless, exclusively materialistic nation. In certain areas—popular culture in particular—this cultural mission of the United States would supersede all expectations. In others, as we shall see, it was confronted with a dilemma whose resolution would prove to be much more difficult than any economic, military, or political measure of influence. Even if many Austrians still had to fetch water from the fountain or from the hallway, they felt superior to "U.S. bathroom culture." Not without reason did Warren Robbins, the former director of the U.S. Information Service in the Federal Republic of Germany, describe the central problem of U.S. cultural diplomacy after the Second World War with the following words: "Yes, America is a country of 50 million bathtubs, but with a humanist in every one!"[118]

# 2

## The Development of United States
## Cultural Foreign Policy

*From the Private and Informal Export of Culture to the
Institutionalization of Culture as a Means of Diplomacy*

Cultures are especially resistant to new patterns of thought, so much so that the
introduction of new ideas usually comes to resemble domestication rather than
assimilation.

    —Frank A. Ninkovich, *The Diplomacy of Ideas* (1981)

Americans are old hands at this sort of thing. . . . We spend half of our lives selling
one another, personally or through a vast system of media outlets, to buy this,
support that, believe her, forget him and accept them. These appeals are not
confined to ourselves. Ideologically we have never paid attention to the twelve
mile limit. We are always shipping our ideas overseas. . . . The fact is that many of
us feel a little Americanization wouldn't hurt the rest of the world. . . . Our
Heavens-to-Betsy protestations about not wanting to impose our ideas on the rest
of the world may convince us but our foreign critics know better.

    —Wilson Dizard, *The Strategy of Truth* (1965)

Every analysis of U.S. foreign policy must begin with the deep-seated
conviction held by the American people that the United States, in all its dealings with other nations, has a special destiny, a particular mission. This belief
distinguishes the United States from all other countries in the world.[1] The
assumption of the worldwide relevance of its social system and the resulting
missionary zeal—as exemplified in the doctrine of Manifest Destiny—were
already a cornerstone of U.S. foreign policy as the nation was founded.[2] Until
the outbreak of the Second World War, however, U.S. diplomacy toward Europe was wrapped in a rhetorical veil of terms such as "isolationism" and
"neutrality," "disinterest" and "nonintervention." These set phrases, which
were already rather unconvincing in the realm of "classic" U.S. power politics
(e.g., in Latin America, the Caribbean, the Pacific, and East Asia), were utterly
irrelevant, especially in the areas of exporting U.S. goods and direct investments at least by the late nineteenth century. This is particularly true in the
field of exporting ideas, especially in the projection of the United States as the

guiding light of freedom for all of humankind. An ideological twelve-mile limit has not been an issue for the United States since the days of Benjamin Franklin.

U.S. cultural exports were not centrally controlled by the government in Washington, D.C., until 1938. A bureaucratically directed cultural diplomacy was most strongly rejected by the representatives of universal internationalism. State interventionism in cultural matters strongly contradicted liberal theories of modernizing and thereby saving the world through private initiative—needless to say, private U.S. initiative. In contrast to the centrally directed cultural initiatives of European states, the cultural internationalists of the United States relied upon the private and voluntary efforts of the new professional and business elites. Only the total freedom of these elites to do business as they chose in "backward" foreign countries—such was the internationalist credo—could guarantee the international modernization based on the U.S. example. The main enemies of international progress were identified as nationalism and ethnocentrism. The internationalists believed that these anti-modernistic evil tendencies could be exterminated through scientific planning and management. Paradoxically, these apostles of modernity did not recognize that the ideology of Western rationality itself offered only nationalist and ethnocentric models. Because made-in-America liberal universalism always fought against local traditions, we can speak here of *anticultural relationships*.[3]

The only exception to this private credo had been the Committee on Public Information, founded in 1917 to coordinate U.S. propaganda during the First World War. Although certain specific measures of this government agency, such as the indirect control of the motion picture market, were significant in later developments, its interventions were limited to a period of just two years. U.S. foreign cultural relations, then, from religious missions to the secularized forms of mission represented by the endowments of large corporations, remained for the most part in the domain of "private" initiative until the Second World War.

This lack of an official cultural export itself became the greatest advantage for the projection of U.S. values abroad because the very absence of governmental intervention seemed to document the victory of individualism. U.S. businessmen, investors, missionaries, doctors, philanthropists, tourists, and corporate foundations brought with them far more than just goods, capital, different forms of the Christian religion, modern medicine, aid, and the latest scientific discoveries. Quite consciously, they exported the social system of the United States—had this not made the other activities possible in the first place?—and thereby also the consumer needs of the United States. The "backward" societies, according to this, need only accept and imitate the blessings of U.S. capitalism. The modernization resulting therefrom—a by-product, as it were, of the subsiding of poverty, sickness, and illiteracy—would guarantee the abolition of social and political conflicts. Societal contradictions should be eliminated through "rational" modernization, or, in other words, through the *pursuit of happiness* as *the pursuit of consumption*. The thin line between universalistic altruism and national egotism shows itself especially in the modernization attempts of the United States in the Far East, especially in China, and in Latin America.[4] As soon as the door for new ideas was opened, it also remained open for American goods. And these goods were accompanied, in turn, by new ideas and demands for ever more American goods.

The International Health Board and the International Health Division, founded by the Rockefeller Foundation in 1913 and 1927, respectively, without question experienced tremendous successes in fighting epidemics in over fifty countries. In addition, they were influential in the development of health care, medical education, and the importation of medical apparatus and medicines. The philanthropic overseas activities of large U.S. corporate foundations, whose management was closely tied to political decision makers, clearly showed the close interconnection between "private" cultural export and the "national" interest of the United States. Under such circumstances, a cultural export offensive controlled by the state had hardly been necessary at all. The long-lasting efforts of the Rockefeller Foundation to initiate the modernization of China through the transplantation of "scientific rationality" toward a liberal capitalistic system shows that "despite its fixation on the scientific ideal, the Rockefeller strategy was guided less by objectivity than by what modern social science, somewhat belatedly, has come to recognize as an ethnocentrically distorted vision of the modernization process."[5]

While the foundations' early programs had been directed primarily toward the foreign elite, the end of the First World War brought completely new circumstances for the cultural exports of the United States. The continually growing influence of the U.S. economy ran parallel to the augmentation of the United States' dominating position in the area of mass communication. This ruling position in the sector of the consciousness industry logically led to the further expansion of the market for U.S. goods and ideas.

Control of the channels of information and of the hegemony of knowledge has always been a prerequisite for political power. It is no coincidence that the world-power status of the United States began at the moment in which it became technically possible to produce and distribute hardware and software of the modern means of communication globally. As a result of European economic problems after 1918, the United States maintained the most advantageous starting point and could secure the most important markets for itself.

The term "isolationism," which characterized U.S. foreign policy during the interwar period, actually conceals the true context. In fact, the economic expansion of the United States—whether in the export of goods, direct investments, or the financing of loans and reparations—was all but isolationist. Until the First World War, French and British news agencies had controlled the South American and Asian markets, and the French motion picture was the primary rival of U.S. productions in American theaters. The economic weakening of Europe after 1918 enabled U.S. corporations to break European monopolies in cable communications and in news gathering agencies, thus securing its dominating position in radio, film, electric products, and the aviation industry.

All-American Cables had already broken the British monopoly in South America as early as 1919. This company was then purchased by International Telephone and Telegraph in 1929, and ITT in turn controlled large portions of the European telephone market. In 1919 General Electric, American Telephone and Telegraph, Western Electric, and the United Fruit Company together founded the Radio Corporation of America, which dominated the development of international radio communications and cooperated closely with the U.S. military. Associated Press significantly weakened its British rival Reuters in Japan in 1927 and also was able to bind to itself the Japanese news agency Kokusai. In the late 1920s United Press International and AP finally broke the regional monopolies of the European agencies Reuters, Havas, and Wolff and thereby established a worldwide news empire. Supported by its leading position in production, distribution, and technical monopolies in the audio-film sector, Hollywood succeeded in weakening the European motion picture industry. In 1927, Pan-American Airways began to spread its mighty wings, secured by exclusive government contracts. Washington supported all of these developments actively and created the legal and political prerequisites for the growth of a global U.S. system of communication. Without a doubt, corporate and state interests were identical in this area. The massive encouragement of Washington transformed these companies into the chosen instruments for the continuation of politics through other means. Emily Rosenberg characterized these corporations quite accurately as quasi-official representatives of national interests abroad. U.S. businessmen and politicians clearly recognized that "American trade and investment seemed to increase or decline along with the expansion and contraction of its communication and culture. If American values were to uplift the world, then, so it seemed, must its capital and its products; and if its goods and capital were to circulate freely, so must American ideas."[6] Already the communication systems of the early modern period had served trading companies and banks with information. Equally, the development of a worldwide information system by U.S. corporations was of similar economic importance in the twentieth century. In addition, the dominant position in the global news market played yet another, even more significant (cultural) political role: because news is by no means value-free information, it itself becomes a major carrier of propaganda.[7]

Even more important, the U.S. culture industry now had the unprecedented opportunity to reach the foreign masses directly. The significance of the consciousness industry's products in conquering the hearts and minds of the public is still underestimated. Only a few critics rise above judgments of aesthetic disdain and evidence of their own arrogance. In 1901, though, John A. Hobson, in his study *The Psychology of Jingoism*, had emphasized that music halls most likely had a greater influence upon public opinion than political debates, churches, and schools combined. The stereotypical propagation of British imperialism in the nostalgic idealized products of mass culture—the term "jingoism," used to characterize the aggressive chauvinism of the British lower classes, itself had originated from a music hall song—aided the ruling classes "to dress economic benefits in idealistic garb, substituting moral crusade for mercenary motive, romance and adventure for political and military aggression."[8] As we know, this strategy did not limit itself only to Great Britain.

## The Development of U.S. Cultural Diplomacy since 1938

After the U.S. information and entertainment networks had achieved worldwide predominance in the 1920s, this expansion became seriously hindered by the developments of the 1930s, especially by the establishment of the "Third Reich," the spreading of (semi)fascist systems in Europe, and the aggressive foreign policy of Japan. During the second half of the 1930s, the propaganda of the Axis powers, but also the influence of socialist ideas, become ever more noticeable in Latin America. For this reason, the informal foreign cultural contacts of the United States no longer seemed sufficient in representing its interests by the eve of the Second World War. In 1938 the U.S. government therefore decided to initiate a cultural offensive and established the Division of Cultural Affairs in the Department of State to coordinate all activities. The other great powers as well as the smaller states had already given their cultural offensives official character. The Alliance Française, the German foreign schools, and the Italian Dante Alighieri Society had already been established prior to the First World War. The Soviet Society for Cultural Relations with Foreign Nations was founded in 1925. In 1934 Czechoslovakia and Switzerland established their official cultural diplomacy programs, as well as Japan with its Society for the Enhancement of International Cultural Relations and Great Britain with the British Committee for Relations with Other Countries, the forerunner of the British Council. The new technical developments to propagate positive and negative images significantly changed the possibilities of cultural self-representation, not only abroad, but also within one's own country. These new means of mass communication created the material basis for a completely new form of diplomacy as the British Foreign Secretary, Anthony Eden, realized in 1937: "It is perfectly true, of course, that good cultural propaganda cannot remedy the damage done by a bad foreign policy, but it is no exaggeration to say that even the best of diplomatic policies may fail, if it neglects the task of interpretation and persuasion which modern conditions impose."[9]

For U.S. cultural diplomacy Latin America became the laboratory for the development of techniques to influence foreign cultures. When Nelson Rockefeller was appointed director of the Office of the Coordinator for Inter-American Affairs in 1940, a certain shyness toward the total bureaucratization of cultural export programs still existed. Yet, his appointment also proved the connection with the private programs of corporate foundations. All possibilities of cultural propaganda that were eventually implemented after the Second World War, from the exchange of scholars and artists to the direct manipulation of the media, were initially tested in Central and South America. Among other measures, Hollywood was pressured to produce motion pictures with Latin American themes and even film new sequences for those films that had stereotypically portrayed Latin Americans as greasy criminals and dirty lazybones. Even Donald Duck was called to the cartoon front in the national interest. To gain sympathy, the Disney Studios produced the film *Saludos Amigos*, in which poor old Gringo Donald was constantly led up the garden path by a Brazilian parrot.

Although Latin American programs officially fell under the heading of rolling back fascist elements, they were also directed toward Communist and socialist tendencies. In addition, these initiatives also had an anti-European undertone, hence "the choice was thus not pro-Nazi or anti-Nazi it was pro-America versus pro-Europe."[10] The available funds for U.S. propaganda in Latin America were just $3.5 million in 1940, but they jumped quickly to $38 million by 1942. This program was expanded to such a great extent by the end of World War II that even the Department of State would refer to it as the largest propaganda campaign of all times.[11]

In light of the massive propaganda efforts of the United States after the beginning of the war against Japan, the "Third Reich," and their European allies, this assessment can be qualified only as an extreme exaggeration. As with the armaments industry, so the seemingly endless resources of the United States—from its Ivy League universities to Hollywood, from opera singers to Tin Pan Alley, from Coca-Cola to Wrigley's chewing gum—were all centrally directed by government agencies. Most important, these initiatives were implemented not only to undermine the fighting spirit of the enemies but also to lift national morale on the home front. In comparison to the U.S. propaganda in the European, Asian, and African war zones between 1941 and 1945, the activities of the Division of Cultural Affairs and the Office of Inter-American Affairs, both founded in 1938, were harmless finger exercises on the propaganda keyboard.

The Office of Facts and Figures was founded in October 1941, only to be incorporated in the Office of War Information in 1942. The Advisory Committee on Cultural Relations and the Liaison Committee on International Education were established in 1942 and 1943, respectively. In addition, the first official cultural relations attaché was appointed in 1943. In 1944 the Division of Cultural Relations was renamed the Division of Science, Education, and Art; also then the Office of Public Information was founded. After the end of the Second World War the agendas of the Office of War Information, the Office of Inter-American Affairs, and the Office of Public Information were pulled together to form the Interim Information Service of the Department of State, which became the Office of International Information and Cultural Affairs in 1946. Since the beginning of the 1950s, the cultural exchange and information programs of the United States have been coordinated by the United States Information Agency (USIA).[12]

Obviously, in the countries that were either completely or partially occupied by the U.S. Army—Japan, South Korea, Germany, and Austria—the U.S. military authorities had a tremendous cultural influence during the postwar years. The culture sections of the U.S. Army were controlled and coordinated by the New York field office of the Civil Affairs Division of the Department of War. These cultural control efforts of the army were then slowly taken over by the Department of State in 1949/50. In addition, the ever-increasing cultural activities of the CIA must also be taken into account.

The U.S. government played yet another significant role in the controlling and guiding of philanthropic and economic relief actions during and after the Second World War, and its influence upon the material culture of the recipient countries has been severely underestimated. These centrally orchestrated actions reached their final culmination in the creation of the Marshall Plan and the Food for Peace Program. The Committee on War Relief Board was already established in 1941 and soon became transformed into the Relief Control Board after the Japanese attack on Pearl Harbor. The Office of Foreign Relief and Rehabilitation Operation followed in 1942, as did the United Nations Relief and Rehabilitation Administration in 1943. Based on the Private Council of Voluntary Aid of 1944 and the Advisory Committee on Voluntary Foreign Aid of 1945, the particularly significant CARE program was established in 1946, whose relief efforts did more than just relieve the extreme need in many European countries. Together with the seemingly endless abundance of goods as flaunted by U.S. GIs, these relief packages in a starving Europe became equated with an overflowing shop window, which displayed the overwhelming achievements of the American economic system. After 1945, philanthropic relief and U.S. foreign policy goals became synonymous.[13]

The concentration of the various cultural contacts abroad, the politics of information, and the propaganda of central government organizations since 1938 did not receive unanimous support in U.S. public opinion; too great was the contradiction with previous practice. Profuse bureaucratic growth, particularly in the area of culture, was simply incongruous with the beliefs of many American citizens. When the Office of Facts and Figures was founded in 1941, the *New York Herald Tribune* in a cover story quickly dubbed it the Office of Fun and Frolic, suggesting that it would not be capable of anything else but "to superimpose its own 'well organized facts' upon the splendid confusion, interpret the interpreters, redigest those who now digest the digesters, explain what those who explain what the explainers of the explanations mean, and co-ordinate the co-ordinators of those appointed to co-ordinate the co-ordination of the co-ordinated."[14]

Only the first propaganda successes during the Second World War—within and without the United States—gradually silenced the critics. And the results were quite staggering. The Office of War Information (OWI) alone spread more than three billion fliers between the landing in Normandy on June 6, 1944, and the end of the war in Europe on May 8, 1945. In addition, by the end of 1944 the OWI already controlled radio stations in London, Tunis, Palermo, and Bari and, most important, Radio Luxembourg, the second strongest transmitter in all of Europe.[15] Even the liberal, internationalist culture experts who repeatedly pushed universalistic, open foreign cultural relations as well as the implementation of "slow media" (education, science, high culture, and especially reciprocity) were slowly taken over by the inherent logic of bureaucratic centralization, which unavoidably subordinated the cultural programs to basic U.S. foreign policy goals.[16]

With their strategy of "fast media" (advertisements through radio, films, and news of all kinds), the Madison Avenue methods promised more than just short-term success. Even more important, the hard-hitting propaganda messages, transmitted via the channels of mass media—the contemporary euphemism being "information"—could, in addition, be portrayed as more "democratic." The traditional programs of the liberal internationalists, whose universalism was essentially based upon an ethnocentric belief that the world should improve according to the American model, had supposedly adhered to highly undemocratic means by addressing only foreign elites. The new Madison Avenue guard, in contrast, wagered upon the attractiveness of the messages of U.S. popular culture, which could easily be spread over the channels of the media networks. Even if the elites raised their brows, this new commercial-through-commercial style created the opportunity to reach the largest possible number of people quickly and directly. In addition, the new strategy had the advantage that it could be unilaterally disseminated. It should not come as a surprise that the concept of the "means of mass communication" is quite simply misleading. Those who control the means of production and distribution can themselves actually communicate with the masses, but the masses do not have the opportunity to communicate with the producers. Within the system of mass communication, the masses thus do not actually communicate. In spite of all objections, U.S. information experts knew, in any event, that the new methods of cultural propaganda "quite simply, gave more bang for the buck than 'culture.' "[17]

Without a doubt, the popular culture of the United States is in this sense "democratic": it elicits a seemingly irresistible attraction for many people above and beyond class barriers and national boundaries. Yet, the frequent artificiality of its products and the horizontal and vertical control of the means of production as well as the concentration of the channels of distribution in few hands exemplify its "undemocratic" nature. This contradiction also characterizes the politics of culture of the United States since the Second World War. U.S. popular culture, then, based on its approval by the masses, could be interpreted as revolutionary, while, at the same time, "by its ritualistic, escapist, and standardized nature, it could also prove profoundly conservative."[18]

The cultural diplomacy of the United States, with its concept of "peoples speaking to peoples," stood completely in the liberal tradition of the four fundamental human freedoms proclaimed by President Roosevelt on January 6, 1941: freedom of opinion, freedom of religion, freedom from want, and freedom from fear. However, Emily Rosenberg has pointed out that the insistence on a completely free flow of information, cited as a fifth fundamental freedom, touched upon an insoluble dilemma. While the United States controlled the networks that made possible the contacts to other nations, these societies had no chance to respond. "The liberal idea of free flow, like that of the economic open door, logically led not to a wide-open market full of varied and competing products but to dominance by the most technologically advanced producers."[19] For exactly this reason the "peoples speaking to peoples" concept quickly acquired the character of "the United States speaking to peoples" programs, which, for the most part, were conceived to fulfill two primary duties. The interests of the U.S. government were to be brought home, first and foremost, by bombarding foreigners with never-ending information broadcasts using all conceivable channels. U.S. culture was always only of secondary importance, even if the rules called for its total representation.[20] Without a doubt, the United States has achieved great victories in both areas since 1945. Yet, the successes in the domain of fast media dominate. Still, U.S. experts were under no illusions when internal discussions turned to the goals of this "information"—or, in plain English, propaganda. They knew quite frankly that the difference between information and propaganda "is largely verbal; but the connotations of 'information' are more palatable to Americans."[21]

Regardless of how foreign cultural programs were defined—as cultural relations, as cultural exchange, as cultural cooperation, as communication of ideas, as public diplomacy, or as a fourth dimension of foreign policy—the ideological offensive of this war of words and images was almost always based upon a blend of political propaganda and cultural self-portrayal, of information *and* disinformation. The dominating position of the United States within the international communication network quite simply was not only politically advantageous, but it also had major cultural implications. Even more, the development of large U.S. civilian, secret service, and military intelligence networks after 1945 clearly showed that the era of a traditional "privately" organized foreign cultural policy was over. The gigantic (dis)information machine that was created after 1945 had one plain mission: to propagate a positive self-portrait of Uncle Sam. At its disposal were (and are) not only the most polished tricks of psychological warfare and advertising but also the latest technological achievements. Contemporary slogans—such as Strategy of Persuasion; Strategy of Truth: Selling the Story of America; Conquest of Spirits; Projection of America Abroad; U.S. Information, Please!; Propaganda Techniques and International Advertising; Commerce in Ideas; Battle of Ideas; War of Ideas; War of Words—clearly denote the warlike character and the political-economic background of these cultural programs. Contrary to public protestations about pursuing a strategy of truth and facts—that rather peculiar Hegelian-Hebrew deity, as Bertrand Russell dubbed it—U.S. information experts in confronting "Communism" placed all their bets on a strategy that, only slightly simplified, may be called dog(ma)-eat-dog(ma).[22]

This sophisticated style of propaganda was more successful with foreign audiences, especially with those Germans and Austrians who had grown more than weary of the propaganda efforts of the Nazis, which in retrospect seemed rather clumsy. It also improved the chances of budgetary approval in the Congress. For as the U.S. Army established its slick cultural-control authorities in their zones of occupation immediately following the Second World War, the future of the civil information machinery that had been set up during the war at first was unclear because of major resistance in Congress. Many congressmen still opposed the notion of government-controlled information programs during times of peace. While the liberals hoped to return to universalist principles, the conservatives especially feared the dominance of New Deal enthusiasts in the cultural programs. In addition, many conservative politicians, whose horizons frequently ended at the borders of their voting districts, were completely convinced that the United States served as a shining example throughout the whole world even without any commercial bustle. Only after the escalation of the Cold War did the Department of State manage to secure the funds that were supposedly needed to win the confrontation with the "Communists." The Smith-Mundt Act of 1947 finally assured the expansion of these programs.

This legislation had been particularly well prepared. Committee members of the Senate and House of Representatives had toured the countries of Western and Eastern Europe in the fall of 1947, being confronted on every hand with the seeming superiority of the Soviet propaganda machine. The political debates surrounding the Smith-Mundt Act clearly show that by 1947 the internationalists had become integrated into the domestic Cold War consensus. The ever-present fears of right-wing congressmen—that cultural diplomacy would be infiltrated by liberal New Dealers—now were defused by the increased attention given instead to its value in fighting Communism. Congressman Howard Smith was not alone in expressing satisfaction over the fact that the legislation would prevent any infiltration by long-haired Communists.[23]

The silent transformation of the style of U.S. cultural diplomacy is also particularly apparent in the selection of its director. The author and librarian of Congress Archibald MacLeish was replaced by William Benton as assistant secretary of state for public affairs in August 1945. Benton's background pre-destined him for the development of the fast media style. Not only had he been vice-president of the Board of Trustees of the University of Chicago for many years, but he also owned advertising agencies, film companies, commercial music publishing companies, and radio stations, the most important known as MUZAK. And Theodore Streiber, the newly appointed director of the USIA in August 1953, brought along significant experience to this organization—the quasi-cultural sector of the Marshall Plan—as the former president of the Mutual Broadcasting Company.[24]

The distribution of revenues appropriated for all foreign activities after World War II shows a preference for the funding of information (international broadcasting, motion pictures, press and publications) as opposed to "pure" cultural programs (educational exchange, libraries and institutions). In the period between 1947 to 1956 the budget exploded approximately 500 percent, with a 300 percent increase in personnel. Although monetary expenditures and personnel initially fell in 1948, their later growth was quite significant, as table 1 shows.

The short-term drop around 1954 reflects the influence of Senator Joseph McCarthy's anti-Communist campaign, which also shook up U.S. cultural diplomacy. The figures in table 1 reflect only the trends in civilian programs. The activities of the U.S. military and the secret services are not included here.

As we can see, the onset of the Cold War shifted the civilian propaganda machine into high gear. Exactly just this additional energy, fueling this continuously accelerating propaganda, in turn generated an even stronger escalation. The foreign cultural programs, which had run under the slogan "Full and fair picture" immediately after the Second World War, soon changed their character. In 1950, the Campaign of Truth was introduced, which institutionalized the tougher approach already apparent since 1947/48. It held its ground until the Great Society Program became the new byword in 1965. The United States might not yet have had the hydrogen bomb in 1950, but it certainly had a bombing propaganda. Dwight D. Eisenhower was not too far off the mark when he commented that the new propaganda line was the "T-Bomb of Truth."[25] One of the more delicate details of the means of financing this Program of Truth must be noted here. Although the U.S. Congress allotted an

TABLE 1. *Funding and Personnel for U.S. Foreign Cultural Programs, 1947–1956*

| Year | Budget (millions) | Personnel |
|------|-------------------|-----------|
| 1947 | $ 19 | 3,008 |
| 1948 | 14 | 1,728 |
| 1949 | 27 | 2,857 |
| 1950 | 37 | 3,834 |
| 1951 | 56 | 5,183 |
| 1952 | 115 | 7,945 |
| 1953 | 129 | 13,054 |
| 1954 | 90 | 10,011 |
| 1955 | 100 | 9,383 |
| 1956 | 110 | 10,038 |

*Source*: Bureau of the Budget, *The Budget of the United States*, 1949–53; Bureau of the Budget, *The Budget of the United States*, 1952 and 1953, 1954 and 1955.

additional $19.3 million for this propaganda offensive in 1950 alone, this was still less than half of the money needed. The rest had to be paid by the participants of the Marshall Plan program from their Counterpart Funds. More than 50 percent of the costs of this American propaganda, therefore, came *directly* from the taxes of those European states in which the United States intensified its propaganda—certainly an exceptional case of surrender of sovereignty.[26]

This raging confrontation with Communism did more than strengthen nationalistic tendencies of U.S. cultural diplomacy at the expense of universalist principles. The new international salesman style also often confused "democratic" culture with aesthetic popularism. More and more, intellectual freedom became associated only with the social system of the United States, and the (not very abundant) domestic critics were stamped with the label "anti-American" and sent, like lepers, into the solitude of domestic exile. "There could, American liberal-expansionists believed, be no truly enlightened dissent against the ultimate acceptance of American ways, and this faith bred an intolerance, a narrowness, that was the very opposite of liberty."[27] In a global setting, the propagation of made-in-America international liberalism more often than not produced exactly its antithesis: social and economic conservatism. This inherent dilemma of U.S. politics became particularly clear in its (non)relationship with UNESCO during the 1980s. The United States' problems with this cultural organization of the United Nations has a long tradition. The discontinuation of cooperation by the Reagan administration was, in a sense, only the last logical step. Already in 1946, the position of the Department of State toward UNESCO showed that the new foreign cultural bureaucracy had discarded international universalism. Instead, the new style was based upon an idealized nationalism "which successfully integrated the concepts of national interest, idealism, and anti-radicalism, while simultaneously identifying this outlook with international well-being."[28]

How could the United States most effectively promote its interests abroad? How could its ideas be best implanted in the minds of others? These questions now were answered quite openly: "Part of the answer lies in intelligent propaganda, much as one may dislike the word. The United States needs the best and subtlest propaganda to carry on the Cold War."[29] This best and most subtle propaganda also included, among others, the creation of a Jewish-Catholic-Lutheran advisory committee that prepared materials stressing the absolute incongruence of Communist ideology with the world's major religions. The American Creed was thereby identified with the Free World Creed; both stood in a secular confrontation with the Devil's Creed, or Communism.[30]

This Madison Avenue style, incorporating the newest scientific findings in sales psychology as well as the latest sales strategies of U.S. media companies and advertising agencies, was swiftly integrated into the political-cultural consensus of the Cold War. If business was a central component of U.S. culture—and, according to the American Creed, to suggest anything else would be un-American blasphemy—then the following argument becomes plausible: "Is it wrong to 'sell' the story of the United States abroad? Not unless all selling is wrong. Should we assume that all people have the intelligence to discover things which are right and good, without being pressured by someone else? Not unless we assume all persuasion is unnecessary."[31] Clearly, U.S. foreign cultural programs had become sucked into the vortex of an aggressive anti-Communist foreign policy "in which the rhetoric of idealism mashed the pursuit of power."[32] At this time, a division of labor had developed within the foreign cultural apparatus. Cultural diplomats, especially the cultural attachés, who often opposed the politics of hard information, implemented "pure" cultural programs; other officers, frequently operating through secret-service channels, concentrated on the hard-hitting propaganda issues.

The following passages taken from "Operating Assumptions" of the USIA show to what great extent U.S. cultural diplomacy became tossed around in the whirlpool of the Cold War and the extent to which it itself had become a tool of the psychological war. The role of America Houses and libraries abroad was stated as follows: "Our libraries have to be objective, but on the other hand, the very definition of our libraries is that they are special purpose libraries. The best we can hope to do is to achieve and maintain the illusion of objectivity. . . . Books must promote USIA objectives. . . . Information Centers are intended to support the interests of the American people, not to furnish recreational material."

A chapter pertaining to music states: "Music is a universal language which can surmount barriers of communication and enable people to identify more closely with the U.S. . . . Musical activity tends to be broad in its targeting. . . . Thus music—particularly jazz or popular music—may be viewed as bait to attract patronage to Information Centers. . . . Popular music makes friends for the U.S."

Yet, nothing came close to the power of the motion picture, which was understood to exert a more universal influence than any other medium:

The film program abroad helps not only American foreign policy or propaganda objectives, but also the American economy. This occurs in two ways: through direct cooperation between USIS and private American companies, and through stimulation of consumer interests by films which document the American style of life. . . . Films effectively convey information. . . . They are an excellent medium to use to expound foreign policy without the audience being aware of it. . . . Films are the best substitute for word of mouth persuasion. The purpose of USIA films is attitude formation, not information.[33]

The importance of the radio for the propaganda strategy of the United States was likewise quite pointedly portrayed: "Five minutes of propaganda with two hours of sugar-coating. Music is the vehicle rather then the end in itself. We wouldn't have more than five minutes of propaganda in one hour. It's like a commercially sponsored program here. Our commercial is our political commentary."[34] This hard-hitting marketing style, which blurred the borders between the promise of democracy and that of a detergent commercial, did not find unanimous support. Especially the cultural diplomats overseas recognized very well that "what sells soap in Indiana can unsell democracy in India."[35]

Even foreign audiences did not demonstrate an undivided enthusiasm. While the anti-Communist majorities in Europe, especially the elites, were extremely thankful for American economic and military support, which essentially guaranteed the continuity of social systems that had been extremely weakened, this gratefulness did not automatically extend to the area of "culture." Especially for the conservatives, the imitation encouraged of the American way of life potentially represented an invitation for cultural suicide. After the Second World War European civilization was confronted by an even more extreme crisis than it had faced in 1918, and "at such a moment we, who have made a business of business and, therefore, as they think, have no civilization, are pressing them to go and do likewise. The medicine is indeed potent; but it is worse than the disease."[36]

Not all European societies outside the power sphere of the Soviet Union were equally affected by these developments, even though similar influences were noticeable (at least eventually) almost everywhere. Not all states were under such massive influence as the Federal Republic of Germany—the mirror image, by the way, of the German Democratic Republic under the dominance of the USSR—whose predecessor, on the one hand, represented the most horrific result of the European crisis after the First World War and, on the other, suicidally initiated the latest collapse of European civilization.

The continuously repeated protestations regarding the necessity of the enormous propaganda efforts of the United States after the Second World War as being absolutely essential in saving at least Western Europe and other parts of the world from Communist aggression cannot be left unchallenged in light of research on the development of the Cold War. Challenges are in order with regard not only to the supposed aggressive military intentions of the government of the Soviet Union but also to the possibilities of its own propaganda efforts.[37] Surely there is no doubt that the government of the USSR attempted everything it could to convince those people living outside of its sphere of power of the truth of its position through the use of propaganda. However, at no point did the USSR possess the financial and technical potential to compete equally with the United States, let alone surpass it. The economic backwardness of the Soviet Union, not least the result of the incredible human and material losses caused by the military aggression of the "Third Reich," provided no material attraction for the vast majority of Europeans. Even more, the establishment of a counterworld, which had been developed in the USSR since 1917, failed to sway the anti-Communism of wide sectors of the populace. With the exception of some success in the export of classic Russian culture, the Soviet (cultural) propaganda saw itself confronted, then, with the insurmountable dilemma that, in paraphrasing Georg Schmid, it failed to present even the outlines of a viable cultural alternative.[38]

This all was well known to U.S. experts and others. A 1957 editorial in *Life* magazine posed a rather significant question. Would not the fact that, in addition to hundreds of thousands of GIs, approximately 580,000 U.S. civilians lived abroad, especially in Europe, have a positive effect on the goals of the United States, especially considering that less than 5,000 Soviet citizens residing outside of the Communist sphere of influence?[39] Even Frederick C. Barghoorn came to the conclusion in his classic work on the Soviet cultural offensive that the USSR was definitely at a disadvantage in any face-off with the United States. Even more, the influence of the Soviet Union "seems almost negligible by comparison, at least in numbers."[40] Secret analyses of Western European reactions toward Soviet propaganda activities, whose threatening effectiveness was always affirmed in public, showed that the differences were not just quantitative in nature. Especially in European countries, Soviet propaganda was confronted with a large anti-Communist public that was extremely skeptical and negatively disposed to these messages. The (cultural) propaganda of the USSR, then, to use the language of Madison Avenue, could hardly surmount the strong sales resistance toward its products.[41] The rather unsophisticated—not to say, malletlike—style of Soviet propaganda did not stand a chance against that of their opponents, who applied their knowledge of the newest advertising psychology and possessed the advantage of controlling the channels of global information distribution. Furthermore, American media—seemingly neutral and serving only the purposes of information and entertainment—also maintained a tremendous advantage in that their messages were not even recognized as propaganda. This formal independence of messages pertained not only to the products of mass media but also often to the official activities of U.S. cultural diplomacy. Its contents, nevertheless, were always measured by the degree of efficiency "to which the program advances the strategic policies of the United States."[42]

The ever-recurring warnings of the superiority of the Soviet propaganda machine did not reflect, therefore, the real power relationship between the United States and the USSR but instead were based on projections of fear and the necessity to justify one's own exaggerated propaganda apparatus. These "stop the thief" slogans had an apologetic function; at the same time, on both sides of the ideological divide, they were also a product as well as a result of a strategy of continuing the Cold War through other means.

The short-lived periods of détente hardly had an effect on the expenditures for the cultural and information programs of the United States. In 1970, USIA alone published 140 magazines with a circulation of 30 million copies. By 1978, the International Communication Agency had a budget of $413 million and employed 12,000 people in 111 countries. The 101 radio stations, including Voice of America, Radio Free Europe, and Radio Liberty, alone were allotted a budget of $85.5 million dollars in 1980. The 2,196 employees in the radio sector saw to it that an additional 4,000 other radio stations were provided with information and complete programs. Often reflecting rather optimistic estimates, official statistics have suggested that these radio programs reached approximately 80 million people daily in the countries of the Warsaw Pact alone. The following self-assessment leaves no doubt as to the power of Western radio stations: they definitely are "The Real Masters of the Black Heavens."[43]

The period of détente, then, by no means ended the ideological offensive via the airwaves and in printed materials, even though the rhetoric in the libraries and exhibits, lecture halls and theaters, lost some of its harshness. This restraint waned after the inauguration of President Ronald Reagan, whose newly appointed propaganda director, Charles Z. Wick, again proclaimed The War of Ideas. As a result, the budget of the USIA grew 74 percent to $796 million in the period between 1981 to 1985. In addition, Congress approved $1.3 billion alone for the modernization of the Voice of America in 1983. By 1985, USIA had 214 branches in 129 countries. It operated 135 libraries in 83 countries and 106 information centers that were managed in conjunction with the host nations. The implementation of a global satellite television coincided with the invasion of Grenada in October 1983. Since 1984, USIA Worldnet-TV has broadcast two to three hours daily, five days a week.[44] This step toward global television constituted, according to Vice-Director of Television Services

Richard C. Levy, the most important advancement for U.S. propaganda since the establishment of the Voice of America. Paradoxically, the new propaganda dimension also shows, however, the inherent problems of technical progress. There are perhaps no legal restrictions for U.S. propaganda overseas; there are, however, restrictions against propaganda within the United States. The juridical question still remains to be answered: Does the transmission of such television programs in the U.S. by USIA satellites violate—at least indirectly—those American laws that prohibit *any* propaganda broadcasts in the United States?[45]

This problem not only impacts official U.S. information politics outside the United States but without a doubt also affects those messages of the U.S. culture industry that are distributed as "infotainment" over global airwaves and that—in the truest sense of the word—cannot be overseen and overheard. While the criticism of "U.S. cultural imperialism," which unfortunately is mostly rather unsophisticated, could be denounced as crude anti-Americanism of Moscow's fellow travelers and useful idiots, American decision makers never doubted the fundamental political power of U.S. media and their promotion of U.S. interests on a worldwide scale. Already in the 1920s, the swaying power of radio, film, records, and other mass-produced goods was recognized as an effective means of propagating the American way of life. After 1945, significant discoveries, especially in the area of electronics, can be seen as yet another twist in the propaganda-information-entertainment spiral. A report published by the Foreign Relations Committee of the House of Representatives, entitled *Winning the Cold War: The U.S. Ideological Offensive*, already summarized these qualitative leaps effectively in 1964:

> For many years military and economic power, used separately, or in conjunction, have served as the pillars of diplomacy. They still serve that function today but the recent increase in influence of the masses of the people over governments, together with greater awareness on the part of the leaders of the aspirations of people, brought about by the concurrent revolutions of the 20th century, has created a new dimension of foreign policy operation. Certain foreign policy objectives can be pursued by dealing directly with the people of foreign countries, rather than with their governments. Through the use of modern instruments and techniques of communications it is possible today to reach large or influential segments of national populations—to inform them, to influence their attitudes, and at times perhaps even to motivate them to a particular course of action. These groups, in turn, are capable of exerting noticeable, even decisive, pressures on their governments.[46]

Since 1964 these developments have rapidly increased their speed, and the self-portrayal of the United States has been hindered by only one border—that of technology. In the sensitive area of propaganda and (dis)information, this study runs into one other boundary: that of verification. We are dealing not only with the official self-portrayal of the U.S. government and the media but also with the activities of the secret service, whose important role in many ways can only be hinted at. These secret activities are carried out not only by the CIA and the military secret-service organizations but also by the National Security Agency, whose 200,000 employees outnumber those of the CIA tenfold. As is the case with other secret services, documentation is exceptionally insufficient and diffuse. In any event, their activities should not be underestimated.[47]

During the hot phase of the Cold War, the CIA supported in particular the anti-Communist stance of the Social Democratic parties in Europe. In Austria, under the guise of the trade unions AFL and CIO, the CIA promoted, among others, the Österreichischen Wander-, Sport- und Geselligkeitsverein (Austrian hiking, sport, and conviviality union) under the leadership of Franz Olah, which trained young trade union members in fighting, shooting, and setting up explosive devices and also had access to a secret network of radio stations throughout the entire country. Even the magazine *Forum* was supported by the CIA via the Congress for Cultural Freedom. It probably is no coincidence that the news agency of the congress was called Forum World Features until 1975.

At the founding meeting of the Congress for Cultural Freedom in Berlin in 1950, Austria was represented, among others, by Peter Strasser, head of the Socialist Youth Organization; Felix Hubalek, deputy editor of the *Arbeiter Zeitung*; and journalist and publisher Fritz Molden. Oscar Pollak, editor-in-chief of the *Arbeiter Zeitung*, was elected to the congress's International Committee. The establishment of the Allgemeinen Jugendwerk-Gesellschaft für Freiheit der Kultur (General youth association for the freedom of culture) was closely tied to the congress and was represented by Peter Strasser in Vienna. Its purpose was to oppose all totalitarian movements, and its chairing board included Christine Busta, Milo Dor, Reinhard Federmann, Alexander Giese, Leopold Gratz, Peter Jankowitsch, Wieland Schmid, and Peter Strasser. Hans Weigel's literature anthology *Stimmen der Zeit* was published because of the encouragement of the Gesellschaft für Freiheit und Kultur (Society for freedom and culture), which also founded the Schriften zur Zeit publishing house. In January 1954, this firm started to publish the well-known intellectual-political journal *Forum*.[48] In addition to the Austrian *Forum*, the CIA financed the British magazines *Encounter* and *New Leader*, the French *Preuves*, the Spanish *Cuadernos*, the Italian *Tempo Presente*, and the *Partisan Review* in the United States. The European International Union of Socialist Youths was also sponsored by the CIA until 1967, as was the International Association of Free Trade Unions.[49]

Even if we may sometimes be tempted to question the intelligence of the Central Intelligence Agency, it definitely surpassed that of many European voters of the postwar period, at least in one point. It was the CIA that saw through the hollowness of the ever-surfacing accusations contained in conservative party platforms that depicted the Socialists as merely a front organization of Communism. Thanks to their militant anti-Communist stance, the

Social Democratic parties—often without the knowledge of their leading politicians—could almost be considered allies of the CIA.[50]

However, not only the European public was fooled. At least until the mid-1970s, the CIA delivered (dis)information through the media giants ABC, NBC, AP, UPI, Hearst, *New York Times*, *New York Herald Tribune*, and Time-Life as well as the British agency Reuters, the Spanish EFEC, and the Chilean Latin. Highly acclaimed institutions, such as the Asian Foundation and the Center for International Studies of the Massachusetts Institute of Technology, were founded by the CIA. Between 1947 and 1967 alone more than a thousand "scientific" books were written and published on behalf of the CIA. At least until 1971, Radio Free Europe, Radio Liberty, Voice of America, and RIAS-Berlin were in part financed by the CIA. Although the political influence of these radio stations has been documented, for example, in the uprisings in the German Democratic Republic in 1953, in Hungary in 1956, and in Czechoslovakia in 1968, we are still lacking studies that analyze the cultural impact of these stations, for example, as a result of their continuous airing of the newest U.S. pop music hits.[51]

One of the most famous deceptions spread worldwide was the manipulation of Nikita Khrushchev's speech at the Twentieth Communist Party Congress; one of the most unappetizing exposés surely must have been the pornographic film that defamed Indonesia's President Sukarno; among the most absurd was the support of Colonel Muammar Gadafi during his climb to power in Libya in 1969.[52] According to conservative estimates, the CIA spent $1 billion for propaganda alone between 1948 and 1974. The logic of this aspect of secret-service activity may be illustrated by a small act, in itself insignificant. During the 1950s, the CIA held thousands of subscriptions to the New York Communist party newspaper *Daily Worker*. Thus, by pointing to the tremendous, yet artificial, increase in circulation numbers, the CIA was able to give the impression that Communism was indeed a real threat to the United States.[53]

When dealing with modern state systems (I emphasize: not only in capitalistic countries), we are confronting propaganda machines that see their system as the one and only solution for crises, which, more often than not, they themselves have actually created. In his study on the Congress for Cultural Freedom, Christopher Lasch demonstrated that the militant anti-Communism of the Cold War, with its dogmatic rejection of historical materialism, projected only a distorted mirror image, which was characterized by exactly the illiberality of which they accused their ideological opponents. This successful strategy is based, on the one hand, upon the identification of absolute intellectual values with the class interests of intellectuals and, on the other, upon the confusion of freedom with the interests of the United States. Therefore, this propaganda strategy required "the cooperation of writers, teachers, and artists not as paid propagandists or state-censored time-servers but as 'free' intellectuals capable of policing their own jurisdiction and of enforcing acceptable standards of responsibility within the various intellectual professions."[54] The English historian Hugh Trevor-Roper summarized his observations of the first conference of the Congress for Cultural Freedom in Berlin in 1950 quite pointedly. According to him, a new alliance had manifested itself in Berlin consisting of the former Communists among the delegation and the German nationalists present in the audience.[55] This Western intellectual alliance was nourished by the amalgamation of the traditional anti-Communism of the conservatives with the new missionary zeal of the former Communist converts. Only this new alliance effectively brought about a change in the position of the Social Democrats, especially in the Federal Republic of Germany, who now accepted rearmament. This, then, became one of the most important prerequisites for a further twist in the weapons spiral.[56]

Developments within the Soviet Union and in the satellite countries, without a doubt, gave enough serious reasons for opposition. Still, proponents of "Western pluralism" quite simply failed to understand the structural significance of the political illiberalism shown by the elimination of Communist parties from Western governments, which ran parallel with the elimination of the political opposition in the satellite states. Stalinism and Communism became the focal points for the establishment of an anti-Communist consensus composed of otherwise divergent political groups. Only this fundamental consensus, then, made possible the safeguarding of the capitalistic social order under the hegemony of the United States in Western Europe; indeed, "if communism had not existed, something like it would have to be invented."[57]

The cultural offensive of the United States, no less than its economic postwar programs, represents, then, "a government-directed effort to integrate others into a new pax Americana."[58] Since the 1970s the multifaceted dimensions of this qualitatively new combination of foreign policy activities have been summarized by the term "public diplomacy."[59] Parallel to supporting a "free" world market for U.S. products, the Cold War intensified the efforts of U.S. foreign policy to achieve a "free" world market for U.S. ideas. The bureaucratization and formalization of these programs during the Second World War made it possible to integrate cultural diplomacy completely into the foreign policy consensus of the Cold War and to use it to further the general goals of U.S. foreign policy. "The Cold War both stimulated and was itself aggravated by new initiatives of the 'cultural dimension' of foreign policy."[60]

The U.S. cultural offensive, nevertheless, was confronted with similar structural contradictions as the U.S. economy was on its way to global economic hegemony. The open door policy did not offer weaker competitors equality of opportunity, not the least reason being that while the power elites of the United States supported a liberal world economy and the opening of foreign markets, they did not feel bound to their own policies when it came to opening their own markets.[61] Many U.S. industrialists and bankers, investors and businessmen simply did not seek a free world market "but a privately owned [one], which they mistakenly labeled as 'free.' "[62]

U.S. cultural diplomacy is characterized by a similar self-deception. Resulting from the cultural consensus of anti-Communism, liberal ideas were often reduced to an apology for political conservatism, thereby fulfilling an important function in maintaining the status quo. Every analysis of the propaganda and information politics of the United States shows that it "was not so much interested in fostering intellectual freedom as in promoting freedom as propaganda—an altogether different proposition."[63]

## The Organization and Tasks of the U.S. Cultural Mission in Austria, 1945–1955

With God's help we will lift Shanghai up and up, ever up until it is just like Kansas City.
  —U.S. Senator Kenneth Wherry, in Eric Goldman, *The Cultural Decade and After, 1945– 1961* (1960)

La nécessité politique d'influence culturelle en Europe Centrale est la raison profonde de notre présence en Autriche.
  —*Le problème autrichien actuel. Pourquoi la France est-elle en Autriche?* Commandement en chef français en Autriche. Secrétariat général. Section d'études. Imprimerie nationale de France en Autriche (undated)

Initially, the defeat of the Axis powers was primarily a military problem for the Allies. The closer the end of the war came, however, the more American planners dealt with the question of establishing a pluralistic, democratic culture in the occupied territories. Many inhabitants of the destroyed "Third Reich," who by the end of the war were confronted with tremendous human grief, material want, moral (self-)accusation, and the collapse of their Weltanschauung, nevertheless were not able to recognize the causes of this chaos in the military and racist megalomania of their own system. The fascist state apparatus, especially National Socialist propaganda, had operated with the total penetration of human consciousness.

For this reason, U.S. experts believed that only one strategy would lead to success; fascist behavior patterns and autocratic attitudes that had been diagnosed as a result of fascist brainwashing could be eliminated only by democratic decontamination. Parallel to the use of DDT for disinfection, the "decontamination of brains" was also necessary. The much-ridiculed and hated slogan for this program, which sought to establish democratic health through the prescription of antiauthoritarian inoculation, was "reeducation." During the first postwar years, the entire U.S. occupation policy in Germany revolved around this task. "Reeducation," in our context, therefore means indoctrination via any means of mass communication and all attempts to democratize the education system and all other areas of culture.[64]

The main reason for reeducation, however, was not any arrogance and foolishness of the occupying powers, as has repeatedly been claimed by those critics who had previously left themselves wide open to fascist indoctrination. The prerequisites for this program lay, more important, in the natural-law principles prevalent in U.S. theories of government, which promote "moralistic" value judgments of actions of other nations. On the one hand, U.S. planners were thoroughly convinced that the "liberal" capitalistic system of the United States could, as it were, be equated with the culmination of all previous human forms of organization, superseding all other social systems not only materially but morally as well. On the other hand, the need of the conquered people to change their culture was equally based upon the unshakable, optimistic faith in progress, assuming that long-range political reforms and the establishment of Western democracy can be achieved only by an open, pluralistic, liberal education.[65]

To succeed, this program of cultural rejuvenation through social management, which was by and large interpreted as thoroughly progressive by local democrats and U.S. authorities alike, after the collapse of fascism had to encompass all social realms. Yet, the antifascist tendencies of these politics of democratization were quickly overshadowed by zealous anti-Communism. Reeducation also, for the most part, focused primarily on political reforms in the areas of personnel, content, and form. In other words, democratization concentrated on reorganizing institutions rather than encouraging a change in social relations. It may be doubted, however, whether an alteration of consciousness can ever be achieved without a change in social relationships that constitute consciousness.[66]

In contrast to the strict reeducation measures implemented in Germany, a softer approach was designated for Austria, involving "reorientation" instead of "reeducation." The U.S. propaganda for Austrians had differed from that for Germans since the Moscow Declaration of 1943.[67] Reorientation policies sought to avoid a certain severity and, as a result, were subject to less criticism in Austria, while reeducation in Germany was quickly branded as brainwashing. Nevertheless, the American plans for Austria still contained a strict program of cultural control, denazification, and cultural reform.

The planners never doubted the cultural importance of the occupation and the singular opportunity offered to the Allies, even though military, political, and economic matters seemed to dominate immediately after the end of the war. For exactly this reason, all four occupation powers used every chance to impress the Austrians with their respective cultural products. In addition to the primary goal of denazification of Austrian cultural life, this competition among the Allies was already apparent in the first phases of occupation. The cultural mission was quite obviously an important means for the strengthening of political power and economic influence.

Immediately following the war, the French Division of Cultural Affairs, the British Council, the Soviet Society for the Preservation of Cultural and Economic Relations between Austria and the USSR, and the U.S. Information Services Branch (ISB) were established in the respective zones of occupation. Apart from the primary duties surrounding the support of the military governments and the circulation of the commanders' proclamations, these culture divisions quickly began with activities in democratic reorientation and control of the Austrian cultural scene.

While French and British cultures and, to a certain degree, also the (traditional) Russian culture were highly respected, many Austrians—like many other Europeans—scorned the United States as a cultural wasteland inhabited by uncivilized nouveaux riches and foolish upstarts. The initial prospects for the cultural representatives of the United States thus were not especially rosy. Ironically, the Allied cultural propaganda initiatives cost huge amounts of money. But this irony only relates to a seeming paradox, one that is caused by "idealistic" minds. While the owners of these minds all too much enjoyed those products of high culture that had been supported by the nobility and the bourgeoisie, they never quite managed to come to grips with the connection between money, power, and culture, between structure and superstructure.

While the French and British cultural programs were always close to financial ruin (the personnel of the British Council had to be reduced by 50 percent between 1947 and 1952), the Soviet Union with its cultural initiatives hardly had a chance to reach more than a minuscule minority in a strongly anti-Communist Austria. Furthermore, the French and British programs hardly carried any mass appeal. Especially the "stiff" French high culture programs, which were embraced by only a small group of elites in Vienna and Innsbruck, were no match for the materially most powerful challenger, the United States.[68] Of all great powers, the United States alone survived the Second World War without suffering total destruction. Furthermore, the economic strength of the United States, which had confronted almost insurmountable problems in the 1930s, now seemed, from the vantage point of a destroyed Europe, to have risen to immeasurable heights as a result of its immense war production.

The attractiveness of this material superiority of the United States, whose cultural message became increasingly drenched in strong doses of anti-Communism, was significant in Austria and elsewhere. In the psyche of the defeated, the United States soon acquired the character of the relatively least harmful (and, as we have seen, foolish) of the victors. In fact, the United States soon became the symbol of the actual winner, on whose side the losers had actually fought. Even though the real behavior of the GIs in many ways was hardly distinguishable from the soldiers of other occupation armies, they had one tremendous advantage—their seemingly endless access to goods. They brought dollars and even harder currencies—food, cigarettes, nylons, penicillin—all the necessities of survival for the plagued, hungry, confused people.

The tremendous fascination of this unlimited wealth of the United States, this fascination with nearly anything "American" itself, actually assisted U.S. cultural propaganda to outwit its competitors, even in those fields that were supposed to be the home turf of the Europeans (i.e., high culture). Although the number of French and British art exhibits exceeded those of the United States, the ISB soon caught up in this field as well. The curators of the 1950 Grandma Moses exhibition in Vienna thus proudly announced that their show had attracted more visitors than any other. Even the works of Pablo Picasso hardly lured half as many guests.[69] This is, without a doubt, just one indicator, though maybe not the least important, for the success of U.S. cultural policies in Austria. These successes embraced more than just popular culture and selected areas of high culture. American initiatives changed not only Austrian material culture but political culture as well, even if we may have our doubts about the depth of democratic convictions in the light of the Austrian presidential campaign of 1986 as well as current xenophobic tendencies. Still, a cynical observer could also point to the Noricum Scandal, involving covert arms exports to Arab nations, as only a sloppy Austrian version of the Iran Contragate scandal.[70]

The organization of reorientation in Austria was directed by the ISB, which began its activities on May 15, 1945. On July 6, 1945, the command of the ISB was transferred from the Supreme Headquarters Allied Expeditionary Forces to the United States Forces in Austria (USFA). The ISB evolved from the Information, News and Censorship Section (INC) and initially comprised employees of the Office of War Information (OWI). Its early independent position was actually strengthened as a consequence of the hesitation involved in the establishment of the Allied Council in Vienna. Hence, the ISB achieved relative organizational independence and thereby decisively dominated the cultural politics of the United States in Austria immediately after the war. In the end, the ISB was subordinated to the Civil Affairs Division (CAD) of the War Department in Washington. The office coordinating the day-to-day activities within the United States was the New York field office of CAD. However, since 1947 the Department of State gained significant influence in the planning and decision-making process. Finally, on October 16, 1950, the Department of State took over all managing control.[71]

The setup of the ISB agencies was carried out by Lieutenant Colonel Robert V. Shinn, James J. Minifie, and Albert van Eerden, under the leadership of Brigadier General A. J. McChrystal. It consisted of the following thirteen sections:

*Press Scrutiny and Austrian Publications Control.* This section granted licenses and screened publications according to limitations contained in Allied decrees.

The allotment of paper for printing was a tremendous leveraging tool. Paper rationing was turned over to the Austrian government in November 1946, and the licensing of publications in May 1947.

*Theater and Music.* This department oversaw the denazification of the art scene, a very delicate and difficult responsibility that was left to the Austrian government in the fall of 1947. Controls regulating the travel of actors and actresses as well as musicians were discontinued in 1949. In addition, this section organized performances of large numbers of U.S. artists and works on Austrian stages and established a library of American compositions for Austrian musicians.

*Films.* Working closely with Hollywood's Motion Picture Export Association (MPEA), this section dealt with the distribution of commercial U.S. films. Together with the British occupation power, the weekly newsreel *Welt im Film* was produced until 1949. The film production properties confiscated in the American zone were returned to the Austrian government in 1946. All German and Austrian films were appropriated and examined as to their political contents. Film licensing rights were then returned to the Austrian authorities in 1948. In addition to the production of propaganda films, this section also dubbed U.S. films. Ernst Haeusserman and Marcel Prawy, two major figures of the Austrian postwar cultural scene, worked for this section.

*Pictorial.* Here, all the necessary photographs and other pictorial material were acquired and distributed to other ISB agencies.

*Communications.* This section controlled the Austrian telegraph and telex communications with other countries. Newspapers and radio stations were supplied with news materials. Furthermore, the radio program Voice of America was tape-recorded, and other foreign stations were monitored. The control of Austrian communication lines with Italy and the Federal Republic of Germany were ceded in 1947 and 1949, respectively.

*News Operations.* All the print media were subordinate to this section. The Amerikanische Nachrichtendienst (AND) supplied the Austrian media with information free of charge. In September 1946, local reporting was left to UPI and AP, but AND continued to play a major role in the training of many Austrian journalists. The Features and Pictures Services translated U.S. articles and placed them in more than 200 Austrian publications with great success.

*Graphic Display.* The Graphic Display department was in charge of the America Houses in Vienna, Linz, and Salzburg as well as nine other information centers and libraries in Wels, Steyr, Ried im Innkreis, Gmunden, Zell am See, Hallein, Innsbruck, Graz, and Klagenfurt.

*American Publications.* This section had three duties: (1) importing and distributing U.S. publications, (2) publishing U.S. books and magazines in Austria, and (3) establishing contacts between U.S. and Austrian publishers.

*Radio Section.* Controlling the U.S. radio station Rot-Weiss-Rot (Red-white-red) with transmission systems and studios in Vienna, Linz, and Salzburg was the responsibility of this section.

*Education Division.* The main duty of this division was the denazification and reform of the education system, from kindergarten to the university.

*Exchange of Persons.* This office controlled the exchange programs and hosted academicians, students, and other official visitors from the United States.

*Youth Clubs.* The most important group of all was entrusted to this department—the youth. Hundreds of 4-H clubs (head, heart, hands, healthy life) in all zones of occupation, including the Soviet zone, guaranteed contact with those youths living in the country. Games and sports programs, gifts of toys and sports equipment (from boxing gloves to baseball bats), the training of youth leaders, the establishment of the AYA (Austrian Youth Activities) Clubs, the publication of magazines, film and dance events, discussions and Christmas parties for schoolchildren in the U.S. zone, as well as support for the rebuilding and new construction of sports facilities ensured continual contact with the young.

*Administration and Financial.* This section managed all administrative, personnel, and financial procedures.[72]

These encompassing duties of the ISB—which were continuously expanded during the period of occupation—are reflected in the personnel figures. It must be noted, however, that the existing documents only approximate the actual numbers. Not only did the employees of the ISB change from month to month, but also the American cultural agenda was not executed by the ISB alone. On certain occasions, members of the diplomatic mission in Vienna, different military agencies, as well as the Marshall Plan Agency (ECA) assisted with projects. The U.S. cultural authorities employed 140 individuals in 1945/46. That number increased to 737 in 1947, to 827 in 1948, reaching its height of 1,060 employees in 1949. Until the end of the period of occupation, the number of employees remained constantly around 900. The greatest majority of those assisting were Austrians. For example, the 1948 staff consisted of 62 Americans and 765 Austrians; in 1952 there were 58 Americans and 879 Austrians.[73]

We confront similar difficulties when trying to compile a reliable budgetary overview for the individual cultural programs. They were financed by more than just various sources of the U.S. Army and the Department of State. While the takeover of the ISB by the State Department in 1950 at least reduced conflicts of jurisdiction, the new budgets still did not exactly cover the costs of many individual programs, the exact revenues in schilling sums, and the financial amounts allotted by the ECA. In any event, the ISB operated at a profit in the first postwar years, for example, through the tax-free profits from the sale of the *Salzburger Nachrichten* and the *Oberösterreichische Nachrichten* (AS 2,632,858), the *Wiener Kurier* (until October 1947 alone, AS 14,093,387), through movie admissions (as German property), through the weekly newsreel *Welt im*

*Film* (until October 1947, AS 4,447,708), and through other publications. This was also especially important because, in the immediate postwar years, the U.S. Congress still disapproved of cultural propaganda. Although the expenditures slowly came closer to the sum of income toward the end of the 1940s, the profit still amounted to AS 7,085,610 between July and September 1949, and AS 1,534,718 between July 1949 and March 1950.[74] The dollar budgets of the ISB as well as the USIE were around one or two million dollars until 1955, from $1,295,481 in 1950 and $1,814,082 in 1951, down to $821,300 in 1952. Yet, these figures reflect only the expenditures in dollars. The local cost amounted to AS 20–30 million per year during the 1950s, with slightly more than AS 100 million planned for 1953 alone.[75] In principle, 90 percent of the programs in Austria were covered by the income of schillings. If we take into consideration the total operating costs, approximately 60 percent of all expenditures could be covered by the income in Austrian schillings.[76]

Throughout the whole occupation period, the ISB controlled enough funds to implement quickly any program considered necessary. In any event, the losses occurred by the ISB were a result of the massive extension of its programs directed toward the audiences in the Communist countries bordering Austria—and that was a completely different story. In contrast to the cultural propaganda of other Allies, the ISB was upwind not only with respect to finances but also in the realm of acceptance by the Austrian public. Martin F. Herz, a diplomat at the U.S. legation in Vienna, noted that "incidentally, as to the payment in Austrian currency, ISB has more Schillings than it knows what to do with."[77]

There was no shortage of opportunity to spend these monies. The duties of the ISB were encompassing, its functions clearly defined. It was founded "to utilize every possible material and psychological means to create respect, if not admiration, for the American attitude, and thereby to vitiate the propaganda of competing political philosophies."[78] During the first years of occupation, the ISB controlled the presentation of films, theater, opera, concerts, newspapers, magazines, books, pamphlets, advertisements, radio, news agencies, the school system, even puppet theaters, circus exhibitions, carnival festivities, balls, religious processions, and local country fairs.[79]

This total control of Austrian cultural life by U.S. authorities reveals structural similarities to the occupation policies of the victorious Union states toward the defeated Confederates during the phase of reconstruction after the Civil War. This control not only constituted the paradox of implementing democratic culture through potentially undemocratic methods. U.S. reorientation, which, at least since 1947, concentrated almost solely on anti-Communism, also dwarfed the more liberal, albeit often utterly clumsy, cultural control and censorship measures of the Soviet occupation power.

Initially, the primary political mission of the ISB was the overcoming of fascist relics in Austrian culture. The most important goal was "to assist in the eradication of Nazism, militarism and GERMAN, Austrian Nazi or Fascist or pan-German sources."[80] Although intense attacks on the Soviet Union were discouraged in the first "Full and Fair Picture" phase, all war reports of U.S. media in Austria show a clear trend: the positive assessment of the war effort of the Western powers, especially the United States, and, at the same time, the playing down of the role of the USSR. The Cold War quickly made this restraint obsolete and led, first through numerous anti-Soviet attacks in 1946, to total confrontation in a new war of words in 1947.[81]

The shift of this main political focus is seen very clearly in the goals set internally by U.S. authorities. The blurring of the differences and polarities between fascism and Communism through the theory of totalitarianism underpinned the new political stance. The much more dangerous opponent stood to the left, as the USIE Country Plan for Austria made clear in 1950. The main objective now was "to counteract totalitarian influences in Austria, whether from the Communist left or the neo-Nazi right, and particularly to encourage democratic stability by exposing and attacking Communist attempts to encroach upon the authority of the Austrian Government."[82] The psychological goals of the USIS Country Plan for Austria for 1953 are even more apparent: "Encourage Austrian will to resist pressures from the East and instill and strengthen kinship with the West. Demonstrate U.S. concern for Austria and its welfare, particularly its independence from interference of influence by the Soviet Union or satellites."[83]

The politics of information and culture were directed, in essence, toward the entire population. The primary target audience, however, was the opinion-forming exponents of the educated middle class. This included teachers, journalists, engineers, scientists, academics, lawyers, and artists. Another principal group was the working class, and especially so because U.S. experts correctly recognized the political leadership of the Socialist Party of Austria (SPÖ) and the Trade Union Association (ÖGB) to be one of the most significant anti-Communist spearheads and the most influential anti-Soviet allies in Austria. (The political absurdity of the Austrian People's Party [ÖVP], which repeatedly spewed warmed-over "Red Cat" slogans, gave U.S. representatives continuous occasion for ironic commentaries until 1955.) Further target groups were the "frequently anti-intellectual" middle class in small cities and in the countryside as well as the youth, especially youth organizations of the political parties, and the Catholic church.[84]

By the spring of 1948, anti-Soviet propaganda in the U.S. media had reached such a high degree of saturation that some American experts in Austria found it advisable to depart from this all too open, negative, and aggressive strategy. Instead, a softer line of information, highlighting the positive sides of the United States, was thought to be more successful. Public-opinion polls had revealed that the great majority of Austrians had clearly shown antipathy toward this malletlike approach. Other reasons, ISB experts felt, made a departure from an aggressive form of propaganda necessary. First, anti-Communist coverage had already largely been taken over and become the norm for Austrian media. Yet, even for liberal ISB representatives one thing remained self-evident: any media whose position was not clearly pro-West were considered Communist and were therefore to be combated whatever the cost. Even though ISB politics were absolutely successful in promoting privately owned newspapers, in reality a *truly independent* media could not exist on the basis of precisely this understanding.[85] Second, the ideological battle in Austria, in any event, had already been decided in favor of the United States. The ISB experts had recognized that political propaganda that could be recognized as such most frequently provoked rejection. In spite of the propagation of different ideological goals, such negative public reactions were, without a doubt, a result of the constant, intensive stream of propaganda that had already existed for more than a decade.

The positive self-projection and persuasiveness of Madison Avenue methods were therefore ideal in this situation. For this reason, the director of the ISB, Ray E. Lee, ordered that anti-Soviet diatribes were to be replaced, because "our real task is to sell America. We doubt that we are selling America by lambasting the Soviets. Putting it another way, someone said that the Austrians dislike the Russians already. It is hardly necessary for us to prove further to the Austrians that they should dislike the Russians."[86] The ISB, therefore, had worked efficiently in the first postwar years. To collect information, the Counter-Propaganda Policy Group had already been established by mid-1946. By mid-1947, the Information Coordinating Board (ICB) had been formed by members of the Intelligence Coordination Branch and the ISB. This new board acted as a central agency for all U.S. departments in the acquisition, development, and media management of anti-Communist propaganda in Austria. Again and again, Soviet propaganda spewed a barrage of anti-American slogans that ricocheted harmlessly off of a largely anti-Communist audience. In contrast, the centrally coordinated information strategy of the ISB, whose approach was thoroughly varied and diverse, experienced major successes. Quick responses to the developments within and without Austria were made even easier by the weekly telephone conferences between the agencies in the Department of State, the Pentagon, and the Information Coordination Committee. The centralization of news acquisition in the ICB was successful in scattering anti-Communist information in the media; it had also even become effective in frequently smuggling certain announcements into the speeches of Austrian politicians and members of government.[87]

During the course of 1947/48, the initial control function of U.S. cultural authorities smoothly changed to that of a directing advisory role, thereby responding more adequately to local circumstances. This change of direction conformed thoroughly with the originally planned phases of U.S. reorientation politics, which had foreseen all facets—from the total ban on Austrian media to the careful loosening of the reins and, finally, to the handing over of all control functions after democracy had been reestablished. Although the American experts in Austria were well aware that culture and information strategies full of variety and diversity had the greatest chance of succeeding in the long run, the higher-ups in the U.S. Army and the Department of State stubbornly opposed any toning down of attacks against the Soviet Union. The representatives of a harder stance in Washington, and especially those in the New York field office, continually demanded not only the retention of the intensity of propaganda but its escalation. Complete disapproval was also voiced toward the practice of those liberal ISB members who rejected total whitewashing as unbelievable and, for this reason, sometimes allowed careful criticism of perhaps less than perfect conditions in the United States (for example, racism) to be discussed in the Austrian media. The controllers in Washington and New York in principle believed that criticism belonged to democracy as such. Criticism could in fact be allowed within the United States, but not in an occupied foreign country, especially at the expense of the American taxpayer.

This latent conflict between the ISB experts who were familiar with local circumstances and the responsible authorities in the United States who wanted to propagate the true American faith sometimes produced strange results. One example will illustrate these opposing positions. In July 1948, an order from New York decreed that the lambasting of the United States would no longer be tolerated, because "when everybody else is criticizing this country and emphasizing its shortcomings, it has become our task to seek out the points which make the American system appear good, sound and the best possible of all systems."[88] According to this logic, the capitalist system also had to be projected in positive terms. In keeping with the command from New York,

it is not official policy to "sell" the capitalistic system under which this country prospered, but the fact remains that it is the only system which has been able, up to this minute, to guarantee the greatest number of individual freedoms which survived anywhere. Now, it is perfectly legitimate for Americans to criticize the American system and to advocate change as, for instance, socialization. Nevertheless, capitalism is basic to the American way of life as it is known today, and secondly, it is attacked from all sides. Therefore, it should be our task to emphasize the good points of capitalism whenever possible.[89]

Such interventions created astonishment, discontent, anger, and rejection among many ISB members in Austria. They realized the ineffectiveness of Soviet propaganda and knew their own flexible advertising strategy to be much more persuasive. Furthermore, they knew all too well what the forceful propagation of the capitalistic U.S. system meant in a country with a strong socialist party and trade unions. If capitalism, then it had to be one à la New Deal, as the newly implemented Marshall Plan required, because

> any attempt to emphasize the good points of capitalism will boomerang, especially in central Europe, where the Social Democratic Party has millions of followers. The suspicion and hostility, which will be engendered by any prating of capitalism's benefits, will go a long way toward making all of our propaganda suspect. Our job is not to "ballyhoo" capitalism, but to sell democracy. Any effort to ram alien economic concepts down the throats of suspicious Europeans will fail. . . . In addition, a frank acknowledgement of our own shortcomings endows our output with that quality of verisimilitude which makes propaganda effective.[90]

As long as the ISB retained relative independence, interventions of this kind could at least be abated. However, in the course of the takeover by the Department of State, the ICB was dissolved, and the ISB soon became the long arm of the USIA. After 1950, the ISB was also given another new important task: it increasingly became the switchboard for coordinating American propaganda toward the Eastern bloc.[91]

The previous achievements of the ISB had, in sum, been quite positively evaluated in the Austria Plan of the USIE for the years 1951 and 1952. Yet, certain drawbacks seemed to remain. The USSR still supported the propaganda apparatus of the Austrian Communist Party (KPÖ) and also controlled the radio station RAVAG. The U.S. media were still confronted with certain difficulties in penetrating the Soviet zone. Because of their experiences with both German and Allied occupation, the Austrians mistrusted every form of obvious propaganda. Beyond the natural resentment of a people toward an occupying power—with their military installations, soldiers, and requisitions—latent fears of becoming a pawn in the conflict between the superpowers and the potential battlefield in a military struggle were also ever-present. Such an exposed position in the case of war as well as fears of revenge by the USSR allowed, in addition, for the rise of apathetic neutralism. Still another factor—and not the least important—had seemed unfavorable for the interests of the United States, namely, Austria's traditional intermediary role in East-West trade.

On balance, however, ISB's work was clearly successful. The U.S. financed newspaper *Wiener Kurier* enjoyed the largest circulation of all Austrian papers. The American radio station Rot-Weiss-Rot not only had the strongest transmitters but also enjoyed, by far, the greatest rate of public acceptance. In addition, the United States maintained eleven exceptionally well frequented information centers. Still further, Austrian mass media were positively disposed toward U.S. policies, and the Austrian government was consistent in endorsing an anti-Communist and anti-Soviet position. Not only were the Communists in Austria quantitatively unimportant, but deep-seated Catholic traditions were still an important part of the society.[92]

In view of these positive conditions for the United States after five years of ISB work, Secretary of State Dean Acheson informed all American offices in Austria during the takeover of the program that it was now time to lay to rest the use of the term "reorientation." Even if there were still groups whose reeducation and reorientation had not yet been achieved, the time had nevertheless arrived in which the instructing role of American media politics in Austria should be officially transformed into a supportive function. The term "reorientation," which contained the undesired connotations of tutelage and imposed reforms, would thereafter be rescinded. It is interesting in this context to note the secretary of state's explanation for taking this step: this policy was implemented precisely to free from the stigma of American tutelage those Austrians who, as opinion makers, had been invited to the United States through exchange programs. Still, precisely these invitations had been an important part of the long-range U.S. strategy in Austria. The travel stipends were mostly given to those individuals who were not chosen "because of any specially urgent need on their part for psychological re-conditioning but because they are considered especially useful in communicating information about the United States and its democratic institutions to their fellow citizens, they themselves being already most favorably disposed in that direction."[93]

This departure from the concept of reorientation did not result, however, in any mitigation of American propaganda. On the contrary, it led to a further intensification. On September 13, 1950, prior to the October trade union strikes in Austria, the Department of State announced a directive for a Psychological Offensive in Austria.[94] The reasons for the augmentation of U.S. activities had nothing to do with an overestimation of the strength of the KPÖ or the Soviet position. Although the actions of the USSR and the Austrian Communists were continuously followed with great suspicion, the experts in the Department of State felt that they could rely upon local anti-Communist defense mechanisms in Austria. In reality, this new propaganda offensive was a particular reaction against two different problems.

First, the long duration of the period of occupation in Austria intensified the ever-growing feelings of helplessness and apathy that were verbalized in growing criticism toward the ÖVP-SPÖ coalition government by the "right-wing" camp. Second, the U.S. government hardly had any direct possibilities of influence in the Eastern bloc countries. As a result, Vienna now increasingly became the forwardmost bridgehead of the U.S. information and propaganda efforts in this direction.

The concerns about strengthened right-wing, authoritarian tendencies in Austria were shown quite clearly in the reports of U.S. officials during these years. In an analysis of the situation between October 1950 and December 1951, after the political success of the Association of Independents (VdU) in the parliamentary elections in 1949 and the relatively strong gains of its presidential candidate, Dr. Burkhart Breitner, in 1951, the revival of antiparliamentarian, traditionalist, and neofascist tendencies was anxiously analyzed. Of particular concern were the trends in rural areas, where such political movements were typically supported especially by local obscurantists, anti-Semites, neo-Nazis, and uneducated nihilists, whose only uniting motive would be the total rejection of the coalition government. Certainly, these groups could lean on the predominantly right-wing-slanted press, which was led by the cleverly produced *Salzburger Nachrichten*. Its antidemocratic and antigovernment position, U.S. analysts noted, was just as notorious as its criticism of U.S. occupation politics.[95]

To counteract these developments, the USIE increased its efforts in all areas within the realm of the Psychological Offensive. Libraries were expanded. A new information center in Gmunden in Upper Austria was established. The translation of children's books was hastened. A new USIE magazine, *Young People*, which was conceived as a learning tool for English classes, was approved by the Ministry of Education and could therefore be used also in the Soviet zone. The Education Section increased its staff, and the program of the magazine *Erziehung* (Education), distributed without charge to all Austrian teachers, was revamped. The Austrian-American Institute for Education and the Austrian-American Society received a U.S. consultant and financial support from the Rockefeller Foundation and from the Marshall Plan office. This way, both societies not only could expand their monthly scope to reach 20,000 persons but also could now establish subdivisions within the Soviet occupation zone.

In addition to the *Wiener Kurier* and other already-existing magazines that were meant to attract a variety of audiences, the publication sector was developed further. The USIE now controlled, besides a news agency, a telegraph network that was connected with U.S. officials and also with the editorial staffs of newspapers in all of Austria. The pamphlet program was expanded, as was the photography section. Picture supplements, photo matrices, and current bulletins were sent to newspapers in rural areas as well as to interested individuals. The quantitative output of this program, which was financed almost solely with Austrian counterpart shillings from the ECA office, was impressive. In the last six months of the year 1951 alone, 2,820,400 political pamphlets were distributed.

Film programs were also increased, as were the political broadcasts of Rot-Weiss-Rot. Discussion programs and political commentaries, directed especially toward workers, received more airing time. The contents of these programs was coordinated by U.S. liaison officers in conjunction with functionaries of the Austrian trade unions. Exchange programs were broadened to include the Fulbright Program, an alumni association was established, and a data collection on all previous participants was prepared. For young academics, training programs were implemented in cooperation with the ECA office. The Visual Media Program now concentrated especially upon the production of posters, particularly the new series Bild der Woche (Picture of the week), which had a weekly circulation of 2,000 issues and was placed on streetcars and train stations, even in the Soviet zone.

Particular attention was given to youth programs. Politically less relevant activities were cut back, only to be substituted by efforts concentrating on more important target groups. Close to the University of Vienna, a cultural center was established for students, seminars for English teachers were intensified, and youth programs became generally more political, particularly stressing the development of anti-Communist sympathies. American youth counselors were explicitly told to "concentrate less on kindergarten and sport activities, as it were, and to devote their energies in developing contacts with a view to indoctrinating Austrian youth leaders with a sense of civic responsibility and to attempt to organize and strengthen a strong anti-Communist front in the Austrian youth organizations."[96]

This escalation of propaganda policies—in other words, the *reorientation* of the reorientation program—created less difficulties for Austrian citizens than for long-standing ISB workers. Liberal U.S. experts thoroughly rejected the sledgehammer approach of the new psychological offensive. Detailed instructions thus were formulated to set them on the right track because "perhaps the chief obstacle in this regard is the reorientation[!] of thinking of the staff members responsible for carrying out the program, who, during the past five years or longer, have become too deeply indoctrinated[!] with the 'full and fair picture' concept of American information work that they completely miss the political meaning and opportunities of the new program."[97]

In contrast, there was no Austrian resistance against increased usage of American and Austrian media as propaganda instruments directed toward the states in the Eastern bloc. Possible Austrian reservations toward an intensification of U.S. propaganda messages originating from Austrian sources were to be overcome by two strategies. On the one hand, the Austrians themselves had to be convinced of the political necessity and long-range benefit for Austria. On the other hand, Austrian opinion makers themselves also had to participate in this process so that the information could be directed in a way in which the actual source remained concealed. In any event, the made-in-America stamp had to be avoided at all cost in a propaganda-saturated Austria. U.S. experts had already gained insights into the soul of the Austrian journalists. They were, after all, convinced of meeting little resistance, so long as articles—completely furnished in the German language—were exclusively molded to fit the needs of the editors. Cooperating journalists not only were privileged with information but, in some cases, also received direct financial support.[98] In the second half of the year 1951 alone, approximately 2,500 American current affairs articles, 5,200 features, and 2,600 pictures were incorporated in Austrian newspapers.[99]

In fact, given the geographic location of Austria and in particular Vienna, every one of these actions fulfilled two purposes. American propaganda experts calculated quite correctly that each and every one of their "Austrian" products "is potentially able to do the double duty of local information and curtain penetration."[100] To intensify the range of broadcasts deep into the Eastern bloc, the transmission capacity of the radio station Rot-Weiss-Rot was increased. In the summer of 1951, two new, more powerful 100-kilowatt transmitters were put into operation in Vienna and Linz "to make deep penetration into neighboring Soviet-dominated areas . . . to make of it a strategic political weapon throughout this Central European area."[101] The facilities of Rot-Weiss-Rot in Salzburg, whose geographic location was not suited for such purposes, were not modernized.

Political propaganda was revamped throughout the programs of Rot-Weiss-Rot. In an effort to reach as many people as possible in Eastern Europe, daily night shows were introduced. World news, information about the Eastern bloc, commentaries, current affairs, and political satire were directed especially toward those listeners behind the Iron Curtain who traditionally felt a cultural affinity with Vienna. Obviously, the USIE experts were, for the most part, concerned neither with this traditional role of Vienna nor with information from and about Austria. In their calculations, Vienna's only function was that of a geographic bridgehead, the "easternmost outpost of western ways and influence [which] lends itself uniquely as an advanced base from which to spread information and exert political attraction."[102]

Without a doubt, these Rot-Weiss-Rot broadcasts let many listeners living beyond the border believe that these shows were actually Austrian programs. In fact, precisely these deceptions made Rot-Weiss-Rot especially valuable, thereby boosting its political credibility. All this, then, had become an important success for the improved and refined propaganda efforts of the psychological offensive. The satisfaction with these successes showed in the reports to Washington: "In this, Red-White-Red has been guided by the method of oblique rather than frontal propaganda—a tactic made possible because of the opportunity of locally blending U.S. information policy into an indigenous-seeming Austrian home network. When heard beyond the border (or rather, 'overheard') the network will continue to appear simply as Vienna speaking to Austria, although much of its content will be selected so as to have special impact upon listeners to the East."[103]

Other American media forms were also drawn upon. A weekly insert was produced for the *Wiener Kurier*, a part of whose circulation was intended especially for the readers in the states of the Eastern bloc. More specifically, an unpolitical magazine certainly "would lend itself also to strategic distribution in the Soviet Zone and in areas beyond the border by special means."[104] In addition, a new pamphlet section, specializing in the adaptation of U.S. texts for local circumstances, was organized. Still further, small brochures written by Austrian authors, especially the reports of exchange program participants, were published.[105] Washington even requested a publication to be titled "Cartoon History of the United States" ("If well done, this could be very useful for Austrian youth, an important target group for which little printed 'ammunition' has been available").[106]

The implementation of these new propaganda strategies obviously cost large sums, especially the building of the new transmitting installations of Rot-Weiss-Rot in Vienna and Linz. While the dollar budget remained almost completely unchanged, the schilling expenditures rose from approximately 30 million in 1952 to over 100 million in 1953.[107] The decisive questions as to what degree the financial expenditures actually paid off for U.S. information politics, or to what degree they had any direct influence upon the Austrians and their neighbors in the Eastern bloc, cannot be precisely answered. It must be kept in mind, however, that the U.S. propaganda strategy in Austria was not conceived as an end in itself but must be understood in a larger, worldwide political context.[108]

One also cannot overlook the fact that the great majority of the Austrian populace was confronted with tremendous material problems, especially in the first years after the war, so that American propaganda *alone* could certainly not achieve any significant changes. Ernst Hanisch correctly asserts that the public mood rose or fell with the intake of calories.[109] Freedom and equality were now, in any event, packaged quite differently—as Liberty Corn, Freedom Grain, and Equality Beans. Without material support, without the Marshall Plan, the success of the reorientation programs would definitely have been much less significant. Yet, the Marshall Plan simply also became *the* outstanding propaganda achievement and *the* psychological victory exactly because of the journalistic support by American media, which increasingly accompanied it. The U.S. media, thereby, accomplished the presentation of the United States as the model of material progress, as the model of modernity as such. "America seemed to represent not merely the future but something futuristic, a technological cornucopia whose products were being poured coruscating on a world accustomed to scrimping and saving but inevitably to be wiped away in the science fiction future for which we were all destined."[110]

Political ideas and ideological patterns that had existed prior to the arrival of U.S. occupation forces, such as anti-Communism, but also the acceptance of a system of parliamentary democracy, were, without a doubt, strongly reinforced by American information policies. In contrast, efforts in overcoming authoritarian thought patterns or anti-Semitic prejudices certainly produced more modest results for reorientation efforts, as all public surveys carried out by the U.S. occupation forces clearly showed.[111] In any event, American experts were satisfied with one decisive point of the outcome of their operation: "The effect of this work cannot precisely be measured. However, its dissemination is believed to contribute in substantial measure to Austria's strongly anti-

Communist attitude, as demonstrated in several elections in which the nation's rejection of Communism has been underwritten by 95% of the voters."[112]

The term "reeducation" had been borrowed from psychiatry. Thus, the Germans were ordered to receive a collective mental healing.[113] The mental condition of the Austrians, in keeping with this image, was seen as less alarming, and therefore only the milder medicine of "reorientation" was prescribed. However the names of the programs may have been called—stressing prohibition and control or highlighting instruction or support—U.S. experts were always confronted with the tricky situation that "one of the more delicate functions of American personnel in Austria is not to encourage people to say what they feel . . . but rather try, as well as we can, to suggest to them the right thing to think."[114]

In Graham Greene's novel *The Quiet American* (1955), U.S. agent Alden Pyle, who began his duties to save Indochina from Communism shortly before the collapse of French colonialism, described a difficult and eventually unsuccessful mission less elegantly: "They'll be forced to believe what they are told, they won't be allowed to think for themselves." In response, note the commentary of Thomas Fowler, whom Greene describes as a hardened, tired, aging, European "rival" in contrast to the young, aggressive, idealistic Pyle: "He was impregnably armored by his good intentions. . . . I never knew a man who had better motives for all the troubles he caused."[115]

According to Frank Ninkovich's thesis, different cultures maintain different levels of permeability toward various foreign influences. That is the reason why material products and technologies, for example, overcome barriers more quickly than new ideas. Hence, states give greater priority to military power, whereas cultural interests will usually come last. Intellectual penetration, according to this paradigm, could gain credibility only after a demonstration of military and economic power and then only in limited scope. Cultural relations, generally speaking, are therefore influenced by a cultural time lag.[116]

The United States had demonstrated its military might during the Second World War and became the leading world power. The continuous reinforcement of material goods from America seemed almost endless, and the United States simply became synonymous with technological progress. Even if pluralistic democracy was nothing new in Europe, the United States still offered particularly powerful illustrative material, especially in a country such as Austria, in which democratic traditions had developed only weakly, only to be broken off by 1933/34. In addition, the United States had its own tradition of high culture (in the European sense, although it was hardly taken seriously in Europe) and, even more important, a popular culture that for many was more attractive and also a well-developed cultural industry whose influence in Europe had been felt already prior to the Second World War.

The presence of millions of GIs in Europe, the control over occupied territories, the dependence of European countries upon U.S. aid, the quick assumption of international political roles abdicated by the former European Great Powers, and especially the taking over of anti-Communist protection as a result of the Cold War—all this gave the United States a brand new opportunity to propagate its ideas and political concepts in Europe.

The U.S. Army did not come to Europe toting only military weapons. By the end of the war, it had distributed millions of copies of American author Stephen Vincent Benét's work *America*. The number of copies published exceeded all other U.S. books of the time. The first few sentences of this book clearly contained the credo of the U.S. missionaries in Europe:

A M E R I C A

There is a country of hope, there is a country of freedom. There is a country where all sorts of different people, drawn from every nation in the world, get along together under the same big sky. They go to any church they choose—Catholic, Protestant, Jewish, Mohammedan, Buddhist—and no man may be persecuted there for his religion. The men and women of this country elect the people they wish to govern them, remove those people by vote—not by revolution—if they feel their representatives have done badly, speak their minds about their government and about the running of their country at all times, stay themselves and yet stay loyal to one cause, one country, and one flag.

The flag is the Stars and Stripes. The country is the United States of America. The cause is the cause of democracy.

It is not an earthly paradise, a Garden of Eden, or a perfect state. It does not pretend to be any of those things.

It has not solved every problem of how men and women should live. It has made mistakes in its own affairs, mistakes in the affairs of the world. But it looks to the future always—to a future of free men and women, where there shall be bread and work, security and liberty for the children of mankind.

It does not want to rule the world or set up an American empire in which Americans will be the master race and other people subject races. If you ask any real American whether he believes in a master race, you will get a long stare or a long laugh. Americans do not believe in master races.[117]

It is more than characteristic for the political climate in the U.S. during the 1950s that Stephen Vincent Benét, whose book *America* embodied the universalistic, liberal faith of American cultural diplomacy, was listed on the index of prohibited authors during the period of McCarthyism.

The following pages will show those areas in which the cultural crusade of the United States enjoyed particular successes as well as those areas in which the coefficient of permeability tended to lie close to zero.

# 3

## United States Press Politics in Austria

### "A Fine Propaganda Medium": The Establishment of Newspapers and Magazines

All news is views.
　　—George Gerbner, *Ideological Perspective and Political Tendencies in News Reporting* (1964)

The control, reform, and reorganization of Austria's press doubtless stood at the center of (cultural) political reorientation programs of the victorious powers. All four allies founded newspapers and issued licenses to politically acceptable publishers. However, U.S. information officers were far more successful than the press officers of the other nations in significantly influencing—directly and indirectly—the Austrian media landscape. They did so not only in the short term, as U.S. press reforms affected Austrian media in many important areas in the long run. This was a result of more intensive planning and material superiority as well as of the internal structure of the Austrian media. Therefore, the great majority of the Austrian press—the most important intensifier of opinions during the first years of the Cold War—became tools for achieving the goals of U.S. information politics.[1]

In spite of its initial total monitoring, the control of the Austrian press was less radical than the plans for the press in Germany. Nevertheless, the first and foremost goal of American press officers was to expropriate all information apparatuses, to rid them of their Nazi functionaries, and to revamp the function of the journalists and the basic workings of the entire press system according to the U.S. model. During the first phase of occupation, the concept for surmounting all fascist remnants certainly also included the former representatives of Austro-fascism. However, these more radical plans were quickly dropped. Such was the case, for example, in the appointment of Gustav A. Canaval, a former chief editor of the newspaper of the Austrian *Sturmscharen Sturm über Österreich*, as copublisher and senior editor of the *Salzburger Nachrichten*. U.S. plans to exclude former Austro-fascists faced total opposition from the ÖVP leadership and the Catholic church and had to be abandoned.[2]

Yet another, more important point was the banishing of all German influence in the new press, or the "de-Germanization" of the entire information machinery. This goal was achieved in the area of personnel. If we look, however, at the impact of the existing German press organizations in Austria since the beginning of the 1950s (as well as similar developments in the publishing industry, in the recording industry, and in television and film distribution) and at the concentration of press ownership in recent years, then we can certainly see a long-term weakening, if not direct failure, of these U.S. goals.

Although U.S. information officers granted some flexibility, the banning of newly established, local antifascist newspapers in Austria demonstrated that they were not prepared to allow the spontaneous growth of a democratic press during the first days following the war. As a result, the reconstruction of the press in the U.S. zone had come exclusively under the control of the U.S. Army. The Austrian public, who had certainly known worse measures of suppression, now experienced another paradox: U.S. censorship as a means of democracy.[3]

In the U.S. occupation zone in Germany, the licensing of newspapers and the appointments of journalists immediately after the war also included some left-leaning applicants (especially Social Democrats but also some Communists). In Austria as well, individual allowances were made to editorial groups that were composed of representatives of the authorized political parties—even though mostly without Communists—and responsible, politically independent persons. Yet, officially nonpartisan, conservative individuals received preferential treatment in the distribution of licenses. They would promote the long-term political interests of the United States in the Cold War because, even without continual direct intervention by the U.S. occupation force, these conservative licensees guaranteed an anti-Communist stance. As a matter of fact, their aggressiveness sometimes surprised American press officers and, in some instances, seemed so primitive that it was detrimental to U.S. goals.

This (neo-)anti-Communism, in any event, really surprised only U.S. authorities. Particularly in the early occupation phase, those officers, who wanted to promote a democratic media culture, sometimes doubted the actual independence of some of the Austrian "independent" journalists. During the reconstruction of the press in Italy, they were impressed when Italian journalists demonstrated tremendous autonomy and were not willing to accept interventions without resistance. In Austria, however, U.S. officers were surprised to find that the new journalists had no qualms about incorporating political suggestions by the U.S. Army without reservations.[4]

To speak here only of Austrian servility would certainly be exaggerated in light of other factors: the enormous material and spiritual needs, many years of political and intellectual suppression, and numerous controls implemented by the victorious powers. In any case, excessive subservience to authority and obsequiousness on the part of the Austrians considerably strengthened the influence of U.S. media officers. The continuously uncritical adoption of styles and forms of American journalism, however, without at the same time gaining a deeper understanding of democracy, also intensified tendencies of restoration.

The young, frequently untrained journalists were the least problem. Even though the year 1945 saw a severing with the Austrian (and German) journalistic traditions, to call it the zero hour of Austrian journalism is still not fitting. The actual break had already occurred in 1933, 1934, and 1938 as first the left, liberal, and Jewish journalists, and finally also the supporters of the Austrian corporate state, had been exiled from the country or had even lost their lives in prisons and concentration camps. Only a few from the first group returned after 1945, and this loss of people and quality still remains to be reappraised by Austrian journalism today. However, while the truncation of one sector of the political spectrum in particular had been effective, surprising continuity can be ascertained with regard to conservative journalists. Fritz Hausjell has shown that not only journalists who had written for the press of the Austro-fascist corporate state but also those who had written for NS papers, in surprisingly large numbers, had been quickly integrated after the war.[5] It may not come as a surprise that this happened particularly often at those newspapers that had been licensed by U.S. authorities. Precisely at such an intersection, the sticky dilemma of U.S. denazification plans and reality diverged.[6]

More than just the lack of qualified, unencumbered applicants had been a decisive factor in tolerating the past histories of certain journalists. Under the circumstances of military occupation, the fundamental democratic goal of incorporating large sections of the Austrian populace back into the political and economic scene had also caused points of conflict during the reconstruction of the democratic community. In addition, considerable motivation for the eventual departure from a stringent denazification course was rooted in the logic of the Cold War. While rallying for a consensus in support of the anti-Communist position of the United States, an already-existing, strong anti-Communist potential could be exploited. In the war of opinions with the Soviet Union, precisely those journalists who had already learned their trade as experts in anti-Communism under fascism could now be used for similar purposes. If this did not correspond with the goals of the "anti-Hitler Coalition," then it could not be helped. According to James A. Clark, the chief of the Interim International Information Service, the U.S. Army in Austria was confronted not only with a difficult and peculiar case but almost with an emergency operation program.[7]

Hence, the intensity of the direct political control of the press by the ISB was noticeably decreased already by the beginning of 1946. And it was exactly the predominant conservative, anti-Communist position of the majority of the papers that had been essential for this easing. The intensification of the Cold War became evident particularly in the area of censorship after 1946. Criticism toward the procedures of the occupation forces was still censored, especially in the Communist party press. Newspapers whose criticism of National Socialism was rather questionable but that compensated with a clearly aggressive anti-Communist stance now could count on the goodwill of U.S. censorship authorities. This slackening of censorship and its eventual discontinuation in

1947 occurred as a result of an ideological "readjustment" toward total anti-Communist propaganda and was by no means an additionally planned step toward antifascist reorientation and democratic redesigning of the Austrian press.[8]

The trends described here were particularly evident in the provincial papers established by the U.S. Army. The *Salzburger Nachrichten*, founded by the ISB on June 7, 1945, was first published under the editorship of Max Dasch and Gustav A. Canaval on October 23, 1945. The latter also acted as chief editor.[9] The U.S. media officers felt that they could be sure that the *Salzburger Nachrichten* would be true to U.S. guidelines, even under Austrian leadership. Albert van Eerden announced to the New York office shortly before he handed the newspaper over that the American way of presenting news had already taken hold in Salzburg. However, editorial freedom should still remain limited because "turning the paper over to the Austrians does not mean complete freedom. They must still follow M[ilitary] G[overnment] regulations on such things as pumping for Nazism in any way, anti-semitism, stories intended to cast reflections on the United Nations, etc."[10] Before long, however, these requirements became meaningless.

In any event, ISB officers clearly asserted themselves against the demands of the ÖVP, SPÖ, and KPÖ for special support of party newspapers. Already on September 19, 1945, a report assessed that it would be virtually suicidal for the intentions of the United States should the newspapers of Salzburg come under exclusive control of the three parties, because "a first class independent newspaper is indispensable if we are to help in the leading of Austrians to a democratic state. . . . Salzburg need not be a provincial town and certainly during U.S. occupation should not be forced to become one. We shall find Salzburg, along with Linz, a very crucial center in which U.S. efforts should be greatest."[11]

U.S. press ideals are impressively encapsulated here. It seems the media officers of the U.S. Army were convinced that Salzburg could not support four respectable newspapers. That assessment had less to do with their clairvoyant abilities than with the intensive support of a press free from party control by the U.S. authorities.[12] The long-term effects upon the Austrian press landscape of this U.S. stance resulted not only in the demise of party newspapers but also in a stronger regionalism.

During the first years of occupation, the relationship between the ISB and the editors of the *Salzburger Nachrichten* remained unspoiled, since the political guidelines of the U.S. Army were mostly upheld even without any pressure. In addition, the *Salzburger Nachrichten* also published countless reports on day-to-day life in the United States, articles on jazz and Hollywood, books and films from the United States, new developments in the arts, travel reports, and articles on the impact of democracy on all aspects of life. Symbolic value can be attributed to the publication of *Gone with the Wind* in December 1945, reflecting the relationship between the victorious and the defeated (yet, the Yankees were not in the Southern states, but in Austria). The "nonpartisanship" of the *Salzburger Nachrichten* went even further. Canaval requested anti-Communist directives and announcements for his newspaper directly from U.S. officers. This wish, however, was a bit too much even for the representatives of the occupation authority.[13]

Nevertheless, this proof of loyalty elicited sympathy for the *Salzburger Nachrichten* from the U.S. authorities, which was of particular importance at this point. On the one hand, the conditions of ownership of the newspaper were anything but clear, and the ÖVP, especially one of its leaders, Josef Rehrl, as representative of the Catholic Press Club, had attempted to take over the paper. On the other hand, these attempts were signs of a power struggle within the Salzburger ÖVP. Salzburg's ÖVP governor, Alois Hochleitner, made it clear in a telephone conversation that had been bugged by U.S. authorities that Rehrl simply wanted to take control of the entire press as a basis for personal power.[14]

Although Rehrl argued against the "irresponsible" reporting of the *Salzburger Nachrichten* (especially that of Viktor Reimann), in particular with regard to the laws controlling the activities of former National Socialists, he could not convince the representatives of the occupation authorities. During this crisis it clearly proved beneficial for the attacked editors that the *Salzburger Nachrichten* "has consistently supported the policy of the United States and has been consistently opposed to the policy and actions of the Soviet Union and of party politics in Austria."[15] The U.S. authorities therefore began to support the interests of Canaval and Dasch behind the scenes, to guarantee the retention of the private ownership structure of the paper. The pressure asserted by U.S. agencies was not limited to the representatives of the ÖVP but included also the archbishop, Andreas Rohracher. Because the U.S. intervention was so drastic, the Austrian opponents of the newspaper were finally forced to concede their positions.[16]

Still, the support of the U.S. Army was restricted to matters of legal authorization of the *Salzburger Nachrichten* and did not include respecting the private profits acquired by the editors. When the paper was finally handed over to Canaval and Dasch on October 23, 1945, the new publishers were obliged by the U.S. authorities to reinvest 50 percent of the profit into the public, cultural, and economic life in Salzburg. Another 25 percent was to be distributed among the employees.[17] The construction of a newspaper with a socialized profit-sharing system was indeed an interesting initiative for the liberal U.S. press officers. In doing so, the intent had been to accomplish two specific goals. First, it was felt that an independent press could be strengthened only through the support of nonpartisan publishers. Second, they were also convinced that the profits, and thereby the economic and opinion-creating power of the editors, most definitely had to be limited to a construction that guaranteed dividends for the general public as well as the employees. This conviction was based on the analysis of the political role of the corporate party structure of the German and Austrian press during the interwar period. The U.S. plans and the first steps of reconstruction for the new press system in Austria, then, were clearly in line with a socialized profit-sharing idea.

These ideas, however, enjoyed only short-lived success. The 50 percent reinvestment of profits that were earmarked for local reconstruction was contributed by the editors of the *Salzburger Nachrichten* for the years 1945–47 only. Only the profit sharing for the staff was maintained until the end of the period of occupation. As of 1956, these payments were also terminated. The board of directors of the *Salzburger Nachrichten*, who were responsible not only for the 50 percent profit distribution but also for overseeing the political stance of the paper (both duties were carried out rather superficially, if at all), benevolently overlooked the breach of contract since 1948 and dissolved itself completely by the end of 1954.[18]

The silent acceptance of the U.S. authorities of these obvious violations and the breach of the original contract shows that American occupation politics were motivated by other social priorities by 1947 at the latest. In addition, this incident also illustrates the fact that the promotion of newspapers that stayed free of political parties received absolute priority in the long-range U.S. media strategy. For this reason, the creeping changes in the legal construction of such newspapers, which clearly favored private publishers, hardly met with criticism.

The unabashed support of American media experts for the publishers of the *Salzburger Nachrichten* against all attempts of intervention by ÖVP politicians would, however, soon cause other problems. The occasion arose not as a result of illegal statutory financial developments but because of changes in news reporting. Even the most experienced secret-service experts could not have foreseen that the editorial stance of a paper founded by the U.S. Army would become more and more critical of the policies of the Austrian coalition government toward the questions of amnesty for former National Socialists. Particularly the support of the *Salzburger Nachrichten* for the German "national" camp and its criticism of U.S. soldiers (especially those who expressed racial prejudice against African-American GIs) made the U.S. authorities nervous. Their own paper had seemingly become an antidemocratic mouthpiece.[19]

Not only the position of the newspaper but the entire political situation in Salzburg was viewed ever more critically by the U.S. authorities. As a result, decisive countermeasures were introduced. Already by September 8, 1952, the questionable situation in Salzburg, a city that in 1945 had been characterized as a "hotbed of political dynamite,"[20] was summarized during a meeting of the Information Projects Committee in Vienna. Salzburg, according to the committee report, existed in a truly Alice-in-Wonderland atmosphere of contradictions in which a Catholic governor had a Communist press agent, a former

National Socialist politician claimed the right to power by trying to reclaim Hitler's glory, the conservative ÖVP was handicapped as a result of the splintering of the party in three factions, SPÖ politicians were suspicious that the U.S. Army supported the VdU, a conservative newspaper had a publisher who had almost daily contact with a Communist, countless influential businessmen and politicians had the personal insurance gained from filling both right- and left-wing party coffers, and the powerful newspaper *Salzburger Nachrichten* actually held a position sharply opposed to the interests of the United States and the coalition government in Vienna.[21]

As a result of the excessive independence of the *Salzburger Nachrichten*, U.S. experts had now reached the decision that the increase of anti-Americanism, anti-Semitism, and neo-Nazism in this city deserved particular propaganda attention.[22] Although all this information was inaccurate, the return of the newspaper to the U.S. Army was now actually being considered. For this purpose, the search for the original October 1945 transmittal contract was ordered in the military archives in Kansas.[23]

Ultimately, the newspaper remained in the hands of Canaval and Dasch. Nevertheless, "Operation Salzburg" commenced on January 26, 1953, with the political objective "to expose obscurantist and Communazi opposition."[24] This special operation foresaw the intensified distribution of the *Wiener Kurier* as competition for the *Salzburger Nachrichten*. The *Kurier*'s enhancement included improved distribution by rapid train transport, increased advertising, and newspaper sales via sidewalk paper vendors in Salzburg. In addition, activities in the America Houses and in theaters, through lectures as well as festivities sponsored jointly by the U.S. Army and the citizens of Salzburg, were strengthened. Even the news and entertainment programs of radio Rot-Weiss-Rot were intensified.[25] As irony will have it, the attacks of the *Salzburger Nachrichten* on America for not being anti-Communist enough arose precisely during the period of McCarthyism and belong to the peculiarities of the "Salzburg climate," whose development was helped along by U.S. authorities.

In any event, the ownership rights of the *Salzburger Nachrichten* remained uncontested. Surely this was not because the transmittal contract had not been found. Although the right-wing politics of the Salzburg paper was not accepted without criticism by U.S. officers, the newspaper could be relied on in one decisive point: it remained a central ally in the propaganda war against the Soviet Union and Communism on a regional level.

The *Oberösterreichischen Nachrichten*, founded in Linz on June 11, 1945, was handed over to Austrian license holders already in October 1945. The legal construction of the Demokratische Druck- und Verlagsgesellschaft m.b.H. again clearly illustrates that the U.S. Army initially aimed at the total transformation of the Austrian press structure. Here, too, party newspapers, which were perceived to be the central instigators of political conflict during the First Republic, were to be weakened.[26] Once again, in an effort to hold the individual interests of the publishers in check, large portions of the profits were to be socialized, distributed among the staff, and used for reconstruction.

While the *Salzburger Nachrichten* had to be handed over to Canaval and Dasch alone because the representatives of the SPÖ and the KPÖ refused to work together with the "Austro-fascist" Canaval, the publishing team (Verlagsgesellschaft) in Linz consisted of six individuals. In addition to the nonpartisan members Hans Behrmann, Franz Lettner, and Otto Nicoleth, three members with political affiliations were appointed: Ernst Koref (SPÖ), Alfred Maleta (ÖVP), and Franz Haider (KPÖ). The paper's line and profit sharing were also controlled by a curatorship.[27]

The *Oberösterreichischen Nachrichten* also evolved into an "independent" newspaper in the U.S. sense because shortly after the authorization of partisan newspapers, Koref and Haider left the group: one went to the *Linzer Tagblatt* (SPÖ), the other to the *Neue Zeit* (KPÖ). Only Maleta, who was thoroughly convinced of the future success of the independents, remained and turned over the editorship of the ÖVP organ *Linzer Volksblatt* to Felix Kern. Maleta thus proved himself not only an intelligent conservative who anticipated new trends in the development of the press but also an ideal editor for U.S. press officers.

In discussions with ISB representatives, Maleta, who was also a parliamentary delegate for the ÖVP, made it clear that as a true "party soldier," he would have had to destroy the *Oberösterreichischen Nachrichten* long ago. He also left no doubt that he had done everything (and would continue in doing so) to save the newspaper from the claws of the ÖVP. As a member of this party, he knew very well how it functioned "and how rotten it was."[28] In illustrating the urgency for the aid of U.S. agencies against the usurpation attempts of the ÖVP, Maleta used the example of the ÖVP printing works in Linz. These, he noted, were actually SPÖ property that had been confiscated by the National Socialists. After the war, they were then taken over by the Americans and left to the ÖVP. Now it was the center for ÖVP publications, which Linz's Catholic bishop had even spoken of as "my printery." Maleta made it quite evident that "the OeVP would never let them revert to the Socialists."[29] The strategy of the editor of the *Oberösterreichischen Nachrichten* was a full success. The U.S. authorities protected the paper from all usurpation attempts, especially by the ÖVP, because they wanted to prevent the strengthening of the party press at all cost.

Alfred Maleta could therefore further develop the *Oberösterreichischen Nachrichten* together with Hans Behrmann. They enjoyed relatively little interference, even though certain similarities with the *Salzburger Nachrichten* existed. Fewer difficulties were registered in the area of the paper's political leanings than in the area of profit-sharing distribution. This problem had actually arisen much earlier in Linz than in Salzburg.

Only energetic resistance on the part of U.S. agencies could hinder the attempts of the owners of the *Oberösterreichischen Nachrichten* to stifle socialization merely one year after the probationary period.[30] The hour of the "private entrepreneur" would, nevertheless, soon come. Since the anti-Communist stance of the majority of the Austrian newspapers was soon obvious, U.S. press officers relinquished any further direct control measures after the summer of 1947. As a consequence, Austrian newspaper publishers soon threw profit sharing overboard and continued to work further without interference.[31] Still, at least Hans Behrmann could not enjoy his new paper for long. In 1948 he was forced to liquidate his independent Zeitschriftenvertriebs-Gesellschaft m.b.H. because of financial irregularities. Finally, in 1952, he resigned completely from the *Oberösterreichischen Nachrichten* after he had been arrested on various charges of professional misconduct in January of the same year. His share of the paper, which had been temporarily managed by Novitas GmbH (Fritz Dickmann and Fritz Molden), was transferred to J. Wimmer GmbH & Co. in 1955. Thereafter, Maleta received only 26 percent of the common stock. However, in a power struggle for the newspaper that lasted more than twenty years, he ultimately emerged victorious in 1975.[32] The foundation stone for his success had been laid by U.S. press officers.

In contrast, the *Wiener Kurier*, founded by the ISB in August 1945, remained under the ownership of U.S. authorities and under the direct control of U.S. press officers. In the first two years of its existence alone, the *Wiener Kurier* made over 14 million schillings in profits, and until the beginning of the 1950s maintained a positive balance.[33] Furthermore, it became—as Austria's newspaper with the highest circulation—not only an important mouthpiece for the United States but especially also the model for other newspapers.

Only toward the end of the period of occupation, when the Austrian press no longer required a directly controlled model and when the remaining propaganda duties could be taken over by radio Rot-Weiss-Rot, did U.S. authorities decide to turn over the *Wiener Kurier*, which had, in the meantime, gone into the red. The paper was then acquired by Ludwig Polsterer after the mediatory assistance of his friend Ernst Haeusserman, a former ISB officer in 1954. The new publisher had promised to maintain the stance supported by the United States. Therefore, the representatives of the U.S. authorities offered no resistance during the last months of occupation as 50 percent of the shares were sold (via Josef Tafler) to the ÖAAB (an organization of the ÖVP), which were then quietly taken over by the ÖVP parliamentary delegate Leopold Helbich. The newspaper hence could be considered nonpartisan merely in a formal legal sense.[34]

Actually, at the time of the founding of the *Wiener Kurier*, its long-term control by the U.S. authorities was not yet completely certain. During the first months, the newspaper was headed by the Austrian editor-in-chief Oskar Maurus Fontana. His objective, in particular, was to incorporate a cultural component. In wanting to reintroduce this traditional European newspaper focus, he quickly collided with U.S. editors. For this reason, Fontana was replaced by the U.S. press officer Hendric J. Burns at the turn of 1946. Political misrepresentation was not the issue here, as Fontana's firing was due solely to his "incompetence" in attempting to make the *Wiener Kurier* a paper in the U.S. style.[35]

Fontana had wanted to reach the intellectual elites with this newspaper. In the eyes of the U.S. experts, however, who wanted to target the middle class, Fontana had thus committed a deadly journalistic sin. According to the ISB officers, it would have clearly been a tremendous mistake to have given the Austrian journalists independent reign, for they would have naturally produced only a mediocre "journal" in the European style. Only after U.S. journalists had taken over command and introduced solid political reports, especially world news printed in bold headlines, would success be possible. There was no doubt that Austrian journalists needed to be guided firmly down the correct path. Theodore Kaghan, one of the most influential U.S. media experts in Austria, pointedly summarized the cardinal sin of the *Wiener Kurier* under Austrian leadership: "Its news coverage was second-rate because the editors were allowed to devote too much space to 'journalism,' European-style, instead of news, American-style. The paper was heavy with culture and light on facts."[36]

Because the "objectivity of facts," compared with the "subjectivity of opinions," had become *the* export hit for U.S. experts, the *Wiener Kurier* had been completely subjugated to American interests; the Austrian staff functioned, at best, as a cover for an inofficial U.S. government organ with potential secret-service duties.[37] This characterization of U.S. newspapers undoubtedly hits the nail on the head, even though liberal internationalists, such as Kaghan, sometimes went beyond publishing hymns of the American way of life to include also critical reports on the inadequacies in the United States, "even when it hurts."[38] This liberal course, however, was not shared by all U.S. agencies, and as a result Kaghan, one of the most important proponents of anti-Communist journalism in Austria, was accused of being a Communist sympathizer by Senator Joe McCarthy in 1953.[39] In the long list of fanciful charges leveled by the senator from Wisconsin, this accusation certainly was one of the most absurd. Not only were such articles criticizing deficiencies in the United States very rare; when they actually did appear, they increased the popularity of the *Wiener Kurier*, thus heightening its political credibility.

Certainly, the newspaper's general political line was anything but painful to U.S. interests. The higher-ups in Washington and New York could point not only to articles dealing favorably with domestic American issues but also to a mass of anti-Communist reports. U.S. diplomats thus followed with satisfaction the development of this daily, which was under the control of U.S. Army press officers, because "the 'Wiener Kurier' is a fine propaganda medium, getting better all the time."[40]

It was not, however, the well-edited combination of news and commentaries with a predominantly pro-American slant that met with the approval of its anti-Communist audience. The idealistic representations of the political and social situation in the United States as well as of the deep, dark, universally lurking threat of Communism were certainly not sufficient to secure the forefront position among the newspapers. For the anti-Communist line surely did not elevate the *Wiener Kurier* above and beyond most of the other trees in the Austrian media forest. Even its privileged position with respect to the allotment of paper, its efficient distribution system, and its access to news developments in advance of others (the *Wiener Kurier* initially enjoyed exclusive access to U.S. public and private news agencies for breaking stories so that it not only published news sooner than its competition but also maintained a monopoly on stories, especially with regard to dramatic developments in domestic matters) still were not enough to make the paper a model in future developments.

Its success depended, rather, on its modern layout, explosive headlines, good photographs, and the perceived division between news and opinion through the introduction of frequent commentaries. Even more important was the packaging of political information in human-interest articles, descriptions of the blessings of the American way of life, and the presentation of U.S. popular culture, which was particularly attractive for the young. Essays on pop music and Hollywood, jazz and Broadway, Cadillacs and Chevrolets, supermarkets and skyscrapers, created an almost exotic appeal. Not only the American standard of living but also the style of life—in many cases still seemingly inconceivable—was constantly presented as the ideal to be emulated by Austrians. In addition, serial novels and reader competitions were an instant hit. The interest in everything American seemed so great that even an English-language course was introduced. In May 1947 the motto "Everyone learns English" appeared.[41]

Certain areas of excess and waste in the United States, however, remained taboo even for the *Wiener Kurier*. In an effort to hinder criticism of declining U.S. aid to Austria and wastefulness, the journalists were instructed in April 1947 to refrain from publishing the following topics: the high caloric intake in the United States, photographs of foodstuffs, recipes, banquets and holiday meals, and atomic tests in the Pacific, which caused a large number of animals to die. Even reports on record harvests were to be omitted unless they were published in combination with official references by U.S. agencies to food shipments for Austria.[42]

To understand fully any paper's stance one must analyze not only the actual printed texts but also the contents of wastepaper baskets of the editors. Even though the press is not always successful in suggesting to the public what it should think, the aforementioned example shows that it was often very successful "in telling its readers what to think about."[43] "Die Stimme Amerikas" (The Voice of America) was the title of one column in the *Wiener Kurier*. This might actually have been a more appropriate name for the publication as a whole.

In addition to the *Wiener Kurier*, the ISB produced and distributed a large number of magazines that targeted important opinion makers and special-interest groups. Between 1948 and 1954, fully 168 editions of the *Gewerkschaftliche Nachrichten aus den USA* (Trade union news from the USA) were distributed twice a month to the leadership of the Austrian Trade Union, its factory committees, and hundreds of thousands of workers. Its reports stressed the high standard of living of American workers, renounced the impression that the United States was the center of capitalistic exploitation, and supported the Social Partnership policies of the ÖGB. Another important task was the support of the Marshall Plan, which meant that the "evangelism of increased productivity" was preached as often as possible. Union interests could also be asserted even without a social-political dimension. This, too, was the tenor of the *Gewerkschaftliche Nachrichten aus den USA* and was especially emphasized by its executive editor, Carl H. Petersen: "I don't believe it is our business to write regretfully about the absence of a major Socialist party in America, to imply that America is backward in social development, or to treat every liberal step with a condescending air, implying that American progress should be measured by the degree to which it accepts Socialist principles."[44]

The 161 issues of *Landwirtschaftliche Nachrichten aus den Vereinigten Staaten* (Agricultural news from the United States) were sent to professors and students of the University of Agriculture, agricultural interests groups, and thousands of farmers between 1947 and 1952. Practical tips were suggested, from avoiding erosion to fighting animal sicknesses, to the massive use of insecticides for combating pests, to irrigation and the introduction of new types of vegetation. Especially highlighted were the advantages of mechanization, electrification, and motorization; the conversion to modern agricultural machinery; the use of chemical fertilizers; and the improvement of methods to increase productivity.[45]

Until 1949, eighty editions of *Medizinische Nachrichten aus den Vereinigten Staaten* (Medical news from the United States) were produced and distributed to approximately 5,000 Viennese doctors and 7,000 medics in the provinces. Only when the place of publication had been moved to Bad Nauheim in West Germany in July 1949 did the number of publications circulated to Austrian doctors decline. The articles dealt especially with the latest developments in operation techniques and healing methods and discussed the advantages and possibilities of the use of new medicines such as penicillin and sulfonamide.[46] The *Verleger Informationen* (Publishers' information) reported on new publications in America, offered Austrian publishers books whose titles had already been translated into German, and introduced new strategies in marketing books according to the U.S. model.

The magazine *Erziehung* was distributed free of charge to Austrian teachers beginning in January 1948, and by 1950 was reaching 30,000 educators. Suggestions addressing school reforms were given much attention. It also examined the introduction of student clubs, student parliaments, group discussions, student newspapers, changes in teaching plans, and modern psychological methods, as well as teaching improvements in individual subjects such as sports, modern languages, physics, and chemistry.

*Deine-4-H-Klub-Zeitung* (Your 4-H Club newspaper) was directed particularly at rural youths. In addition to information on sports and entertainment programs that were sponsored by the U.S. Army, the boys and girls in the country were officially made familiar with the newest advances in American agriculture. In this magazine, reinforcement of traditional gender roles was particularly evident. While articles on agricultural machines, modern livestock breeding techniques, and the attainment of greater harvest via the use of chemicals were dedicated to young men, young women learned almost solely about sewing, knitting, cooking, how to improve one's vegetable garden, and—a key point—the importance of hygiene.

Even U.S. GIs stationed in Austria had their own periodical. Yet, other soldiers enjoyed the U.S. magazine as well. The journal *Amerika*, which was also published in Russian and was directed toward the soldiers of the Red Army, was distributed in the Soviet zone with a circulation of 1,500 to 3,000 issues.

Still further, the ISB also circulated other magazines that had been produced by the U.S. Army in the German occupation zone. This included *Heute* (Today, with a circulation in Austria between 38,000 and 75,000), *Die amerikanische Rundschau* (The American review, circulation between 2,500 and 50,000), and *Der Monat* (The month, circulation between 2,000 and 5,000). Also the British-American coproductions *Die neue Auslese* (The new digest, circulation between 5,000 and 15,000) and *Das Tor* (The door) were distributed. The latter magazine was discontinued only after four issues because it was considered too left-wing.

The U.S. version of *Reader's Digest* was circulated until 1948, only to be directly replaced by a German-language edition that was introduced by the ISB. As a result of certain import privileges as well as the preferential distribution through the system established by the U.S. Army, other U.S. newspapers and magazines, such as the *New York Times, Time,* and the *New York Herald Tribune,* also profited.[47]

The finances for the Magazines for Friendship Program were certainly well invested. Public-opinion polls and studies on the popularity of the American publications produced between 1946 and 1954 show that they were read "until they literally fell to pieces."[48] Those especially falling to pieces were mostly publications characterized as "Their Masters' Voices."[49] Although *Heute, Die amerikanische Rundschau,* and *Die neue Auslese* were obviously copies of *Life, Harper's,* and *Reader's Digest,* American criticism of these German copies was not long in coming. U.S. press experts lamented especially the complacent, professorial, and unjournalistic style, which even all development aid for the press by the U.S. Army could not eradicate. The U.S. magazines in Germany, according to a biting commentary, were similar to the *New Yorker*, which published articles from the *Philological Quarterly*.[50]

## Licenses for Publications

The ISB was not only exerting influence on its own press products. Even more important, until mid-1947 all publications appearing in the U.S. zone— from the most important to the most unassuming—required a permit issued by the occupation power. Even the magazines *Das Wüstenroter Eigenheim* (A homeowners' journal), *Die bunte Kinderwelt* (The colorful world of children), and *Der oberösterreichische Imker* (The Upper Austrian beekeeper) were ordered to obtain American approval.[51]

In total, U.S. press officers issued permits to 214 publications and publishers until this requirement was repealed in mid-1947. The press politics in Austria were, without a doubt, much more liberal than in Germany, where licensing was maintained until 1949. This stricter policy, therefore, had stronger and more long-term implications for the press landscape of the Federal Republic of Germany.[52]

The relatively more liberal posture in Austria by no means suggests a relinquishing of all influence and control. In addition to censorship measures, which had been initially implemented against all forms of fascist activities, and which became directed almost wholly toward Communist newspapers after 1947, the ISB had other forms of pressure, including paper allotments, news blockages, access to information, and preferential treatment. And U.S. occupation authorities had another trump card, which can by no means be quantified: the fear of interference, which caused most Austrian editors to avoid publishing articles critical of the United States.

It is just as difficult to measure exactly the impact of U.S. media politics on the popular press in Austria. However, the lifting of the press import tax on German publications in 1951 gave the popular boulevard press in Austria all it needed to flourish.[53] To interpret this, however, as the surmounting of American influence would surely be incorrect. For precisely the new permeability of the once-shielded border between the U.S. zone in Germany and Austria until the end of the 1940s would soon catapult the Federal Republic into the position of being the most important transmission vehicle and intensifier of American influence in Austria—and not only with respect to the media. Obviously, the German interpretation of information coming out of the United States through Wenzel Lüdecke and Co. resulted in a twice-filtered image of the United States in Austria.[54]

## Information as Public Relations:
## The Duties of the News and Features Division

The central turnstile and point of coordination for communications between the ISB and the Austrian press was the News and Features division. The U.S. Features and Pictures Services supplied up to 200 Austrian newspapers and magazines—even in the Soviet zone—with reports and pictures from the United States free of charge and also familiarized Austrian journalists with the practices of the U.S. press. Particular attention was devoted to newspapers in rural areas. Approximately 120 local papers were serviced with news and information each week. The selection of material had to appear as uncontroversial as possible, for not only could Austrians supposedly smell propaganda a mile away, but it was essential to incorporate as many articles in newspapers as possible, for they might in turn also appear in the Soviet zone. Therefore, "loud beating of drums for Uncle Sam" was consciously avoided.[55]

Quarterly analyses of the printing of American news reports in Austrian newspapers document the sweeping success of these programs. Already by the end of the 1940s, hundreds of articles could be placed in papers every month, and by the summer of 1950, the program was expanded even further. Because the British occupation power had discontinued its local press activities, the ISB assumed authority over all British news installations and also exclusively supplied local papers in the British occupation zone in Styria and in Carinthia. With that, the breadth of American news was increased significantly. Through a newly organized special service, dealing primarily with local newspapers, it had now become possible to publish more than 550 lengthy and 230 shorter news articles each month. Fully 90 percent of the articles translated by AND (American News Service) were so accommodated.

The ISB was now successful in distributing 3,500 photos and also picture matrices and print forms as a result of improvements of the Austrian infrastructure. These services were also free of charge and were particularly appreciated by local papers. In addition to quantity, the quality of photos was also increased because the ISB now received the rights from AP, INP, and UPI to use photographic materials from these agencies free of charge outside Vienna. From 1950 onward, 75 percent of the Austrian press could be reached directly, and approximately 50 percent of the photos offered were printed. These numbers, however, do not include the press in Vienna. The *Wiener Illustrierte* (Vienna illustrated) alone published four pages of American material each week, presenting, in particular, reports and photos highlighting the blessings of the Marshall Plan in Austria.[56]

This psychological offensive no longer dealt exclusively with influencing Austrian newspapers. Its potential reverberations in neighboring Communist countries had been elevated to a principal component of the plan. This "curtain penetration" was possible with the help of "special means."[57] The new media offensive made increases in circulation possible for the *Gewerkschaftliche Nachrichten aus den USA* from 10,000 to 46,000, the *Landwirtschaftliche Nachrichten aus den Vereinigten Staaten* from 9,000 to 11,000, and *Erziehung* from 20,000 to 30,000.[58] The intensification of U.S. press activities was closely coordinated with the ECA Mission. The Marshall Plan office was not granted advisory rights without reason, for a portion of the media program was also financed by this office—via Austrian counterpart schillings.[59]

However, more than just the tremendous financial leeway and the anti-Communism of the majority of the Austrian readership and journalists expedited the success of U.S. press politics. The ISB still had two further trump cards at their disposal: the large interest in American literature after years of isolation, and especially the craving for information concerning the daily life and the standard of living in the United States.

For this reason, it was quite simple to accommodate Austrian editors with short works of fiction. However, the most important criterion in choosing such works was not always their literary quality. The decisive factor, according to the leading editor of the News Services in Vienna, Carl H. Peterson, was, more important, that every printed story reflected "typical" life in the United States—and not "that it should please high critics. Without ruling out stories of social significance, I prefer little yarns about home, or school, or farm life, or Christmas, or a good western, to depressing things of the 'Tobacco Road' type."[60] Theodore Kaghan was thoroughly convinced of the attractiveness of short stories because "the Austrian editors are very hungry for good American fiction, and we exploit this hunger to pull a 'package' deal. In other words, we can often get an editor to run what we consider to be one or two good implementers by offering him a short story as a bribe."[61]

Primarily those features that seemingly carried no political content and informed quite generally about the United States were particularly effective tools of this press strategy. Stories achieving the greatest resonance dealt with the American way of life, technical advances, human-interest stories, and the sensational and unusual in everyday American life. Newspapers in all three Western zones of occupation and in Vienna published these special articles. Approximately 5 percent of the material offered was even published in papers originating in the Soviet zone. Every month, the ISB placed between 600 and 1,500 features in the Austrian press. Exact figures of the special articles published until 1955 cannot be compiled because the archival materials are spotty. In any event, each and every article was strictly recorded. Therefore, on the basis of the enormous amounts of available materials, one can estimate that approximately 60,000 to 100,000 features were published until the end of the occupation period.[62] These items ranged from "Who Was Uncle Sam?" to "America, the Land of Milk and Honey," from "Miss America 1947—a Versatile Woman" to "How America Celebrates Christmas," from "Walt Disney" to "Bing Crosby Adopts an Orphan."[63]

## Austrian Journalism on the Side of the "Forces of Freedom": U.S. News Agencies and the Training of Austrian Journalists

This free and vast supply of features was, without a doubt, one of the most important and successful programs of American press politics. The wide range of topics and large number of articles was more than the ISB staff could produce by itself. During the first months of occupation, the ISB received support in the compilation of news and the creation and selection of special articles from AND in particular. The services of the private U.S. agencies Associated Press (AP) and United Press International (UPI) were also called upon beginning in the summer of 1946, even though AND alone distributed news to newspapers, amounting to 6,000 to 10,000 words per day.

The interweaving of U.S. state and private interests had long-lasting consequences for the Austrian news market. The situation was similar to that in Japan and in the German western zone, where the monopolies of Domei and Wolff were broken. In Austria as well, the U.S. agencies AP and UPI set up shop, as did, to some extent, the British Reuters. With this, a decisive change had been instigated, and the prewar monopolies of French and German news agencies were taken over by their Anglo-American counterparts. As a matter of fact, the American agencies also played a significant role in the establishment of the Austrian Press Association (APA) in 1946, and AP and Reuters, as a result, became the most important deliverers of foreign news for APA.[64]

The influence of U.S. news agencies was by no means limited to Austria but also included all of Western Europe. While AP only had 469 customers in the whole of Europe in 1939, this number swelled to 1,493 by 1949. During the same period, UPI's clients also rose from 485 to 1,058.[65] The market in telephotography has been dominated by AP and UPI since this time as well and could, with exception of the former Communist states, expand worldwide. Reuters was also successful in consolidating its position primarily in the area of data communications for international financial markets. The increasingly important video news market was shared between the British Visnews and the Anglo-American conglomerate UPITV and the U.S. news firm CBS. With this, these agencies achieved—worldwide—significant influence not only on the selection and contents of news but also on its form. The way in which information was presented had an especially exemplary and long-lasting effect. The title of Jeremy Tunstall's book *The Media Are American* is by no means an exaggeration.[66]

Still, U.S. press politics in Austria were limited neither to the spreading of a flood of general information concerning the United States nor to the propagation of direct political news that was to support the interests of the United States. They also focused on the training of Austrian journalists. Already by the end of 1946, the ISB and AND employed 200 Austrians, and many hundred more journalists had been trained in American journalism by the end of the occupation period. AND had become what one might consider a schooling center for young Austrians. American media experts were primarily concerned that the continuity of this work should not be endangered by the end of the period of occupation. Already in October 1946 the first successes made the leading press officer, Albert van Eerden, optimistic. The most important groundwork had been laid. In any event, the ISB would "leave behind a fairly substantial cadre of young Austrian men and women experienced in the American type of journalism and indoctrinated in the democratic approach to news. Time may prove that AND's 'school of journalism' was a valuable factor in whatever democratization Austria may attain."[67] A daily example of the great success of U.S. journalism was the *Wiener Kurier*. The ISB was continually reassured that its paper was having the strongest influence on the Austrian press in decades.[68]

Even though U.S. media officers could soon notify Washington that "it is gratifying to note that the larger part of the Austrian press has aligned with the forces of freedom,"[69] they nevertheless felt that a significant portion of the Austrian papers were still very provincial and old-fashioned. Furthermore, they assessed the influence of party newspapers as being still too great, although they were on their way out. To effectively secure long-term changes, young, talented, and particularly promising journalists were chosen to participate in ongoing exchange programs and went to the United States. Upon arrival, they were educated in U.S. journalism at various universities and thereafter could participate in internships at prestigious newspapers. Of all Austrian participants in these exchange programs during the first years, between 10 and 20 percent were journalists. They included not only practicing journalists but also students of this discipline as well as other newspaper specialists, such as the future chairman of the Journalism Institute at the University of Vienna, Kurt Paupié. The main goal of these exchange programs was "U.S. indoctrination in basic newspaper principles."

## The Role of the Picture: Photography, Advertisements, Comics

More than just the journalistic word, report, and column were influenced by the U.S. model. Press photography also took many examples from the (prefabricated) images of American photojournalism, which no doubt reached its zenith in the "documentary style" of the New Deal.[70] The chief photographer of the ISB and the head of the USIS photo post in Vienna, Yoichi R. Okamoto, trained forty Austrians alone and worked with many of the most important Austrian photographers in the postwar period, such as Gottfried Rainer, Fritz Mayr, Ferdinand Schreiber, Ernst Haas, Lothar Rübelt, Herbert Bayer, and Heini Mayr. Some of these photographers, in turn, were influential in the United States, such as Ernst Haas in his series for *Heute* and Heini Mayr, who was with the *Salzburger Nachrichten* from 1945 to 1955, in his later work for *Time* and *Life* in New York.[71]

The angle of vision and focus of U.S. photography, however, was nothing new for Austrian photographers. Already directly after the First World War, the press photography of AP, Wide World Photos, and UPI had flooded the Austrian market. Between 1933 and 1938 an important representative of this photographic style had been Kurt Korff, once head of the *Berliner Illustrierte* and then head of *Wiener Illustrierte*. After being forced to emigrate from Austria, Korff later became one of the cofounders of the magazine *Life*.[72]

This reciprocal influence in postwar artistic projects between U.S. and European photography—for example, in the founding of *Magnum* magazine in 1954—was quite obvious. The mutual influence was weaker in the illustrated tabloids, these twentieth-century poor-man's Bibles, which generally focused only on the dramatic.[73] The photographic documentations of the Austrian illustrated *Wiener Bildwoche* (1945–60), *Wiener Wochenblatt* (1945–51), *Alpenland Illustrierte* (1945–47), but also *Heute* (1945–51) and *Wiener Kurier* (1945–54), had become more and more like their U.S. counterparts in their photography. It is clear that these developments were hastened considerably through the free distribution of American photographic materials. This trend was even more intensified when German illustrated magazines began to flood the Austrian market after 1951. The viewpoint of *Welt Illustrierte*, which was published by the Soviet occupation power between 1946 and 1955, could only be called out of focus in comparison.[74]

Austrian press photography in the postwar era increasingly adjusted its focus and perspectives according to the U.S. model. This was a change in focal length that was not limited to the pictorial representation of "political" news, general information, and the sensational. It also had an impact on advertisements, which gained greater importance and expanse ever since the beginning of the 1950s.[75] If we look at the period of reconstruction through the lens of published advertising photos and compare it with earlier ones, we can see another system in the visual landscape of possibilities. Certainly, during the early years after the war, photos often showed a collage of destitution and the new beginnings of wealth, a kaleidoscopic rejection of poverty and embracing of newly created abundance. In the same vein, the images of a better life and the supposed advantages of consumption also grew in intensity and focus.

Especially after the commencement of Marshall Plan aid, these developments in Austria were codirected, for the most part, by advertising agencies and opinion-research institutes that were established either as sister companies of U.S. firms or by indigenous companies utilizing the models and methods developed in the United States. As in many other areas of the media, the ISB also set important guidelines for using public-opinion studies on Austrian acceptance of U.S. cultural policies.[76] These investigations were carried out under the supervision and direction of ISB by Austrian coworkers. The

Gallup company could fall back on this trained personnel when it opened an Austrian office only several years later. With respect to commercials, the ECA Mission was exemplary because its control of the purse strings made it the most important customer in this newly established branch.

In total, the development of advertising had already been strongly influenced through American agencies based in the United States and Europe before the Second World War. Even though the war and the first few years of need thereafter caused a short period of stagnation, the end of the war brought with it once again a tremendous increase in the possibilities of influence, so that the sign language of advertising in all of Western Europe was soon American. The new methods of advertisement in the press were certainly not limited to layout, form, and subject matter. Because of a lower level of prosperity, different structures of ownership, but also the different roles of the media in the respective societies, the importance of advertising in the print media in Austria, at least in the early 1950s, only slowly blossomed. Only since the 1960s has the Austrian press fully followed the American example, where "the larger the number of advertising pages carried, the more space there was to be filled 'to keep the advertisements apart.' "[77]

One possibility to fill the space between the advertisements was the incorporation of comics, which became increasingly popular with young audiences. Already in 1950, two authors of Ph.D. dissertations in journalism pointed an accusing finger at these "corrupting" U.S. imports. The so-called comic strips, which they felt were by no means comical but instead served their undemanding readers sensational serial stories, seemed to be growing like weeds.[78] The authors shook their heads and asked themselves where the humor was. They maintained that although it could be rather arrogant, and even simply untrue, to categorize all Americans merely as children, it still remained a fact that the American mentality was fundamentally different from that of the Austrian.[79]

The difference in mentality, at least in this area, was not so great, as even Benito Mussolini had come to learn. When the Italian government attempted to keep U.S. comic strips out of Italian newspapers prior to the Second World War, the public was outraged. The removal of *Popeye* created such unrest that the government felt itself forced to allow once again the publishing of the adventures of the spinach-craving sailor.[80] Even after the official banishment of comics under the "Third Reich," the cultural battle was continued against this "cultureless poison" and not only because these series still continued to enjoy underground circulation. Obviously when Superman destroyed the Siegfried line and threw bombs on Berlin, it became completely clear to the S.S. paper *Das Schwarze Korps* to which "race" the flying world-policeman Clark Kent belonged.[81] As Joseph Goebbels announced in the German Reichstag, Superman is a Jew.[82]

Even official U.S. agencies took the warlike heroic actions of comic strip characters completely seriously. From October 17, 1943, to the end of the war, the series *Terry and the Pirates* thus was recorded in the *Congressional Record*.[83] Flash Gordon, Prince Valiant, Joe Palooka, Jungle Jim, Scorchy Smith, Dick Tracy, X-9, Tarzan, Buz Sawyer, and Johnny Hazard all carried out such patriotic duties that they too were entitled to participate in the victory of the Allies, thereafter to concentrate on the Communist enemy. In 1955, already fifty-three comic strip series were available in Austria, most of which were imported from the Federal Republic of Germany.[84]

This popularity, of course, meant that the professional protectors of the youth had no rest. With the help of legislation, they tried to build a wall that even Superman could not leap over. To prohibit the "seduction of the innocent" through comic strips, a "volunteer control group for comic strips" was established in West Germany, analogous to the U.S. Comic Strip Code Authority. In Austria, even more far-reaching measures were installed. Whereas the Buchklub der Jugend saw itself called upon to develop an effective counter-poison, the infamous Smut and Trash Law was passed to assist in strengthening the foundations of the protection. This piece of legislation proposed a radical cure for the "comic pest." Therefore, Walt Disney Productions, whose Mickey Mouse became the most popular comic strip magazine, saw itself called into action, and, in a highly publicized trial, it managed to overturn these censorship measures.[85]

Only twenty years after this attempt to vilify Mickey Mouse and Donald Duck as seducers of children had failed, U.S. comic strips were reaching approximately 200 million readers in sixty countries daily. By the middle of the 1980s, Walt Disney Productions took in $350 million in Austria and Germany alone.[86]

The frustrated defenders of youths' morals perhaps were unaware that these highly respected series from the United States were simply outgrowths of the work of Gustave Doré, William Hogarth, Heinrich Hoffmann, and Wilhelm Busch. This connection is exemplified by the two series that are seen as the first models of the modern comic strip.

Richard Felton Outcalt's strip *The Yellow Kid*, published first on February 16, 1896, in *New Yorker World* (owned by the Hungarian immigrant Joseph Pulitzer), had definite parallels with the nasty boys from Europe, Max and Moritz, and the tricks of the protagonist were a particular delight for recent immigrants. And the *Katzenjammer Kids*, by Rudolph Dirks, whose pranks first appeared on December 16, 1897, in *New York Journal*, satisfied a child's dream of William Randolph Hearst, who, during a trip to Europe, had become acquainted with the work of Wilhelm Busch. The Katzies, Hans and Fritz, were therefore at least cousins—if not brothers—of the German Max and Moritz.[87]

Whereas the pranks of Wilhelm Busch's protagonists even appealed to the opponents of comic strips—surely also because of the "pedagogical value" of their eventual punishment—their counterparts in the United States could see no sure value, for Hans and Fritz got away with it all. Without a doubt, it was not in the interest of the conservative Hearst press to jeopardize the U.S. system by publishing these comics. Just the opposite is true. The Katzenjammer Kids, this duo of destruction and disrespect for every authority, practiced their pranks in the milieu of German immigrants, and the laughs were almost solely at the expense of ethnic minorities and "un-American" nonconformists. Still, Hans and Fritz rhymed with "society is nix," a message that was especially understood by the ridiculed and humiliated.

This ambivalence, or tension between conformity and criticism, surely contributed to the enormous success of comic strips. Undoubtedly, they also contributed to the dissemination and reinforcement of basic ideological positions. It is not surprising, then, that Ariel Dorfman and Armand Mattelart, based on a study of the "upright" Walt Disney comics, could show how individual adventurers operated with the supposed backwardness and cultural inferiority of the countries of the so-called Third World. Solutions to problems were always reached by a First World victory over the "exotic" and by technological superiority over nature.[88]

Even comic strips, which had a reciprocal influential relationship with serious art, helped to see the world a bit differently, although they sometimes remained a frequently amusing, sometimes annoying, phenomenon in comparison to photography. Since its development in the nineteenth century, photography had prided itself as the technological possibility to reflect "reality" and unquestionably introduced another type of visualization of the world. Yet, further technological advancements in the twentieth century subsequently led to hiding the evident artificiality of every photographic image from the consciousness of the viewer.

Particularly the distrust toward the propaganda aims of photography in the "Third Reich" and in the Soviet Union during the period of Stalinism enabled American photography to become a dominating model in Austria after 1945. Now the new style was the program. The name "photorealism" alone promised technological professionalism and the total reproduction of "reality"—in other words, the surmounting of subjectivity through the absolute objective portrayal of "fact."

Semiological studies, which unmasked the powers operating in the symbolic and the subconscious, have shown that this claim is not valid. How we interpret truth is just as much a result of cultural preconditions as it is of our impressions of any external "reality." Symbols of systems lend themselves as the ideal starting point for control, subservience, and exploitation precisely because they seem so self-evident; manipulation is most successful where it is seemingly not present.[89]

Even though this political meaning of photography is not (always) conscious for some artists and connoisseurs of art, the power brokers are always aware of it. They routinely operate with the old adage "Seeing is believing." In anticipation of McCarthyism, as it were, critical New York photographers had already been subjects of the blacklist by December 1947. Even the Photo League, which publicly portrayed the *other* reality existing in the United States through their New Deal social documentaries, was dissolved.[90] "Realism" was not allowed to show socially hidden facts but instead had to suggest "the interesting."[91] Not only in the United States, however, did the "objective" reporting of the cameras fail to guarantee the objectivity of views.

## Objectivity and Professionalism of Journalism as the Goal of U.S. Press Politics in Austria

The central priorities of all activities of the U.S. press officers in Austria—in their own newspapers and magazines or in the placement of news, special articles and photographs, or with the training of Austrian journalists—were first and foremost the long-term stability of a democratic press and the battle against Communism. The American press served as the model and example with its supposed objectivity, impartiality, and incorruptibility—that is, with its separation of news from opinion. The U.S. press became in this process the ideal prototype. Without a doubt, Austrian journalism had to play catch-up in these areas, and the aid of American experts was quite beneficial in some respects. Press politics of this kind reflected an absolute belief in the representation of "reality" that was beyond the influence of human subjectivity and selectivity. Partiality, viewed as unscientific, was supposedly to be overcome through journalistic professionalism. In reality, this U.S. position, as one of the last bastions of positivism, meant the establishment of a new type of "new" journalism. Inculcated in an artificial aura of fact, the "masters of facts" were able to conceal that "there is no fundamentally non-ideological, apolitical, non partisan news gathering and reporting system."[92] The possibility of a selection of news and the placement of information through the "captains of consciousness" had, in any event, only little to do with the sworn objectivity, for every news necessarily conveys its own ideology.[93]

The media not only reports occurrences but also creates public opinion through the compilation of its daily agendas. More than a few social problems have thereby been made peripheral in the name of objectivity, and "social conflicts have been disguised, contained, and displaced through the imposition of news objectivity, a framework legitimizing the exercise of social power over the interpretation of reality."[94]

Although the concept of freedom of the press should actually guarantee the right of every individual to have access to all available information, it is more accurately a question of the freedom of opinion for those who have the money to own newspapers and radio or television stations.[95] The problem of social hegemony through the control over the interpretation of "reality" and the interpretation of fact is mostly acknowledged when media manipulations from "outside" become public. The press feeding of the CIA, with its many years of orchestration with regard to the contents of various newspapers, has caused quite an uproar.[96] The fundamental impossibility of objectivity of journalism seems, in contrast, to receive less attention. Even though modern journalism in the Western democracies is no longer confronted with clumsy, transparent, and therefore old-fashioned methods of censorship through official government agencies, this situation does not guarantee either objectivity or the absence of other forms of censorship. Edward R. Murrow highlighted this fact when he said, "News is not censored; it is merely omitted."[97]

Journalism à la the United States by far has improved the earlier practices of the Austrian press, especially during the period of Austro-fascism and the "Third Reich." The massive investment of U.S. press officers brought with it a necessary flow of fresh air into the Austrian newspaper landscape after years of deterioration. Many positive developments in Austrian journalism are certainly attributable to the long-range activities of American press politics. The legacy of these press officers, however, was not limited only to formal changes in styles of reporting and in the self-understanding of journalistic professionalism and language but also involved content.

For the most part, the United States achieved two political goals in its press politics. On the one hand, the influence of the Communist press was almost completely suppressed through the increased aggravation of preexisting anti-Communist sentiments. On the other hand, U.S. press officers left a press landscape behind in which the majority of journalists were not only clearly anti-Communist but also pronouncedly pro-American. The large majority of the Austrian newspapers conformed with the foreign policy positions of the United States during the Cold War. This same majority sympathizingly commented on U.S. interventions in Indochina, even during the phase in which the large liberal newspapers in the United States and in other NATO countries began their criticism of the U.S. government politics and began to distance themselves from it.

Although the recent Waldheim case briefly dampened the enthusiastic reports of a part of the Austrian press toward the United States, this by no means points to a change in trend. In any event, a public-opinion poll that evaluated the position of twelve Western European nations toward the United States in the first months of 1987 produced quite interesting results. Of all the nations surveyed, the Austrians had the most positive attitude toward the United States.[98] The massive commitment of U.S. press reforms has paid off—at least for forty years.

# 4

## "Howling and Noise":
## United States Radio Politics in Austria

Pecos Bill, the King of Cowboys.

An interesting picture of the cowboy will be given to listeners during the American part of the Allied Hour. Folktales almost always have a grain of truth, and why should it not be so that the cowboy and his profession were invented overnight. And who really was the first cowboy? It was Pecos Bill, the adventurous orphan adopted and raised by a pack of prairie dogs, finding it very difficult to once again return to civilization and people. As a result of his animal-like intelligence, he invented the lasso to capture and herd cattle, and it is even said that cowboy songs can be traced back to him.

   —Press release of the station Rot-Weiss-Rot for the program transmitted on
      May 21, 1949

Voice of America Will Tell Reds about Santa

U.S. plans to show Soviets what a fine season Christmas is in a land Russians are taught to hate. . . . Even Santa Claus is in on the conflict with Russia. Jolly St. Nick will play a leading role in the Voice of America broadcasts to the Russians this Christmas.

   —*New York Sun*, December 22, 1949

Not only was the propaganda Cold War fought with black ink, but the airwaves also were used in the information battle. Just as significant as U.S. press politics was the influence of U.S. radio officers on the development of radio in Austria.[1] Already by the beginning of June 1945, the U.S. radio group Rot-Weiss-Rot (named after the colors of the Austrian flag) began transmissions from Salzburg (first in the Landestheater, then in the Franziskaner Cloister) and from Linz (in the provincial parliament). By July 1945, the Viennese radio studio (located in the Waldheim-Eberle Press) had also begun its broadcasts. Only in October 1946 were the headquarters of radio Rot-Weiss-Rot finally moved to Vienna from Salzburg, and this initial concentration in Salzburg was also a signal from U.S. radio reformers to regionalize and federalize Austrian radio. Even though the implementation of this initiative was hindered by the Austrian government during the occupation period, the development of strong stations in Salzburg and Linz set the course that finally led to a national radio plebiscite and the reorganization of Austrian Radio (ORF).

The continually growing importance of this medium gave grounds for U.S. authorities to assert control over the radio until the end of the period of occupation. Not only did Rot-Weiss-Rot broadcast for Austria, but it also played an important role in the U.S. propaganda effort toward its Communist neighbors. The facilities in Salzburg and Linz were therefore turned over to the Austrians as late as March 1954; the stations and studios in Vienna, only after the signing of the state treaty on July 26, 1955.[2]

While the *Wiener Kurier* played first fiddle in the concerted American information efforts immediately following the war, Rot-Weiss-Rot became the most important propaganda medium for the United States in Austria by at least 1950. The modernization of transmission facilities (the transmitters in Vienna and Kronsdorf, which in 1951 had increased their capabilities from 50,000 to 225,000 watts, were especially important) was just as decisive as the ever-increasing distribution of radios (754,239 were licensed in Austria in 1945, and 1,629,000 in 1955).[3]

The post-Gutenberg epoch was ultimately dominated by television, but the radio, as a modern tribal drum (in the words of Marshall McLuhan), also had revolutionized the world of information since the 1920s. No other medium was better suited to penetrate political boundaries or other man-made barriers.[4] The vast range of possibilities that the radio created was quite advantageous to U.S. planners in Austria, for it reached not only the national populace but the peoples in the neighboring Communist states as well.

Information cast to the winds permeated the Iron Curtain, and thus, between 1946 and 1949, Rot-Weiss-Rot was broadcast in the Hungarian, Serbo-Croatian, Czech, and Slovak languages.[5] The taking over of these foreign-language transmissions by Radio Free Europe in Munich actually increased the propaganda effectiveness of Rot-Weiss-Rot. The voice of Austria, as it were, now could project an image without an obvious American touch. In the same light, the U.S. broadcast group was only one link in the American radio station chain that surrounded the Soviet Union and its sphere of influence like a ring and untiringly transmitted its political mission. The radio became one of the most important political instruments; its cultural power was superseded only by that of Hollywood.

The special magic of radio turned U.S. radio evangelism into a significantly new dimension of foreign policy, because "Hearing is believing" too.[6] Therefore, all developed industrialized nations utilize this instrument, including the former Soviet Union. But even though the influence of Radio Moscow was continuously cited in the budgetary debates in the United States, the "real masters of the black heavens" were no doubt the propaganda stations of the United States (Voice of America, Radio Liberty, Radio Free Europe), supported by its NATO partner stations (BBC External Services, Radio Canada International, Deutsche Welle, Deutschlandfunk, RIAS-Berlin). The Voice of America alone maintained a network of fifty-two transmitters that broadcast in twenty of the languages spoken in the former Soviet Union and had a combined transmission power of 4,331,000 watts, making all disruption attempts of the Soviets obsolete.[7] However this politico-cultural power of the radio is interpreted—militarily (word bombs), idealistically (beams of hope), sarcastically (le pick-up Américain), or realistically (electronic colonialism)—the radio was the vanguard of those electronic apparatuses that would shatter the foundations of the age of the "cuius regio—eius informatio."[8]

It should not be forgotten that U.S. radio plans for Austria were, for the most part, a by-product of a general press strategy and were by no means free of contradictions.[9] Beginning in 1944, the Office of War Information developed its own radio program for Austrians as a reaction to the Moscow Declaration, in which the liberation of Austria had become an Allied war aim. It was broadcast three times daily and was clearly differentiated in style, tone, and language from the programs for the Germans.[10] The first director of Rot-Weiss-Rot, U.S. officer Hans Cohrssen, initially even demanded the autonomy of the radio station. This position, however, quickly was rejected by his military superiors.

By the end of 1945, Cohrssen was consequently replaced by Joseph Savalle and Ernst Haeusserman. They were succeeded by Josef Sills and W. Stuart Green in 1948, William Stricker in 1951, Harry J. Skonia in 1952, and, finally, Fred G. Taylor in 1953.[11] The U.S. radio officers certainly deserve credit for the reconstruction and professionalization of radio in Austria. Even though Rot-Weiss-Rot soon gained an Austrian image through the introduction of modern program techniques and by incorporating increasing numbers of Austrians into the broadcast process, the coordinates of political control remained tightly fixed until 1955. For the U.S. Army, Rot-Weiss-Rot was "an army radio [which] should feed the Austrians pure American stuff."[12] Rot-Weiss-Rot therefore could have easily been called Red-White-Blue. As the Department of State took over the reins in the beginning of the 1950s, this situation did not fundamentally change.

Official justification for the strong control of the U.S. broadcast group was always the supposed total influence of the Soviet occupation power on the Austrian Radio Company (RAVAG). The administration of this station, however, was de jure fully in the hands of the Austrians. Soviet officers no doubt censored its programs, and pressure was also sometimes levied upon its Austrian staff. Nevertheless, the regulating measures implemented by the Soviets upon the RAVAG were, with the exception of the years from 1947 to 1950, significantly less severe than those with which Rot-Weiss-Rot had been tied.

Naturally, U.S. agencies were cognizant of these facts. The American minister to Austria, John J. Erhardt, for example, reported to the Department of State in October of 1947 that the Soviet control over RAVAG "is paralleled by outright control by the other occupation powers of separate radio networks in their zones. . . . In the case of RAVAG, Russian control is not yet complete."[13]

And this control would never be complete! During none of the phases of occupation was RAVAG completely dominated by Soviet occupation authorities.

While the demands of the Soviets upon RAVAG broadcast time had been only 5 percent in 1945 and only 6 percent in 1948, the ISB, in contrast, received 32 percent in 1946 and 24 percent of Rot-Weiss-Rot air time in 1949. However, the percentage reduction in programs had been accompanied by an increase in direct propaganda transmissions. Even the great majority of RAVAG information transmissions did not originate solely from Soviet sources, but from Reuters. Three percent of RAVAG stories were delivered by Tass between 1946 and 1947, and even in 1950, the year of the strongest Soviet influence, this figure was only 20 percent. In contrast, AND had a complete monopoly of all news and information for Rot-Weiss-Rot until the beginning of April 1946. Even after the licensing of private agencies, the average amount of news originating from U.S. sources was still 40 to 50 percent.[14] U.S. propaganda transmissions were developed still further within the realm of the psychological offensive even after Soviet interventions receded following the October trade union strikes in 1950. In addition, blacklists were established for those artists who worked for RAVAG or were suspected of sympathizing with the KPÖ.[15]

The continually increasing influence of U.S. radio officers actually led to the resignation of the superintendent of Rot-Weiss-Rot, Andreas Reischek, in July 1950. The well-hidden escalation of control of the radio groups by U.S. authorities was sarcastically commented upon by Reischek to the head of ISB, Ray E. Lee: "Even today the bulk of the listeners is of the opinion that Red-White-Red is an Austrian network and only as far as certain programmes are concerned it is adviced [sic] and controlled by responsible Americans."[16]

Criticism toward the programming was voiced quite early in the western provinces. The displeasure was particularly great in Salzburg, and public-opinion polls of 1946 to 1948 showed that especially jazz—or "negroid dance music," as it was called in the magazine *Berichte und Informationen* (Reports and information)—was explicitly disavowed, and showed "that the United States had not yet given its best."[17] Especially a "so-called modern American Christmas show" of December 25, 1947, provoked tremendous indignation. The critique was scathing: "The zenith of—mildly put—tastelessness was reached when the authors let Mary say: 'Look at what the three brought me. Gold, perfume, and baby powder.' We urgently ask our American friends to save us from such eccentricities."[18] In an effort to clarify just who was responsible for these "eccentricities," *Berichte und Informationen* made it quite obvious that the idioms of the speaker certainly allowed the conclusion that they were dealing with people who were far, far removed from Christian thought and tradition.[19]

Also, the program *Music of the West* ("a mixture of kitsch and noise") or Sunday chats with Peggy Sanford were—at best—laughed at by those defenders of the Occident who, as a result, were getting new impetus.[20] Concrete political interests were hidden behind these squabbles over "good taste," and this criticism became more and more concentrated in the western Austrian provinces between Linz and Bregenz by the late 1940s. People found offensive not only the increasing direct control of Rot-Weiss-Rot by U.S. officers but also certain denazification measures, the escalation of the hard propaganda programs during prime airing times, the funding for propaganda (which was derived in part from Austrian public radio fees), and the disregard for regional interests in spite of high radio tariffs in Upper Austria and Salzburg.[21] It is a notable fact that these critics in no way attacked anti-Communist propaganda as such but solely that which they held to be *inefficient* because it did not correspond to the Austrian taste.

Already during the first years of occupation, between 14 and 20 percent of Rot-Weiss-Rot's air time was reserved for news (two hours daily) and information from the Voice of America. Approximately one-third of the programs were directly related to U.S. topics, such as *America Calls Austria, America Helps Austria, This Is America, America in Word and Sound, The American Voice, Radio Forum, Radio Parliament,* and *Radio University.* In addition, numerous other entertainment programs were designed to attract Austrians (so-called coverage with a U.S. slant), such as *Metropolitan Hour,* which discussed everything from a visit to Broadway and the latest news from Hollywood to reports on soapbox car races that had been organized by American officers for Austrian children. More and more American entertainment programs began to be imported and adapted for the Austrian market. Prime examples were the much-loved quiz shows. All programs had one thing in common: they conveyed propaganda messages in the interest of the United States according to four variations—"top" or "heavy play," "good play," "straight play," or "played down."[22]

Austrian criticism of Rot-Weiss-Rot was noted carefully by U.S. authorities and taken quite seriously, for only a program that was taken seriously by its audience would achieve its intended political effect. In the fall of 1950, the Department of State therefore ordered the revamping of Rot-Weiss-Rot during its psychological offensive campaign. Three main goals were to be reached. First, improved programming would entice the average listener and thereby elevate the prestige of this radio station over RAVAG. Second, through the intensification of political output, Rot-Weiss-Rot would be an even more effective "ideological weapon of major impact throughout this area." Finally, of particular importance were also "the strategic possibilities inherent in RWR as a network broadcasting in German nominally for domestic Austrian consumption only, but actually able to spread its message through the use of new high-power transmitters to German-speaking peoples deep behind the iron curtain."[23]

Because neither the Austrian nor the foreign listener was supposed to recognize the transformation of Rot-Weiss-Rot, in accordance with the psychological offensive, particular attention was given to incorporate "high-caliber Austrian talent in political and other programming under overall American guidance." To increase the attractiveness of Vienna as a cultural magnet, the salaries of the Austrian personnel were dramatically increased, as were the budgets for radio plays, radio dramas, readings of novels, news, education, music, and other entertainment programs.

Program improvements were significant. To heighten the effectiveness of education programming, Rot-Weiss-Rot departed from RAVAG's *Schulfunk* (the daily education hour) and developed its own agenda. In addition, weekly radio lectures held by school experts were stopped, replaced by discussion rounds of youth leaders. And the music program *For the Homemaker* as well as *Radio University* and *Night Studio* were reorganized. Weekly concerts of the Vienna Philharmonic held in the Konzerthaus were taped and aired to improve the selection of broadcast music. These attractive performances were actually sponsored by the ECA Mission in Vienna. And to distinguish itself from RAVAG's Saturday *Russian Hour*, which offered classical entertainment, the program *1,000 Austrian Words* was conceived. This was a combination of classical music, operettas, radio plays, and short documentaries. Even the *Reading Hour* won over new listeners, for example, with Daphne du Maurier's "Rebecca." Finally, Austrians who had participated in the U.S. exchange programs also became increasingly active in the programming of shows. They were often asked to discuss their overseas experiences, especially on a program called *Mirror of the Times.*

The main emphasis of modification clearly focused on the area of news and information programming. Deviation from the strict and formal presentation of the reading of bulletins made this a more interesting and exciting instrument. At the same time, Rot-Weiss-Rot imported forms of the integrated news programs from the United States that were broadcast at 7:00 A.M., 12:30 P.M., and 8:00 P.M. In total, air time was increased by 25 percent, and after March 1951, news updates were broadcast every hour on the hour between 6:00 A.M. and midnight.

The reform of the information sector was, however, not limited to news alone. On February 14, 1951, the voice of "Karli Frei" was first heard at 6:05 A.M. In a humorous yet hard-hitting fashion, Karli revealed the real concerns of a true Austrian worker. This spot followed a RAVAG program for workers (*Listening to Colleagues*) at 6:00 A.M. and effectively countered its pro-Communist union message. The U.S. radio officers, by the way, received the background information for "Karli Frei" directly from socialist ÖGB members.[24] Even new cabaret programs ("combining ideological content with a light, entertaining touch"), including *What's Up, What's New*, served in the battle against Communism.

In addition, as of May 1951, an entire one-hour segment between 12:05 A.M. and 1:05 A.M. was reserved in which "the entire period [was] to be used for material primarily designed for (but not openly directed at) German-speaking listeners in iron curtain areas adjoining on Austria."[25] The structure of the program from this outwardly Austrian radio station was developed especially for the putative needs of listeners across the border. A news block followed press commentaries from Austrian and foreign newspapers, in which reports on cultural and sport activities were mixed together with the political. This was then followed by current information from the Eastern bloc and the recapitulation of the most important bulletins of the day from Voice of America. Finally, the main commentaries or the most significant political reports of Rot-Weiss-Rot were repeated.

The Voice of America became increasingly incorporated into the program. Because many radio owners received shortwave programs poorly, if at all, more programs were transmitted directly by Rot-Weiss-Rot. Three fifteen-minute news shows were included in the standard program, in which five of the week's most important programs were recapitulated. Also, the Monday night program *America in Word and Sound* was produced.

The particular appeal of the music programs of Voice of America proved to be very strong.[26] As a result, Rot-Weiss-Rot thereby significantly boosted the "unpolitical" lure of music in its programming. Two-thirds of the shows now included music, with one-third reserved for spoken programs. In Vienna, the Rot-Weiss-Rot station broadcast approximately 200 hours per month, in Salzburg 160 hours, and in Linz 100 hours. A third of the programs were produced by the radio group itself, and two-thirds originated from other "Austrian" (the British Radio Alpenland and the French Radio West) and foreign stations, especially Voice of America.[27]

The reforms were a tremendous success. On the one hand, the effects of the propaganda—a central concern of the entire campaign—were augmented. It became even easier "to exert an attracting influence over a wide region which in spite of national and ideological barriers still remains uniquely responsive to the historic focus of Vienna."[28] On the other hand, the transformation also initiated a change in attitude in the western Austrian newspapers that had previously criticized the radio group most vehemently. This was perhaps the greatest success for U.S. reformers and was, to a certain extent, a masterpiece in public relations. While the Austrian commentators celebrated the "retreat" of U.S. authorities, the supposed yielding to Austrian wishes and the increased consideration for local needs, the true background for these reforms—the beginning of the psychological offensive—remained hidden. The Austrian triumph over the United States was therefore rather pathetic. For the deference toward Austrian sensitivity ("it was felt that the best way of disarming them was by drastically revised performance")[29] did not cost much, created sympathy in general, and strengthened the effectiveness (because it was now carried out more intelligently) of anti-Communist propaganda.

Rot-Weiss-Rot had undoubtedly fulfilled these duties already prior to the reforms of 1950/51, even though its programs could not be received in several areas before new transmission stations were put in operation. While RAVAG broadcast classical, traditional radio and was therefore lauded by some commentators as being the more demanding station, Rot-Weiss-Rot bet on modern U.S. radio practices that were primarily appealing to the youth. The new entertainment programs brought a fresh wind into the Austrian radio landscape, and the star principle was also introduced into classical music programs. The Austrification of U.S. shows, the expansion of entertainment such as quiz shows and other programs soliciting audience participation, the innovations in entire programming areas, formal rejuvenation such as the introduction of series and easily identifiable programs at set times, as well as technical modernization, all made the American station the model for later radio developments in Austria.

No less important was the fact that the popularity of Rot-Weiss-Rot was also a result of the efforts of qualified artists and journalists. Peter Wehle, Karl Farkas, Helmut Qualtinger, Carl Merz, and Gerhard Bronner (in *Radio Rendezvous, Farkas Laughter Parade, Radio Brettl, Der Watschenmann, Radio Family*, and *Brettl vorm Kopf*) provided for intelligent and (sometimes) biting entertainment. None of these programs could, however, surpass the popularity of Maxi Böhm's *Versuch Dein Glück*, a copy of the American quiz show *Take It or Leave It*. A report by the *Salzkammergut Zeitung* on a quiz evening in Gmunden in May 1947 may suffice: "And then he came, the greatest of them all: Maxi Böhm! The applause took on a tumultuous form! Shortly before, the announcer Fredy Schmelz, with his soft, lulling voice gave a praeparatio gaudentiae, and the audience participated gleefully."[30]

During the entire period of occupation, Rot-Weiss-Rot remained the most popular and influential radio station. Already the first public-opinion polls of 1946 showed as much, and the favorable trend increased consistently until 1955. RAVAG, in comparison, lost its popularity. In 1948, of those surveyed in Salzburg 99.5 percent listened to news broadcasts on Rot-Weiss-Rot, as did 99 percent in Linz. For Vienna the numbers were less impressive in 1948: Rot-Weiss-Rot, 42 percent, RAVAG, 31 percent. The reason for this was that many older radios could not receive the Viennese Rot-Weiss-Rot station.[31] A survey taken by *Funk und Film* magazine at the end of 1949 reported that 62 percent of those asked felt that Rot-Weiss-Rot had the best programs, while only 17 percent preferred RAVAG.[32] This trend remained consistent over the years to come, until finally by 1954, fully 82 percent of the radio listeners favored Rot-Weiss-Rot over its competition; RAVAG received only a meager 8 percent.[33] These dream results, however, were not published, for continued strict control over the radio group Rot-Weiss-Rot would not have been justifiable without the ongoing threat of a putatively influential, Communist-dominated RAVAG. Internally, RAVAG had not been taken seriously for quite some time because it was very well known that since 1945 it "has been going steadily down the hill."[34]

Even the introduction of radio commercials (whose initiation was not completely coincidental with the commencement of the Marshall Plan) did not lessen the popularity of Rot-Weiss-Rot. The success of the U.S. radio officers was even that much more remarkable, for the incorporation of advertisements was implemented against the strong resistance of the Austrian coworkers, who insisted that commercials on the radio were sacrilegious. For this reason, the ISB's commission for the establishment of radio advertisements moved quite slowly. Nevertheless, they decided to break with tradition for primarily one reason: a financial basis was to be secured that would guarantee the independence of Rot-Weiss-Rot after the period of occupation had ended.

Although even the power of the United States of America could not achieve the authorization of private radio stations in Austria, at least commercials were to remain a legacy. In an effort not to elicit overly negative reactions toward advertising, experiments were carried out using sponsored programs. However, more than just the (supposed) sensitivity of the Austrian public was taken into consideration. Because commercials in the United States are inseparable from the star system of entertainers and because, according to the opinion of U.S. radio officers, the European radio system still remained in its infancy, the advertising experts believed that no other path was open for them to take. In any event, sponsored programs proved to be an excellent means for dismantling the aversion toward radio commercials in general. For: "(1) It would create a psychological wedge which could slowly break down prejudices against advertising on the part of the Austrian listeners; (2) it would provide revenue which could contribute to the effectiveness of spot-advertising programs, when they are introduced on the air; (3) most important of all, it would permit time to make necessary preparations for all-out advertising."[35]

The preparation time was well used. Similar to public-opinion polls, which had been introduced by the U.S. Army, then to be taken over by Gallup, U.S. examples and agencies soon dominated in advertising as well. Not only did the most important agencies come from the United States, but so too did its most important customer—the U.S. authorities in Vienna. Serving as an ice-breaker, so to speak, they were effective in motivating skeptical Austrian firms. Until the early 1950s, the ECA Mission was the most important sponsor of advertising time, as it was quite consciously attempted to balance the potentially negative impression of commercials during the airing of high-culture programs (e.g., *Vienna Philharmonic Concerts* and *Orchestras of This World*). It may not be all too surprising that many of the Austrian firms that bought commercial time from the U.S. radio station had previously enjoyed Marshall Plan funds. The resistance toward radio advertising was soon broken, and the efficiency of advertising spots as demonstrated during the 1950 Fall Trade Fair in Vienna was soon to win over more customers.[36]

As the forerunner in the introduction of radio advertising, the ECA Mission, in keeping in line with the economic modernization concept of the Marshall

Plan, did more than just assist the firms and listeners in gradually getting used to commercials. Through the increased use of the radio as a medium for seemingly unpolitical purposes (e.g., in airing the Vienna Philharmonic), it in turn served as advertising for the Marshall Plan (ERP).

The integrated use of ISB budgetary means, ERP funds and income from Rot-Weiss-Rot, radio service fees, and profits from advertising for the development of studios and transmitter stations made particularly clear the close interaction of U.S. radio politics with general political, economic, and social plans for the U.S. occupation power. On the one hand, the efficiency and productivity, hastened by the Marshall Plan's push for modernization of the Austrian economy, could be ensured only if, at the same time, the infrastructure of the communications system was developed. On the other hand, the improvement of the communication network, for example, by proceeding with countrywide electrification, would in turn guarantee increased efficiency and productivity of propaganda for Marshall Plan politics.

The transmitter behind Salzburg's Pass Lueg had poor reception until 1948/49. In addition, Radio Saarbrücken's strong frequency interfered. A change in wave lengths brought relief, even though the *Demokratische Volksblatt* skeptically noted in 1948 that "even in the twentieth century, modern technology will not be successful in conquering the everlasting Alps."[37] Still, the expansion of Rot-Weiss-Rot was the initial step for improvements, and the financial means of ERP funds were also later implemented for further improvements in the reception density of the Austrian radio network.

Those radio listeners who had received Rot-Weiss-Rot poorly, if at all, during the first years of its transmission, still were able to receive made-in-America messages over the airwaves. Many radio owners could tune into the wavelengths of Voice of America, Blue Danube Radio (the GI station in Austria), American Armed Forces Network, and later also Radio Free Europe—and quite a number of listeners took advantage of these opportunities. While many of the listeners did not yet completely understand the English-language news broadcasts (the Voice of America, in any event, also had German programs), the propagation of U.S. popular culture, especially music, was of eminent political importance. In this scheme, the radio played an extremely decisive role. Audience reactions, which the stations received in bundles, exemplify the impact of music in the creation of generally positive attitudes toward the United States. Therefore, music had also been a significant component in the propaganda concept, for:

1. It is emotional.
2. It is well liked, and establishes a pleasant association with the United States.
3. It demonstrates that the Voice of America does not merely concentrate on official announcements.

4. It shows that the United States has a cultural side.
5. It attracts an audience and makes total output more pleasant.
6. Musical signatures serve as a necessary identification. . . .
7. An hour of solid talk, basically political, is a strain for the listeners; music acts as a contrast and as a bridge in programming.[38]

A letter of thanks from a teacher in the small alpine village of Mühlbach am Hochkönig to the editors of Voice of America in February of 1949 represents the sentiments of many others: "We are so devoted to American culture and ideals and are grateful for any and all assistance."[39]

The strongest opponents of the new methods of programming proved to be those Austrian radio experts who could not be weaned from the official announcements and instructive radio broadcasts of the interwar period. We can safely assume that the development of the radio in Austria would have taken a completely different course if it had not been for the often-forceful pressure of U.S. radio officers to modernize. Rudolf Henz's opinion on the programs of Blue Danube Radio clearly demonstrates the fronts of this Kulturkampf: "Twenty hours of noise and howling inflames enthusiastic teenagers, but also all avant-gardists with and without a beard. For us program people, who were idiotically concerned with broadcasting philharmonic concerts, all we received was a sympathizing smile."[40] The difficulties with the superintendent of Rot-Weiss-Rot, Andreas Reischek, were laconically assessed by U.S. radio officer W. Stuart Green: "What he can't stand is modern radio."[41]

Modern radio was most definitely necessary in efficiently representing the interests of the United States in Austria, and the U.S. officers were thoroughly convinced (how could it be any other way?) that only America had a modern radio system. The "old-fashioned" kind, as illustrated by RAVAG, received their total rejection and provoked condescending disregard. Rot-Weiss-Rot's success with its audience was rather a strong argument in favor of American radio.

The influence of U.S. radio politics in Austria could not be ignored. The situation with which U.S. radio officers were confronted in 1945 as they began their activities was anything but favorable. (The material difficulties themselves were not a primary hindrance.) In 1950, the head of U.S. radio, W. Stuart Green, accurately characterized the problems of U.S. radio politics in Austria. The ISB had to begin their work starting at square one because there was no trained personnel to assist them. The training of new coworkers was very difficult, but Rot-Weiss-Rot now had the best team in all of Austria. Starting at square one also especially included the fundamental rejection of the Austrian radio tradition from which they had radically deviated:

The methods advocated by RWR's Americans seemed radical, controversial and even undignified to a generation of Austrians whose entire radio experience had been in listening (or working for) the type of radio offered by Austria's schoolteacher-politicians with its traditional lack of color.

To sum up briefly, the development of RWR brought one radical and basic change in radio practice which stands out above all others—the planning of program material in accordance with listener wishes. Before RWR, the government radio, with no competition to worry it, fed listeners what it wanted them to hear—spinach because it was good for them. Since one of the reasons for RWR's existence is to disseminate news in an area where straight news is hard to get, it is only natural that the program content should be aimed at attracting as many listeners as possible so they'll hear the news.

This "popular program" notion was a difficult idea to put over, especially in a land where new or different ideas are often rejected if they conflict with traditional ways of doing things. But the project was carried out over the past three years and without sacrificing the Austrian flavor of the network's offerings.[42]

The popularizing of radio programs is the decisive legacy left by Rot-Weiss-Rot to Austrian radio. These modifications were by no means an end in themselves. Precisely as in the case of the U.S. radio system, in which popular broadcasts serve as commercials for the (actual) commercials, U.S. radio officers campaigned for the politics of the United States with the well-loved Rot-Weiss-Rot programs. The genuine advertisements aired on Rot-Weiss-Rot thus were the news and political commentaries.

Esto es la Voz América . . . Ici la Voix d'Amérique . . . Here is the Voice of America. Without a doubt, the Rot-Weiss-Rot radio voice had an American accent.[43] Radio Rot-Weiss-Rot not only spread political (dis)information but also familiarized its listeners with untraditional methods and changed listeners' habits. Yet, one decisive contradiction was not resolved by these program alterations. Although technological advancements, forms of programs, and radio idioms revolutionized Rot-Weiss-Rot, the program contents ran in the direction of stabilizing and conserving existing social relationships and structures.

Particularly significant in this respect were not so much news and political commentaries (top or heavy play) but, instead, the types of entertainment and information programs that portrayed the United States in a favorable light or elevated it to the model of civilized humankind (good play). The press release introducing this chapter lets us clearly recognize that the nation that was the most forward looking in the world could not dispense with long-kept patterns—equivalent to classical mythology—in projecting its image. Hence, Pecos Bill confronts us as king of the cowboys. And this founder of the cowboy imperium was also immediately adopted and raised by prairie dogs. If we replace the pack of prairie dogs with wolves, then we come to Romulus and

Remus and the fundamental myth of Roman antiquity. The only true difference is that Pecos Bill—and how could it be any different for a cowboy?—was a loner, an individualist.

In a slightly modified form, the made-in-America myth, which was gladly believed by Europeans, of the dishwasher turned millionaire was shown in the program *Lebensbilder aus USA/Lives in America*, with Martin Kennelly. Born in a slum, Kennelly began his career as a transportation clerk and, through diligence and decency, cleanliness and correctness, rose to become the mayor of Chicago. While the romantic reputation of Chicago as the U.S. center for gangsters was used to acquire the interest of the listeners, they were promptly informed that Mayor Kennelly had exterminated this disease at its roots. This is an example of the liberal ISB media strategy that sometimes reported on problems in the United States, especially those, as in the case of gangsters, that supposedly belonged to the past.

The majority of Rot-Weiss-Rot programs are unfortunately unavailable, since neither recordings nor scripts have been systematically archived. A detailed analysis of these programs can therefore not be delivered. One small view of the self-projection of the United States is, however, depicted in the following two radio scripts, which, surely exemplary, denote two main directions of U.S. cultural propaganda: on the one hand, the land with enormous political freedoms, the highest standard of living, and the most advanced technology; on the other hand, a nation that, counter to European prejudices, has not sacrificed leading a refined lifestyle through high culture. Emphasizing the existence of high culture, especially in the area of music, was quite important, particularly in Austria. However, these efforts remained mostly unsuccessful. The entire problem of American cultural self-portrayal is clearly shown in the following text of a Rot-Weiss-Rot broadcast discussing the music library at the Information Center in Linz. Interestingly enough, even the protagonists of U.S. high culture were seemingly unsympathetic to one of America's greatest cultural achievements, namely, jazz. With that, they surely gained the approval of the majority of Austrian listeners.


*Radio Script 1*

Series: *The Information Center Linz Speaks*[44]
Dialogue: Librarian, Dr. Elfriede Reinhold, and a visitor to the library
Theme: Music (books, magazines, sheet music, records)
(Noises in a room like those created by the presence of many people who are trying to be quiet. Place: U.S. Information Center Linz, Reading Room, ground floor)
V: Good morning. Do you have any books on music history and theory, perhaps even sheet music and other materials for the professional musician?

Female Voice: Oh, yes. Our collection is greater than you think. Please speak with our librarian, Dr. Reinhold, in the Reading Room on the ground floor. She will gladly direct you to the desired materials.

(Record—William Schuman: Three Score Set; begins in third section—the quick part; quiet—loud—quiet, play for half a minute)

V: Oh, how wonderful, one is welcomed by music. Frau Dr. Reinhold?

Dr. R.: Yes?

V: My name is Ferry Hofer. I am a professional musician and would like to know what kinds of serious American music you have in your library.

Dr. R.: Certainly, Mr. Hofer. I am just in the process of trying out a few new records. We just recently received them from the archives of the Library of Congress in Washington, D.C.

V: The history of serious American music is so young that it is difficult to get acquainted with it.

Dr. R.: Certainly, it is not easy to find the rules, musical directions, and isms. In my opinion, though, it is more essential to listen to a few artists and to judge them individually. A fundamental philosophy will develop from there.

V: That's true, Frau Dr. Reinhold. Oh, there is a copy of Charles Ives's "Harmony Piano Sonata" on the table. Do you think it's worth playing the piece yourself? There really is so much here.

Dr. R.: If you think you can manage the technical difficulties that are present even in this, the shortest piece of Ives, then it is most definitely worth the effort. You see, Charles Ives is a problem even in America. The man wrote quite a lot, but not much of it has been played. As I said, the technical difficulties make him almost unplayable, not to mention difficult to perform. Charles Ives is, nevertheless, one of the most original composers of his generation.

V: Who should I look at, Frau Dr., to get an impression of contemporary American music?

Dr. R.: I certainly don't want to give you a detailed lecture, but with the help of the sheet music and records I would gladly give you a general look at contemporary music. One of the most famous composers who is, without argument, at the forefront in America is Aaron Copland. One must mention him, here and there, when speaking of modern music. I am sure you must have heard of his suite *Our City*?

V: Wasn't also a book of his, *Music of Today*, recently published?

Dr. R.: Yes. There are, however, many more in addition to him that are all well known in America. Samuel Barber, William Schuman (you just heard a piece by him), Walter Piston, Roger Sessions, Virgil Thomson—they are all, more or less, distinctive musical personalities. Do you know the music style of Roy Harris?

V: Unfortunately not.

Dr. R.: We find Roy Harris's melodic talent particularly pleasant. His music comes closest to a national *melos*. Listen for yourself to his piano piece "The Birds."

(Record—quiet after half a minute, then blend out; play record after first half!)

V: I see a piano piece here by William Schuman, and here is the record. This is a wonderful aid for learning if one can use both eyes and ears.

Dr. R.: You will discover much more that you will enjoy as a musician. Just look at our rich collection of string quartets of modern America, chamber music in various combinations. Here, for example, is Walter Piston's String Quartet no. 2.

V: Isn't that the well-known composition teacher from Harvard University? I have come into contact with his music on several occasions and find it very pleasant.

Dr. R.: You are correct. Piston is a moderate for the European ear. He is comparable to a musician of the eighteenth century with his intellectual clarity.

V: Do you have any folk music in stock?

Dr. R.: Here you will see songs by Virgil Thomson, which have been successfully performed in concert halls for some time now. This is based primarily on his talent to let the English language sound natural when it is sung. Thomson is, however, also one of the best in American opera.

V: I thought I heard that he gave the impression of being disconcerting through his moderation, he seems all too "normal." I am not familiar with his songs, but I remember Thomson's opera *Four Saints in Three Acts*. This opera received much positive attention and gave Thomson his reputation.

Dr. R.: Because we are already at the new classical direction in America. Roger Sessions is also one of these composers and wrote a very fitting article a few years ago:

(Record—Roger Sessions: out of a diary; quiet background while the following lines are read until the cue "its contribution," then blend out immediately)

"Young people dream of a completely different type of music—a music that takes its strength from forms that are more appealing through content than expression, that gets its impulse from the reality of a passionate logic, and that thereafter strives to create form, goal and a vision of order and harmony as its contribution."

V: A new road was taken. First out of spite for German Romanticism, then with the credo "Back to Bach" taking a turn in the direction of the eighteenth century, then again impressions and expressions; it is a complicated net of directions and has changed again since Schönberg.

Dr. R.: That is interesting! The creative musician hears beyond his time. The unprepared listener will simply find it difficult to establish a relationship with modern music. Nevertheless, it is precisely folk music that is turned into modern music.

V: And that brings us to folk music. Do you have any material on that, Frau Dr.?

Dr. R.: Certainly, and quite encompassing at that. You can look up the so-called folk songs from all parts of America in our library. You can read the sheet music or listen to the records. In addition, I would like to emphasize that you may borrow our records at any time.

V: That is very generous. May I listen to an American folk song now or perhaps a real Indian song?

Dr. R.: With pleasure. I have here, for example, the "Eagle Dance," accompanied by water drum and rattle.

(Record—blend out after less than one minute)

Dr. R.: I could play examples from the North as well as from the South for you, but we do not have enough time for that. All of these recorded songs are genuine and easily remembered; the accompanying printed texts make understanding easier.

V: This really is valuable material for the folklorist.

Dr. R.: You will even find folklore collections from America in book form here. We have numerous editions, for children and adults. They belong to the most-loved volumes for music lovers, and even the smallest ones in the children's hours are always happy when they are taught a new song from one of these books.

V: I understand. I suppose you are also a kind of musical fairy-story teller! (*laughter*)

Dr. R.: The small ones cannot be raised early enough with music. The loveliest childhood melodies become the best folk songs, and some of the most eternal works by composers have been developed out of folk music.

V: Our literary knowledge of modern America is unfortunately not all that great, especially in the last years.

Dr. R.: Don't worry, the connection will soon be made and will be permanent. The novelty of the unknown is over; the era is beginning to establish itself clearly. In addition, we have here on the shelf some excellent encyclopedias that will answer all your questions on music.

V: And these many anthologies, musician's biographies, compendiums, and theoretical works!

Dr. R.: I can see that you will soon find your favorite book. *Theme and Variation,* the autobiography of Bruno Walter, is excellently written. Or here, the history of music by Marion Bauer—*How America Grew*—a particularly good and serious work.

V: Yes, but unfortunately in English. I must admit that my English is not good enough to read such a book for pleasure. Fortunately, the sheet music is international, so it does not create any barriers. But the word is more difficult to handle when it comes from across the ocean.

Dr. R.: (*laughing*) Don't say that! Even musical expression is dependent on the mentality of the people to which the composer belongs. In any event, jazz rhythms are eating up the entire world. One who has the necessary patience can hold out without being negative. To say no would be stubborn, yes, even narrow-minded. It is our duty to deal with all contemporary movements.

V: That is a very respectful point of view and to be supported wholly. Everyone who demonstrates the strength to be objective will soon be able to distinguish between valuable creations and bad imitations.

Dr. R.: But for you, Herr Hofer, to make you feel better about your language problem: we have lovely books in the German language from Switzerland. Here, too, the most modern writings.

V: My God, there is the old Karl Nef with his history of music!

Dr. R.: And here a valuable aesthetic of music for the spiritual connoisseur.

V: And this marvelous Mozart biography by Bernhard Paumgartner, which I did not think I would see again so quickly. This music corner, with its biographies and music histories, is one that I truly find enjoyable.

Dr. R.: I gladly believe you. Frequently read is, for example, Berta Geissmar's book *In the Shadow of Politics*. The secretary of Furtwängler wrote about her work together with the cherished master during the difficult Nazi years.

V: Truly a treasure chest, this music corner!

Dr. R.: Now all that is left is to acquaint you with our music magazines. The entire theater, concert, and music life in America is reflected impressively in word and picture. Those theater enthusiasts who read these magazines regularly get to know the productions at the Metropolitan Opera and its stars better than those in some of the local Austrian theaters.

V: Are these magazines published regularly?

Dr. R.: So far, yes. *Musical America, Musical Courier,* and *Opera News* (a weekly report from the Metropolitan Opera) are in demand by our readers and are highly praised.

V: And what is this here? A magazine called *Die Etüde*?

Dr. R.: That brings us back to serious music. It is a collection of easy-to-play pieces that one always wanted to play, especially on the piano at home, to get an impression of how they sound. But one could only play it in a simplified version. That is the purpose of *The Etude*.

V: It has gotten late. Time has passed so quickly while we have been speaking, Frau Dr., May I thank you for your valuable time and information. Would you mind playing a nice exit piece for me?

Dr. R.: With pleasure. Listen to a rhythmically interesting piece by Paul

Bowles, "La Cuelga." Hopefully many music enthusiasts listened to our talk and will evaluate our available materials properly.

(Record—Paul Bowles's "La Cuelga"; blend in record at cue "hopefully many music," then turn down slowly; blend out)


## Radio Script 2

Series: *The Automobile in America*, aired October 1950[45]

(Noise of a busy intersection—cars driving by, brakes sounding, horns blowing, etc. Noises are always in the background during the entire program.)

Reporter: (*blend in, quick reporting style, excited speaking voice*) . . . we are standing here with our microphone on a terrace high over the intersection of Fifth Avenue and Forty-sixth Street. Below us are the deep ravines through which the stream of cars push. Car roofs glistening in the sun look like a pearl necklace from here. It is an unusual and strange view. (*surprised*) What have I discovered! Among the first cars stopped at an intersection, next to a big shiny Buick, a small, boxy Ford Model T! A highly unusually sight here in New York . . .

Voice: (*interrupts reporter*) Excuse me, please, for interrupting you, but I have a little question.

Reporter: Sure, what's it about?

Voice: You are talking about a Model T down there. The term is not clear to me. Where does it come from?

Reporter: Well, we are dealing with one of the first cars produced by the Fords, who have diligently been in business for over twenty-five years. This car is colloquially called the Tin Lizzie. . . . Wagging tongues will say that it was built with as much tin as necessary to make a tin can. This is a bit exaggerated, but the body is really only an irrelevant issue because the Model T had a high, strong chassis with a strong motor. The car was designed to handle the most difficult road conditions and has proved itself exceptional for that. The Tin Lizzie was the first car in the world that was produced in a series on a production line . . .

Voice: Production line, do you mean . . .

Reporter: Yes, exactly what it sounds like. The production process was dissected into the smallest steps, and a worker was made responsible for only one repetitive movement in the assembling of the car, which moves past on a production line. Ford used this method in his factory, which stems from the Pittsburgh steel factory engineer Taylor. Thereby, auto production as a whole was withdrawn from the manual workers. That is how Ford became the founder of the auto industry. Production lines saved time and therefore cost less, and Ford put a good, reliable, and inexpensive car on the market.

Voice: Ford is the king of cars, as the Americans say.

Reporter: The title may be correct, but he no longer limitlessly reigns over the broad field of car production. He must now compete with new factories and production companies, for example, General Motors. This development is best understood by looking at the following figures: in 1918, Ford produced sixty out of every hundred cars; by 1941, only twenty out of a hundred cars carried the Ford name.

Voice: You can hardly think of America without cars . . .

Reporter: You are right. The distances that have separated people from one another in America, which until recently was still very sparsely populated, called for an inexpensive and fast means of transportation. That is how the automobile became the most important tool for the Americans. On every four Americans, one car falls. (*laughing*) And this is not meant in the sense of accidents, but only statistically speaking. If groups of four Americans all got into cars at the same time, then all houses and apartments would be empty and the entire country would be on wheels. A "nation on wheels," as Americans are called.

Voice: With this tremendous amount of cars, the auto industry must be of great economic importance in the United States.

Reporter: Naturally, it holds first place among all industries. In terms of the monetary value of the total yearly industrial production, $10 out of every $100 comes from auto production. The importance of the car is even more significant if one takes into consideration that every seventh person in the United States is employed by an occupation that is connected to the production, maintenance, or distribution of automobiles.

Voice: America produces so many cars. Can they all be sold in the United States, or does export play an important role?

Reporter: The United States produced more than 5¼ million vehicles of all kinds in 1948. Of this enormous amount, only ½ million were exported. In other words, for every 200 cars that were built, 17 were exported. You will surely ask why, because American cars are so well known and famous. As a result of the long war, the world has a long list of important, demanding needs for industrial production. All cars that were produced in 1948 could, without difficulty, be sold domestically. A number of buyers were even forced to postpone their wishes for a new model until 1949.

Voice: Since we are speaking about models—there really is a big difference between an American and a European car, don't you think?

Reporter: Certainly there is! The reason for this is that America is a country with enormous distances that are preferably traveled quickly and safely. For that, one requires a car that can perform for long stretches and is therefore also heavy. Luxury and comfort also play an important role. In comparison, the European construction increasingly aims for economic feasibility, keeping always in mind the cost of the vehicle per kilometer and the relationship between motor performance and the weight of the car. The new American models are now also aiming for better economic feasibility. For this reason, we can admire the advances of the American auto industry on the streets of the world.

Voice: Yes, the magnificent limousines, which everyone loves, the jeeps, and many more.

Reporter: Since you mention the jeep: that is a typical example of a car that met the demands of the war and was produced as a coproduction of the American auto industry. In addition to the jeep, there are still many other, multifaceted, and particularly purposeful vehicles. At the moment, European engineers are in the process of incorporating the most successful aspects of the American auto industry, as the Americans increasingly look to European performances in this area as well.

Voice: Yes, but . . .

Reporter: (*interrupting*) Excuse me, please, but my time is up, and I really must get on with my report.

(motor sounds increase)

Reporter: In the meantime, the streets below us have a new face. The sun is setting, and the first billboard lights are going on . . .

(The voice of the reporter is slowly drowned out by the sound of the street. Program slowly fades out.)

Speaker: This has been a program of the U.S. Information Center, informing you about America, its people, land, and life. If you have a particular question regarding American life, please direct your questions to the American Information Centers in Vienna, Linz, Salzburg, Steyr, Wels, and Zell am See.

# 5

## The U.S. Information Centers,
## the U.S. Publications Section, and
## U.S. Literature in Austria

### "Our Propaganda Shops": The America Houses

New Books from America.

Salzburg (AND). New books from America have just arrived. With this, the wishes of many Austrians to learn more about the United States are fulfilled. Of particular interest is a thorough and objective representation of life in America for Austrian readers who have been held in intellectual isolation for the last seven years.

—*Salzburger Tagblatt*, March 23, 1946

One of the most difficult duties of the ISB was the softening of predominantly negative clichés depicting the United States as a cultural wasteland. Challenges abounded, particularly in a country in which cultural self-confidence (even self-overestimation) hardly seemed broken, in spite of (or perhaps because of?) the experiences of fascism, National Socialism, destruction through war, and postwar disparity. In a country in which the ownership of nicely bound books already served as a symbol of culture, the America Houses and the distribution of U.S. literature—yes, even proving that literature existed at all in America—quite naturally, maintained a high priority. The height of these barriers, which U.S. cultural officers had to surmount, is illustrated by the following announcement regarding the Information Center in Linz, which appeared in the *Linzer Volksblatt* on November 29, 1945.

USA Culture for Austria: For us Austrians, America is really an unknown country, of which some feel that it confuses culture with technological achievements. This is not so. Even America can offer us something culturally and scientifically. Yet, we Austrians would be very happy if the American soldiers now living in our country would get to know Austrian culture and lifestyles, and learned to respect this small but culturally important country. Victors are easily susceptible to the danger of deducing their intellectual superiority only from their military strength.[1]

Because the losers, in turn, did not seem to associate intellectual defeat with their military defeat, the ISB truly faced a difficult task. The presentation of U.S. (high) culture through U.S. Information Centers (the term "America House" did not come into use until the end of the 1940s) was therefore a particularly important goal of American foreign policy. However significant the cultural purpose of the Information Centers seemed, the "Propaganda Shops" (as the military jargon dubbed them) most notably bore two specific political functions: "To provide the ideological and informational support of American foreign policy; and to provide the means of a broad commerce of ideas that can contribute to the actuality of a unity of culture and purpose among nations."[2] The two inseparable goals of the America Houses were therefore also called "projecting democratic ideals and the American way of life."[3] To describe them in the frontier language of the U.S. politico-evangelism as "the first outposts in the revival of American culture in Austria" is rather appropriate.[4]

In total, twelve such foreign posts of U.S. culture were established in Austria between 1945 and 1955: the first three in Salzburg, Linz, and Vienna in 1945. They were followed by Steyr, Wels, and Zell am See in 1948; Innsbruck and Hallein in 1949; Graz and Ried im Innkreis in 1950. Within the framework of the psychological offensive, the opening of additional branches in Braunau am Inn, Gmunden, Leoben, Klagenfurt, and Bregenz was considered. In 1951 it was decided to erect another center in Gmunden (because it was visited by many guests from the Soviet zone of occupation during the summer), and then in 1953 in Klagenfurt. These branch centers were all closed at the end of the occupation period; the America House in Klagenfurt was terminated only in 1958, Graz in 1961, Salzburg in 1963, and Linz in 1965.[5] Only the America House in Vienna, which became the most important information center for American Studies since the period of occupation, still remains in operation today.

The activities of the America Houses were not limited to the occupied territories (Germany, Japan, Korea, and Austria). Forty-four Information Centers existed worldwide by 1945 (of these, 24 in Europe); by 1951 this figure grew to 195 (94 in Europe), and then to 197 by 1955 (69 in Europe). If one takes into consideration not only the America Houses but also the affiliated branches, then 300 of these cultural centers had been founded globally already by 1949. Approximately 23 million guests had visited these establishments.[6]

The America Houses fulfilled a variety of functions. They were libraries, reading rooms, concert halls, galleries, theaters, lecture halls, lenders of records and films, and information centers for all questions relating to the United States. Many decisions to emigrate were reached after such visits. The implications for the economy and culture in Austria after 1945 of the loss of thousands of mostly highly qualified individuals, the effects of this brain drain, still require their own study.

## „EI, EI, WER HÄTTE DAS GEDACHT!"
### MANFRED LIMMROTH (1955)

Cartoon commenting on the ubiquity of America Houses; the caption reads
"Well, well, who would have thought!" (*Forum* 38 [February 1957]: 78)

The engraving of a positive image of the United States was realized in the
America Houses via slide shows as well as popular academic lectures, classical
music evenings, and gospel concerts. Countless lectures discussed the history
and political system of the United States. Particularly popular were events
covering topics such as American freeways and trains, the Pacific Coast and
Hawaii, the American kitchen, cowboys, and the development of American
jazz. In addition, the America Houses offered a large assortment of courses,
from language classes to stenography, from seminars on U.S. libraries to continued education for teachers, from modern management methods to advertising.[7]

These lectures reached thousands of weekly listeners in the America Houses
alone. By the end of the 1940s, lecturers held more and more presentations also
in small villages and rural areas that were not directly served by official Information Centers. These lecture series grew even more in 1950–51 under the
auspices of the psychological offensive. More and more lecture teams were
active in Vienna, two were also established in both Linz and Salzburg, and one
in Innsbruck. During the last years of occupation, up to 600 events monthly
were organized from Linz, Salzburg, and Innsbruck, and each lecturer addressed 10,000 people per month on the average. This means that approximately 100,000 Austrians were reached monthly.[8]

In addition, America Houses organized countless photography exhibits, which could also be requested by Austrian institutions. Every show was presented so that it "tells a part of the American story, with photographs of things American, with maps, animated exhibits, diagrams, cartoons, art displays, showing America to the Austrian people in every possible pictorial and graphic way."[9] Especially favored were the picture series entitled "Automobile Superhighways in America," "Gone with the Wind," and "Walt Disney Cartoons and American Humor." Some explicit propaganda exhibits were also highly esteemed, such as "America Calls Austria," "America Helps Austria," "The Marshall Plan," "Where Do the Americans in Austria Get Their Food From?," and "Atlantic Pact."[10] These photo series were offered free of charge to the schools in all Austrian provinces. As a result of the large demand for such shows, the Kosmos Theater in Vienna had been rented in June 1951, allowing for a decisive expansion of the events.

America Houses also distributed posters and placed slides and short propaganda films in theaters. In the first three months of 1950 alone, more than 4,000 films were shown. The propaganda/information power of the film medium was certainly an important trump card for the U.S. Information Centers, and surely not only because many schoolchildren regarded it as a welcome change in the monotony of a school day.

In a study for the Department of State, the Institute of Communications Research suggested utilizing the implementation of film programs extensively because "films are especially suitable for unsophisticated audiences. . . . It makes no difference what we have to show them. You will find this true almost anywhere except perhaps among intellectual groups where they are blasé about it. There is a fascination that films have for people. Even among intellectuals there, they come to be critical. . . . You can do anything you want with them as long as you don't drive them away."[11] The ISB films that were lent from America Houses to state institutes, private associations, and also businesses addressed a broad range of themes. In addition to the hard-hitting messages of the political films, the weekly *Welt im Film*, coproduced with the British occupation power, was once again circulated in the America Houses.[12] The films were so popular that the Viennese Room of the Mozarteum in Salzburg, holding 400 people, was filled to capacity during the semiweekly showings from 1950 onward. Visitors were inevitably sent away at each show.[13]

*A Door Stands Open* (directed by Karl Sztollar and moderated by Paul Hörbiger, with music by Robert Stolz) was the title of a film produced by the ISB in 1948 that advertised the America Houses, and this open door was entered by more and more Austrians. Already by the beginning of 1947, the ISB reported to Washington that "the thirst of the Austrian people for information and news and facts about America has brought them storming into U.S.-Information Centers by the tens of thousands."[14] The first visitors after the Second World War had predominantly sought information on prisoners of war, missing family members, emigration possibilities, as well as help in solving personal survival problems. This, however, changed quickly. More and more Austrians borrowed books, read displayed newspapers and magazines, referred to the rich subject library, informed themselves on stipends, cultivated business contacts with U.S. firms, asked questions on obscure details concerning America, or borrowed films, pictures, education materials, and records.

The record collections of U.S. Information Centers included recordings of works by American composers and the major orchestras that were otherwise nowhere to be found in Austria.[15] They specialized in folk music, cowboy songs, spirituals, musicals, and jazz. It was, however, a further duty of the America Houses to demonstrate "America's unique contribution in these art forms [through] a serious and intelligent presentation of pure jazz and musicals."[16] The (younger) public's demand for jazz, moreover, overshadowed that for all other forms of music; one of the most desired books was Paul Whiteman's *How to Be a Bandleader*.[17]

Even if the *Salzburger Nachrichten* had reported in July 1947 about the still "hidden treasures in the Information Center,"[18] the wave of visitors in Vienna with genuine interests in the culture of the United States already had swelled much earlier. Nevertheless, the reading rooms in Linz and Salzburg soon also announced increased usage. This demand was augmented significantly through the specific advertisements in all U.S. media and in the *U.S. Information Center News*, of which 5,500 copies were distributed to schools alone.

By the middle of 1946, the Vienna library catered to approximately 600 registered borrowers, 3,000 in 1947, 10,500 in 1949, and 20,000 by the end of the occupation. Its chambers housed 7,000 volumes in 1947. By 1949, this figure had grown to 30,000, and 40,000 by 1955. In Salzburg, the number of volumes also grew from 5,200 in 1947 to 20,000 by 1955. Even in the Information Center in Innsbruck, which opened its doors only in 1949, the figures continuously rose from 5,500 volumes to 20,000 in 1955. The collection of newspapers and magazines contained approximately 400 titles in Vienna and 200 in Linz and Salzburg, respectively. In the years to follow, these selections doubled and even tripled in Vienna. The America House in Vienna only had 1,300 monthly visitors by mid-1946, but the average rose dramatically to more than 60,000 per month by 1950.[19] In sum, the total visitor count stood at 332,706 between July 1946 and August 1947 (187,664 in Vienna, 91,681 in Salzburg, 53,361 in Linz). By the budget year 1950, already 1,923,117 Austrians had taken advantage of the services of the U.S. Centers: 751,987 in Vienna, 320,598 in Linz, 440,076 in Salzburg, 254,332 in Innsbruck (in only nine months), 3,235 in Ried im Innkreis (in one month only), 68,520 in Steyr, 61,671 in Wels, 64,215 in Zell am See, and 90,152 in Hallein. It had soon been demonstrated that the branch centers were relatively inexpensive to maintain, for the visitor figures in these smaller towns were proportionately higher than in the major cities. All in all, the cost-benefit ratio was extremely successful. The total cost for 1,992,117 visitors came to 1,751,320 schillings in 1950, which meant that one visitor cost only 88 groschen (or two cents).[20]

During the last years of occupation the amount of visitors stagnated at two million. The largest increase was registered in 1948 and 1949, when in Vienna alone the readership grew 81 percent and the number of borrowed books jumped 90 percent. The reason for this tremendous interest was the increased supply of German translations of U.S. works. Whereas 60 percent of the borrowed books were in English in 1948, by 1949 only 33 percent were. The 27,000 volumes in the America House in Vienna were borrowed 218,000 times, meaning that each book on the average was borrowed eight times.[21]

Children and teens were not forgotten. Since 1948, the American Institute of Education in Vienna held a children's hour every Saturday, and a "Young People's Literary Club" was developed for boys and girls between twelve and sixteen. While the programs of the children's hour, which introduced them to America, were carried out in a rather casual fashion ("American children's stories will first be told in German and then read in American picture books. Children's songs, which are particularly loved by the little ones, will also be taught. Films will enhance the appeal of the children's hour"),[22] the Young People's Literary Club organized slide shows and discussions with U.S. youths of the same age.[23]

To cultivate the interest of these important target groups in American literature, a library catering to the young was opened in Vienna in March 1950. The other U.S. Information Centers also built reading rooms for the youth. The library in Vienna, the first library of this kind ever in Austria, offered 1,500 children's books and also free admission to film features, entertainment programs, and presents at Christmas parties from Santa Claus. Already during the first month, 900 children came. By the last years of occupation, entire school classes were taken to the youth library. These activities represented an important, long-range success.[24]

The final balance sheet of the U.S. Information Centers was certainly positive. Their effectiveness, however, was limited to a relatively small radius around the libraries, especially during the first years. To counteract this limitation, and also to reach people in the Soviet zone in particular, a large number of books were made available as permanent loans to universities, schools, museums, libraries (especially in rural areas), churches, political and trade union organizations, private associations, and youth clubs. By 1950, already 102,151 volumes had been distributed on loan throughout all of Austria.[25]

During the fist years, the ISB had initial difficulties in placing these books in the Soviet zone. Therefore, extension libraries were established. From September 1949 onward, boxes containing up to 100 books each were sent to public institutions as well as hotels located in tourist vacation areas and businesses, which had not been reached until then. By the commencement of the psychological offensive in October 1950, already 436 book boxes with a total of 34,886 books were in circulation. Although no data as to the use of these books are available, for these extension libraries were given to new users after some time had elapsed, one can certainly assume their wide scattering. Numerous thank-you notes from all corners of Austria confirm, in any event, their great appeal. The fact that more than 20 percent of these book boxes ended up in the Soviet zone was seen as a particularly significant success.[26]

The America Houses in Graz, Linz, and Salzburg also introduced the *book-mobile*. Each bus transported more than 4,000 books every week to the most remote corners of the provinces. In addition, these American vehicles were complete with record players and film and slide projectors in an attempt to bring also the rural population closer to the pictures and music of the United States. The Salzburger bookmobile alone regularly serviced approximately 20,000 people in Salzburg, Upper Austria, and the Tyrol. From December 1952 to 1955, about 240,000 loans were made. The bus was finally handed over to the city of Salzburg in 1958, which has used bookmobiles to supply individual districts with materials ever since.[27]

All these activities had an effect upon the clientele of Austrian libraries, which, in contrast to the U.S. Information Centers, levied fees. Already by the end of 1949, the Austrian Library Association protested because U.S. programs had created a ruinous loss of patrons of more than 50 percent. In an effort to curb this "unfair" competition, it was demanded that the America Houses should uphold Austrian laws. The protests naturally had no impact. As the director of the U.S. Information Center, A. N. Hopman, noted, giving in to these wishes would "defeat the implementation of our entire program and make our efforts less effective."[28]

The America Houses not only abolished library fees but also sold books without having a trade permit. The protests of the book trade again remained without consequence. The U.S. officials simply went ahead with their system of "free trade," ignoring any efforts to hinder their competitive advantage.[29]

A public-opinion survey from 1948 shows the popularity of the America Houses. Whereas only 4 percent of the population in the U.S. zone in Germany knew what the America Houses had to offer, 22.8 percent in Vienna, 37.2 percent in Linz, and 23.6 percent in Salzburg were familiar with them. Approximately 9.6 percent of Vienna's population had visited the America Houses, as had 15.4 in Linz, and 15.6 in Salzburg, and between 29.6 and 54.4 percent were even informed about the photography series. Two-thirds of these visitors were men, and only one-third were women. For the most part, they were young, had a higher education, and tended to sympathize with the conservative ÖVP. The age group between eighteen and twenty made up 16 percent of the visitors, while the group over sixty represented only 3.5 percent of the guests. The upper- and middle-class visitors totaled 41.9 percent, and only 2.3 percent belonged to the lower class. High school students and graduates represented 49 percent, whereas visitors with only a grammar school (*Volksschule*) education were only 1.4 percent.[30] The most significant result of this ISB poll was that the great majority of those surveyed were clearly positively disposed to the America Houses in Austria. Only an absolute minority of 4.5 percent disapproved of them as U.S. propaganda.[31]

The preferences of the guests were also carefully registered. The most-read newspapers included the *New York Times, New York Herald Tribune, Washington Post,* and *Wall Street Journal.* The most popular magazines were *Life, Time, Newsweek, Reader's Digest, Saturday Evening Post, Colliers, Esquire, Look, Art and Architecture, Art Digest,* and *National Geographic.* Female readers preferred *Vogue, Harper's Bazaar, Ladies Home Journal, Good Housekeeping,* and *Better Homes and Gardens.*[32]

While the U.S. librarians strove to portray the image of the United States as a land of high culture by introducing "serious" literary texts, the majority of Austrian readers demanded crime novels (the most popular included Ellery Queen and Mickey Spillane), comic books, and Wild West novels, which were particularly popular with young readers. Austrian authors who had emigrated, such as Franz Werfel and Stefan Zweig, were especially interesting for the Austrian audience. The most-read American authors were Ernest Hemingway, Louis Bromfield, John Steinbeck, Sinclair Lewis, John Marquand, William Saroyan, and Pearl S. Buck.[33]

Many books were so popular that they were literally grabbed out of the hand of the previous readers in the overcrowded reading rooms.[34] Some books were not always returned completely, as in the case of a father who lamented that his baby had eaten a part of Dr. Spock's book on caring for children.[35] Even if a guest could not be satisfied with the desired book, the staff tried to assist in other ways. On one occasion, one staff member even came to the assistance of a well-known Viennese dentist who was searching futilely for a new standard work on dentistry in the United States. "All in the aid of better Austro-American understanding, one of the American staff gave the researching dentist a private glimpse of her own brand-new dental work done in America just before her voyage to Europe. The dentist was delighted beyond words; it was just what he wanted to learn about American dental technique and he inspected it thoroughly. With gratitude and admiration for the American dental profession, he hurried off to adapt his new knowledge to a waiting clientele."[36]

Even when a desired title was available, certain problems arose, often because English was not yet the lingua franca in Austria. A librarian, for example, held the following conversation with a client in Vienna: " 'Please, I want a book by Saroyan.' '"My Name is Aram"?,' asked the librarian. 'Is it really?,' replied the inquirer. 'Mine's Prochaska. I want a book by Saroyan.' 'Yes. "My Name is Aram"?' 'And mine's Prochaska.' "[37]

Still, selecting the politically correct books for the libraries was a much less humorous endeavor. U.S. press headlines indicated the direction: "Uncle Sam's Bookstack," "Books Perform Vital Service in Campaign of Truth,"

"Books That Tell the Story of America," and—not to be outdone in its clarity—"Our Fighting Books."[38] If the duty of "democratic reorientation" had been in the foreground until the middle of 1947, "anti-Communist orientation" became the priority thereafter. The America Houses became more and more a weapon of the cultural front of the Cold War. "The kid gloves had to be taken off"[39]—even in U.S. libraries abroad.

All publications—16 million of them were in the America Houses in Austria and Germany in 1950 alone—were examined with a fine-tooth comb. The publishing of anti-Communist literature was also drastically augmented. By 1953, some 6.5 million anti-Communist titles were housed in these stacks in Europe alone. The particularly aggressive anti-Communism that characterized the German America Houses was much less evident in Austria. The reason for this is not so much a more liberal attitude as it is the realization that there was no longer any need for vehement attacks against Communism in Austria. For by the end of the 1940s, the point of anti-Communist saturation had been reached. Any further intensification of obvious U.S. propaganda would have been counterproductive.

Nevertheless, all volumes contained in the Austrian America Houses were carefully examined, and works by authors who were considered too "liberal" or "left" were taken out of circulation. As a matter of fact, the criteria used to eliminate certain pieces became more and more narrow, until the State Department finally asserted in 1953 that "no materials shall be selected which, as judged by their content, advocate destruction of free institutions, promote or reinforce communist propaganda, or are of inferior literary quality, as evidenced by malicious pornographic, sensational, cheap or shoddy treatment, or matter inherently offensive."[40]

In keeping with the administrator of the International Information Agency, Robert L. Johnson, the first and foremost program of the U.S. library program was "to disclose the danger of Soviet Communism by every possible means. This was accomplished through the utilization of materials speaking directly for democracy and forthrightly against communism." Of essential importance, Johnson continued, was that "we have been anxious to avoid an impression abroad that our primary purpose was propaganda rather than information."[41]

Although the anti-Communist course was hereby intensified, it did not, in any event, signify a fundamental change in course. Already by 1947, Assistant Secretary of State William Benton had defined the function of the America Houses: "They cannot be regarded as libraries in the same sense in which we think of a library in this country. They are really information centers about the United States, to which we give the name of libraries as a more convenient and exploratory name."[42]

Even though some librarians may have protested, the domestic political situation in the United States tolerated only unambiguous anti-Communist foreign cultural programs. This was more than apparent during a 1952 hearing of the

Committee on Foreign Relations of the Senate, which heard the following testimony: "Culture for culture's sake has no place in the U.S. Information and Educational Exchange Program. The value of international cultural interchange is to win support for the cultural achievements of our free society, where that respect is necessary to inspire cooperation with us in world affairs. In such a situation, cultural activities are an indispensable tool of propaganda."[43]

Although the anti-Communist tendency of the America Houses had already reached its initial heights between 1947 and 1952, this had not been sufficient for the supporters of Senator Joseph McCarthy. In February 1953, therefore, a further mandate to purge the U.S. Information Centers was issued. Many works were taken from the shelves, and some books were even burned.[44] The protests of American librarians initially bore no fruit. They pointed out that these excesses, with their parallels in the burning heaps of literature of days not long past, were hardly appropriate in furthering the democratic image of the United States.

Two of the most enthusiastic coworkers of the senator from Wisconsin, Roy Cohn and G. David Schine, even personally made their way on a clean-up expedition through the U.S. Information Centers in Europe in April 1953. Their visit was very critically reviewed in the commentaries of many European newspapers. While thumbing through the card catalogs, they found eighteen titles of Communist authors and seventy-eight works of authors who had denied cooperation with the Congressional Committee on Un-American Activities. On the one hand, this was certainly not a dramatic result when one considers that more than six million volumes existed at the time. On the other hand, the limited results of this book inquisition made it quite clear that the America Houses, even prior to the outbreak of McCarthyism, had already been true outposts of America.[45]

However, banned now were not only the works of Communist party members, supposed fellow travelers, or those authors who took the Fifth Amendment during their hearing of the House Un-American Activities Committee and had long been on the blacklist but also books by authors who were generally considered too critical and who were therefore automatically labeled un-American. Gray lists were introduced for these categories, which became the source for great insecurity among the librarians—and almost completely strangled the program. Whereas approximately 120,000 books were sent to the U.S. Information Centers each month prior to the McCarthy attacks, this number dwindled to only 340 copies during the height of the onslaught. A memorandum of September 1953 made this precarious situation more than obvious: "Book selection at the present is still confused, and seems to be based on fear rather than logic."[46]

A hardly complete list of authors, academics, and composers whose works were removed from the America Houses looks like a who's who of postwar culture: Sherwood Anderson, Charles Beard, Leonard Bernstein, Pearl S. Buck,

Erskine Caldwell, Aaron Copland, John Dewey, John Dos Passos, Theodore Dreiser, W. E. B. DuBois, Albert Einstein, Howard Fast, Philip S. Foner, George Gershwin, Dashiell Hammett, Lillian Hellman, Ernest Hemingway, Stefan Heym, Langston Hughes, Julian Huxley, Harold Ickes, Archibald MacLeish, Norman Mailer, Thomas Mann, Arthur Miller, Alberto Moravia, Lewis Mumford, Reinhold Niebuhr, Saul K. Padover, Jean-Paul Sartre, Arthur M. Schlesinger, Roger Sessions, Georges Simenon, Upton Sinclair, Edgar Snow, Mickey Spillane, Virgil Thomson, Henry Wallace, and Frank Lloyd Wright.[47]

The search for the most dangerous underminers of the free world went even further and produced some surprising results. Honoré de Balzac's *Comédie humaine*, Boccaccio's *Decameron*, Gustave Flaubert's *Madame Bovary*, and Stendhal's works were all removed, although it may seem difficult to understand what was so un-American about these classics of literature. The apex of absurdity was reached in the banning of those authors whose books had assisted in establishing the democratic reputation of U.S. literature, such as Thomas Paine's *Common Sense* and Henry Thoreau's *Walden*. Even standard works of academic publishing were not spared by these purging acts. All copies of the *Annals of the American Academy of Political and Social Sciences* for 1946 were eliminated simply because they included deliberation of the pros and cons of a world government.[48]

Although these extremes were gradually discontinued after the political fall of McCarthy, this epoch of anti-Communist hysteria left behind obvious scars, for, as one American critic sarcastically noted, judgment was passed on a book according to "whether its author's great-grand-mother liked red caviar or whether in childhood the author himself read 'Little Red Riding Hood.' "[49] By 1955, the U.S. foreign libraries held a catalog of 18,000 titles that had even been blessed by the American Foreign Legion. The once-liberal image of the America Houses was so badly damaged that the *Chicago Daily News* warned only a few weeks after the signing of the Austrian State Treaty that the United States could loose the "Battle of Books."[50]

A special task force was therefore organized in June 1955 to revive the distribution of American books.[51] Great care had to be taken, for the public suspicion of supposed "red" books in these "expensive American centers of infection" was by no means ended.[52] Interventions of this kind obviously intimidated the librarians of the America Houses, who kept a low profile by mostly collecting "germ-free fare."

During the 1960 visit of the U.S. Fulbright scholar Helmut Bonheim to the America House library in Vienna, he noted that the collection between 1948 and 1955 had been extensively purged. He found a large number of magazines, such as *Reader's Digest* and *Better Homes and Gardens*, "but of the more liberal magazines there was hardly a trace."[53] The practices of U.S. foreign libraries led to serious questioning of the democratic legitimacy of these institutions. On the basis of what he saw, Bonheim could only lament that "the resulting collection, safe and unobjectionable, could hardly be called a monument to the freedom which is our boast and our claim to leadership. . . . At present we run the risk of presenting as typical of our culture that which foreign intellectuals most fear and despise in their own."[54]

Nevertheless, the political damage remained within bounds in Austria. Still, the great success of the America Houses in Austria was never officially acknowledged in the United States, because the yearly renewal of the congressional support for further program security was dependent upon the Communist threat, which supposedly continued to grow. Yet, the positive effect of the houses was unquestioned internally. Direct comparison between the efforts of the Soviet Union and those of the United States in Austria clearly showed that "communist information centers—in Austria, for example—are highly unsuccessful compared with USIA centers."[55]

The quantitative influence of the America Houses in Austria also should not be overestimated. Besides offering intellectual stimulation after many years of isolation, they also satisfied apolitical curiosity, offered a warm escape during the cold winters after the war, acted as a meeting place for a rendezvous, and also served as a shelter for black market activities.[56] In any event, the qualitative importance should also not be underestimated. The most avid users were a part of the group that can be counted among the most important opinion makers: academics and members of the upper and middle classes, especially university and high school students, the reservoir of future opinion leaders.

Without a doubt, the influence of the printed page is often exaggerated. It also does not allow for exact quantification, as do most of the areas of human (self-)understanding. Still, a complete disregard for the impact of the printed word could possibly lead to another distortion, especially in a country whose postwar leaders were still fixed upon the written word. Most important in our context, at least *one* thing was made obvious by all surveys, namely, those Austrians who knew American books judged, not only the United States, but also American politics, more positively.[57]

## "Books Follow the Jeep": The U.S. Publication Service

The phase of German and Austrian dependence upon the occupation powers surprisingly corresponded with a literary image of America that tried to hide this dependence and glorified the occupying nation rather than attacked it. A means to this end was especially the return to myths about America, with which one could avoid the historic reality.

— Rainer Götz, "Der Wandel des Amerikabildes in der deutschsprachigen Literatur seit 1945" (1979)

Perhaps we can best comprehend the present vogue of American letters in Europe by remembering three brusque words used by Thomas Hobbes to account for the authority of the classics: "Colonies and Conquests." . . . Local color, the Wild West, highways and byways of the Jack London territory make a stronger impression on them than upon ourselves.

—Harry Levin, "Some European Views of Contemporary American Literature" (1949)

When the British essayist Sydney Smith posed the condescending question in 1821, "In the four quarters of the earth, who reads an American book?," the success of Harriet Beecher Stowe's *Uncle Tom's Cabin* could not yet be known. By 1884 in Great Britain alone, however, more than 100,000 copies had been sold, more than any book before.[58] Already in 1850, Herman Melville had countered Smith's provocation by asking if the period might not be all too far away "when you shall say: who reads a book by an Englishman that is modern?" However, it still needed a victory of the U.S. Army in the Second World War before the British critic Cyril Connolly would come to acknowledge that "the fort has collapsed and the difficulty now would be to name any major English writers who are not deeply influenced by America."[59] The headline of the *New York Times Book Review* of December 1949 stated laconically, "On Englishmen Who Write American."[60]

The works of countless postwar European authors are, in any event, literary witnesses that Henry James's *Lesson of the Master* had been transformed into a *lesson by the student*. Although the works of the Lost Generation had already excited many European intellectuals during the interwar period, only after 1945 had the literary market become flooded with works by American authors. What a curious irony of history, states John Lehmann, "that Europe should search for its lost secrets in an American mirror—only fifty years later."[61]

Certainly, the Second World War was not won with books alone, but the U.S. Army had armed itself with literary weapons extremely well. Courtesy of the Armed Services Edition, GIs were the recipients of more than 122 million books (1,342 titles) during the war, and millions of copies of overseas editions were being prepared in all the languages of the liberated and occupied countries. Books could actually serve as paper projectiles, and the Council of Books in Wartime quite openly used as its slogan "Books are bullets" and, more notable in the long-run, "Books follow the jeep."[62]

The literature programs of the U.S. Army functioned as more than just a fortifier of the morale of one's own troops. These wartime editions also led to the breakthrough of the paperback and guaranteed the U.S. publishing system a dominating position by the end of the war. They were also only a slight muscle-flexing of what was to come in the postwar era. The American cultural experts set the goal, in particular, to elevate the image of U.S. literature, which was significantly below the prestige of European literature. Next to this rallying for status, another consideration played an important role as well, namely, the idea that "English must replace German as lingua franca of scholarship."[63]

These responsibilities were of particular importance in Austria, for the climate of reception for U.S. literature was definitely cooler than in Italy, France, Great Britain, Scandinavia, and even in Germany before 1938. With but few exceptions, the works of American authors had the reputation of being the cheapest trash and superficial, mass-produced goods. Even those authors who were acknowledged as showing a certain literary standard of quality were criticized for lacking essential moral consciousness and depth, which was supposedly a "typically American" quality. Although Eugenie Zäckel admitted in 1940, in a dissertation on James Fenimore Cooper and Washington Irving, that both authors had a certain influence upon German literature in the nineteenth century, she did, however, come to the conclusion that the essence of the United States could really be comprehended only by a European, and at best by a "German": "Both authors describe for us their country and its inhabitants in a way, but both lack the ability of the master to illustrate significant features. Strangely enough, this was left to a German. Karl Postl [Charles Sealsfield] loved this young country across the Atlantic as his second home, but he was certainly not blind to its limits. With superior control, he captures the country and people and develops pictures for us of incredible vitality and reality."[64]

The point of departure for the "Projection-of-America-Business" was thus surely not simple in Austria. Shortly after the war ended, the ISB saw to it that National Socialist literature was banned and also—wherever possible—hindered the publication of works by politically disfavored American authors.[65] The distribution of the overseas editions in Austria initially had some difficulties as a result of bottlenecks in supplies.[66] At least until the middle of 1947, U.S. officers were also able to influence significantly the development of the Austrian publishing industry through licensing and paper distribution.

Austrian publishers did incorporate an ever-increasing amount of American literature in their programs, with the most-preferred authors being Thomas Wolfe, John Steinbeck, Upton Sinclair, Theodore Dreiser, Irving Stone, William Faulkner, John Dos Passos, Ernest Hemingway, and Sinclair Lewis. However, they were almost completely unyielding in refusing to publish U.S. propaganda. In an effort to reduce the publisher's risks, the ISB frequently took over the responsibility of subsidizing these titles. In addition, in 1946 the U.S. authority founded its own publishing house, Verlag Neue Welt, whose assortment of anti-Communist literature was continuously on the rise.

The ISB also organized the acquisition of books for the America Houses and the advertisements and distribution of the U.S. magazines *Heute*, *Neue Auslese*, *Amerikanische Rundschau*, *Amerika*, and *Der Monat*. The distribution of these magazines amounted to between 50,000 and 175,000 copies monthly.[67] For example, the magazine *Erziehung* was sent free of charge to 6,000 Austrian schools and to between 20,000 and 30,000 teachers.

The U.S. Publications Section also extensively controlled all American works published in Austria resulting from its entitlement to publication and translation rights, options, and contracts. It essentially improved the private business relationships between U.S. and Austrian publishers, especially after 1948. This in turn influenced in many cases the selection of works published; in other words, the types of works offered were entertaining literature and hymns on the American way of life. Nevertheless, control measures against "undesirable" American literature were not completely effective.

The book program, at least until the end of the 1940s, did confront many obstacles. In a sense, it always remained a stepchild of ISB activities, one of the "worst bottlenecks in our program."[68] The blossoming postwar book market was nipped in the bud as a result of the currency reform of late 1947. In addition, the Austrian schilling was nonconvertible, making the Austrian market uninteresting for U.S. publishers, who did not receive subsidies. Still further, the lack of access to the German market was yet another problem. Consequently, Austrian publications were not cost effective, causing great difficulties for Austrian publishers. The Association of Austrian Publishers, therefore, made a clever move in 1948, when it forced U.S. representatives into action as a result of the favorable export offer by the Soviet zone of occupation in Germany.[69]

To counter these overtures, the ISB started an initiative that was to spur the success of the U.S. book program through a variety of new measures. Immediate aid was given to the export of Austrian books in the amount of $125,000 to the Bi-zone of Germany (American and British zones). Tremendous relief also came with the Media Guarantee Program of the Marshall Plan, which made dollar credits from the ERP Fund available to subsidize those U.S. publishers who released their rights for Austria. This program, whose support made possible the publication of additionally large numbers of U.S. books in Austria, initially was opposed by many Austrians. As Charles A. Hoffman reported in June 1950, difficulties existed as a result of the predominating opinion that "pocket books were trash and not desired in Austria."[70]

Furthermore, the ISB credited Austrian editions of U.S. titles with AS 624,000 in 1948 and AS 157,500 in 1949. The money went only to those publishing houses that had, until this time, supported the goals of the ISB, "enabling some of our most important supporters to take firm root in the present barren soil of the industry."[71] Investment in the publication of "overt books" was also intensified, and the long-term fortification of the U.S. position was also meant as a support for some specific Austrian authors. Considered were only those authors "who are favorably oriented toward the West, with the purpose in view not only of reaching a wider reading public and eliminating skepticism on the part of the reading public concerning 'propaganda' by American authors, but also of encouraging and strengthening a corps of native writers oriented toward us."[72]

The ISB's *Verleger Informationen*, which was published between late 1948 and 1956, also served to improve its contacts with the Austrian book market. This magazine, with a monthly circulation of between 500 and 1,000 copies, informed publishers and booksellers of the newest trends in the American book market, published completed contract agreements and sales successes of U.S. literature in Austria, introduced lesser-known American authors to Europe, offered an overview of current U.S. titles, and made new publication rights known.

In spite of the above-mentioned difficulties, the U.S. Publication Section had already been a success by the end of 1948. It completed contracts with more than 120 Austrian publishing houses, a figure that does not include private contracts. Not without reason did a proud note in the first issue of *Verleger Informationen* announce a record number of applications for translation rights that had to be processed.[73] Even if this announcement served as self-advertisement, the U.S. Publications Section, which supplied the Austrian publishers with much other information on the U.S. book market, was all but idle. Each month between three and twelve contracts were signed, and although not all titles were completed in the anticipated production time, up to twelve titles by U.S. authors were published during peak months in Austria.[74]

The initiatives were accompanied by a massive advertising campaign that, for the first time in Austria, demonstrated modern book promotion. The U.S. Publications Section used *Verleger Informationen* for advertisements, and also the new books of American authors were prominently displayed in the windows of the America Houses. Prospectuses were distributed to all bookstores possible, amounting to the use of up to 4,000 kilos of paper per month. In addition, the announcements and book shows on Rot-Weiss-Rot as well as the advertisements and serial novels in the *Wiener Kurier* and other Austrian newspapers also served to popularize U.S. books. Last but not least, the ISB organized a series of book presentations and saw to it that these books were continually present at book fairs.[75]

The U.S. Publications Section was still further active in the founding of Austrian book clubs, especially the youth book club. For the most part, these activities served two goals: "to obtain better distribution of American books and to illustrate to Austrians new methods of selling and distributing books."[76] While the works of John Steinbeck, Herman Wouk, Louis Bromfield, James Jones, Taylor Caldwell, and Pearl S. Buck were among the most-sold novels in the 1950s at the book club Donauland, the book association Gutenberg, the Europäische Buchklub (European book club), Welt im Buch (World of books), and the book union Alpenland, the books most in demand in Austria in 1955 were Herbert Tichy's *Cho Oyu*, *The Esquire Cocktail Book*, and Walt Disney's *The Desert Lives* and *The Wonders of the Prairie*.[77] Translations of American books also played an important role in the selection of the youth book club titles.[78]

The best self-presentation of the United States was an anthology developed especially for children and youths entitled *Eine neue Welt für unsere Jugend* (A new world for our youth), compiled by U.S. cultural officers in Germany and published in 1953 by the Verlag für Jugend und Volk. On 480 pages the United States was portrayed in the best possible light through reports, stories, verses, and letters, with over 500 photographs and pictures. No other youth book can better illustrate the ISB's efforts toward reaching young Austrians (and Germans). No book from this period documents better the unquestionable attractiveness of the United States. Just how many childhood yearnings for trips, dreams of exotic adventures and unknown challenges, or wishes for a better life and modernity were furthered or even first ignited by this work can hardly be estimated. The big sales success of this quite elaborately produced, yet still affordable, book allows the conclusion that many young readers enthusiastically reached for the fascinating expedition to the New World that seemed attainable, at least here between two book covers.

Only by reading the complete volume can one truly grasp the dramaturgy and the fascination of this attractively produced book. Only a few of its high points can be mentioned here. In it, New York opens the door to the New World, not only with pictures of the night skyline of Manhattan and the radiant Statue of Liberty, but also with lightning around the Empire State Building (shown touching down on its lightening rod). New Orleans, Chicago, Florida, Los Angeles, and Hawaii lured, as did the cowboys, who rode the prairie daily; fights with grizzly bears fascinated, as did the black citizens of the United States. Adventurous, and by no means boring, was the history of the United States that then followed: presidential legends, the pony express, Buffalo Bill as scout, the vestiges of native Americans, the rejuvenation of Europe, the banker of the poor, the rodeo victor, a powwow and the fire dance, a sixteen-year-old general executive, the largest department store in the world, the art of commercials, a mail-order warehouse, Margaret becomes a Camp Fire Girl, Ann works in America's fashion center, chewing gum celebrates its seventy-fifth anniversary, from the peace pipe to the cigarette, Sing Sing yesterday and today, the world power of petroleum, the B-36 at the altitude of 15,000 meters, an "army" without military "drill," Wild West heroes help mothers—the message was insistent and easy to understand, for "the heroes do not exist only in history books." Furthermore, baseball excites a continent, a black team dazzles with a basketball, man struggles against man in football, motors whine in Indianapolis, a magical boxing arena in New York fascinates, Mickey Mouse comes of age, even little people can be big, and music from spirituals to bebop could be enjoyed. The United States was conquered by automobiles and airplanes, and now even a ticket to the moon seemed at hand. No wonder the reader was attracted by this country, which also produced the man who "discovered electricity"! Even the first atomic bomb explosion was fascinating—"the desert melted into green glass." Now, however, the fearful could calmly lean back after this impressive tour de force because they were assured that now the philosophers' stone for peace had finally been found in the form of atomic energy.[79]

The impression given to the children and youths in a predominantly poor Austria by this form of reading material, coupled with other types of media presentations, should not be underestimated. Typically, the tremendous success of U.S. culture called the protectors of the Occident into action at the beginning of the 1950s. Although the Schmutz und Schund (Smut and trash) campaign was seemingly directed "only" against "the new flood of comics," which "undid the art of book printing,"[80] and other "abnormalities" of modernity, the cultural debate of the 1950s, with its undifferentiated attacks against eroticism, alcoholism, rowdies, and the consumption craze, was actually steered against the putative aberrations of U.S. culture. It attacked "the consumption dictate of life's joys,"[81] meaning the "subversive" cultural imports from the United States.

If this campaign, with its structural similarities to earlier autos-da-fé, were not typical of some rather questionable developments of the Austrian postwar culture, especially since the 1980s, they could surely be forgotten, belonging to the realm of the absurd. The veil of silence—the campaign against Ingmar Bergman's film *The Silence* was also among these unspeakable incidents—must, however, be uncovered, if for no other reason than to insist that the German edition of Mickey Mouse in the translation (better: re-creation) of word-wizard Erika Fuchs represented a tremendous literary success. Her work stands the test of comparison with any other children's and youth literature of the period.

Although a 1952 survey showed that Austrian children between six and ten years old preferred Wilhelm Busch's Max und Moritz two to one over Walt Disney's Bambi, those in the age group between ten and fourteen overwhelmingly favored Karl May's Wild West stories. And Mark Twain's *Tom Sawyer* and Jack London's adventure stories already rivaled Daniel Defoe's *Robinson Crusoe* and Erich Kästner's children's books.[82] The popularity of Karl May's novels was no secret to U.S. authorities. In an effort to counter the images depicted in May's works, the Department of State actually handed down an order urging that future U.S. diplomats sent to Germany and Austria be prepared to deal with the prejudices illustrated in May's books.[83]

The sale of books by American authors in Austria did develop very positively during the 1950s. The opening of the market by the ISB was a tremendous success. Already in 1952, there were 112 titles published in Austria that were translations from English (the majority were U.S. titles), and translations of all other languages together (including ancient Latin and Greek) amounted to only 95 works. The number of translations from English grew to 132 in 1952; the others, in comparison, fell to 88. This trend continued in the years to follow.[84]

The U.S. book program, however, could not achieve this success without running into conflicts with Austrian publishers and book dealers. The Verband der österreichischen Verleger (Association of Austrian publishers) opposed some ISB programs, but not only because of the "unfair" competition. It was especially the form of implementing this campaign that met with rejection. For a segment of the publishers and book dealers were unsympathetic toward the ISB's daily demonstrations of new methods in sales and advertising. Although this opposition did not have a political character, the ISB nevertheless attempted to assert covert influence on the composition of the association's board of directors, thereby strongly pressuring its president, Hans Urban. Only those members who actively supported the goals of the United States in Austria were acceptable; neutral publishers were automatically tools of the political opponent. "Is it expecting too much if we ask that the men leading such an important organization for reaching the reading public take sides with us? . . . I think we ought to confer with Urban and tell him where we stand and that we expect positive cooperation from the Association. . . . What I think advisable is that our power and prestige be used to put in positions of influence those men who positively think and act as we do. Either men like Urban will come out on a limb with us—or they should be deprived of the fruit of the tree. . . . If the present leaders of the Austrian book trade don't have foresight then we have to act to find leaders who do."[85]

Actually, the benefits of ISB credits were enjoyed only by those publishing houses that not only reflected U.S. prerequisites with regard to content but also went along with the ideas of the experts for structural modernization. In addition, a reorganization of the Austrian publishing system occurred after the liberalization of trade with the Federal Republic of Germany. Here, especially, those publishers not wanting to conform to this system ran into difficulties. Pressured by the ISB and threatened through statewide competition, an ever-increasing segment of the publishers and book dealers—assessed as being exceptionally inflexible, antireformist, even reactionary by the ISB[86]—chose to incorporate modern production and management methods, advertising strategies, and forms of presentation. Even a best-seller list was introduced in 1951, and the victory of the paperback could not be restrained any longer.[87]

The influence of the United States was not limited only to the types of book imports allowed, the modernization of the publishing system, and the practice of book sales. In addition, the myth of America itself was tremendously fascinating for Austrian authors, a development that occurred similarly in the Federal Republic of Germany and in other European countries. The combination of three factors—the end of many years of intellectual isolation, the presence of U.S. occupation troops, and the simultaneous support of American literature within the framework of a U.S. foreign cultural offensive—created an exceptionally favorable reception for the works of American authors. The interest in literary developments in the United States was strong in all of Europe, although its impact seems greater in the countries occupied by the U.S. Army. Not without reason had the U.S. prisoner-of-war camps been characterized as the cradle of West German literature.[88]

A 1949 public-opinion survey made quite clear that Ernest Hemingway was the model for the majority of West German authors. The long isolation from new developments in U.S. literature—only a few U.S. authors who were critical of the United States had been published during the "Third Reich," especially after 1939—led to an unusual phenomenon. The works that had been written by Thomas Wolfe, John Dos Passos, William Faulkner, and Ernest Hemingway during the interwar period were reviewed at the same time as the pieces by postwar authors, such as Norman Mailer and James Jones.[89] The same was true not only in the area of prose but also of drama.[90] Something else is notable in this context, namely, that "the writers most celebrated in postwar Europe for their 'Americanness,' like Hemingway, Dos Passos, or Faulkner, were usually the same people [U.S.] prewar nationalist critics had condemned for being false to basic American virtues and values."[91]

Although it can be shown just how great the stylistic influence of U.S. literature was for many German-language authors after the war, the clichés depicting the United States frequently did not differ from earlier images. For the most part, the United States maintained a quasi-mythical character that still had little relation to the American reality. With only a few exceptions in East German literature and a few critical works, which appeared during the 1960s and 1970s, the majority of German-language postwar literature represented America as a metaphor for a place that existed outside the perimeters of history.[92]

Rainer Götz has shown that it is not essential who embodies the American myth, whether Pocahontas or Marilyn Monroe. The America pictures of these works (from Wolfgang Koeppen to Peter Handke, from Ilse Aichinger to Ingeborg Bachman, from Max Frisch to Herbert Achternbusch) stand in a long tradition in which "America was invented long before Columbus set sail."[93] In spite of the real presence of the United States in Europe, in spite of the reduction in travel time between both continents, America still remained a product of fantasy and a projection screen for European dreams.

Flight from reality and praise of the United States by appealing to the mythical was, without a doubt, especially widespread during the first years of the Cold War and greater in Austria than in the Federal Republic of Germany and Switzerland.[94] Even East German authors did not escape the reference to the fantastic. Günter Kunert, for example, felt that he was on a trip on another planet during a U.S. excursion. He had the impression that humanity was followed by an extraterrestrial civilization that had taken over the symbols and forms of a civilization long lost and adapted it for its own purposes without true understanding.[95]

At the same time, when so many authors were succumbing to the "Myth America," the United States was also being discovered more and more in the nonfiction sector. Until the middle of the 1960s alone, more than 150 travel guides of America had been published. And something else became of even greater importance. America, concealed by clichés, became the inevitable setting for German-language "trivial literature." This refers not only to Westerns, where it is to be expected, but also to genres such as pornography, science fiction, and crime novels.[96]

A comparable change of position had already taken place at the turn of the century as the topos of "the city" was less and less represented by Paris, London, Berlin, or Vienna but instead was replaced increasingly by New York and Chicago. Although it seemed thoroughly possible at the time of Jules Verne and H. G. Wells that Europeans could travel as pioneers to the moon or to distant planets, the years after 1945 changed this fundamentally. Not only had Europe lost its political and military importance through forced emigration, annihilation, war destruction, and the growing brain drain following the war (including numerous experts who had previously served in the "Third Reich"), but it also lost economic substance and scientific prestige. The continual repression of the Soviet Union from the European consciousness elevated the United States as the only synonym for modern science. The United States quite logically had to become the show stage for science fiction.[97] It is surely only an example for the complexity of the shift in (inter)national connotations when one of the most interesting authors of crime stories, the American Patricia Highsmith, caused yet another inversion of the myth (or perhaps only built upon a tradition that began with Edgar Allan Poe) as she chose Europe as the setting of most of her books.[98]

Although these "trivial genres" dominated the literary export market for U.S. books, they received hardly any academic attention in the German-speaking countries. However, even in the rare cases in which they did, their status as "cheap literary mass-produced articles" led to serious misjudgments and misleading conclusions of unbelievable naïveté. The following assessment is typical: "But this is purely user literature that cannot even spoil or influence the image of America abroad. . . . Therefore, one cannot attribute any influence to these works and their distribution."[99] Even though the cinema and television have functioned as the most significant means of transporting "trivial myths" in the twentieth century, it would be more than wrong to assert that the influence of those literary genres was minimal for the propagation of pictures and clichés about the United States, particularly during the period between 1945 and 1955. Simplifications of this sort are just as ineffective as blanket condemnations, particularly because there is a great lack of analysis of how this literature is perceived and understood. For aesthetic preferences are surely not "questions of good taste." Rather, they reflect real political power and social stratification.[100]

We are dealing here not only with fine distinctions but especially with the fact that seemingly trivial cultural products have by no means trivial effects. Even if their utilization must still be examined more closely, there can be no doubt that precisely the products of the culture industry can be stimulating in periods of cultural stagnation—both positively and negatively. Whatever the intentions of the transmitter may be, the receiver can surely interpret and use the conveyed messages in another way. In his study on the reception of U.S. science fiction literature in Europe, Gérard Cordese has pointed out this important problem: "For European intellectuals the formal contribution far outweighed the naive content—the mystique of science or the American middle-class ideology. In this model formula for international trade, one side bought what the other side never suspected it was selling."[101]

After World War II, hardly anybody knowledgeable of the literary scene could have taken seriously Sydney Smith's question, whether there was anyone in the four corners of the world who had actually read an American book—not even in Austria. The ISB had taken care of that. But the success of American literature was not limited only to the occupied territories. The worldwide export of U.S. books increased tenfold between 1949 and 1963. In contrast, the United States had exported only five million books a year between 1919 and 1939, a comparatively low figure. These statistics show both an absolute and also a relative increase in U.S. book exports. Only 1 percent of American book production had been exported between 1919 and 1939, whereas this total had risen to 8 percent by 1961. The value of these exports was $157 million in 1968, which can be compared with an import figure of only $69 million.[102]

In any event, these large export successes were not achieved without some governmental assistance. As predicted, the books followed the jeep. The Media Guarantee Program alone, as a part of the Marshall Plan (1948–67), distributed 15,162 editions of U.S. books in fifty-six languages, totaling 134 million copies. In addition, 36 editions were published especially for students, amounting to 800,000 volumes.[103] There is no mitigation of the value and attractiveness of the works of many U.S. authors intended when I assert here that these politically motivated book-export programs were essential in contributing to the establishment of the United States' dominating position in the literary market of the postwar world.

# 6

## Psychology instead of a Teacher's Pedestal: The U.S. Education Division, Exchange Programs, and the Propagation of the English Language

Soap and education are not as sudden as a massacre, but they are more deadly in the long run.

    —Mark Twain, *Sketches New and Old* (1900)

The rise of English is a remarkable success story. When Julius Caesar landed in Britain nearly two thousand years ago, English did not exist. Five hundred years later, English, incomprehensible to modern ears, was probably spoken by about as few people as currently speak Cherokee—and with about as little influence. Nearly a thousand years later, at the end of the sixteenth century, when William Shakespeare was in his prime, English was the native speech of between five and seven million Englishmen and it was, in the words of a contemporary, "of small reatch, it stretcheth no further than this iland of ours, naie not there over all."

Four hundred years later, the contrast is extraordinary. Between 1600 and the present, in armies, navies, companies and expeditions, the speakers of English—including Scots, Irish, Welsh, American and many more—travelled into every corner of the globe, carrying their language and culture with them. Today, English is used by at least 750 million people, and barely half of those speak it as a mother tongue. Some estimates have put that figure closer to one billion. Whatever the total, English at the end of the twentieth century is more widely scattered, more widely spoken and written, than any other language has ever been. It has become the language of the planet, the first truly global language.

    —Robert McCrum, William Cran, and Robert MacNeil, *The Story of English* (1986)

Reforms of the education system in the occupied territories were highly important for the long-term securing of a positive climate of reception for U.S. culture. Most notably, this included the democratization of the school system, the development of English-language classes, the augmentation of U.S. topics in teaching curricula, and the support of American Studies. In total, the reform plans were exceptionally detailed and encompassed the following areas:

1. school organization and administration;
2. parent-teacher associations and local school committees;
3. curriculum reforms;
4. U.S. model schools;
5. teacher training;
6. teaching materials;
7. exams, grades, and special consideration for the individual development of the children;
8. student and teacher advising through teachers;
9. student organizations and extracurricular activities;
10. teacher associations and education journals;
11. the liberalization of higher education;
12. the support of the social sciences at universities;
13. the liberalization of career possibilities for academics;
14. career training in trade and industry;
15. student exchange programs;
16. library and museum reforms;
17. cultural exchange through theater, music, and applied art;
18. the training of youth leaders;
19. adult education;
20. training in local democracy; and
21. the development of local democratic organizations.[1]

Except for the period immediately following the war, the Austrian school system experienced less stringent treatment than its German counterpart.[2] Did this occur because the U.S. Education Division encountered in Austria a thoroughly democratic school system, few material problems, and teachers who had a good knowledge of U.S. topics? By no means!

The lack of politically unblemished teachers represented a definite problem during the first phase of reorientation. For denazification had a more severe effect, quantitatively, upon the Austrian school system than in any other area of the society. By the end of 1946, out of the 18,108 primary school teachers, 2,943 were dismissed and 5,170 were suspended. Of the 3,410 secondary school instructors, 477 were fired and 859 were temporarily expelled. And in the universities, of the 327 university professors, 243 were deferred and 27 were suspended. Teacher training colleges saw 69 dismissals and 106 suspensions.[3] Not only was there a lack of qualified teachers, but also schoolrooms, teaching materials, clothes, and, especially in urban areas, heating materials and food were in short supply. Consequently, the filling of empty stomachs was initially just as important as stuffing the heads of teachers and students with democratic scholastic ideals. School meals contributed by the U.S. Army (and the other Allies) certainly aided in relieving the first needs; they actually also paved the way for creating an acceptable environment for instruction. In the province of Salzburg alone, 18,400 children enjoyed these donations in 1946; by 1949 the number reached 30,000.[4] The U.S. Army allowed for the acquisition of further material aid for the schools.[5] By the end of 1949, the expenses of the U.S. Education Division alone amounted to $72,362 for supplying machines, teaching materials, books, school furniture ("for demonstration of typical American classrooms"), and film projectors.[6]

U.S. school experts saw themselves confronted not only with the remains of National Socialist indoctrination, human anguish, destroyed schools, and many other material needs, but also, in their eyes, with an antiquated school system. The contents of the curricula were not the only facets that required democratization. More important, the entire Austrian school system was to be redesigned according to the newest scientific findings in the United States. Next to the predominance of traditional curricula, the U.S. school reformers especially criticized the fact that the children in Austrian schools were not prepared to deal with social problems and therefore were not adequately instructed about the social abilities that were necessary for a working democracy.[7]

These views were based on the surely correct assessment that Austrian and German pedagogy—and not only that of fascism—had been instrumental in the shaping of authoritarian personality patterns, which had made the success of National Socialism possible in the first place. That was the main reason that the U.S. Education Division wanted to break the scientific dominance of idealism and subjectivism and replace it with empirical-analytical thought patterns. This meant, in a scientific-theoretical sense, nothing more than that the U.S. reformers were committed to introducing the methods of Anglo-Saxon empiricism and rationalism; thereby they in effect interpreted German historical thinking prior to 1945 as irrational and foreign.[8]

In order to make this paradigm transformation possible, all areas of the educational system had to be incorporated into the reforms. Particular attention was given to the modernization of curricula in all school types as well as the course offerings at the universities and academies. In this effort, new social-scientific areas of study and the development of English-language teaching certainly received greatest support. The distribution of U.S. schoolbooks and their propagation as models for Austrian schoolbook authors also served this goal. The pedagogical and psychological training of Austrian teachers was to be notably intensified and modernized. Not completely without basis, the pedagogical-educational standards of *Gymnasium* (high school) teachers, in particular, had been described as elementary, dull, and hollow.[9]

Discussion evenings and continuing education training for teachers were intended to familiarize instructors with the developments of U.S. pedagogy, as were the educational programs on radio Rot-Weiss-Rot, reports in the *Wiener Kurier*, lecture series in the America Houses, and book donations. Only a few primary and high school teachers received the opportunity to experience the education system in the U.S. firsthand through exchange programs. Yet, the experiences of the returnees not only were exploited by U.S. media in Austria but strongly influenced their future work. Of course, especially those teachers were chosen who had particularly good career chances and who could therefore be expected to influence their peers.

In an effort to reach all teachers, even those in the Soviet zone, the U.S. authorities published the magazine *Erziehung* beginning in January 1948. As a matter of fact, it was financed with profits from the *Wiener Kurier*. This publication was sent free of charge to 6,000 schools and 35,000 teachers.[10] The contents of the individual issues show the program followed by the U.S. Education Division in their efforts to win over Austrian instructors for the desired reforms. The first issue opened with the introduction to the pedagogy of John Dewey.[11] The magazine continuously emphasized the notion of a democratic school with student parliaments, student newspapers, student clubs, group discussions, practical education, the use of modern methods of developmental and teacher psychology, and the improvement of communication between teachers and parents. The modernization of school furniture belonged just as much to the program as the abolishing of the teacher's lectern, which was seen as a superfluous symbol of authoritarian thought and was to have no place in the modern school. Education minister Felix Hurdes certified that *Erziehung* found "extraordinary good reception among the Austrian teachers."[12]

To demonstrate concretely the practicality of these suggestions, three schools were equipped with the latest in school furniture (one in the Albertgasse in Vienna, in Nussbaum in Upper Austria, and in Golling in Salzburg). Furthermore, Austrian teachers were invited to attend lectures at the American Dependents School in Vienna, which had also been provided with the most modern audiovisual equipment. Closer contacts with U.S. institutions were ensured through school adoption programs that included more than a hundred Austrian schools.[13]

In total, this reform package aimed especially at the creation of an integrated system for junior high and high schools based on the U.S. model. The U.S. Education Division had hoped to solve two school and political problems simultaneously with the reform of the secondary level. These obstacles were seen as the central hindrance blocking the democratization of the school system—indeed, they stood in the way of the democratization of Austrian society as a whole. The reforms were intended, first, to dismantle the intellectual snobbery of academics and graduates of higher education and, second, to make higher education available for children of the lower classes.

Yet, the limits of influence of the U.S. Education Division became particularly apparent in this specific case, and not only because the possibilities for U.S. lower-class children to gain admittance to college education were somewhat theoretical. While the U.S. education reformers were quite successful with their suggestions for material improvements (the new Austrian school buildings and furniture soon mirrored their U.S. models), the reform plans for integrating the Austrian junior high and high school were, however, destined for failure. Not even the mighty U.S. Army was capable of implementing the comprehensive school in Austria.

Only socialist school experts supported these U.S. plans, probably because they foresaw that the integration of the secondary level would remain only a futuristic vision without the pressure of U.S. experts. Yet, the U.S. school reformers were confronted with the total rejection of the ÖVP and the Catholic church. And this opposition quite simply could not be broken. The U.S. Education Division quite accurately unmasked the school politics of the ÖVP and the Catholic church as "the preservation of existing practices and . . . the restriction of education opportunities to the masses."[14] In addition, these reforms were categorically rejected by the majority of the teachers, who had feared a loss of status. Not without reason, Austrian teachers were categorized as "typically provincial" by U.S. education experts.[15]

Under Minister Felix Hurdes as a bulwark of the Catholic fraternity Cartell Verein, the Ministry of Education became the central bastion of conservative-Catholic cultural politics. The "Christian Occident" had to be defended against "materialism," with a crusade against psychoanalysis and "logical positivism." And this was also true with respect to the unwelcome school reform suggestions of the U.S. Education Division, which certainly had an air of Communist leveling. The U.S. diplomat Martin F. Herz, in his final report from Austria, commented laconically and with resignation: "Part, at least of the appalling decline of Austrian learning must be charged to the narrowly conservative orientation of these personalities."[16] This intellectual climate of cultural provincialism provoked a new derisive nickname for Austria—Hurdistan.

In such a climate, it becomes understandable that the introduction of a psychological service in the Ministry of Education could be interpreted as a great success by U.S. education reformers. All far-reaching plans for formal democratization of the system of education had to be withdrawn already by 1948, so as not to irritate further the ÖVP. The general support of the ÖVP for the interests of the United States in Austria was certainly more important in the long term than the implementation of specific educational reforms.

Although these reform plans had been also a central part of the U.S. education policies for Austria, relinquishing their execution did not constitute a total failure. Socialist school reformers were strongly influenced and stimulated. Also, the English language became the leading foreign language in Austrian schools. Especially when seen in a larger context of general aversion toward innovation in Austria, the incorporation of more topics relating to the United States in Austrian school curricula can also be interpreted as a success for U.S. educational politics.

The universities of Vienna and Graz had already offered courses in U.S.

history and geography in the second half of the nineteenth century. Between 1919 and 1945, almost fifty courses on American topics were taught at the University of Vienna, and a dozen at the Interpreters Institute alone between 1940 and 1945.[17] Still, although the United States was not totally missing from the list of Austrian course offerings, it was hardly a focal point of academic interest when compared with the courses on literature, history, geography, and the laws of other countries.

It would be a total exaggeration to state that the United States has become the center of Austrian academic research since the years of occupation; yet, it has moved from the periphery in this direction. Only fifteen years after the end of the war the well-known Americanist Sigmund Skard came to the conclusion in his comparative analysis of American Studies in Europe that the situation in Austria had improved considerably; more important, "in view of the relative scarcity of course material in present-day Vienna, there is hardly any place in Europe where the available material is being put into more use effectively. . . . In the picture of American Studies in post-war Europe, Austria is a pivotal point in more than one sense. With their limited means the Austrians are living up to that responsibility in a way which demands respect, and may well serve as a model to other nations. . . . Few European universities today can compete with Vienna in the extent and variety of its American teaching."[18] Future developments were already signified in 1945, when the Englisch Institut of the University of Vienna was rebaptized as the Englisch-amerikanisches Institut shortly after the arrival of the U.S. Army. While the students' interest in U.S. topics rapidly rose, the professors, with few exceptions, were neither prepared nor competent to deal academically with the United States. As a result, Austrian and German professors were certified in an official U.S. report as still almost absolutely ignorant in all questions of intellectual and scientific developments in America. This study, which was based upon hundreds of interviews with academics in Austria and in Western occupation zones of Germany, demonstrated the absolute unfamiliarity of the interviewed professors with U.S. philosophy and social sciences.

This void of information can hardly be surprising. The upswing of the social sciences in the United States had been partially based upon the contributions of those European exiles whose scientific-theoretical positions in Nazi Germany and Austria had been a reason for their forced exile. Traditional academia had not needed the geographic distance of the United States to silence, write off completely, or, still worse, ignore to death these new approaches. But even after the defeat of the "Third Reich," the intellectual narrowness of the universities could not be automatically overcome. Should the academic elite continue to limit themselves to the antiquated curricula and academic methods, which in the period after Hiroshima could only be characterized as escapism, then the Austrian intellectual community was threatened "to be the victim of a policy based upon thinking of the years prior to the airplane, the rocket, and the atomic bomb," because "the German and Austrian academicians are the first victim of their own intellectual training."[19]

Although the temptation to hold a mirror up to the authors of the study with regard to the last sentence might be great, the development of the Austrian universities since 1945 has proved that these words of warning were not articulated without reason. The U.S. authorities reluctantly went along with many of these restorative tendencies in Austrian intellectual life. Therefore, they developed various exchange programs in an effort to help break through the many years of isolation and hinder the retreat of academia to traditional theoretical positions. Austrian opinion leaders were to be especially won over for the politics of the United States; "the exchange program must be designed to indoctrinate as well as educate."[20]

These exchange programs not only offered scientists desperately needed contacts with U.S. research but also enhanced the position of U.S. scientists worldwide. For, as Frank Ninkovich has stated in connection with the establishment of the Fulbright Commission, "whether or not it is admitted, or even recognized, the Fulbright Bill provided for the creation of an overseas American educational imperium through the system of binational 'foundations.'"[21] Because of the complicated organization—not only did political screening require time, but also transportation was difficult in the first postwar years—the exchange programs demanded a longer preparatory phase. In 1947, then, the first two students made their way to the United States for one year of study.[22] These student programs, which were developed further in the years to come, were not limited to the occupied territories. Only 10,000 foreign students had studied in the United States in 1939, but this figure rose to over 50,000 in 1960.[23] High school students were not ignored, for "the ideological plasticity of the teenage group might single them out as an ideal point of entry for introducing democratic ideas."[24] The American Field Service assisted eighty-eight Austrian secondary school students in acquiring a yearlong stay in the U.S. between 1949 and 1956. In contrast, thirteen U.S. teenagers had made a countervisit to Austria by 1955.[25]

In addition, exchange programs for "Austrian Leaders and Specialists" and "American Experts Visiting Austria" were introduced, with a budget of $115,000 in 1950. This program as well as the others was not primarily interested in extending education but stressed the political means of influence, "aiding not the physical, but the ideological reorientation of Austria."[26]

To allow the political fruits of these exchange programs to ripen to the fullest possible degree, particularly young, promising leaders who had not yet reached the zenith of their careers were chosen to participate. Also university professors and students were especially targeted. The "Programming the Foreign Leader" initiative was not limited only to scientific areas[27] but also included leaders in politics, trade unions, professional guilds, journalism, and church and youth organizations, as well as artists and civil servants. Members of the universities therefore composed only a minority of all participants. Approximately 500 Austrians took part under this program. Between 1948 and 1960, some 12,000 foreign opinion leaders came to the United States, most for a two- to three-month visit. Slightly over 10,000 came from the Federal Republic of Germany. This personal form of U.S. developmental aid indeed had quite another center of gravity. Besides the approximately 50,000 foreign students that studied in the United States in 1960, also over 75,000 foreign officers and soldiers were trained by the U.S. Army in the same time.[28]

As important as these various exchange programs were, the intensification of scientific contacts between the United States and Austria was furthered by one program in particular. Developed by Senator William J. Fulbright in 1946, the Fulbright Program's significance in intellectual matters may equal the economic influence of the Marshall Plan.[29] In Austria, the program, which was financed by the sale of surplus materials of the U.S. Army, began in June of 1950. Since then, it has become the most important financial and organizing motor for scientific communication with the United States.

Until 1963, the Fulbright Program was financed only with American means, totaling approximately $3 million. For the academic years 1951/52 to 1955/56 alone, $1.25 million was made available. This amounted to a yearly budget of $250,000, and the total sum came to 33.5 million schillings, according to the rate of exchange at the time. After the right of disposal of ERP counterpart funds was turned over to the Austrian government in 1961, a new financial agreement between the United States and the Republic of Austria was reached in June 1963. Austria now would be responsible for 67 percent of the expense, which was to be backed by the ERP Fund. The United States has since financed the additional 33 percent. In total, 136 million schillings were applied to the Fulbright Program in Austria between 1950 and 1975.[30]

Already by 1975, the Fulbright Program had offered approximately 78,000 scientists, academics, teachers, and students from 110 countries the opportunity to travel to the United States. During the same period, 39,000 U.S. professors and students taught, carried out research, and studied abroad as participants in this program. Between 1948 and 1958, the travels of 22,066 Europeans to the United States and 9,888 Americans to Europe were financed by these means.[31] From Austria alone, 2,654 stipends were granted between 1950 and 1958. Austrian guest professors, researchers, teachers, and students were scattered among more than one hundred universities and colleges throughout the United States. In addition, the Fulbright Program made it possible for 130 Austrians to study at the Bologna Center and at the Salzburg Seminar in American Studies as well as participating in the Cleveland Youth Leaders Program. American guest professors and students taught and studied at all Austrian universities and academies. Course offerings included almost all areas of the natural sciences, the humanities, and the arts. A main focal point for the participants from both countries was the study of language and literature.[32] In this context, the activities of private U.S. foundations, especially the Ford Foundation and the Rockefeller Foundation, must be mentioned, for they were extremely important in the establishment of modern social science research in Austria.[33]

A quantitative overview of these intensive scientific and academic exchanges, which are still growing, certainly allows us to estimate the long-term qualitative impact of the Fulbright Program. The total repercussions for the further development of many scientific areas of study in Austria and for the establishment of personal contacts in the United States were indeed significant. And it is certainly not an exaggeration to assert that it created the first prerequisites for modern American Studies. The Fulbright Commission not only financed American guest professors in American Studies (since 1951 at the University of Innsbruck, since 1953 in Graz, since 1954 in Vienna, and since 1968 in Salzburg) and historians (1984–89 in Salzburg) but also assisted with the development of area libraries and the improvement of the infrastructure of academic institutes.

The extension of Austrian research libraries with works from the United States was initiated by the ISB in 1945. Material needs, war destruction, but especially previous disinterest had resulted in the fact that the libraries of the respective university institutes did not even hold the most important standard works of American literature. As a matter of fact, the Anglistic and Interpreter Institutes of the University of Vienna together had only one American English dictionary—actually only the first volume (from A to D) of this dictionary! The entire collection of books on U.S. subject matters at both institutes could be housed without difficulty in a small bookcase; in contrast, the library had 18,000 volumes on British topics.[34] The English Seminar of the University of Innsbruck had not even acquired complete collections of works by Edgar Allan Poe, Ralph Waldo Emerson, Walt Whitman, Theodore Dreiser, Carl Sandburg, Robert Frost, Edgar Lee Masters, and Thomas Wolfe by 1949.[35] Even if the ISB did not have access to the means to fill all of these gaps, the reference materials, literary works, monographs, and newspaper subscriptions it did supply certainly made possible the beginning of serious academic discussions of U.S. literature in the Austrian universities.

Countless book donations, exchange programs, U.S. guest professors, and the increasing interest of students resulted, then, in an unparalleled explosion of course offerings and academic research on U.S. topics at Austrian universities, at first mostly in Vienna. Compared with the fifty courses relating to the United States held between 1919 and 1945, more than one hundred courses with U.S. themes were held between 1946 and 1954 alone.[36] Between 1919 and 1945, no more than two dozen dissertations on the United States were completed; between 1945 and 1955, this number rose to almost one hundred.[37] This trend could also be found with respect to master's theses that were written in

English Language and Literature Studies, although not to the same magnitude. Nevertheless, more than a third of the theses involved U.S. topics between 1946 and 1955, whereas such studies had been extremely rare during the interwar period. In addition, more than eighty theses with U.S. topics were approved at the Business School of the University of Vienna between 1946 and 1954 alone.[38]

Of equal importance was the further development of the teaching of English at secondary schools and high schools, a trend that actually was noticed already in the 1920s. Even the National Socialist education experts favored English over French in foreign-language instruction. English, after all, was an Anglo-Saxon language, whereas the latter belonged to the "alien" Romance group. Only after 1945, however, did English finally become the dominating foreign language in Austrian schools. Of the 61,600 students that had foreign-language lessons in 1952, some 51,400 studied English, 29,400 Latin, 11,400 French, 5,000 classical Greek, and 2,200 Russian.[39] In 1946, twelve U.S. authors were for the first time incorporated into the last year of high school curricula, and even the writers of school textbooks could not any longer avoid including information about the United States in their works, even though it was still hardly of adequate proportion.[40]

Although the dictionary *Amerikanisch in Abkürzungen* had already appeared on the market in 1946,[41] the ISB still had to battle almost insurmountable mental barriers against U.S.-American English and U.S. literature perpetuated by most Austrian English teachers.[42] ISB officials repeatedly noted that "there exists a decided bias towards British accent and CULTURE among Austrian English teachers."[43] As surveys in the years to follow have shown, these preferences certainly had an effect upon the knowledge of the students, who "are developing a surprising knowledge of England and its way of life. On the other hand, they are hopelessly ignorant of life in the United States."[44] Based on a combination of ignorance and European cultural arrogance in the tradition of the century-old prejudice that the United States is a nation without culture, most teachers at best demoted U.S. English to the status of an inferior dialect.

This attitude existed not only in Austrian secondary schools and high schools but, for a long time, in the universities. An especially vivid example of this mental tradition is the dissertation entitled "The Infiltration and Adoption of Americanisms in Contemporary British," which was approved at the University of Vienna in 1943. According to this, Great Britain actually had to lead a defensive war against the "foreign thought patterns" from the United States. The "hurricane-like expansion" of U.S.-American English into the "blood line" of British English, caused primarily through the intellectually flat products of opinion factories and "nigger minstrels," also demanded a well-aimed defensive attack by all British classes and professions; what was needed was "a fanatical gunner with the heaviest language artillery." Yet, England had not been completely lost. A chance still existed, for it was still a European country, and only in a society that had been erected upon cultural misconceptions could such desolate monotony and standardization abide.[45]

The lack of any sense of reality in this work, which was written during a period when hundreds of thousands of GIs were in Great Britain in preparation for the invasion of Normandy together with British soldiers, is surprising. The appeal for an aggressive renunciation of American English and its culture in a war dissertation would hardly be that unusual, however, except that its author was Louis Heinrich Paulovsky, who later became the chairperson of the English Institute and the Institute for Translation and Interpreter Training at the University of Vienna after the Second World War. *This* connection is certainly interesting.

Nevertheless, Austrian teachers at least no longer disregarded British English, as had many of their predecessors. Nationalism and the ideology of the folk had already demanded the construction of a cultural front to repel all that was "foreign" in the second half of the nineteenth century, especially the "Anglo-Saxon." The Allgemeine Deutsche Sprachverein (General German language union) thus proclaimed the following resolution in 1899, at the height of imperialism, at a time in which the English language still followed the Royal Navy: "With the growing influence of the English, the number of foreign words from the English language is growing at an alarming rate. In this modern language development, the old hereditary defect of the German people has once again risen: overestimation of that which is foreign, lack of self-esteem, disrespect for one's own language."[46]

These "hereditary defects of the German people" were rather probably an *underestimation* of that which was foreign and an *overabundance* of self-esteem, otherwise the Allies surely would not have been victorious in 1945. In any event, the British as well as the U.S. Army both utilized the opportunity to encourage the growing interest in English study, and the difficulties faced by the U.S. Education Section were mitigated by the parallel efforts of the British occupation power. In 1948 only 20 percent of the Austrians demonstrated some knowledge of English, a figure that rose to 50 percent by the end of the occupation period.[47] The support for the English language was absolutely successful, and French fell more and more to a minority position in the schools. Even in the French zone, only one-third of the students learned French, whereas two-thirds studied English. Between 1947 and 1952, the number of students of French actually declined, in spite of the presence of French occupation troops.[48]

Although the development of language courses clearly improved the opportunity to propagate the fundamental knowledge of English, the school was not the only—perhaps not even the most important—window of opportunity for Anglicisms and Americanisms. Austrian students probably did not learn the new hip vocabulary in school, yet they understood the following perfectly: sex appeal, pin-up girl, black market, nylons, jazz, publicity, boogie-woogie, jitter-bug, swing, bar, star, do it yourself, safety first, service, hobby, manager, corned beef, candy, striptease. English words, especially U.S. idioms (did not a "dandy" turn into a "playboy"?), became more and more common in Austria, and not only with regard to words that had no substitutes in German (count-down, comics, fallout, babysitter), but also partial substitutes (Hitparade, Partyraum, Jazzsänger) and complete literal substitutes (Marktforschung, Meinungsumfrage, Kalter Krieg).

The use of English expressions gave the speaker an aura of victory and success, of modernity and progressiveness, but also—and this was essential after the long years of the glorification of discipline—slickness and coolness; to use another complete substitution, the new words were quite simply used as a *Statussymbol*. The press belonged to the most important propagators of these new expressions, a consistently increasing trend since the late 1940s. The use of the expressions taken over from English grew 793 percent between 1963 and 1974 alone.[49] Only 900 lexically defined Anglicisms appeared in the German language in 1909;[50] by the mid-1980s, one-twentieth of the colloquial German vocabulary included Anglicisms, but especially Americanisms.[51] In 1963 only one Americanism on the average could be found in German and Austrian newspapers and magazines; by 1974, the number had already risen to four-teen.[52] Next to the influence of the print media, the radio, television, film, and records significantly contributed to these developments. A great number of Americanisms infiltrated particularly the language of the young as well as the technical terminology of the entertainment industry, pop music, jazz, the sci-ences, the military and the armaments industry, politics, economics, technol-ogy, sports, transportation (in particular, automobiles and airplanes), tourism, and fashion.[53]

At the beginning of the 1950s, "mode" had still not been renamed "fashion," and Christian Dior was still "couturier" and not "designer." His newest "cre-ation" was not yet part of a "line," but it nevertheless was called the "new look." The rapidly expanding advertising companies, which were in part owned by U.S. firms, not only copied "marketing" and "public relations," "product placing," and the "image" of their American models, but also some-times offered some refreshing (Sexy Flower Power, Super Pop-Op Cola), often unspeakable (If Kostensenkung, go to Deutsche Leasing), language-development assistance. Although these developments were not as rapid in Austria as in the Federal Republic of Germany, the future potential of the advertising industry was clearly represented in a dissertation of the University of Vienna in 1947 entitled "Modern American Language in the Service of Present Day Advertising: A Survey of Linguistic Means Available for the Psy-chology of Selling."[54]

Most recently, German has added *Joggers* and *Bodybuilders*, *High-Fidelity-Fans*, *High-Tech-Maniacs*, and *Computer-Freaks*. When German *Computer-Kids* hit the *Reset-Knopf* with the command *Pac Man's an*, then it only remains a question of time until the partial substitution *Computerwitwe* (computer widow) will also find its way into Austria.[55]

This language phenomenon is not unique to Austria. "Deutschlish" is in good company with "Franglais" and "Spanglish," and "Japlish" has even acquired a vocabulary of more than 20,000 Americanisms since the end of the Second World War. Even though "Russlish" is not yet as widespread, developments have recently accelerated dramatically; *seaksapil* and *noh-khau* had ceased being foreign words even before "glasnost" and "perestroika."

Although only approximately one-tenth of the world's population has English as its mother tongue, around one billion people have some sort of knowledge of English. It has become the most important medium for scientific and academic publications and is most frequently spoken at conferences. More than half of all scientific journals are published in English. Even in France, almost a third of all natural science research appears in English. English is the official language of sea and air traffic and of the World Council of Churches. Approximately three-fourths of all messages sent by post, telegram, and telex and more than half of all newspapers and magazines are written in English. Over half of all radio stations and the most important television stations broadcast their programs in English. More significant for the future is perhaps the fact that over 80 percent of computer information worldwide is stored in, or at least based on, the English language.[56] The British Empire had certainly created the best conditions for this expansion. Yet, without question only the superpower position of the United States after the Second World War made the English language into the lingua franca of the second half of the twentieth century.

This advancement of the U.S. version of the English language has even provoked opposition from the protectors of Queen's English in the United Kingdom. The late 1970s saw the beginning of the Plain English Campaign, which even preoccupied the House of Lords. These debates, which ran parallel to the French campaign against Franglais, in themselves were rather unimportant. It is notable, however, that the arguments used against the penetration of American English by British Lords were not structurally different from the concerns vented by critics during the "Third Reich" against the American "Un-language." Lord Somers surely would have found widespread support above and beyond that of the House of Lords for his contribution to this debate on November 21, 1979, which concluded with the following: "If there is a more hideous language on the face of the earth than the American form of English, I should like to know what it is!"[57]

If the shadowboxing of the language nationalists can be compared to a hopeless fencing battle in which they have their backs to the wall against the most modern weapons, then at least one thing is certainly amusing. The expansion of U.S. English was most stringently resisted by precisely those social groups that, at the same time, advocated the military, political, and economic presence of the United States around the world. The penetration of American English, however, is not based only upon the position of the United States as world power. It is also a result of the vitality of the language itself, whose pragmatism often offers the occasion for rather unwarranted mockery. One is, by no means, a naive handyman of cultural imperialistic ambitions when one ascertains that the language police is simply one form of thought police, and language nationalism is just a particular version of nationalism. Furthermore, language imperialism can also turn into a boomerang, namely, when the inhabitants of a colony command not only their own language but that of the imperial metropole, requiring the colonizer to seek the assistance of foreign interpreters to understand their affairs.

Questions of good taste are based on class and power, as the use of the phrase "language purity" illustrates all too well. Another particularly wise British lord, the philosopher Bertrand Russell, pointed precisely to the historic determinedness as he sarcastically stated in 1950: "The only good thing about the American language is the slang. Fortunately, it is just this that the English are most disposed to copy. I console myself with the reflection that French, now such a beautiful language, was in origin the argot of uneducated Roman soldiers. Perhaps in fifteen hundred years American will become equally admirable."[58]

Although Austrian ski teachers and Chinese economic experts, Peruvian students and Polish jazz enthusiasts, Japanese rock fans and Egyptian computer kids seem to be speaking the same idiom, one should not overlook the fact that to describe new situations, new vocabulary is simply necessary. The hybridization of language, which will no doubt be pushed still further through modern communication technology, and the continually noticeable shifts in meaning of adopted slang expressions allow the conclusion that English is "A Language That Has *Ausgeflippt*."[59]

Without a doubt, these factors are just as important for the propagation of the U.S. version of English as is the wide support of English-language courses in the schools. Because of the pro-British leaning of the teachers long after the end of the war, one could almost suggest that U.S. idioms spread as they did, not because of, but in spite of, school. However, the Austrian youth did become more or less familiar with the foundations of English in school. Even though the teachers may have insisted upon the putative cultural superiority and absolute correctness of Queen's English or Oxford English (forms that, by the way, are hardly spoken in Great Britain), the young people had more linguistic armor with which they could adapt, if not create, "slanglish." And many did precisely this out of conscious opposition toward their instructors.

The efforts of the U.S. Education Division were therefore not without long-term influence, in spite of some difficulties resulting from moments of institutional and mental lethargy. These endeavors were also supported by the

Austro-American Society, the Austro-American Friendship Society, the Austro-American Institute of Education, the Austro-American Club, the Austro-American Circle, the Rainbow University in Zell am See, and a long list of private and public youth organizations. Last but not least, the daily contacts with GIs were also an important source for language practice.

Yet, more than just the pervasion of the American English language was criticized. The propagation of American Studies offered occasion for critical commentary as well. Marcus Cunliffe may have been correct when he asserted that in dealing with the expansion of American Studies in Europe after 1945, we are confronted with a functionally more intelligent and refined form of U.S. cultural imperialism, which "was drumming home the ideology of the frontier thesis and demanding room in the curriculum for a purportedly brilliant national culture."[60] However, in the case of Austria, one decisive qualification must be made. The augmentation of American Studies certainly served as another means for pressing the Cold War. Nevertheless, the deficit in Austria of scientific and academic information with respect to the United States made the development of American Studies an absolutely necessary desideratum of a modern, scientific development that was open to the world. In other words, an academic analysis of the United States would have been desperately necessary, even without the presence of the U.S. Army and the Cold War. It may be questioned, however, whether this would have occurred without the initiatives of the ISB, even more so when one takes into consideration that scientific discourse dealing with the United States is still in need of further development, although certain improvements have been achieved.

One significant center for American Studies is housed in Austria: the Salzburg Seminar in American Studies. The establishment of the Harvard Summer School in Schloss Leopoldskron in the summer of 1947 was surely not a component of official U.S. education politics. The Salzburg Seminar, more accurately, was an initiative of the Harvard University Council and marks certainly one of the most important individual contributions to the improvement of the quality of American Studies, not only in Austria, but throughout all of Europe.

However, not even the private character of the Salzburg Seminar, which quickly evolved into the "most efficient center for the dissemination of American ideas in Europe,"[61] protected its initiators from political interventions. Even the Salzburg Seminar, which attempted to promote the exchange of ideas between European and U.S. intellectuals through direct personal contacts, was caught in the pull of the Cold War. Merely the fact that mild criticism of the United States had been voiced in the stimulating discussions during the first session in 1947 caused the secret service of the U.S. Army to intervene. The organizers of the seminar quickly recognized that their support for the free expression of ideas could not include openness to critical analysis of the United States, for "the presence of an American army of occupation imposed a certain realism on the seminar."[62]

This realism meant the refusal of entry for U.S. citizens whom the U.S. Army deemed to be supporters of the former U.S. vice-president Henry Wallace and supposed fellow travelers. This ban included not only Clemens Heller, the founder of the seminar, who for no reason was denounced as a Communist, but also the prominent Harvard University professor F. O. Matthiessen, who had participated in the first session in 1947.[63] This expert of literature, whose book *From the Heart of Europe* not only dealt with the fascinating years of the founding of the Salzburg Seminar but also contributed significant insights to the cultural situation in postwar Central Europe, withdrew himself through suicide from the ever-increasing pursuit against critical intelligence in the United States.[64]

This control of the Salzburg Seminar by the U.S. Army, which amounted, more or less, to ideological conformity, was at first observed with uneasiness by the Department of State. In particular, its reservations were based upon the realization that it was precisely the intellectual and political openness of U.S. professors that impressed the European participants the most. But even the State Department, which increasingly found itself in the crossfire of criticism because of its putative soft stance toward the "Communist world conspiracy," was soon to acquire a more rigid posture. Even if its goals could hardly be differentiated from those of the U.S. Army, its methods were certainly different, for "there is a difference between an intelligent and an unintelligent defense of American policy."[65]

Although the U.S. foreign cultural experts still overwhelmingly espoused the concept of cultural universalism during the Second World War, the Cold War brought a distinct about-face. This meant simply that "the State Department now took the position that universality would have to reflect American national values, and not the reverse."[66]

The slow mitigation of political difficulties as a result of the self-censorship of the seminar management was not, however, the seminar's only obstacle. For even here U.S. intellectuals were again and again confronted with the phenomenon that proved itself to be a continual handicap for the foreign cultural politics of the United States during the Cold War. Henry Nash Smith certainly did not exaggerate when he stated, "No one could stay at Leopoldskron without realizing that the conceptions of the American character held even by cultivated Europeans are vastly oversimplified if not downright misleading."[67] Exactly for this reason, those U.S. cultural officers who had taken over the duty of demonstrating to Austrians that even the United States maintained a high culture with an impressive niveau were hardly to be envied.

# 7

## Drama and Music from the United States

And so our view of American influence on European music must really depend, in the last resort, on our attitude to the democratization of taste. Can a whole new educated public be aesthetically enfranchised without lowering aesthetic standards? If not, then American influence has been harmful, for it has already begun the scaling down of aesthetic values so as to be within the intellectual grasp of the average city dweller, beside whom Stendhal's "average sensual man" would have seemed highly civilized. This is a revolution not merely in taste but in the very concept of taste . . . which will end, not with the debasement of taste, but with the disappearance of the word from our vocabulary.

—Martin Cooper, "Revolution in Musical Taste" (1951)

### The Theatre and Music Section

Certainly the most difficult duty of U.S. cultural diplomacy was the presentation of the artistic achievements of U.S. high culture in the most advantageous light. Particularly in this area, the observation is hardly exaggerated that Europeans were possessed by overwhelming negative clichés and prejudices toward the supposed cultural inferiority of the United States (according to the motto "Europe has culture, the United States has civilization"). These attitudes actually had led to the necessity of U.S. foreign cultural programs in the first place. The cultural efforts of the U.S. governments to impress the Europeans with the manifestations of American high culture via the mitigation of European cultural hybrids were an integral component of the political strategy to integrate Europe into "one world," the "Western world" of the Pax Americana. It is significant, however, that even many U.S. cultural diplomats had not removed themselves from Eurocentrism. They, too, thought in the stereotypical dimensions of the superiority of European culture—including its American form; they, too, could not withdraw themselves from the prejudices of the supposed superiority of "white" culture. This fact, in particular, certainly did not help the democratic legitimation of U.S. programs.

Although the programs of high culture, by definition, did not make a significant difference quantitatively, their qualitative potential was that much more important. Directed toward an "elite" target group, the products of high culture (at least officially) had traditionally been attributed greater value. The performance of artistic works of high standing and the demonstration that the United States also possessed an aura of high culture were to assist in breaking down the negative cultural stereotypes, thereby winning over the political sympathies of specific social groups. In short, in an effort to solidify the political claim to leadership, it was essential to prove that the United States was no longer in its infancy and that it had reached "cultural and artistic maturity."[1]

Notwithstanding a few exceptions involving younger intellectuals, European "elites," generally speaking, did not seem to be particularly impressed, and the "masses" were in actuality hardly addressed by these programs of high culture. The long-lived prejudices were too strong to be definitively altered during the few years of occupation, in spite of the intensive efforts of U.S. cultural diplomacy.

In addition, the individual activities of the different sectors of the U.S. Army were almost certain actually to intensify negative attitudes during the first months of occupation. While the Red Army had supported the recommencement of cultural activities in Vienna immediately after the end of fighting through the reconstruction of destroyed theaters and the distribution of special rations for artists, the U.S. Army requisitioned similar buildings for housing its own troops. Had not the U.S. troops shown their barbarism by transforming the holy halls of the Salzburg Festival House into a variety stage, whose glittering Las Vegas–style name Roxy's was blasphemous on this temple of high culture? Here the UFA star Marika Rökk, whose experience had been founded in entertaining rather different troops, now sang and danced Judy Garland numbers for the GIs. Furthermore, the confiscation of the Provincial Theater of Salzburg for the purpose of screening films, performing the musical review *Glory Road*, as well as the holding of boxing competitions in the Great Hall of the Mozarteum had not particularly aided in diminishing local prejudices. These unfortunate preliminary actions certainly hindered the activities of U.S. high culture officers so significantly that the ISB music expert Margot Pinter complained already in November 1945 that "the Russians are actually the only power now interested in re-establishing Viennese musical life."[2]

In particular, the Theatre and Music Section of the ISB had to deal with this difficult point of departure. Its most important responsibilities were the following:

1. To make the Austrians acquainted with representative American plays and music, spreading hereby in an unobtrusive way the meaning of democracy.
2. To rehabilitate theatrical and musical life in the U.S. Zone of Austria.
3. To take part in the denazification of theatrical and musical activities in Austria.[3]

The ISB section for high culture, then, combined political occupation duties, such as denazification, de-Germanization, licensing of directors, and banning pieces with fascist and militaristic tendencies, with initiatives for cultural self-advertisement through the propagation of works by U.S. authors and composers as well as facilitating performances by American artists. Its aim was to open finally the eyes and ears of Austrian theater and music lovers to the achievements of U.S. high culture. This section was headed by the Austro-Americans Otto de Pasetti, Henry C. Alter, and Ernst Lothar, in cooperation with Music Officers Margot Pinter and Virginia D. Pleasants, until the end of 1947. Edward Hogan took over the section in April 1948, followed in 1950 by Ernst Haeusserman, who then ran the Theatre and Music Section as an appendage of the Motion Picture Section.

The high culture section of the ISB alone, with its headquarters in Vienna and subdivisions in Linz and Salzburg, controlled seventeen theaters, one opera house, a festival house, twenty-four concert halls, and forty-six variety theaters; it also had, on an inter-Allied basis, additional influence upon eleven theaters and two opera houses.[4] Consequently, it fulfilled the duty of a state-controlled cultural management authority. This was actually nothing extraordinary in the Austrian state-run cultural tradition. One must recognize, however, that this entailed cultural management by another state, whose official credo—precisely in the cultural sector—was private initiative and supply and demand.

The Theatre and Music Section took care of all details. It clarified copyright questions, organized the completion of translations, distributed books and scores, organized tours by U.S. artists, and allocated performance rights of U.S. works to Austrian stages, sometimes stipulating even the directors and the cast. Not only the large theaters but the small ones as well were affected by these activities. Already by mid-1946, contracts involving the performance of U.S. dramas had been completed with Vienna's Burgtheater, the Akademietheater, Theater "Die Insel," Theater in der Josefstadt, the Kammerspiele, the Neues Schauspielhaus, the Volkstheater, and the provincial theaters in Salzburg, Linz, Graz, Klagenfurt, and Eisenstadt. The section also arranged contracts with the city theaters in Bad Aussee, Braunau, and Steyr, as well as with the Volksbühne Bludenz and the performance groups Die Stephansspieler, Studio junger Schauspieler, and Die Tribüne.[5]

The selection of pieces was first prescribed by the Reorientation Branch of the U.S. Army. In contrast to the U.S. zone in Germany, the ISB officers in Austria enjoyed a certain amount of flexibility in their right to suggest the inclusion of certain works. However, all performances required further authorization by the appropriate authorities of the U.S. Army.[6] "Classics" of modern American drama, pieces preaching democracy, exaltations of the American way of life, and popular theater were, for the most part, released. Socially critical works could hardly expect to pass the army's preliminary censorship. However high their artistic value may have been, the positive self-portrayal of the United States was not to be endangered by the presentation of the dark side of life, for "on a long range basis this Section is concerned directly with the projection of the United States upon Austria with the supplying of U.S. music and plays to Austrian musical organizations and theatres. . . . As far as the plays go, only such plays are chosen which emphasize the American way of life . . . only those plays are policy-cleared which in every respect give a true and clear picture of the American way of life."[7]

These rigid practices of selection by no means eased the tasks of U.S. high culture officers. Although it initially served the function of curtailing the purchase of critical pieces, this censorship limited not only the artistic freedom of the ISB, which had actually been instituted to guarantee that precisely these freedoms be nurtured in Austria. It also drastically reduced the number of pieces that were appropriate for this particular country of occupation. For although some dramas by U.S. authors (including Robert Audry, Eugene O'Neill, and Paul Osborne) and other foreign pieces had most certainly been favorably viewed by the Austrian theater audience during the first postwar years, it was soon apparent that the pieces allowed by the army were often unsuited in achieving the goals of reorientation. Even Thornton Wilder's *Our Town* and William Saroyan's *Time of Your Life* found little resonance, and it was therefore foreseeable that other pieces included in the list of the Periodical Unit would also hardly be successful. According to Ernst Lothar, the reason was quite simple: "The local audiences, bewildered by characters and conditions wholly alien to them, not only refuse to be carried away but rather feel encouraged to air their barely hidden ill-will towards productions which they consider as forced upon them. In other words, we would fail in our mission to show America at her best and to make her understood in the field of creative art if we would not take into consideration that our offerings have to correspond, to some extent at least, to the mentality and the background of the local authorities."[8] In spite of a short liberalization in 1947 / 48, the flexibility of the Reorientation Branch would remain within certain bounds.

The experts of the Theatre and Music Section were initially confronted with more than just great material difficulties. The execution of projects was also made particularly tiresome through censorship measures. Yet, these problems were comparatively unimportant in the long term, and even competition from the Soviet Union and the other occupation forces did not represent an insurmountable barrier. The greatest hindrance for the success of the U.S. Theatre and Music program proved, however, to be the existing attitude in Austria, which prescribed exactly how any true product of high culture must look at this supposed center of the cultural world.

Although the Viennese Burgtheater had been forced to perform in the variety theater Ronacher because of the destruction incurred by the war, it could at least begin its first postwar season with Franz Grillparzer's *Sappho* on April 30, 1945, thanks to the support of the Soviets. The selection of this piece had symbolic value and can certainly be interpreted as a metaphor for significant trends in the Austrian high culture scene since 1945. In any event, the support of the Soviets for local cultural initiatives was clearly distinguishable from the rigid U.S. politics of total cultural control—and Soviet measures of support were primarily concerned precisely with the sector of high culture. Was this not at least proof enough that the Russians, who unfortunately were Communists, were nevertheless Europeans?

Furthermore, the question of the denazification of the Austrian art scene also caused great difficulties for U.S. cultural officers. The Soviet authorities, in contrast, transferred this area of responsibility for the most part to Austrian officials. The question of the "political cleansing" of Austrian society had in itself become a difficult problem in the postwar period, and it had been particularly delicate in the area of the arts.[9] In addition to other obstacles, the U.S. officers saw themselves confronted with the following dilemma: while only 8 musicians of the 110-member Berliner Philharmonic had been members of the NSDAP, 45 musicians of the 117-member Viennese Philharmonic were party members—22 were even illegal supporters before 1938, as were 2 others members of the SS.[10] "Militaristic" Berlin versus "friendly" Vienna?

Although the responsible officers of the army had initially attempted to change the Austrian high culture scene through serious denazification measures, the interventions were limited to short-term performance bans for certain individuals. For the most part, however, the structures remained intact. In addition, the public acceptance of the denazification decisions, which were often quite subjective, also suffered. This is especially true when one takes into consideration that the evaluation of an individual's political responsibility had frequently not been a decisive factor. The prime motive instead was whether an individual artist could be useful for U.S. occupation policies.[11]

Obviously, the exponents of left-wing, antifascist art were "artistically" useless for U.S. aims. Nevertheless, this group was somewhat effective in establishing itself in Vienna, especially in the Neues Theater in der Scala. Because these artists were suspected of being Communist sympathizers—and some of them were actually "true" Communists—they were disqualified by the ISB as representatives of another understanding of high culture. Political affiliation with "the East" or "the West" had become a reliable gauge of artistic qualification during the Cold War.[12]

The mostly inconsequential implementation of denazification measures was therefore sacrificed for two more important concerns of U.S. politics: the restoration of "bourgeois high culture" and anti-Communism. Harsh denazification measures not only could jeopardize the long-term goals of the United States, but they also could have a counterproductive effect, which was lamented by Henry C. Alter already in November 1945: "We have not succeeded in cleaning out Nazi influence but have severely impaired cultural activities through indiscriminate de-nazification measures."[13] In light of the traditional affinity of Austrian high culture artists with the political powers that be, there can be no doubt that a true denazification in this sector through the U.S. Army, at least in the short and middle term, could have meant the total collapse of those cultural activities that Austrian elites understood as High Culture—and this cultural vacuum could not be risked because of political reasons.

## U.S. Drama

The leading genre on Broadway was psychological drama, advanced especially in the intense, demanding plays of Tennessee Williams and later of Edward Albee. It was safer to concentrate on inner realities, however outlandish and grotesque they might be, in a period that saw repeated congressional investigations of Communist influence in the arts and entertainment media and the general acceptance of the practice of blacklisting present or former political radicals.

—Charles C. Alexander, *Here the Country Lies: Nationalism and the Arts in Twentieth-Century America* (1980)

Prior to the Second World War, theater performances of plays by U.S. authors had been very infrequent in Austria. This short list includes works by Theodore Dreiser, Samuel Raphaelson, Maxwell Anderson, and Zoe Akins. Shortly before the Anschluss, in February 1938, Eugene O'Neill's *Mourning Becomes Electra* had its German theater debut at the Burgtheater in Vienna. The Anschluss, however, brought an abrupt end to these timid beginnings. Consequentially, U.S. dramas performed in the German language, such as those by Irwin Shaw, Moss Hart, George S. Kaufmann, Samuel Raphaelson, John Steinbeck, Robert Sherwood, Eugene O'Neill, and Thornton Wilder, would only be staged in Switzerland between 1938 and the end of the war. This situation changed fundamentally after the defeat of the "Third Reich," and the sudden, unusually strong presence of American dramas on European stages has correctly been characterized as the penetration of North American drama in German-language theater programs.[14]

Certainly, the preparation of theater productions required a considerate period of preparation. During the first term of occupation, the ISB even had difficulties supplying enough suitable books. Pieces had to be chosen and examined for political correctness, questions of copyright had to be cleared, translations prepared, and, finally, performance contracts had to be negotiated. The latter contained a "Special Regulations" clause—especially in conjunction with performances in larger theaters—which had direct influence upon the presentations.[15]

It can therefore hardly be surprising that by the end of 1945, only nine plays, which had not yet been translated into German, were available for performances in Vienna. It is rather more amazing that Thornton Wilder's *Our Town* could already be premiered on February 15, 1946, although the rehearsals had begun just two weeks earlier, on January 31. By the beginning of December 1946, Ernst Lothar was finally given a list of over forty-one plays deemed appropriate.[16]

By January 1950, at the point when the main duties of the Theatre and Music Section were already completed, the ISB had access to the rights for a total of sixty-seven theater pieces. If one were to take into consideration not only the initial material difficulties and the complicated selection process but also the fact that these theater programs were by no means the true focal point of U.S. cultural politics in Austria, then one would recognize that the ISB did actually have access to a considerable pool of plays.[17] Here it may be interesting to note the names of those authors not included in this list, such as John Steinbeck and Arthur Miller.

Even though only three pieces by American authors could be presented by the middle of 1946, the efforts of the Theatre and Music Section gradually blossomed. *The First Legion*, a production by Emmet Lavery, was staged at the Theater der Stephansspieler by the end of the same year, as were Eugene O'Neill's *Mourning Becomes Electra* at the Akademietheater, William Saroyan's *Time of Your Life* at the Theater in der Josefstadt, Paul Osborn's *On Borrowed Time* at the Volkstheater, and Clifford Odets's *Awake and Sing* at the Theater "Die Insel" in der Komödie. This was quite a representative program of U.S. drama produced by the most important stages. In addition, already twelve further contracts had been concluded with theaters in Vienna, Linz, Salzburg, Steyr, and Innsbruck by the end of 1946, and negotiations on the production of a large number of other dramas were just on the verge of completion. The great success of *Mourning Becomes Electra* and *On Borrowed Time* was also attributable to its leading actors Helene Thimig-Reinhardt and Albert Bassermann (who was "greeted with an applause unequaled in Vienna's theatre history"). The comeback of these prewar stars (and this is meant in more than one sense) was sponsored by the ISB.[18]

The years to come brought considerable successes. By the end of 1947, eighteen American dramas were performed, and contracts had been signed for staging seven further productions.[19] By the end of September, eighteen Austrian theaters had played twenty-five pieces in 945 performances, and the profits collected by the ISB, which were always 10 percent of the evening's gross income, had already amounted to 183,052 schillings. One year later, these profits had risen to 253,731.51 schillings.[20]

The quantitative success of the ISB is clearly represented in the performance statistics of the Landestheater in Salzburg. The Theatre and Music Section was able to encourage the staging of twenty-one pieces by U.S. authors in Salzburg alone between 1945 and 1955. This meant that 12 percent of all pieces and 18 percent of their authors had originated in the United States.[21] In contrast, it is also interesting to note that during the entire period of occupation, no plays by Russian authors were performed. Furthermore, the directors of Salzburg's

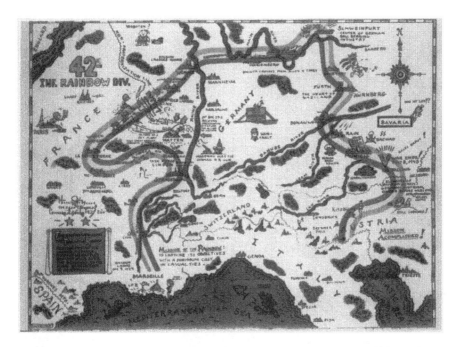

"Mission Accomplished—Alles Kaput!—Germany under a New Management: U.S.A. Fräuleins Verboten?" Inscriptions on a cartoon map in the official booklet on the contribution of the Forty-second U.S. Infantry (Rainbow) Division in the liberation of France, Germany, and Austria in the Second World War (*Mission Accomplished* [Salzburg, 1945])

Front of Amerika Haus in the Kärntnerstrasse, Vienna, decorated with stars representing each of the states of the United States (Washington National Record Center, Suitland, Maryland, 260/105/44)

Reading room of Amerika Haus, Vienna
(Washington National Record Center, Suitland, Maryland, 260/105/44)

A shop window for America at Amerika Haus, Vienna
(Washington National Record Center, Suitland, Maryland, 260/105/44)

GENERAL COLLINS GIVES A CARE-PARCEL TO A WOMAN

GENERAL COLLINS BESCHENKT EINE ALTE FRAU

GENERAL COLLINS BRINGS GIFTS FOR THE CHILDREN

GENERAL COLLINS BRINGT GESCHENKE FÜR DIE KINDE

Drawings in which children from Salzburg thank U.S. General Collins for food assistance in 1947 (Private collection of the widow of General Collins in the archive of the Karl-Steinocher-Fonds zur Erforschung der Geschichte der Arbeiterbewegung im Lande Salzburg)

The U.S. Army as a combination of Santa Claus and Saint Nicholas with spurs in a drawing from Salzburg children thanking General Collins for food assistance in 1947 (Private collection of the widow of General Collins in the archive of the Karl-Steinocher-Fonds zur Erforschung der Geschichte der Arbeiterbewegung im Lande Salzburg)

Poems, some accompanied by illustrations, by pupils from the Kevenhüller School, Linz, thanking the U.S. Army for its assistance program, Christmas 1947 (Archive of the Karl-Steinocher-Fonds zur Erforschung der Geschichte der Arbeiterbewegung im Lande Salzburg)

This poem reads, in part, "The Ami is a good man / He does for us what he can. . . . A little boy from Austria / Thanks the Mister from America."

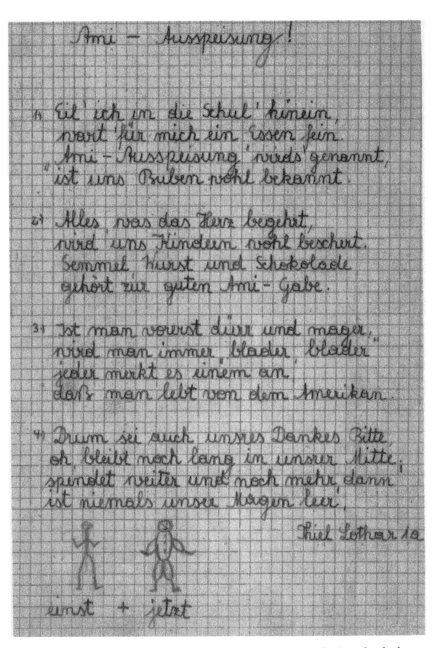

**Ami – Ausspeisung!**

1) Eil' ich in die Schul' hinein,
wart' für mich ein Essen fein.
„Ami – Ausspeisung" wird' genannt,
ist uns Buben wohl bekannt.

2) Alles, was das Herz begehrt,
wird uns Kindern wohl beschert.
Semmel, Wurst und Schokolade
gehört zur guten Ami – Gabe.

3) Ist man vorerst dürr und mager,
wird man immer „bläder, bläder"
jeder merkt es einem an,
daß man lebt von dem Amerikan.

4) Drum sei auch unsres Dankes Bitte,
oh, bleibt noch lang in unsrer Mitte;
spendet weiter und noch mehr, dann
ist niemals unser Magen leer.

Thiel Lothar 1a

einst + jetzt

A boy, who had been starving before U.S. food assistance arrived, gives thanks for having gone "fat" again with the help of American bread, sausages, and chocolate. He adds before-and-after pictures of himself at the bottom.

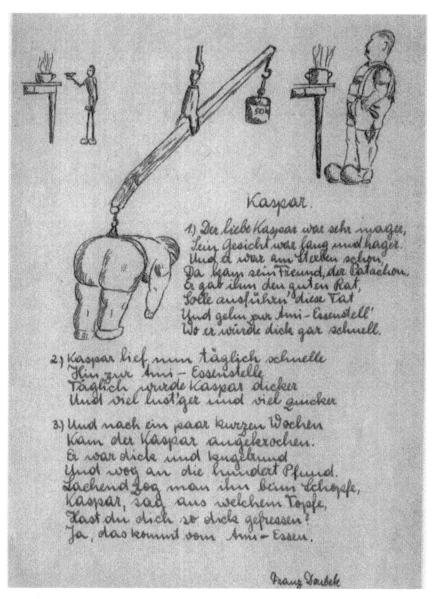

Kaspar.

1) Der liebe Kaspar war sehr magere,
Sein Gesicht war lang und hager.
Und er war am Sterben schon
Da kam sein Freund, der Patachon.
Er gab ihm den guten Rat,
Solle ausführen diese Tat
Und gehn zur Ami-Essenstell'
Wo er würde dick gar schnell.

2) Kaspar lief nun täglich schnelle
Hin zur Ami-Essenstelle
Täglich wurde Kaspar dicker
Und viel lust'ger und viel quicker

3) Und nach ein paar kurzen Wochen
Kam der Kaspar angekrochen.
Er war dick und kugelrund
Und wog an die hundert Pfund.
Lachend zog man ihn beim Schopfe,
Kaspar, sag aus welchem Topfe,
Hast du dich so dick gefressen?
Ja, das kommt vom Ami-Essen.

Franz Doubek

Another before-and-after poem and illustration, referring to the miraculous qualities of U.S. food assistance

This poem lightly pokes fun at the fattening effects of the 800-calorie daily ration of dried milk and eggs provided with American help.

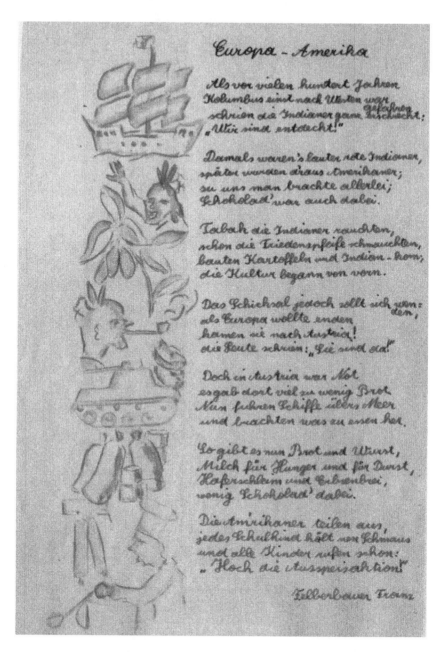

Hundreds of years ago, this poem points out, Europeans discovered America, Indians, tobacco, and potatoes; but now, when Austria is in dire need, the ships are sailing back from America, bringing much-needed food.

"Do you already dance the Creep?" from a picture story on this modern dance craze
(*Wiener Kurier*, February 20, 1954)

# AFHQ
## INCOMING MESSAGE

LXAM

filed 291032B

AFSC K 282/30
30052GB
hgt

### NATOUSA MESSAGE
### ROUTINE

FROM    SOS NATOUSA SIGNED LARKIN

TO      PEMBARK RPT FOR INFO TO CG NATOUSA

NO      L-8096 - P-46 June 29, 1943

On early convoy request shipment three million bottled Coca-Cola, (filled), and complete equipment for bottling, washing capping same quantity twice monthly. (CITE SSQMC-599). Preference as to equipment is 10 separate machines for installation in different localities, each complete for bottling twenty thousand bottles per day. Also sufficient syrup and caps for 6 million refills. Syrup, caps and sixty thousand bottles monthly should be on automatic supply. Monthly shipment bottles is to cover estimated breakage and losses. Estimate ship tons initial shipment 5 thousand . Ship without displacing other military cargo. Data available here very meager as to these installations and operations. Request they be checked by fully qualified sources and this Headquarters advised promptly recommended installation to meet the two hundred thousand bottle daily demand and when same can be shipped. Destination later.

ACTION:        QM

INFORMATION:   SGS
               G-4
               DTC
               M & TN
               SPEC SERV
               AG RECORDS
               SUMMARY

MC IN 13331   30 June 43  1530B   Ref No. L-8096  rht

Telegram of the supreme commander of the Allied forces in Europe, General Dwight D. Eisenhower, on the need for Coca-Cola among U.S. troops in Europe, June 29, 1943 (National Archives, Washington, D.C.)

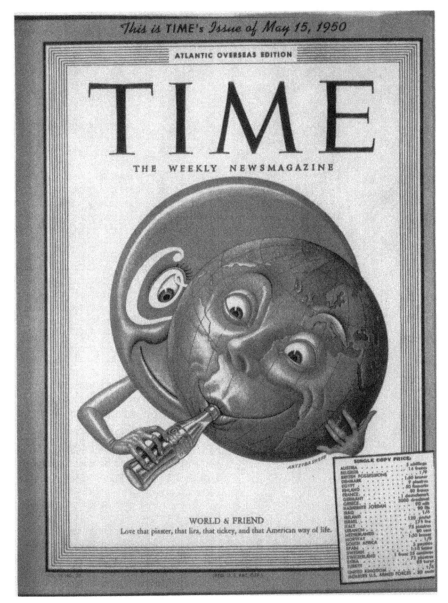

*Time* magazine cover announcing inside story on global popularity of Coca-Cola (*Time*, May 15, 1950). Copyright 1950 Time Inc. Reprinted by permission.

Photographic evidence from one
Austrian family of how U.S. cultural
imperialism turned traditional Austrian
citizens into chewing-gum-chomping,
Coca-Cola-drinking desperadoes
completely corrupted by the music from
hell, the "Jailhouse Rock" (Collection of
Felix Wagnleitner)

Landestheater who were not quick enough in incorporating more U.S. pieces in their programs, such as Johannes von Hamme and Alfred Bernau, were relieved of their posts. The lack of cooperation of these directors was clearly not a result of their opposition to U.S. dramas as such but more accurately a consequence of the rude mannerisms of some ISB officers, who acted like colonial masters, especially toward the representatives of the smaller theaters.[22]

Although the ISB was quite successful in controlling the political orientation of the theaters, it had been particularly ineffective in convincing the Salzburg audience of the quality of these dramas. Even the spring 1950 performance of the *Glass Menagerie*, by Tennessee Williams, which was celebrated in other cities, received a reaction of indifference in Salzburg. While neither the piece nor the production was inferior, theater officers based its qualitative failure on circumstances specific to Salzburg: "The theatre there suffers not only from a dull-witted, hide-bound public but also from capricious interference on the part of the provincial government."[23] As a result, the repertoire of the Landestheater was dominated by operettas, "which are as old as possible,"[24] while "the most abysmally hammy troupe in all of Austria" could be engaged as guest performers. The conservative policies, however, were well received by the audience: "Needless to say their ancient and horrible dialect folk comedies cleaned up. The management thereupon formally opened the season with a shoddy production of Schiller's *Wilhelm Tell*, which was the extent of its imagination."[25]

The ISB in response offered support for the establishment of independent theater groups, such as Die Tribüne in Salzburg. This group held its first performance in the cloister St. Peter on October 12, 1946, with the piece *The Adding Machine* by Elmer Rice.[26] Quite successful were the regular performances of U.S. drama readings. Also, the radio productions of Rot-Weiss-Rot in particular won many listeners not only as a result of modern recording technology but also because of their prominent cast lists. In June 1951 a real radio sensation, which swept the streets clear of people, was the dramatized version of Thornton Wilder's *Bridge of San Luis Rey* (translation and adaption: Friedrich Schreyvogel; music: Franz Salmhofer; cast: Helene Thimig-Reinhardt, Marianne Hoppe, Hedwig Bleibtreu, Aglaja Schmidt, Oskar Werner, Raoul Aslan, Anton Edthofer, Peter Lorre, and Gustav Waldau).[27]

Contacts with young, up-and-coming actors were maintained through close connections with Helene Thimig-Reinhardt and through the support of the Reinhardt Seminar in Vienna. Especially those artists who had participated in an exchange program were incorporated into all facets of the media after their return from the United States "to do informative missionary work."[28] Dramas were even staged in the Viennese Kosmos film theater beginning in 1950, broadcast on Rot-Weiss-Rot to make them available to a broad audience.[29]

Because these productions were generally free of charge, the unfair competition of the ISB was severely criticized by the managers of the theaters in Vienna. In an effort not to jeopardize the good relationship with the Austrian stage, fewer performances were held at the Kosmos Theater after 1951. Nevertheless, this self-limitation occurred only in larger cities, for the U.S. theater activities now had discovered a generally ignored audience in rural areas. Therefore, in an effort to reach the inhabitants of the smaller cities and towns, which did not have their own theaters, the USIS Travelling Stage was established in January 1951. Until the end of occupation, the "travelling stage" held two- to three-month tours each year, reaching many small villages in Upper Austria, Salzburg, Tyrol, Vorarlberg, Carinthia, and Styria. Already during the first tour, this traveling group performed Thornton Wilder's *Our Town* and John van Druten's *Voice of the Turtle* a total of ninety times in forty-five towns, and was a tremendous success. "Halls and theatres were crowded beyond capacity and the press reaction was a hundred per cent enthusiastic," stated a report describing this rural theater sensation.[30] In 1952, the USIS Travelling Stage held 101 performances (*My Sister Eileen* and a puppet version of *Tom Sawyer*), performing for approximately 55,000 people. "By far the most successful and, propagandawise, the most effective" were actually its last three programs—*Musical Trip through America* (1953), *The History of America* (1954), and *From the American Operetta* (1955). Carrying the central responsibility for these successes was the master of ceremonies and U.S. cultural officer Marcel Prawy,[31] who later became one of the most influential interpreters of classical music for Austrian radio and TV audiences.

Naturally, in the course of the period of occupation, the theater work of the ISB became more and more characterized by anti-Communism. The U.S. Army implemented performance bans not only on pieces that were openly directed against the politics of the United States but also against antimilitary dramas, such as Ferdinand Bruckner's *Liberated*, which was assessed as follows: "The author's treatment and presentation of the conflict and his opinion of the military [are] considered unsuitable for the program."[32] Although the ISB presented *The Adding Machine* by Elmer Rice as one of the best examples of modern U.S. theater in Austria until 1947, the piece was withdrawn in 1948.[33] And even the director of the Theatre and Music Section, Ernst Lothar, who wanted to stage Arthur Miller's *All My Sons* in Vienna, could not alter the opinion of the War Department. This ban naturally had nothing to do with the quality of Miller's work, which had been especially praised in New York as the best drama of the year. The contents of the play, offering an extremely critical, yet realistic, portrayal of American war profiteers, had been the true grounds for disqualification.[34]

Ernst Lothar was not to be trusted with the implementation of a more hardline political stance, and therefore his contract was not extended beyond 1947. Only an American "of long standing" would be eligible here, and thus Edward Hogan, a former "story-scout" for the motion picture company Metro-

Goldwyn-Mayer, was called upon to head the Theatre and Music Section.[35] Hogan also obviously concentrated on the best possible commercial use of politically acceptable pieces and prepared the transition of ISB agendas to private American agencies. Yet, even Hogan did not allow himself to be completely directed by commercial issues. He had reservations with regard to "politically harmless" pieces because the Austrian public was not yet seemingly mature enough for them. For this reason, in 1949 he opposed the production of the successful criminal comedy *Arsenic and Old Lace* in the Theater in der Josefstadt because "the times have not yet returned in these parts of the world, when an audience can laugh for three hours at wholesale murder. In future years this fine farce will doubtless duplicate its world-wide success on the German-speaking stage."[36] This paternalistic cultural control, however, became obsolete as private U.S. agencies began to take over the ISB agenda. Yet, even after the Department of State had decided to end the theater programs in West Germany and in Austria in 1950, the U.S. high culture division was not dissolved. It was then integrated into the Film Section, where Ernst Haeusserman would implement it for two main purposes: to observe "left-wing" artists, and to hinder all attempts of a feared Communist undermining of Austrian cultural life.[37]

While the Theatre and Music officers were extremely cautious that their activities—excluding bans of pieces with National Socialist and militaristic contents—did not smell of censorship during the first period of the occupation, political manipulation by the Reorientation Branch became ever more apparent after 1947/48. ISB officers were now even interfering in the selection process. Their activities were, however, mostly discreet—their democratic reputation was still on the line—and inquiries concerning plays by discredited authors could quite simply be evaded with a reference to not-yet-cleared performance rights.

Relatively liberal politics no longer fit into the concept of the U.S. occupation power during the time of Cold War escalation. Therefore, in establishing selection criteria another barrier was erected, which could be used to exclude "materials of controversial nature or of any subversive connection or otherwise not conducive to the reeducation program consistent with our government."[38] The ban was, however, aimed only in one political direction and, for the most part, affected socially critical pieces. As a disciplinary measure, a boycott of artists was also implemented, and from 1953 to 1955, a blacklist actually existed. This meant not only a performance ban on the majority of Austrian stages but also a broadcast ban on radio Rot-Weiss-Rot. The blacklist affected not only the members of the ensemble at the Neues Theater in der Scala and artists who sometimes worked for RAVAG but also singers and musicians who had performed at the recently reopened Oper Unter den Linden in East Berlin.[39]

The U.S. Army was once again able to rely upon the indigenous cultural cold warriors, whose anti-Communist verve—for example, in boycotting Bertolt

Brecht—often astonished even U.S. cultural officers. Illustrative is the following report of Ernst Haeusserman of the ISB:

> In September an event of considerable artistic importance was shrugged off with indifference by the Viennese. The Berliner Ensemble is an aggregation of theater idealists which for more than two years has been providing the Prussian capital with some of its most stimulating productions. It is strongly left-wing. It came to the Communist-subsidized Scala Theater in Vienna for a guest engagement, with "Der Hofmeister," a curiously powerful satire written in 1774 by Reinhold Lenz and recently adapted by Bert Brecht. Such smooth trooping is and has been, since Reinhardt left, unknown in Vienna. It was painful to observe, after the usual opening night hoopla for Communist Party bigwigs, a performance by this fine troupe in a worthwhile play (no matter what its politics) to an audience of a handful in a 1,200 seat house.[40]

This acknowledgment of the artistic achievements of ideological dissenters by a U.S. cultural officer may seem surprising. For Austrian leaders on the anti-Communist cultural front, no such differentiations would be at all acceptable. Perhaps for exactly that reason Hans Weigel insisted that the fight against Communism was an all too serious matter to be left to the Americans.[41]

But of course cultural anti-Communism in Austria was not left to the Americans, even though it was in part financed by them. From 1954 onward, the magazine *Das Forum*, which was cofinanced by the CIA, became the most important intellectual mouthpiece for those Austrians attempting to hinder Brecht. This could certainly not come as a surprise for the politically initiated. Shortly prior to the publication of the first issue of *Forum*, its editor, Friedrich Torberg, explained quite clearly the purpose and goals of the new magazine in a report to Laurence Dalcher, the information officer at the U.S. embassy in Vienna: "The first half will be devoted mainly to political topics and the second half mainly to cultural ones, that is to theater, literature, music, film, etc. This is something not only the Viennese intellectuals, but the Viennese public in general is always interested in, particularly if well established names go with it. We hope to lure our readers via the cultural part into the political one. Brutally spoken, we want to sell them politics under the pretext of culture, and I don't have to tell you what sort of politics it will be."[42] Few documents better describe the duties of U.S. cultural diplomacy than these few sentences by Torberg.

In any event, while the political contents of U.S. cultural diplomacy were happily accepted and further developed by the dominating Austrian cultural elites, the cultural component of ISB theater initiatives enjoyed less success. Of course, this was also a result of the ban on a series of the best U.S. plays, which could be performed only much later through the mediation of private agencies and against the will of U.S. authorities.

There is certainly no doubt that the ISB initially created an important bridgehead for U.S. drama and theater in Austria. Nevertheless, in spite of all efforts, it was not possible to secure a dominating position for American works compared with pieces from other countries. Between 1945 and 1949, 25 plays by nineteen U.S. authors were performed at the Burgtheater, Akademietheater, Theater in der Josefstadt, Theater "Die Insel" in der Komödie, and Volkstheater. During this same period they were competing against 120 productions of works by forty-three Austrian playwrights, 53 performances of plays by twenty-five Germans, 57 productions of works by twenty-four British authors, 53 presentations of dramas by twenty-nine French authors, and even 29 stagings of plays by seventeen Russian authors.[43]

Many U.S. dramas were torn apart by Austrian critics or, perhaps even worse, dismissed according to the belief that the development of the problems discussed in U.S. drama is not sufficiently brought to a satisfactory conclusion; U.S. plays established only the direction, which is perhaps typically American.[44] What could explain better the lack of understanding and the hubris of the Austrian theater critics of the period than the use of the stereotype "typically American"? And on the occasion that an American author, such as Thornton Wilder, did find recognition, it was certainly not because he was American. Quite the contrary: "One knows Thornton Wilder's novels, works of an author with personality and importance. In addition to being typically American, he radiates supersensory hunger for knowledge, a brooding drive for success: a creator, a poet full of his own world, his own message, his own architecture—certainly an American, but one with a view transcending American worldliness toward the cosmic heaven."[45]

These plays, which had washed up on shore with the U.S. Army from the other side of the Atlantic, had lacked essence, depth, and soul according to the nearly unanimous opinions of the critics. Such a criticism was leveled apart from all political reservations, for this judgment was not levied against Russian authors. "Typically American" meant (and means) "Made in America." While this label signified quality with respect to an automobile, at least in the 1940s and 1950s, this description indicated the old ideological conflict in the area of high culture: culture versus civilization. What could be expected from an author such as William Saroyan, who, instead of behaving like a "true" poet, was supposedly a carefree individual? Actually, Saroyan could not even be a poet, for he acted worse: he was a person who had no social graces, drank too much, gambled, and played tennis and poker. Furthermore, he even fraternized with simple, uneducated, and vulgar people.[46]

In costuming the character of the student in a production of Goethe's *Faust*, one of the most holy of all German dramas, in the garb of a youth rebel, Oskar Werner provoked unanimous protestations against the modern, uncivilized, rotten (i.e., U.S.) youth in February 1948. Just three years after the end of the "Third Reich," more and more voices could once again be heard in the Austrian press against the flood of foreign (un)culture.[47] This was just one variation of the cultural leitmotif of the central organ of the protectors of Western civilization, which already in February 1947 had issued a by no means new (but "typically Austrian") proclamation of cultural war in the paper *Die Presse* and rallied against the total foreign infiltration of the theaters, which was causing a lack of cultural dignity and artistic bankruptcy.[48] To which could this attack have been referring: the German Goethe or the U.S. youth rebel?

Although the number of foreign theater pieces still increased at the beginning of the 1950s (of the seventy-eight productions on the larger Viennese stages between 1952 and 1953, only ten were written by Austrian authors), American dramas, with few exceptions, still had difficulty in receiving positive recognition.[49] The most successful authors on German-language stages were Tennessee Williams, Thornton Wilder, Arthur Miller, Clifford Odets, Herman Wouk, and John Patrick. Of all U.S. dramas after the war, one achieved a particularly dramatic success indeed: John Patrick's *Teahouse of the August Moon*. During the theater seasons of 1955 / 56 and 1956 / 57 alone, Patrick's work was performed 2,800 times in 790 productions.[50] But the unusual success of this play on West German and Austrian stages was based on a seemingly reassuring message; its amusing depiction of the clumsiness of the American occupiers and the cultural superiority of the liberated Japanese played to the feelings of cultural superiority of the losers of the Second World War[51]—were not "old Asia" and "old Europe" in the same situation?

Many "cultured" Europeans thus remained rigid in their conviction of cultural superiority vis-à-vis the United States. Although these judgments were rather unwarranted, the European withdrawal into the ivory tower of high culture is psychologically understandable. Because inferiority in all other areas had become more than drastically apparent, it was certainly more pleasant to discuss Max Reinhardt's influence on the theater in the United States than to attribute depth, soul, and "true" culture to American dramas.[52] And although Ernst Haeusserman and Marcel Prawy, who had officially returned to Austria after the Second World War as ISB cultural officers, were certainly among the most important personalities exercising great influence upon Austrian theater and music in the Second Republic—in spite of their efforts to support works by U.S. authors—there can be no doubt that they stood primarily in the European theater tradition.

U.S. theater export politics thus found themselves in the defensive, and their main duty—to demonstrate the legitimacy and artistic maturity of U.S. dramas—could only be fulfilled in part. Even the European tour of Players from Abroad (with Elisabeth Bergner, Albert Bassermann, and Uta Hagen) and the American National Theater Academy, financed by the Department of State, were seen less as examples for the maturity of U.S. theater than as a triumph of European tradition in the United States.[53]

The public affairs officer of the U.S. embassy in Vienna, E. Wilder Spaulding, summarized these difficulties for American Theater in Austria with resignation:

> While the American element may be congratulated upon the large number of American plays that are appearing in Austrian theaters it is perhaps unfortunate that so many of them are successful in bringing only the drab side of American life to the Austrians. . . . These plays tend to confirm the impression which American motion pictures give to so many Austrians that America is a land of degeneracy and gangsterism. The American element of course no longer controls even the American content of the Austrian stage and we can be only thankful that plays like *27 Wagonloads of Cotton* [Tennessee Williams] and *Der Gangster* [Irwin Shaw] are having short runs. Even plays like *The Glass Menagerie*, which played in Salzburg as well as in Vienna, do not do very much to relieve the unfortunate impression that Austrians are receiving of America through the legitimate stage.[54]

It seems that not only Austrian politics has problems with authors of the "legitimate" theater.

## Music

### "SERIOUS" MUSIC AND THE MUSICAL

Today, although the millennium has certainly not arrived, we can confidently say that the concept of music as part of international relations is firmly established and that it is doubtless here to stay. . . . Every encouragement is given for live performances of American works in the belief that one of the best ways to demonstrate our culture is to present the work of our creative musicians. . . . All over the world we are watching a growing interest in American Music. This interest must be studied and capitalized upon.
—David S. Cooper, "American Music Abroad" (1956)

It's a new strategy in the fight against Communism, and it's going over big. . . . Europeans and Asians are eating it up. . . . It is almost like an old-fashioned band contest, with the trumpets of one side trying to drown out the horns of the other.
—U.S. News and World Report (1955)

In the light of countless human tragedies, it may seem macabre to interpret the Second World War and the Cold War as old-fashioned band competitions in which the main objective was to produce the loudest note. Yet, one thing is certain: these conflicts were not just world conflicts in which only the trump cards of military, economic, and political power were newly shuffled, but they also included the cards of *cultural hegemony*. For the clashing together of these "worlds" was much more encompassing than their destructive military dimension.

Even though it might seem, superficially speaking, as if we are dealing with an unimportant peripheral war zone in the area of high culture, it was, by definition, actually at the center of the conflict. Hence, according to the National Socialists, the Second World War was, on the one hand, a direct result of the struggle of European culture, whose highest form was supposedly "Germanness," against the "Jewish contamination" of modern mass civilization represented by Hollywood, Wall Street, and Communism. For the Allies, this fight, on the other hand, represented the defense of all central values of "Western culture" against the barbarian powers of fascism, which had thrown all common cultural ties overboard. As the Anti-Hitler Coalition broke apart, this latter accusation was consequently transferred to the government of the Soviet Union, now under the stamp of totalitarianism. One can therefore not quite ignore the irony contained in the fact that Beethoven's Fifth Symphony served the National Socialists as a symbol of the highest expression of German genius, while the BBC implemented it as a theme song for their German propaganda transmissions during the Second World War, U.S. orchestras used it as proof of having reached cultural maturity, and Communist cultural politicians employed it as evidence to show just who the legitimate heir and protector of the progressive and humanistic tradition of European high culture was.

The modern war is total, and not only the "Third Reich" utilized "serious" music as a propaganda weapon. "Music at War" was the slogan even in the United States, and "thus the propagandist must regard music. A sponsor of mass emotions, in his responsibility for popular reaction he must consider music a necessary weapon."[55] And even if this music at war had not been composed by U.S. composers, we are still dealing with a cultural declaration of independence of the United States and, even more, with the question of the *business* of music. It must not be forgotten that until the beginning of the Second World War, the opera and concert business and the management of artists in the United States had been dominated by European—in particular, German—agencies. The war had decisively changed this situation, and now American agencies, such as Columbia Concerts, also increased their control in the business of "serious music."[56]

The warlike mood was not just limited, by the way, to the actual enemies, but also contained clear symptoms of anti-European cultural xenophobia. The politics of the American Federation of Music (AFM) and the American Society of Composers, Authors and Publishers (ASCAP), two of the most important copyright organizations, clearly demonstrate this trend. AFM and ASCAP, which dominated the U.S. market in a quasi-monopolistic fashion, not only supported nationalist cultural trends but also preferred cultural isolationism, which, in its limitations to the Western Hemisphere, was equal to a cultural Monroe Doctrine. According to a programmatic statement of ASCAP, European culture should be treated as follows: "We must give less and less attention to the culture of Europe. This culture has begot strange ideologies, and it is becoming more and more important to us that the impact of these cultures upon our citizenship does not breed here what it has bred there."[57] This cultural provincialism by no means corresponded with the universalistic attitude of the culture experts in the Department of State, and the outcome of the Second World War obviously did not change "serious" music as such. Yet, it had a significant impact on its commercial control. It can therefore hardly be surprising that not only the Götterdämmerung of National Socialism but also the downfall of German musical hegemony had been discussed in the United States since 1942.[58] Consequently, it seemed only logical that "serious" music had been incorporated into the agendas of U.S. cultural diplomacy.

The Theatre and Music Section of the ISB pursued politico-cultural and commercial goals at the same time. On the one hand, the presentation of works by U.S. composers, possibly through performances of conductors, singers, and musicians from the United States, would represent the cultural equality of the United States. On the other hand, this mediator role was to also pave the way for American artists onto the stages of Austrian concert halls and opera houses.

Consequently, the ISB brokered artists and performance rights; supplied sheet music and records; dealt with cultural managers, conductors, and orchestras; worked closely with music colleges; organized seminars for musicians; placed "serious" American music on the radio station Rot-Weiss-Rot; and held its own concerts and tours. All this stood under the motto "Contribution of U.S. Music to the Democratization of Austria."

> Works by leading American composers will be performed this season in both public concerts and house concerts. . . . It is specifically requested of each American conductor to whom an invitation is extended to conduct in Austria that they include one good representative American work on their program. The exchange of artists will emphasize the fact that all people have the opportunity to work and establish themselves in the artistic field. Outstanding conductors and artists will come to Austria and we shall be able to show and tell what has developed in music in America especially during the past ten years when Europe was cut off from the outside world.[59]

One of the more important partners dealing with the ISB in the United States was the artist agency Columbia Concerts. However, their demands did not always conform with the occupation policies and goals of the U.S. Army in Austria. Therefore, the patriotism of the agency leadership was frequently appealed to, with reminders of the most important goal: "In brief—we are here to make the Austrians acquainted with American music and American performers. In order to do so we depend not only on the preparedness of American composers and performers but also on their patriotism. They have to realize that Austria is a ruined country. She can't afford to pay high salaries in her present condition. In other words, the whole matter cannot and should not be looked upon as a commercial proposition."[60]

Obviously, this task was anything but simple because many Austrians who received this musical development aid of the Theatre and Music Section felt hardly more than contempt for it. Even though the war had been lost, was not Austria still the land of music? Therefore, those ISB officers who attempted to enrich the musical life in Austria through the propagation of American works and artists, first in Salzburg, then in Vienna and Linz, always saw their efforts confronted with the question: "Please, what 'serious' music from the United States?" This last bastion of supposed European superiority had to be defended with all means, and the issue was quite heatedly debated. The magazine *Der Turm*, for example, posed the question in February 1946 whether American music existed *at all*.[61] Certainly, Igor Stravinsky, Béla Bartók, Arnold Schönberg, and Paul Hindemith were seen now as half-American. But did not the inferior quality of the newer pieces of these composers quite clearly show that the cultural wasteland of the United States had dehydrated their artistic spirit? Granted, some U.S. orchestras had gained a certain reputation. Yet, was their performance not too technically oriented, their playing too standardized, flat, and unoriginal? Nicolas Nabokov summarized these sentiments quite explicitly by stating that American music suffered from the un-spirit of cultural mass production and reflected the taste of the average American, who is more enthused about the musical than about music.[62]

These problems of the ISB were most clearly apparent at the Salzburg Festival. The effective support of the U.S. Army, for example, through foreign transmissions via Rot-Weiss-Rot, facilitated the reestablishment of the festival only a few months after the end of the war. The American musical contribution was, however, limited to the open-air performance of the U.S. Military Choir and the Vienna Boys Choir singing "My Bonnie Lies over the Ocean" and "Yankee Doodle" in the Great Festival House, which displayed the power of its new masters with its name Roxy's.[63] Moreover, the news of the death of the Austrian composer Anton von Webern, who had mistakenly been shot by a GI on September 15, 1945, did not help to improve the reputation of the United States as a music power.

The ISB was nevertheless strongly interested in making the U.S. presence more apparent in Austria, at least in the program of the Salzburg Festival of 1946. In countless conversations with the festival organizers, U.S. officers tried to point to the important role of modern American composers. Yet, again and again, they were confronted with ignorance and lack of willingness. Ernst Lothar therefore reported that "it must, however, be stated frankly that the influential musical circles in Austria were not only unaware of this but seemed rather opposed to it. . . . Though the Salzburg Festival was taking place in an entirely American zone it never occurred to its directors to include one single

American work."[64] Only at the last minute, and with great distaste, did the festival succumb to the pressure of the ISB, so that finally on August 30, 1946, Samuel Barber's Adagio for Strings was performed. In addition, the ISB sponsored the performances of Yehudi Menuhin, Antal Dorati, Gilbert Winkler, and Grace Moore as well as the presentation of Aaron Copland's *Quiet City* on September 2, 1946, making "an all-American conclusion" for the festival.[65]

Also in 1947, the works of Roy Harris, Paul Hindemith, Arnold Schönberg, and Ernst Krenek were incorporated into the program of the festival, again only after countless interventions. Even the performances of Otto Klemperer, Helene Thimig, Lothar Wallerstein, Yehudi Menuhin, Paul Hindemith, Charles Munch, John Barbisolli, and Ernst Deutsch were organized and financed by the Theatre and Music Section. During the negotiations with Otto Klemperer, Charles Munch, John Barbirolli, Josef Krips, Karl Böhm, and Herbert von Karajan, the ISB was also successful in persuading these artists to include U.S. works in their programs.[66]

Yet, the ISB in the long term again would remain powerless in the face of the politics of the festival management and the taste of the audience. To be sure, star performers from the United States could establish themselves if they demonstrated the ability to master the European music tradition. An exceptional phenomenon even prior to the Second World War, Yehudi Menuhin was once again enthusiastically celebrated—"Mr. Menuhin did for America in one hour more than all the diplomats have done in years."[67] Yet, the works of American composers enjoyed no comparable success. Increasingly nervous reports by humiliated ISB officers stressed the fact that when dealing with Salzburg (and Austria, in general), one was confronting the most conservative audience in the world, which could not be shied away even by the typical characteristic of the Salzburg business world, the financial exploitation of the visitors.[68]

Nevertheless, the ISB succeeded in bringing twenty works of U.S. composers to Austria between August 1946 and May 1947. This list of performances in Salzburg, Graz, and Vienna included Samuel Barber, Aaron Copland, William Schuman, George Gershwin, Walter Piston, Harl McDonald, Virgil Thomson, Ernest Bacon, Kent Kennan, Henry Cowell, Randall Thompson, Leonard Bernstein, and John Alden Carpenter. With the exception of George Gershwin's *Rhapsody in Blue*, none of the compositions had ever before been performed in Austria.[69]

Already by the end of spring 1946, the ISB had brought Arturo Toscanini, Bruno Walter, and Erich Kleiber to Vienna. They were followed a year later by Eugene Ormandy, Otto Klemperer, George Szell, and Leonard Bernstein. The great successes of these conductors, however, were achieved through the performance of European works. The minor success of the "All-American Concert" was attributed to the Tonkünstler Orchestra and the pianist George von Szemere under the direction of George Robert in Vienna on December 1, 1946, who played pieces by Schuman, Gershwin, Piston, and McDonald. Yet, the reaction of the audience was no more than "favorable."[70] As it turned out, McCarthyism's shadow was cast also upon the Bernstein invitation. The ISB had trouble obtaining an entry permit from the U.S. Army for this artist, who had been denounced as a Communist. Only with a reference to the uncalculated negative repercussions resulting from a refusal was a permit issued.[71]

These respectable successes, nevertheless, were rare. Even in Vienna, the ISB again and again reported that their failure was due to the fact that modern music just did not have a chance "because the Viennese are perhaps the most conservative people in the world."[72] Yet, this observation was not completely fair to the Viennese audience, especially when one considers the even worse situation existing in the provinces. For the first time in October 1947, for example, an audience had to be lured by the offer of free tickets into listening to two U.S. chamber music concerts in Linz. "American music on its own," lamented the report, "is a sort of scarecrow to a provincial Austrian audience."[73] "Suggestions for Projection of American Music" thus insisted that the selection of U.S. music had to follow very strict criteria: "Selections from American music should for the most part be conservative. They should contain allusions to classical music if the taste of this public is to be satisfied."[74] In addition, it also had to be taken into consideration that the pieces of U.S. composers should no longer be too obvious but instead should be discreetly placed between generally accepted pieces. This meant they would be "sandwiched in between two works [to guarantee] better digestion to Austrian audiences."[75]

In an effort to acquaint musicians and the public with the American works of "serious" music, music sections were further developed at the America Houses. Initial difficulties with supplies were surmounted in 1946, and by 1947 the ISB had scores and sheet music from 164 symphonies, concerts and other orchestra pieces, and vocal and chamber music by U.S. composers. Over 3,000 records, which could be played at the U.S. Information Centers themselves and also could be taken home, were also made available to the public.[76] Still further, the ISB presented music by U.S. composers in the weekly broadcasts from radio Rot-Weiss-Rot in Vienna;[77] Salzburg and Linz also continuously transmitted "serious" U.S. music in their programs.[78]

While this was effective in maintaining the presence of "serious" American music during the occupation period as at no other time before, a large portion of the Austrian audience simply played deaf. Even music pedagogues, who had been confronted with U.S. works in ISB seminars, proved to be resistant, and the ISB experts could only wonder that "Austrian music teachers were [still] unaware of the extent of American progress in composition."[79] It is tempting to note that this astonishment of the ISB officers was itself surely rather astonishing, as it showed unwavering optimism at best, if not total misunderstanding, about the musical taste of the majority of Austrians. There truly was no reason for optimism, and this became quite obvious in the negotiations with the most prominent Austrian music managers. George Hogan thus commented on a conversation with the director of the Gesellschaft für Musikfreunde (Society for music friends) that "Rudolf Gamsjäger is pro-American. He is, however, rather skeptical about our conductors!"[80] Reports with similar contents were not unusual. It was one thing to win over the Austrians for the political relationships of the Pax Americana, and yet another when dealing with high culture, the last refuge of supposed superiority.

Certainly, the great majority of the public similarly rejected the "serious" music of modern European composers as those by Americans. Arthur Honegger's sarcastic comment that contemporary music was only tolerated as the uninvited invader between Beethoven and Brahms applied to modern compositions from both sides of the Atlantic; still the "typically American" provenance of "serious" music certainly constituted an additional handicap.[81] It seemed as though creativity and life in the United States completely negated each other, and the U.S. orchestras were always accused of producing stream-lined, soft glamour through their emphasis on perfectionism and technical ability and of completely missing the essential technique of classical performance.

Therefore it was only logical that those U.S. composers whose quality could simply not be overlooked were consequently seen as pioneers of European music in the United States. The British music critic Martin Cooper was sure of wide agreement in his judgment of, for example, Roger Sessions, Walter Piston, William Schuman, Aaron Copland, Virgil Thomson, and Roy Harris as he wrote: "Their artistic foundation was European and even when they retrieved a really personal or—if there is such a thing—a really American style, they played no reciprocal part in influencing the music of Europe. On the creative side, then, we can discount American influence, and America's creative poverty partly explains, as it has also qualified, that concentration on performance natural among a people preoccupied with means rather than ends."[82] This devastating criticism is hardly worth mentioning, since far too many similar European manifestations of cultural hubris exist, especially in the area of music. Yet, these sentences are interesting because they were published for purposes of propaganda in the brochure *The Impact of America on European Culture*, financed by the U.S. government. This was not, by the way, an especially manipulative and clever public relations ploy in which political points could be won through the playing up to European cultural stereotypes. Rather, more decisive was the fact that also many Americans who were particularly interested in "serious" music had shamefully shared the opinions of their European critics and repaid European cultural condescension with feelings of inferiority.

Even the majority of U.S. music propagandists in Austria may be included in this group as well. For most of the ISB experts were not interested in supporting that which was truly unique about the high music culture in the United States, namely, jazz. More important, they wanted to demonstrate that even the United States had successfully achieved classical European high culture. It is not unimportant for our discussion that those representatives of the U.S. "to whom this propaganda was entrusted worked from a traditional European concept of culture and from a European assessment of cultural values centered upon European accomplishments, assuming, apparently, that our purpose was to prove ourselves as good Europeans as any."[83] Obviously, such a strategy could hardly be successful in Europe. Clearly, it was not those works that (supposedly) stood in the tradition of European music that had been decisive in gaining acclaim for "serious" U.S. music, but works like Gershwin's *Porgy and Bess*. The production of this piece, which had become synonymous with U.S. opera and whose appeal was due especially to its jazz elements, was a sensation in Vienna in September 1952. And the following tours became like a victory march through all the countries of Europe. "An American Opera Conquers Europe" exclaimed the headlines of *Theatre Arts*, and even the reserved *New York Times* left no doubt "that Porgy and Bess constitutes America's Ambassador at large."[84] Gershwin's *An American in Paris*, Piano Concerto in F, and *Rhapsody in Blue* even made the performance of a USIS-supported concert of the Viennese Philharmonic under the direction of the Fulbright scholar William Strickland possible in the Soviet zone for the first time on November 30, 1952. The audience of Wiener Neustadt was thrilled, and the Soviet cultural officer also "was very enthusiastic."[85]

Yet, not only Gershwin's music was effective. Very soon after the Second World War, the English musical play and the French opéra comique were seriously challenged by the competition of the musical. It is surely a clear, and in this case more than understandable, indicator of the resistance of the Austrian audience as well as of the disinterest of most of the U.S. cultural diplomats that the ISB and the USIS were not able to produce one musical in Austria during the entire ten-year period of occupation. One ISB expert, Marcel Prawy, who did not shy away from "light" music, became a pioneer of the musical in Austria. Already in 1953, Prawy had introduced many Austrians to the melodies of musicals during his *Musical Trip through America*, and the program *From America's Operetta* enjoyed approximately 400 performances in Austria and Germany in 1955/56.[86] These early preparations slowly gave the Austrian audience a taste for this art form, and in 1956 the time was ripe. Marcel Prawy's production of Cole Porter's *Kiss Me, Kate* premiered at the Volksoper under the direction of Julius Rudel, ". . . and nobody missed the waltz."[87] Quite the contrary, the musical took Vienna by storm and became such a box-office hit that the director Julius Rudel sarcastically commented: "The learned and bearded men who had opposed Prawy's doing a musical with government funds, are now spending their time counting the tremendous box-office receipts."[88]

Although the management of the Volksoper immediately set aside 100,000 schillings for an "Austrian musical," the Austrian artists had to acknowledge that *it was not that simple* to perform a work of "light" music from America. For Julius Rudel had to deal not only with musicians in the rehearsals of *Kiss Me, Kate* who felt that the essence of jazz was exhausted with a blue note, but also with singers and dancers who were, respectively, not accustomed to dancing and singing. *Kiss Me, Kate* presented, then, a new type of performance style in Austria. Even though its influence was slow in coming, this form had an impact on theater and music productions as well as on the training of actors and singers, making the immobile opera tenor an anachronism. *Kiss Me, Kate* was the pioneer, and "it served to acquaint the Viennese with the use of music of many different forms in a single show, with the careful integration of music and book, with the sustaining of a constant performance without long pauses, and with the use of a singing chorus that is moving all the time, always participating, never standing around. These were the basic revolutions in 'operetta' production that Vienna witnessed and loved, and which doubtlessly will affect the future of its musical stage."[89] These are certainly prophetic words in light of the successes of *My Fair Lady*, *The Man of La Mancha*, and *Cats*, to name only a few. Since 1956, the Austrian operetta, to a certain degree, had to live in peaceful coexistence with the musical, and especially the most recent developments clearly show that musicals are enjoying growing popularity even in Austria.

## "NEGROID DANCE MUSIC"—JAZZ

The Voice of America got a juke-box accent six months ago—and they're eating it up in the far away places! Sometimes the "voice" is Bing Crosby. Sometimes it's Frank Sinatra. And sometimes it's "My Heart Belongs to Daddy."

Because baby, even if it's a cold war outside, you gotta tell 'em how things are in Glocca-morra. Which proves that what's good for East St. Louis will work in Surinam— and there are lots of old cowhands along the Rio Danube.

—*Christian Science Monitor*, October 27, 1949

Hallo! Swing, Swing!
Es spielt das Neue Wiener Tanzorchester unter Ludwig Babinski; das Original Swingtett—die Swingboys.

—Advertisement in the *Arbeiter-Zeitung*, September 12, 1945

Jazz was born. But the unique thing about it is not its existence—there have been plenty of specialized musical idioms—but its extraordinary expansion, which has practically no cultural parallel for speed and scope except the early expansion of Mohammedanism.

—Francis Newton [Eric Hobsbawm], *The Jazz Scene* (1959)

While the lovers of "serious" music asked questions about the existence of "serious" music in the New World, U.S. pop music swept onto the shores of old Europe in waves, not to be curtailed by any western wall. Even jazz, which in my opinion is the most important contribution of the United States to world culture, impetuously crossed the Atlantic, and—*this cannot be stressed enough*—much to the surprise of the cultural diplomats, developed into one of the "most exportable commodities—second, perhaps, only to dollars."[90]

Because jazz was increasingly popular not only in Western Europe but in the Communist states as well, it can hardly be surprising that it was implemented as a weapon in the Cold War, much to the dislike of many musicians and most U.S. cultural diplomats.

Three reasons were responsible for the rejection of jazz by U.S. cultural diplomacy. First, jazz had originally been the exclusive music of African-Americans. It thus embodied their cry for freedom and equality and could, as a consequence, be understood as the fanfare for the cultural rebellion of the exploited in America. Second, the multifaceted rhythm and melody of jazz symbolized also the democratic equality of the African, American, and European cultures, cultural diversity and interdependence, the freedom of improvisation and the equality of all musicians and listeners. This stood in sharp contrast to the restrictions of the European tradition of art. Theodor W. Adorno stated this quite pointedly: not without reason does the rule of the successful conductor remind us of a totalitarian leader.[91] Finally, jazz also signified the rebellion of syncopation against the four-four measure of military marching music and therefore threatened, at least potentially, the regimented marching not only of the Red Army but also of all military, including the U.S. Army.

Of course, jazz styles did exist that contained fewer of these characteristics, far fewer than did bebop and free jazz. The many attempts to cloak jazz with a "European," symphonic, or chamber-music-like robe most of the time were musically hopeless. Even further, these endeavors did not change the fundamental rebellious image of jazz, as has been demonstrated all too clearly by the continuing attacks of jazz opponents.

Although the foes of jazz varied, the contents of the attacks always remained the same. In this tradition are Otto Basil's insistent warnings to the readers of *Neues Österreich* in December 1950: "black" music was in the process of conquering Vienna. His central criticism was that jazz represented Africa plus America—more simply, jungle plus machine.[92] This reoccurring cliché clearly shows only the ignorance of the critics and the irrelevance of their critique. Whatever jazz seemed to connote, it certainly did *not* represent a machine. More accurately, the essence of jazz lies in something quite opposite, namely, that it is not standardized and mass-produced music.[93] This is, however, also an indicator for the ambivalence of a world music like jazz as well as the fundamental political availability of every cultural manifestation. The *New York Times* thus labeled jazz as the new secret weapon in the Cold War on August 6, 1955: "United States Has Secret Sonic Weapon—Jazz."[94]

Actually, this secret weapon was neither a secret nor all that new. It was new insofar as its use for political purposes had only recently been recognized by the U.S. "elites." Already in 1918, as the Thirty-sixth U.S. Army Infantry Regiment (The Hellfighters) demonstrated their new music on the occasion of the victory celebration at the Paris Tuileries, jazz's victory march through Europe had begun. This phenomenon had been initially signaled by the enthusiasm for ragtime during the first decade of the twentieth century. Even then, contemporary critics set the tone for future jazz adversaries. J. B. Priestley, after hearing the American Ragtime Octet in 1912, led off the round of upholders of Western civilization that in this music he recognized "the menace to old Europe, the domination of America, the emergence of Africa."[95]

In spite of all warnings, jazz spread like a brushfire. The European tours of American jazz artists laid the foundation for this great enthusiasm, among others the Original Dixieland Band, Louis Mitchell's Jazz Kings, the Southern Syncopated Orchestra, Sydney Bechet, Louis Armstrong, Duke Ellington, Fats Waller, Ted Lewis, Cab Calloway, Coleman Hawkins, Benny Carter, Dickey Wells, and Bill Coleman. But also new developments in radio and recording technology gave jazz a ubiquitous venue. The (pseudo)jazz of white bands had an enormous influence upon European jazz until the outbreak of the Second World War, especially Paul Whiteman, Red Nichols, Jean Goldkette, and the Casa Loma Orchestra. This is a development that, in light of the corresponding enthusiasm of many European intellectuals for black culture, is not uninteresting in a historico-cultural perspective, for the majority of European jazz musicians (re)discovered African-American music for the first time only after the commencement of the Second World War.[96]

The most important centers for jazz in Europe during the interwar period had been Great Britain, France, Denmark, Sweden, and Holland. Germany, Czechoslovakia, and Italy also had local jazz scenes, and even the Soviet Union and Austria were not left completely unaffected by this music form. For the most part, jazz was interpreted as dance music, which was stylistically veiled with some jazz elements. Some European musicians could, by the way, measure their talents against those of black musicians who had emigrated to Europe as a result of less severe racial prejudices existing in France and England or as a result of the lack of performance possibilities after the worldwide economic crisis in the United States. The list of the most significant European jazz pioneers, most of whom had favored swing, includes the Quintet of the Hot Club de France with Django Reinhardt and Stéphane Grappelli, Hubert Rostaing, Nat Gonella, George Chisholm, Tommy McQuater, Spike Hughes, Sven Asmussen, Ulrik Neumann, Pietro Carlini, Enzo Ceragioli, the Maestri del Ritmo, Adi Rosner, Alexander Tsfasman, Leonis Utiosov, Valeri Ponomarev, and Romano Kunsman.

Typically, the first jazz critics and theoreticians were not Americans but Europeans. A Belgian, Robert Goffin, was actually the first publisher of a jazz magazine, *Music*, in 1921. However, it was European artists and intellectuals who made jazz socially acceptable—eventually even in the United States. They included Hugues Panassié, Charles Delaunay, Max Jocob, Jean Cocteau, and Boris Vian. Yet the intellectual discourse about jazz was not limited to France alone. Samuel Beckett's first published work was a review of Duke Ellington's music. Also, European collectors were the ones who first systematically ordered and cataloged the new music and published the magazine *Discography*.

Still, the development of black jazz was, more often than not, well ahead of the critics and was frequently misunderstood by the popes of criticism, like Hugues Panassié and André Hodeir. The humorless overenthusiasm and mania bordering on meticulousness with which some European jazz lovers collected, stored, and mummified black music caused many musicians just to shake their head. Frequent wars of words were bitterly fought with the intensity of crusades over what constituted "real" jazz and "true" jazz. Not without irony did Satchmo Armstrong once exclaim that European jazz lovers knew more about his records than he did himself.[97]

By the outbreak of the Second World War, British intellectuals had been the first to interpret the traditional jazz of New Orleans as the only true form of jazz. As a result of the exposure to the U.S. Army presence, Continental Europeans were soon to follow in this understanding. Consequential to this romanticizing of jazz as slave music, they ignored the new jazz styles exactly at the moment when young black musicians had emancipated themselves from the paternalism of white tastes through bebop. The European jazz scene following the war was therefore mainly dominated by traditional jazz bands like Claude Abadie, Claude Luter, George Webb, Alex Welsh, Humphrey Lyttleton, Ken Colyer, Chris Barber, the Dutch Swing College Band, and Carlo Loffredo's Roman NO Jazz Band. The fans of Dixieland consciously turned to jazz archaeology because they accused—not always without reason—the swing bands, especially those of Benny Goodman (whose arrangements were by Fletcher Henderson), Stan Kenton, and Claude Thornhill, of destroying the spontaneity of jazz through their polished, quasi-symphonic, postimpressionistic arrangements, and burying its "true" roots through their conformity with majority taste and Europeanization of the music.[98]

One consequence of this tendency toward music mummification was the discovery of the blues in Europe—the first Leadbelly performances took place during the intermissions of traditional jazz concerts in London and Paris in 1949. The blues led to the skiffle boom of the 1950s and, in turn, spurned the British beat explosion of the 1960s. While those developments were quite positive as such, one more fundamental fact became more than apparent in the music business. For when the blues boom had ended, it was the white rock stars "who had the Rolls Royces, the film contracts, the big houses with the swimming pools, and their profiles in Vogue; not the blues singers. It was no coincidence that the black audiences quit the blues like it had never been, when the Beatles and the Stones topped the charts."[99] Ironically, the white pop music audience in the United States would first be exposed to the blues through the reimports of white British bands.

While Dixieland, then, became ersatz folk music at Sunday morning visits to the local bar, at riverboat shuffles, and country festivals, especially in Great Britain and in West Germany, it would take until the late 1950s until the modern forms of black jazz would begin to become familiar in Europe. The European concerts of Dizzie Gillespie in 1948 and Charlie Parker in 1949 had only a limited influence upon a small group of jazz avant-gardists.

Austria most certainly had only a marginal impact on the development of European jazz during the interwar period. The small jazz scene was restricted especially to Vienna, and most jazz musicians seemed to appreciate only the watered-down versions of white U.S. jazz orchestras and, only in rare cases, hot jazz. Economic hardships, the emigration of many musicians, and the extreme opposition with strong racial undertones certainly had their effect upon the assessment of jazz already prior to 1938. Finally, the banning of "swing music," "Anglo-Saxon hot music," and the music of Jewish composers after the Anschluss must not be overlooked.

Although the tours of the major jazz artists never came to Austria, some African-American musicians repeatedly found their way to Vienna. Ragtime had already been performed in the Ronacher in Vienna in 1903, and a black group of thirty artists presented the cakewalk to a Viennese audience in 1905. After the First World War, the Syncopated Orchestra also created a real sensation at the Vienna Prater in 1922. The Chocolate Kiddies Show of Sam Woody's Jazz Symphonic Orchestra at the Raimund Theater in 1925 was a major success, as were the performances, often held in the Weihburgbar, of Arthur Bugg's Savoy Syncops Orchestra, the Seven Michigan Jazz, Leon Abbey, Eddie South, Teddy Sinclair's Original Orpheans Band, Bobbie Hind's London Sonora Band, and Babe Egan's Hollywood Redheads. Influential for the Viennese jazz scene were also the Weintraub Syncopaters from Germany and the Jack Hylton Orchestra from Great Britain. Even RAVAG did not ignore jazz completely. Finally, the greatest vehicle for the propagation of jazz was, without a doubt, the record.[100]

The first record that was produced with jazzlike music in Austria was the Chamber Choir of Karl Haupt with "O That Yankiana Rag" in Vienna in 1910. The most significant groups of the interwar period included the big bands of Frank Fox, Hugo Gottwald, and Hans R. Krongold, as well as the Stella Polaris Band, the Sonora Band, the Eric Gehrens Orchestra, the Jazzkapelle Charly Gaudriot, Hot Jazz Ernst Holzer, the Vier Rhythmiker, the Bobby Sax Hot Five and Bobby Sax and His Band, the Florida Band, Charlie Sekor's Happiness Boys, the Edi von Csoka Band, Heinz Sandauer and His Orchestra, and the Jazzkapelle Charley Kaufmann. Most of these bands played "jazzy" dance music. And although jazz was accepted only by a small minority, a "Contest for Viennese Jazz Bands and Jazz Singers for the Golden Band" was held in the Konzerthaus as early as the 1930s. Charles Kaufmann, who directed a course of study for jazz music and headed a department for jazz piano, even introduced jazz to the hallowed halls of the Viennese Schubertkonservatorium.[101]

When the *Neues Wiener Abendblatt* announced the performance of the lady of jazz, Erna Rosell, who had dazzled Europe, daily at 8:00 P.M. in the café-restaurant Hübner on March 10, 1938, just two days before the Anschluss,[102] obviously, the end was near. German jazz racism would soon produce rather peculiar blossoms. In 1940, the Reich's Ministry of Propaganda decreed a defensive battle against syncopated rhythm and even gave explicit instructions directing that melodies and horn segments could not be repeated more than three times by a soloist and no more than sixteen times by one or more horn groups.[103] Although the leaders of the "Third Reich" banned what they called "nigger music" as decadent, foreign, racially inferior, and subversive, Joseph Goebbels had swing bands flown into Berlin from London for film balls until the beginning of the war. Even during the war, he employed several jazz bands, such as Charlie and His Orchestra in Berlin and the dance band of the Deutscher Europa Sender (Reichssender Wien) under the direction of Ludwig Babinski. While they were only used for foreign propaganda, it should be noted that even Goebbels could not deny the attraction of jazz. The text of the propaganda song "So You Left Me . . . ," performed by Charlie and His Orchestra in July 1942, in an upbeat swing tempo and transmitted in the direction of Great Britain, is certainly worth quoting here.

> Lady Skinner's husband has joined the communists
> She is furious about it
> Now listen to her
> Swinging appeal.
>
> So you left me for the leader of the Soviet
> You don't like my social parties anymore
> Though you broke my heart in two
> I'll be waitin' here for you
> Till your Soviet days are over with and through.
>
> Communism is now spreading over England
> And we'll all be bloody communists one day
> But my comrade, don't forget
> England is not beaten yet
> Why play traitor and why join the Soviets?
>
> Though you think you're mighty cute
> I think you're just a brute
> The Soviets got you dipsy-doodle-oo
> When you hear of all their faults

You learn to do the English Waltz
Come back to me and I will waltz with you.

I am worried 'bout the leader of the Soviets
'Cause they call him killer-diller-swingaroo
If that killer-diller means
What I think it really means
Then I'm all prepared to come and rescue you.[104]

This text surely must be one of the most curious that was ever sung to a jazz accompaniment. For the population of the "Third Reich," it was hazardous to attempt to circumvent the regime's total ban on jazz during the Second World War. Yet, jazz did not die completely. Jazz musicians and jazz fans were a too greatly dedicated community. In Vienna, for example, the Steffldiele bar was the insider's tip. Here the most important Austrian jazz musicians, such as Herbert Mytteis (violin), Ernst Landl (piano), and Rudy Kregcyk (saxophone), played with the Italian guitarist Vittorio Ducchini, the Belgian trumpeter Bob Pauwels, and the French drummer Arthur Motta, holding the jazz banner high. Especially private jam sessions were hard to control. Virtually legendary were those that took place in the apartment of the Belgian pianist and singer Jeff Palme. Still, the Germanization of titles and the use of agile bouncers guarding the door were precautions well worth taking in order to avoid possible trouble. Swing also became the secret code for the "unpolitical" protests of a group of youths, mostly from the upper middle class. The cultural provocation of these swing clubs, which were formed only in the larger cities, was quite logically called *hotten*.[105]

Shortly after the liberation of Vienna through the Red Army, the jazz musicians once again crawled out of their basements, and in spite of the sorry state of the material situation, there was a surprising renaissance of the jazz scene. Especially during the years of its banishment, jazz had symbolized a particular freedom, and this freedom could now once again be enjoyed. Those U.S. officers who now arrived as the vanguard of the U.S. Army in Vienna obviously had expected a completely different Viennese music scene. Colonel Arthur E. Sutherland regretfully acknowledged that "at the hot spots it is rather disconcerting to expect to hear Johann Strauss waltzes played and, instead, to be greeted by some slightly faded American dance pieces. Viennese music will, however, be played as a concession for Allied visitors."[106] Colonel Sutherland clearly found himself in the proverbial tourist trap, in the position of the alien, for whom supposedly authentic folk music was played. At least he did not have to listen to old-fashioned U.S. hits for too long. For shortly after the arrival of U.S. troops, the establishment of the soldiers' radio station, and not to be forgotten, the coming of the legendary Victory Discs, the Viennese jazz musicians were once again at the cutting edge. The jazz musicians certainly belonged to the group of Austrians that regretted the occupation the least. The countless GI clubs provided them not only with endless opportunities to perform and earn money but also, even more important, numerous possibilities to jam with U.S. musicians.

Without a doubt, Austrian jazz experienced a tremendous blossoming during the occupation period. It was especially important for the future that small, yet active, jazz scenes could develop in the provinces, particularly in the U.S. zone. The most significant groups of this jazz explosion were Ludwig Babinski's New Vienna Dance Orchestra (with Fred Gallosch and Erwin Halletz), the Rhythmic Seven, Ernst Landl and the Hot Club Vienna (with Theo Ferstl, Hans Koller, and Joe Doleschal), Horst Winter's Vienna Dance Orchestra, the Nine Serenaders, the Orchestra Joe Ribari, Vera Auer and Her Soloists (with, among others, Attila Zoller), and the Gert Steffens Dance Band. The most important groups, who established Austria's reputation in the international jazz scene for the first time, included Johannes Fehring and His Orchestra (with Joseph Zawinul, Karl Drewo, Hans Salomon, and Erich Kleinschuster), Hans Koller's New Jazz Stars (with Roland Kovacs and Rudi Schering), and the Fatty George Band (with Bill Grah, Oscar Klein, Heinz Grah, and Bob Blumenhoven).[107]

Friedrich Gulda also played an important part in the establishment of jazz in Austria. Gulda's love for jazz and his open commitment naturally aroused the sentiments of the lovers of "serious" music, who played deaf to the quality of jazz for reasons of cultural hubris or, even worse, racism. That jazz, however, had been like a transfusion for the anemic music of Western civilization[108] had been recognized already during the first decades of the twentieth century by composers such as Igor Stravinsky (*Histoire de Soldat, Ragtime pour onze instruments, Piano Rag Music*), Paul Hindemith, Kurt Weill, Ernst Krenek, and Eric Satie. In France, a virtual *fureur nègre* had been provoked for jazz by Claude Debussy's "Golliwog's Cakewalk," Maurice Ravel's "L'Enfant et les Sortilèges" and the "Blues in the Violin Sonata," Darius Milhaud's *La Création du Monde*, George Auric's "Adieu New York," and Francis Poulenc's "Rapsodie Nègre."

When, however, Ernst Krenek's opera *Jonny spielt auf* premiered at the Vienna State Opera in 1927, it created one of the greatest cultural scandals of the First Austrian Republic. The National Socialists called upon "all Christian Viennese, artists, musicians, singers, and anti-Semites" to participate in a "huge protest demonstration" because "our *Staatsoper*, the premier art and education center in the world, the pride of all Viennese, has fallen to impudent, Jewish-Negroid defamers." For "the shameful work of a Czech half-Jew, *Jonny spielt auf*, in which society and nation, custom, morals, and culture are brutally stepped upon, was forced upon the *Staatsoper*. A foreign pack of business Jews and Freemasons have done everything to diminish our *Staatsoper* to a toilet for their Jewish-Negroid crimes. Bolshevist art brazenly rears its head."[109] What had actually reared its head here had been anything but Bolshevist art. The shadow of the repression of "nigger music" had thus been cast a decade before the Anschluss.

Although the National Socialists quite definitely were the most violent opponents of jazz, the opposition to that musical form was by no means limited only to them. In 1927, the "jazz expert" Gustav Stresemann opined that jazz was not music at all. And Emmerich Kalman's operetta *Die Herzogin von Chicago* riled the spirits of so many Viennese in 1928 that even the *New York Times*, under the headline "Vienna Is Alarmed by Inroads of Jazz," felt compelled to report about the illuminating concerns of a Viennese critic who was racking his brains on how to *humanize* jazz.[110]

Even more important, the rejection of jazz quite definitely was not limited to Europe. Jazz was particularly controversial precisely in its country of origin. Jazz's most militant opponents were not only members of the Ku Klux Klan, veterans' associations, southern racists and fundamentalists, women's organizations and prohibitionists, but also many members of the liberal East Coast establishment, who saw the cultural hegemony of white, Anglo-Saxon Protestantism threatened. The subversive potential of jazz must have been threatening indeed. The Illinois Vigilance Association seriously asserted that in 1921–22 alone, the "honor" of more than a thousand girls in Chicago had been lost to jazz.[111] And Dr. Florence Richards, school doctor at a high school for girls in Philadelphia, published a widely respected "scientific" warning against dance music in the early 1920s: "Continued exposure to this influence may tear to pieces our whole social fabric."[112]

The embittered opposition to jazz easily surmounted the distance between continents as well as ideological barriers. Certainly, young socialist and Communist intellectuals belonged to the most important supporters of jazz in Europe. Yet, the jazz politics of the Stalinists clearly showed that—under the international fighting slogan "Jazz opponents of the world unite"—they represented the "left" avant-garde of the antijazz front. However, the position toward jazz was not uniform during the period of Stalinism. While Soviet music ideologues sometimes acknowledged jazz as a cultural manifestation of repression of African-Americans, they mostly tended to interpret the music only as an expression of bourgeois decadence and as a strategy of demoralization, a tool of U.S. cultural imperialism. In any event, the *stiliagi* and *tarzansti* who played and danced the *dzahz* were often recklessly persecuted.[113]

No matter where the elites were positioned politically, they were an intercontinental, quasi supra-ideological international of jazz enemies. For the majority of U.S. cultural diplomats and politicians secretly agreed with the announcer of the East German radio on the occasion of a Bach concert directed by Dimitri Shostakovich: "Bach or boogie-woogie—take your pick!"[114] However, both sides misunderstood the basic premise because the difference between Bach and boogie-woogie is not musical but only ideological. The solution to the problem is quite simple. The question is not Bach *or* boogie-woogie, but Bach *and* boogie-woogie.

Jazz and pop music with jazz elements did not require the support of either highfalutin U.S. cultural diplomats or their European colleagues to succeed. Quite the contrary: it was not the music that required the propaganda, "it was propaganda that needed the music."[115] All those who owned a radio could tune in to the American Forces Network, and many youths shifted into continual reception. Much to his disappointment, U.S. literature professor F. O. Matthiessen had to acknowledge after the first session of the Salzburg Seminar in 1947 that the European students had evidently confused the session with a jam session. The European participants wanted to listen to only one kind of music, namely, "the programs of recorded jazz provided by the American army so that one of the American assistants, a step ahead still on the Europeans at least on the insides of radios, had to 'fix' ours so it wouldn't go."[116] Private contacts with GIs, the many GI clubs, records, tapes, and the music boxes of the early 1950s, which soon became standard equipment in Austrian restaurants and cafés, even in the most secluded areas, also contributed to the spreading of jazz.

Only very slowly did the State Department recognize that the great acceptance of jazz and pop music could be used abroad to raise the popularity of the United States. Most U.S. cultural diplomats, who swore to high culture, followed the new guidelines from Washington only reluctantly. Even the programmers of the Voice of America hesitated for some time until they allowed jazz and modern pop music to be incorporated into its program. This hesitation was especially significant, since listeners' mail after the end of the war quite clearly indicated the popularity of this music. Not until the spring of 1949 was the Voice of America prepared to give in to the wishes of its foreign audience to a greater degree. It now acquired a music-box accent, with which it became tremendously successful. The flood of fan mail from all parts of the globe approving of the programs of the disk jockeys Martin Block and Jo Stafford reached such dimensions that the *New York Herald Tribune* reported with complete surprise: "Disk Jockey of 'Voice' Is Winning Good Will for U.S. World Over."[117]

The despised jazz now was discovered as a means of propaganda, and it was therefore only logical that one of the most important jazz critics in the U.S., Leonard Feather, proclaimed a whole new type of Cold War: "Let Hot Jazz Melt Joe's Iron Curtain. How about parachuting some real cool tenor sax men and a couple of crazy trumpets into strategical Eastern European points, to start their own Iron Curtain concert tour. Heck, we could turn the cold war into a Cool War overnight!"[118] And in *Down Beat*, the most influential U.S. jazz magazine, Feather announced the new mission of jazz: "Here's bad news for the Kremlin—music is fighting communism."[119]

The great achievements caused the Voice of America to further develop its music program during the first half of the 1950s. On January 6, 1955, the show *Music U.S.A.* began, moderated by Willis Conover, which became probably the most effective propaganda coup in its whole history. This hour-and-a-half music program, in which any direct political advertisement was discreetly avoided, was broadcast every evening in the prime time slot, right between the two most important evening news programs. Before the program began, Dinah Shore sang an advertising jingle to the melody of a former auto advertisement:

> Hear the U.S.A. on the V.O.A.
> America is asking you to call:
> Tune to V.O.A., for the U.S.A.
> There is something on the air for one and all.[120]

*Music U.S.A.*, whose program was half dance music and half jazz, became the most listened-to broadcast of the Voice of America. More than thirty million listeners, a large portion in the Communist states, could be reached every evening during the second half of the 1950s, and within a year, more than 1,400 fan clubs in over ninety countries were founded. The disk jockey of *Music U.S.A.* established more than just the "Conover accent." When George Wein, the producer of the Newport Jazz Festival, traveled to the states of the Warsaw Pact in 1959, he reported aghast that "Eastern Europe's entire concept of jazz comes from Willis Conover."[121] A survey in Poland had resulted in proclaiming Conover the "best-known living American," and visitors traveling to Poland in the 1960s were surprised that Conover's likeness was displayed as often and with as much affection as pictures of John F. Kennedy.[122]

The popularity of jazz abroad superseded by far the recognition that this music form received in the United States. This positive influence of a minority music (referring here to the quantitative impact of the jazz scene in the United States and not to the ethnic group of African-Americans) surprised not only the American public but even more the U.S. propagandists. The *Wichita Eagle* announced in a special report in 1955, "'Voice' Rocks World Jazz Fans: Somewhat to its own surprise the *Voice of America* finds itself playing Pied Piper to the jazz devotees of the world."[123] The directors of the Voice of America even felt it necessary to convey an apology to *Time*: "Like it or not, jazz is a valuable exportable U.S. commodity."[124]

No matter what the majority of U.S. diplomats individually felt about jazz, the propaganda effect of the music was more important than personal prejudices. The music was, as *Look* magazine recognized, an international trump card: "Jazz is a door opener everywhere, a Pandora's box full of friendliness totalitarians won't easily be able to close."[125] Contrary to the original strategy, jazz bands now had to be incorporated into the Cultural Presentations Program and were sent abroad as cultural ambassadors of the United States. The artists chosen included Dizzy Gillespie, Benny Goodman, and Louis Armstrong.

As expected, this official revaluation of jazz met with hefty resistance in Congress. The opposition no longer focused on the export of "good jazz" (e.g., Duke Ellington or Louis Armstrong). However, the sympathies for the necessity of cultural foreign propaganda ended with state subsidies for the export of bebop. In contrast to swing, this new style obviously came too close to a cultural rebellion of the black populace. The selection of the Dizzy Gillespie Band, in particular, caused tempers to heat, and Senator Allen J. Ellender's sentiments exemplified the direction of the criticism: "I never heard so much pure noise in my life. . . . To send such jazz as Mr. Gillespie, I can assure you that instead of doing good it will do harm and the people will really believe we are barbarians."[126] Dizzy Gillespie nevertheless went on tour, and it would soon be apparent that Senator Ellender's assessment was gravely mistaken. As the Gillespie Band performed in Athens, it became clear that a large sector of the audience was composed of students, who had thrown stones at the U.S. embassy to protest America's Cyprus policy only a day earlier. One headline quite fittingly reported: "Greek Students Lay Down Rocks and Roll with Dizz."[127] Marshall W. Stearn's report on the Gillespie tour in the *Saturday Review* documents the surprise—even more, the incomprehension—of many Americans of the fact that the success of jazz could have anything to do with culture and art. "It has never dawned upon Americans that many people in foreign lands consider jazz a new and impressive contribution to culture. It is the old story of finding the bluebird in your own garden. Thus, the concrete example of one good jazz band may communicate more of the sincerity, joy and vigor of the American way of life than several other American creations inspired by Europe. Jazz was born and grew up in the US and nowhere else. As a European composer remarked to me, 'Jazz is one of America's best-loved artistic exports.' "[128]

Stearn's question "Is Jazz Good Propaganda?" seems to have answered itself. As one elegant lady told him in Zagreb, "What this country needs . . . is fewer ambassadors and more jam sessions."[129] Although congressional critics might have shaken their heads in disbelief, the tremendous success of jazz as foreign propaganda would soon put them to silence. Even the most vocal opponents of jazz had to come to terms with the fact that "in most parts of the world, jazz is a kind of Esperanto to the young generation from 15 to 25, and even countries with boiling anti-American prejudices enjoy and respond to it."[130]

Those who were particularly consternated about this new trend of cultural self-presentation were quite obviously those members of the American elites who had until then attempted to portray the United States as a nation with high culture. Allen Hughes's article in the magazine *Music America*, one of the most influential American publications dealing with the subject of "serious" music, illustrates this clearly: "*Music U.S.A.* is simply more of the same sort of thing that clutters up our own airways ad nauseam. . . . The immediate response of serious American music-lovers to this fact is likely to be despair coupled with anger."[131] Yet, criticism against the propagandist dissemination of black music could also be heard from the sector of American society that produced the music. This was especially important because the sudden discovery of jazz by the Voice of America was by no means a correct representation of the situation with which African-Americans were confronted in their daily lives. An analysis of the Voice of America broadcasts, as presented by the magazine *Afro-American*, complained quite explicitly in 1950 "that they are sugarcoating the facts of life as we live it, misrepresenting the work of our militant organizations, and serving as apologists for the Dixiecrat South in the eyes of the world."[132] (In all the controversy, the musicians themselves were obviously never asked for their opinion.)

In spite of all the criticism, jazz had been established as a central component of U.S. foreign cultural programs. However, the next horror for the plagued U.S. cultural presenters was not long in waiting, for by the mid-1950s, rock 'n' roll began to call attention to itself louder and louder. This new music damaged the ears of the programmers of the Voice of America so much that they were quite willing to sacrifice its potential propaganda value. Willis Conover exclaimed: "I see no reason to poison the ears of overseas listeners."[133] Although other propaganda transmitters such as Radio Free Europe and RIAS-Berlin soon showed themselves to be less selective than Voice of America,[134] the same would be true for rock 'n' roll as for jazz. Both forms of music were at first labeled as "noisy fads," and both succeeded in asserting themselves *against* official U.S. cultural diplomacy. It was just a matter of time until, around the late 1950s, even the Voice of America had to abandon its boycott of rock 'n' roll.

Had U.S. cultural diplomats, in general, been quite reserved toward jazz, then especially those who were active in Austria after the Second World War had specific grounds for caution. They were thoroughly convinced, and not without reason, that the majority of the (adult) population, which had long denounced jazz as "nigger music," would never welcome it with open arms. Therefore, radio Rot-Weiss-Rot hardly incorporated jazz and dance music with jazz elements into its program, and the reactions of its listeners seemed to confirm the wisdom of this policy. A public-opinion survey of April 1948 showed that 10 percent of the listeners in Vienna, 15.5 percent in Linz, and 20.5 percent in Salzburg complained mostly about "American jazz"—and this was the case even though it was heard only 2 percent of the broadcast time. Another postscript to the music land Austria: 5.5 percent of the Viennese, 16.5 percent of the Linzers, and 17 percent of the Salzburgers also disapproved of "serious music."[135]

Already in 1946, similar results were also published in the magazine *Berichte und Informationen*. The accompanying commentary clearly shows the background of these prejudices: "Negroid dance music is rejected. Dance music is rejected especially because of its specific American elements . . . its preference for foreign rhythms without a clear melody."[136] Just how deep-seated this prejudice actually was, is illustrated in an article by Joachim-Ernst Berendt entitled "The Origin and Horizon of Jazz" that was published in the journal *Der Turm* at approximately the same time. The author categorically asserted that every true melody of jazz was of European origin and that jazz was therefore only an "interpretation swing" of old European music.[137] Surely, this erroneous assessment would hardly be worth mentioning if its author were not to become one of the most influential authors on jazz in the Federal Republic of Germany.

It can hardly be surprising that a type of magazine such as *Berichte und Informationen* would announce in another article on U.S. radio politics that "America has not yet given its best,"[138] when the official press organ of the U.S. Army remained in the dark about jazz itself. An indicator for the misinterpretation and the playing down of jazz was explicitly demonstrated in the *Salzburger Nachrichten*, a publication of the U.S. Army, in calling it "America's folk music" on July 31, 1945. And in the most important mouthpiece of the ISB, the *Wiener Kurier*, one could read on January 20, 1949, that jazz, surprisingly according to the latest research, now had to be considered to be music.[139]

Nevertheless, the fact that jazz enjoyed great popularity especially with urban youths could not remain hidden from U.S. cultural diplomats for very long. The unusual success of concert evenings with black spiritual singers caused even the ISB to consider if it should not cater to the wishes of the audience. Modern jazz, of course, did not come into question. The ISB was of the opinion, however, that an exception should be made for the world-renowned swing bands à la Benny Goodman.[140] By 1950, traditional jazz would also find a niche in the program of the Kosmos Theater in Vienna. And the lectures and record evenings held there by Günther Schifter became one of the most-loved events of the USIS.

It cannot be stressed enough in this context that the ISB, which did all it could to convince the Austrian public of the cultural achievements of the United States, showed anything but initiative in introducing perhaps the most important American cultural creation. Instead, the ISB only reacted to already-existing audience desires. The way in which an ISB jazz brochure was compiled is a good example. Only after an enormous flood of questions did the ISB produce a small book of information on the history of jazz in early 1948. This volume, entitled *The Development of Jazz*, was eventually reissued under the title *Jazz erobert die Welt* (Jazz conquers the world).[141] The ISB experts were anything but enthused that their own creation became a natural success.

The rejection of jazz by adults was of course an additional appeal for the young in claiming this music for themselves. Whether these authority figures were parents, teachers, or U.S. cultural officers, the result of their bans was frequently disavowal by youths. Harald Staube's comments on the relationship between jazz and school are, therefore, paradigmatic for the relationship between jazz and U.S. cultural propaganda. He asserts that although jazz was halted in front of school gates, it did not stop at the ears of those who *are* the school, namely, the students.[142]

Already when the Institut für Jazzmusik was founded by Johannes Fehring in Vienna in 1948, Austria was no total jazz province anymore.[143] Even though it was a slow process, jazz found its way into the music academies in the decades to follow, especially in Graz. Although Austrian jazz musicians are appreciated only by a minority, it can be said that since the Second World War Austrian jazz has developed, quantitatively and qualitatively, to a degree hardly imaginable in 1945. This includes not only musicians but also the audience, jazz research, education, performance possibilities, and festivals. The establishment of the European Jazz Federation in Vienna in 1969 is only one example of this development. Certainly, U.S. cultural diplomacy had little to do with this, yet the presence of the U.S. Army surely did. For it is definitely not a coincidence that the most significant Austrian jazz festival is located in a place where over 10,000 GIs were stationed between 1945 and 1955—in the little town of Saalfelden.

## POP MUSIC AND ROCK 'N' ROLL

*Kathpress.* Cardinal Ratzinger, prefect of the Vatican congregation, explained at the beginning of a congress on church music in Rome on Sunday that rock and pop music would not be allowed in the Catholic church. These music forms attempt to convey a form of redemption and freedom that contradict Christian expectations. They attempt to lift the barriers of day-to-day life and to cause the illusion of redemption through the freeing of the individual "in the wild ecstasy of noise and the masses." Music has today become the "decisive vehicle of an antireligion."
    —*Salzburger Nachrichten*, November 19, 1985

The contradiction in the contribution of black music to American popular culture lies in the fact that the music of the slaves is a forceful expression of human freedom and human desires. The reaction of the slave owners is pleasure mixed with feelings of guilt. When the most pleasing form of entertainment rests upon the worst human humiliation, then the enjoyment of this entertainment contains a secret fight with reality.
    —Simon Frith, *Jugendkultur und Rockmusik* (1981)

Goodbye, Momma, I'm Off to Yokohama
We Are the Sons of the Rising Guns

Oh, You Little Son of an Oriental
Slap the Jap Right Off the Map
To Be Specific, It's Our Pacific

When Those Little Yellow Bellies
Meet the Cohens and the Kelleys

Put the Heat on Hitler,
Muss Up Mussolini and
Tie a Can to Japan

Let's Put the Axe to the Axis

You're a Sap, Mr. Jap, to Make a Yankee Cranky
Uncle Sam Is Gonna Spanky

Praise the Lord and Pass the Ammunition
We Are the Janes Who Make the Planes
Stalin Wasn't Stallin'
   —Title lines from U.S. pop songs during the Second World War, in Richard Lingeman,
     *Don't You Know There's a War On? The American Home Front, 1941–1945* (1970)

In only a few decades, jazz was successful in revolutionizing the musical taste of a relatively small yet, for the development of music, nevertheless important minority. Much more successful was U.S. pop music, containing popularized jazz elements. Its victory march could not be stopped—until today we are pursued by its parody Muzak into elevators, shopping centers, restaurants, and even bathrooms. Simon Frith correctly stated that Anglo-American mass music reigns the world more effectively than any other mass media and that jazz and its derivative have developed into the "Sound of the Century" without any competition.[144]

Although the taste of the majority of Austrian and German music consumers seemed to change only slowly after the Second World War, the trend clearly is in favor of a cosmopolitan, homogenized, canned music.[145] German hits dreamed primarily of fishing on Capri, of the South Sea Islands, and of the old home (*Heimat*, which had been lost by the millions as a result of the war), but—consciously or unconsciously—they still reflected U.S. trends and fashions and copied rhythms and arrangement techniques that had been successful in "Hitsville U.S.A." "Let's Knock the Hit Out of Hitler" was the title of a popular American song during the war. Not only the German military leaders but also the German record industry should have taken this warning seriously. It would not take long after the war had ended before the German *Schlager* became the German *Hit*.

Not only the presence of occupation troops but also the economic situation of the German record industry, which also dominated the Austrian market, played an important role in this development. Because the majority of production companies had been destroyed during the war—only German Grammophon (Siemens, Polydor) was able to reestablish itself quickly—American and British firms had gained speedy access to the (West) German and Austrian record market. And even the German companies were soon to be incorporated into a tight network of a few major enterprises because of capital linkage, in spite of the fact that the number of record labels seemed endless. Hence, EMI (Electrola) distributed the U.S. labels Ember, ABC-Paramount, Roulette, and King, while Teldec cooperated with RCA, and Deutsche Philips cooperated with Columbia Recording.

In 1947 alone, 400 million records were sold in the United States. In contrast, the sales trends developed slower in the western German zones and in Austria. Yet, the profits made especially since the beginning of the *Wirtschaftswunder* (economic miracle) are still considerable. While only 5 million records were sold in West Germany in 1949, the earlier sales zenith of 1929—when 30 million were sold—was reached already by 1955. In 1960, this figure more than doubled. However, not only sales figures grew proportionally to the size of the market, as they did in the United States. Also, the market segments of individual music styles showed parallel trends of development. While still 25 percent of the German production had been allocated to "serious" music in 1929, of the records produced in 1953, already 90 percent were "entertainment" music. And in 1958, the category "hits" alone composed 88 percent of the entire sales volume in West Germany.[146]

One decisive factor for the unusually rapid penetration of the newest fashions of U.S. pop music in Germany and Austria was certainly the (seemingly) coincidental reception of the "latest crazes," both through technical means (radio, records, tapes, film, television) and through the examples of the GIs. This immediacy of participation in the newest pop music fashion, *as it happened*, reflected the undeniable "ideological" demand of this music. In addition, this immediacy was also a fundamental requirement for the most rapid and universal marketing of any "latest craze," which had to be consumed before the next fashion could be marketed—again, *as it happened*.[147]

The economic basis for this development of a transatlantic music taste was the dominating position of U.S. media companies. Now, the U.S. hit parades became the most-copied model, and many German-language authors spent a great deal of their time "Germanizing" U.S. hits. This development consequently led to quite a paradoxical but significant trend, as in the case of Wolfgang Sauer's "Glaube mir" of 1952. While Sauer's original interpretation initially received no recognition in the Federal Republic of Germany, "Glaube mir" suddenly became a huge sales success—after Nat King Cole's cover version had climbed the U.S. charts.[148]

Already in the late 1940s, individual English words had been incorporated into German-language hits. Completely in line with the intentions of the modernization politics of the Marshall Plan, many German and Austrian *country boys* and *country girls* identified themselves more with the life of a *farmer* on a *ranch* than with the difficult reality of most European *Bauern*. Yet, German-language hits still needed the infusion of rock 'n' roll until the titles of the hits would read like the first lesson of a crash course in Pidgin English: "I Love You, Baby" (Conny, 1957), "Hey Boys—How Do You Do?" (Conny, 1957), "Hey, Mr. Music" (Conny, 1958), "Sugar Baby" (Peter Kraus, 1959), and "Crazy Boy" (Ted Herold, 1959). Naturally, German-language rock 'n' roll was predominantly ersatz rock 'n' roll, a particularly sterile version of the already-diffused white U.S. copy of the black originals. Artists' names also experienced the fitting transmutation to *stars* and *starlets*: Ernst Bjelke became Bruce Low, Manfred Nidl-Petz became Freddy Quinn, Rainer Müller was Ray Miller, Ditta Zuza Einzinger became Lolita, Rudy and Riem de Wolff were the Blue Diamonds, and Evelyn van Ophuisen became Daisy Door. And the sound of the name Ralf Bendix was simply *cooler* than his original name: Dr. Karl Heinz Schwab. Quite fittingly, these artists' names, then, also possessed the "magic" of the countless products of the whole palette of the Marshall Plan *Wirtschaftswunder*.[149]

In any event, the integration difficulties and language problems of the GIs stationed in West Germany seemed to be even greater. While Elvis Presley brought audible evidence that the seemingly hardest rock 'n' roller could be brought to his knees by the armed service ("Muss i denn, muss i denn, zum Städtele hinaus"), Johnny Cash and Tom T. Hall dreamed "I wish I could sprechen sie Deutsch!" while washing down their "Krautland Blues" with "3,000 Gallons of Beer."[150]

Analogous to the jazz phobia of the 1920s, the rock 'n' roll whirlwind in the United States and its wildfirelike sweep across Europe provoked an almost unanimous defensive front of adults on both sides of the Atlantic, again superseding all ideological barriers. No other cultural phenomenon even came close to unifying NATO opponents and supporters, conservatives and Communists, liberals and socialists, monarchists and republicans, believers and atheists, as did the "jungle music" from the United States. Organization men, ambitious *Wirtschaftswunder* makers, and the (dis)organizers of real socialism saw their peace equally disturbed. Hence, no matter how loud rock 'n' roll was, the screams of its opponents seemed almost louder.

Three short examples may suffice, one from the United States, one from Austria, and the third from the German Democratic Republic. *Time* magazine could not abstain from warning its readers in 1956 that "Rock 'n' Roll is based on Negro blues, but in a self-conscious style which underlines the primitive qualities of the blues with malice aforethought. . . . Psychologists feel that Rock 'n' Roll's deepest appeal is to the teener's need to belong; the results bear passing resemblance to Hitler mass meetings."[151] *Neues Österreich*, too, saw the customs and morals of the young in great danger as a result of the "exciting dance acts" and the "sensuality of the jungle." It seemed rather typical that the new dance was closely tied to the arousal and unbridled enthusiasm of large sectors of the young. Furthermore, there obviously was no musician who did not hate rock 'n' roll.[152] It could hardly be surprising that the East German author Kurt Barthel unmasked rock 'n' roll as no less than the "most modern American psychological preparation for war," when even a policeman from Oakland formulated the following thought after a concert by Elvis "The Pelvis" Presley: "If he did that in the street, we'd arrest him."[153]

Racism and bigotry, provincialism and prudery, ignorance and overestimation of one's own culture, anticapitalism and anti-Communism—from these various mixtures of ingredients the arguments of the international rock 'n' roll opponents were formed. Yet, these arguments were not new—many other dances, such as the waltz or the tango, were initially outcast and rejected—nor was the supposed sexual dimension of the dance rock 'n' roll. Is not every dance, as George Bernard Shaw pointedly asserted, "a perpendicular expression of a horizontal desire?"[154] Unfortunately, the astute Irishman did not live long enough to be able to analyze the issue of rock 'n' roll. This is especially unfortunate because the quality of academic literature on mass culture, generally speaking, and on pop music, in particular, is frequently rather depressing. Not including the often-mediocre artist hagiographies, most works deal with protests against, and not studies of, the subject matter. "If a literary man puts together two words about music," said Aaron Copland, "one of them will be wrong."[155] Had Copland studied the literature on rock 'n' roll more closely, his assessment would have been even less flattering.

Rock 'n' roll became many things at the same time: it was seen as a part of the Communist world conspiracy and as an anti-Communist war propaganda, as a revolt against capitalism and as cultural capitulation in the face of capitalist profit interests, as political revolutionary stimulant and as depoliticizing tranquilizer, as a stimulus for aggression and as a social safety valve, as a part of a strategy led by "world Communists" to corrupt the young of the "free world" and as a part of the imperialistic strategy for total social control and weakening of any revolutionary potential. These contradictions only reflect the ambiguity of the music—mostly resulting from its marketing by the culture industry—whose emancipating demand has been frequently used only as an excuse and as a veil for its product character.[156] "Pop acts out revolt rather than provokes it. It's almost a substitute for revolution in the social sense and is anyway geared, even these days, to the capitalist system," stated the British jazz singer and culture critic George Melly. One can only agree with him when he adds that pop culture is a "Revolt into Style."[157] The only thing "revolutionary" in a song like "Juke-Box Baby" (and if we meet again at ten in front of the jukebox it would be wonderful) was the German pronunciation of such a machine (*Juck*-Box), which had become a meeting place for the young.

Without a doubt, rock 'n' roll was incorporated, molded, and domesticated as one of the most important leisure-time products of the culture industry. By no means, however, does this imply that all artists indulge in escapism or that all statements of rock 'n' roll are only passively consumed. Like all capitalistic cultural forms, rock 'n' roll represents both repressive as well as emancipating elements. The question of authenticity must be raised, as it must be for any mass-produced, technical reproductions in any area of artistic expression, just as the problem of commerce and corruption must be considered not only for rock concerts but also for the Salzburg Festival.

Rock 'n' roll clearly is a component of capitalistic mass culture. It cannot, however, be truly understood if the innate dialectical tension between release and control is not considered. Although the supply of capitalist mass culture is often "false," the original needs that it seeks to fulfill, as Simon Frith correctly stresses, are "true." As Frith notes, cultural reproduction means that the ruling class forces its hegemonic discourse upon the exploited. For this reason, the ideology of rock music can be understood only if one takes into consideration its role in the reproduction of cultural capital as well as its resistance to cultural capital. The contradictions of rock music therefore are a sign of the class struggle.[158] Under the system of capitalism, the supply and demand of popular culture are at the same time always "commercial" and "anticommercial." It is one of the most misunderstood contradictions that with enough demand the "anticommercial," according to the immanent logic of the system, quasi-automatically becomes "commercial."[159]

Since the middle of the 1950s, rock 'n' roll has become the dominating music of the young in the industrialized world. Almost every country has its Johnny Hallidays, and even in former East Germany, Hootenanny Clubs shot up out of the socialist ground like mushrooms, offering more than just ideologically acceptable protest songs.[160] It is no secret that the breakthrough of rock 'n' roll as *the* global soundtrack is not only based on its sometimes terrific musical quality. But rock 'n' roll still was rather more than just a coincidental background music to the Pax Americana, for the ideological components of both phenomena were often mutually complementary, in spite of all seeming and actual contrasts. Robert Pattison pointed to this connection as he noted in his study *The Triumph of Vulgarity*: "Rock grew up in the 1950s during America's postwar supremacy and is the musical compliment to the naive democratic sentiments that underline the political doctrine of manifest destiny. In the myth of American imperialism, the United States leads a world eager to be swept into the ambit of democratic order. . . . Like the American imperialist, the rocker wants not just the world, but the world's reciprocal love."[161] As we know, rock music does indeed have more success than the government of the United States has with its foreign and economic politics; U.S. pop culture exports have become, in the meantime, one of the most important assets of the American foreign trade balance.

Jazz and rock 'n' roll are, on the one hand, certainly the cultural results of the capitalist world system based on colonialism and imperialism, slavery and exploitation, industrialization and standardization, de-individualization and the triumph of the image over being. On the other hand, these styles also represent the rebellion against the main profiteers of this situation. The success of jazz and rock 'n' roll definitely are not explained only through their quality—or, according to some critics, their lack of quality.

Eric Hobsbawm perhaps came closest to explaining this phenomenon when he stated that both U.S. folk music in the nineteenth century and jazz and pop music in the twentieth century differ in their meaningfulness and vitality from the music of Europe in that these American styles were "never swamped by the cultural standards of the upper class."[162] Surely the victory march of rock music was also the triumph of vulgarity, and "vulgarity in its rock incarnation is America's most powerful weapon and most successful export, an export with all the political and cultural significance of American vulgarity itself. Rock and vulgarity are well on the way to conquering the sensibilities of the entire planet."[163] To counter any misunderstandings, however, those who carry the word "democracy" on their lips and who turn up their noses at the triumph of vulgarity would be well advised to pause and to refer to the etymology of the term *vulgus*.

This pause would also be appropriate especially for the propagandists of U.S. democracy abroad. For, quite contrary to the intentions of U.S. cultural diplomacy, it was precisely that "Negro music," "race music," and "jungle music," which horrified all supporters of high culture on *both* sides of the Atlantic, that was able to assert itself. It is certainly telling that the champions of U.S. capitalism in Europe saw their cultural propaganda efforts threatened the most by the products of their *own* capitalistic culture industry.

Here we are not dealing only with the overestimation of "Western high culture" by many Europeans and those quasi-Europeans whose ancestors had emigrated to other continents but also with another paradox of the system of capitalism. Exactly those "elites" are usually most embarrassed by the cultural manifestations of capitalism who not only profit from it in economic, political, and social terms but who also own its means of production and who make the products of mass culture available in the first place.

In attempting a survey of the Cultural Presentations Program of the Department of State in 1963, Lucius D. Battle, assistant secretary of state for educational and cultural affairs, categorically stated that U.S. composers of "serious" music, such as Henry Cowell, Aaron Copland, and Virgil Thomson, were the true "music missionaries" and, more than any other group of U.S. citizens in Europe, had helped "to convey our cultural maturity and to give the lie to the diehard cliché that America is a materialistic and culturally underdeveloped nation."[164] But Lucius D. Battle erred. To become aware of the uniqueness of American music culture, a keen listener did not need the "serious" music from the United States—in spite of all its good qualities. The quality of American music was ascertained by Louis Armstrong and Duke Ellington, Charlie Parker and Miles Davis, Dizzy Gillespie and John Coltrane, Ray Charles and—yes, at his best—Elvis Presley. Once again, history fooled the experts, and "it fooled them in the usual way. It didn't repeat. Only the experts repeated."[165]

# 8

## The Influence of Hollywood

I meet people occasionally who think that motion pictures, the product that
Hollywood makes, is merely entertainment, has nothing to do with education.
That's one of the darndest fool fallacies that is current. When I was a motion picture
editor on the *Chicago Daily News* we used to report what was a four-handkerchief
picture as distinguished from the two-handkerchief picture. Anything that brings
you to tears by way of drama does something to the deepest roots of your
personality. All movies good or bad are educational and Hollywood is the foremost
educational institute on earth, an audience that runs into an estimated 800 million
to a billion. What, Hollywood's more important than Harvard? The answer is, not
as clean as Harvard, but nevertheless, farther reaching.

—Carl Sandburg, as quoted by Edward R. Murrow in a speech for the leading
managers of the U.S. film industry on November 5, 1961

By our asinine emphasis on the material goodies we have seemed, by implication,
to deny the existence of anything else in American life worth bragging about.
Even during the most desperate days of the war we got our message of hope so
tangled up with refrigerators and cars that, as one Office of War Information
worker put it, we could have billed it as "The War That Refreshes." The
commercial projection of America has gone a step further; while our information
people spend millions trying to demonstrate that we are really cultural after all,
the biggest information agency in the world, Hollywood, has been exporting
films that seem to demonstrate the opposite—so persuasively, it might be noted,
that in Austria the Russians have been saving their breath by letting several of our
gangster films quietly circulate in their occupation zone.

—*Fortune*, February 1951

This conception sees the popular artist as an enforcer of conformity, and reveals
the views of art taken by the Hollywood mass producer and by the rigid
communist not as things opposed, as both would like to believe them to be, but as
essentially the same. They both have gone to the same lengths through their belief
that thought is dangerous. The Hollywood producer measures the danger solely
in terms of money, since any deviation from the approved and expected formula
may mean the loss of a million at the box office. Both are committed to official
versions of life, and must, therefore, be resisted at every point by anyone
concerned with breaking through the official to the real.

—F. O. Matthiessen, *From the Heart of Europe* (1948)

There have been people at all points on the political and cultural spectrum who have been contemptuous of the messages American movies have delivered, who have found fault with their formulas, evasions and untruths. The value of such criticism depends, in the perspective of cultural history, on a number of related issues, among them the comparative formulas, myths, evasions and untruths of textbooks, sermons, newspapers, political statements and other modes of disseminating information in the society. . . .

That so many American movies have been mediocre or venal or false has to do with the profit motive that dominates them, and it is short-sighted to speak of transforming commercial entertainment without first transforming social ideologies.

—Robert Sklar, *Movie-Made America: A Cultural History of American Movies*
(1975)

## The Hollywood Film as the Text of Power

Motion picture history is world history,[1] and this history has been dominated by Hollywood at least since the First World War. Hollywood, which in this context stands for film and television production in the United States, has become—not without reason—synonymous with and symbolic for the capitalist culture industry per se. The economic significance of the new medium of film, the Esperanto for the eye, clearly came to light already during the heyday of the silent movie.[2] For this reason, the governments and industries of the United States, Great Britain, France, Italy, and Germany engaged in a quasi trade war in an effort to control the world's film markets.

The talkie not only revolutionized the entire film language and the film as text but also fundamentally changed the ownership structures of the film industry as a result of ever-increasing financial extravagances. Hence, these economic conflicts escalated. The exceptionally capital-intensive film production and technical equipment required for film theaters meant a fundamental deterioration of the market position of smaller countries competing with the United States because the amortization of films, especially large costly productions, could hardly be guaranteed in the limited domestic market. However, European producers were not the only ones confronted with this dilemma. Even Hollywood, which had access to the largest domestic market, became dependent upon the export of films. The costs of production and distribution were frequently recovered in the large film market of the United States. Yet, true profits could only rarely be achieved even in this huge market. At least in the understanding of capitalist economics, this situation consequently led to an intensified battle for foreign markets, and this film export war has been decided in favor of Hollywood.

The U.S. film industry had been effective in asserting itself worldwide not only because the U.S. government—under the supposedly democratic slogan "Freedom of information"—made the allocation of immensely needed foreign credits in war-ravaged European countries dependent upon the free-market access for Hollywood films. Ironically, even the attempts of European governments to limit the stream of American films through import quotas were counterproductive—in the true sense of the word—because they often led to the intensification of direct investments of Hollywood firms in the respective states. And when one of these protective measures stipulated that the number of movies exported by the United States had to correspond with the import of a certain number of domestic European films, it actually enabled Hollywood sister-companies in Europe to increase the amount of pseudolocal film productions, which in turn increased the import quotas for U.S. films. The paradoxes created through the quota laws were numerous. On the one hand, the relatively modest box office receipts of these "quota quickies" (such was the Hollywood term for low-budget films) amounted to significant profits for U.S. companies. On the other hand, these U.S. direct investments enabled more accurate assessment of foreign markets, the development of distribution chains, and the dividing up of the market. In addition, local film firms not only were dependent upon capital and technical cooperation from the United States but often also assumed the Hollywood *perspective*.

After the Second World War, which cut off the European film market for U.S. movies in all of the states occupied by the German army, a further irony appeared. In an effort to boost domestic film production, quota measures were introduced, for example in France, Great Britain, and Italy. However, because these import restrictions had been hindered by frequent threats of credit restrictions by the U.S. government, individual governments then attempted to introduce taxes on movie tickets. These monies were to be earmarked for film funds to subsidize productions. Yet, Hollywood, which had experienced a dramatic crisis at the end of the 1940s, took the opportunity to step up the production activities of its sister firms in Europe. And now the amount of state subsidies for the national film industries in Italy, Great Britain, and France suddenly played a significant role in deciding what (U.S.) films would be made in which European atelier. While the box office results of Hollywood films abroad during the interwar period had made real profits possible, these markets now became even more important. "By the 1950s, overseas locations and American investment in foreign productions had become essential elements in Hollywood's financial survival."[3]

As a consequence, 18 percent of the production costs of "British" U.S. films, such as *Lawrence of Arabia*, *Bridge on the River Kwai*, *The World of Suzie Wong*, *Tom Jones*, *From Russia with Love*, *Goldfinger*, and *A Hard Day's Night*, were financed by the British taxpayers. In 1966 alone, 80 percent of the subsidies in the British Production Fund, approximately $10 million, went to Hollywood firms. These state monies only rounded out total profits, which were derived from the following: "American films in Britain, earnings in Britain of British films financed by American interests, earnings in Britain of non-American foreign films financed by American companies, commissions for distributing films, earnings from film theaters, etc."[4] It may not come as a surprise that the name of the British film center is Pine*wood*, and the British film producer Tony Garnett hardly exaggerated when he stated, "To be an Englishman in the film industry is to know what it's like to be colonized."[5] The British film industry may represent one of the most extreme examples of economic dependence upon Hollywood, yet the difference to the other important film countries of Western Europe is only slight. In light of these economic connections, it would be quite absurd to speak of any "national" film production.

Hollywood's rule over the celluloid imperium has implications beyond just economic dominance. Georg Schmid correctly pointed out that, especially with film, not only economic but also symbolic capital circulates.[6] Analogous to the loss of political, military, and economic power, the European (film) powers also lost a part of their sovereignty in the production and distribution of movies after the First World War. They thereby forfeited control over a decisive channel of cultural self-interpretation and self-definition. This is especially significant, for film—according to the theory of technical primacy, whereby all art forms of an epoch come under the influence of the technically dominating—"has technical primacy during the years between the rise of cubism and the present."[7] The paradigm change from the printed text to the visual stimulants of film—to a certain extent the beginning of the end of the "Gutenberg galaxy" (in the words of Marshall McLuhan)—thus had the greatest implications. The assertion of a new medium not only changes the way in which a society interprets itself but also "restructures the agenda of those things which we deem to be important. . . . The movie thus becomes a quasi-encyclopedia in which one finds the visual repository of much of our culture."[8]

And this encyclopedia filled itself, with the speed of visual stenography, with more and more pictures and articles produced in the United States. Since the First World War, Hollywood has developed (or plagiarized) the leitmotif, the fundamental themes of film, while all other forms of film were given only the role of variation. The Hollywood film took over, in a certain sense, the function of the traditional novel, while the non-Hollywood film acted the role of the *roman nouveau*.[9]

Hollywood's triumph meant, however, far more than just the victory of the narrative. The massively distributed reflections of film developed the character of a mystification, and this mystification provided the cultural conceptions of the lower middle class with, so to speak, the natural insignia of universal truth.[10] The Hollywood film—with its emphasis on individualism, competition, the cleansing forces of the market, the freedom of choice, and especially the melting pot—became the most influential iconographic inventory of the capitalist ethos and U.S. democracy in the twentieth century.[11] These films as a commodity are similar to reality, as other wares are to true needs, because "if the consumer society has occasionally been defined as the commercial exploitation of false needs, then the commercial cinema could be called the aesthetic exploitation of false consciousness."[12]

Yet even though social problems degenerate to genres in most films, these genres are actually a metatext, a system of orientations, expectations, and conventions that circulates between the film industry, the text, and the public.[13] The netlike disposition of these relations, therefore, does not allow a clear answer to the question as to whether film reflects reality or reality imitates film. One can certainly agree with Pierre Sorlin's assessment that each film that speaks of the past depicts only the time in which it was produced; in other words, it represents yet another past.[14] Similarly, another question is left unanswered: Is this *restaging of the past* through film not really (and this would be much more decisive) a license for the creation of the future as a result of the history-shaping power of pictures? In any event, it does not matter whether we are speaking of an entertainment film or a documentary. Studies have shown that there are no significant distinctions between either métiers with respect to their credibility and influence upon the creation of opinions. For *seeing is believing*, and English allows the very fitting play on words: *reel facts* become *real facts*.[15]

Without a doubt, in dealing with film, we are dealing with a complex institution of social control and socialization that represents concrete economic interests.[16] Nevertheless, film is not only cunning manipulation; it is actually reality as well, representing at least fragments of realities and not only of the hegemonic ideology, class, and culture of the time of production, but also exactly that which it subconsciously signifies.[17] Finally, it also symbolizes the absence of the powerless or their belittled reality. Film, then, is both the means *and* the vehicle, the product *and* the source of history, and film analysis therefore also allows the analysis of societies.[18]

In light of the image imperium of Hollywood, we can be sure that we are dealing not only with a *Movie-Made America*[19] but also with a whole world produced by film. In this context, I do not only refer to the creation of national stereotypes but also especially to the matter of "historical films," whose alternative description as "monumental films" is more than telling. After viewing the movie *El Cid*, it would not hurt to consult a Turkish film interpreting the Crusades.

In both cases, the audience not only is confronted with a collective form of representation but also itself introduces collective forms of images. In other words, movies represent a collective phantasm, or, according to Georg Schmid, the collective mechanics of association, which creates needs as much as it gives in to needs as a result of commercial considerations. Hence, according to Siegfried Kraucauer, films represent "the collective dream material of a given culture, and can be psychoanalyzed like an individual's dreams."[20] Because this collective dream material has been processed more and more by Hollywood and spread worldwide, Carl Sandberg's assertion that the Southern Californian film metropolis is one of the most important pedagogical institutions on earth can certainly be affirmed. Hollywood is one of the largest information agencies, probably the number one center in the twentieth century for image production and distribution and therefore also "the most pervasive and successful agent of cultural imperialism there has ever been."[21]

This assertion by no means represents only the ideologically or economically motivated assessments of opponents of the United States. The attractiveness and international propaganda influence of American films is certainly apparent to the managers of the film industry as well as to the political power brokers in the United States. This was also the essential reason why Hollywood's representatives could always count on full political support from Washington in their efforts in opening and securing foreign markets. Joseph H. Hazen, the leading manager of Warner Bros., described this symbiosis clearly in 1943: "The motion picture is truly an 'invisible'[!] arm of our Government and the industry has dedicated itself to an everlasting cooperation in the present fight and in the future peace."[22]

The close cooperation between the U.S. government and the motion picture industry has been equally profitable for both partners. Gerald M. Mayer, the head of the International Division of the Motion Picture Association, summarized the importance of the export of Hollywood products quite accurately:

The modern American motion picture, almost beyond any possible comparison with other items of export, combines considerations of economic, cultural and political significance. . . . No one has ever attempted to calculate—and it probably would be an impossible task—the indirect effect of American motion pictures on the sale of American products, not only on display, as it were, but in actual demonstrated use. Scenes laid in American kitchens, for example, have probably done as much to acquaint the people of foreign lands with American electric refrigerators, electric washing machines, eggbeaters, window screens, and so on, as any other medium. . . . There has never been a more effective salesman for American products in foreign countries than the American motion picture.[23]

Yet, it was not only the economic commercial effect that counted. Mayer also anticipated newer results of film studies, as he concluded: "The motion picture is one product which is never completely consumed for the very good reason that it is never entirely forgotten by those who see it. It leaves behind a residue, or deposit of imagery and association, and this fact makes it a product unique in our tremendous list of export items."[24]

If this analysis only alludes to the political usefulness of Hollywood exports and almost modestly ignores its importance next to economic and cultural aspects, then this can be explained as a result of the contemporary domestic political situation in the United States: precisely at this time the House Committee on Un-American Activities was scrutinizing Hollywood for its supposed Communist undermining. These exercises not only exemplified the clearly paranoid characteristics of a witch-hunt but definitely made one thing perfectly clear: the U.S. political elite had full awareness of the potential political power of Hollywood.[25]

Any analysis of its political influence on foreign markets makes especially clear the groundlessness of the accusations against putative left-wing tendencies of Hollywood products. While Hollywood was now forced to market its films as completely politically harmless within the United States, these same films were consciously implemented abroad as perhaps the most important components of U.S. foreign propaganda.

In an effort to guarantee the defeat of the Italian Communists in the parliamentary elections in April 1948, not only had massive political and economic pressure been imposed by the U.S. government during the election, but Hollywood also added its contribution. In the last months of the campaign, all large U.S. distribution firms in Italy formed a consortium and saw to it that all U.S. weekly newsreels, documentaries, and propaganda films were most optimally disseminated. In addition, three films on the positive effects of U.S. aid to Italy were circulated in cooperation with the Italian motion picture industry, and the leading Italian weekly news program, INCOM, was also persuaded to produce its own pieces on this topic as well. In order that these messages reach the largest possible audience, these films, wherever possible, were coupled with those movies that promised to be the most popular. Still further, theaters that were frequented by poorer people were predominantly chosen for such screenings. All such endeavors cost the U.S. government not one single cent. American propaganda films reached more than 600,000 individuals per week, those produced by U.S. distribution companies five million, and INCOM eight million viewers. Finally, Hollywood firms also organized a donation drive via radio for Italian war orphans. The success of these concerted actions was so overwhelming that the chief correspondent of the *New York Times* in Italy, Arnold Cortesi, contentedly reported: "Throughout the pre-electoral period the cooperation of the leading American distributors put films of positive propaganda value in virtually every Italian screen and so helped powerfully to save the day for the anti-Communist side. The success scored by the movies on this occasion suggests a new direction in which a continued American propaganda effort should work."[26] Still, the main responsibility for this success cannot actually be attributed to the propaganda films themselves but instead to the "harmless" entertainment movies. Especially popular was Ernst Lubitsch's comedy *Ninotchka*, in which Greta Garbo and Melvyn Douglas deliver a pointed satire about Communism. A disappointed Italian Communist party functionary realized defeat when he saw it: "What licked us was *Ninotchka*."[27]

*Ninotchka*'s struggle against Communism was not only limited to the Italian elections of 1948. This film was also implemented in Austria directly after the trade union strikes in October 1950, being shown concurrently in the two large theaters within the international zone. In November 1950 alone, more than 70,000 Viennese saw this film, and Public Affairs Officer Charles K. Moffly could report to Washington that "considerable persuasion and reassurances of American interests" had paid off with respect to the film audience. "The enthusiastic reception accorded this U.S.-produced satire on Communism is proof of the high effectiveness of the proper type of commercial motion picture presentation when used in support of USIE's psychological campaign."[28]

It would surely be too simplistic to attribute the election defeat of the Italian left or the predominantly anti-Communist position of the Austrian populace only to the impact of U.S. films, even if Josef Stalin stressed to Wendell Willkie in 1942 that he needed nothing more than control over Hollywood to convert the whole world to Communism.[29] The opinion of the Soviet dictator on the formative power of the entertainment film hardly differed from that of the director of the OWI, Elmer Davis, who at the same time commented: "The easiest way to inject a propaganda idea into most people's minds is to let it go in through the medium of an entertainment picture when they do not realize that they are being propagandized."[30] This strategy was definitely mastered better by Hollywood than by the Soviet film industry, and it is undisputed that the products of the U.S. media firms represented an extremely important component of the anti-Communist propaganda offensive.

The films of Hollywood should therefore play an important role in the future within the foreign cultural initiatives of the United States. If the Cold War did not have so many victims, it would be tempting to assert that the domestic political developments in the United States in the 1950s merely followed the script of a cynical, ironic Hollywood screwball comedy. While the ridiculous activities of the HUAC severely damaged the reputation of U.S. democracy abroad as no other domestic issue in the United States, the HUAC witch-hunt concentrated on precisely the artists and films that have come to be known abroad as the best propagandists for the American way of life.

Motion pictures do not merely depict just any moving images. These images also represent a fascinating weapon of the silver screen. Above and beyond this, the Hollywood melodrama and the Communist hunters of the HUAC seemed to be created especially for one another.[31] The president of the Motion Picture Association, Eric Johnston, clearly illustrated this irony in his talk at the Foreign Policy Committee of the U.S. Senate in 1953: "Pictures give an idea of America which is difficult to portray in any other way, and the reason, the main reason, we think, is because our pictures are not obvious propaganda."[32]

## The Economic Imperium of Hollywood

"The film is to America what the flag was once to Britain. By its means Uncle Sam may hope some day, if he be not checked in time, to Americanize the world." This warning by the *London Morning Post* in 1923 was answered by Edward G. Lowry in the *Saturday Evening Post* on November 7, 1925, with the statement: "The sun, it now appears, never sets on the British Empire and the American motion picture."[33] This laconic as well as fitting assessment on the condition of the world film market of the mid-1920s would have been completely wrong only a dozen years earlier. The U.S. film industry may have become more and more consolidated since the fights for patents and distribution rights of 1907, but the Europeans, especially the French, had dominated not only the European market but the American as well until 1914/15. In 1912, up to 90 percent of all films on the world market came from France, and the Pathe Frères were still the largest film producers in the world.[34] For this reason, U.S. film producers were the *first* to demand import quotas to shield the U.S. market against foreign films, complaining that the competitive advantage of foreign films was due only to greater quantities of productions. Yet, when some of the most important European film nations wanted to implement similar measures against the now-dominating Hollywood motion picture after the First World War, the same American film moguls naturally fought angrily against all import limitations for films—this time, however, appealing to the inviolability of the free market.

The First World War was also a decisive turnabout for the power relationships within the world of motion pictures. As a result of the war—the loss of lives, the destruction of production facilities and theaters, the economic problems in general, and the monetary shortages in particular—the European film industry would never recover completely, in spite of individual successes. And while Europe experienced its demise, Hollywood not only drove out the European film from the American market through intensive development of production and distribution networks but also prepared for the domination of the foreign markets.

Essential to this strategy was the elimination of the European film from the American market. The conquering of the domestic film market and its horizontal and vertical cartel-like control through its own large companies guaranteed at least the possibility of amortization also of expensive megaproductions in American theaters. In contrast, the point of departure for European producers had dramatically worsened because the U.S. motion picture market had remained closed since the First World War—with the exception of a few "European" films which were financed with American capital and cast with American stars. The intensified presence of Hollywood in Europe especially meant that the respective national film industries abdicated not only decisive portions of past European export markets to U.S. competitors but also important market segments in their own countries.

While the European audience increasingly found pleasure in the expensively made, elaborate films from Hollywood, the ruined European motion picture industry could hardly cover the costs of producing relatively inexpensive and therefore less attractive films for a smaller market. The attempts to create a Continental film market that was to be competitive with its U.S. counterpart—for example, Film Europa, launched by the Germans—did not improve the situation until the introduction of the sound film, and even then brought little effective long-term relief. Even the import quotas for talkies, introduced in the second half of the 1920s, could not fundamentally change the situation because "at best their efforts had a negligible effect; at worst they encouraged American producers to seek power over European production as well as their own."[35] Only the German film industry profited from the quota regulations to some extent, while the other European film nations were only able to reduce their losses. In 1927, the British film industry was "well on the way to extinction." Just how extreme its situation actually was can be seen in the film law of the same year; according to this, only a meager 5 percent of the playing time in British theaters was to be reserved for the British film.[36]

The crisis of the European motion picture industry not only was a consequence of the specific changes in the world film market but was also due to general economic and financial-political developments. The extreme devaluation of the German mark vis-à-vis the U.S. dollar created short-term easing of exports for the German film industry at the beginning of the 1920s. Yet, the stabilization of the European currencies altered this situation decisively. For example, prior to the League of Nations loans for Austria, 90 percent of the imported films came from Germany; immediately after the stabilization of the Austrian currency, however, forty films from Hollywood were purchased for every five German motion pictures. The head of distribution for Paramount analyzed this side effect of stabilization of European currencies quite precisely: "They have this disadvantage in producing, that as money becomes stabilized on the other side their negative costs approach the basis that we are operating on here, but their revenue is limited, compared with ours. If they make a motion picture that costs $150,000, they have only one-fifth of the market in which to get their negative cost back."[37]

The European film industry could counter this economic onslaught only with a different cinema aesthetic—at least in the best cases. Yet, the European film industry could not be restored with a few of its own artistic, high-quality motion pictures, for more and more people in Europe were becoming accustomed to Hollywood's movie grammar. It is especially important to note in this context that U.S. motion pictures were successful not only as a result of American economic dominance. Even the star system, the lavishly created sets, and the action-packed films could not alone explain the far-reaching impact of Hollywood outside of the United States. The U.S. motion picture industry held two further trump cards.

The American movie was diametrically opposed to the European film, which stood in the tradition of an elitist high culture and was therefore often too demanding as a mass media form. At least during the first decades, the U.S. film operated in an open and uninhibited manner, frequently vulgar, yet often biting and accurate, and consciously making fun of the taste of American elites. Until the taming of Hollywood—a result of the influence of the large banks after the introduction of the talkie—U.S. films were therefore still despised and avoided by the tone-setting WASPs just as much as the immigrant slums of the metropoles from where the new mass medium recruited its film moguls, artists, and technicians as well as its audience. "No cultural force as strong as movies had ever established itself so independently of the proprietors of American culture,"[38] and this was one of the most important cultural prerequisites for Hollywood's success not only in the United States but also for its worldwide march to victory.

Yet the American motion picture was not only free from the sales-stifling burden of high culture. It had yet another far-reaching, underestimated advantage. For the U.S. film to succeed in its domestic context, with America's numerous ethnic groups, it had to create a pictorial grammar that could be understood across more than one "national" context. Emily Rosenberg correctly pointed to this important phenomenon in noting, "Created not out of the traditions of elite art but designed to entertain a diverse, multi-ethnic patronage at home, early American films were perfectly suited to a world market."[39]

Only the consideration of all of these factors makes the following statistics understandable. In 1912, most films were French productions. By 1918, however, 85 percent of all films came from the United States; by 1926, U.S. films made up 75 percent and, according to other sources, by 1928, actually reached 90 percent.[40] Between 1915 and 1916 alone, the U.S. film export grew 45 percent. While the European film still dominated the U.S. market until 1914/15, by 1918, fully 98 percent of all films shown in the United States had been produced in domestic studios. In 1925, 95 percent of all film showings in Great Britain and Canada, 80 percent in Latin America, and 70 percent in France were of American origin. In Italy, the portion of U.S. films grew from 30 percent in 1923 to 75 percent by 1930, and in the Netherlands, 85 percent of the films shown were from the United States by 1929. The newsreel market experienced similar tendencies with the dominating Movietone News by 20th Century Fox and Paramount News. In addition, Kodak controlled approximately 75 percent of the world market for negative film.[41]

Still further, Hollywood's dominance was supported also by its leading position in the film distribution sector and the ownership of numerous film theaters. In 1918, all movie houses in the United States were owned by U.S.

firms, and this alone constituted 50 percent of the world's theaters. In 1938, of all theaters worldwide, 40 percent were American, and these belonged for the most part to only a few media companies. This economic potential of the U.S. market, in itself, was enough to secure an unchallenged power position for Hollywood. The horizontal intertwining of the celluloid imperium, however, was more far-reaching than the American borders. Hollywood's film companies not only built up their production and distribution networks after the First World War but also opened or purchased a large number of theaters. By 1925, approximately 1,200 theaters in Australia, Canada, and South Africa were under American control, as were also three-quarters of the best movie houses in France and at least half of the best venues in Great Britain. In total, more than half of the leading theaters in the world were owned by U.S. companies.[42]

It certainly belongs to Hollywood's central legends and achievements to attribute the development of its international position only to the quality of its products, which supposedly won only because of free-market forces and prospered without state subsidies. It is surely difficult to disprove legends, especially when a media imperium like Hollywood, which—quite clearly—continually reproduces such tales in new variations, stands behind them. Nevertheless, the facts speak another language, and the growth of the Hollywood empire can be understood only in the whole context of the foreign economic politics of the United States after the First World War. Within this context, the American motion picture plays a frequently underestimated role. In light of the long-term economic, cultural, and political relevance of its far-reaching impact, it certainly also can be included in the most decisive triumphs of these politics.

Even though the majority of American elites detested the U.S. film—at least at a time when Washington had not yet become an outpost of Hollywood—they did not want to ignore the economic and propagandistic possibilities of this new medium. For this reason, the U.S. government supported measures to open foreign markets for U.S. films in negotiations for bilateral trade treaties and the allocation of monetary credits already in the early 1920s. Thereby, Hollywood's export business as well as its foreign investments were secured. Already by the mid-1920s, Hollywood's film exports reached such significant dimensions that it seemed necessary to formalize its informal support on a legal basis. According to a decision made by the U.S. Congress, a Motion Picture Section was consequently added to Herbert Hoover's Department of Commerce in 1926.[43] This step meant, on the one hand, that Hollywood would be accepted as an increasingly respectable component of culture and therefore would become more and more integrated into the U.S. mainstream. On the other hand, because the U.S. government intervened intensively on behalf of the interests of the motion picture industry through its foreign representatives, thereby giving the interests of U.S. movies an official character, this was equivalent to the quasi-diplomatic acknowledgment of Hollywood.

The economic development of the American film would justify these efforts. Already by 1929, the film industry was one of the most important economic sectors of the United States, third only to the steel and oil industries. The strength of Hollywood's position after the First World War is exemplified by the following statistics: according to estimations, the worldwide film industry amounted to $2.25 billion of invested capital in 1931. Of this sum, $2 billion was American and the remaining $250 million was shared by all other nations together.[44]

The greatest challenge for Hollywood in the 1920s was not foreign competition but the introduction of the sound motion picture. The massive increase in production costs and investments for theater equipment could no longer be carried by the film industry alone. Hollywood would become more and more dependent upon outside capital as well as the electronics companies, such as General Electric and Western Electric, that controlled the patent rights of these new technological developments. While some film moguls were degraded to minor feudal lords of large banks and corporations, the U.S. film industry profited on the whole from the introduction of the talkie. The initial losses of foreign-language markets could be gradually recouped by U.S. productions abroad, stock market shares, and especially through the ever-increasing implementation of dubbing.

It is self-evident that the film industries of smaller states did not stand a chance against the American competitors. For the sound film introduced an almost insurmountable problem: insofar as films were not produced in a world language, the languages spoken by smaller nationalities would automatically become a sales hindrance. Only the German market was successful in competing with Hollywood in the sound film system in Europe.

Analogous to the United States, the character of the German film industry had also changed. The German motion picture industry, in which Dutch interests were represented, was essentially under the control of Siemens & Halske and AEG, the most important sound film patent holders. In order now to participate in the German market controlled by German industry, General Electric bought shares of AEG in 1929, and Warner Bros. took over a fifth of Tobis-Klangfilm in 1930. *Der blaue Engel/The Blue Angel* was produced simultaneously in German and English by UFA and Paramount in 1930 after Adolph Zukor and Marcus Loew had invested $4 million in UFA. Finally, the largest sound motion picture producers in Germany and in the United States actually amalgamated to form an international cartel in the Paris Treaty of July 22, 1930. Here, we are dealing with a true imperialistic segmentation of the world market: German-Dutch interests were to control Germany, Gdansk, the Saarland, the Memel area, Austria, Hungary, Switzerland, Czechoslovakia, Holland, Denmark, Sweden, Norway, Finland, Yugoslavia, Romania, Bulgaria, and Indonesia; while the United States, Canada, Newfoundland, Australia, New Zealand, Singapore, Malaysia, India, and the Soviet Union[!] would be reserved for U.S. firms. The rest of the world, according to a generous clause, would remain open to the patents of both countries.[45]

This cartel did not remain intact for very long, and not only because the Soviet Union would not bow to these demands, consequently developing its own sound motion picture system. The increase of import quotas in Germany and the circumventing of cartel regulations through the Hollywood film companies that did not belong to the General Electric group and were therefore at a disadvantage created inconsistencies within the system as well. For those countries that did not have access to their own sound film system, the cartel's strength simply meant yet another weakening of the domestic film industry. The French industry was again disadvantaged in that it was not only subjected to overpriced payments for the use of sound film projectors but was also required to pay for the rights to show their own films on these machines.[46]

The introduction of the talkie not only had far-reaching economic implications. It can concurrently be understood as part of a political and cultural strategy as well. Hollywood decided to implement this new film technique, which had already been accessible for some time, just at the point when the Soviet films of Sergei Eisenstein and W. I. Pudowkin were about to win over the masses with a new film aesthetic. The continuously praised "talkie revolution," therefore, was actually more of a technological counterrevolution, for the Soviet film could not offer an alternative because of financial and technical hindrances. "Hollywood switched to sound at precisely the same period that Soviet silents captured world-wide attention. Along with the financial and industrial imperatives that made the shift necessary and desirable there may also have been aesthetic imperatives: to recapture the center stage by a technological counterrevolution that reformulated the elements of cinema expression and gave new vitality and validity to the familiar mode of capitalist commercial cinema."[47]

The film export industry thus became a part of a complex strategy in which box office results were no longer the only consideration. More important, it also encompassed the establishment of large electronics companies in foreign markets. The title of an approved dissertation at the University of Bern of 1933 was rather appropriate: "The Development of the Sound Film Industry: A Contribution to Create a World Electro-Monopoly."[48] The main actors—as competitors and as cartel partners—were primarily the U.S. and German firms. Although the economic imperialism of the German film industry was at least as aggressive as that of Hollywood, the U.S. motion picture industry was still able to improve its world position in the 1930s, in spite of some individual losses.[49]

Even in those countries in which the influence of the German film industry was strong, such as in Austria and Holland, Hollywood still maintained a market share between 25 and 55 percent in the 1930s. Until the establishment of National Socialist control, over one-third of the films shown even in Germany originated in the United States, and in fascist Italy, 75 percent of the motion pictures screened were American, even in 1937! Statistically speaking, U.S. films dominated the theaters in most countries in the period from 1918 to 1939 with a market share between 75 and 90 percent.[50] The films from Hollywood, which were consumer products, commercials, and a propaganda medium all rolled into one, demonstrated the new world position of the United States like no other U.S. product—even more so, they were in certain respects its avant-garde. Consequently, already two decades "before Henry Luce's famous *Life* editorial proclaimed the American Century, Hollywood helped lay the groundwork for America's awakening desire to assume the imperial role."[51]

Not even the world economic crisis harmed Hollywood in the long term. Although exports contracted sharply in 1930/31, profitable results were again reached by 1935, comparable to the boom years of 1927/28. Only the beginning of the Second World War brought drastic reductions in foreign markets. U.S. films had already been successively suppressed from the German market since 1933, but from 1939 onward, all markets that had been conquered by the German army were automatically lost. And those nations conquered by Japan would also remain sealed from Hollywood's influence. Exports of the U.S. motion picture industry, therefore, fell to a low point in the period between 1940 and 1942. Yet, by 1943, they quickly rose again to the 1938/39 level.[52]

This rapid recovery is attributable to the fact that Hollywood now concentrated completely on Latin America as a reaction to its losses in important European and Asian markets. Through the significant political and financial support of the Department of State, the U.S. film industry was able to expand its position massively in Central and South America to such a degree that the U.S. share of the market was just under 100 percent in many countries.[53] Although this market drive occurred under the seal of antifascism and anti-Communism, German and Italian films in Latin America were not the only ones to be ousted. Included in the same mopping up process were also films by the Allied competition from Great Britain and France.

Hollywood's war activities were by no means limited to the expansion into new markets. It also actively participated in the recapturing of lost ones. Already during the First World War, the U.S. film industry fulfilled its patriotic duty by supporting the Committee on Public Information, and thereby it laid an important foundation for future expansion. Since that time, Hollywood had become a respectable and exceptionally influential foreign and domestic power factor with whose "war service" the U.S. government could not dispense. Washington and Hollywood were thus in certain respects "natural" allies because both were dependent upon one another. While the U.S. government, on the one hand, desperately required the propaganda force of Hollywood—both abroad and nationally—the American motion picture industry, on the other hand, certainly depended again upon the strong arm of Washington to conquer and secure foreign markets. This perfectly reciprocal constellation of interests led to extremely intensive cooperation, lasting well beyond the end of the war. In the fight against fascism, as later in the war against Communism, all means were needed, and the Hollywood products were an important weapon in the arsenal of the United States. The director of the International Motion Pictures Division of the State Department therefore correctly asserted that "during the war 'millimeter' referred not only to the size of guns, but also to the gauge of a new weapon—the motion picture."[54]

The war became one of the most significant subjects of the U.S. motion picture industry. Immediately after the Japanese attack on Pearl Harbor, the studios plunged to a "new" theme: in the period between 1942 and 1945 approximately 500 war films were made, out of a total production of 1,700 movies. These were not meant only for the civilian audiences in the United States and in the Allied countries but were also produced for the U.S. Army. Already in 1943, over 630,000 GIs could see at least one Hollywood movie *daily*. And until the end of the war, the War Activities Committee, which organized and coordinated all activities of the U.S. film industry, put 43,306 reels at the disposal of the U.S. Army free of charge.[55] In addition, training films played an increasingly important role in the education of soldiers and workers in the military industries, and in this area as well, Hollywood made an important contribution. The Hollywood Canteen, under the direction of Bette Davis, became one of the most important entertainment centers for U.S. troops in the United States. Still further, the Hollywood Victory Committee made available 3,805 artists for a total of 45,468 performances at 7,633 events for GIs in all war locations. The Hollywood Motion Picture War Finance Committee sold war bonds valued at over $838 million already in 1942, in other words, more than one-sixth of all bonds sold during that year. The members of the American film industry alone bought $94 million war bonds until 1945 and collected $1,970,672 for war invalids and orphans through the Permanent Charities Committee.[56]

Hollywood's support for U.S. war efforts by far exceeded what was visible on the silver screen. The war contribution of the new weapon—with its 16mm and 35mm calibers—was not limited to the production and selection of patriotic entertainment and training films to strengthen the morale of the troops and to demonstrate the necessity and purpose of the United States' participation in the war, for troop entertainment, for the sale of war bonds, and for the organization of charity collections. The cooperation between Washington and Hollywood's War Activities Committee resulting from international conflicts was so intensive that there were hardly any more important government departments and agencies in which the film industry was not represented. Hollywood's access thus reached not only to institutionalized relationships in all government offices but even to the White House. The official recognition of Hollywood in this common fight was also visually apparent. The U.S. government allowed approximately 4,000 members of the U.S. film industry—including directors and actors, studio bosses and sales managers—to wear military uniforms (predominantly officers uniforms at that!). This number by no means included those Hollywood artists who either had been drafted or enlisted and who served as active soldiers. The specially created officers, who could enjoy their ranks as a sign of masculinity, mostly were those Hollywood civilians who could enjoy the privilege of fighting the war only on a movie set.[57]

Clearly the most important U.S. government agency for Hollywood's plans to reconquer the European and Asian film market was the Bureau of Motion Pictures of the OWI, founded in 1942. Information experts of the government and Hollywood managers coordinated all film propaganda activities for the national and international markets; here, the export offensive of the American motion picture industry, which trailed right behind the victorious troops, was mutually planned and carried through. In return for the government's support, Hollywood agreed to a new Film Export Code at the end of 1942, which allowed the Office of Censorship to ban the export of all films that were critical of certain less favorable circumstances in the United States. The films that were particularly affected were those that dealt with racial or labor conflicts. Films discussing war rationing measures were confronted with the export ban as well. Wild West and crime films could be exported only when law and order were victorious and when the bad guy finally got what he deserved.[58] Because censorship measures could conceivably hinder each and every film, they exerted an influence upon the decision about which films should actually be produced in the future.

Hollywood films stood at the top of the priority list for the Department of State with respect to their propaganda possibilities for the time following the war. However, it required the film industry in turn to take the general interests of the United States into consideration. "Especially in the post-war period, the Department desires to cooperate fully in the protection of American motion picture interests abroad," read the instructions for U.S. missions abroad. "It expects in return that the industry will cooperate whole-heartedly with the government with a view to insuring that the pictures distributed abroad will reflect credit on the good name and reputation of this country and its institutions."[59]

The owners and managers of the motion picture industry more than warmly welcomed government support. They knew only too well, as the magazine *Film Daily* wrote only a day before the end of the war, that Hollywood would not be able to assert itself without the intervention of the U.S. government with regard to expected import limitations abroad. But it was not only Hollywood that required the support of the government; Washington also needed the aid of the film industry. And its leaders were self-confident enough to demand state support for film exports, which they regarded as a hereditary right. The *Film Daily* correctly pointed out on May 7, 1945, that "managers of foreign, or international, departments believe they have a right to expect aid of the Government on the sale of American pictures in foreign countries. The American picture, they point out, sells not only entertainment but a way of life. It has been called the greatest salesman of American goods. For these reasons, the Government has a direct stake in maintaining foreign markets."[60]

This completely justified estimation of the identity of interests at stake was supported by the interwar experience but especially also by Hollywood's role during the war, and in particular within the framework of its activities in the Bureau of Motion Pictures. Since 1943, this government agency, with several dozen carefully chosen films dubbed in numerous languages, made it possible for Hollywood once again to regain sure footing abroad by allowing films to be shown in the theaters behind the lines of the victorious U.S. troops: first in North Africa, then in Italy and France, and later in all liberated areas.[61] Hollywood's productions therefore clearly maintained a special position. *Variety* commented already on September 9, 1943, that "the motion picture industry is the only commercial setup that has been permitted to operate in the North African and European war zones."[62] This privileged starting point finally made it possible for Hollywood, whose invasion plans for foreign markets were just as intensely calculated as the military landing operations of the Allies, to develop indispensable bridgeheads for the film business of the postwar era. In the view of the American motion picture industry, the Allied invasion of the coast of Normandy, which had the code name Operation Overlord, certainly had the character of an Operation Celluloid.[63]

It can therefore hardly be surprising that the *Film Daily* again noted, only two days after the war in Europe had ended, exactly just what the victory of the Allies meant for Hollywood, namely, "Opening Europe to Film Company Rep[resentative]s."[64] Actually, the first official invitation extended by the U.S. Army to American businessmen in an effort to sound out the recaptured market in June 1945 was to the representatives of the film industry, including Jack Warner. This invitation was made by no one less than General Dwight D. Eisenhower.[65]

The condition of the recaptured market presented itself in an ambivalent light. On the one hand, no import restrictions were expected at least in the areas occupied by the United States, and this was of significant importance especially with respect to the German film industry. On the other hand, the destruction of the national economies in most European countries, in particular dollar shortages, would hardly allow any solution other than the introduction of import quotas in order to let these economies get back on their feet.

But securing the export markets had become an extreme priority for Hollywood after 1945. The profitability of most films now could be guaranteed only by box office receipts from foreign markets because of the doubling of the production costs and the gradual decline of profits in the United States in the late 1940s. Because the interwar experience had shown that competition only weakened the position of individual U.S. film firms and reduced export profits, the leading film companies chose to form a cartel in August 1945. The Motion Picture Export Association (MPEA) represented the interests of the firms Allied Artists, Columbia Pictures, Metro-Goldwyn-Mayer, Paramount Pictures, RKO Pictures, 20th Century Fox, United Artists, Universal International, and Warner Bros., and it controlled more than 90 percent of the entire U.S. film export market.

The individual European film industries were powerless against the united front of this concentrated film power, which still enjoyed the energetic support of the Department of State. In addition, the protectionist measures of the European governments could not hold their ground against the Hollywood phalanx and Washington.[66] These nations were too greatly dependent upon U.S. economic and financial aid in 1945 to risk this desperately needed support for reconstruction as a consequence of protective measures for local film industries. The instrument of pressure—the denial of credit—proved to be exceptionally effective: either the U.S. negotiators were immediately successful in hindering the implementation of effective quotas, or existing quotas would be rescinded by the completion of finance, economic, and trade treaties at the latest.

Hence, under the pressure of the U.S. embassy in Rome, the Italian government was forced to withdraw all plans for the reintroduction of import quotas for American films. The importance that U.S. diplomacy attributed to Hollywood's interests can be highlighted by the following detail. Although accredited only on January 8, 1945, the new U.S. ambassador to Italy, Alexander Kirk, began his interventions in matters involving U.S. films as early as January 10, and these efforts would soon bear fruit. For U.S. diplomacy operated against more than simply all plans for the union, consolidation, and nationalization of the divided Italian film industry. Its influence extended above and beyond this. The government in Rome saw itself confronted with a situation in which all draft legislation relevant to the film industry had to be presented secretly to the U.S. embassy as well as to representatives of the MPEA *even prior to* parliamentary debate. This preliminary access to information and the resulting influence forced upon the Italian film legislation is interesting well beyond the question of Italy's sovereignty *after* the peace treaty. As a result, the American motion picture industry achieved a clear competitive advantage over all other (Allied) film-exporting nations as well. Hollywood thus enjoyed a special position in Italy. The U.S. embassy in Rome benignly reported on November 27, 1948, that this privilege "is [a] favor not conceded to other foreign interests."[67]

The developments in the other Allied film markets were hardly any different from those in the former enemy nation Italy. In liberated France, measures reserving 55 percent of all performance days for French films were again enacted. Yet, this action met with the strongest opposition from Hollywood, and the U.S. embassy in Paris therefore continuously intervened against such statutes since the beginning of 1945. The following telegram distinctly shows that we are dealing not only with Hollywood's interests but with those of Washington as well. "Aside from the purely commercial considerations involved, the Embassy is convinced of the importance of American films as one of the most effective media for the dissemination of information regarding the United States, and it is logical to assume that barriers may be raised in foreign countries designed to restrict their free distribution. It is also aware of the possible influence in other European countries of trends and developments in France tending to restrict or discriminate against American made films."[68]

Although the French government initially refused to rescind import restrictions, it would soon come to understand its limitations. This moment occurred as the French government had to approach Washington with a request for urgently needed economic aid at the end of 1945. Negotiators left no doubt that U.S. support could be expected only if trade restrictions were dismantled, which naturally included the elimination of film quotas. The completion of the Blum-Byrnes Treaty of May 28, 1946, then, also meant the reduction of days reserved for performance days of French films from 55 to 30 percent. The result was a 50 percent decline in French film production within one year alone.[69]

Great Britain, too, stood on the verge of economic ruin in 1945. The immense war costs could be financed only through the sale of a large amount of foreign assets and through loans from the United States. Still further, the British government lost economic leverage as a result of surrendering the pound sterling as a leading currency in the former empire. This relinquishment was, by the way, not a voluntary action. One of the requirements made by the U.S. government during the negotiations for the first postwar loans and the subsequent strengthening of the dollar vis-à-vis the pound brought the Labour government of Clement Attlee into extreme balance-of-payments difficulties. The British finance minister, Stafford Cripps, and the president of the Board of Trade, Harold Wilson, reacted with an austerity program, which allowed the expenditure of foreign currencies only for vital products.

Hollywood films, according to the interpretation of the Labour government, certainly did not belong to this category. Because such films had caused the loss of over $50 million in one year alone, Sir Stafford decreed an import tax upon 75 percent of all new U.S. films in August 1947. This *second battle for England*, as Prime Minister Attlee labeled it on August 6, 1947, would, however, not be victorious. The Washington-Hollywood axis functioned effectively, even with respect to Whitehall. The austerity measures levied against Hollywood would actually prove to be especially counterproductive. The British government saw itself confronted not only with continual interventions from the Department of State but also with an export boycott from the U.S. motion picture industry. And this boycott would show just who the actual leader of the British film market was. On the one hand, the position of Hollywood's distribution firms was strong enough to flood the market with old films, which were exempt from the new import tax. On the other hand, the British audience was already so used to Hollywood films that, if they had to make a choice, they would certainly decide in favor of American heroes over the government in London. Hollywood's power thus could not be broken. "The exhibitor's eagerness pointed to the essentially colonial nature of American control of the British film industry and the British film audience—both had conspired against the dictates of their own government. National economic policy might require that precious dollars go to pay for necessities, but ultimately it was found that so far as the rank and file of the British cinema audience was concerned, American films were a necessity."[70]

The Attlee government consequently had to concede defeat in March 1948, and Hollywood's stipulations virtually meant the capitulation of the British film industry. The compromise that was reached—to end the import tax, to transfer currency in the amount of $17 million to the United States, and to facilitate investment possibilities for the remaining U.S. film profits in the British film industry—ultimately sealed the dependence of British film production. As a result of the Second World War, not only did Great Britain become the junior partner of the United States, but the British government also had to deal with a new contracting partner in California. The true power relationship is shown most clearly in the preamble of the following treaty: "Memorandum of Agreement Between His Majesty's Government in the United Kingdom of Great Britain and Northern Ireland and the Motion Picture Industry of the United States dated 1st October 1950."[71]

Hollywood's power was so far-reaching that it was not only in a position to dictate conditions to the governments of *other* nations. The example of the film politics in occupied Germany—where extreme conflicts of interest between U.S. authorities and the American motion picture industry existed—demonstrates that Hollywood was also effective in asserting itself against the expectations of *its own* government. In dealing with the question of the future of the German film industry, Washington's and Hollywood's plans were diametrically opposed. Although the U.S. Army practiced complete control over the movie industry in its zone during the first years of occupation, the character of these measures was fundamentally limited in time. The reintroduction of a democratically oriented German film industry was thoroughly in the interest of Washington's goals. In contrast, Hollywood was expecting much more from the Allies' victory, namely, the total elimination of an economically strong competitor in Europe. Therefore, prestigious exponents of the American film, such as the studio boss of 20th Century Fox, Darryl F. Zanuck, pressured the U.S. government already during the Second World War to ensure that the German film industry would be completely dissolved and banned for an undefined period. Furthermore, all future film activities were to be reserved only for the film companies of the Allies, especially those of the United States. Just what the responsible Germany-planners in Washington thought about the wishes of Hollywood is made clear in the report of the future high commissioner John J. McCloy to the special adviser to President Roosevelt, Harry Hopkins, on January 8, 1944: "I do not see why they should not have their own movies if they want to make them, as well as their own theaters and their own books. The logical outcome of this almost amounts to continuous Allied control of all their industry and culture and I think that approaches nonsense."[72]

The refusal of Hollywood's maximum demands by no means meant that now the U.S. Army would completely deny the solicitations of American film interests in Germany—as long as these coincided with the greater goals of the occupations politics. For this reason, the Information Services Division (ISD) laid the foundation for the reconstruction of the U.S. distribution network and thereby assisted Hollywood against British and French competition.[73] However, this aid was not far-reaching enough for Hollywood—and not only because of its rejection of the difficult screening process involved in selecting politically sound films for Germany. Because the U.S. government had decided to strengthen all anti-Communist forces and therefore proposed to take all possible steps against a further destabilization of the German economy, Hollywood too was to bow to these occupation policy decisions. For the American film industry, this would have meant a preliminary abandonment of immediate profit transfers because the earnings from box office sales would be managed by the U.S. Army in a blocked account trust. Because vehement opposition toward these measures bore no results, the film companies attempted to receive permission at least to utilize the frozen assets to purchase German theaters. This, too, was not permitted. Such an exception, according to an economic adviser in the State Department, would mean nothing other than "economic imperialism under the guise of wishing to assist in the reeducation of Germany."[74]

As a consequence of the failure of this effort, the American motion picture industry decided upon a drastic step. Because Hollywood thought itself cheated of acquiring immediate access to its profits through U.S. occupation politics, they now subjected Washington to painful pressure: they quite simply held back the films intended for Germany. This blackmailing of its own government ultimately proved successful. Washington was much more dependent upon the propaganda impact of American films in the German west zone than Hollywood was on the profits from the German film market. Hence, already in February 1948, the duties of the ISD were relinquished to the MPEA.

Although not all demands of the U.S. film industry could be fulfilled by 1948, Hollywood nevertheless was granted yet another concession—in the framework of the Marshall Plan. The Informational Media Guaranty (IMG) Program, which was formed within the context of the ECA, was to assist in breaking down the export boycott of Hollywood through the creation of an economic incentive. Consequently, the IMG Program saw to it that U.S. companies would be compensated for at least the distribution, copy, and raw material costs of all films exported to Germany—and this in dollars from Marshall Plan funds. However, Hollywood was not yet completely satisfied with this solution. Therefore, the MPEA announced that it would discontinue fully the export of films to Japan and Germany by mid-1949, and this continual pressure was soon to bear fruits. For the U.S. government, "virtually faced with a situation of 'either . . . or . . . ,'"[75] saw itself forced to revamp the ECA law. This brought a decisive improvement for Hollywood in 1949. Now the U.S. motion picture industry not only would be compensated for the costs accrued in the export of films but in addition was guaranteed the amount of approximately $25,000 of Marshall Plan funds for each film exported under the IMG Program. Washington's only requirement for this subsidizing of Hollywood was a consultation right in the selection of exported films, because the money should only be given to those films that "reflected the best elements of American life."[76]

The U.S. film industry was certainly not idle. Although Hollywood exported only 170 films to Germany between 1945 and the end of 1949, this number jumped to 278 films shown in the German movie houses between January 1950 and March 1951 alone. The financial incentive of the IMG Program should not be underestimated. Already by 1955, the IMG payments for exports to West Germany alone amounted to $5.1 million. In total, Hollywood received $16 million from this program until 1966.[77]

Although this measure may not represent the complete compensation for the direct takeover of the (West) German film industry, it created the best possible prerequisites for the recapturing of its film market. The roundabout way of the IMG Program nevertheless still brought the American film industry a few steps closer to its original plans. The economic effect of Hollywood's privileges were, as Albert Norman stated in 1951, that "the industry's conditions did not fall short of virtual ownership of the studios and control of the film market in Germany."[78] And Henry Pilgert's assertion with regard to the newsreel market surely pertains to the entire film industry in West Germany: "The German producers were thus clearly not able to compete and secure their share of the business."[79]

No other example makes the power of Hollywood as apparent as the change in the official film policies of the United States toward the Western occupation zones in Germany and later in the Federal Republic. In light of the developments outlined here, it can hardly be surprising that the MPEA with the aid of the State Department stifled all efforts to erect import quotas in the FRG. "Discussion in Washington between MPEA representatives and the State Department resulted in an order to the U.S. High Commissioner in Germany that the Department wanted no quota on importation of American films. An official German quota never materialized."[80] Such was the laconic assessment.

The official support of Hollywood through the government of the United States was more than a symbol of the amalgamation of politics, economy, and culture during the Cold War. This cooperation also changed the significance of the film (as a symbol) itself. By acknowledging its function as the most important foreign propaganda medium, Hollywood's products were assigned the official duty of enlightening the world about the advantages of the American way of life as a continuously entertaining video sound track of U.S. politics. Politics thus were turned not only into film but into the symbol of politics as well. Thomas H. Guback correctly pointed out in connection with the IMG Program that it "implicitly . . . expanded the number of markets which could be exploited by the American industry, and put an 'official' label on Hollywood's work. American film could then go forward with the rank of ambassador. . . . The stimulus to release came from the availability of dollars, and the availability of dollars stemmed from a need for propaganda."[81]

There is no question that both parties profited from the close symbiosis of U.S. politics and U.S. film. Washington did not unconditionally surrender to Hollywood, for the U.S. government had a filter through the Advisory Committee on Motion Picture Guarantees, which fulfilled a double function. Because the sought-after export subsidies were issued only for those films that depicted America in the best possible light (Group I—suitable), more than just an intensification of a positive propaganda effect was achieved.[82] At the same time, export restrictions applied to those films that expressed predominantly negative judgments of the United States (Group II—not advisable; Group III—unsuitable). This category was not limited only to socially critical films. Export restrictions were levied also against movies that portrayed the United States as the nation of organized crime and depraved decadence. Even those films of poor and cheap quality that could be ridiculed abroad were now, as was the case during the war, barred as well. Such controls in turn had a direct influence upon film production. Because only actual foreign business guaranteed the large profits, the U.S. motion picture industry initially had to conform its production to export guidelines.

Hollywood's self-censorship was beneficial in another way as well. Already in the first postwar years, the Department of State instructed its embassies to report on the patrons' reactions and attitudes toward U.S. films.[83] This information was consequently passed on to Hollywood, which enabled the film industry to improve its export chances. On the one hand, it was now better equipped to adapt to the positive expectations and tastes of foreign audiences. On the other hand, this information made it possible to avoid film subject matter or individual sequences that were seen as particularly insulting or degrading. By the beginning of the 1950s, the USIA took over this audience-service function for Hollywood. The USIA—with its more than 200 film libraries worldwide and with its 500-million-strong audience annually, making it the largest *governmental* film propaganda organization—collected and transmitted all information concerning local occurrences, morals and traditions, national prejudices and cultural values. This knowledge was beneficial to film producers with respect to their impact in the respective countries. It was clear that this merging of politics and film had nothing to do with propaganda or even censorship, in both parties' self-estimation; "this is not censorship but rather a healthy cooperation between government and the film industry that results in products more acceptable to overseas audiences."[84]

Yet another consequence of this cooperation is worth noting. Because the most positive presentation of the United States was no longer enough, the film industry was now obligated to serve a further purpose. While the inquisitors of the HUAC concentrated upon the political cleansing of Hollywood, the U.S. film producers received yet another signal from Washington. (These HUAC show trials diverted attention from what could have been a relevant inquisition of the cartel-like ownership structures of the U.S. motion picture industry.) This meant in clear context "that the rifle the film industry had shouldered in World War II could not be put down; it had to keep marching to the drums of another martial conflict—the Cold War with international and domestic communism."[85]

The film studios reacted quickly. Between 1948 and 1952 alone, forty-eight Cold War movies were produced in which the fight against Communism was the direct theme. In the period between 1948 and 1962, the total of these films amounted to 107.[86] Only one month after February 9, 1950, in which Senator McCarthy announced that supposedly 257 Communists were undermining the Department of State, Elizabeth Taylor was married to the Communist Robert Taylor in the film *Conspirators*. Personifying American innocence, Elizabeth's first doubts toward the integrity of her husband occurred when he refused to help an injured rabbit. A further, tragic discovery, however, finally led to the happy ending, for "the discovery of a letter requesting a meeting with a party superior finally brings into focus her husband's insidious views and his unpatriotic attitude towards rabbits. It all connects and she no longer loves him."[87]

Gregory Peck, in contrast, immediately recognized in the film *Night People* (1954) just what the Communists were really up to: "These are cannibals, Mr. Leatherby . . . head-hunting, blood-thirsty cannibals to eat us up."[88] And only a year later, Jack Palance, as a disillusioned liberal author in *The Big Knife*, proved that—better late than never—the once politically confused could also learn a thing or two. "You used to believe in the New Deal, or the Fair Deal, or some deal. What do you believe in now?" This was the decisive question. But Jack did not want to hear anything more about this blatantly un-American deal: "I believe in . . . rare roast beef and good scripts."[89]

In an epoch in which even the New Deal and the Fair Deal of Presidents Roosevelt and Truman could be denounced as a part of the undermining strategy of the "Communist world conspiracy," especially the intellectuals had to be stopped (*I Married a Communist*, 1949). One also had to be cautious when meeting strangers on a train (*Strangers on a Train*, 1951). The Communist underminers would not even stop at the holiest of all institutions, the family (*My Son John*, 1952). Although the FBI tried everything it could, legally and illegally (*I Was a Communist for the FBI*, 1952), only by summoning all its forces could it keep the icy hand of the world revolution from taking over the United States through Communist Eskimos (*Red Snow*, 1952). Even in Hawaii the Communist threat was impending, and even John Wayne had to be pulled out of the Wild West (*Big Jim McLain*, 1952). Although the fight had taken on interplanetary dimensions (*Red Planet Mars*, 1952), Hollywood continuously and urgently demonstrated the superiority of capitalism. How else could the capitalist seducers win over the iron Russian Katherine Hepburn in *The Iron Petticoat* (1956) than with expensive gifts ranging from negligés to champagne? *Especially* when the U.S. daredevil was named Bob Hope? Cyd Charisse would be convinced by similar means one year later in *Silk Stockings* to run over to the right side—the heartthrob this time at least was Fred Astair.[90]

On television the Cold War also was fought in the series *Crusade in Europe* (1949), *Crusade in the Pacific* (1951), *Victory at Sea* (1952), *The Big Picture* (1951–72), *I Led Three Lives* (1953), and *Pentagon, U.S.A.* (1953). In *Biff Baker, U.S.A.* (1952–53) the protagonist, a U.S. businessman abroad, demonstrated that a little spying was a thoroughly acceptable patriotic duty. Why even bother about such little things as national sovereignty when every successful adventure brought the anti-Communist crusade just one step closer to victory? As Mr. Baker, in the course of an episode during an Austrian vacation, discovers a secret Communist radio station that disrupted the broadcasts of the Voice of America, it certainly became apparent that the true anti-Communist never had time to relax. *Biff Baker, U.S.A.* came to the aid of Austria. He destroyed the transmitter—"in the name of all people who seek freedom behind the Iron Curtain."[91]

With these productions, Hollywood would again and again deviate from the path of subtle convincing. Yet, Communism seemed to be a threat everywhere, and "for the matters of anti-communist Cold War films of the late 1940s and 1950s persuasion was too mild. In films like *The Woman on Pier 13* they figuratively hit audiences over the head with a hammer and a sickle."[92]

The anti-Communist paranoia was so strong that even the children's animated film *Ferdinand the Bull*—in which the flower-loving cartoon bull, Ferdinand, refuses to battle the matador—could be denounced as a defenseless, pacifist, left-wing propaganda tool.[93] The message of the cartoon *Red Fox*, produced by the USIA, in which a strikingly red fox terrorizes a chicken coop, had, in contrast, nothing to do with the indoctrination of children, even when the USIA happily noted that "the audience gets the point."[94]

In this context, the films that quite openly propagated the Cold War position of the U.S. government are not the only ones of significance. These blatant political movies actually may have been even less efficient than many other films that, supposedly independent of the Cold War theme, still indirectly propagated the American way of life at every fitting (or unfitting) opportunity. For example, John Steinbeck's original script of *Viva Zapata* (1953) clearly highlighted the necessity of social change in Mexico. Yet, the text could not pass Hollywood's censors without decisive alterations. In the final product, Marlon Brando's Zapata was therefore mutated to an unbelievable liberal democrat, who now had to battle the left-wing villain Fernando.[95]

Other, less-studied film genres also reflect the heated climate of anti-Communist hysteria, especially science fiction and monster films. *Invasion of the Body Snatchers* by no means warned only of the attack from another planet, and in the wonderfully unsuccessful production *The Return of the Killer Tomatoes* the color red itself gave its viewers the actual terrestrial origin of only seemingly foreign cannibals.[96] The thesis that science fiction and monster films well represented the Zeitgeist of the United States certainly has a true basis.

Even the noticeable boom in *the* genre of the U.S. film—the putatively completely unpolitical Western—very obviously reflects the political tendencies of the Cold War. The Western not only showed the victory of the brave, capitalistic individual over the dark forces of (mass) bandits—and the red man. It also offered Hollywood the excellent opportunity to free itself from the accusations of the HUAC. Not without reason did Kyle Chrichton in his review of *Red River* in 1948 point precisely to the following connection: "When things get tough in Hollywood they start the horses galloping. . . . Nobody can yell 'propaganda' at a motion picture full of cows, horses, gun play, brave women and daring men."[97]

The difference in the essential message between the supposedly left-wing Western, like *High Noon* (1952), with its contempt for conformity of the citizens of Hadleyville, and a supposedly right-wing production like *Rio Bravo* (1959) was hardly distinguishable. Hence, at the decisive moment when Gary Cooper is left high and dry by the citizens of Hadleyville in his lonely showdown with the Miller brothers at 12:00 noon, his wife, Grace Kelly, finally fulfills her patriotic duty. Although the members of the Quakers are actually committed to peacefulness, she can overcome the weakness of pacifism at the last moment—and supports her husband, as it should be, with weapon in hand against the lawless intruders.

*High Noon* was not only played in Hadleyville. It became *High Noon* also for the European film industry, and individual countries had less success in the invasion from Hollywood than Cooper and Kelly did against the Miller brothers. The U.S. film industry did, however, have access to the most effective gun: its most important weapon was the MPEA. It is certainly part and parcel of the curiosities of postwar economic history that precisely those companies came together in an exceptionally important cartel that were among the loudest missionaries of the free market.

"If one were to write the history of economic imperialism, then American film production would be one of the most interesting chapters."[98] This sentence by Rudolf Oertel describes the role of the MPEA quite precisely. And the way in which the export profits were balanced between the individual member companies constitutes the most interesting chapter in this classic cartel construction. The division of box office results from all foreign markets was done in a manner in which all members of the MPEA profited, regardless of the success or failure of their own productions. The MPEA not only transferred foreign profits for individual films; it centrally collected, more important, all foreign profits. The individual member companies were given exactly those shares of all profits that corresponded with their gross portion *of the U.S. market*.[99]

This decreased the distribution costs and production risks considerably because now each individual cartel member, in any event, participated in foreign profits, even if none of its own films had profited abroad. In addition, all partners profited from the situation whereby the cartel owned a pool of more than 2,000 films from productions since 1940. Because the nine largest film producers in the world avoided competition with one another, all information on the individual film markets came together through the MPEA. Such precise knowledge of the market, in turn, made possible the best selection of the most promising film successes. Therefore, it was also feasible to take into consideration the regional and timely placement of the most expensive productions of the individual member firms and thus avoid competing with each other. This, too, created a considerable increase in profits.[100]

The methods of this export offensive notably contradicted the slogan that Hollywood declared as its motto—"Freedom of world markets, freedom of communication." The degree to which the politics of the MPEA attempted to achieve market dominance abroad can also be detected in terminology. At the MPEA central headquarters, which not without reason was called "the little Department of State," one did not speak of the individual foreign markets or even sovereign states but of MPEA *territories*, a term that certainly reflects actual power relationships. The territories in which the MPEA had exclusive distribution rights included Austria, Hungary, Germany, Bulgaria, Czechoslovakia, the Netherlands, Poland, Romania, Yugoslavia, the Soviet Union, Korea, Japan, and Indonesia. But also in those states in which the export monopoly of the MPEA did not come to complete fruition, the cartel could increase its dominating position after 1945. The figures for the year 1951 are impressive.

In all of (Western) Europe, 61 percent of the movie days of all running films were U.S. films; 85 percent in Ireland, 80 percent in Malta, 75 percent in Belgium, Denmark, Gibraltar, and Luxembourg, 70 percent in Great Britain, Greece, Finland, Turkey, and the Netherlands, 65 percent in Italy and Portugal, 63 percent in Norway, 60 percent in Sweden, 50 percent in France and Switzerland, and even 40 percent in Yugoslavia. In Africa, the MPEA controlled approximately 50 percent of the films in Ethiopia and over 70 percent in Mozambique and South Africa. In all of South America, 65 percent were MPEA films; 75 percent in Ecuador, 70 percent in Brazil and Chile, 65 percent in Bolivia and Venezuela. In Mexico and Middle America, the MPEA films amounted to 76 percent, in the Caribbean 80 percent. In the entire South Pacific, the MPEA's market shares were 65 percent, and in the most important markets, Australia and New Zealand, 75 and 80 percent, respectively. In the Middle East the MPEA distributed 57 percent (80 in Iran, 70 in Israel, 60 in Syria and Iraq), and in the Middle and Far East, 48 percent (90 in Thailand, 85 in Indonesia, 75 in Burma, 70 in the Philippines, 40 in India and Indochina). The only exceptions to this worldwide film empire were the Communist states, whose curtains, with only a few exceptions, were closed to MPEA films in an ironlike fashion. The "development of Socialism in one country" actually meant the loss of a territory for the MPEA. And these losses were rather important. For example, the MPEA had still distributed approximately 50 percent of all films to Hungary and China in the first postwar years.[101]

Already in 1947, approximately 235 million people saw films from Hollywood weekly: 90 million in the United States, and 145 million abroad. And the latter would become increasingly important in the 1950s because the box office profits in American theaters tended to decline as a result of the introduction of television. Still, this meant no real losses but actually resulted only in a shift in the entertainment sector. One the one hand, the U.S. film industry entered the TV business; on the other hand, to fill program times, television resorted to Hollywood productions. This development would also repeat itself in the victory march of television in Western Europe in the mid-1950s. Although the film market declined here, the MPEA could do more than simply hold on to its market shares in smaller markets. The television also gave Hollywood the chance once again to utilize even the oldest films.

The leading position of the MPEA again remained unchallenged. A 1979 report of the European Council stated: "One of the main obstacles to the free circulation of films stems from the dominant position of a few companies. For example, the American firms which are members of the MPEA are in a position to apply certain pressures. The cold calculations of commercial profit and the play of world economics are thus a constant threat to European cultural identity."[102] The development of foreign film profits immediately following the Second World War was of decisive significance for securing and further augmenting the international dominance of the U.S. film industry. In the best export year of the interwar period, 1937, Hollywood earned only 40 percent of its profits abroad. By 1958, this figure had grown to 50 percent. A comparison of all data from the time of the outbreak of the Second World War to the end of the 1950s clearly shows how the relationship between domestic and foreign profits developed. In 1939, as the beginning of the war decreased the opportunities abroad, 65 percent of their profits were made on the U.S. market; by 1959, it was only 50 percent. The profit share from foreign markets grew proportionally, from 35 to 50 percent. And in 1987, worldwide 79 percent of all film and television exports were produced in the United States![103]

Even though the sun might have set on the British Empire, it certainly was continuously shining in the world empire of Hollywood. Operation Celluloid was a complete success.

## The Austrian Film Market

Similar to its activities in many other European countries, Hollywood was successful in establishing itself as the strongest film power in Austria after the First World War. Nevertheless, its position did not remain unchallenged. As a result of the introduction of the sound film, the dominance of U.S. movies was threatened by the German competition. The talkie not only posed language problems but also resulted in a monopoly-like control of the Austrian film market by German-screening patents. The aggressive film politics of the "Third Reich" and the anxious obedience of Austrian film managers and politicians finally led to the fact that the German film relegated Hollywood products to second place even before the Anschluss.

In Austria we are dealing not only with one "film imperialism" but with two, which makes the analysis of the cultural implications of this phenomenon especially complex. Furthermore, this situation is by no means a result only of the struggle for power and of the assertiveness of the U.S. and German film industries. Initially, it also was a consequence of the economic, cultural, and political circumstances within Austria.

By the time of the introduction of the sound film at the latest, the size of the Austrian market made it difficult to produce films without thinking of the German market. Only between 10 and 15 percent of the production costs, at best, could be recovered in Austria, while the German market brought in 80 percent. Therefore, Austrian films were dependent not only upon German patents and German capital but also upon German taste. An Austrian film could, as a result, cover the cost of production only if it could be exported to Germany. The degree to which the Austrian film industry was economically extorted by Germany is clearly shown by the situation in the 1930s. If the economic consequences of this dependency alone were repressive enough, the cultural and film-political implications were even more difficult. As a consequence, the development of an independent Austrian film culture was impossible.

Certainly, the conditions in Austria never had been particularly favorable, especially because the majority of the ruling "elites," in contrast to those in France and Italy, found film to be barbarian and lacking culture. Hence, their ignorance torpedoed individual artistic developments. From the beginning, film in Austria was something foreign, exotic—even un-Austrian. Until 1907, only foreign directors and producers worked in Austria, and until 1911 Emperor Francis Joseph allowed himself to be filmed only by foreign firms. It may be only a curious note, but the founder of the Sascha-Filmfabrik, the most important producer in Austria, was Baron Alexander Joseph Sascha Kolowrat-Krakowski, who was born in the United States in 1886. The reputation that the Austrian film industry maintained may also be assessed by the fact that cinematographers were categorized under the vagabond laws.[104]

In connection with an extreme dependence in production on export possibilities to Germany, these negative conditions allow the question to be asked whether an Austrian film industry had any chance at all even to exist under such circumstances. Georg Schmid correctly pointed to this often-ignored problem of cultural identity in the supposed Austrian film: "Austrian film production is unthinkable without the German market; it is unimaginable without constantly reminding oneself of this condition. Thereby, all artistic codes are set in such a way that they have to justify this situation; the Austrian film will therefore remain foreign to itself, foreign in its own country."[105] The underdevelopment of Austrian film culture, the dependence of the very existence of the Austrian film upon the German market, and Hollywood's dominating position in film distribution—these three intertwining components are the key to understanding film in Austria. Each analysis of the Austrian motion picture must therefore result in the conclusion that the term "Filmland Austria" is only a euphemism.

This assessment is also relevant for the situation after both world wars. Even the popularity of the Austrian film until the 1950s cannot hide the fact that domestic production could, in actuality, never compete quantitatively with the imports, especially those from the United States and (West) Germany. A few numbers support this: 27 Austrian films competed with 286 imported films in 1935; of these 126 were from the United States and 116 from Germany. In 1955, only 28 films were produced in Austria, which competed with 440 imports, including 229 from the United States, 105 from West Germany, 42 from France, 31 from Italy, and 18 from Great Britain. Since the 1960s, U.S. films make up one-third of the imported films, and Germany composes one-fifth. Between 1970 and 1980, 1,236 films originated from the United States (32.39 percent), 760 from Germany (19.92 percent), 532 from Italy (13.94 percent), 394 from France (10.32 percent), 237 from Great Britain (7.15 percent), and 161 from Hong Kong (4.22 percent). During the same period, only 80 films were Austrian productions—or 2.1 percent![106] With the exception of the period between 1936 and 1945, the data for each randomly chosen year confirm the above-shown dimensions; in certain years, Hollywood proved to be even stronger than noted above.

In any event, these numbers lead to the conclusion that Austrian film production has played only a marginal and limited role. Without a doubt, the poor quality of most of these films was also a determining factor. With only a few exceptions, Austrian films were neither formally nor artistically innovative, nor did they address relevant social problems. Analogous to the sentiment of many people, who dreamed of the past glory of a no longer existing monarchy, the Austrian film emigrated into the idyllic preserve of trivial, aggrandized, and historically concocted films in which the "good old days" were praised, in which each pretty servant girl found her baron and each attractive milliner found her proper officer. It is certainly not by chance that the title of the first Austrian sound film in 1929 was called *G'schichten aus der Steiermark* (Stories from Styria).

Axel Corti was certainly correct in commenting that perhaps the world knows so little about Austria because so many films were made about a nation that never existed.[107] This judgment of prewar movies is also fitting for the majority of films that were produced after 1945. The Austrian film industry still did not find it necessary to change its course and continued to deliver tear-jerking pieces "as if nothing else had happened."[108] The flood of pictures with sentimental portraits depicting Viennese schmalz, *Heimat* (the homeland), and operettas found their well-deserved end in the late 1950s and early 1960s because of the film crisis.

Not only the brutality of National Socialism but also the desolate condition of the Austrian film culture lay behind the emigration of many great artists: Josef von Sternberg, G. W. Pabst, Michael Curtiz, Fritz Lang, Hedi Lamarr, Elisabeth Bergner, Elissa Landi, Luise Rainer, Vanessa Brown, Oscar Homalka, Ricardo Cortez, Erich von Stroheim, Billy Wilder, Paul Henreid, Otto Preminger, Fred Zinnemann, and others. Austrian film thus ultimately lost its potential, and the infusion of talented individuals meant a great gain for Hollywood.[109] We are dealing with an often-ignored phenomenon here; especially because the Austrian film culture—as a result of cultural and political intolerance, incompetence, and racial prejudice—defused *itself*, the U.S. film was strengthened and in turn could affect Austria more effectively. Still another point: precisely those who are particularly riled about Hollywood's cultural imperialism thought nothing of opening the Austrian gate to the cultural imperialism of the "Third Reich." In light of this situation, it can hardly be surprising that the Austrian film is hardly discussed in international specialist literature. Agnes Brody-Bleier described this situation fittingly: "In most film encyclopedias the category can be summarized as: 'Austria—see Germany.' "[110] While this is certainly true for film productions in Austria, films *shown* in Austria could run under the category "Austria—see Hollywood."

The Austrian film industry, whose exports profited from inflation in the short term after the First World War, was extremely weakened by the currency rehabilitation through the League of Nations loan. While the production of films between 1919 and 1925 sank from 130 to 35, the Austrian market was flooded with more and more foreign films after 1923, the majority from the United States. Metro-Goldwyn-Mayer, Paramount, 20th Century Fox, and RKO Pictures immediately opened their own film distribution firms in Vienna;

in addition, United Artists, Universal, Warner Bros., and Columbia were represented through Austrian agencies. Because of favorable currency exchange rates, the U.S. firms could now place their already-amortized films in Austria and also in the successor states of the Habsburg monarchy under advantageous conditions. The capital-lacking Austrian film industry, in contrast, was hard-hit by the currency rehabilitation, and this was a beating from which it would never recover. The production of an Austrian film required similarly high investments as did the Hollywood film, and because of the limited domestic market, only a further export expansion would have helped. Yet, precisely those export advantages were now lost that existed until 1922. The Austrian film was therefore no longer internationally competitive and slid into a deep crisis. After production had come almost to a standstill in 1925, the government finally reacted to the pressure of the domestic film industry and in May 1926 passed a quota law for film imports.[111]

This improved the situation somewhat. Yet the suffocating power of foreign films still remained, with Hollywood films being surpassed by German imports in the early 1930s. In 1927, of all films shown in Austria 75 percent had originated in the United States and only 18 percent from Germany. By 1929, this gap was reduced to 54 and 37 percent, respectively. This trend continued: in 1930, German films comprised 47 percent, and U.S. films were only 43 percent of pictures imported, and by 1934 the ratio of 50:40 was clearly in favor of the German film. This was a result not only of a reduction of U.S. imports vis-à-vis those from Germany—even in 1937, each country was the source of 38 percent of all imports—but also of a distinct improvement in the box office returns of German pictures. Even though the number of U.S. motion pictures was larger than German imports (115:112), the German films accounted for 70 percent of the returns, and Hollywood brought in only 15 percent.[112] The increase in profits for German films was due to two factors. On the one hand, together with the rise of the National Socialist movement, German films enjoyed great popularity especially in the provinces. Hollywood films were hardly successful in rural areas, although they did make up over 80 percent of all profits in cosmopolitan Vienna. On the other hand, all foreign films—*with the exception of German films*—required registration approval, which let the profits of German movies explode.

The exception of German movies from registration would not be the only compromise that Austrian film politics made prior to the Anschluss. The reasons for this were not only material and economic in nature, but also political and cultural. The crisis-ridden film industry could not achieve the transition to the sound film by its own means, and the necessary financial backing came, for the most part, from Germany. Already since 1916, the Sascha-Filmfabrik had been forced to cooperate with the Berlin company Messter, yet the influence of the German film industry grew enormously after the First World War. The most apparent indicator for this was the inception of the German Tobis AG as part owner of Sascha in 1932. In addition to economic coercion, ideological pressure increased after the taking over of power by the NSDAP in Germany.

The intertwining of the Austrian film industry with the German film industry and its dependence upon National Socialist film politics, as well as the enormous compromises it was required to make, were recently analyzed by Gerhard Renner.[113] The Anschluss of the Austrian film had already occurred between 1934 and 1937. Its repression happened in many stages: from self-censorship in the selection of topics and scripts, to not employing emigrants from Germany and the repression of Jewish stockholders in the Tobis Sascha AG, to the exclusion of Jewish actors, directors, and even extras. This "Aryan clause" governing the workers in the Austrian film industry had begun in 1934 and was complete by 1937. Hence, the Austrian film had already capitulated one year *prior* to the Anschluss. The subtitle of a new study on the Austrian motion picture in the 1930s is not without reason called "A Product of Economic and Political Dependencies."[114]

As a result of all of the above, Hollywood's position in Austria was considerably weakened. Already in 1934 the U.S. film trade papers had reached the conclusion that Austria was no longer a good market for U.S. films.[115] However, hope for recapturing the market was not given up completely because Hollywood was still in second place. A column in the *Film Daily Year Book* for 1938 described this situation clearly: even though the German film had surpassed its U.S. counterpart, the "competition from other countries and from domestic production is unimportant."[116]

Only shortly after this article had been published was the temporary end of Hollywood's activities in Austria heralded by the invasion of German troops. A few U.S. films were still being shown in some Viennese theaters, but the films from Hollywood became more and more rare. The forced confiscation of theaters with Jewish owners, distributors, and producers; the concentration of the Austrian film industry in the Wien-Film; the relocation of U.S. distribution agencies from Vienna to Berlin and their closing after the beginning of the war—all this meant the end of the last remnants of independence that the Austrian film had been able to maintain until 1938. It also resulted in the banishing of Hollywood films from the "German Reich." If Austria had already been scratched off the film export lists in U.S. film papers in 1938, then yet another export market also had to be eliminated after 1940: Germany.

As a matter of fact, Austria's defeat was laconically acknowledged in the Southern California film metropole. Only a few days after the Anschluss, the *Film Daily* now stated that the "latest Nazi reshuffle of the European map, in so far as the U.S. film industry goes, makes little difference, but a threat to the excellent American pix markets in Czechoslovakia and Poland, where business is good and has been steadily improving during the past two years."[117] And a top manager of a large film studio actually stated: "Domination of Austria by Germany means that we now have one lame duck on our hands instead of two. . . . We haven't been able to get any real money from either country and now we simply won't get any money from one country."[118] Well, *real money* would once again be made only after the defeat of the Axis powers.

### The ISB Film Section and the MPEA in Austria

The more obvious the Allied victory had appeared during the Second World War, the more intensive the preparation of the U.S. film industry had become for the recapturing of film markets lost to the German aggression. One important result of the military downfall of the "Third Reich" was the long-term weakening of German film, Hollywood's strongest economic competitor.

The reestablishment of the U.S. film industry's dominant position in the small Austrian market was well prepared. In contrast to the German case, a ban on the production of films was not demanded—according to experience, Austrian film production had proved to be of little threat. Therefore, the U.S. film industry aimed for absolute uninhibited access to the market. This was to be achieved, on the one hand, through the prohibiting of all discriminating laws and import restrictions for U.S. film, and on the other hand, through the banning of all future preferences for German films. In addition, the distribution network was once again to be rehabilitated whereby Vienna would become the turntable for other film markets in Czechoslovakia, Poland, Hungary, Romania, Bulgaria, and Yugoslavia. To guarantee the implementation of these goals, the Hays Organization (Motion Picture Producers and Distributors of America, Inc.) in its detailed "Austrian Country Memorandum" of January 29, 1945, demanded that the U.S. government insist that future Austrian governments agree to the following measures:

1. No limitation on the importation of American films, or the number of copies of each film imported, whether in the original or dubbed versions, either by license or by quota systems.
2. Most-favored-nation treatment with foreign and national films.
3. No obligation to purchase and / or release national films in Austria or abroad.
4. No obligation to dub films in Austria, but freedom to dub films for the Austrian market, if desired, wherever practical.
5. No requirement to title or print films in Austria.
6. All regulations governing the importation and release of American films in Austria should be definitized in an agreement between the American and Austrian governments and not subject to the arbitrary decisions of any ministerial or trade body, as was the case before the war.[119]

The Hays Organization, which furnished the Department of State with a fully developed contract proposal, would see its wishes fulfilled. Hollywood received a onetime opportunity in 1945, by the liberation of Austria and the ten-year period of occupation through the Allies. With the help of the Film Section of the ISB the once-predominant position of the U.S. motion picture industry in the distribution sector could be not only reestablished but even extended. As the Hays memorandum had made clear: "It is very probable that Austria, under normal conditions and not subject to German pressure, would be an excellent market for American motion pictures."[120]

In this context it is certainly worth noting that although the Film Section was still an official organ of the U.S. Army in Austria, it represented in reality the elongated arm of Hollywood during the first years of occupation. This conclusion is supported by the example of personnel politics within the ISB. The first director of the Film Section, civilian Eugen Sharin, was an export manager for various Hollywood companies. His successor in 1947, Wolfgang Wolf, moved directly from ISB services to heading the distribution section of the newly opened Austrian office of the MPEA.[121] This was nonetheless a logical step because the U.S. Army was responsible for the reconstruction of the U.S. distribution system in Austria until March 1947 and consequently relieved the MPEA of a most difficult duty.

The chaos during the first postwar days certainly did not make the immediate showing of U.S. films a priority. All theaters were closed, all films confiscated, and the examination of the political content of German films required time. More important, there was still a lack of Hollywood productions. The operations director of the ISB, James J. Minifie, therefore let out a helpless cry on July 7, 1945: "Films: Nothing to report. No films!"[122] A sarcastic note only one week later to the Office of War Information made this even clearer: "We have two American films in stock: *Cowboy* and *The Battle of the Mariannas*. Suggest entry to Vienna with a flot whereon are raft and cowboy with legend 'This is America.' "[123] There was not only a lack of American films but also a lack of professional film managers. This deficiency was relieved through the appointment of Eugen Sharin at the end of July 1945, from whom the ISB expected a great deal ("The Film Section in the hands of Mr. Sharin will see to it that our United States interests are very well taken care of").[124]

This assessment was certainly justified—at least when we equate the interests of the United States with those of Hollywood. Sharin would soon be successful in building a theater empire, which took a special place even within Hollywood's success story. Initially, "German properties" in Salzburg and Upper Austria, including confiscated buildings, machines, film materials, film copies, and bank assets of all film production and distribution firms formed the basis for this film empire. While there were hardly any film activities worth mentioning in the U.S. zone, these confiscated funds nevertheless constituted the greatest portion of the film property in Austria because the film companies and authorities in Vienna had evacuated a significant part of their assets to western Austria toward the end of the war. This included the Deutsche-Film-

Vertriebs Gesellschaft, Reichsfilm Chamber, Filmtreuhandgesellschaft Süd-Ost, Wien-Film, Prag-Film, Tobis-Film, Terra-Film, Universal-Film, UFA, Gaufilmstelle of the NSDAP, Mars-Film (German Army), Bavaria Filmdienst, and Fink-Film. The property of the Leni-Riefenstahl-Film-Gesellschaft, which was requisitioned in Kitzbühel, was turned over to the French army. More than 1,500 copies of 700 films alone were confiscated in the U.S. zone. Film censorship, licensing of all film activities, and an import and distribution monopoly completed the absolute control of the ISB over the entire film sector, which was initially limited only to the U.S. occupation zone.[125]

As the Film Section began its duties in Vienna in August 1945, it significantly augmented its radius of action and, through this, its influence—and not only in its own sector, but also in those of the other Allies, including the Soviet zone. Although the Viennese film production companies were divided among the four zones—the Sieveringer Atelier was in the U.S. zone, Rosenhügel in the Soviet, the Atelier Schönbrunn in the British, and the largest film warehouse in the French—the ISB was soon successful in securing the leading role in the reconstruction of the film business in Vienna and thereby in all of Austria.

The activities of the Film Section under Eugen Sharin are more than exemplary for Hollywood's plans for Austria. The Red Army may have confiscated a large portion of the existing film production facilities in Vienna before the arrival of the Western Allies. Yet, it also made two essential concessions to the Austrian government with regard to movies. It allowed the government not only the takeover of Wien-Film as the centralized production monopoly but also the establishment of the Austria Film-Verleih und Vertriebsgesellschaft (Austrian film distribution and marketing association) to operate as a state-controlled monopoly—even for foreign films, including those from the Soviet Union.[126] However, neither a strong, centrally directed state-owned film production nor the competition in the distribution sector was acceptable for Hollywood. It was therefore only consistent that the U.S. Army—against the protests of the Soviet Allies—now confiscated all film property in its occupation sector in Vienna. And because the Neubaugasse, the Viennese *Film Row* accommodating the offices of all the most important film companies, happened to be in the U.S. zone, these measures affected almost all production and distribution companies. In addition, the Film Section could now levy pressure on film producers and not only through the allocation of licenses. Through the weakening of the Austria Film-Verleih und Vertriebsgesellschaft the ISB was also able to eliminate the only possible valid competitor on the distribution sector. In addition, it now also had access to the bank assets of the state-owned marketing company—in other words, to the box office profits of German and Austrian films, which amounted to a respectable ten million schillings![127]

This process illustrates the collaboration between Hollywood and the Film Section quite neatly. In this context, it is especially important to understand that these confiscation measures of the U.S. Army were only tactical in nature.

It had not even been planned to definitively lay claim to confiscated property in Austria. Rather, the confiscated values were to be steered into an Austrian film fund on an appropriate occasion. The necessary guidelines for this procedure, however, were still to be established. Ultimately, the confiscated properties served as an appropriate means of pressure, which in turn would secure Hollywood's future position. The plan was quite simple and straightforward: U.S. film interests in Austria were not to be hindered, and confiscated film property was carefully employed as a security deposit by U.S. negotiators in dealing with the Austrian government. The negotiations determining the transition of properties to Austria had only one goal: to achieve an official governmental guarantee for *unlimited* access of U.S. films to Austria. More on this later.

But the Film Section was successful not simply in asserting itself against the Austrian government. It bypassed the other Allies as well. Even Soviet film officers let themselves be persuaded by the professional film politics of the ISB, and toward the end of 1945, the ISB de facto controlled the entire film industry in Austria. Through the newly established Sieveringer Atelier made up of Salzburger stock, the ISB thereby controlled not only the sole functioning production facility in Austria but also its counterpart studio in the Soviet zone through their main office. This position was more than just nominal. Until spring 1946, all workers on the Rosenhügel were on the payroll of the U.S. Army, and the film laboratory in the atelier in the Soviet zone produced film copies for the ISB free of charge! In light of this fact, it is hardly worth mentioning that the Film Section also controlled the Schönbrunner Studio in the British zone. In total, the ISB employed 80 people in the office of Wien-Film, 48 in the Sieveringer Atelier, and 250 at Rosenhügel and Schönbrunn. A similar picture can be painted in the marketing sector. The Vienna office of the Film Section (eighty-four employees) was responsible for all occupation sectors in Vienna and the Soviet zone, whereby it was concerned not only with the distribution of confiscated German films and U.S. movies but also with the marketing of British, French, and Soviet films. In November 1945, Sharin was successful in carrying out a sensational coup by establishing an ISB depot in Amstetten—a town in the Soviet zone. He reported with pride that "this is especially noteworthy, because it constitutes an ISB Sub-Branch in the Russian zone proper."[128]

The bureau in Salzburg (twenty-four employees) supplied the movie houses in city and province and, because of an informal agreement with the French occupation power, also those in the French zone. The office in Linz (twenty employees) was responsible not only for all theaters in the U.S. zone in Upper Austria but also for the theaters in the Soviet-occupied Mühlviertel. In addition, the ISB also controlled the distribution of the weekly newsreel *Welt im Film*—a coproduction of the U.S. and British armies in Germany with camera teams in Austria—and the marketing of its French counterpart.

The unusual success of the ISB did not go unnoticed. A fitting comment of

U.S. General Arthur McChrystal must be noted here: "As situation developed all distribution of Allied films has been taken over, with each nation represented. However, we are running the show."[129] According to the untiring Eugen Sharin: "As far as the Motion Picture Industry is concerned, American leadership has been established beyond any doubt. . . . It is up to us to evolve a policy that will ultimately reserve all reasonable influence for American informational activities and all reasonable opportunities for American business."[130] The prerequisite for this had already been created. Because the French and British system of distribution was not established before 1946, the strong position of U.S. films could not be threatened. And competition was hardly expected from the Soviet industry because of its low production as well as its rejection by the Austrian audience. The ISB had little respect for the film competence of the Soviet Union to begin with, and just who felt that they were the actual masters of the Austrian film business becomes quite clear in the following. When General Scheltow protested against the confiscation of Wien-Film and the Austria-Film by the ISB and supported Austrian interests, Eugen Sharin's response was simple: "The Russians have made a great gesture by handing over to the Austrian State 160,000 meters of negative 'in order to assure the start of production.' Needless to say, this is a hollow gesture as no production can be started without the equipment ISB is holding at present."[131]

The Soviet occupation power might not have been a competitor for Hollywood, but it at least could hinder the activities of the ISB—if not completely repress them—in its zone. As the tensions between the Allies intensified, the Soviet authorities placed film distribution under the control of the company Sovexport on March 15, 1946. Then on June 15, 1946, the Wien-Film on the Rosenhügel fell under direct Soviet control as German property. Also, their own film production would now commence. Yet, the films, many of which were worth viewing, hardly found distribution possibilities outside of the Soviet sector.[132] In addition, the majority of films were boycotted by the Austrian public, even in the Soviet zone, while U.S. films found great approval.

In this context the following assertion almost forces itself upon us: with respect to the cultural situation in occupied Austria, no other prejudice was quite as strong as the reigning sentiments ironically equating the U.S. occupier with cultural liberalism and the Soviet occupier with cultural repression. That these preconceptions themselves were part of anti-Communist propaganda is evident precisely with regard to the film sector in the respective zones of occupation. It is not contested that censorship measures, screening hindrances, and the banning of U.S. films had again and again been introduced in the Soviet sector. In most cases, however, these acts were arbitrarily implemented only by local commandants. In spite of all difficulties, the ISB (and later the MPEA) was still effective in placing not only a large number of U.S. films but also U.S. newsreels in the Soviet zone after the founding of Sovexport. Conversely, these opportunities were denied for Soviet films in the U.S. sector because the issuing of permits was only a rare exception. Therefore, U.S. film officers frequently defended themselves against Soviet demands to implement quota measures for a film exchange: for they would have led to the unavoidable situation that a small number of Soviet films had to be allowed into the U.S. zone, while the large number of U.S. films in the Soviet zone would have to be reduced. Wolfgang Wolf, as the leading ISB film officer, noted in October 1946:

> Despite repeated difficulties and the fact that there is no agreement between the American and the Russian Film Section, I have been able to keep up distributing a substantial amount of American films in the Russian zone of Austria, without any compensation whatsoever in our zone.
> The balance for the present week (18–24 October [1946]) is as follows:
>
> 1. American films played in the Russian Zone (Russian sector of Vienna not included):
>    Features in 29 Theaters
>    Shorts in 11 Theaters
>    Newsreel in 161 Theaters
> 2. Russian films played in the American Zone:
>    None.
>
> All in all, we have been playing several hundred hours of American films in the Russian Zone for every hour of Russian films in the American Zone.[133]

Wolfgang Wolf, now the MPEA's representative to Austria, also informed the ISB in July 1947 that nothing had changed: U.S. films could still be unofficially distributed within the entire Soviet zone, and 150 of 250 theaters (still 60 percent!) showed the weekly newsreel *Welt im Film*. "Our films have gained tremendous popularity in the Soviet Zone and are stiff competition to the Russian films."[134] The situation involving the screening possibilities of films produced by the individual Allies in the other zones of occupation could not be formulated more explicitly than in a meeting of the Film Section of August 1947: "At present Russian films or films produced by Russian directed firms are not allowed in the British and US Zone whereas the Russians do not have such a ban."[135] And U.S. diplomat Martin F. Herz noted in June 1948: "By coincidence, I learned that films, including films made in Austria, require a US license before they can be shown in the US zone. The only zone where such censorship doesn't exist is the Soviet zone. It does not seem that we would lose anything if we left it to the Austrians to decide what films should or should not be shown."[136] The ISB license would be canceled already within that same month; the boycott of Soviet films would not. This was seen to by the power of the MPEA and the taste of the Austrian public.

Hollywood's actual business is the business of creating (ersatz) dreams, and the business in Austria, thanks to the activities of the Film Section, was a dream in itself: "Business is booming. In the larger cities all the shows are sold out," Eugen Sharin reported in September 1945.[137] Only a few weeks later he announced that Hollywood's plans for Austria came closer and closer to their realization: "Extremely unusual and interesting developments may be expected from the fact that ISB FILMS, Vienna, is the sole distribution outlet of any consequence in the region. . . . We are in an excellent position to safeguard American interests by allowing no legislation directed against imports; this position the undersigned intends to use in full all times. Otherwise we shall encourage private industry, and discourage interference by the Government of Austria."[138]

Although the export of hard currency had not yet been clarified, Sharin transferred $17,500 *in cold cash* already in September 1945. His only problem seemed to be that he could not get enough films, for "we have a beautiful, unequalled, monopolistic opportunity for the dissemination of information to say nothing of doing some business in the Motion Picture field."[139] Reinforcements of U.S. films became stabilized in the first months of 1946, and by the end of February 1946, the Film Section already had transferred more than two million schillings to its bank account as a result of the box office profits from U.S. entertainment films and documentaries as well as the weekly newsreel *Welt im Film*. If one takes into consideration that a large number of theaters had been destroyed and that this sum had been the profits of only six months of activities in Salzburg and Upper Austria and only four months in Vienna, then the most positive annual returns of Hollywood films in Austria during the 1930s were already surpassed. The U.S. films earned only 50,000 schillings in August 1945, a total that rose to 650,000 schillings in April 1946. The ISB film business had indeed developed "in the most satisfactory way."[140]

Less satisfactory, however, was the fact that the profits could no longer be transferred abroad as a result of the schilling law of December 1945. But the ISB now took over the management of MPEA-member bank accounts. In total, the profits for U.S. films in Austria came to 7,765,582.08 schillings in 1946; for politically acceptable German films, 6,856,878.34—at least according to the statistics available.[141] This latter indication is especially important at this juncture because the data available are more than fragmented. This was apparent already in 1947, during the examination of the Film Section's bookkeeping. This audit was requisitioned by the legal branch of the U.S. Army after suspicions grew that Eugen Sharin had not always followed the guidelines of U.S. occupation politics in the course of his duties, but instead those of Hollywood (and his own). Sharin's high-handed measures as well as other irregularities had led to his dismissal in May 1946.[142] His attempt, together with General Arthur McChrystal, to rent the Wien-Film studios hardly enhanced his film career in Austria.[143]

Yet, Sharin had served Hollywood well. Developments within the Austrian film structure, in his words, were "extremely unusual and interesting," which did not refer only to the predominant position of the Film Section in the distribution sector.[144] Certainly, this position alone was unusual in a country occupied by four powers. Even more unusual as well as interesting, however, is another delicate detail in the ISB's business dealings.

Immediately at the beginning of the occupation, the Film Section had attempted to create a favorable starting position for U.S. films. It thus ordered the theaters in the U.S. zone to remain closed until enough Hollywood films had arrived in Austria. These supplies, however, were very slow in coming during the first months after the war ended. In an effort to lift public morale and show the goodwill of the ISB, the leadership of the U.S. Army insisted that the theaters, in the meantime, be once again opened to show politically neutral German and Austrian films. Here, the ISB reached for a surprisingly simple instrument: if the competition could not be hindered, then the development of Hollywood's position should at least be aided. This quite clearly meant that, at least in the first year, all expenses of the Film Section would be financed by the box office profits of the confiscated German films alone.

These profits allowed the Film Section to settle all distribution costs of the films from Allied states, which were predominantly from the United States. Also the development of the entire U.S. distribution network, the costs for production and distribution of the newsreel *Welt im Film*, the distribution of all American documentaries and propaganda films, and even the salaries of the Film Section in management, distribution, production, reproduction, censorship, and advertising were paid for by the monies in this pot. Because import tariffs could not be levied by the Austrian government, the turnover corresponded to net profits, and gross profits were the same as net profits. We are speaking here of a monthly income of more than one million schillings beginning in 1946. Of this sum, between 60 and 70 percent of all profits came from German films. This reinforcement of Hollywood's position by building on the proceeds from confiscated German films was surely a creative idea as well as a once-in-a-lifetime opportunity. The unique character of this situation was definitely apparent to Eugen Sharin. "Not one cent was ever charged against any American picture" he would state in October 1945. Furthermore, "We truly believe that this is the only operation in the history of motion pictures where business was done, and still is being done, for Uncle Sam and the American Motion Picture Industry without any expense whatever."[145]

This assessment was shared by the Film Committee which had been established in 1946 to control the business behavior of the Film Section—yet, without Sharin's enthusiasm. When the Film Committee learned that "all expenses incurred by the Film Section were met from the income of the German films," it immediately attempted to stop this practice.[146] This unusual means of profit maximization not only contradicted the duties of the ISB, which, as a trust, was to secure confiscated German property, but it also brought with it the great danger of causing irreparable damage to the image of the United States in Austria. It speaks for the political correctness and intelligence of the members of the Film Committee that they not only put an end to this practice but also tried to return the diverted monies as far as possible. The emphasis here is on "as far as possible" because the Film Committee was not able to come close to the sum of the profits that came into question, in spite of an intensive investigation lasting one and a half years. Such an assessment was not possible because of the chaotic condition of the records kept by the Film Section. In any event, we are dealing with profits of "several million schillings."[147]

Nevertheless, the position of American films had become so solidified through the activities of the Film Section that a normalization of the situation was estimated for the summer of 1946. Consequently, the distribution duties of the Film Section were to be taken over as soon as possible by the MPEA, and the question of the transfer of confiscated film assets into a trust managed by the Austrian government was tied to securing the position of the MPEA. The discussions held in the fall of 1946 showed quite explicitly that these values only served to secure the U.S. negotiating position. The Department of State agreed in principle to this transfer but insisted that it be made clear to the Austrian government in informal talks that it would have to agree not to implement any measures that would raise restrictions for U.S. films in the future.[148] The negotiations, entitled "Protection of U.S. Film Interests in Austria," were successfully concluded on December 14, 1946. *All* of Hollywood's goals were achieved. It was certainly no coincidence that only three days after the signing of the transfer contract, the U.S. high commissioner, General Mark W. Clark, received a document in which the Austrian federal chancellor Leopold Figl announced:

Neither the Austrian government nor its political subordinated agencies for the duration of this treaty will, with respect to films partly or fully produced by the United States or other members of the United Nations or their nationals:

1. levy any higher or different kinds of tariffs, conditions, limitations, or bans for the import of such films to Austria other than those for the import of films that are produced in or belong to some country or their nationals that have been decreed or will be established in the future;
2. prescribe any licenses or censorship measures or other regulations, limitations, or fees for the distribution or showing of such films in Austria, which do not equally correspond with films that are produced in or belong to Austria or its nationals; or
3. treat differently, either directly or indirectly, the films of the United States or other members of the United Nations or their nationals with respect to the distribution and airing of films in Austria.[149]

The Austrian government completely subordinated itself to the demands of the U.S. film industry with this declaration. Furthermore, it guaranteed that the film plans of the minister for trade and development, Eduard Heinl, were disturbed. Heinl, who had been the president of the Tobis-Sascha-Filmgesellschaft prior to the Anschluss, was keen on regaining control over the film industry. U.S. negotiators, who were aware of this, thus firmly demanded that the Ministry for Protection of Property and Economic Planning act as the manager of the trust and not Heinl's ministry.[150]

The U.S. position in the Austrian movie business was secured even further. In an additional secret protocol, the Austrian government had to agree to numerous other conditions. This included the submission of a semiannual financial report, the soliciting of approval for personnel changes, as well as a report of monthly accomplishments, a summary of operations planned for the following month, and other pertinent facts concerning current plant operations, including any transfer of inventories.[151] This compulsory recounting of information secured U.S. representatives with further indirect control of the Austrian film industry.

Only after the Austrian government had submitted this written agreement did Hollywood's path become free of obstacles. Therefore, the ISB suggested that all distribution agendas should be turned over to the MPEA at the beginning of 1947. The MPEA, however, requested a three-month delay in this process in order better to prepare itself. The degree of importance that the MPEA attributed to the direct control of the film market is demonstrated by the following detail. As the representatives of the U.S. Army considered the idea of allowing an Austrian company to look after the distribution of U.S. films *only in the interim period*, they ran up against total rejection. The MPEA would have rather pulled all U.S. films from Austria immediately.[152] The Film Section could not risk this and therefore accommodated the wishes of the MPEA by continuing to manage distribution until the export cartel was thoroughly prepared for the takeover. This occurred on March 28, 1947, and the MPEA now organized, in addition to the management of its members' films, also the distribution of the Wien-Film. The distribution of German films was transferred to the Austrian Filmvertriebs- und Verwertungsgesellschaft. The assets of the MPEA member firms, which amounted to 5,862,530.60 schillings on March 27, 1947, were handed over to the MPEA (Austria) by the ISB on August 22, 1947.[153]

The MPEA, in turn, also served the ISB well. It took over, with profit sharing, the distribution of U.S. educational and propaganda films as well as the newsreel *Welt im Film*. The latter, which enjoyed great popularity, was one the most significant propaganda tools of the Film Section in Austria.[154] *Welt im Film* had avoided all appearances of obvious propaganda and could therefore increase its efficiency. Ernst Haeusserman, who headed the Film Section in April 1947, stressed the following: "Without ever producing open propaganda, we have in each reel inserted stories informing the Austrians about US aims in Austria, US contribution to Austrian recovery, cultural and intellectual representatives of America in Austria, the work of the US Relief Mission and the European Recovery Program with its effects upon Austria. Again, an addition of all these stories would result in a film history of US activities in Austria."[155]

*Welt im Film*, according to this, was based on the "sandwich principle," which was wonderfully described by a USIA expert: "We make it up like a sandwich, take a good international story to lead off with, then put in a slightly slanted story and a local story and a typical neat newsreel story. Then you put in another big international story, then maybe another of definite State Department interest. If we can get one story in there with a hook in it we are satisfied. It might be nothing more than getting something into the lines. If you put too much of the State Department thing in there, it will immediately become suspect."[156]

Putting this "sandwich principle" into practice is beautifully illustrated by two typical issues of *Welt im Film* of December 1948:

Number 182:
   More on the reelection of President Truman
   Japan: flood catastrophe destroys a city
   The smallest camera
   Four-legged export
   A house in Vienna collapses
   The famous film and theater actor Hans Jaray comes back from the
      United States
   The Austria book
   The reopening of the Christmas market in Vienna
   Ice Follies 1948.

Number 183:
   President Truman in Washington
   Suspension bridges in England
   Record flight London-Rome
   The new head of the ECA Mission in Austria, Mr. King in Vienna
   Carol Reed films in Austria
   Departure of Jewish displaced persons to Israel
   A "nice party"
   Football in the United States
   Ski races on the Zugspitze.[157]

No matter how efficient the propaganda effect of *Welt im Film* might have been, for Hollywood, which was certainly convinced that it was the best propagandist of the American way of life, this newsreel would soon represent troublesome competition. In spite of initial cooperation between the MPEA and the ISB (the Civil Affairs Division lifted the law requiring scrutiny of all

American films exported to Austria), it would soon become apparent that the "thankfulness" of Hollywood would end when it came to business—even toward the U.S. Army. Although the MPEA received greater profits from the distribution of *Welt im Film* than the ISB and although all the necessary fuel for the cars distributing the films was issued to the MPEA by the U.S. Army, the MPEA attempted to eliminate the official weekly newsreel produced by the U.S. occupation power from the Austrian market with its own weekly *Fox Tönende Wochenschau*.

The measures implemented by the Austrian representative of the MPEA, Wolfgang Wolf, toward his former employer, the ISB, were anything but subtle. He enticed theater owners with dumping offers, and also spread rumors in advertisements and newspapers that *Welt im Film* would soon be discontinued. The ISB's reaction was outrage. It demanded from U.S. Army superiors that Wolf's work permit be immediately retracted. This insistence was founded upon numerous accusations. According to this, Wolf had "*a.* Lied unconscionably; *b.* Adopted Soviet tactics of creating confusion; *c.* Taken actions prejudicial to the United States interests as an occupying force."[158] Yet, all these accusations did not bear fruit, and this conflict demonstrates clearly just who had more power in Austria—the ISB or Hollywood. Wolf remained in his job, and the ISB would discontinue *Welt im Film* before the end of the year, on October 15, 1949. The semiofficial newsreel *Austria-Wochenschau*, which was launched at the same time, was no real competition, and the *Fox Tönende Wochenschau* quite conveniently took over the contracts of *Welt im Film*.[159]

The duties of the Film Section now were limited to propaganda activities that were not covered by Hollywood. By mid-1949, it concentrated completely on the distribution and marketing of documentaries, such as *Facts—Tatsachen*, *Das Lied von Morgen* (about the AYA youth programs in cooperation with the Viennese Boys' Choir), *Helfende Hände* (U.S. aid programs in Austria), *Offene Türen* (America Houses), *Mit vereinten Kräften* (Marshall Plan aid). The titles certainly speak for themselves. Even though the Film Section reduced its personnel considerably, it completed its duties with great success. For example, U.S. propaganda films had more than 4,200 screenings in the first three months of 1950 alone, and by February 1950, the taking over of the Kosmos Theater in Vienna presented a new excellent venue.[160]

Ernst Haeusserman and his assistant Marcel Prawy were also concerned about the next Austrian film generation and consequently opened a film seminar in which each course had more than fifty participants. When the program was taken over by the Department of State in the second half of 1950, the evaluation was exceptionally positive. "Film utilization in Austria is as advanced as in Germany and is undoubtedly, therefore, superior to utilization in other counties." And: "As evidenced by this program's large monthly attendance figures, the program is well-known in both countries as a mild propaganda and information endeavor of the American Government."[161]

In total, the U.S. propaganda films reached more than approximately 200,000 people per month, 70,000 alone in Vienna. The films were shown not only in commercial theaters, in the Kosmos Theater, and in the America Houses. Nine film operators traveled continuously with their movie projectors through the provinces and showed films in schools, church halls, trade union homes, restaurants, and even in market squares. In one decisive point the U.S. Film Program in Austria was clearly superior to its German counterpart. In Austria, the distribution of films was uninhibited—even in the Soviet zone. "To a large extent they are sent into the Soviet Zone," read the aforementioned review of the ISB film program, and "the Soviet Zone of Austria is very different from the Soviet Zone of Germany."[162] The difference was substantial as the U.S. Film Program reached an average of 10,000 people in the Soviet sector.

Success was also ensured during the last years of occupation. USIS films reached an average of more than 1.5 million people per year in commercial theaters. As a result of the distribution to other venues, another 700,000 viewers could be reached. The most important target groups were the youths and the trade unions. On a statistical average, U.S. propaganda films thus reached approximately one-third of the Austrian public per year until 1955. Yet, the quantitative success was not all that counted. In Department of State reports the qualitative results of the Film Program were again and again stressed. A report of the cultural affairs officer of the U.S. embassy in Vienna, E. Wilder Spaulding, of June 19, 1953, is a typical example: "Because of the success of USIS films in Austria, little criticism has been expressed concerning the propaganda content. . . . Furthermore, it must be taken into consideration that USIS showings in commercial theaters and otherwise (35mm and 16mm respectively) in the Russian occupied zone in Austria have been and continue to be most encouraging."[163] This estimation can be interpreted as *the* typical positive assessment of the political efficiency of U.S. film activities during the entire occupation period. It must again be stressed that the United States was extremely successful in Austria exactly because it avoided blatant propaganda— and this was in actuality the best prerequisite for truly effective propaganda.

Yet, not only the political but the commercial tasks were optimally solved as well. All economic restrictions on U.S. films could be prevented, and the (West) German films were again behind Hollywood films in second place. The status quo ante was thus resumed. Table 2 is revealing. Actual audience successes cannot, however, be determined from the number of imported films alone. But Hollywood nevertheless came off well ahead of the rest. U.S. films alone achieved almost the same number of film days as (West) German and Austrian films together.[164] And they could maintain their dominant position in Austria until the end of the occupation. The slow death of the Austrian cinemas would certainly have been that much more rapid without the films from Hollywood. Still, without a doubt, the Austrian films of the 1940s and 1950s still ranked first with Austrian audiences. The reason for this was pointedly analyzed by

TABLE 2. *Films Shown in Austria, 1946–1955, by Country of Origin*

| Country of Origin | Year | | | | | | | | | |
|---|---|---|---|---|---|---|---|---|---|---|
| | 1946 | 1947 | 1948 | 1949 | 1950 | 1951 | 1952 | 1953 | 1954 | 1955 |
| United States | 52 | 31 | 59 | 150 | 204 | 184 | 192 | 180 | 219 | 229 |
| Britain | 21 | 11 | 30 | 34 | 40 | 32 | 26 | 25 | 25 | 18 |
| France | 43 | 39 | 36 | 19 | 22 | 23 | 28 | 25 | 32 | 42 |
| Italy | 7 | — | — | 3 | 11 | 11 | 27 | 10 | 25 | 31 |
| West Germany | 135 | 2 | 17 | 40 | 108 | 98 | 71 | 106 | 105 | 105 |
| Other | 84 | 39 | 44 | 34 | 40 | 35 | 48 | 44 | 25 | 15 |
| Total Foreign | 342 | 122 | 186 | 280 | 425 | 383 | 392 | 390 | 431 | 440 |
| Austria | 29 | 14 | 24 | 26 | 17 | 23 | 19 | 25 | 22 | 29 |
| Total | 371 | 136 | 210 | 306 | 442 | 406 | 411 | 415 | 453 | 469 |

*Source*: Guback, *The International Film Industry*, p. 48. Also see the annual volumes of the *International Motion Picture Almanac*, 1942–52 and 1957–81; *International Motion Picture and Television Almanac*, 1952–56; *Motion Picture Herald*, 1945–50; *British Film Year Book*, 1947–50; *Index de la Cinématographie Française*, 1947–55.

Marcel Prawy, who noted with respect the propaganda impact of the ISB film *Offene Türen*:

> To get a maximum number of theatres to play the film and to appeal to the Austrians with a basically dry subject we have followed one system in the approved script: to disguise propaganda for the Centers within the framework of a light musical of popular Viennese style. Austria is a country of "Schmalz." "Schmalz" is what they want. "Schmalz" is what they are producing themselves to get their houses packed. If we give them the desired "Schmalz" in one part of the film, they will be considerably more receptive to the things which we want to tell them and which we are telling them in the other part of the film.[165]

In second place were still the German films, especially for rural audiences. But precisely here, the dominant distribution position of the ISB and the MPEA and the resulting strong presence in numbers of U.S. films, and, in turn, the simultaneous limiting of German films, achieved a long-term alteration in patron preferences. In any event, the films from the United States had fended off all other film imports for the goodwill of the public soon after the end of the Second World War. Especially luxurious productions and masterfully staged action films attracted audiences. The most-loved genres included musicals and action films, especially gangster and Wild West films, but also sex films.[166] And the popularity of the last three genres caused strong headaches for the U.S.

occupation authorities. They even suspected that the Soviet authorities allowed the showing of U.S. films in their zone only because these films again and again included portrayals of the United States in an unfavorable light. For this reason, the ISB was instructed to "carefully screen and select the films destined for showing in the Russian Zone of Austria to insure the elimination of gangster, cowboy and sex pictures from the films supplied to Austrian theaters in the Russian Zone. The films selected by ISB should depict US life in its most favorable light."[167]

Here, were are truly dealing with the height of irony of the cultural Cold War: not the Red Army but the U.S. Army itself censored the films from Hollywood that were to be shown in the Soviet zone. This censorship was not limited only to the Soviet zone but included all U.S. film imports—with less success, however, in the western sectors. Under Secretary of State Dean Acheson lamented already in mid-1946 that nothing effective could be done about the import of unwanted U.S. films to Austria, although "from the viewpoint of information program objectives the exhibition of such films in Austria as *Dillinger* are considered harmful."[168] Even though the commercial interests of Hollywood might not have always corresponded with the expectations of the U.S. occupying authorities, they could assert themselves in most cases. Still, the U.S. Army was nevertheless successful in keeping a large number of U.S. films out of Austria. These included not only socially critical films such as *Grapes of Wrath* but also *Hunchback of Notre Dame*, *Babes in Arms*, *Son of Dracula*, *Ghost of Frankenstein*, *The Devil and Miss Jones*, *Tarzan's Secret Treasure*, and *Casablanca*![169] Even the film classic *Key Largo* was not allowed in Germany and Austria in 1948. The reason given is revealing:

> This gangster film, based on the highly successful stage play of the same name, builds up terrific excitement from its first moments in a style which American producers often do best at and which pleases the American public tremendously. This film will be one of the biggest public hits of the year and one of the biggest box-office successes.
>
> KEY LARGO is not a film to export to any country where we may be interested in either reeducation, reorientation or giving a positive and constructive picture of American life. To show such a picture in Germany would open both Military Government and the American Motion Picture industry to concerted and bitter attacks from church, state, city and school. The newspapers and the magazines which are so ready to criticize American films would shower criticisms upon a gangster picture such as have not been published since 1945.[170]

Yet, the ban affected more than just entertainment films. Even a documentary about Franklin D. Roosevelt, only four years after his death, was not allowed to be shown in 1949. The reason: the film contained too many scenes portraying the economic depression in the United States in the 1930s and too much praise for the success of the Red Army in the Second World War.[171] Neither the German nor the Austrian populations seemed to be "mature" enough to interpret these films—in the politically correct sense.

Whatever these bans achieved, the massive influence of U.S. pictures provided entertaining tutorials and socialization assistance in (West) German and Austrian theaters in order to make especially the youth of both countries "mature" enough for the central message of the American way of life: *the culture of consumption*.[172] Hollywood's power and the attractiveness of its products certainly made the United States the visually best known country on earth. Toward the end of the 1950s, U.S. films already enjoyed 50 to 90 percent of all film days globally. A massive study by the USIA, which included the film markets in Europe, Africa, Asia, and Latin America in 1961, shows quite clearly that "a considerable number of people who have never seen an American movie are nevertheless ready to venture an opinion of the impression of America left by these movies. . . . Hollywood movies are cited as a major source more frequently than any of the American media in these countries."[173]

Whether Hollywood actually contributed to a true understanding abroad of the real essence of democracy in the United States remains an open question indeed. "We need the voice of Thomas Jefferson and we have been given the voice of Hollywood . . . the cult of the happy ending, and the equally vicious cult of easy tears," lamented J. E. Morpurgo at the beginning of the 1950s.[174] It may be suspected that Jefferson would not have had a chance against Hollywood, even under more favorable circumstances.

Vistavision, Cinemascope, Wunderama, Cinerama: are the memories of the 1950s perhaps so flat because the 3-D movies were not successful? Still, one thing is certain: Hollywood indeed received its happy ending.

## Appendix

UNITAS-FILM Gesellschaft MBH Vienna I, Stubenring 6[175]

Vienna, June 20, 1947

To:
ISB Film Section
Attn.: Mr. Haeusserman
Neubaugasse 1
Vienna VII

Dear Mr. Haeusserman,

In our film *Gottes Engel sind überall* an American soldier has a conversation with a boy, 6 years old. The scene contains a benevolent and friendly dialogue of the American soldier and the boy. The part of the American soldier is very sympathetic and purely human and we attach a copy of the scenario.

The part will be given by a first class film actor.

We request to kindly allow that an American soldier's uniform is used for this purpose and ask for your kind cooperation in this matter.

Very truly yours:

Anton Profes
UNITAS-FILM

1 Enclosure


Enclosure:

73. Picture

Garden of the inn "Zum Eichkatzl" at Traunkirchen

A small, idyllic situated restaurant garden at Traunsee. An iron railing borders the bank-wall. In some distance, opposite the restaurant-garden, on a romantic cliff in the sea, a small church is situated. On one side of the garden on the street is an inn, a bright, friendly looking building. Not far away from the house a big cage in Barock [sic] style is erected, a sort of Barock voliere, containing a squirrel, the escutcheon of the house.

(Outside—Day-Time)

255. Total
The waitress Anni, a very healthy, nice looking girl wearing a "Dirndl" dress and a white apron, walks between the tables in the direction of the camera.
The playing of an accordion can be heard.                              (accordion)
Anni looks up, her face lights up, she
nearly shouts:                                     Jessass! . . . [Jesus]

256. Semi-Close
Josef and Flo are coming into the garden and behind them they drag a trailer.
Anni's voice joyful:                               It is Joschi—!
Josef smiles and calls:                            How do you do, Squirrel! . . .
Camera turns with them.
Flo, disappointed:                                 That's the squirrel? . . .
Josef, smiling:                                     Silly boy, she is only called thus. . . .
Josef looks sideways and says:                     Look there!
Flo cries:                                         Oooohh!
He runs out of the picture.
Camera drives nearer.
Anni shakes hand with Josef and
says heartily:                                     How do you do, Joschi! . . .

Josef, warmly:
That you have recognized me again.

Anni, it can be seen, is impressed by
him and says candidly:
In civilian dress I like you better. . . .

Josef skeptically looks down his
clothes:
I don't know, in this suit! . . .

Anni, enamored:
It always depends who is inside the
clothes! . . . come on, put away the
trailer! . . . I shall bring you
something to eat. . . .

257. Very Close
A squirrel is hopping merrily in the
cage to and fro—drolly it sits down
on a branch. Flo is standing before
the cage—low and tender he says:
Squirrel . . . wait a minute. . . . I shall
bring you some bread. . . .

A nut falls into the cage—the squirrel
leaps after it.
Flo looks up.

258. Close
An American soldier, a good and
friendly looking young man, stands
at the other side of the cage.
The American soldier chews gum,
turns to Flo, and says with a
pronunciation enforced by chewing:
How do you call this animal?

Flo:
This is a squirrel! . . .

The American soldier repeats:
Aischkatzl? . . . [squirrel?]

Flo:
No, E i c h-katzl! . . .

The American soldier:
Well, I say: Aischkatzl! . . .

Flo:
Not A i s c h, E i c h-katzl! . . . That's
not so easy. . . . How do you call
Eichkatzl in the American language?
. . .

The American soldier:
Squirrel! . . .

Flo:
Squörl!

The American soldier:
No—squirrel!

Flo:
I say: Squörl . . .

The American soldier:
Not "squörl"—squirrel! That's not
easy!

Flo and the American soldier are
laughing.

259. Close

| | |
|---|---|
| The American soldier: | What's your name? . . . Uuie haischt Du? . . . |
| Flo repeats: | Flo . . . and you? |
| The American soldier: | Me? . . . |
| Flo nods. | |
| The American soldier: | Joe . . . ! |

260. Close

Flo, enthusiastic:              That rhymes . . . Joe and Flo . . .
                                fine! . . . Have you toothaches?
Joe, not understanding:         What's that? Tsaanschmertsen?
Flo:                            Zahnschmerzen? . . . [toothaches]
                                that's thus—

He blows up the left cheek, makes a
painful face and holds the cheek.
Joe, smiling:                   I see—tooth-ache . . . no—I'm
                                chewing . . . ich kaue . . .
Flo, curious:                   All the time? . . . (Was denn) . . . and
                                what? . . .
Joe, smiling:                   Bubble-gum!
Flo repeats correctly:          Babblegam?
Joe, pleased:                   That's right! . . . Will you have some?
He takes out of the pocket a bubble-
gum and hands it to Flo.
Flo, delighted:                 Thank you, Joe! . . .
He opens the small package.
Joe regards him, smiling—then he
shoves a big piece into his mouth.

261. Big
Flo chews—a morsel goes the wrong
way, and he coughs. A little gum-
bubble is on his lips.
Joe laughs:                     (Laugh)

262. Close
Josef is sitting on a table—there are
on it a bellied coffee-pot, a plate fully
covered with bread and butterpieces,
and a big glass of honey stands
between two covers.
Anni takes place at his side, but has
no cover before her.
The laughing of Joe and Flo is heard.  (Laughing)

# 9

## The Result: The Children of
## Schmal(t)z and Coca-Cola

In a consumer society, the language and meaning of objects are fused with those
of the market-place.
—Stuart Ewen and Elizabeth Ewen, *Channels of Desire* (1982)

On the way back [from Innsbruck] I taught the Soviet general how to chew gum
which he did with much gnashing and uneasy chomping. The Soviets have no
idea of it at all.
—Guirey to Santford (1946)

To refer to Austria, the land on the *stream* according to the national
anthem, as a *streamlined land* in the 1950s may seem somewhat exaggerated
when one takes into consideration the typical resistance toward all innovation
unique to this country. Nevertheless, the influence of that which is generally
described as "American" culture was so vast that an anthropologist would
have good reason to say that the United States had unleashed a new form of
the Monroe Doctrine, namely, of the *Marilyn Monroe Doctrine*. The period of
occupation may have perhaps opened great possibilities for the victorious
powers, yet only the United States could exploit this situation to its fullest. On
the one hand, it could build upon the old European dream of U.S. democracy
as a way of life that secured a standard of living for the masses; on the other
hand, the United States alone possessed the necessary financial means to organize a comprehensive cultural program that embraced all facets of life.[1]

Between 1945 and 1955, the U.S. authorities in Austria and the Austrians
themselves set the course for trends that would completely unfold only after
the end of the 1950s. However, in certain areas of industrial culture and in the
consciousness industry, some of those developments had already become apparent during the interwar period.

The hundreds of thousands of GIs, those "vaccinated Crusaders" (in the
words of Wolfgang Koeppen), were living examples of America's abundance
and its way of life, which the Austrian populace could study and, in many
cases, learn to love (the last phrase is by no means directed against the so-called
chocolate girls). U.S. authorities, in addition, had prepared a powerful cultural
agency of the U.S. Army—the ISB. Its mission was simple—the most positive
presentation of all that was "American"—and its impact was invaluable.

The influence of U.S. culture officers on the Austrian media landscape was immense. A new kind of boulevard journalism was introduced in the *Wiener Kurier* that was frequently imitated. Furthermore, many of today's most prominent Austrian journalists were trained by experienced U.S. colleagues. Almost all Austrian papers continuously printed countless ISB articles and pictures. Individual publications were directed toward workers and farmers, teachers and doctors, the youth and intellectuals. Finally, it cannot be forgotten that U.S. agencies held a leading position in the Austrian news market.

The U.S. radio station Rot-Weiss-Rot, the most popular broadcasting organization in Austria, would fundamentally influence developments in radio. News programming slanted toward U.S. politics was obvious. The popularity of the station, however, resulted more likely from its program structure, which imitated its U.S. counterparts. Programs successfully tested in the United States were Austrianized, and quiz shows as well as others including listener participation were particularly loved. News would soon be aired every hour on the hour. Program series were introduced, as were script departments staffed by talented young Austrians. In 1948, one could hear the first advertisements. Then in 1949, the first disc jockeys, Fred Ziller and Günther Schifter, followed, and in 1952, Rot-Weiss-Rot left the radio show business catering to schools only to establish the pop show *Vergnügt um Elf*. Those who were not yet satisfied could tune their dials to American Forces Network, Voice of America, Blue Danube Network, and Radio Free Europe, where young listeners could hear the newest U.S. hits.

Hundreds of thousands of visitors became familiar with America through books, magazines, newspapers, films, posters, slides, paintings, music, sports, entertainment, and science in the twelve America Houses and Information Centers. Many thousands of volumes were given or loaned to schools. Publishers who published unprofitable, yet politically important, U.S. books were subsidized. American bookmobiles brought books, records, and films to the markets and villages. U.S. theater pieces and compositions were supported and sometimes even performed against the will of Austrian directors. Performances by artists and even entire productions, including *Porgy and Bess*, were also organized.

Thanks to U.S. school experts, Austrian schoolbooks were now dedicated to U.S. topics for the first time, and English finally asserted itself as the first choice of a foreign language in the schools. A bona fide explosion of dissertations and theses on U.S. topics could be seen at the universities. Not only could Austrian students hear many U.S. guest professors, but professors and students also profited from stipends that were granted within the perimeters of exchange programs.

A great selection of programs was constructed for children and teens ranging from school festivals, Christmas parties, youth clubs, summer camps, and sporting events to the establishment of playgrounds and swimming pools.

U.S. youth officers, operating under the auspices of the Austrian Youth Activities (AYA), were concerned with the spiritual and physical happiness of the young whom they were to supervise—and this in the truest sense. For example, *the* American drink, Coca-Cola, was initially not available for purchase during the first years of the occupation. Instead, it was produced exclusively for GI consumption. Therefore, a rather special incentive for participating in AYA events for Austrian children was the free distribution of Coca-Cola rations. The AYA expenditures for the Coca-Cola gifts amounted to no less than between 30,000 and 50,000 schillings monthly in 1949.[2] These investments served two purposes: on the one hand, they improved the reputation of the U.S. Army with Austrian youths, an important group for long-term political goals; on the other hand, they also simultaneously laid the groundwork for a new market.

Another example of the successful work of the ISB is demonstrated by the introduction of 4-H Clubs. Based upon the U.S. model, these clubs for rural youths were to familiarize the next agricultural generation in Austria with the newest developments in American agriculture through educational activities, excursions, and competitions. By 1950, *Deine-4-H-Klub-Zeitung* (Your 4-H Club newspaper) reached a publication figure of 28,500 copies. The brochure *Was sind 4-H-Klubs?* (What are 4-H Clubs?) was distributed by the hundreds of thousands. It is particularly interesting that of the 577 clubs with 14,700 members, only 95 (16.5 percent) were located in the U.S. zone of occupation, while the Chamber of Agriculture in Lower Austria—in the Soviet zone!—organized 264 clubs with 6,400 members (45.8 percent). In Austria, by the way, "4-H" stood for head (*Haupt*), heart (*Herz*), hands (*Hände*), and—in place of health (*Heil*, which U.S. officers found still all too familiar)—healthy living (*heilsames Leben*).

Finally, in light of the desperate needs of the populace, the immense propaganda impact of countless material aid measures, especially the Marshall Plan (ERP), cannot be forgotten. In addition, a small percentage of ERP funds to be expended for cultural propaganda purposes was also directly and contractually secured. It is not necessary to repeat here in detail the impact that Marshall Plan funds had upon the reconstruction of Austria, as did its side effects in the fight against Communism, strengthening the parliamentary system according to the Western image, establishing the Social Partnership with pro-American trade unions, supporting certain production lines such as primary industries and industries producing semifinished goods and introducing U.S. products, productions systems, and management methods, thereby decreasing the strains on the U.S. economy. *This* billion dollars proved to be a wise investment.

It hardly seems too presumptuous to assert that the dreams of the "American dream" (nightmares were not included, there were already enough of those) played an absolutely decisive role in the political developments of the

Second Republic. Regardless of how much the Austrian population actually knew about the United States, regardless of how twisted the images might have been (and still are), the United States stood for wealth, a comfortable standard of living for the masses, freedom, modernity, the culture of consumption, and a peaceful life. America was somewhere between paradise and the land of milk and honey on the cognitive maps of the Austrians.

Official U.S. cultural propaganda, which soon after the end of the war turned from antifascism to anti-Communism, certainly acted as a motor and a catalyst. But even those groups of the populace who did not have direct contact with this information were constantly confronted with the United States, even after the end of the occupation: in the newspapers; on the radio; in advertisements, which were almost completely oriented toward U.S. images and, in part, created by U.S. agencies; in records; on the television, which would first play an increasing role at the end of the 1950s; and especially in the movies. Particularly toward the end of the Second World War, the world of mass media had become American; there was hardly a part of the world that could withdraw itself from made-in-America messages.

In 1921 Hugo von Hofmannsthal defined film as an ersatz for dreams. In the 1950s these (ersatz) dreams were predominantly American, even in Austria. Furthermore, between 1950 and 1960, 40 to 50 percent of all films shown in Austria were American. These figures do not even include those European films that were produced with U.S. capital, which include a large number of "independent" films that were poor reproductions of American flicks, with the exception of a few such as *Lemmy Caution* with Eddie Constantine. The desperate situation of the Austrian film industry strengthened this trend. However, even the wife of the forest ranger of Silberwald wore makeup from the United States (à la américain), and Hans Moser, too, had to deal with the problems of an inheritance from the United States in the movie *Ober, zahlen*. ("Pride nowadays stops at $5,000 and not at $20,000!," as stated by his waiter-colleague Paul Hörbiger.)

Let us look at a few titles of U.S. films and examples from the world of advertising in the 1950s. Their slogans, in particular, showed that no matter where the extolled products came from, American-sounding names were highly attractive and helped increase sales figures. The following examples have been randomly chosen from thousands.

While *Hurricane, The Wizard of Oz, The Paleface*, and *For Whom the Bell Tolls* were shown in Austrian theaters with great success in 1950, the hour had come for a "new" piece of clothing, the "lumberjack" (or, as it was colloquially pronounced, *Lempatscheck*). On the marketing front, anti-Communist hysteria could certainly be compared with only one other phenomenon—an invasion of dandruff, which all of Austria seemed to be plagued by. Fortunately, to their aid came U.S. cosmetics; the beauty treatment of tomorrow was Max Factor,

Helena Rubinstein, Cutex, Atkinson, Sherks Cold Cream, and H. J. B. Williams Aqua Velva Aftershave.

In 1951, *Colorado, Station West, A Streetcar Named Desire* (Vivian Leigh and Marlon Brando), and *How Green Is My Valley* (Sonja Ziemann and Rudolf Prack) were shown. In advertising, Christian Dior's "New Look" (from Paris!), U.S. nylons, and underwear made of perlon would make people wonder. "Sex appeal," "vamp," and "pin-up girl" were no longer foreign terms, and obviously disturbed viewers complained about the all-too-manicured appearance of many schoolgirls as Rita Hayworth and Esther Williams during the ball season.

While French colonial troops could hardly protect themselves from the rebellion in Morocco, *Casablanca* was shown in Austria in 1952. In addition, Walt Disney's *Grand Parade, Viva Zapata, Two Flags West* (and *Wild West in Upper Bavaria*), *Bambi, Zorro's Fighting Legion*, the 3-D film *Bwana Devil*, the long-awaited *Gone with the Wind, Montana, Rio Grande, Stagecoach, South of St. Louis, Drums along the Mohawk, Texas Carnival*, and *Rock Island Trail* were unusually successful—and what a lesson in U.S. geography! There is no way to find out whether *The Hasty Heart* (Ronald Reagan) was to be a success. Austria countered *Harlem Dances Voodoo in Harlem* with *Sensation in San Remo* (Marika Rökk), *The Private Lives of Elizabeth and Essex* (Errol Flynn and Bette Davis) with *Maria Theresia* (Paula Wessely), *Love Manoeuver* with *Du bist die Rose vom Wörthersee* (You are the flower of the Wörther Lake). These woods-and-meadow films coaxed a sigh from the troubled critic: "It's too bad for the nice scenery." One even tried to let the water out of the pool for Esther Williams; during the Christmas season, the film *Seesterne* (Starfish) began running, the first Austrian underwater revue film, with Eva Kerbler and Rudolf Carl.

The elegant gentleman wore Tarr-Rasierbox aftershave, a Palm Beach cravat, a touring coat, and city shoes to accompany his hairstyle à la Burt Lancaster while reading a "best-seller," watching "quiz" shows, using Mobiloil Arctic (heavy duty) in his car, watching the Johnnies, Charlies, Bobbies, and Frankies at the first Austrian bartender competition, where one was amused by Santa Claus, LPs, and the Philips Changer, Pullman caps (continuously sold out), nylons, and "kinder-overalls." The ladies dreamed of kitchen appliances and the American bedroom, which (how exciting) was comparable to a laboratory. The "smart" youngster could not yet afford Lucky Strike or Chesterfield ("die Ami") and therefore reached for Jonny or Old Splendor, the newest cigarettes of the American type, which slowly drove out the Oriental cigarettes from the market.

By 1953, the U.S. films *Titanic, Robber's Roost, Hellfire, Zorro Rides Again, That Wonderful Urge, Cleopatra, The Racket, Scared Stiff, Rose of Cimarron, Thunder Bay*, and the 3-D film *The Charge at Feather River* competed with the Sascha-Film *Auf der grünen Wiese* (On the green field). The box office hit *Lili* (Leslie Caron) was soon to follow, as well as the Semperit-Lili doll (ERP made this possible). The smart person wore the Combi-Trench, which they would more than likely purchase in Austria's first boutique. Appropriate for the Chevrolet, the most-driven American car in Austria, was the Trenchcoat Traveller, Williams Luxury Shaving Cream, umbrellas called Darling, baby slippers, kiddy chewing gum, Rowdies, the five o'clock tea in "The Open Gate," the Kardex organizer from Remington Rand, and the first complaints about the growing noise problems. The Christ Child and Santa Claus could both congregate in the "Hoover School" of democracy, enjoying electrification studies under the motto "All for Hoover, a Hoover for all."

And speaking of electrification: the power-station structures of the period—true concrete monuments to the Marshall Plan in Austria—delivered more than just the necessary energy basis for the modernization of the country alone. These power stations could also be seen as *energy centers* that, together with the nerves extending from them—the cables—made it first possible to incorporate all households into a central network that finally also enabled the culture industry to reach all people and to offer illusions as wares.

Between 1953 and 1962, the number of electric gadgets increased dramatically. The number of electric stoves increased from 115,000 to 514,000, refrigerators from 30,000 to 591,000, and washing machines from 8,000 to 280,000. The number of radios, which had to be registered with the communication authorities, grew from 1,318,039 in 1950 to 1,988,267 in 1960; telephones increased from 260,000 to 428,807. Even synthetics were now more frequently used in Austria, although still relatively less when compared with international consumption figures. While already 7.5 kilograms were consumed, statistically speaking, by each inhabitant of the United States and 4.5 kilos in Germany, the figures in Austria were only one kilo per person. From electronic heating pads to irons, from record players to electric feeding cribs for cows—all of these products enjoyed the reputation that these were common goods for each U.S. citizen and had been accessible already for many years.

In 1954, the following films made their way to Austrian theaters: *From Here to Eternity, How to Marry a Millionaire, Mutiny on the Caine, Escape from Fort Bravo, Rails into Laramie, Red Hell, Goodbye, Mr. Chips, Forever Female, White Christmas*, and *Warner Bros. Great Jazz Parade* (with Harry James, Woodie Herman, Cab Calloway, Doris Day, and Lester Young). German producers countered the last one with *Grosse Starparade* (Great star parade, starring Evelyn Künecke, Horst Winter, and Bully Buhlan).

In an effort to marry one of the few millionaires in Austria, Plasto-Sein ("your breasts will look wonderful") as well as Mirodent gum ("chew your teeth healthy") would surely be useful. Scientific studies were awaited by men and women from the newly established Austrian Society for Sexual Research. The greatest Christmas cheer for many a woman was sure to have been the Star-Mix hand mixer. Children were delighted by the "Texas-Farmer-Hose

Advertisement for American-style merchandise
(*Wiener Kurier*, February 27, 1954)

(Pants)-Jim," teens by the "Cowboyhemd Jacky," the "Ami-Hose Jonny," and the "orig.-amerik. Steave-Jean-Hose"[!]; those who were still not satisfied could purchase an "Ami-Texas-Farmerhose Jim." For the chic father we had the "Ami-Arbeitsanzug First Work," and the continuous news about Caryl W. Chessman's fight in death cell 2455 created the corresponding ambience.

In addition to the U.S. films *The Dolly Sisters, The Siege at Red River, Vera Cruz, The Glenn Miller Story, The Vanishing Prairie, Overland Pacific, Svengali,* and *Holiday Inn* (Lionel Hampton), audiences were introduced to American youth culture in *East of Eden* (James Dean) and *The Wild One* (Marlon Brando) in 1955. Interestingly enough, *The Wild One* was hardly successful until the Austrian media began to react hysterically. The film was shown in Vienna for only one week in August and five days in October. The West German film industry answered with *Lass die Sonne wieder scheinin* (Let the sun shine again), and Austrian producers hit back hard with the seemingly appropriate hammer: *Sissi*, a quaint tale of the Austrian empress Elizabeth.

Fashion news stressed the Belly-Cap, Helena Rubinstein's "Opaline Make-up und Barrett" ("removes the hair from your legs, arms, underarms, and face"). Women hoped to replace the increasingly scarce number of servants with the Kitchen-Aid ("the girl for everything in the kitchen"). He who thought of the refrigerator, thought of Frigidaire (by GE), and the "Original American Permanent Wave" crowned the Happy-End Make-up, which went over just fine in the "Adebar" with "Just Jazz." The stressed *Wirtschaftswunder* manager, who just introduced the newest IBM-EDPM mainframe computing machine, time clock, and electric typewriter based on the newest American standards, all of a sudden also became confronted with the manager's disease. For factory and office workers, who had to conform to the new electronic time-control instruments, there remained only a hobby, Do-it-Yourself—and yet another consolation: the chance to buy things on installment. The best-sellers of 1955 were Herbert Tichy's *Cho Oyu*, followed by Esquire's *Cocktail Book* and Walt Disney's *The Desert Lives* and *The Wonders of the Prairie*.

In addition to the 1956 films *Moby Dick, Meet Me in Las Vegas, The Harder They Fall, Lady and the Tramp, Trapeze, The Seven-Year Itch, Rhapsody in Blue, The Benny Goodman Story*, and *Love Me or Leave Me*, a new type of U.S. film was introduced that would give an entire generation (or the part that would later come to write about it) new cult figures: *Giants* and *Rock around the Clock*. Even a visual accompaniment to the most heart-breaking romance of the decade—Soraya and the Shah—was provided by Hollywood: the Grace Kelly film week in the cinemas. Austria confronted this challenge stoically not only with *Kitty und die grosse Welt* (Kitty and the great wide world, starring Romy Schneider and Karlheinz Böhm) and *Musikparade* (Peter Alexander and "jazz trumpeter" Peterli Hinnen), but also with a new production of the Viennese Ice Follies (music: Robert Stolz) in which Jirina Nekalowa, called "sex appeal on ice skates," would prove her honorable reputation during a leopard-skin number surrounded by Indians. The number *Dangerous Love* was announced as a "super-American film production in 3-D and Technicolor," in which the Cold War was represented by the conflict between the red man and the trappers.

Those who got too hot in the auditorium of this ice show could reach for Air-Fresh, a true air pollutant; Anti-Svet looked after your underarms, and Bryl-creem, Mennen Skin Bracer and Lather Shave, Gillette Rasier Creme, Fit, Brisk, and Lanol Spray also aided the "New Look." Fashions for the "career" girl included a Set, lipstick from Margret Astor, nylon clothes (in dots, stripes, and flower patterns), and nylons from the stocking bar (and for a friend, a Gentleman-Slip). For most women, however, the dream to own a dryer was just that; the reality remained hand lotion.

General Motors still rode on top of progress, and the revolution was completed by the Hoover "wonder ball" vacuum cleaner. The hand-formed paper bag uselessly resisted its demise with the plastic bag (presentation: the good industrial form—more attractive, more hygienic). And while a thief made off with the regional medical insurance fund in the town of Enns, mirroring a Wild West or gangster film, the skeleton of Salzburg's first high-rise, Hotel Europa, was finally erected. Even in Vienna's Prater, streamlined U.S. cars and motorcycles replaced the boring wood carousel horses, as recorded tapes did the announcers, and U.S. shooting apparatuses with electronic contacts successfully competed with old-fashioned carnival booths. Naturally, loop-the-loop and scooters could not be missing. From now on, even during winter, only the best of the best would accompany the most delicious grilled specialties: since late fall of 1956, the entire Austrian population knew "thirst knows no season: drink Coca-Cola (ice cold)."

Nevertheless, not all that came out of the United States was welcomed in Austria. When the African-American singer Theresa Greene, who had been invited to perform by the Viennese Konzerthausgesellschaft in October 1956, wanted to retire to her hotel after her performance, all rooms were suddenly occupied. Was this typically Austrian? Soft drinks OK, but "foreign"-looking people stay out?

In 1957, Hollywood's films included *Three Violent People, Gun Glory, Will Success Spoil Rock Hunter?* (Jayne Mansfield), *High Society, Illegal, The Songs of Satchmo, Border Feud, Four Guns to the Border,* and, just in time for the sweltering summer heat, *Calypso Heat Wave. Rebel without a Cause* was countered with the Austrian films *Winzerin von Langenlois* (The lady vinedresser from Langenlois), *Skandal in Ischl,* and the Paula-Wessely-Film *Unter Achtzehn* (Under eighteen, starring Vera Tschechowa; music: Carl de Groof). Above and beyond this, a pyromaniac from Apetlon demonstrated the impressive power of the film medium: he lit the theater on fire during the presentation of *Something of Value,* whose title in German ironically was "Flames over Africa." Even Gunther Philipp, as *Der kühne Schwimmer* (The courageous swimmer), could not come to the rescue.

But at least one's thirst could be quenched—with Sunkist oranges from California. The Austrian media may have always poked fun at "American gadget mania," but the Bar-Secretary (naturally filled with whisky bottles), the waterproof tourists' watch Everlight, the Florida heating method, the full transistor, the Radio Gross-Super, the Calculator 99, the Skyriter(!), the Flu-Defensor, and the electric squirt-gun Champion Super were all the latest craze. And the "American kitchen" and the "practical American sideboard" remained the desire of many a housewife—in H. C. Artmann's 1958 dialect poem *med ana schwoazzn dintn* they already stood in every communal apartment. W. F. Adlmüller designed the "Dream-Line," Teddy Plaids protected against the cold, Socketts absorbed sweat, Rock 'n' Roll pants could be purchased for 195 schillings, which could be worn with the poplin blouse and the vest based on the "American Façon" and "new from Paris with Viennese charm"—the Belly-Calypso cap. While the electronic stove introduced the new age of kitchens (baked chicken, ready to serve in four minutes), the first new parking garage with an automatic elevator and escalator was to counter the newly ensuing parking difficulties at Vienna's General Shopping Center (AEZ). In the same way, a typical Austrian answer to the provocation of Sputnik and the beginning world arms race was found: the *Schlurfraketen* (rockers' rockets).

Against this, even Hollywood's *Twelve Angry Men* were helpless in the following year. And the confusion was perfect with the promotion of the British rock 'n' roll film *The Tommy Steele Story*, airing the slogan "England's Jazz Star Nr. 1." But even the police now followed the streamline trend. The summer uniform shirts of 1958 were now Sanforized, the summer caps were made of indanthren: watch out, you Schlurfs! Coca-Cola—finally—put the practical family bottle on the market, perhaps to help the ever-increasing latchkey children, whose lives were also made less difficult through instant coffee, infragrill, and Relax-Fauteuil. The petticoat was seen on the streets and at parties, and technically produced music was no longer tied to the wall socket. At last we had the "Party 59 (Philips)" full transistor and the "Hornyphon Siesta" full transistor portable with integrated record player. One's rest surely ended with the Hornyphon Siesta, and the dancers, bathed in sweat, now reached for the Anti-Svet-Stick. For the athletic tan, now Spray-Tan was available, and at the Salzburg Festival, Fritz Hochwälder's drama *Donnerstag* introduced a contemporary, modern version of Faust aptly named Niklas Manuel *Pomfrit* (French fry).

In 1959, film showings included *Invaders from Mars, The Ten Commandments, North by Northwest, Rio Bravo, Some Like It Hot, The Geisha Boy, Pal Joey,* and *Gunsmoke in Tucson*. Yet, neither these U.S. films nor the Viennese Boys' Choir in *Wenn die Glocken hell erklingen* (When the bells ring) and *Die Nacht vor der Premiere* (The night before the premiere, with the ideal combination of Marika Rökk, Louis Armstrong, Helmut Zacharias, Billy Mo, and the Sunnies), as well as Vistavision, Cinemascope, Wunderama, Cinerama, 3-D, and not even *Tom & Jerry in Cine-Maus-Cope* could hinder the fact that the heyday of the film was also nearing its end in Austria. Statistics on motion picture audiences show an increase in visits from 92.5 to 114 million between 1950 and 1955; yet, in 1960, the figure had decreased to 106.5 million. In Vienna alone, two million tickets less had been sold than in 1959. The scapegoat for these developments was quickly found: television and motorization. Few faulted the films themselves, for example, perhaps in the (self-)castration of Hollywood, which had already begun prior to McCarthyism, or in the expulsion of Austrian films from their Eden of forest, field, homeland, and Viennese wine bar. Even with respect to the future of cinema, Austrian developments followed U.S. developments— ten years removed, as usual. If theaters had once been turned into movie houses, then movie houses would be transformed into parking garages.

Even pimps, who thought well of themselves, now appeared as auto gangsters (Charly K.). The "autoradio" traveler aired the appropriate sounds, and the bride let herself be seduced by a Coca-Cola and rum. The Super-Sex-Revue elicited hair-raising excitement and, still better, so did the risqué American Sex-Revue with Dorothi Neal, "The Venus of Striptease." Gentlemen would feel comfortable in the briefs and T-shirts of the international underwear producer Jockey, while the ladies, under their vacation dress "Holiday," skirts and clothes made of denim (Modell Blue-Jeans-Girl), could don perhaps "the most successful elastic stocking in the world: little X (made of Heathcoats Twylex-Nylon-Elastic tulle decorated with lurex braid trimming)." Teenagers and Twens were "up-to-date" at parties with black nylons, "Petticoats," the "Party-dress," "Slippers," and straight-leg pants while "Dancing." In the best case, the music had a "cool Beat" and "Drive" in stereophonics and Hi-Fi from record desks with "Flip-Over" diamond needles. The "Juice" was in the "Grill-Room," the "Car-A-Van" waited outside with the "Auto-Bag," and "Make-up for the floor" allowed for "After-Party" cleanliness.

The bank Raiffeisenkasse let the George S. May International Company give it a new image: their contracts perhaps would be signed with a "Fountain-Ball" pen. Products influenced by industrial design were again and again found wrapped in "Austrophan" (the ideal clear plastic wrap) and packaged in a gift box. For an automatic shine one could go to "Putzboy," the first shoe-shine machine, and the Viennese Electronics Institute proudly presented Austria's contribution to the automation age: the electronic mouse "Niki." In the area of television, which officially began in January 1956, developments were contrary to those in film. The number of registered TV sets grew rapidly: 73 in 1954, 457 in 1955, 1,415 in 1956, 3,975 in 1957, 16,324 in 1958, 49,238 in 1959, 112,223 in 1960, and 192,553 in 1961. By 1961, only 45 percent of the country had access to television reception, yet already 63 percent of the population took advantage of it. The developments in registration figures during the second half of the 1950s may seem low in absolute terms. Yet, if the percentage figures are also taken into consideration, the tremendous success of this mass medium was quite clear in the 1960s. Still there were some difficulties. While approximately 13,000 televisions were sold in 1957, only 9,000 were registered. A small taste of the television craze in the decades to follow could be seen in the latest fad in women's fashions in August 1955, when the trial run had only just begun—a pantsuit called "Television-Set," and this with only one thousand televisions in all of Austria.

A television broadcast system such as that in Austria could never be maintained without foreign program contributions, especially during the initial years. Indeed, programs from the Federal Republic of Germany and the United States filled up almost the entire air time. The popularity of future programs such as *Dallas* and *Dynasty* could already be presumed on the basis of the television imports from America between 1956 and 1960. In the early years, many of the most successful children and family programs were produced in U.S. studios and dubbed in Germany, including *Corky, Lady and the Tramp*, various adventure series, Walt Disney's nature films, and *Father Knows*

*Best* (Robert Young and Jane Wyatt)—which introduced not only the soap opera format but also the concept of the television family. The list continues with the *Perry Como Show, Hawaii 5-O, Fury*, an Alfred Hitchcock series, *Texas Rangers, Nat King Cole Show*, and *Jazz at the Philharmonic*. Also dramas by Arthur Miller, Clifford Odets, and Eugene O'Neill were included. The most-favored quiz shows were based on their U.S. counterparts: *21, Jede Sekunde einen Schilling, Wer spielt mit?, Sieben auf einen Streich*, and *Was bin ich?* This popularity was enhanced by entertainers and quizmasters such as Lou van Burg and Peter Frankenfel. U.S. idioms, even if they were often parodied, were used in Austrian productions such as *Spiegel vorm Gesicht* and the series *Es gibt immer drei Moeglichkeiten* (by Fritz Eckhardt, Carl Merz, Gerhard Bronner, and Peter Wehle).

Television is the medium that, more than any other, was (and is) best suited for the "American image." And yet, television technology was by no means exclusively developed in the United States. But the head start of the United States in the development of the television as a mass medium had a decisive influence upon the fact that television *language* became American. The visual presence of the United States allowed *Reports from America* to become a kind of luxurious, national history lesson.

In the twentieth century Europe lost not only its dominating economic position but also its leading position as a radiating center for music. Developed just about the same time as jazz, the record made it possible for jazz to become the most important enriching of music culture of the century. By the 1920s at the latest, recorded music became cosmopolitan, and the United States became its most important transmitter. As the first jazz band, colloquially known as "Die Neger," played in the Kaisergarten in Vienna's Prater in 1922, Vienna's chic, including Conrad Veidt, Sebastian Droste, and Adolf Loos, pilgrimaged to the concerts almost daily. Loos had already created a stylish ambiance with his American Bar in the Kärntnerstrasse passageway in 1908/9. Even during the Second World War, the enthusiasm (of a minority) for jazz blossomed in Vienna, and during the 1950s, Hans Koller, Fatty George, Friedrich Gulda, Joseph Zawinul, and others held some rather "hot" sessions. Zawinul, now known as Joe, became the most significant Austrian jazz export to the United States at the beginning of the 1960s.

After the Second Word War, the U.S. companies RCA-Victor, Columbia, Capital, Decca, and Mercury not only dominated the American market but divided up the Western European market with the four firms EMI-Lindström (= Electric and Musical Industries), Philips, AEG-Teldec, and Siemens-Elektro A.G.-Deutsche Grammophon, with which they were incorporated through complicated legal arrangements. The market was clearly rigged, and only the large number of subsidiary labels hid their true owners. For example, Deutsche Grammophon owned the labels DGG, Archiv Produktion, Literarisches Archiv, Polydor, Heliodor MGM, United Artists, Veroc, and Commond. Only toward the end of the 1950s would new developments take place on the record market. At the beginning of the decade, the 78 record still dominated; it was slowly replaced by the 45 and then by the 33. In addition, pop music outsold all other musical forms. At the end of the 1950s, popular hits amounted to 90 percent of all records sold.

Already after the First World War, the fox-trot, slow fox, Charleston, English waltz, one-step, and tango had triumphed in Europe. Now one danced the rumba, jitterbug, boogie-woogie, mambo, samba, cha-cha, badminton, rock 'n' roll, calypso, stroll, hoola-hoop, hawk, and twist and reveled in the guitar playback tricks by Les Paul. No matter where the rhythms had originated (e.g., from Latin America or the Caribbean), they came to Europe clad in the U.S. sound. Dominating the Austrian market were especially the record companies Elite-Special, Decca (The Supreme Sound), Columbia, Austrophon, Polydor, Harmona, Telefunken, Popular, and Standard. Austrian record buyers found themselves in a rather interesting situation. Not only popular Austrian singers such as Freddy, Peter Alexander, or Lolita but also recordings by local orchestras and musicians faced import taxes because the artists' market was dominated by German agencies and companies. In 1938, the relationship between foreign profits made on the performance rights of works by Austrian composers to royalties exported still had been 40:1; in 1950, this relationship was 1:1. Furthermore, Austrian authors frequently had to accept West Germans as coauthors of their songs just to be accepted by German publishing houses—and these coauthors automatically received 50 percent of the rights. It is more than ironic that cries denouncing "American cultural imperialism" were frequently made by these same businesspeople.

Already long before the so-called Ami wail annoyed many adults' ears, songs of *Heimat* (home) and yearnings for exotic places had copied U.S. arrangements, rhythms, and sounds. The cover versions of U.S. titles were innumerable. "Die Geisterreiter" (The ghost riders) rode with Harry Count, "Zwei Gitarren am Meer" (Two guitars at the sea) were played by the Ruwiro Hawaiians, Gerhard Wendland wanted to go to "Santa Fé," the Texas Duo let "Cowboys durch die Nacht zieh'n" (Cowboys ride through the night), and the Standard Jazz Band and Erwin Halletz hoped for "Ich und Du und ein Haufen Geld dazu" (You and I and a ton of money). Even the interpreter of the "Herz-Schmerz Polka," Johannes Fehring, compiled a jazz book soon after the end of the war.

The names of German and Austrian singers experienced a magical metamorphosis into English. Names that sounded particularly American (Jack, Joe, Bill, Johnny, Jimmy, Freddy, Macky, Charly, Jenny, Rosalie, Lou) appeared more frequently in German lyrics than did Southern European names, by a ratio of 5 to 1. Even geographic locations in the United States were referred to more often than European ones. And let us not forget Pidgin English vocabulary, which grew to include boy, girl, baby, darling, yeah, okay, hello, yes, goodbye, sweetheart, daddy, ranch, farmer, sweet, happy, moonlight (the night is beautiful!), kiss, money, old, young, little, fans, quick, and playboy. Obviously, the pop hit was not the only medium in which American jargons were used: for the lingoes of show business, technology, sports, fashion, business, mass media, and, in particular, advertising and science certainly made contributions as well.

After 1954 / 55, a new specter appeared before the eyes of parents in America: rock 'n' roll. And—as Chuck Berry expressed the insistence of a generation when he sang, "It's gonna be Rock and Roll music / If you wanna dance with me"—European adults would soon learn to fear that specter, just as their American contemporaries did. English-language abilities were sufficient to understand its proclamations, and its hammering rhythms even penetrated noise-polluted ears. According to the opinion of an Austrian critic, this *Shaking and Squirming* would lead even an objective viewer to understand that this was only a dancing version of highly explicit acts—and that was also *thoroughly* intended. A desperate American journalist commented on Paul Anka's singing: "It is as if a soldier shot in the neck was saying his last prayer."

Such accusations were by no means new. New, however, was the fact that this product of acculturation from Africa, America, *and* Europe had developed into the cultural statement of a single generational group, namely, the young— who owned the music but not the profits. The success of this music is based on various reasons. First, the breakup of the American Society of Composers, Authors and Publishers (ASCAP) and the Tin Pan Alley monopolies allowed the breakthrough of African-American music, termed "race music" on white radio stations. The African-Americans now brought the essential musical impulses, while the white businessmen reaped its fruits. Besides the presence of countless, undoubtedly exceptionally talented artists, the development of the general standard of living and the changes within the technical-material sector played a large role as well. And, not to be forgotten, *for the first time*, money could be found in the pockets of teenagers![3]

Rock 'n' roll is a music of quotes, of blues, rhythm and blues, country and western, bluegrass, and much more; an antiart that was particularly well suited for emigration into a revolutionary idyll. It especially caused the proletarian, inner-city youths to "Rock around the Clock." As this movie with Bill Haley and the Comets was shown in Vienna in December 1956, the film distribution firm could proudly report on its success: "If the atmosphere gets too hot, please keep on your skirts and blouses." And: "The cinema's seats are determined to survive this film." Vienna's police force was nevertheless well prepared for this "subversive" presentation and constituted—in civilian dress—a not unimportant part of the audience. This was also surely the reason why—according to Otto F. Beer—the rockers in Vienna's dancing schools maintained the elegant reservation of British Members of Parliament. For Beer, the film evoked screaming dervishes, ritual tribal dances, and bars that could be compared to an insane asylum that was run by its patients. Beer also delivered a description of the shaking and squirming that was both classic as well as lacking in understanding: "At the first trumpet sob[!], couples fell into convulsive twitches, the gentleman threw the lady and caught her again on his back, hardly moving around his own axis; to his surprise, he pulls her through his legs, even prefers to stand her on her head or throws her around his neck, and the music plays on."[4] By the way, don't fear! The dreaded excesses occurred a week later—at a soccer game between Real Madrid and Rapid (won by the former, 2-0) in which Happel and Lesmes had to be excluded.

University Professor Dr. Richard Wolfram even saw the recommencement of medieval dance sickness. Rock 'n' roll and "Comic Stripes" [sic], according to this expert, lead not only to rage, madness, complete lack of restraint and control—"a crazy scream of the clarinet[!] ends the phrase, and the tuba[!!!!] wails romm-romm-romm-romm"—no, this recipe for the intoxication of primitive people was, in addition, perhaps much more brutal and clever than common drugs.[5] Now, certainly this was no longer the established in-step march, but "this introduction to sexual urges" in the daily radio program and a few wild syncopations nevertheless did not mean a real revolt. The number of fights related to rock 'n' roll in cities like Vienna and Linz remained insignificant, and most of the protagonists were consumers of rebellion anyway, a position that the oh-so-rebellious generation of the 1960s expertly repeated.

A revolt of quite other dimensions was concurrently taking place in Little Rock, Arkansas; but what does that have to do with rock 'n' roll? Nevertheless, even though the emancipating character of rock 'n' roll increasingly reverted to a commercial slogan under the control of the media industry, the fact that the system knew how to make money with a musical rebellion does not necessarily lead to the conclusion that all the shaking and squirming was corrupt. In the words of Helmut Salzinger, it showed, at best, that the system of late capitalism felt (and feels) secure enough to make a profit even out of a revolution.

Certainly, the black ghetto outcry, which had already been diluted in the white version of rock 'n' roll, was soon debased to "Sugar, Sugar Baby" (Peter Kraus, which sold 500,000 records in 1956/57) in the German language. Elvis Presley's first film *Love Me Tender* is a glowing example of the German art of dubbing. The German title was the sentimental "Gunsmoke and Hot Songs." And Presley's *Jailhouse Rock* appeared in German as "Texas Cellar," in which something was going on. Surely this phenomenon could not really be all that dangerous. Was not "Papa's in the ice-box looking for a can of ale, Mama's in the backyard learning how to jive an' wail" (Louis Prima, 1957) thoroughly in the interest of the electricity industry? And did one not see explicit signs of rock 'n' roll attractively contrasting with the grand gowns and tuxedos even at the Viennese Philharmonic Ball already in 1959?

The musical quality of the early Elvis numbers as well as those by Chuck

Berry, Louis Prima, Sam Cooke, Fats Domino, Little Richard, and, especially, Ray Charles is beyond doubt, while very little comes to mind when thinking of Bill Haley and Fred Bertelmann. And should the accusation of inauthenticity even be made of the aforementioned artists, how would one assess folk music and traditional marching band music? Are we not dealing with the artificial creation of traditions and of the Germanization of Turkish military music?

Since the victory march of rock 'n' roll, distinctive changes in the instrumentation and in the sound of all genres of popular music have occurred, even in Austria. The blond Günter played the Ha-ha-ha-ha-harmonica (Duo Hepp-Scheib and Norbert Pawlicki and His Soloists) less frequently; dominating was now the sound of the Hammond organ and the Fender guitar, the electric bass and the drums, to be followed later (and in part replaced) by the synthesizer. Music teachers would soon pull out their hair.

Finally, a perhaps peripheral, yet certainly informative mass phenomenon that occurred toward the end of the 1950s, thrilling hundreds of thousands even in Austria, must be mentioned: the hoola-hoop. The hoopers prepared themselves for regional as well as for national competitions and had already preempted the future fitness craze. In the Orwellian year of 1984, the mind-watchers would no longer be enough in Austria and instead were supplemented by Weight Watchers. The only assessment of the hoola-hoop phenomenon that occurred to Theodore Ottawa, surely confused while watching too long, was, "Oja, one could say, that Austria swings in this hoop."

The music consumption of the 1950s was also influenced by jukeboxes imported from the United States, of which 2,790 had been put into operation by 1957 (800 in Vienna, 800 in Upper Austria, 400 in Lower Austria, 400 in Styria, 130 in Vorarlberg, 80 in Carinthia, 80 in Tyrol, 70 in Salzburg, and 30 in Burgenland). These jukeboxes, each costing between 40,000 and 80,000 schillings—a Steyr-Puch 500 car cost under 30,000 schillings—served as a popular investment for doctors, attorneys, and other well-to-do individuals, who mostly opted for the record "Silentium." While the "boxing music" and "American entertainment through noise" resounding from music machines or Wurlitzer organs were especially criticized by those who had no difficulty in counting the schillings that youths threw into these machines, vending machines for newspapers, shoeshines, tissues, candies, chewing gum, cigarettes, coffee and cocoa, milk, nylons, flowers, food, film, and drinks were thoroughly welcomed as aids to modernization. Even a (less-successful) book-vending machine at the Porrhausplatz in Vienna ideally embodied the game of economic catchup in Austria. Quite obviously, Austrian businessmen felt up to date only when they copied the model of the U.S. Sales Executive Club. Vending machines were, in any event, the latest craze. Had not the new ten-schilling coin been created especially for this service? And should automation have found its end only with respect to music?

The first comprehensive study of Viennese and Lower Austrian youths—a sociological analysis also imported from the United States—carried out by a team under the direction of Leopold Rosenmayr, took place at the end of the 1950s and beginning of the 1960s. It showed with exceptional clarity the surprising, far-reaching leveling of the tastes of Western youths: Pat Boone was favored over Perry Como and Elvis Presley in the United States, Elvis was more popular than Freddy Quinn and Pat Boone in Austria.[6] It can therefore hardly be surprising that the prize for an Austrian musical competition was set at 100,000 schillings already in 1956. Even the Austrian army understood the sign of the times. Since 1957, its marching bands could play hot marches for the Austrian soldiers—the introduction of the saxophone showed that the Austrian army was at least prepared for a musical arms race.

But there were still those unruly youths—aptly called *Halbstarke*—who sucked up Coca-Cola as if it were their mother's milk. Only a few years earlier, a large segment of male youths had marched in uniform lines and destroyed wide areas of Europe—these surely had been the really strong men. By the 1950s, however (reconstruction as well as the loss of the collective memory had long become the state doctrine), a few rowdies now destroyed some theater chairs, caused scooter noise, wore long sideburns and ponytails for excitement, and certainly endangered Western society. And yet, neither the phenomenon nor the description was new. In northern Germany, the term *Halbstarke* (rowdy) was already used at the turn of the century, and the *Schlurfs*, *Bubenplatten*, and *Swingjugend* were nothing new.

In Vienna and also in some smaller industrial cities, some fights indeed occasionally took place between rowdies. The media, however, turned these fights into grotesque gang wars in which "Joe" and his gang in their corduroy pants and plaid jackets destroyed a café because of losing a rock 'n' roll competition. The Café Colosseum in Meidling/Vienna, the Espresso Putzi on Märzstrasse, the restaurant Zum Sonnenaufgang in Hernals, and the Prater had similar reputations of disorderliness. The "geschupfte Ferdl"—a wonderful parody of the phenomenon of the Austrian rowdy—was at home at all of these places, but only a few armchair analysts considered the correlation between these disturbances and their location in the poorest neighborhoods. And only the seasoned observer would discover that in almost all fights, rowdy laborers battled it out with foremen. The newspapers declared that the Wild West had broken out in the district of Meidling in Vienna; the rowdies did not seem to fear the "cops" or the "can" but instead dashed away at the first call of "Watch it, the sheriff's coming!" After a conference in police headquarters in July 1957, Vienna's top sheriff, Josef Holaubek, expressly announced that the "disturbances" had been nipped in the bud. Youth clubs, such as the Schwarze Panther (Black panthers)—where else but in the *Wurlitzer*gasse?—would again scoop the young up from the streets.

By the end of 1958, it could finally be proudly announced that there were no more rowdies in Vienna. The majority of the youths were much happier to enjoy themselves, whenever financially possible, at gatherings at Partyland or the Jazzkeller or even at jam sessions at the ruins of the castle Dürnstein. In 1959, hopes once again were on the rise because of reports that in those places where teenagers danced, good manners were making a comeback. It seemed particularly positive that almost two hundred visitors at one dance club consumed only two liters of wine, half a bottle of brandy, and twenty-five bottles of beer. In contrast to the limited quantity of alcohol, approximately two hundred bottles of Coca-Cola were consumed.

Decisive for the existence of these new youth subcultures were distinct social changes: the slow repression of traditional ways of life through the culture of consumption and modern economic development; the changes in family structures with smaller families, more households, and the increase of two-income families; the (sub)urbanization (and at the same time the disappearance of urbanity); motorization and mobility (replacing the political movements of past decades); the growth of mass income, with resulting embourgeoisement and standardization; and especially also the modernization in the agricultural sector. Between 1951 and 1964, the share of those employed in agrarian economy declined from 32 to 21 percent, which meant a loss of 380,000 agricultural jobs. In contrast, the number of tractors grew steadily, from 234 in 1937 to 11,702 in 1948, 17,763 in 1950, 86,395 in 1957, and 125,718 in 1960. In short, even in Austria all signs pointed to a rapidly industrializing society.

Because these radical social changes had increasingly occurred during the interwar period in the United States and because the U.S. culture industry controlled the cultural capital, *the codes of modernity*, these modernization phenomena were generally understood as "American." The aforementioned study by Leopold Rosenmayr shows that more than just the music tastes of the Austrian and American youths had become similar. Austrian youths also preferred film and pop-hits magazines (*Bravo, Funk und Film*), comics (*Mickey Mouse, Fix und Foxi, Akim*), illustrated magazines (*Quick, Hobby, Neue Illustrierte Wochenschau, Stern*), suspense, and Wild West novels. The most popular novels were the ones that had already been filmed.

To be sure, there were definitely subtle differences. One must consider not only the geographic differences between Vienna and the provinces, between industrial, agricultural, and tourist areas, but also between areas in the (former) Soviet sector and the "Golden West." Likewise, subtle distinctions could also be seen in social areas, between students in the cities and rural youths, between secondary and high school children, between young workers and students. It is nevertheless decisive that the wishes for ownership and consumption of all youths were astoundingly similar: three-quarters of those asked wished for blue jeans, and 77 percent of the high school and university students wished for a tape recorder, as did 64 percent of students in vocational training. Although no truly uniform youth culture existed in Austria during the 1950s, such as the high school culture in the United States, the consumption wishes—and also actual ownership (already almost 40 percent owned portable radios and records)—pointed in this direction: the establishment of the *culture of consumption* was definitely in high gear.[7]

In all areas of sociocultural changes, the Austrian population rarely was directly confronted with the United States, except perhaps with the ever-decreasing presence of GIs until 1955. Instead, they anxiously stared at its mirror image—the Federal Republic of Germany. West Germany, which was always a few steps behind the United States, but miles ahead of Austria, became the transmission belt, catalyst, intensifier, and transfer mechanism for American developments in Austria. Particularly in the area of mass media, Austria became a subcolony of the colony. As such, the import of newspapers and magazines from West Germany tripled until 1957 after the freeing of the newspaper import taxes in 1951. This development forced all Austrian illustrated magazines to concede defeat. Almost all comics were imported from the Federal Republic as well.

The Austrian saviors of Western culture showed their true colors particularly when combating comics in their campaign against "smut and trash." As the iconoclasts attempted in 1956 simply to declare all publications in which picture material predominated as smut in an amendment to the Federal Law on the Fight against Indecent Publications and the Protection of the Young against Moral Dangers, Wilhelm Busch and the Struwwelpeter were not the only ones in danger. For this reason, Walt Disney Productions hired Christian Broda as their representative in an effort to save the honor of Donald Duck. Broda consequently brought the assessment of constitutional expert Josef Korn into a parliamentary committee debate; it hardly requires any comment: "Only when it is proven that Donald Duck inspires youths to commit dangerous acts or other punishable actions, or stimulate lecherousness or sexual urges, then a general limitation on the proliferation of Mickey Mouse magazines would actually be justified."[8] Oh, Daisy!

Jack Kerouac's novel *On the Road* was hardly known in Austria in the 1950s. Nevertheless, the title of the book sounded like a battle cry and motto of the ensuing wave of motorization. In its first edition of August 1, 1953, the *Wiener Bildwoche* featured Will Quadflieg, who had played the part of Jedermann in the Salzburg Festival, and his wife sitting on a Puch scooter, and the message was clear: everyone should be motorized. Between 1948 and 1960, Austria's road network (including federal and province roads) grew from 28,521 to 31,093 kilometers, with a strong trend in federal road construction, increasing approximately 80 percent from 5,072 to 9,234 kilometers. The motorways were anything but developed, yet the first part of the network to be completed, slowly winding through the countryside, was none other than the "West Autobahn"; it may not have been a Route 66 from Chicago to L.A., but an increasing number of drivers would use this supposed race track to get their kicks.

In 1937, 13,817 trucks were registered in Austria, 35,869 in 1948, 43,970 in 1950, 65,422 in 1957, and 73,856 in 1960. Registration figures of motorcycles (including scooters until 1950) also increased from 65,481 in 1937, 96,715 in 1948, 136,830 in 1950, 247,405 in 1957, only to decline to 213,060 in 1960. In contrast the number of scooters grew from 77,783 in 1957 to 91,029 in 1960; and mopeds from 40,000 in 1953 to 440,000 in 1962. The development of car registrations made all other statistics look unimpressive: 32,373 in 1937, 34,382 in 1938, 51,314 in 1950, 70,000 in 1953, 233,175 in 1957, and 404,042 in 1960. The automobile, though, was still a luxury item. Only during the decade to follow would it become a means of mass transportation (registration in 1966: 876,913). Nevertheless, in Vienna alone the number grew from 49,436 in 1955 to 60,981 in 1956. Many driver's license candidates had to emigrate to neighboring Lower Austria because the Viennese examiners could no longer handle the flood of applicants. (By the way, at the same time the public also demanded that it was now time for the examiners to possess driving skills as well!) Austria never did manage to construct a drive-in theater—the first opened in Europe was in Rome in 1957—but at least one could partake in an automobile blessing by Catholic priests. And this was surely essential, for the rapid increase of traffic accidents necessitated more than just the widening of the auto cemeteries. During the latter part of May 1959, a "noise-free week" was proclaimed, which was only to be countered by a demonstration under the motto "We are driving quietly," on Vienna's Ringstrasse. However, for the noise-polluted Austrians, there was no happy end. The frustrated organizers of the anti-noise-pollution protest had to acknowledge that their appeal fell upon deaf ears—perhaps the noise level was already too high?

Even if one sat in a Lloyd 600, a Goggomobil, a Steyr-Puch 500, a Volkswagen, a Kabinenroller, or a Three-Wheeled Isetta (BMW), or on a KTM-"Mecky," a Puch S4, or a "Sissy," it was very difficult to repress the dream of owning a Chevrolet, a Cadillac, or a Harley Davidson. Many European chrome monsters, mostly produced by U.S. subsidiaries, offered a relatively inexpensive ersatz, and the particularly clever built small, gasoline-efficient motors into old "Ami-sleds"; this, then, was colloquially known as a car's sex-change operation.

Of course, Helmut Qualtinger looked for his "baby" still traveling the national railway during the mid-1950s: "Is she in Oberlaa, is she in Unterlaa, is she in Erlaa, or is she in Laa an der Thaya—dann schrei i Feuer! Is she in Bruck an der Mur, an der Ybbs, an der Donau, or is she in Bruck an der Leitha, and so weiter." The "Bundesbahn Blues" (by Gerhard Bronner) was more than a brilliant blues parody. In retrospect, was it not also a swan song for the Bundesbahn, which would slowly sing the blues itself? How would Helmut Qualtinger have made his trip from Lunz to lovely Wieselbruck only ten years later?

Certainly, Austria was hardly the center or the forerunner of the Coca-Colonization of Europe in the 1950s. It did, however, experience decisive steps on the path to the late capitalist culture of consumption, a path that most individuals took more than voluntarily after the incredible losses and tragedies of the war. And hereby, the activities of U.S. cultural officers had opened unimaginable possibilities for the U.S. culture industry. The massive influence of this consciousness industry, which had access to the decisive (symbolic) capital, allowed the path to modernization to seem, on the whole, to be an "American" one.

With few exceptions, the term "Americanization" is just as thoroughly confusing as the concept of transatlantic culture. For, in a true sense, both are actually unhistoric. The first coyly suppresses the fact that, in dealing with the United States, we are first confronted with a product of *European imperialism*— including the genocide of most Americans and the enslavement of millions of Africans. The second also suppresses a decisive component, namely, the economic, military, and political dominance of the United States, which made its cultural hegemony (as Antonio Gramsci has labeled it) first possible. In addition, how many Europeans have given much thought to the fact that nineteenth-century opera houses from Valparaiso to Milwaukee and from Tiflis to Sydney played standard European music?[9]

Precisely those who were not able to make the world exist in their (supposedly German) image now screamed the loudest against the unacceptable side effect of prosperity à la Americana. Naturally, the military aggression of the "Third Reich" had nothing to do with the U.S. presence in Europe, absolutely nothing. Also the accusation that Austrian youths became addicted to an imported mass culture in the 1950s sounds—at least coming from the mouths of those who a few years before had enthusiastically welcomed the destruction of everything Austrian by the German occupiers—mildly put, macabre.

Could it still be surprising that after the preparatory work of the 1950s, a great portion of disillusioned European youths increasingly turned to the subcultures of their U.S. counterparts? These subcultures, which not only show the problems of modern society most clearly but are almost always also immediately exploited by the culture industry, certainly delivered many highly original artistic commentaries. And even if it was only a late retribution, it seems worth noting that the most important African-American influence on European music arrived through the harbor that not only gave an entire music trend its name but also had been the most important slave harbor of Europe in the seventeenth and eighteenth centuries: Liverpool.

The cultural hegemony of the United States was felt not only in the area of popular culture, for also the artistic avant-garde anxiously stared to the West. The establishment of New York as the center of modern art also had a political character, serving the cultural legitimation of the Pax Americana. Would the CIA have assisted in presenting exhibits of abstract expressionists in Europe if it had not represented a countertrend to the social engagement of the realism of the New Deal? "How New York Stole the Idea of Modern Art" is the provocative title by Serge Guilbaut's study on the political role of abstract expressionism in the Cold War.[10] In this area, too, we see that cultural hegemony could be achieved only through economic, military, and political dominance. The made-in-America stamp of U.S. painting fought the cliché of provincialism prior to the Second World War, and now abstract expressionism signified internationalism, modernity, and freedom. In any event, this art trend literally stole the show from European painting in the 1950s.

In the United States—no, in America—everything was better, fresher, younger, more colorful, more glowing, sassier, more technically perfect, more streamlined, simpler, richer, cleaner, more hygienic, sexier, more modern, more practical, easier, faster, more comfortable, and freer. Above and beyond this, however, *everything was possible*. Obviously, even in Austria, these advantages had to be copied.

Or perhaps not?

P.S. Is it an irony of history, or only another dimension of Star Wars? After twelve years of voodoo economics, only three of the seven major studios in Hollywood are controlled by U.S. companies: Disney, Paramount, and Warner Bros. The others are all in foreign hands: 20th Century Fox was taken over by Rupert Murdoch's Australian Firma News Corp, Columbia Pictures is owned by Sony, MGM/UA was bought by the Italian financier Giancarlo Parretti, and Universal Pictures is owned by Matsushita Electric Industrial Company. And by 1994, in the area of recorded music, most of the important U.S. companies had been taken over by foreign competitors in unprecedented megadeals as well: Sony now owns Columbia and Epic, Matsushita bought MCA and Geffen, Thorn EMI owns Capitol, Bertelsmann bought Arista and RCA, and Polygram controls Mercury, PLG, and A&M.

P.P.S. Study the historian before you begin to study the facts (Edward Hallett Carr).

# Notes

## FOREWORD TO THE AMERICAN EDITION

1. For an intelligent divergent view from the inside, see John Tomlinson, *Cultural Imperialism* (Baltimore, 1991).

2. Geir Lundestad, "Empire by Invitation? The United States and Western Europe, 1945–1952," *Journal of Peace Research* 23 (September 1986): 263–77.

3. Archiv der Republik, Vienna, Kabinett des Ministers, Karton 12, 110.031-K/50. I am grateful to Günter Bischof for pointing out this document to me.

4. For a recent discussion of this phenomenon, see "Special Report: The Controversy about Popular Culture," *American Enterprise*, May–June 1992, pp. 72–90.

## INTRODUCTION

1. Baudrillard, *America*.

2. Boyd-Barrett, "Media Imperialism," pp. 116–35.

3. Maier, "The Politics of Productivity," pp. 607–33.

4. Eco, *Über Gott und die Welt*, p. 146.

5. *Time*, June 16, 1986, p. 53.

6. Könenkamp, "Die Hosen des Siegers," pp. 17–22; Bigsby, *Superculture*; Portelli, "The Paper Tiger," pp. 88–89.

7. Lyrics by Rolling Stones in "Mother's Little Helper" from the album *Aftermath*.

8. Ravault, "L'imperialism boomerang," pp. 291–311.

9. Geiss, *Geschichte des Rassismus*; Mazrui, "Uncle Sam's Hearing Aid," pp. 181–92.

10. Bitterli, *Alte Welt—neue Welt*; Gewecke, *Wie die neue Welt in die alte kam*.

11. Bachmann, *Die Hörspiele*, p. 104.

12. Washington National Record Center (hereafter WNRC), Record Group 260, Box 92, File 34 (hereafter 260/92/34), Letter: Jim Clark to Albert van Eerden and James Minifie, New York, November 2, 1945.

13. Henningsen, *Der Fall Amerika*.

14. Eltis, "Free and Coerced," pp. 251–80.

15. Ibid.

16. Bitterli, *Alte Welt—neue Welt*, p. 37.

17. Bradbury, *All Dressed Up*, pp. 127–62; Schüler, *Erfindergeist*.

18. Ewen and Ewen, *Channels of Desire*, p. 53.

19. This is not a play on words of Robert A. Heinlein's novel but a song by Leon Russell and Don Preston, from the album *Leon Russell and the Shelter People*, abc Records, SRL-52008.

## CHAPTER ONE

1. Commager, *America in Perspective*; Galantiére, *America in the Minds of Europe*; Joseph, *As Others See Us*; Skard, *American Myth*; Axtell, Baker, and Överland, *America Perceived*.

2. Commager and Giordanetti, *Was America a Mistake?*.

3. Echeverria, *Mirage in the West*; O'Gorman, *The Invention of America*.

4. Quotation in Annie Kriegel, "Consistent Misapprehension: European Views of America and Their Logic," *Daedalus* 101 (Fall 1972): 87–88.

5. Lerner, "World Imagery and American Propaganda Strategy," pp. 13–26.

6. Raeithel et al., "Europäische Amerika-Urteile im 20. Jahrhundert," pp. 333–41; Fischer, *Nationale Images als Gegenstand vergleichender Literaturgeschichte*.

7. Elizabeth Todd, "National Image-Research and International Understanding," in *As Others See Us*, edited by F. Joseph (Princeton, N.J., 1959), pp. 355–60.

8. Thaller, "Studien zum europäischen Amerikabild."

9. C. Jönssen, ed., *Cognitive Dynamics and International Politics* (London, 1982); Piaget and Weil, "The Development in Children of the Idea of the Homeland," pp. 561–78.

10. Herskovits, *Les bases de l'anthropologie culturelle*; Bastide, *Le proche et le lointain*.

11. Downs and Shea, *Kognitive Karten*, p. 143.

12. "Europe's Film Industry: Sleeping with the Enemy," *Economist*, October 26, 1991, p. 91.

13. Durzak, "Perspektiven des Amerikabildes," pp. 297–305.

14. Baritz, "The Idea of the West," pp. 618–40; Ruland, *America in Modern European Literature*; Pauline Moffitt Watts, "Prophecy and Discovery: On the Spiritual Origins of Christopher Columbus' 'Enterprise of the Indies,'" *American Historical Review* 90 (February 1985): 73–102.

15. Quoted in Baritz, "The Idea of the West," p. 638.

16. Bitterli, *Die "Wilden" und die "Zivilisierten"*; Gewecke, *Wie die neue Welt in die alte kam*.

17. Todorov, *Die Eroberung Amerikas*; Kohl, *Entzauberter Blick*.

18. Arciniegas, *America in Europe*, pp. 60–89.

19. Quoted in Mintz, *Sweetness and Power*.

20. Earl J. Hamilton, "American Treasure and the Rise of Capitalism," *Economica* 9 (1929): 338–57; Chaunu and Chaunu, *Séville et l'Atlantique*; Braudel, *Sozialgeschichte des 15.–18. Jahrhunderts*.

21. Smith, *The Wealth of Nations*.

22. Marx and Engels, "Manifest der Kommunistischen Partei," pp. 459–93.

23. Garcilaso de la Vega, *Royal Commentaries of the Incas*, 2 vols. (Austin, Tex., 1966), pp. 638–48.

24. Quoted in J. H. Elliott, *The Old World and the New*, p. 61.

25. Todorov, *Die Eroberung Amerikas*, p. 229.

26. Crosby, *The Columbian Exchange*; Salaman, *The History and Social Influence of the Potato*; Henry Hobhouse, *Seeds of Change: Five Plants That Transformed Mankind* (New York, 1986); Herman J. Viola and Carolyn Margolis, eds., *Seeds of Change: A Quincentennial Commemoration* (Washington, D.C.: Smithsonian Institution Press, 1991); Ruffié and Sournia, *Die Seuchen in der Geschichte der Menschheit*.

27. Clément, "Amerika als Herausforderung des Westens," pp. 325–30.

28. Evans, *America: The View from Europe*.

29. Arciniegas, *America in Europe*, pp. 240–45.

30. Ibid., pp. 148–55 and 240–45.

31. Barraclough, "Europa, Amerika und Russland," p. 285.

32. Mandrillon, "Philosophical Investigations," p. 176.

33. Günter Kahle, *Simon Bolívar und die Deutschen* (Berlin, 1980).

34. Arciniegas, *America in Europe*, p. 290.

35. Dippel, *Americana Germanica 1770–1800*; idem, *Germany and the American Revolution*; Strauss, *Menace in the West*; Blumenthal, *America and French Culture*.

36. Eisermann, *Crèvecoeur*.

37. Billington, *Land of Savagery*, p. 30.

38. Ruland, *America in Modern European Literature*, p. 31; Woodward, *The Old World's New World*.

39. Dickens, *American Notes*; idem, *Martin Chuzzlewit* (London, 1844); Evans, *America: The View from Europe*.

40. Trollope, *Domestic Manners of the Americans*, p. 362.

41. Arnold, *Civilization in the United States*.

42. Burckhardt, *Weltgeschichtliche Betrachtungen*.

43. Marx and Engels, "Vorwort zur ersten Auflage des 'Kapitals,'" p. 15; Weiner, *Das Amerikabild von Karl Marx*.

44. Sombart, *Warum gibt es keinen Sozialismus?*, p. 126.

45. Evans, *America: The View from Europe*, pp. 21–79; Seliger, *Das Amerikabild Bertolt Brechts*; Reilly, *America in Contemporary Soviet Literature*; Donald Heiney, ed., *America in Modern Italian Literature* (New Brunswick, N.J., 1964).

46. Stead, *The Americanization of the World*.

47. Ludlow, "The Growth of American Influence over England," pp. 618–23; George W. Steevens, *The Land of the Dollar* (London, 1898); Brooks Adams, *America's Economic Supremacy* (London, 1900); Lenschau, *Die amerikanische Gefahr*; Wells, *The Future in America*.

48. Costigliola, *Awkward Dominion*, p. 24.

49. Grünwald and Lacina, *Auslandskapital*, p. 72. The entire U.S. foreign ownership grew in the same period from $2.7 to $7.6 billion.

50. Costigliola, *Awkward Dominion*, p. 153; Sarah Elbert, "'Anywhere with Jesus, Everywhere with Jesus': American Women's Foreign Mission," *American Quarterly* 37 (Winter 1985): 755–61; Hill, *The World Their Household*.

51. Rosenberg, *Spreading the American Dream*, p. 86.

52. Costigliola, *Awkward Dominion*, pp. 140–66.

53. Ibid., p. 157.

54. Chesterton, *What I Saw in America*; Kisch, *Beehrt sich darzubieten*; Shaw, *The Political Madhouse*; Gorer, *Hot Strip Tease*; Elliott, *Hell! I'm British*; Woodruff, *America's Impact*.

55. Lethen, *Neue Sachlichkeit*; Giese, *Girlkultur*; Allen, *French Views of America*; Sommer, *Die Weltmacht USA*.

56. Halfeld, *Amerika und der Amerikanismus*, pp. x–xi, 9–11, 27–43, 53–75, 103–4, 134–35, 217–20; Colyer, *Americanism*; Lüddecke, *Amerikanisches Wirtschaftstempo*; Voechting, *Über den amerikanischen Frauenkult*.

57. Lethen, *Neue Sachlichkeit*, p. 26.

58. Siegfried Kracauer, *Das Ornament der Masse. Essays* (Frankfurt am Main, 1963), p. 54.

59. Theodor W. Adorno, "Aldous Huxley und die Utopie," in *Prismen, Kulturkritik und Gesellschaft* (Munich, 1963), p. 92; Gramsci, *Philosophie der Praxis*.

60. Thaller, "Studien zum europäischen Amerikabild"; *The Times*, May 19, 1939, p. 18, as quoted in Reynolds, "Whitehall, Washington," p. 171.

61. Reynolds, "Whitehall, Washington," p. 171.

62. Ibid.

63. Skard, *The United States in Norwegian History*; Franklin D. Scott, "American Influences in Norway and Sweden," *Journal of Modern History* 18 (March 1946): 37–44.

64. Marias, "From Spain," p. 32; José de Onis, *The United States As Seen by Spanish Writers* (New York, 1952); Madariaga, *Americans*.

65. Braunschvig, *La vie américaine*; Pomaret, *L'Amérique*; Soupault, *The American Influence*; Gibson, "French Impressions."

66. Winkler, *The Politics of Propaganda*.

67. Faenza, *Gli Americani*; Iurlano, "La Cultura," pp. 671–706; A. Donno, *La cultura americano nelle riviste italiano de dopoguerra. "Tempo Presente" (1956–1968)* (Lecce, 1978).

68. Thaller, "Studien zum europäischen Amerikabild," p. 344.

69. See Baurichter, *Amerika trocken?*; Walcher, *Ford oder Marx*; Wirsing, *Der masslose Kontinent*; L. F. Hausleitner, ed., *Quo Vadis Amerika?* (Hamburg, 1941); Hedin, *Amerika im Kampf der Kontinente*; Hans-Jürgen Schröder, *Deutschland und die Vereinigten Staaten 1933–1939* (Wiesbaden, 1970); Weinberg, "Hitler's Image of the United States," pp. 1006–21; Knapp et al., *Die USA und Deutschland 1918–1975*; Adams and Krakau, *Deutschland und Amerika*.

70. Peter von Zahn, "From Germany," in *As Others See Us*, edited by F. Joseph (Princeton, N.J., 1959), p. 96.

71. See three documents prepared for Division of Radio Program Evaluation, Department of State, by International Public Opinion Research, all published in New York in 1952 and now located in the United States Information Agency Library, Historical Collection (hereafter USIAL/HC), Washington, D.C.: *Media of Communication and the Free World As Seen by Hungarian Refugees*; *Media of Communication and the Free World As Seen by Czechoslovak Refugees*; and *Media of Communication and the Free World As Seen by Polish Refugees*.

72. Deckardt, "Die wissenschaftliche Arbeit Kinos."

73. Benna, *Contemporary Austrian Views*.

74. Ibid., pp. 20–30; Sprunck, "Zwei österreichische Forschungsreisende," pp. 414–26.

75. Josef Karl Mayr, "Die Emigration der Salzburger Protestanten von 1731–32," parts 1 and 3, *Mitteilungen der Gesellschaft für Salzburger Landeskunde* 69 (1929): 65–128 and 71 (1931): 129–99; Jones, *The Salzburger Saga*.

76. Luebke, "Austrians," p. 165; Schlag, "A Survey of Austrian Emigration," pp. 139–96; Spaulding, *The Quiet Invaders*; Déak, "Auswanderung aus Österreich," pp. 163–98.

77. Chmelar, *Höhepunkte der österreichischen Auswanderung*; Dujmovits, *Die Amerikawanderung der Burgenländer*; Monika Glettler, *Pittsburgh—Wien—Budapest* (Vienna, 1980).

78. Steiner, "How Returning Emigrants Are Americanizing Europe," pp. 701–3; Alfred Farau, *Der Einfluss der österreichischen Tiefenpsychologie auf die amerikanische Psychotherapie der Gegenwart* (Vienna, 1953).

79. Palmer, *The Age of Democratic Revolution*.

80. Benna, *Contemporary Austrian Views*, pp. 30–48; Houtte, "Documents on Commercial Conditions and Negotiations," pp. 567–78.

81. Benna, "Österreichs erste diplomatische Vertretung," pp. 215–40; Fichtner, "Viennese Perspectives," pp. 19–29.

82. Schmid, "Wenzel Philip Leopold von Mareschal"; Friebel, "Österreich und die Vereinigten Staaten"; Efroymson, "Österreichs Beziehungen zu den Vereinigten Staaten."

83. Hülsemann, *Geschichte der Demokratie in den Vereinigten Staaten*, p. vii; Schweikert, "Dr. Johann Georg Ritter von Hülsemann"; Schachner, "Das Bild von den Vereinigten Staaten."

84. Baerbl Hanzlik, "Ludwig Kossuth und die ungarischen Emigranten in Amerika nach der Revolution von 1848/49" (Ph.D. diss., University of Vienna, 1966); Salzbacher, *Meine Reise nach Nord-Amerika*.

85. Paul Nettl, "Beethoven's American Connections," in *Österreich und die angelsächsische Welt*, edited by Otto Hietsch (Vienna, 1961), pp. 424–35.

86. Sidons [Karl Postl], *Die Vereinigten Staaten*; Duden, *Bericht über eine Reise*; Grünzweig, "Das demokratische Kanaan"; François Furet, "Naissance d'un paradigme: Tocqueville et le voyage en Amérique (1825–1831)," *Annales* 39 (March–April 1984): 225–39.

87. Gottas, "A Hungarian Traveler's View," pp. 213–33.

88. Ghega, *Über die Baltimore-Ohio-Eisenbahn*.

89. Papen, "Die Rolle der Presse."

90. Lympius, "Die diplomatischen Beziehungen"; Marshall, "Der amerikanische Bürgerkrieg"; Fabritz, "Der amerikanische Bürgerkrieg"; Portisch, "Das Zeitungswesen"; Ursula Rachbauer, "Die Aussenpolitik Österreich-Ungarns 1870–1871 im Spiegel der amerikanischen Gesandtschaftsberichte John Jays," *Mitteilungen des österreichischen Staatsarchiv* 21 (1968): 331–87.

91. Peez, *Die Amerikanische Concurrenz*, p. 95; Meier, "American Technology," pp. 116–30.

92. Peez, *Die Amerikanische Concurrenz*, pp. 94–100; Andrew C. Jewell, "The Impact of America on English Agriculture," *Agricultural History* 50 (January 1976): 125–36.

93. Josef Grunzel, *Handelspolitik und Ausgleich Österreich-Ungarn* (Vienna, 1912).

94. Grünwald and Lacina, *Auslandskapital*, pp. 71–74.

95. Stern, "Machinery and Liberty," p. 2.

96. *Brother Jonathan's Epistle to His Relations Both Sides of the Atlantic, but Chiefly to His Father, John Bull, Brother Jonathan Being a Leetle Riled by the Remarks Made by John Bull at His Small Wares Displayed at the Opening of the Grand Exhibition* (Boston, 1852), as quoted in Meier, *American Technology*, p. 128.

97. Blaich, *Amerikanische Firmen*; Southard, *American Industry*.

98. Peez, *Die amerikanische Concurrenz*, p. 118.

99. Sterne, "Presidents of the United States," pp. 153–71; Szilassy, *L'empire du travail*.

100. Lesky, "American Medicine," pp. 368–76.

101. Donald G. Daviau, "Hermann Bahr's Cultural Relations," in *Österreich und die angelsächsische Welt*, edited by Otto Hietsch (Vienna, 1961), pp. 482–522; Fellner, *Dichter und Gelehrter*.

102. Zeltner, "Die Politik des Präsidenten Woodrow Wilson."

103. Martin, "Österreichisch-ungarische Propagandatätigkeit."

104. Fellner, "Der Plan," pp. 469–88; Stephan Verosta, "Alfred Frieds Denkschrift (1917) an Ottokar Czernin über amerikanische Bemühungen zur Friedenssicherung und zur Gründung eines Völkerbunds," in *Beiträge zur Zeitgeschichte. Festschrift für Ludwig Jedlicka zum 60. Geburtstag*, edited by Rudolf Neck and Adam Wandruszka (St. Pölten, 1976), pp. 11–36.

105. Meisels, "Die Beziehungen zwischen Österreich-Ungarn"; Angelo Ara, "Die Vereinigten Staaten zwischen Italien und Österreich von der amerikanischen Kriegserklärung an Österreich-Ungarn bis zur Friedenskonferenz," in *Innsbruck-Venedig: Österreichisch-italienische Historikertreffen 1971 und 1972*, edited by Adam Wandruszka and Ludwig Jedlicka (Vienna, 1975), pp. 47–60.

106. Hausmann, "Die amerikanische Aussenpolitik"; Schmid, "Amerikanische Österreichpolitik"; Hanns Haas, "Österreich als Friedensproblem" (Ph.D. diss., University of Salzburg, 1968); Claudia Kromer, "Diplomatie und Volksabstimmung. Die Fragen Kärntens 1918–1920 in amerikanischer Sicht," *Geschichte und Literatur* 14 (1970): 401–13; Claudia Kromer, *Die Vereinigten Staaten von Amerika und die Frage Kärnten 1918–1920* (Klagenfurt, 1970); Jon D. Berlin, *Akten und Dokumente des Aussenamtes (State Department) der USA zur Burgenland-Anschlussfrage 1919–1920* (Eisenstadt, 1977).

107. Ursula Freise, "Die Tätigkeit der alliierten Kommissionen in Wien nach dem Ersten Weltkrieg" (Ph.D. diss., University of Vienna, 1963); Haas, "Die Vereinigten Staaten," pp. 233–55; Adlgasser, "Brot für Kinder."

108. Costigliola, *Awkward Dominion*, pp. 48–50 and 112–14; Buckingham, "Diplomatic and Economic Normalcy."

109. Stiefel, "The Reconstruction," pp. 415–30; Herbert Matis, "Disintegration and Multinational Enterprises in Central Europe during the Post-War Years (1918–23)," in *International Business*, edited by Alice Teichova and P. L. Cottrell (Leicester, 1983), pp. 73–96.

110. März, *Österreichische Bankpolitik*, pp. 410–23.

111. Ernst Fischer, "Der Geist des Amerikanertums," in *Ernst Fischer. Kultur, Literatur, Politik*, edited by Karl-Markus Gauss (Frankfurt am Main, 1984), pp. 25 and 28.

112. Ernst Fischer, "Al Capone im Heimwehrkostüm," in *Ernst Fischer*, edited by Karl-Markus Gauss (Frankfurt am Main, 1984), pp. 106–10.

113. Meisels, "Die politischen Beziehungen"; Fritz Fellner, "Die aussenpolitische und völkerrechtliche Situation," in *Österreich. Die Zweite Republik*, edited by Erika Weinzierl and Kurt

Skalnik, vol. 1 (Graz, 1972), pp. 53–90; Gerald Stourzh, *Die Geschichte des Staatsvertrags 1945–1955* (Graz, 1980); Keyserlingk, *Austria in World War II*.

114. Siegwald Ganglmair, "Amerikanische Kriegspropaganda gegen das Deutsche Reich in den Jahren 1944/45" (Ph.D. diss., University of Vienna, 1978).

115. *Punch* 22 (1852): 218, as quoted in Thaller, "Studien zum europäischen Amerikabild," p. 1049.

116. Bronner, "Eine amerikanische Philosophie," pp. 29–30.

117. *Der Turm* 1 (November–December 1945): 84–86.

118. Robbins, *Report on the USIS*.


CHAPTER TWO

1. Heald and Kaplan, *Culture and Diplomacy*, p. 4.

2. Knud Krakau, *Missionsbewusstsein und Völkerrechtsdoktrin in den Vereinigten Staaten von Amerika* (Frankfurt am Main, 1967).

3. Ninkovich, "The Trajectory of Cultural Internationalism."

4. Heald and Kaplan, *Culture and Diplomacy*, pp. 9 and 92–123.

5. Ninkovich, "The Rockefeller Foundation," p. 817.

6. Rosenberg, *Spreading the American Dream*, pp. 87–107, 203–4, 213–14; Wagnleitner, "Propagating the American Dream," pp. 61–62.

7. Stephens, *Facts to a Candid World*, p. 109.

8. MacKenzie, *Propaganda and Empire*, p. 258.

9. As quoted in Eastment, "The Policies and Position of the British Council," p. 2; Ellwood, *Europe and America in Cultural Diplomacy*.

10. Ninkovich, *Diplomacy of Ideas*, p. 42; Espinosa, *Inter-American Beginnings of United States Cultural Diplomacy*; Smith, "The United States and the Cultural Crusade in Mexico."

11. Haines, "Under the Eagle's Wing," pp. 373–88.

12. The development of the organization of U.S. cultural diplomacy has been best analyzed in Winkler, *The Politics of Propaganda*; Ninkovich, *Diplomacy of Ideas*; Rosenberg, *Spreading the American Dream*.

13. Rosenberg, *Spreading the American Dream*, p. 322.

14. *New York Herald Tribune*, October 9, 1941, p. 1.

15. Winkler, *The Politics of Propaganda*, pp. 78–172.

16. Ninkovich, *Diplomacy of Ideas*, pp. 63–115.

17. Rosenberg, *Spreading the American Dream*, p. 217.

18. Ibid., p. 36; see Schiller, *Communication and Cultural Domination*; idem, *Mass Communications and American Empire*.

19. Rosenberg, *Spreading the American Dream*, p. 219.

20. Deibel and Roberts, *Culture and Information*.

21. Leonard W. Doob, "Communication of Information about the United States," *Journal of Consulting Psychology* 10 (1946): 45–50.

22. Macmahon, *Memorandum on the Post-War International Information Program of the United States*; White and Leigh, *Peoples Speaking to Peoples*; Beloff, "The Projection of America Abroad," pp. 23–29; Department of State, *The World Audience for America's Story*; Morris, "U.S. Information Please!," pp. 1–5; Peters, "American Culture and the State Department," pp. 265–74; Merle Curti and Kendall Birr, *Prelude to Point Four* (Washington, D.C., 1954); E. Grant Meade, "Dogma-Eat-Dogma" (M.A. thesis, War College, Maxwell Air Force Base, 1961); Blum, *Cultural Affairs and Foreign Relations*; Rubin, *The Objectives of the U.S. Information Agency*; Braisted, *Cultural Affairs and Foreign Relations*; C. T. Sorensen, *Auch wenn sie uns nicht lieben* (Freiburg im Breisgau, 1969); Kellermann, *Cultural Relations as an Instrument of U.S.*

*Foreign Policy*; Horton, *Understanding U.S. Information Policy*; English, "United States Media-Diplomacy"; Elder, *The Information Machine*; Coombs, *The Fourth Dimension of Foreign Policy*.

23. Ninkovich, *Diplomacy of Ideas*, p. 132.

24. Catherine D. Williston, "The Development of Propaganda as an Instrument of Foreign Policy, 1945–1959" (Ph.D. diss., Radcliffe College, 1959); William Benton, "Self-Portrait by Uncle Sam," *New York Times*, Magazine Section 2, December 2, 1945, p. 13; Milton Lehman, "We Must Sell America Abroad," *Saturday Evening Post*, November 15, 1947, p. 6.

25. "The T-Bomb of Truth," *New York Herald Tribune*, July 27, 1950; also USIAL/HC, Historical Background of USIS Library Programs, October 19, 1967.

26. "A Truth Program," *Christian Science Monitor*, September 14, 1950.

27. Ninkovich, *Diplomacy of Ideas*, pp. 234, 172–75.

28. Ibid., pp. 136–37.

29. USIAL/HC, Smith and Neff, *Bi- and Multi-National Cooperation in Germany*.

30. Barrett, "Truth Is Our Weapon," pp. 10-1–10-8.

31. Meyerhoff, *The Strategy of Persuasion*, p. 149; Frankel, *The Neglected Aspect of Foreign Affairs*.

32. Ninkovich, *Diplomacy of Ideas*, p. 168.

33. USIAL/HC, *A Study of USIA Operating Assumptions* (Washington, D.C., 1954); USICA e 744. 5 13 v. 4.c.2, Institute of Communications Research, Inc., pp. L-24–L-26, PA-22–PA-23, IM-1–IM-4.

34. Bogart, *Premises for Propaganda*, p. 44.

35. Terrence H. Qualter, *Propaganda and Psychological Warfare* (New York, 1962), pp. 123–24; Steven Pfeiffer, "The USIA and the Private News Media" (Research project, The American University, May 1968); Coarse, "The Market for Goods," pp. 384–91.

36. Russell, "The Impact of America on European Culture"; Kenneth L. Kornher, "The Truman Administration Foreign Information Program" (M.A. thesis, Georgetown University, 1960); Harold Snyder, "Neglected Aspects of International Cultural Relations," *School and Society* 74 (November 24, 1951): 384–91.

37. The best synopsis of these results in the German language is Loth, *Die Teilung der Welt*.

38. Schmid, "Die 'Falschen' Fuffziger," pp. 7–23.

39. Editorial, *Life*, December 23, 1957, p. 21.

40. Barghoorn, *The Soviet Cultural Offensive*, p. 214; idem, *Soviet Foreign Propaganda*; V. Kortunow, *The Battle of Ideas in the Modern World* (Moscow, 1979); J. Samuel Walker, " 'No More Cold War': American Foreign Policy and the 1948 Soviet Peace Offensive," *Diplomatic History* 5 (Winter 1981): 75–91.

41. Barghoorn, *The Soviet Cultural Offensive*, p. 229.

42. Dizard, *Strategy of Truth*, p. 187.

43. Schulz, *Die geheime Internationale*, pp. 146–49; Short, *Western Broadcasting*, pp. 1–11.

44. Charles Wick, "The War of Ideas," *Vital Speeches of the Day* 52 (October 15, 1985): 16–21.

45. "U.S.I.A. Plans Satellite News Parleys," *New York Times*, February 3, 1984, p. 3.

46. U.S. Congress, House, Committee on Foreign Affairs, *Winning the Cold War*, pp. 6–7.

47. James Bamford, *The Puzzle Palace: Technological Frontiers and Foreign Relations* (Washington, D.C., 1985); Dallek, *The American Style of Foreign Policy*; Hansen, *USIA*.

48. Keller and Hirth, "Die CIA als Mäzen," pp. 311–18; Schulz, *Die geheime Internationale*, pp. 160 and 326.

49. Marchetti and Marks, *The CIA and the Cult of Intelligence*.

50. Schulz, *Die geheime Internationale*, p. 160; Hirsch and Fletcher, *The CIA and the Labour Movement*; Prader and Unterleitner, "Das 'Trade Union Recovery Program' der amerikanischen Gewerkschaften in Westeuropa und Österreich," pp. 89–106; Gene Sensenig, "Die neue Rolle der Gewerkschaften in der Aussenpolitik des staatsmonopolistischen Kapitalismus. Am Beispiel der Beziehungen des AFL und des CIO zum ÖGB zwischen 1945 und 1950"

(Ph.D. diss., University of Salzburg, 1984); Joesten, *C.I.A.*; Agee, *Inside the Company*; Christopher Andrew and David Dilks, eds., *Missing Dimension: Governments and Intelligence Communities in the Twentieth Century* (London, 1984).

51. The list noted here does not pretend to be complete. See Schulz, *Die geheime Internationale*, pp. 146–47.

52. Powers, *CIA*; Rositzke, *The CIA's Secret Operations*.

53. Marchetti and Marks, *The CIA and the Cult of Intelligence*, p. 165.

54. Lasch, "The Cultural Cold War," p. 344. See also *New York Times*, International Edition, April 28, 1966, p. 3.

55. Lasch, "The Cultural Cold War," p. 326.

56. Axel Frohn, *Neutralisierung als Alternative zur Westintegration. Die Deutschlandpolitik der Vereinigten Staaten von Amerika 1945–1955* (Frankfurt am Main, 1985); Andrew James Birtle, "Rearming the Phoenix: American Military Assistance to the Federal Republic of Germany, 1950–1960" (Ph.D. diss., Ohio State University, 1985); Joseph Bernard Egan, "The Struggle for the Soul of Faust: The American Drive for German Rearmament, 1950–1955" (Ph.D. diss., University of Connecticut, 1985).

57. Ninkovich, *Diplomacy of Ideas*, p. 179.

58. Rosenberg, *Spreading the American Dream*, p. 228.

59. GAO Report to Congress, May 5, 1977, *Public Diplomacy in the Years Ahead* (Washington, D.C., 1977).

60. Rosenberg, *Spreading the American Dream*, p. 228.

61. Junker, *Der unteilbare Weltmarkt*.

62. Rosenberg, *Spreading the American Dream*, p. 233.

63. Ninkovich. *Diplomacy of Ideas*, p. 163.

64. Bungenstab, *Umerziehung zur Demokratie?*, p. 190.

65. Breen, "Das deutsch-amerikanische Austauschprogramm im Rahmen der Umorientierung Westdeutschlands"; Schlander, *Reeducation*; Knapp et al., *Die USA und Deutschland 1918–1975*; Lange-Quassowski, *Neuordnung oder Restaurierung?*; Tent, *Mission on the Rhine*; Lutz Niethammer, *Die Mitläuferfabrik* (Berlin, 1982); Prinz, *Trümmerzeit*; Jonas, *The United States and Germany*; Siegfried Quandt and Gerhard Schult, eds., *Die USA und Deutschland seit dem Zweiten Weltkrieg* (Paderborn, 1985); Adams and Krakau, *Deutschland und Amerika*; Nicholas Pronay and Keith Wilson, eds., *The Political Re-Education of Germany and Her Allies after World War II* (Beckenham, Kent, 1985); Ludolf Herbst, ed., *Westdeutschland 1945–1955* (Munich, 1986); Frei, *Amerikanische Lizenzpolitik*.

66. Mettler-Meibom, *Demokratisierung und Kalter Krieg*, p. 11.

67. See USIAL/HC, Office of War Information, June 10, 1944, Radio: General 1943–1950, Development of German Section; Wagnleitner, "Die kulturelle Reorientierung Österreichs," pp. 326–44.

68. Lettner, "Die französische Österreichpolitik," pp. 313–51; G. Arnoldsen, "Französischer Geist und Österreich," *Die Bastei* 8 (1946/47): 3–5.

69. Richard Hiscocks, *Österreichs Wiedergeburt* (Vienna, 1954), pp. 218–42.

70. Hanisch, "Historische Überhänge," pp. 15–19.

71. Rathkolb, "Politische Propaganda"; Hiller, "Amerikanische Medien"; Schönberg, "Amerikanische Informations- und Medienpolitik"; Sieder, "Die Alliierten Zensurmassnahmen"; Leidenfrost, "Die amerikanische Besatzungsmacht."

72. WNRC 260/889/43, Memorandum: Connaughton, February 16, 1950, Responsibilities Turned Over to the Austrians.

73. National Archives (hereafter NA) 511.63/2-1252, Department of State to the Officer in Charge of the American Mission Vienna, February 12, 1952; USIE Country Paper, 1951–1952; NA 511.63/12-952, Department of State to Officer in Charge of the American Mission in Vienna, December 9, 1952; USIE Country Plan, Austria 1953.

74. WNRC 260/889/40, Memorandum: Col. Pesch to War Department and Department of State, Vienna, September 15, 1947. See also Rathkolb, "U.S.-Medienpolitik in Österreich," p. 3.

75. WNRC 260/862/93, total estimated cost for fiscal year 1951.

76. WNRC 260/889/40, Telegram: General Keyes to War Department, January 1948.

77. "Memorandum: Herz to Denby, Vienna, June 2, 1948," in *Understanding Austria*, edited by R. Wagnleitner (Salzburg, 1984), p. 398.

78. WNRC 260/59372-1, ISB Policy. See Hiller, "Amerikanische Medien," p. 25.

79. See Rathkolb, "Politische Propaganda," p. 265; Hiller, "Amerikanische Medien," pp. 20–23; Sieder, "Die alliierten Zensurmassnahmen," pp. 12–88.

80. WNRC 260/102/11, USFA, ISB, Memorandum: Control of Austrian Informational Services, August 6, 1945.

81. Rathkolb, "Politische Propaganda," pp. 31–124; Hiller, "Amerikanische Medien," p. 52.

82. WNRC 260/889/43, USIE Country Paper on Austria 1950.

83. NA 511.63/12-952, USIS Country Plan, Austria 1953.

84. Ibid.

85. Rathkolb, "Politische Propaganda," pp. 143 and 161.

86. WNRC 260/889/43, Memorandum: Lee: Distribution of Anti-Soviet Material, Vienna, March 22, 1949.

87. Rathkolb, "Politische Propaganda," pp. 146–80.

88. WNRC 260/41/6, Chief, New York Field Office, to Chief, CAD, July 20, 1948.

89. Ibid.

90. WNRC 260/41/6, Memorandum: Grossman to Kaghan, Vienna, August 18, 1948.

91. Rathkolb, "Politische Propaganda," pp. 233–45; Hiller, "Amerikanische Medien," p. 24.

92. NA 511.63/2-1252, USIE Plan for Austria, 1951–1952, February 12, 1952.

93. NA 511.63/4-1050, Department of State to Officer in Charge of American Mission in Vienna, April 7, 1950.

94. NA 511.63/5-1551.

95. NA 511.63/3-1252, USIE Semi-annual Evaluation Report, Vienna, March 12, 1952; USIE Semi-annual Evaluation Report, Vienna, June 1, 1951; NA 511.63/6-1953, Minutes: Information Projects Committee, Vienna, June 15, 1953.

96. NA 511.63/5-1551, U.S. Legation, Vienna, to Department of State, May 15, 1951, Subject: Development of Psychological Offensive by U.S. Information and Cultural Media in Austria.

97. Ibid.

98. NA 511.63/4-1251, Department of State to Officer in Charge, U.S. Legation, Vienna, April 12, 1951.

99. NA 511.63/3-1252, U.S. Legation, Vienna, to Department of State. Semi-annual Evaluation Report, March 12, 1952.

100. NA 511.63/5-1551, U.S. Legation, Vienna, to Department of State, May 15, 1951.

101. Ibid.

102. Ibid.

103. Ibid.

104. Ibid.

105. See USIS, ed., *Sozialversicherung in den USA* (Vienna, n.d.); U.S. Archiv-Dienst Frankfurt, ed., *Der Neger im amerikanischen Leben* (Frankfurt am Main, n.d.); USIS, ed., *Quellen der Produktivität* (Vienna, 1953); USIS, ed., *TVA: Wandlung eines Flusstales* (Vienna, n.d.); Pressereferat des ÖGB, ed., *Fünf Gewerkschafter sehen Amerika* (Vienna, 1951); Amerikanische Wirtschaftsmission Wien, ed., *Besser Leben: Frauen lösen das Problem* (Vienna, n.d.); USIS, ed., *Der österreichische Staatsvertrag: Eine Darstellung der westlichen Bemühungen und der Obstruktion der Sowjets* (Vienna, 1952).

106. NA 511.63/1-852, U.S. Legation, Vienna, to Department of State, Subject: Pamphlets Adapted to Austria Program, January 8, 1952.

107. NA 511.63/12-952, Department of State to U.S. Mission, Vienna, December 9, 1952.

108. Rathkolb, "Politische Propaganda," p. 200.

109. Ernst Hanisch, "Von den schwierigen Jahren der Zweiten Republik—Salzburg im Wiederaufbau," in *Salzburg und das Werden der Zweiten Republik. VI. Landessymposium am 4. Mai 1985*, edited by Eberhard Zwink (Salzburg, 1985), p. 23.

110. Temperley, "Anglo-American Images," p. 333.

111. Hiller, "Amerikanische Medien," pp. 159–65.

112. NA 511.63/3-1252, U.S. Legation, Vienna, to Department of State. Semi-annual Evaluation Report, March 12, 1952.

113. See *Zeitschrift für Kulturgeschichte* 37 (1987).

114. WNRC 260/52/72, undated ISB Memorandum, in Rathkolb, "Politische Propaganda," p. 452.

115. Greene, *The Quiet American*, p. 95.

116. Ninkovich, *Diplomacy of Ideas*, p. 6.

117. Benét, *America*, pp. 7–8.


CHAPTER THREE

1. Rathkolb, "Politische Propaganda," p. 12.

2. Rathkolb, "U.S.-Medienpolitik und die neue österreichische Journalistenelite," pp. 6–7.

3. Rathkolb, "U.S.-Medienpolitik und die neue österreichische Journalistenelite."

4. Minifie, "At an Alarming Rate," p. 9.

5. Fritz Hausjell, "Österreichische Tageszeitungsjournalisten am Beginn der Zweiten Republik (1945–1947)" (Ph.D. diss., University of Salzburg, 1985); idem, "Entnazifizierung der Presse in Österreich."

6. Meissl, Mulley, and Rathkolb, *Verdrängte Schuld*.

7. WNRC 260/92/34, Letter: J. A. Clark to van Eerden and Minifie, New York, November 2, 1945.

8. Rathkolb, "U.S.-Medienpolitik und die neue österreichische Journalistenelite," p. 9.

9. Wagnleitner, "Der kulturelle Einfluss der amerikanischen Besatzung," pp. 47–58.

10. WNRC 260/49/25, Letter: Van Eerden to Clark, Vienna, October 10, 1945.

11. Ibid., September 19, 1945.

12. Wagnleitner, *Diplomatie zwischen Parteiproporz und Weltkonflikt*, pp. 92–93.

13. Rathkolb, "Politische Propaganda," pp. 34–35.

14. WNRC 260/98/IF-SN, Civil Censorship Group Austria (US), May 20, 1947.

15. WNRC 260/98/IF-SN, Memorandum: Pettegrove to Eberle, June 1, 1947.

16. WNRC 260/98/IF-SN, Memorandum: Fox to Kaghan, Vienna, September 21, 1948.

17. WNRC 260/ACA Austria/98.

18. Hausjell, "Die gescheiterte Alternative," pp. 17–30.

19. NA 511.63/3-1252, USIE: Semi-Annual Evaluation Report, Vienna, March 12, 1952.

20. WNRC 260/48/13, Letter: Van Eerden to McChrystal, Vienna, September 19, 1945.

21. NA 511.63/9-1052, Protocol: Information Projects Committee Meeting, Vienna, September 8, 1952.

22. Ibid.

23. Ibid.

24. NA 511.63/11-452, Telegram: Thompson to Department of State, February 11, 1952.

25. NA 511.63/2-1153, Telegram: U.S. Embassy, Vienna, to Department of State, February 11, 1953.

26. See the report "The Press in Austria" by Martin F. Herz, in *Understanding Austria*, edited by R. Wagnleitner (Salzburg, 1984), pp. 156–97.

27. Hausjell, "Die gescheiterte Alternative," pp. 17–18.

28. WNRC 260/196/72, Minutes by Mr. Fox: Meeting with Dr. [sic] Behrmann and Nationalrat Dr. Maleta, February 25, 1947, 11:45–13:00.

29. Ibid.

30. WNRC 260/ACA Austria/99/214, Interview: Fox with Behrmann, January 31, 1947.

31. Hausjell, "Die gescheiterte Alternative," p. 27.

32. "Die Oberösterreichischen Nachrichten-Story," *Profil*, January 20, 1976, pp. 30–34.

33. WNRC 260/889/40.

34. Florijan Sablatschan, "Kurier—Glanz und Elend einer Zeitung," *Cash-Flow*, December 12, 1987, pp. 24–30, especially pp. 25–26.

35. Reininghaus, "Oskar Maurus Fontana."

36. WNRC 260/862/92, History of the *Wiener Kurier*, by Ted Kaghan; WNRC 260/86/2/91; Schönberg, "Amerikanische Informations- und Medienpolitik," p. 165.

37. Rathkolb, "Politische Propaganda," p. 218.

38. WNRC 260/55/5, Memorandum: Kaghan to van Eerden, Projection of Democracy through the *Wiener Kurier*, October 10, 1946.

39. Rathkolb, "Politische Propaganda," pp. 134–36.

40. NA 800 Soc/84/2534, Memorandum: Denby and Erhardt, Vienna, April 20, 1948.

41. WNRC 260/88/33, Statistical Review, June 1949; Hiller, "Amerikanische Medien," p. 48.

42. Rathkolb, "Politische Propaganda," p. 144.

43. B. C. Cohen, *The Press, the Public, and Foreign Policy* (Princeton, N.J., 1963), p. 13.

44. WNRC 260/60/81, Letter: Peterson to Sanders, Vienna, November 16, 1949; WNRC 260/75/41.

45. WNRC 260/75/5.

46. Ibid.; Hiller, "Amerikanische Medien," p. 97.

47. NA 511.6321/6-2751, Telegram: Dowling to Secretary of State, Vienna, June 27, 1951.

48. Cook, "Magazines for Friendship," pp. 36–39.

49. Joachim Joesten, *German Periodicals in 1947* (New York, 1947).

50. Breitenkamp, *The U.S. Information Control Division*, p. 79.

51. Pilgert and Dobbert, *Press, Radio, and Film*; Matz, *Die Zeitungen der US-Armee*; Hurwitz, *Die Stunde Null*; Borchers and Vowe, *Die zarte Pflanze Demokratie*; Frei, *Amerikanische Linzenzpolitik*.

52. Frei, "Die Presse," pp. 275–354.

53. "Zwei Millionen für die Förderung des Imports von Sex-Appeal und Schafzimmergeschichten," *Neues Österreich*, January 4, 1959, p. 3; Jacques Hannak, "Die Zeitung—Opium oder Heilmittel," in *Bestandaufnahme Österreich 1945 bis 1963*, edited by Jacques Hannak (Vienna, 1963), pp. 327–52; Tschögl, "Tagespresse."

54. Wagnleitner, "Die kulturelle Reorientierung Österreichs," p. 330.

55. WNRC 260/60/81, Letter: Petersen to Sanders, Vienna, November 16, 1949.

56. WNRC 260/65/82, Quarterly Historical Report, ISB, October 2, 1949.

57. NA 511.63/5-1551, Airgram: U.S. Legation, Vienna, to the Department of State, May 15, 1951.

58. WNRC 260/65/82, Quarterly Historical Report, ISB, October 2, 1949.

59. NA 511.63/3-1252, Semi-Annual Evaluation Report, March 12, 1952.

60. WNRC 260/65/82, Letter: Petersen to Sanders, Vienna, November 16, 1949.

61. WNRC 260/890/72, Memorandum: Kaghan to Nathan, Vienna, August 13, 1946.

62. Quarterly ISB Reports in WNRC.

63. In addition to the Quarterly ISB Reports, see also WNRC 260/35/24, Features Section, Salzburg to Petersen, Salzburg, September 25, 1949; WNRC 260/35/24, Features 1948.

64. UNESCO, *World Communications* (1951); Hauptfeld, "Österreich und die grossen europäischen Nachrichtenagenturen"; Fett, "America's Role in International News Exchange"; Dizard, *Strategy of Truth*; Tunstall, *The Media Are American*; "The Selling of Reuters," *Time*, June 11, 1984, pp. 54–60.

65. Fett, "America's Role in International News Exchange."

66. Tunstall, *The Media Are American*, p. 34.

67. WNRC 260/58886-2, Albert van Eerden: "How the USFA Projects America and the Democratic Life in Austria through the ISB," October 11, 1946, as quoted in Hiller, "Amerikanische Medien," pp. 67–68.

68. WNRC 260/35/24, Memorandum: Training of Journalists.

69. Ibid.; see also quotation at the end of the paragraph. Also, NA 511.63/3-1450, Report of Public Affairs Office, February 1–28, 1950; WNRC 260/101, Project in Journalism, September 26, 1950; Rathkolb, "U.S.-Medienpolitik und die neue österreichische Journalistenelite."

70. Stott, *Documentary Expression and Thirties America*.

71. Kandl, "Pressefotografie und Fotojournalismus," pp. 311–24; Mangelberger, "Die Verwendung der Photogrgaphie"; Kemp, "Nach '45," pp. 215–20.

72. Kandl, "Pressefotografie und Fotojournalismus," pp. 215–20.

73. Pauer, "Bildkunde und Geschichtswissenschaft," p. 201.

74. Kaindl, "Das Tor zur weiten Welt," pp. 222–31; idem, "Völkerverbindende Sprache: Fotografie in Österreich von 1945 bis zum Beginn der 70er Jahre," in *150 Jahre Fotografie*, Sondernummer des Lesezirkels der *Wiener Zeitung*, January 1988, pp. 8–9.

75. Nussbaum, "Der Anzeigenmarkt der österreichischen Tagespresse."

76. WNRC 260/41/12, Memorandum: Van Eerden to McChrystal, Vienna, September 19, 1945.

77. Tunstall, *The Media Are American*, p. 73.

78. Smekal, "Die Stellung der amerikanischen Presse- und Aussenpolitik," p. 427.

79. Künewalder, "Die historische Darstellung," pp. 160–61.

80. Roger Lewis, "Captain America Meets the Bash Street Kids," in *Superculture*, edited by C. W. E. Bigsby (Bowling Green, Ohio, 1975), pp. 175–89.

81. Philip Melling, "American Popular Culture in the Thirties," in *Approaches to Popular Culture*, edited by C. W. E. Bigsby (Bowling Green, Ohio, 1976), pp. 241–63.

82. Metken, *Comics*, p. 77.

83. Ibid.

84. Ibid., p. 70; *Comic Strips. Vom Geist der Superhelden. Colloquium zur Theorie der Bildergeschichte. Schriftenreihe der Akademie der Künste*, vol. 8 (Berlin, 1970); Hans Dieter Zimmerman, ed., *Comic Strips* (Berlin, 1970).

85. "Ehrenrettung für Donald Duck: Schmutz- und Schundgesetz gegen Walt Disney. Eine Gesetzesnovelle will alle 'Comics' in Bausch und Bogen verdammen," *Neues Österreich*, November 11, 1956, p. 9.

86. Lewis, "Captain America Meets the Bash Street Kids," p. 180; "Linzenzen," *Der Spiegel* 38 (May 21, 1984): 60–62.

87. Metken, *Comics*, pp. 25–26.

88. Dorfman and Mattelart, *How to Read Donald Duck*; Dorfman, *The Empire's Old Clothes*.

89. Ralph Werner, *Das gefundene Auge. Mit Essays von George Schmid* (Salzburg, 1985); Barthes, *Elemente der Semiologie*; Bourdieu et al., *Eine illegitime Kunst*; Freund, *Photographie und Gesellschaft*; Aigner, "Die Blicke im Zeitalter," pp. 163–71; Luc Boltanski, *Rhetorik des Bildes* (Frankfurt am Main, 1981).

90. Caute, *The Great Fear*.

91. Werner, *Das gefundene Auge*.

92. George Gerbner, "Ideological Perspectives and Political Tendencies in News Report-ing," *Journalism Quarterly* 41 (1964): 508; Schiller, *Objectivity and the News*; Herbert J. Gans, *Deciding What's News* (New York, 1979); Ewen, *Captains of Consciousness*.

93. Gerbner, "Ideological Perspectives," p. 495.

94. Schiller, *Objectivity and the News*, p. 196; Paul F. Lazarsfeld and Robert K. Merton, "Mass Communication, Popular Taste, and Organized Social Action," in *The Processes and Effects of Mass Communication*, edited by Wilbur Schramm and Donald D. Roberts (Urbana, Ill., 1971), pp. 554–78.

95. Vance, "Freedom of the Press for Whom?," pp. 340–54.

96. Loory, "The CIA's Use of the Press," pp. 9–18.

97. Robert J. Landry, "Edward R. Murrow," *Scribner's Magazine*, December 1938, p. 10.

98. *Die Presse*, April 10, 1987; Rathkolb, "U.S.-Medienpolitik und die neue österreichische Journalistenelite," p. 14.

CHAPTER FOUR

1. Because Austrian television first aired only after the end of occupation, its development will not be discussed further here. See Franz Rest, "Die Explosion der Bilder: Entwicklung der Programmstrukturen im österreichischen Fernsehen," in *Medienkultur in Österreich*, ed-ited by Hans H. Fabris and Kurt Luger (Vienna, 1988), pp. 265–315; Pluch, *Grosser Bruder Fernsehen*.

2. Ergert, *Fünfzig Jahre Rundfunk*, p. 124.

3. Department of State, *The World Audience for America's Story*; UNESCO, *World Communica-tions* (1950 and 1956); NA 511.63/5-1551, Airgram: U.S. Embassy, Austria, to Department of State, May 1, 1951, Subject: Development of Psychological Offensive by U.S. Information and Cultural Media in Austria.

4. The disruption of foreign programs alone cost the Soviet Union up to $300 million yearly and employed between 7,500 and 10,000 technicians. See Alan Heil and Barbara Schiele, "The Voice Past," in *Western Broadcasting*, edited by K. R. M. Short (London, 1986), pp. 98–112.

5. Rathkolb, "Politische Propaganda," pp. 491–500.

6. Dixon Wecter, "Hearing Is Believing," *Atlantic*, July 1945, pp. 37–43; Pelt, "The Cold War on the Air," pp. 97–110; Ingeborg Winter, "Radio Liberty" (Ph.D diss., University of Vienna, 1986); Short, *Western Broadcasting*.

7. Short, *Western Broadcasting*.

8. " 'Voice' Crashes the Iron Curtain," *New York World Telegram and Sun*, June 2, 1951, p. 15; "Le Pick-Up Americain: Voice of America," *Time*, October 11, 1948, p. 69; McPhail, *Electronic Colonialism*; "Mitchel Airman Beams Hope to Austria," *Mitchel Field Newspaper*, December 1951; Roth, *Cuius regio—eius informatio*; Tyson, *U.S. International Broadcasting and National Security*; Hansen, *USIA*.

9. For general information regarding U.S. radio politics, see USIAL/HC, Radio: General 1943–1950, 1951–1953, 1954–1959; and Radio: History of Voice of America. For U.S. radio plans, see Rathkolb, "Politische Propaganda," pp. 31–64; Hans Bausch, "Rundfunkpolitik nach 1945," in *Trümmerzeit*, edited by F. Prinz (Munich, 1983); L. A. Hartenian, "Propaganda and the Control Division of Radio Frankfurt, 1945–1949" (Ph.D. diss., State University of New Jersey, 1984).

10. USIAL/HC, U.S. Office of War Information, June 10, 1944, Radio: General 1943–1950, Development of the German Section.

11. Ergert, *Fünfzig Jahre Rundfunk*, pp. 124–91.

12. Abbey to Cohrssen, May 15, 1946, p. 1, private archive of Hans Cohrssen, as quoted in Rathkolb, "Politische Propaganda," p. 452.

13. "Despatch: The American Minister (Erhardt) to the Secretary of State, Vienna, October 22, 1947," in *Understanding Austria*, edited by R. Wagnleitner (Salzburg, 1984), p. 261. The name RAVAG is used in line with the terminology of U.S. media experts, although the company had been deleted in the Wiener Handelsregister (Vienna Trade Registry) in August 1938. See Michael Schmolke, "Normalität und Terror, Verlockung und Gewalt," *Medien Journal* 4 (1988): 179–82; Venus, "Die Entstehung eines Massenmediums."

14. Rathkolb, "Politische Propaganda," pp. 461–569.

15. NA 511.63/5-1551, Airgram: Dowling to Department of State, Vienna, May 15, 1951, Subject: Development of Psychological Offensive by U.S. Information and Cultural Media in Austria.

16. WNRC 260/66/16, Letter: Reischek to Lee, September 15, 1950.

17. "Amerika hat noch nicht sein Bestes gegeben," *Berichte und Informationen* 2 (February 14, 1947): 11–12; "Kritik am Sender Rot-Weiss-Rot. Ergebnisse einer Publikumsumfrage," *Berichte und Informationen* 1 (November 8, 1946): 15–16.

18. Hans Hanke, "Auf- oder Abbau der Sendergruppe Rot-Weiss-Rot?," *Berichte und Informationen* 3 (February 13, 1948): 1–3.

19. Ibid.; WNRC 260/891/11, Pettegrove to Eberle, Linz, February 16, 1948.

20. *Die Radiowoche*, February 15, 1948, p. 11; *Die Neue Front*, September 5, 1953; NA 511.634/9-1453, Telegram: USIS Vienna to USIA Washington, D.C., September 14, 1953.

21. WNRC 260/888/26, Green to CIC Denazification Section, August 23, 1950, Subject: Request for Reconsideration of the Dismissal Order on Dr. Geza Rech.

22. Mettler-Meibom, *Demokratisierung und Kalter Krieg*; idem, "Der Besatzungsrundfunk als Medium der amerikanischen Umerziehungspolitik," *Rundfunk und Fernsehen* 2/3 (September 1973): 166–83.

23. NA 511/634/3-2751, Airgram: Legation, Vienna, to Department of State, March 27, 1951, Subject: Red-White-Red Programming Changes and Public Reactions Thereto.

24. Ibid.

25. Ibid.

26. Bogart, *Premises for Propaganda*.

27. WNRC 260/65/82, Quarterly Historical Report, ISB, October 2, 1950.

28. See n. 23.

29. Ibid.

30. "'Versuch Dein Glück' auch in Gmunden," *Salzkammergut Zeitung*, May 25, 1947, p. 3.

31. Rathkolb, "Politische Propaganda," p. 488; Schönberg, "Amerikanische Informations- und Medienpolitik," pp. 126–31; WNRC 260/891/17, USFA in Austria, Survey Section, Report no. 18, January 9, 1948; Merritt and Merritt, *Public Opinion in Occupied Germany: The OMGUS Surveys*, pp. 115–16 and 128–30.

32. *Funk und Film*, December 15, 1949.

33. Merritt and Merritt, *Public Opinion in Semisovereign Germany: The HICOG Surveys*, Special Report no. 196-S1, "The Status of Red-White-Red among Austrian Listeners," May 17, 1954.

34. WNRC 260/65/82, Quarterly Historical Report, ISB, October 2, 1950.

35. WNRC 260/92/39, Memorandum: Stern to Lee, December 23, 1948, Subject: ISB Radio Advertising.

36. See n. 34 and WNRC 260/66/59040-1, Green to Struck, September 20, 1950.

37. "Radiohören soll wieder Vergnügen werden," *Demokratisches Volksblatt*, December 29, 1948.

38. USIAL/HC, *A Study of USIA Operating Assumptions*, vol. 4 (Washington, D.C., 1954). For information concerning foreign radio programs, see Holt, *Radio Free Europe*; Browne,

"The History and Programming Policies of RIAS"; Greaser, "The Role of the Voice of America in the Hungarian Revolt of 1956"; Pirsein, "The Voice of America"; Scheel, *Krieg über Ätherwellen*; Hansen, *Radio Free Europe*; Maurey Lisann, *Broadcasting to the Soviet Union* (New York, 1975); Browne, *The Voice of America*; Browne, *International Radio Broadcasting*; Mickelson, *America's Other Voice*.

39. USIAL / HC, A Study of Operating Assumptions, What the Listeners Say, February 7, 1949, p. 122.

40. Ergert, *Fünfzig Jahre Rundfunk*, p. 132.

41. WNRC 260 / 66 / 16, Memorandum: Green, not dated.

42. See n. 21.

43. Dizard, *Strategy of Truth*.

44. WNRC 260 / 88 / 30, Program series: *Das Information Center Linz spricht*.

45. WNRC 260 / 88 / 30, Program series: *Das Auto in Amerika*.


CHAPTER FIVE

1. "USA-Kultur für Österreich," *Linzer Volksblatt*, November 29, 1945.

2. USIAL / HC, Memorandum, U.S. Information Centers IIA, ICS A, Goodwin, May 3, 1953.

3. WNRC 260 / 32 / 59, Activities: Graphic Display and Publications Section, Vienna, no date.

4. WNRC 260 / 92 / 14, Publicity Material: U.S.-Information Center, Vienna, ISB, March 6, 1947, J. B. Wilson, Publications and Graphic Display Officer.

5. See the contents of USIAL / HC Libraries, 1942–56; Libraries: Philosophy, Goals, and Operating Principles of U.S. Libraries Overseas; Libraries: Studies; USIAL / HC, Initial Establishment Dates of U.S. Information Centers, April 1, 1966; USIAL / HC, Study of USIS Libraries, August 1967; WNRC 260 / 65 / 86, Draft for Extending Reading Rooms to Smaller Cities of Austria, September 21, 1950.

6. USIAL / HC, Study of USIS Libraries, August 1967; Alexander, "The Relationship between United States Foreign Policy Aims"; Pilgert, *The History of the Development of Information Services*; "An Appraisal of the America Houses in Germany: A Program Guidance Study of Effectiveness of the U.S. Information Centers," Report no. 210, Series no. 2, April 15, 1955.

7. WNRC 260 / 92 / 12, Lectures held in cooperation with the US-Information Center, no date; USIAL / HC, Study of Amerika Haus Vienna, Washington, D.C., 1955.

8. WNRC 260 / 65 / 86, Plan for Extending Reading Rooms to Smaller Cities of Austria, September 21, 1950; ibid., Report of Activities for Information Centers for the Month of September, October 2, 1950.

9. WNRC 260 / 92 / 12, Publicity Material: US-Information Centers, Vienna, March 6, 1947.

10. WNRC 260 / 32 / 59, Report: Information Centers—Austria, September 1, 1947.

11. USIAL / HC, Study by Institute of Communications Research: International Motion Picture Services.

12. WNRC 260 / 88 / 22, Monthly Report, Film Loan List, April 21–May 20, 1949.

13. WNRC 260 / 88 / 22, A. N. Hopman: Report of Activities for Quarter April–June 1950, June 27, 1950.

14. WNRC 260 / 92 / 12, Publicity Material: US-Information Centers, Vienna, March 6, 1947.

15. USIAL / HC, The America Houses: A Study of the U.S. Information Centers in Germany, Office of the U.S. High Commissioner for Germany, September 1953; WNRC 260 / 40 / Libraries, Stocks 1949; WNRC 260 / 66, Office Supply, List of Records, September 20, 1950; *Wiener Kurier*, June 25, 1949.

16. USIAL / HC, The America Houses.

17. WNRC 260/31, General Report on Lending Library-US-Information Center, Vienna, October 1, 1947.

18. "Verborgene Schätze im Information Center," *Salzburger Nachrichten*, July 8, 1947, p. 4.

19. See WNRC 260/31/Reports, Vienna, General Report on Lending Library-US-Information Center, Vienna, September 20, 1947; WNRC 260/40/Reports, ISB, Report for the Month of November, Vienna, November 26, 1948; ibid., Activities of the Information Centers, November 1948.

20. WNRC 260/65/85, Plan for Extending Reading Rooms to Smaller Cities of Austria, September 21, 1950.

21. See n. 19.

22. *Verleger Informationen* 6 (May 1949): 8.

23. Ibid.

24. WNRC 260/88/34, Opening of Young People's Library, March 28, 1950.

25. WNRC 260/632/Chief, Public Affairs, Statistical Tables.

26. Ibid.; WNRC 260/88/22, Report of Activities for Quarter April–June 1950, June 27, 1950; ibid., Loans to Rural Areas, First Supplement, January 13, 1950; WNRC 260/65/86, Book Loans to Factories and Trade Unions, September 21, 1950; ibid., Report of Activities for Information Center for the Month of September, October 2, 1950; WNRC 260/65/82, Quarterly Historical Report, ISB, October 2, 1950; WNRC 260/93/Statistical Table: Permanent Loans.

27. "Amerikawagen: USIS Library on Wheels," US-IIA Newsletter, May 1953; *Die Stadt Salzburg in Wort, Bild und Zahl 1959/1960* (Salzburg, 1960), p. 51.

28. WNRC 260/35/44, Memorandum: A. N. Hopman, Conference with Representatives of Lending Library Association, December 27, 1948; *Volksstimme*, May 26, 1949.

29. WNRC 260/632/Chief, Public Affairs, Letter: Haslauer to Information Center; ibid., Memorandum: Hopman to Connaughton, June 20, 1950.

30. WNRC 260/35/Surveys, Headquarters USF in Austria, ISB Survey Section, Report no. 44, US-Information Center, May 17, 1948.

31. Ibid.; WNRC 260/40/Reports, ISB, Monthly Report of the US-Information Center, Vienna, November 25, 1948.

32. WNRC 260/35/22; 260/49/25; 260/102/39; Hiller, "Amerikanische Medien," pp. 130–48.

33. WNRC 260/32/59, Report: Information Centers—Austria, September 1, 1947.

34. See Schmidt, "Training for Democracy," pp. 224–29; Howard, "Letter from Austria," pp. 615–17.

35. Dizard, *Strategy of Truth*, p. 138.

36. WNRC 260/92/22, Publicity Material, US-Information Center, Vienna, March 6, 1947.

37. "Austria Keeps Briefed at U.S. Information Centers," *Christian Science Monitor*, August 10, 1950.

38. *Christian Science Monitor*, August 5, 1950; *Publisher's Weekly*, November 18, 1950; *The Pantagraph* (Bloomington, Ill.), December 27, 1955; *Watertown* (New York) *Times*, December 30, 1953; Crowell and Carpenter, *Supplementary Reports on the Use of Books*; "American Books in Overseas Libraries," *Publisher's Weekly*, October 28, 1950.

39. *Milwaukee Journal* 20 (June 1948), as quoted in Bungenstab, "Entstehung, Bedeutungs- und Funktionswandel," pp. 191–203.

40. USIAL/HC, Circular Airgram, no. 1692, IIA, Department of State: Instructions for Selection and Retention of Material in Book and Library Program, July 15, 1953.

41. Rita E. Moskowitz, "A Study of the Historical Development of the Program of the Overseas Libraries of the United States Information Agency" (M.A. thesis, Washington, 1950), p. 16.

42. U.S. Congress, House, U.S. Information and Educational Exchange Act of 1947, *Hearings*, p. 164; Babin, "The Book Selection Policy."

43. U.S. Congress, Senate, Committee on Foreign Relations, *Overseas Information Programs*, part 1, p. 112.

44. Mary Trembour, "Some Political Aspects of United States Information Agency Book Selection Policies" (Research paper, University of Denver, 1971); "Who Are the Book Burners?," *New Republic*, June 29, 1953, p. 8.

45. Louthan, "The McCarthy Sub-Committee."

46. USIAL/HC, Memorandum: Francis R. St. John for Richard A. Humphrey, September 12, 1953. See also Scrutineer, "Secret Blacklist," pp. 376–79; "Schnuffles and Flourishes," *Time*, April 20, 1953, p. 26; "Book Order Survives Sen. McCarthy's Blast," *Washington News*, July 10, 1953.

47. USIAL/HC, *Report on the Operations of the Overseas Book and Library Program*, Department of State, July 15, 1953; *Publisher's Weekly*, December 13, 1952.

48. WNRC 260/88/3, ISB-Austria, List: Out Books; USIAL/HC, *Report on the Operations of the Overseas Book Library Program*; Dizard, *Strategy of Truth*, pp. 140–41; Criscietello, "The Role of American Books," pp. 106–12.

49. Scrutineer, "Secret Blacklist."

50. "U.S. Losing Battle of Books," *Chicago Daily News*, June 6, 1955.

51. USIAL/HC, Report: The Task Force for Increasing the Distribution of American Books Abroad, November 30, 1955.

52. "Those Red Books Still on Shelves," *Albany Times-Union*, September 26, 1955.

53. Bonheim, "American Books in Vienna," p. 37.

54. Ibid., p. 38.

55. Bogart, *Premises for Propaganda*, p. 83.

56. WNRC 260/41/13, Memorandum: Pettegrove to Col. Eberle, Salzburg, May 3, 1948.

57. Gehring, *Amerikanische Literaturpolitik in Deutschland*, p. 108; see also Evans, "United States Libraries Abroad," pp. 6–7.

58. Williams, "Who Reads an American Book?," pp. 518–31.

59. Cyril Connolly, "On Englishmen Who Write American," *New York Times Book Review*, December 18, 1949; Mottram, "American Studies in Europe"; Ludlow, "The Growth of American Influence," pp. 618–23.

60. Connolly, "On Englishmen."

61. Lehmann, "The Lesson of the Pupil," pp. 23–33.

62. William M. Leary, Jr., "Books, Soldiers, and Censorship during the Second World War," *American Quarterly* 2 (Spring 1968): 237–45; Lingeman, *Don't You Know There's a War On?*, pp. 278–80; Brooks, "Books Follow the Jeep," pp. 25–28; Jamieson, *Books for the Army*.

63. Ninkovich, *Diplomacy of Ideas*, p. 89.

64. Zäckel, "Der Einfluss James Fenimore Coopers."

65. Bundesministerium für Unterricht, *Liste der gesperrten Autoren und Bücher*; WNRC 260/35/24, Letter: Henry E. Jackson, CAD New York, to Chief ISB, November 4, 1947.

66. WNRC 260/93/99, Overseas Editions; USIAL/HC, Department of the Army, Special Staff, US Army, CAD, Reorientation Branch, November 15, 1948, Printed Materials for Occupied Areas.

67. WNRC 260/40/Publicity, Memorandum: Hoffman for Chief, ISB, Vienna, April 30, 1948.

68. WNRC 260/40/25, Memorandum: Hoffman to D. C. Fox, Vienna, August 16, 1949; Rathkolb, "Der Kalte Krieg," p. 50; Gehring, *Amerikanische Literaturpolitik*, p. 87.

69. Rathkolb, "Der Kalte Krieg," pp. 50–52.

70. WNRC 260/63/Publications Section, Memorandum: Hoffman to Chief, ISB, Vienna,

June 20, 1950; ibid., Report for Publications Section for Month of February 1949, February 25, 1949.

71. WNRC 260/63/Publications Section, Report of Publications Section for the Month of September 1949, September 23, 1949.

72. Ibid., Memorandum: Comments of U.S. Publishers Report on Austrian Book Publishing, October 22, 1948.

73. *Verleger Informationen* 1 (December 1948): 1.

74. See *Verleger Informationen* from December 1948 to 1955.

75. WNRC 260/63/Publications Section, Memorandum: Hoffman to Fox, Vienna, August 16, 1949.

76. Ibid., June 20, 1950.

77. *Forum* 26 (February 1956): 68; "Die Buchgemeinschaften in Österreich," *Berichte und Informationen* 619 (May 1958): 12–14.

78. Buchklub der Jugend, *Zehn Jahre Österreichischer Buchklub der Jugend*; Internationales Institut für Kinder-, Jugend- und Volksliteratur und Österreichischer Buchklub der Jugend, *Zwanzig Jahre Österreichischer Buchklub der Jugend*.

79. *Eine Neue Welt für unsere Jugend*. I thank Leopold Radauer for introducing this work to me.

80. Bamberger, *Jugendlektüre*, p. 183; "Bundesgesetz über die Bekämpfung unzüchtiger Veröffentlichungen und den Schutz der Jugend gegen sittliche Gefährdung," March 31, 1950.

81. Joseph McVeigh, *Kontinuität und Vergangenheitsbewältigung in der österreichischen Literatur nach 1945* (Vienna, 1988), p. 70.

82. Bamberger, *Jugendlektüre*, pp. 42–44.

83. Cracroft, "The American West of Karl May," p. 258.

84. Lunzer, "Der literarische Markt," pp. 24–45; UNESCO, *Index Translationum*; Milo, "La bourse mondiale de la traduction," pp. 92–115.

85. WNRC 260/63/Publications Section, Memorandum: Hoffman to Wilson, Vienna, August 31, 1948.

86. Ibid., Memorandum: Hoffman to Chief, ISB, June 20, 1950.

87. Franz Kroller, "Der Siegeszug der Taschenbücher durch alle Welt," *Berichte und Informationen* 622 (June 20, 1958): 13–14.

88. Wehdeking, *Der Nullpunkt*; Sigmund Skard, *The Study of American Literature* (Philadelphia, 1949); Ruland, *America in Modern European Literature*; Mönning, *Amerika und England im deutschen, österreichischen und schweizerischen Schrifttum*; Breitenkamp, *The U.S. Information Control Division*; Price, *The Reception of United States Literature in Germany*; Galinsky, *Amerikanisch-deutsche Sprach- und Literaturbeziehungen*; Frenz and Lang, *Nordamerikanische Literatur im deutschen Sprachraum*; Denkler, *Amerika in der deutschen Literatur*; Ritter, *Deutschlands literarisches Amerikabild*.

89. Götz, "Der Wandel des Amerikabildes," p. 14.

90. U.S. drama is dealt with in connection with the U.S. Theatre and Music Section.

91. Alexander, *Here the Country Lies*, p. 261.

92. Götz, "Der Wandel des Amerikabildes," pp. 12–14 and 299; Durzak, "Abrechnung mit einer Utopie?," pp. 98–121.

93. Ruland, *America in Modern European Literature*, p. 4.

94. Götz, "Der Wandel des Amerikabildes," p. 32.

95. Kunert, *Der andere Planet*, p. 150.

96. Langenbucher, *Der aktuelle Unterhaltungsroman*; Ashliman, "The Study of Popular Literature in Germany," pp. 332–38; Stadler, "Der Heftroman"; Mann, "Karl May," pp. 391–400; Gassman, *The Literary Evolution*; Cracroft, "The American West of Karl May," pp. 249–58; Shippey, "The Cold War in Science Fiction," pp. 308–22; Ernest Mandel, *A Social History of the Crime Story* (Minneapolis, 1985).

97. Gérard Cordese, "The Impact of American Science Fiction on Europe," in *Superculture*, edited by C. W. E. Bigsby (Bowling Green, Ohio, 1975), pp. 160–74.

98. Götz, "Der Wandel des Amerikabildes," p. 36.

99. Kühnelt, "Die Aufnahme der nordamerikanischen Literatur in Österreich," pp. 200 and 203.

100. Bourdieu, *Die feinen Unterschiede*; Eco, *Apokalyptiker und Integrierte*; Lefebvre, *Kritik des Alltagslebens*; Levin L. Schucking, *Soziologie der literarischen Geschmacksbildung* (Bern, 1961).

101. Cordese, "The Impact of American Science Fiction," p. 170.

102. Criscietello, "The Role of American Books," pp. 106–12.

103. McNeil and Hooker, "The Role of the Arts and Humanities," p. 67.

CHAPTER SIX

1. USIAL/HC, Interdivisional Reorientation Committee: Cultural Exchange Programs, February 1949; Louis Albee, "Education as an Implement of U.S. Foreign Policy" (Ph.D. diss., Yale University, 1948).

2. Rudolf Haas, "Amerikanische Einflüsse auf das deutsche Bildungswesen nach 1945," *Jahrbuch für Amerikastudien* 8 (1963): 24–33; Bungenstab, *Umerziehung zur Demokratie?*; Thron, "Schulreform im besiegten Deutschland"; Kellermann, *Cultural Relations*; Heineman, *Umerziehung und Wiederaufbau*.

3. Engelbrecht, "Die Eingriffe der Alliierten," pp. 278–308; idem, *Lehrervereine im Kampf um Status und Einfluss*, pp. 130–34; Spachinger et al., *Die österreichische Schule 1945–1957*.

4. *Zehn Jahre Aufbau 1945–1955.*

5. Hiller, "Amerikanische Medien," p. 201.

6. WNRC 260/88/16, Memorandum: Education Division to USACA, Educational Supplies on Loan to Austria, Vienna, October 24, 1949.

7. WNRC 260/58888-1, Dexter G. Tilroe: Goals and Methods in Social Education for Austrian Schools, as quoted in Hiller, "Amerikanische Medien," p. 249.

8. Kotthorst, "Geschichtsverlust"; Armytage, *The American Influence on English Education.*

9. WNRC 260/58888-1, Henry Brechbill, Recommendations for Teacher Education in Austria, 1947, as quoted in Hiller, "Amerikanische Medien," p. 227.

10. Hiller, "Amerikanische Medien," pp. 286–98.

11. "Ein grosser amerikanischer Pädagoge und Philosoph," *Erziehung* 1 (January 1948).

12. See individual issues of *Erziehung.*

13. Hiller, "Amerikanische Medien," pp. 200 and 316–17.

14. Ibid., p. 270.

15. Ibid., p. 286.

16. Martin F. Herz, "Compendium of Austrian Politics, Vienna, December 2, 1948," in *Understanding Austria*, edited by R. Wagnleitner (Salzburg, 1984), p. 573.

17. Skard, *American Myth*, p. 409.

18. Ibid., pp. 415–16; Beer, "The Development of Teaching and Research," pp. 177–93.

19. Anderson, *The Humanities in the German and Austrian Universities*, pp. 86–97; Lewis Coser, *Refugee Scholars in America: Their Impact and Their Experiences* (New Haven, Conn., 1984); Stadler, *Vertriebene Vernunft*, vol. 1.

20. Memorandum: U.S. Informational and Educational Exchange Objectives in Next Five Years, January 1950, as quoted in Ninkovich, *Diplomacy of Ideas*, p. 148.

21. Ibid., p. 141.

22. WNRC 260/40/2, Report: Austro-American Institute of Education, July 1948; USIAL/HC, The Army's Educational Exchange Program, Reorientation Branch, Office of the Under-Secretary, Department of the Army, May 1950.

23. Dizard, *Strategy of Truth*, pp. 153–70; John W. Gardner, "The Foreign Student in America," *Foreign Affairs* 30, no. 4 (July 1952): 637–50; Norton, "The United States Department of State International Visitor Program"; USIAL/HC, Two Way Street: Report of the United States Advisory Commission on Educational Exchange, June 30, 1950; Department of State, *Cross-Cultural Education*.

24. Wilson and Bonilla, "Evaluating Exchange of Persons Programs," p. 24.

25. Rock, *The History of the American Field Service*, pp. 589–607.

26. WNRC 260/96/ISB-199, Memorandum: Herz to Kellermann, Present Status of Exchange-of-Persons Program for Austria, and policy considerations in connection therewith, Washington, D.C., April 18, 1949; NA 511.63/4-450; WNRC 260/861/89.

27. Elder, *The Information Machine*, pp. 31–34.

28. Dizard, *Strategy of Truth*, p. 154; USIAL/HC, American Embassy: Report on a Survey of the Department of State Exchange of Persons in Austria, Vienna, 1955; USIAL/HC, A Beacon of Hope: The Exchange-of-Persons Program, Washington, D.C., 1963; George A. Mastroianni, "A Study of Attitudes toward the United States Held by Former Participants in a United States Educational Exchange Project in Radio and Television" (Ph.D. diss., Syracuse University, 1971); USIAL/HC, West German Receptivity and Reactions to the Exchange of Persons Program, Report no. 151, August 25, 1952; Committee on Educational Interchange Policy, *Twenty Years of United States Government Programs in Cultural Relations*.

29. Department of State, *Educational Exchanges under the Fulbright Act*.

30. Obergottsberger and Berthold, *25 Jahre Fulbright-Programm in Österreich*, pp. 22–25 and 37–39; *The Fulbright Program in Austria*.

31. Schulmann, "United States Government Educational, Literary, and Artistic Cultural Exchange Programs," p. 99.

32. Obergottsberger and Berthold, *25 Jahre Fulbright-Programm in Österreich*, pp. 30–34; Johnson and Colligan, *The Fulbright Program*; Special Supplement: "New York," *Salzburger Nachrichten*, March 23, 1990, p. iv.

33. WNRC 260/632/Chief, Public Affairs, Memorandum: Hopman to Lesser, December 14, 1950; Snyder and Beauchamp, *An Experiment in International Cultural Relations*, pp. 58–79; C. I. Barnard, *The Rockefeller Foundation Directory of Fellowship Awards for the Years 1917–1958* (New York, 1959); D. L. Revoldt, "Raymond B. Fosdick: Reform, Internationalism, and the Rockefeller-Foundation" (Ph.D. diss., University of Akron, 1982).

34. WNRC 260/88/14, Letter: Paulovsky to Commission for International Educational Reconstruction, Vienna, May 20, 1947; NA 511.63/1-550, Airgram: E. Wilder Spaulding, Report of Public Affairs Officer, December 1949, Vienna, January 5, 1950; Hillway, "American Studies in Austria," pp. 89–94; Gleason, "World War II and the Development of American Studies," pp. 343–58; Bradford Smith, "European Fulbrighters Back Home," *Institute of International Education News Bulletin*, April 1959, pp. 7–8; USIAL/HC, Jean Joyce, An Overview of International Educational Exchange, 1946–1966, August 10, 1966.

35. WNRC 260/581/12, Letter: Brunner to Chief, ISB, Innsbruck, May 9, 1949.

36. Skard, *American Myth*, p. 413.

37. *Verzeichnis über die seit dem Jahre 1872 an der philosophischen Fakultät der Universität Wien eingereichten und approbierten Dissertationen*, vol. 1 (Vienna, 1935); *Verzeichnis der 1934 bis 1937 an der philosophischen Fakultät Wien und der 1872 bis 1937 an der philosophischen Fakultät der Universität Innsbruck eingereichten und approbierten Dissertationen*, vol. 4 (Vienna, 1937); *Verzeichnis der an der Universität Wien approbierten Dissertationen 1945–1949* (Vienna, 1952); *Verzeichnis der an der Universität Wien approbierten Dissertationen 1950–1957* (Vienna, 1959); Skard, *American Myth*, p. 416.

38. Skard, *American Myth*, p. 416.

39. *Zahlenmässige Darstellung des Schulwesens in Österreich. Schuljahr 1951/52. Heft 1, Stück 6, 1952*.

40. Baschiera, Hassfurthner, and Reitterer, *A British and American Reader*; Stammler, *Amerika im Spiegel seiner Literatur*; Tacke, "Die Bedeutung der westlichen Fremdsprachen für den demokratischen Schulunterricht," pp. 66–72.

41. Rudolf, *Amerikanisch in Abkürzungen*.

42. USIAL/HC, USIA's English Language Teaching Program, Historical Source Book, June 15, 1964.

43. WNRC 260/32/83, Memorandum: Pettegrove to van Eerden, May 24, 1946.

44. WNRC 260/75/ISB, Letter: Williams, Chief Education Division, to Petersen, Vienna, October 7, 1948.

45. Paulovsky, "Das Eindringen und die Aufnahme von Amerikanismen," pp. 2–3, 48, 73, 87, 147, 201.

46. Joachim Stave, "Über Ursprung und Geschichte des Wortes 'Jazz,'" *Muttersprache* 68 (1958): 80–87.

47. WNRC 260/35/Surveys, Headquarters USF in Austria, ISB Survey Section, Report no. 44, May 17, 1948.

48. Lettner, "Die französische Österreichpolitik," p. 341.

49. Viereck, "Englisches Wortgut," p. 209; Blanke, *Yankeetum*; P. Ganz, *Der Einfluss des Englischen auf den deutschen Wortschatz 1640–1850* (Berlin, 1957); Zindler, "Anglizismen in der deutschen Presse"; Viereck, Viereck, and Winter, "Wie Englisch ist unsere Pressesprache?," pp. 205–26.

50. Ortner, "Untersuchungen zum Vokabular deutscher Popmusikzeitschriften," pp. 257–58.

51. McCrum, Cran, and MacNeil, *The Story of English*.

52. Ortner, "Untersuchungen zum Vokabular deutscher Popmusikzeitschriften," pp. 257–58.

53. Carstensen, "Amerikanische Einflüsse auf die deutsche Sprache," pp. 34–35; Welter, *Die Sprache der Teenager und Twens*; Bungert, "Zum Einfluss des englischen auf die deutsche Sprache," pp. 703–17; Urbanová, "Zum Einfluss des amerikanischen Englisch," pp. 97–114; David Crystal, "American English in Europe," in *Superculture*, edited by C. W. E. Bigsby (Bowling Green, Ohio, 1975), pp. 57–68; Viereck, *Studien zum Einfluss der englischen Sprache auf das Deutsche*; Otto F. Beer, "Des Playboys Ahne war grösser. Vom Untergang des Dandys," *Die Zeit*, October 12, 1962.

54. Frank, "Modern American Language"; Wendelken, "Der Einfluss des Englischen," pp. 289–308.

55. "Von Software Gurus und Computerwitwen," *Deutscher Forschungsdienst*, September 11, 1985.

56. Wallace K. Ferguson and Geoffrey Brunn, *A Survey of European Civilization* (Boston, 1964), p. 944; "English, English Everywhere," *Newsweek*, November 15, 1982.

57. Hansard, "House of Lords Debates," November 21, 1979; McCrum, Cran, and MacNeil, *The Story of English*, pp. 343–44.

58. Bertrand Russell, *The Political and Cultural Influence of America* (Boston, 1951), p. 14.

59. "A Language That Has Ausgeflippt: The Word around the World Is English, More or Less," *Time*, June 16, 1986, p. 27.

60. Cunliffe, "American Studies in Europe," p. 47.

61. Peters, "American Culture and the State Department," p. 273; Mottram, *American Studies in Europe*, p. 9; Herbert Gleason, "Amerika und Europa trifft sich auf Schloss Leopoldskron," *Erziehung* 4 (October 1951): 14; Williams, "Who Reads an American Book?," p. 519.

62. Smith, "The Salzburg Seminar," p. 31.

63. WNRC 260/59/Salzburg Seminar, Letter: Lt. Col. Creighton, Jr., to Allied Permit Office, U.S. Element, Subject: Matthiessen, F.O., March 17, 1950; ibid., Disposition Form: USACA Education Division, Lewis E. Perry, Deputy Director of Intelligence, March 6, 1950,

Subject: Matthiessen, F.O.; ibid., Salzburg Seminar in American Studies, 1948, A Report; WNRC 260/59/6630, Telegram: Erhardt to Secretary of State, February 4, 1949; NA 740.00119, Control (A) 9-849, Report of Public Affairs Officer (E. Wilder Spaulding), August 1–31, 1949; WNRC 260/885/10, Salzburg Seminar, July 26, 1947; Rathkolb, "Die Entwicklung der US-Besatzungspolitik," pp. 39–40.

64. Mathiessen, *From the Heart of Europe*.

65. "Memorandum: Martin F. Herz, Vienna, August 16, 1948. Subject: Observations on Salzburg Seminar," in *Understanding Austria*, edited by R. Wagnleitner (Salzburg, 1984), pp. 443–46, also pp. 306–9, 413–15.

66. Ninkovich, *Diplomacy of Ideas*, p. 105.

67. Smith, *The Salzburg Seminar*, p. 34.


CHAPTER SEVEN

1. Mellinger, *Das Theater am Broadway*, p. 71.

2. WNRC 260/892/Music and Theatre Reports, 1945–1947, Pinter to van Eerden, November 13, 1945.

3. WNRC 260/35/89, Letter: Virginia D. Pleasants to National Music Council, Vienna, November 25, 1946; Szanto, *Theater and Propaganda*; Soucek, "The Use of Theater Abroad"; "Arts and Entertainment: Latest 'Cold War' Weapon for the U.S.," *U.S. News and World Report*, July 1, 1955, pp. 57–59; Müller, "Theater im Zeichen des Kalten Krieges."

4. WNRC 260/35/89.

5. WNRC 260/636/10, Theatre and Music Section, Contracts.

6. Gehring, *Amerikanische Literaturpolitik*, pp. 62–73; Lothar, *Die Rückkehr*; Haeusserman, *Mein Freund Henry*.

7. WNRC 260/58886-2, Memorandum: van Eerden, How the USFA projects America and the democratic life in Austria through the Information Services Branch, October 11, 1946.

8. WNRC 260/35/19, Letter: Lothar to Lorenz, Periodical Unit, November 1946.

9. WNRC 260/96/ISB-191, De-nazification of Austrian Actors.

10. Rathkolb, "Politische Propaganda," pp. 395–405.

11. Rathkolb, "Die Entwicklung der US-Besatzungspolitik," p. 37.

12. Wilhelm Pellert, "Neues Theater in der Scala (1948–1956)" (Ph.D. diss., University of Vienna, 1978).

13. WNRC 260/892/Music and Theatre Reports, 1945–47, Bi-Weekly Report, November 24, 1945; Rathkolb, "Politische Propaganda," p. 344.

14. Felsenreich, "Der Einbruch der nordamerikanischen Dramatik," pp. 10–36; Brünnig, "Amerikanische Dramen," pp. 246–69; Woess, "Die Rezeption der Dramen Eugene O'Neills."

15. WNRC 260/892/Music and Theatre Reports, 1945–47.

16. WNRC 260/892/57, Music and Theatre Reports, November 10, 1945–December 31, 1947; WNRC 260/35/12, Memorandum: Lothar to Chief of Branch, December 2, 1946.

17. WNRC 260/632/ISB Reports, List of U.S. plays represented by ISB, Vienna, January 1, 1950.

18. WNRC 260/35/12, Memorandum: Lothar to Chief of Branch, December 2, 1946; WNRC 260/820/ISB.

19. Rathkolb, "Politische Propaganda," p. 420.

20. WNRC 260/41/30, Memorandum: Hogan to Chief of Branch, September 30, 1948; WNRC 260/632/ISB Miscellaneous Reports, Monthly Report, Theatre Section, December 14, 1949.

21. Andrea Schneider, "Das Theater als Medium der Kulturpolitik der amerikanischen

Besatzungsmacht in Österreich am Beispiel Salzburgs" (Seminar paper, University of Salzburg, Winter Semester 1984/85).

22. WNRC 260/35/11; 260/49/20.

23. WNRC 260/58/59027-21, Quarterly Activities Report for the U.S. High Commissioner, June 30, 1950.

24. WNRC 260/51/14, Report covering the period from October 22 through December 13, 1949.

25. WNRC 260/65/82, Quarterly Historical Report, ISB, October 2, 1950.

26. WNRC 820/2/ISB, Semi-Monthly Report, Theatre and Music Section, September 30, 1946.

27. WNRC 260/65/82, Quarterly Historical Report, ISB, October 2, 1950; NA 511.63/7-1051, Haeusserman to Moffly, July 10, 1951.

28. WNRC 260/72/ISB, Memorandum: Hogan to Fox, May 15, 1950.

29. NA 511.63/4-2553, Airgram: Hale to Department of State, Vienna, April 25, 1953.

30. NA 511.63/7-1051, Memorandum: Haeusserman to Moffly, Vienna, July 10, 1951; NA 511.632/11-751, Airgram: April 30, 1951.

31. NA 511.63/7-2453, Airgram: US-Embassy to Department of State, July 24, 1953.

32. WNRC 260/72/ISB Telecon.

33. WNRC 260/632/ISB Reports, List of U.S. Plays represented by ISB, Vienna, January 1, 1950.

34. WNRC 260/35/10, Letter: Smith to Secretary of State, September 17, 1947, as quoted in Rathkolb, "Politische Propaganda," p. 413; Miller, Timebends.

35. Rathkolb, "Politische Propaganda," p. 424; Müller, "Theater im Zeichen des Kalten Krieges."

36. WNCR 260/59/63, Memorandum: Hogan to Lee, Vienna, December 6, 1949.

37. NA 511.63/2-150, Telegram: Acheson to US-Legation Vienna, Washington, D.C., January 30, 1950; NA 511.63/5-2251.

38. WNRC 260/72/ISB Telecon, April 27, 1948; "American Plays Used by Communists in Austria for Propaganda," New York Times, February 18, 1951, sec. 2, p. 3.

39. Rathkolb, "Die Entwicklung der US-Besatzungspolitik," pp. 40–41.

40. WNRC 260/65/82, ISB, Quarterly Historical Report, October 2, 1950.

41. Hans Weigel, "Taktlos gegen Deutschland," Salzburger Nachrichten, July 15, 1954, p. 4; idem, "Ora et collabora," Salzburger Nachrichten, June 14/15, 1952, p. 12.

42. Friedrich Torberg to Laurence Dalcher, Information Officer, PAD, U.S. Embassy, Vienna, November 5, 1953. Frank Tichy called this letter in the Torberg Papers to my attention. See Tichy, "Ein fauler Hund," pp. 60–67; Robert Kriechbaumer, "Der Fall Bert Brecht—Gottfried von Einem. Zu einem Kapitel Kulturgeschichte des Kalten Krieges," Zeitgeschichte 8 (April 1981): 292–300; Palm, Vom Boykott zur Anerkennung.

43. Sadofsky, "Die Geschmacksbildung an den Wiener Theatern."

44. Ibid., p. 40.

45. Ibid., p. 63.

46. Ibid., p. 64.

47. NA 511.63/7-1051, Haeusserman to Moffly, Vienna, July 10, 1951.

48. Die Presse, February 8, 1947.

49. Lunzer, "Der literarische Markt," p. 35, n. 51.

50. Felsenreich, "Der Einbruch der nordamerikanischen Dramatik," pp. 152–55.

51. Ibid., p. 132.

52. Ludwig Ullmann, "Max Reinhardt und das amerikanische Theater," Der Turm 2 (1946): 121–25.

53. "U.S. Legits as European Envoy," Variety, July 20, 1949, p. 1; Harrison Smith, "American Culture for Export," Saturday Review 38 (July 30, 1955): 22.

54. NA 511.63/4450, Airgram: Spaulding to Department of State, Report of Public Affairs Officer, March 1 to 31, 1950, Vienna, April 4, 1950.

55. Pearson, "Music at War"; idem, *The Pattern of Propaganda in Music*; Sinclair and Levin, *Music and Politics*.

56. Ninkovich, *Diplomacy of Ideas*, p. 87.

57. ASCAP-Pamphlet 1944, as quoted in Ninkovich, *Diplomacy of Ideas*, p. 89.

58. Freymann, "The Eclipse of German Musical Hegemony," p. 185.

59. WNRC 260/35/12, Memorandum: Contribution of U.S. Music to the democratization of Austria [late 1946].

60. WNRC 260/35/12, Letter: Lothar to Mertens, Vienna, November 14, 1946.

61. "Gibt es eine amerikanische Musik?," *Der Turm* 1 (February 1946): 189; Barbara A. Zuck, *A History of Musical Americanism* (Chicago, 1980); Hamm, *Music in the New World*; Tischler, *An American Music*.

62. Nabokov, "Musiker und Komponisten," pp. 32–44.

63. *Salzburger Nachrichten*, August 2, 1945, p. 2.

64. WNRC 260/35/10, Theatre and Music Report, August 31, 1946.

65. WNRC 260/892/57, Lothar to Chief ISB, Semi-Monthly Report, August 31, 1946; WNRC 260/49/63, May 16, 1946.

66. WNRC 250/35/10, Theatre and Music Report, August 31, 1947.

67. WNRC 260/35/12, Letter: Lothar to Mertens, Vienna, November 14, 1946.

68. WNRC 260/65/82, ISB, Quarterly Historical Report, October 2, 1950.

69. WNRC 260/35/10, Theatre and Music Report, April 30, 1947.

70. WNRC 250/35/12, Memorandum: Pleasants, December 3, 1946.

71. WNRC 260/35/3, Notes, Leonard Bernstein, Director N.Y. Symphony, May 17–18, 1947, Concert.

72. WNRC 260/35/20, Memorandum: Eberle, January 14, 1948.

73. WNRC 260/41/29, Memorandum: Pettegrove to Eberle, Linz, December 26, 1947, Subject: Suggestions for Projection of American Music.

74. Ibid.

75. WNRC 260/632, Info-Reports 1950, Report October.

76. WNRC 260/892/57, Theatre and Music Report, April 30, 1947, American Compositions in the ISB Music Library; WNRC 260/195/20; 260/40/Music 1947–48.

77. WNRC 260/65/82, ISB Quarterly Historical Report, October 2, 1950.

78. WNRC 260/65/82, Quarterly Report, Theatre and Music Section, Salzburg, June 15, 1950.

79. WNRC 260/591/63, Memorandum: Fox to Chief of Branch, August 23, 1949.

80. WNRC 260/632/Current Correspondence, Letter: Hogen to Spaulding, May 18, 1949.

81. Arthur Honegger, *Je suis compositeur* (Paris, 1951).

82. Cooper, "Revolution in Musical Taste," pp. 67–78.

83. Pleasants, *Serious Music*, p. 95.

84. Stewart, "An American Opera Conquers Europe," pp. 30–34 and 94; Jack Raymond, "Porgy Delights Belgrade Crowd," *New York Times*, December 17, 1954, p. 36; Cooper, "American Music in Europe," pp. 10–11; NA 511.63/4-2453, Airgram: April 24, 1953.

85. NA 511.63/12-252, Airgram: Spaulding to Department of State, December 2, 1952.

86. NA 511.63/7-2453, Airgram: Madeen to Department of State, July 24, 1953.

87. Rudel, ". . . and Nobody Missed the Waltz," pp. 78–80 and 92–93.

88. Ibid., p. 93; Prawy, "Der Text macht die Musik," pp. 110–13; Spaulding, *The Quiet Invaders*, p. 143.

89. Rudel, ". . . and Nobody Missed the Waltz," pp. 80 and 92.

90. *New York Herald Tribune*, October 29, 1949.

91. Adorno, *Dissonanzen*, p. 72.

92. Otto Basil, "Schwarze Musik erobert Wien," *Neues Österreich*, December 24, 1950, p. 9.

93. Newton [Hobsbawm], *The Jazz Scene*, p. 15.

94. Felix Helair, Jr., "United States Has Secret Sonic Weapon—Jazz," *New York Times*, August 6, 1955, p. 1.

95. Paul Oliver, "Jazz Is Where You Find It: The European Experience of Jazz," in *Superculture*, edited by C. W. E. Bigsby (Bowling Green, Ohio, 1975), pp. 140–51; Bornemann, "The Jazz Cult," part 1, pp. 141–47; idem, "The Jazz Cult," part 2, pp. 261–73; Collier, *The Making of Jazz*; Bernhard, *Jazz, eine musikalische Zeitfrage*; Burian, *Jazz*; "Jazz All Over Europe," *New York Times*, April 30, 1929, p. 14; Pleasants, *Death of a Music?*; Reginald Rudorf, *Jazz in der Zone* (Cologne, 1964); Viera, *Jazz in Europa*; Lange, *Jazz in Deutschland*; Lubomir Doruzka and Ivan Polednák, *Der tschechoslowakische Jazz* (Prague, 1967); Godholt, *A History of Jazz in Britain*.

96. Collier, *The Making of Jazz*, p. 317.

97. "Jazz on the Voice," *New York Herald Tribune*, October 29, 1949.

98. H. F. Mooney, "Popular Music since the 1920s: The Significance of Shifting Taste," *American Quarterly* 10 (Spring 1968): 67–85; Goody, "New Orleans to London," pp. 173–94.

99. Oliver, "Blue-eyed Blues," pp. 227–39.

100. A look at early developments in jazz in Austria is offered in the LPs *Jazz and Hot Dance in Austria*, vol. 5, Harlequin, 2014 (1984), and *Jazz in Austria, 1933–1959: Swing into Bop into Cool*, Black Jack, LP 3019; Klaus Schultz, "Making Records—Austrian Jazz History on Disc," *Danube Weekly*, February 12, 1985, p. 14.

101. Glanz, " 'Jazz' in Österreich," pp. 46–48.

102. *Neues Wiener Abendblatt*, March 10, 1938, p. 1.

103. Zwerin, *La Tristesse de Saint Louis*; Blume, *Das Rasseproblem in der Musik*.

104. Music cassette *Musik der Stunde Null*, compiled by Werner Burkhardt, Walter Haas, and Heinz Wunderlich for *Die Zeit*.

105. Peukert, "Edelweisspiraten, Meuten, Swing," pp. 307–27.

106. NA 740.00119 Control (A)/10-1645, Report: Sutherland, Jr., to Erhardt, September 1945.

107. I am grateful to my brother, Günter Wagnleitner, for much of the information on the development of jazz in Austria after the Second World War.

108. Wolfgang Sandner, "Saxophone lachen nicht," *Frankfurter Allgemeine Zeitung*, July 15, 1988, pp. 28–34.

109. Rathkolb, "Bürokratie und Musikalltag," pp. 26–29.

110. "Jazz Is Not Music, Stresemann Asserts," *New York Times*, June 12, 1927, p. 19; "Vienna Is Alarmed by Inroads of Jazz," *New York Times*, April 15, 1928; Decsey, "Jazz in Vienna," pp. 441–45.

111. H. O. Brunn, *The Original Dixieland Jazz Band* (Baton Rouge, La., 1960), p. 173.

112. Paul Whiteman and Mary MacBride, *Jazz* (New York, 1926); Jones, *Blues People*; Leonard, *Jazz and the White Americans*.

113. Starr, *Red and Hot*.

114. Peters, "American Culture and the State Department," pp. 265–74.

115. Pleasants, *Serious Music*, p. 98.

116. Matthiessen, *From the Heart of Europe*, p. 60.

117. *New York Herald Tribune*, October 27, 1949, p. 1; "The Voice of America: What It Tells the World," *Time*, May 1, 1950, pp. 22–23; USIAL/HC, A Statement on the Voice of America Program Schedule, May 3, 1950; "Beat Me Ivan: Popular Music on the Voice of America Broadcasts," *Newsweek*, August 4, 1947, p. 30; "America Gets Letters from 140,000," *New York Herald Tribune*, May 4, 1947; "Uncle Sam Tells the World," *Scholastic*, February 18, 1946; "Swinging Voice," *Time*, December 9, 1966, p. 21.

118. Feather, "Let Hot Jazz Melt Joe's Iron Curtain."

119. Feather, "Music Is Combatting Communism," pp. 1 and 19.

120. "Special Report," *Wichita* (Kansas) *Eagle*, December 2, 1955.

121. Dizard, *Strategy of Truth*, p. 76.

122. Sorensen. *The Word War*, p. 230.

123. "Special Report," *Wichita* (Kansas) *Eagle*, December 2, 1955.

124. "Jazz around the World," *Time*, June 25, 1956, p. 47.

125. "Big Jazz behind the Iron Curtain," *Look*, November 20, 1962; Rogers Warren, "America's Voice Swings a Little," *Look*, November 15, 1966, pp. 46–49.

126. Acinapura, "The Cultural Presentations Program of the United States," p. 73.

127. *Saturday Review*, July 14, 1956, pp. 28–31; "Benny Goodman Sways Thailand," *New York Times*, December 23, 1958, p. 8; Hal Davis, "Benny and the King of Siam," *Saturday Review*, January 12, 1957, pp. 64–65; Willie Ruff, "Jazz Mission to Moscow," *Down Beat*, January 14, 1960, pp. 16–20.

128. *Saturday Review*, July 14, 1956, p. 30.

129. Ibid., p. 29.

130. "Jazz around the World," *Time*, June 25, 1956, p. 47.

131. Allen Hughes, "The Voice of America," *Musical America*, April 1960, pp. 16–21.

132. "Voice of America Broadcasts Southern Myths on Racial Issue," *Afro-American*, July 15, 1950, p. 14.

133. "Jazz around the World," *Time*, June 25, 1956, p. 47.

134. Browne, "The History and Programming Policies of RIAS," pp. 323–25.

135. WNRC 260/891/25, Headquarters USFA, Survey Section, Das Programm des Senders Rot-Weiss-Rot, Bericht no. 38, Vienna, April 20, 1948; WNRC 260/891/34.

136. "Kritik am Sender Rot-Weiss-Rot. Ergebnisse einer Publikumsumfrage," *Berichte und Informationen* 1 (November 8, 1946): 15–16.

137. Joachim-Ernst Berendt, "Ursprung und Horizont des Jazz," *Der Turm* 2 (1946): 287–88.

138. "Amerika hat noch nicht sein Bestes gegeben," *Berichte und Informationen* 2 (February 14, 1947): 11–12.

139. *Salzburger Nachrichten*, July 31, 1945; *Wiener Kurier*, January 20, 1949, p. 4.

140. WNRC 260/58/46, Memorandum: Fox to Buttler, May 6, 1949; WNRC 260/93/77.

141. Information Services Branch, *Jazz erobert die Welt*; WNRC 260/50/49.

142. Straube, "Jazz und Schule," p. 184.

143. Fehring and Heidrich, *Der neue Jazzstil*; see also the individual issues of *jazzforschung/jazzresearch* since 1969.

144. Frith, *Jugendkultur und Rockmusik*, p. 11.

145. Reichardt, "Die Schallplatte," pp. 44–56 and 108–28; Kraushaar, *Rote Lippen*; Haupt, "Stil- und sprachkundliche Untersuchungen"; Schmidt-Joos, *Geschäfte mit Schlagern*; Scholz-Wanckel, *Pop-Import*; Dietrich Kayser, *Schlager—das Lied als Ware* (Stuttgart, 1975); Ratzenböck, "Expeditionen in eine exotische Heimat," pp. 264–73.

146. Reichardt, "Die Schallplatte," pp. 108–28.

147. Michael Watts, "The Call and Response of Popular Music: The Impact of American Pop Music in Europe," in *Superculture*, edited by C. W. E. Bigsby (Bowling Green, Ohio, 1975), pp. 123–32.

148. Kraushaar, *Rote Lippen*, p. 34.

149. Ibid., pp. 26–27; Stölting, *Deutsche Schlager*; Ortner, "Untersuchungen zum Vokabular."

150. Helt, "A German Bluegrass Festival," pp. 821–32.

151. "Yeh-Heh-Heh-Hes, Baby," *Time*, June 18, 1956, p. 37.

152. *Neues Österreich*, August 10, 1955, p. 3.

153. DPA announcement, April 22, 1957; Geoffrey Gorer, "Gedanken über den Rock 'n' Roll," *Der Monat*, May 1957, pp. 88–92.

154. Melly, *Revolt into Style*, p. 63.

155. Pattison, *The Triumph of Vulgarity*, p. vii.

156. Zimmer, *Popmusik*, p. 156; Braacke, *Beat*; Trevor Fisher, *We're Only in It for the Money* (Birmingham, 1972); Salzinger, *Swinging*; Siegfried Schmidt-Joos and Barry Graves, *Rock-Lexikon*, 2nd ed. (Reinbek bei Hamburg, 1990); Chapple and Garofalo, *Rock 'n' Roll Is Here to Pay*; Marcus, *Mystery Train*.

157. Melly, *Revolt into Style*, p. 120.

158. Frith, *Jugendkultur und Rockmusik*, pp. 50, 82, 302.

159. Newton [Hobsbawm], *The Jazz Scene*, p. 22.

160. Günther Mayer, "Popular Music in Cultural Exchange," *Journal of Popular Culture* 18 (Winter 1984): 145–58.

161. Pattison, *The Triumph of Vulgarity*, p. 12.

162. Newton [Hobsbawm], *The Jazz Scene*, p. 43.

163. Pattison, *The Triumph of Vulgarity*, p. 12.

164. Battle, "The Role of Music in Cultural Exchange," pp. 915–17.

165. Pleasants, *Serious Music*, p. 111.


CHAPTER EIGHT

1. Oertel, *Macht und Magie*.

2. Sklar, *Movie-Made America*, pp. 33–157; Seldes, *The Movies Come from America*; Lewis Jacobs, *The Rise of American Film* (New York, 1939); Thompson, *Exporting Entertainment*.

3. Sklar, *Movie-Made America*, p. 276; William Lynch, *The Image Industries* (New York, 1959); Chauvet, Fayard, and Mazars, *Le cinéma à travers le monde*; Monaco, "Movies and National Consciousness," pp. 62–75.

4. Guback, "American Interests," pp. 7–21; Swann, *The Hollywood Feature Film*.

5. Walker, *Hollywood, England*.

6. Schmid, *Die Figuren des Kaleidoskops*, p. 13; Stanley, *The Celluloid Empire*.

7. Sypher, *Rococo to Cubism in Art and Literature*, p. 266; Robert Friedel, *Pioneer Plastic: The Making and Selling of Celluloid* (Madison, Wis., 1983).

8. Garth Jowett and James M. Linton, *Movies as Mass Communication* (Beverly Hills, Calif., 1980), p. 15.

9. Bart Testa, "Sorting Out the Muddle of Modern Cinema," *Globe and Mail*, September 27, 1983, p. 15.

10. See Sklar, *Movie-Made America*, p. 197.

11. Reader, *Cultures on Celluloid*, pp. 86–92; Ralph C. Croizier, "Beyond East and West: The American Western and the Rise of the Chinese Swordplay Movie," *Journal of Popular Film* 1 (1972): 229–43.

12. Thomas Elsaesser, "Screen Violence," in *Approaches to Popular Culture*, edited by C. W. E. Bigsby (Bowling Green, Ohio, 1976), p. 172.

13. Stephen Neale, *Genre* (London, 1980), p. 19; Schmid, *Die Figuren des Kaleidoskops*, pp. 13 and 70; Thomas Schatz, *Hollywood Genres* (Philadelphia, 1981); Kaminsky, *American Film Genres*; Barry K. Grant, ed., *Film Genre: Theory and Criticism* (Metuchen, N.J., 1977); Richard Slotkin, "Prologue to a Study of Myth and Genre in American Movies," *Prospects* 9 (1984): 407–32.

14. Sorlin, *The Film in History*; Grenville, *Film as History*; Lebel, *Cinéma et idéologie*; Dowdy, *Films of the Fifties*; Smith, *The Historian and the Film*; O'Connor and Jackson, *American History/American Film*; Philip Davies and Brian Neve, eds., *Cinema, Politics, and Society in America* (Manchester, 1981); Gerald Mast, ed., *The Movies in Our Midst* (Chicago, 1982); Lary May, *Screening Out the Past* (Chicago, 1983); Wolfgang Ernst, "DIStory: Cinema and Historical Discourse," *Journal of Contemporary History* 18 (July 1983): 397–410; Biskind, *Seeing Is Believ-*

ing; Michael R. Pitts, *Hollywood and American History* (Jefferson, N.C., 1984); Ray, *A Certain Tendency of the Hollywood Cinema*; Gabriele Jutz, "Der Historizitäts-(Kon)Text im Film," in *Die Zeichen der Historie*, edited by Georg Schmid (Vienna, 1986), pp. 257–77; Bernd Hey, "Geschichte und Film: Grundsätzliches und ein Beispiel: Der Western," *Geschichte in Wissenschaft und Unterricht* 39 (1988): 17–33.

15. Steinberg, *Reel Facts*.

16. Elsaesser, *Screen Violence*, p. 172.

17. Marwick, "Der Film ist Realität," pp. 297–310.

18. Ferro, *Cinéma et histoire*; Ferro, "Film as an Agent," pp. 357–64; Metz, *Sprache und Film*; Andrew Tudor, *Theories of Film* (London, 1974); Jurij Lotman, *Semiotics of Cinema* (Ann Arbor, Mich., 1976); Monaco, *How to Read a Film*; Peter Roffman and Jim Purdy, *The Hollywood Social Problem Film: Madness, Despair, and Politics from the Depression to the Fifties* (Bloomington, Ind., 1981).

19. Sklar, *Movie-Made America*.

20. Martin Esslin, "The Television Series as Folk Epic," in *Superculture*, edited by C. W. E. Bigsby (Bowling Green, Ohio, 1975), p. 194; Siegfried Kracauer, *Von Caligari bis Hitler* (Hamburg, 1958); Jochen Beyse, *Film und Widerspiegelung: Interpretation und Kritik der Theorie Siegfried Kracauers* (Cologne, 1977).

21. Reader, *Cultures on Celluloid*, p. 11.

22. As quoted in Pütz, "Business or Propaganda?," pp. 394–415.

23. Mayer, "American Motion Pictures in World Trade," pp. 31–36.

24. Ibid., p. 34.

25. U.S. Congress, House, Committee on Un-American Activities, *Hearings*; Gordon Kalm, *Hollywood on Trial* (New York, 1948); Robert Griffith and Athan Theoharis, eds., *The Specter* (New York, 1974); Caute, *The Great Fear*; Ceplair and Englund, *Inquisition in Hollywood*.

26. Arnold Cortesi and "Observer," "Two Vital Case Histories," in *Public Opinion and Foreign Policy*, edited by Lester Markel (New York, 1949), p. 203.

27. Ibid., p. 202.

28. NA 511.635/2-2351, Telegram: Moffly to Department of State, Vienna, February 23, 1951.

29. Dizard, *Strategy of Truth*, p. 88.

30. Koopes and Black, "What to Show the World," pp. 87–105.

31. Richard Maltby, "Made for Each Other: The Melodrama of Hollywood and the HCUAA, 1947," in *Cinema, Politics, and Society*, edited by Philip Davies and Brian Neve (Manchester, 1981), pp. 82–84; Puig, *Etude de films américains*.

32. U.S. Congress, Senate, Committee on Foreign Relations, *Overseas Information Programs*, part 2, p. 272.

33. Lowry, "Trade Follows the Film," p. 12.

34. Oertel, *Macht und Magie*, p. 173; Sklar, *Movie-Made America*, p. 106. All of the statistics quoted here have been verified. However, because film statistics from individual countries are compiled differently, we are dealing only with relatively exact estimated values in these percent figures. The margin of error resides less in the area of exports and imports than in the number of showing days and, perhaps even more important, the number of tickets sold.

35. Sklar, *Movie-Made America*, p. 219; North, "Our Foreign Trade in Motion Pictures," pp. 100–108; U.S. Department of Commerce, *Review of Foreign Film Markets*; Harley, *World-Wide Influence of the Cinema*.

36. *Political and Economic Planning: The British Film Industry* (London, 1952), p. 41.

37. As quoted in Thompson, *Exporting Entertainment*, p. 104.

38. Sklar, *Movie-Made America*, p. 131.

39. Rosenberg, *Spreading the American Dream*, p. 100.

40. Oertel, *Macht und Magie*, p. 173; Sklar, *Movie-Made America*, p. 47; North, "Our Foreign Trade in Motion Pictures," p. 100.

41. Sklar, *Movie-Made America*, pp. 47 and 107; Rosenberg, *Spreading the American Dream*, pp. 100–102; Thompson, *Exporting Entertainment*, pp. 130–31; Shi, "Transatlantic Visions," pp. 583–96.

42. Strauss, "The Rise of Anti-Americanism in France," pp. 821–32.

43. Rosenberg, *Spreading the American Dream*, p. 102.

44. Oertel, *Macht und Magie*, p. 173.

45. Thompson, *Exporting Entertainment*, pp. 153–70.

46. Ibid.

47. Sklar, *Movie-Made America*, p. 156.

48. Beijerinck, "Die Entwicklung der Tonfilmindustrie."

49. Curt Belling, *Der Film in Staat und Partei* (Berlin, 1936); David Stewart Hull, *Film in the Third Reich* (Berkeley, Calif., 1969); Pierre Cadars and Francis Courtade, *Le cinéma Nazi* (Paris, 1972); Erwin Leiser, *Nazi Cinema* (New York, 1975); Julian Petley, *Capital and Culture: German Cinema, 1933–1945* (Colchester, 1979); David Welch, *Propaganda and the German Cinema, 1933–1945* (Oxford, 1983).

50. Sklar, *Movie-Made America*, p. 217; Thompson, *Exporting Entertainment*, pp. 153–70.

51. Sklar, *Movie-Made America*, p. 216.

52. Thompson, *Exporting Entertainment*, pp. 167–68.

53. Ninkovich, *Diplomacy of Ideas*, pp. 43–50, 63–73, and 118; Rosenberg, *Spreading the American Dream*, pp. 62–63; Woll, "Hollywood's Good Neighbor Policy," pp. 278–93.

54. Edwards, "Films in the U.S. Overseas Information Program"; see also Cohen, "Film Is a Weapon," pp. 43, 72, 74; Ralph R. Donald, "Hollywood and World War II: Enlisting Feature Films as Propaganda" (Ph.D. diss., University of Massachusetts, 1987).

55. McClure, "Hollywood at War," pp. 123–35.

56. "The Motion Picture Industry in the War during 1944–45," *International Motion Picture Almanac*, 1945–46, pp. 483–92; Lingeman, *Don't You Know There's a War On?*, p. 173.

57. "The Motion Picture Industry in the War during 1944–45"; "Hollywood in Uniform," *Fortune* 25 (April 1942): 92–95.

58. Walter Wanger, "OWI and Motion Pictures," *Public Opinion Quarterly*, Spring 1943, pp. 407–14; Rosten, "Movies and Propaganda," pp. 116–24; Larsen, "The Domestic Motion Picture," pp. 434–43; Mackay, "Domestic Operations of the Office of War Information"; Claudia Schreiner-Seip, *Film und Informationspolitik als Mittel der Nationalen Verteidigung in den USA, 1939–1941* (Frankfurt am Main, 1985).

59. Ceplair and Englund, *Inquisition in Hollywood*, p. 248.

60. *Film Daily*, May 7, 1945; Macmahon, *Memorandum on the Postwar International Information Program of the United States*.

61. Ceplair and Englund, *Inquisition in Hollywood*, p. 247.

62. *Variety*, September 9, 1945, pp. 1 and 5.

63. Koopes and Black, "What to Show the World," pp. 100–104; Gordon, "Operation Celluloid," pp. 416–19.

64. *Film Daily*, May 10, 1945, pp. 1 and 8.

65. Culbert, "American Film Policy," pp. 173–202.

66. *Film Daily*, May 14, 1945, pp. 1 and 3; Tunstall, *The Media Are American*, p. 70.

67. NA 865.4061 MP / 11-2748, Telegram: Dunn to Department of State, Rome, November 27, 1948; NA 865.4061 MP / 1-1945, Telegram: Kirk to Department of State, Rome, January 19, 1945; NA 865.4061 MP / 3-2145, Minutes of an Informational Meeting held in Mr. Brown's office, March 10, 1945; NA 865.4061 MP / 2-745, Ministero degli Affari Esteri, February 3, 1945.

68. NA 851.4061 MP / 2-1045, Memorandum: Labouisse to Department of State, Paris, February 10, 1945, Subject: Treatment of American Motion Pictures in France.

69. NA 851.4061 MP / 6-1846, Telegram: Caffery to Department of State, Paris, June 18, 1946; Annie Lacroix-Riz, "Négation et signature des accords Blum-Byrnes (october 1945–mai 1946) d'après les archives du ministère des affairs étranères," *Revue d'histoire moderne et contemporaine* 31 (1984): 417–47; Hubert-Lacombe, "L'accueil des Films américains en France," pp. 301–13; Portes, "Le origines de la légende noire des accords Blum-Byrnes," pp. 314–29.

70. NA 862.4061 MP / 6-1346, Canty to Milliken, Washington, June 13, 1946; NA 841.4061 MP / 3-2847, Mayer to Wilcox, New York, March 28, 1947; NA 841.4061 MP / 12-2347, Bliss to Secretary of State, December 23, 1947; Swann, *The Hollywood Feature Film*, pp. 81–115; "Mr. Rank and Dollars," *Financial Times*, July 26, 1947.

71. Cmd. 8113 (London, 1950).

72. NA 862.4961 MP / 11-1145, Letter: McCloy to Hopkins, January 8, 1944.

73. NA 862.4061 MP / 1-446, Telegram: Byrnes to U.S. Embassy, Paris, February 13, 1946; NA 862.4061 MP / 10-2447, Telegram: Mayer to Byrnes, Baden-Baden, November 21, 1946, French Plans to Exploit German Motion Picture Market.

74. NA 862.4061 MP / 11-3046, Memorandum: Anderson to Begg, Washington, February 7, 1947; ibid., J. Kenneth Galbraith to Bernstein, March 27, 1946.

75. Norman, *Our German Policy*, p. 63.

76. Guback, *The International Film Industry*, pp. 132 and 124–41; Pütz, *Business or Propaganda?*, pp. 405–7; NA 862.406 MP / 12-2049, Guarantees for Motion Picture Projects, Policy Regarding Dollar Amount for Each Guarantee.

77. Guback, *The International Film Industry*, pp. 133–34.

78. Norman, *Our German Policy*, p. 134.

79. Pilgert, *Press, Radio, and Film in West Germany*; Joesten, "The German Film Industry"; Klaus Kreimeier, *Kino und Filmindustrie in der BRD* (Kronberg, 1973); Alfred Bauer, *Deutscher Spielfilm-Almanach 1929–1950* (Munich, 1976); Hoenisch, Kämpfe, and Pütz, *Amerikanische Kulturpolitik*.

80. Guback, *The International Film Industry*, p. 134.

81. Ibid., pp. 132 and 133.

82. NA 862.4061 MP / 10-2049, Memorandum: Herz to Kellerman. First Meeting of the Advisory Committee on Motion Picture Guarantees, Washington, D.C., October 18, 1948.

83. Paul J. Vanderwood, "An American Cold Warrior: Viva Zapata! (1952)," in *American History/American Film*, edited by John E. O'Connor and Martin A. Jackson (New York, 1979), pp. 183–201.

84. Dizard, *Strategy of Truth*, p. 93.

85. Ceplair and Englund, *Inquisition in Hollywood*, p. 249; Adler, "The Politics of Culture"; Sayre, *Running Time*; Lary May, "Movie Star Politics: The Screen Actor's Guild, Cultural Conversion, and the Hollywood Red Scare," in *Recasting America: Culture and Politics in the Age of Cold War*, edited by Lary May (Chicago, 1989), pp. 125–53.

86. Shain, "Cold War Films," pp. 365–72; idem, "Hollywood's Cold War," pp. 334–50.

87. Dowdy, *Films of the Fifties*, pp. 16–17.

88. Shain, "Hollywood's Cold War," pp. 341–42.

89. Dowdy, *Films of the Fifties*, p. 32.

90. Shain, "Hollywood's Cold War," pp. 341–42.

91. MacDonald, "The Cold War as Entertainment in Fifties Television," pp. 3–31; idem, *Television and the Red Menace*.

92. Leab, "How Red Was My Valley," p. 82.

93. Sayre, *Running Time*, p. 29.

94. Eugene W. Castle, *Billions, Blunders, and Baloney: The Fantastic Story of How Uncle Sam Is Squandering Your Money Overseas* (New York, 1955), p. 103.

95. Vanderwood, "An American Cold Warrior," p. 189.

96. Murphy, "Monster Movies," pp. 31–44; Wolf, "Dr. Strangelove," pp. 57–67; Stuart Samuels, "The Age of Conspiracy and Conformity: Invasion of the Body Snatchers (1956)," in *American History/American Film*, edited by John E. O'Connor and Martin A. Jackson (New York, 1979), pp. 203–27.

97. Sklar, "Empire to the West," p. 168.

98. Oertel, *Macht und Magie*, p. 172.

99. Hansen, "Hollywood and International Understanding," pp. 28–45; Film Centre/UNESCO, *The Film Industry in Six European Countries*; Mercillon, *Cinéma et monopoles*; Jones, "Hollywood's International Relations," pp. 362–74; Berton, *Hollywood's Canada*; Balio, *The American Film Industry*; Guback, "Film as International Business," pp. 90–101.

100. Hansen, "Hollywood and International Understanding," pp. 28–45.

101. Ibid., p. 42; see also the individual editions of the *International Motion Picture Almanac*; Anthony H. Dawnson, "Motion Picture Economics," *Quarterly of Film, Radio, and Television* 3 (1948): 217–40; U.S. Congress, Senate, Select Committee on Small Business, *Motion Picture Distribution Trade Practices*; Guback, "Theatrical Film," pp. 199–298.

102. "Cinema and the State." Report of the Committee on Culture and Education, Lisbon Symposium, June 14–16, 1978, Strasbourg, Council of Europe, 1979; see also Nicholas Garnham, *The Economics of the U.S. Motion Picture Industry* (Brussels, 1980).

103. Dizard, *Strategy of Truth*, p. 90; Swann, *Hollywood Feature Film*, p. 115; C. D. Jackson, "Assignment for the Press," in *Public Opinion and Foreign Policy*, edited by Lester Markel (New York, 1949), p. 188; "TV Boom in Europe Aids U.S. Producers," *New York Times*, December 28, 1987.

104. Fritz, *Kino in Österreich*, pp. 1–63.

105. Schmid, "Kinogeschichte der Zwischenkriegszeit," p. 713; idem, "Die 'Falschen' Fuffziger," pp. 7–23.

106. The statistics originate from the annual editions of the *Motion Picture Almanac*, *Motion Picture and Television Almanac*, *Film Daily Year Book*, and *Österreichischen Jahrbücher*; Thompson, *Exporting Entertainment*; Gesek, "Kleines Lexikon des österreichischen Films"; Institut für Publizistik und Kommunikationswissenschaft der Universität Salzburg, ed., *Massenmedien in Österreich—Medienbericht II. Berichtzeitraum 1976–1982* (Vienna, 1983).

107. Axel Corti, "Geleitwort," in *Kino in Österreich*, edited by Walter Fritz (Vienna, 1981), p. 7.

108. Fritz, *Geschichte des österreichischen Films*, p. 145; Fritz et al., *Österreichische Film- und Fernsehchronik 1945–1955*; Fritz, "Entwicklungsgeschichte des österreichischen Spielfilms"; Wagner and Stangl, "Die Filmwirtschaft in Österreich"; Agnes Bleier-Brody, ed., *Geschichte des Filmes in Österreich* (Vienna, 1966); Bernhard Frankfurter, "Die Wien-Film," in *Medienkultur in Österreich*, edited by Hans H. Fabris and Kurt Luger (Vienna, 1988), pp. 103–16; Gertraud Steiner, "Der österreichische Heimatfilm" (Ph.D. diss., University of Vienna, 1985); Schmid, "Zur Geschichte asymmetrischer Kulturbeziehungen," pp. 27–36.

109. Fritz, *Kino in Österreich*; Spaulding, *Quiet Invaders*, pp. 293–303.

110. Agnes Bleier-Brody, "Österreich in der ausländischen Filmliteratur," *Österreichische Zeitschrift für Soziologie* 4 (1979): 143.

111. Fritz, *Kino in Österreich*, pp. 96–135.

112. Thompson, *Exporting Entertainment*, p. 131; *Motion Picture Almanac*; *Film Daily Year Book*.

113. Renner, "Der Anschluss der österreichischen Filmindustrie seit 1934," p. 1.

114. Schnürer, "Der österreichische Film der dreissiger Jahre."

115. *International Motion Picture Almanac*, 1935–36, p. 1002; *International Motion Picture Almanac*, 1937–38, pp. 1115–17; *International Motion Picture Almanac*, 1938–39, pp. 1028–30.

116. *Film Daily Year Book*, 1938, p. 1167.

117. *Film Daily*, March 16, 1938, p. 1.

118. Ibid., p. 10.

119. NA 863.4061/6-2045, Memorandum: Hays Organization, Austria, Market for American Motion Pictures, January 29, 1945.

120. Ibid.

121. WNRC 260/894/5 and WNRC/894/Sharin Personal File.

122. WNRC 260/890/85, Report on Operations of ISB (Austria) for week ending July 7, 1945.

123. WNRC 260/64/12, Letter: Minifie to Clark, July 13, 1945.

124. WNRC 260/890/80, Memorandum: Eerden to McChrystal, September 19, 1945 (italics in original).

125. WNRC 260/65/93, Film Section, Report to State Department, October 24, 1945; ibid., Report on Recommendations of the Movie Committee, March 30, 1946.

126. Rathkolb, "Die 'Wien-Film'-Produktion," pp. 117–32.

127. WNRC 260/65/93, ISB Film Section, Report to State Department, October 24, 1945; *Wiener Zeitung*, October 10, 1945, p. 1.

128. WNRC 260/65/81/Film Division, Semi-Monthly Activities Report, November 15–30, 1945, November 30, 1945.

129. WNRC 260/65/93, Memorandum: McChrystal for Brann, Vienna, October 29, 1945.

130. WNRC 260/65/93, Eugen Sharin, Report to State Department, October 24, 1945.

131. WNRC 260/64/21, Memorandum: Sharin to Shinn, Vienna, November 7, 1945; ibid., Letter: Scheltow to Brann, Vienna, November 2, 1945.

132. Rathkolb, "Die 'Wien-Film'-Produktion," pp. 123–32.

133. WNRC 260/65/82, Memorandum: Wolf to Ladue, Vienna, October 24, 1946.

134. WNRC 260/65/94, Memorandum: Various Matters Discussed with Wolfgang Wolf, Representative of MPEA (Austria), Inc.

135. WNRC 260/888/19, Minutes of Meeting held in ISB Film Section Office, Vienna VII, Neubaugasse 1, August 18, 1947.

136. "Memorandum: Herz to Erhardt," in *Understanding Austria*, edited by R. Wagnleitner (Salzburg, 1984), p. 415.

137. WNRC 260/65/46, Films Division, Weekly Activities Report, August 26–September 1, 1945, Vienna, September 1, 1945.

138. WNRC 260/65/93, Films Division, Weekly Activities Report, September 23–30, 1945, Vienna, September 30, 1945.

139. WNRC 260/65/93, Films Division, Weekly Activities Report, September 16–22, 1945, Vienna, September 22, 1945.

140. WNRC 260/65/96, Films Division, Semi-Monthly Activities Report, February 15–28, 1946, Vienna, February 28, 1946.

141. WNRC 260/452/90, Profit figures of American and German films as based on available data on July 28, 1947.

142. See n. 121.

143. Rathkolb, "Die 'Wien-Film'-Produktion," p. 123.

144. See n. 138.

145. WNRC 260/64/Films, Letter: Sharin to B. Frank Smith and Hans Lefebre, OWI, Motion Pictures Bureau, Vienna, October 11, 1946; "Army Snafu's Own 1,000,000 Film Setup in Austria via Manager Switch," *Variety*, May 15, 1946.

146. WNRC 260/35/Film Committee, Financial Report on the Liquidation of ISB Film Section, Vienna, October 3, 1947.

147. Ibid.

148. NA 863.4061 MP/7-1846, Telegram: Department of State to Erhardt, Washington, D.C., August 9, 1946.

149. NA 863.4061 MP / 2-2747, Letter: Figl to Clark, Vienna, December 17, 1946.

150. Rathkolb, "Die 'Wien-Film'-Produktion," pp. 118–22.

151. NA 863.4061 MP / 2-2747, Annex A to Agreement, July 16, 1946 (Transferring German Assets in Austria to Federal Government of Austria as Trustee).

152. WNRC 260 / 64 / Films, Meeting of the ISB Film Section Committee, Vienna, July 26, 1946.

153. WNRC 260 / 35 / 10, Letter: Van Eerden to MPEA (Austria), Vienna, August 22, 1947.

154. WNRC 260 / 46 / 41, Survey Section, Report no. 45, Vienna, May 19, 1948, "Die Bevölkerung und der Film" / "The Citizens and the Film." This survey showed the following: 62 percent of the residents of Vienna, 91.5 percent of Linz, and 86 percent of Salzburg preferred the *Welt im Film* newsreel to all other weeklies; *Welt im Film 1945–1950*; Smither, "Welt im Film," pp. 151–71; Gesek, "Zur Geschichte der Wochenschau in Österreich."

155. WNRC 260 / 452 / ISB-Films 1949, Memorandum: Haeusserman to Deputy Chief of Branch, Vienna, May 25, 1949.

156. USIAL / HC, Institute of Communications Research, International Motion Picture Service, Survey 1950.

157. WNRC 260 / 42 / Newsreels.

158. WNRC 260 / 42 / 60, Letter: Ray E. Lee, Chief ISB, to Director USACA, Vienna, December 29, 1948.

159. For information concerning the Austria Wochenschau, see Petschar and Schmid, *Erinnerungen und Visionen*.

160. Hiller, "Amerikanische Medien," pp. 93 and 145.

161. NA 511.635 / 1-2451, HICOG Frankfurt to Department of State, Austrian Film Program: Report on Survey Trip made by IMP—P. C. Kirkbride, January 2–9, 1951, Frankfurt am Main, January 25, 1951; NA 511.635 / 1-2351, Telegram: HICOG Frankfurt to Department of State, Austrian Film Program, January 23, 1951.

162. NA 511.635 / 1-2451, HICOG Frankfurt to Department of State, Austrian Film Program.

163. NA 511.635 / 6-1553, Telegram: Spaulding to Department of State, Vienna, June 15, 1953; NA 511.635 / 12 / 2452, Telegram: Acheson to U.S. Embassy Vienna, Washington, D.C., December 24, 1952.

164. Statistisches Zentralamt: Theater, Film, Rundfunk, Fernsehen, Vienna, 1959 (Beiträge zur Statistik, 39).

165. WNRC 260 / 42 / 51, Memorandum: Prawy to Chief of Branch, Vienna, August 19, 1948.

166. WNRC 260 / 65 / 93, Films Division, Audience Reaction Report, Vienna, October 26, 1945; WNRC 260 / 46 / 41, Memorandum: Hauesserman to Chief of Branch, Vienna, March 3, 1948.

167. WNRC 260 / 42 / 52, Telegram: Headquarters Zone Command Austria to Commanding General USFA, Salzburg, January 12, 1948.

168. NA 820.02-ISB, Telegram: Acheson to Erhardt, Washington, D.C., June 18, 1946.

169. WNRC 260 / 35 / 2, WDSCA to Commanding General OMG Germany, Films: Germany and Austria, not dated.

170. WNRC 260 / 42 / 51, Letter: Brigadier General Robert A. McClure to Colonel Sidney Eberle, New York, August 13, 1948.

171. NA 862.4061 MP / 12-1649, Memorandum: The Roosevelt Story, December 16, 1949.

172. See Maltby, *Harmless Entertainment*; Luger, "Es ist alles irgendwie so vorbeigezogen," pp. 45–101.

173. USIAL / HC, Opinion Survey Conducted in 17 Countries in Europe, Latin America, the Far East, and Africa, The Impact of Hollywood Films Abroad, July 1961.

174. Morpurgo, "Hollywood: America's Voice," p. 60.

175. WNRC 260/452/90.

CHAPTER NINE

1. This chapter is a revised version of my article "Die Kinder von Schmal(t)z und Coca-Cola." The advertising texts and the stories are taken from *Neues Österreich, Wiener Kurier, Salzburger Nachrichten, Wiener Bildwoche, Berichte und Informationen,* and *Forum.* The statistical data come from the Bundespressedienst, ed., *Österreichische Jahrbücher;* Otruba, *Österreichs Wirtschaft im 20. Jahrhundert;* and März, *Österreichs Wirtschaft zwischen Ost und West.*

2. The financial costs of the AYA for the distribution and sale of Coca-Cola bottles are found in the monthly listings in WNRC 260/624/AYA-Vouchers.

3. Münster, *Geld in Nietenhosen;* Italiaander, *Teenagers;* Helmut Lamprecht, *Teenager und Manager* (Munich, 1965); Schmidt-Joos, *Geschäfte mit Schlagern.*

4. Otto F. Beer, "Rock and Roll ante portas," *Neues Österreich,* December 11, 1956, p. 5.

5. Richard Wolfram, "Die Tanzkrankheit des Mittelalters wieder ausgebrochen?," *Berichte und Informationen* 11 (October 26, 1956): 15.

6. Rosenmayr, Köckeis, and Kreutz, *Kulturelle Interessen;* Rieger, "Änderungen in den Lebensverhältnissen"; *Grosstadtjugend und Kino;* Kammer für Arbeiter und Angestellte, "Freizeitgestaltung der Arbeiter und Angestellten Wiens"; Heinz Bonfadelli, *Die Sozialisationsperspektive in Massenkommunikationsforschung* (Berlin, 1981); Preuss-Lausitz et al., *Kriegskinder, Krisenkinder, Konsumkinder;* Mitterauer, *Sozialgeschichte der Jugend.*

7. Bourdieu, *Die feinen Unterschiede;* Enzensberger, *Einzelheiten;* Haug, *Kritik der Warenästhetik;* Donald M. Lowe, *History of Bourgeois Perception* (Brighton, 1982).

8. *Neues Österreich,* November 11, 1956, p. 9.

9. Hobsbawm, *The Age of Capital.*

10. Guilbaut, *How New York Stole the Idea of Modern Art;* Matthews, "Art and Politics in Cold War America," pp. 762–87; Ninkovich, "The Currents of Cultural Diplomacy," pp. 215–37; Wagnleitner, "Propagating the American Dream," pp. 60–84; Stich, *Made in USA;* Doss, "The Art of Cultural Politics," pp. 195–220.

# Bibliography

ARCHIVAL SOURCES

The majority of the archive sources are located in the National Archives in Washington, D.C., and the Washington National Record Center, Suitland, Md. The extensive archives and library resources of the U.S. Information Agency Library Historical Collection in Washington, D.C., were also used.

The following boxes from Record Group 260 of the National Archives were used: Boxes 31–32, 35–46, 49–50, 57–76, 88–103, 105–7, 185, 195–96, 202–4, 221, 369–70, 384–85, 618–19, 624–26, 630–32, 636–37, 657–59, 855, 861–62, 885, 887–90, 892, 894–95, 899, 902, 916–17, and 66741-1-3.

The following boxes from Record Group 59 of the National Archives were used: Boxes 110–16, 321, 502, 532, 1199, 2985, 3713–17, 3719–20, 4480, 4653, 4655, 4692, 4696, 4699, 4702–3, 4705, 4777, 5369, 5817, 6126–27, 6519, 6548, 6629–30, 6691, 6816, 6847, and 7095.

PRIMARY SOURCES

*The America Houses: A Study of the U.S. Information Centers in Germany.* Prepared by the Management and Budget Division and the Office of Public Affairs. Office of the U.S. High Commissioner for Germany. September 1953.

*The Budget of the United States.* Bureau of the Budget, fiscal years 1949 through 1953. Washington, D.C., 1953.

*The Budget of the United States, 1952 and 1953, 1954 and 1955.* Washington, D.C., 1955.

Bundesministerium für Unterricht, ed. *Liste der gesperrten Autoren und Bücher. Massgeblich für Buchhandel und Büchereien.* Vienna, 1946.

"Cinema and the State." Report of the Committee on Culture and Education, Lisbon Symposium, June 14–16, 1978. Strasbourg, Council of Europe, 1979.

Commandement en Chef Français en Allemagne. Direction de l'education publique, ed. *L'oeuvre culturelle française en Allemagne.* Baden-Baden, 1947.

Committee on Educational Interchange Policy. *Twenty Years of United States Government Programs in Cultural Relations.* New York, 1959.

Common Council for American Unity, ed. *European Beliefs regarding the United States.* New York, 1949.

Department of State, ed. *Cross-Cultural Education: A Bibliography of Government-Sponsored and Private Research on Foreign Students and Trainees in the United States and Other Countries, 1946–1964.* Washington, D.C., 1965.

——. *The Cultural Cooperation Programs, 1938–1943.* Washington, D.C., 1944.

——. *Educational Exchanges under the Fulbright Act.* Washington, D.C., 1948.

——. *Program of the Department of State in Cultural Relations.* Washington, D.C., 1940.

——. *The World Audience for America's Story.* Publication 3485. Washington, D.C., 1949.

*The Fulbright Program in Austria.* Vienna, 1959.

Macmahon, Arthur W. *Memorandum on the Post-War International Information Program of the United States.* Washington, D.C., 1945.

*Report on the Operations of the Overseas Book and Library Program.* Issued by the International Information Administration. Department of State, July 15, 1953.

UNESCO, ed. *Index Translationum.* Paris, 1950.

——. *World Communications: Press, Radio, Film, Television.* New York, 1950, 1951, 1956.

U.S. Congress. House. Committee on Foreign Affairs. Report no. 2. *Winning the Cold War: The U.S. Ideological Offensive.* 88th Cong., 2nd sess., April 27, 1964. House Report 1352.

——. Committee on Un-American Activities. *Hearings regarding the Communist Infiltration of the Motion Picture Industry.* 80th Cong., 1st sess., October 1947.

——. U.S. Information and Educational Exchange Act of 1947. *Hearings before the Special Subcommittee on Foreign Affairs.* 80th Cong., 1st sess., May 13–20, 1947.

U.S. Congress. Senate. Committee on Foreign Relations. *Overseas Information Programs of the United States,* part 1. 82nd Cong., 1st sess., 1952.

——. Committee on Foreign Relations. *Overseas Information Programs of the United States,* part 2. 83rd Cong., 1st sess., 1953.

——. Select Committee on Small Business. *Motion Picture Distribution Trade Practices.* 84th Cong., 2nd sess., 1956.

U.S. Department of Commerce, ed. *Review of Foreign Film Markets.* Washington, D.C., 1937.

*Winning the Cold War: The U.S. Ideological Offensive.* Hearing before the Subcommittee on International Organizations and Movements of the House Committee of Foreign Affairs. Part 1. Washington, D.C., 1963.

*Zahlenmässige Darstellung des Schulwesens in Österreich. Schuljahr 1951/52.* Heft 1. "Sonderbeilage des Bundesministeriums für Unterricht." Stück 6. 1952.


## SECONDARY SOURCES

### BOOKS

Abshire, David. *International Broadcasting: A New Dimension of Western Diplomacy.* Beverly Hills, Calif., 1976.

Adams, Benjamin P., ed. *You Americans: Fifteen Foreign Press Correspondents Report Their Impressions of the United States and Its People.* New York, 1939.

Adams, Walter, ed. *The Brain Drain.* New York, 1968.

Adams, Willi Paul, and Knud Krakau, eds. *Deutschland und Amerika: Rezeption und historische Realität.* Berlin, 1985.

Adorno, Theodor W. *Dissonanzen. Musik in der verwalteten Welt.* 4th ed. Göttingen, 1969.

Agee, Philip. *Inside the Company: CIA Diary.* London, 1975.

Alexander, Charles C. *Here the Country Lies: Nationalism and the Arts in Twentieth-Century America.* Bloomington, Ind., 1980.

Allen, Donald Roy. *French Views of America in the 1930s.* New York, 1979.

Allen, H. C. *American History in Britain.* London, 1956.

——. *Great Britain and the United States: A History of Anglo-American Relations (1783–1952).* New York, 1955.

Allen, H. C., and Roger Thompson, eds. *Contrast and Connection: Bicentennial Essays in Anglo-American History.* London, 1976.

Anderson, Eugene N. *The Humanities in the German and Austrian Universities.* Washington, D.C., 1950.

Arciniegas, Germán. *America in Europe: A History of the New World in Reverse.* San Diego, Calif., 1986.

Armytage, Walter. *The American Influence on English Education.* London, 1967.

Arnold, Matthew. *Civilization in the United States.* London, 1888.

Austin, James C. *American Humor in France.* Ames, Iowa, 1978.

Axtell, James, William J. Baker, and Orm Överland. *America Perceived.* 4 vols. West Haven, Conn., 1974.

Ayman, Iraj. *An Evaluation of U.S.I.S.-Sponsored Programs in the United States of America for Iranian Participants.* Tehran, 1963.

Bach, Julian. *America's Germany.* New York, 1946.

Bachmann, Ingeborg. *Die Hörspiele.* Munich, 1985.

Baerns, Barbara. *Ost und West. Eine Zeitschrift zwischen den Fronten.* Münster, 1968.

Balio, Tino, ed. *The American Film Industry.* Madison, Wis., 1976.

Bamberger, Richard. *Jugendlektüre.* Bonn, 1955.

———. *Jugendschriftenkunde.* Vienna, 1975.

Barghoorn, Frederick C. *The Soviet Cultural Offensive: The Role of Cultural Diplomacy in Soviet Foreign Policy.* Princeton, N.J., 1964.

———. *Soviet Foreign Propaganda.* Princeton, N.J., 1964.

———. *The Soviet Image of the United States: A Study in Distortion.* Port Washington, N.Y., 1969.

Barker, Ronald E., and Robert Escarpit, eds. *The Book Hunger.* Paris, 1973.

Barnouw, Erik. *The Image Empire.* New York, 1970.

———. *The Magician and the Cinema.* New York, 1981.

Barrett, Edward. *Truth Is Our Weapon.* New York, 1953.

Barthes, Roland. *Elemente der Semiologie.* Frankfurt am Main, 1979.

Barzini, Luigi. *Americans Are Alone in the World.* New York, 1953.

Baschiera, Karl, Richard Hassfurthner, and Theodor Reitterer. *A British and American Reader.* Vienna, 1950.

Bastide, Roger. *Le proche et le lointain.* Paris, 1970.

Baudrillard, Jean. *America.* London, 1988.

Baurichter, Kurt, ed. *Amerika trocken? Deutsche Urteile über das Alkoholverbot.* Berlin, 1929.

Beissel, Rudolf. *Von Atala bis Winnetou. Die Väter des Western-Romans.* Bamberg, 1978.

Benét, Stephen Vincent. *America.* Vienna, 1947.

Benjamin, Walter. *Illuminationen.* Frankfurt am Main, 1977.

Benna, Anna. *Contemporary Austrian Views of American Independence: A Documentary on the Occasion of the Bicentennial.* Vienna, 1976.

Berg, Peter. *Deutschland und Amerika, 1918–1929. Über das deutsche Amerikabild der Zwanziger Jahre.* Lübeck, 1963.

Bernhard, Paul. *Jazz, eine musikalische Zeitfrage.* Munich, 1927.

Berton, Pierre. *Hollywood's Canada: The Americanization of Our National Image.* Toronto, 1975.

Bigsby, C. W. E., ed. *Approaches to Popular Culture.* Bowling Green, Ohio, 1976.

———. *Superculture: American Popular Culture and Europe.* Bowling Green, Ohio, 1975.

Billington, Ray Allen. *Land of Savagery, Land of Promise: The European Image of the American Frontier.* New York, 1981.

Biskind, Peter. *Seeing Is Believing: How Hollywood Taught Us to Stop Worrying and Love the Fifties.* New York, 1983.

Bitterli, Urs. *Alte Welt—neue Welt.* Munich, 1986.

———. *Die "Wilden" und die "Zivilisierten": Grundzüge einer Geistes- und Kulturgeschichte der europäisch-überseeischen Begegnung.* Munich, 1976.

Blaich, Fritz. *Amerikanische Firmen in Deutschland 1890–1918. US-Direktinvestitionen im deutschen Maschinenbau.* Wiesbaden, 1984.

Blanke, Gustav. *Yankeetum: Tendenzen der modernen amerikanischen Zivilisation nach amerikanischen Quellen.* Leipzig, 1943.

Bloom, Salomon F. *Europe and America: The Western World in Modern Times.* New York, 1961.

Blum, Robert, ed. *Cultural Affairs and Foreign Relations.* Englewood Cliffs, N.J., 1963.

Blume, Friedrich. *Das Rasseproblem in der Musik.* Berlin, 1939.

Blumenthal, Henry. *American and French Culture, 1800–1900: Interchanges in Art, Science, Literature, and Society.* Baton Rouge, La., 1977.

Boehmer, Konrad. *Zwischen Reihe und Pop. Musik und Klassengesellschaft.* Vienna, 1970.

Bogart, Leo. *Premises for Propaganda: The United States Information Agency's Operating Assumptions in the Cold War.* New York, 1976.

Borchers, Hans, and Klaus W. Vowe. *Die zarte Pflanze Demokratie. Amerikanische Re-education in Deutschland im Spiegel ausgewählter politischer und literarischer Zeitschriften (1945–1949).* Tübingen, 1979.

Bourdieu, Pierre. *Die feinen Unterschiede: Kritik der gesellschaftlichen Urteilskraft.* Frankfurt am Main, 1984.

Bourdieu, Pierre, et al. *Eine illegitime Kunst. Die sozialen Gebrauchsweisen der Photographie.* Frankfurt am Main, 1981.

Bozeman, Adda B. *Politics and Culture in International History.* Princeton, N.J., 1960.

Braacke, D. *Beat—die sprachlose Opposition.* Munich, 1968.

Bradbury, Malcolm. *All Dressed Up and Nowhere to Go.* London, 1983.

Braisted, Paul J., ed. *Cultural Affairs and Foreign Relations.* Washington, D.C., 1968.

Braudel, Fernand. *Sozialgeschichte des 15.–18. Jahrhunderts: Der Handel.* Munich, 1986.

Braunschvig, Marcel. *La vie américaine.* Paris, 1931.

Breffka, C. *Amerika in der deutschen Literatur.* Cologne, 1917.

Breitenkamp, Edward C. *The U.S. Information Control Division and Its Effect on German Publishers and Writers, 1945 to 1949.* Grand Forks, N.D., 1953.

British Broadcasting Corporation. *Monitoring Service: Summary of World Broadcasts.* Vol. 3, *Germany and Austria.* Reading, 1950.

Brogan, Denis W. *Der amerikanische Charakter.* Vienna, 1949.

Browne, Donald R. *International Radio Broadcasting.* New York, 1982.

——. *The Voice of America.* Minneapolis, 1976.

Brunner Emil. *Was hat Amerika uns, was haben wir Amerika zu geben?.* Zurich, 1945.

Bryson, L. *The Communication of Ideas.* New York, 1948.

Buchanan, William, and Hadley Cantril. *How Nations See Each Other.* Urbana, Ill., 1953.

Bullock, Mary Brown. *An American Transplant: The Rockefeller Foundation and Peking Union Medical College.* Berkeley, Calif., 1980.

Bungenstab, Karl-Ernst. *Umerziehung zur Demokratie? Re-education Politik im Bildungswesen der US-Zone 1945–1949.* Düsseldorf, 1970.

Burckhardt, Jacob. *Weltgeschichtliche Betrachtungen.* Edited by Werner Kaegi. Bern, 1947.

Burian, E. F. *Jazz.* Prague, 1928.

Carr, Ian. *Music Outside: Contemporary Jazz in Britain.* London, 1973.

Carstensen, Broderson. *Englische Einflüsse auf die deutsche Sprache nach 1945.* Beihefte zum Jahrbuch für Amerikastudien 13. Heidelberg, 1965.

Cartier, Raymond. *L'Europe à la conquête de l'Amérique.* Paris, 1956.

Caute, David. *The Great Fear: The Anti-Communist Purge under Truman and Eisenhower.* New York, 1979.

Cauter, T., and J. S. Downham. *The Communication of Ideas.* London, 1954.

Ceplair, Larry, and Steven Englund. *The Inquisition in Hollywood: Politics in the Film Community, 1930–1960.* Garden City, N.Y., 1980.

Chapple, Steeve, and Reebee Garofalo. *Rock 'n' Roll Is Here to Pay: The History and Politics of the Music Industry.* Chicago, 1977.

Chaunu, Huguette, and Pierre Chaunu. *Séville et l'Atlantique.* 8 vols. Paris, 1955–59.

Chauvet, Louis, Jean Fayard, and Pierre Mazars. *Le cinéma à travers le monde.* Paris, 1961.

Chester, E. W. *Europe Views America.* Washington, D.C., 1962.

Chesterton, Gilbert K. *What I Saw in America.* London, 1922.

Chmelar, Hans. *Höhepunkte der österreichischen Auswanderung. Die Auswanderung aus den im Reichsrat vertretenen Königreichen und Ländern in den Jahren 1905–1914.* Vienna, 1974.

Collier, James Lincoln. *The Making of Jazz.* New York, 1978.

Colyer, Ken. *New Orleans and Back.* Delph, 1967.

Colyer, W. T. *Americanism: A World Menace.* London, 1922.

*Comic Strips. Vom Geist der Superhelden. Colloquium zur Theorie der Bildergeschichte.* Schriftenreihe der Akademie der Künste. Vol. 8. Berlin, 1970.

Commager, Henry S., ed. *America in Perspective: The United States through Foreign Eyes.* New York, 1947.

Commager, Henry S., and Elmo Giordanetti. *Was America a Mistake?.* Columbia, S.C., 1967.

Coombs, Philip H. *The Fourth Dimension of Foreign Policy: Educational and Cultural Affairs.* New York, 1964.

Costigliola, Frank. *Awkward Dominion: American Political, Economic, and Cultural Relations with Europe, 1919–1933.* Ithaca, N.Y., 1984.

Crèvecoeur, Michel-Guillaume Jean de. *Letters from an American Farmer.* London, 1782.

Crosby, Alfred W. *The Columbian Exchange: Biological and Cultural Consequences of 1492.* Westport, Conn., 1972.

Crowell, Robert L., and Harland A. Carpenter. *Supplementary Reports on the Use of Books in the Department of State's Overseas Information Program.* Washington, D.C., 1952.

Curtin, Philip D. *Cross-Cultural Trade in World History.* New York, 1984.

Czerny, Peter, and Heinz P. Hofmann. *Der Schlager. Ein Panorama der leichten Musik.* Berlin, 1968.

Dallek, Robert. *The American Style of Foreign Policy: Cultural Politics and Foreign Affairs.* New York, 1983.

Deibel, Terry L., and Walter Roberts. *Culture and Information: Two Foreign Policy Functions.* Washington, D.C., 1976.

Denkler, H., ed. *Amerika in der deutschen Literatur.* Stuttgart, 1975.

Dickens, Charles. *American Notes.* London, 1842.

Dippel, Horst. *Americana Germanica 1770–1800: Bibliographie deutscher Amerikaliteratur.* Stuttgart, 1976.

——. *Germany and the American Revolution.* Wiesbaden, 1978.

Dizard, Wilson. *The Strategy of Truth.* Washington, D.C., 1965.

Dorfman, Ariel. *The Empire's Old Clothes: What the Lone Ranger, Babar, and Other Innocent Heroes Do to Our Minds.* New York, 1983.

Dorfman, Ariel, and Armand Mattelart. *How to Read Donald Duck: Imperialist Ideology in the Disney Comic.* New York, 1975.

Dowdy, Andrew. *The Films of the Fifties: The American State of Mind.* New York, 1973.

Downs, Roger M., and David Shea. *Kognitive Karten. Die Welt in unseren Köpfen.* New York, 1982.

Duden, Gottfried. *Bericht über eine Reise nach den westlichen Staaten Nordamerikas und einen mehrjährigen Aufenthalt am Missouri.* Elberfeld, 1829.

Dujmovits, Walter. *Die Amerikawanderung der Burgenländer.* Stegersbach, 1975.

Echeverria, Durand. *Mirage in the West: A History of the French Images of American Society to 1815.* Princeton, N.J., 1968.

Eco, Umberto. *Apokalyptiker und Integrierte. Zur kritischen Kritik der Massenkultur.* Frankfurt am Main, 1984.

——. *Über Gott und die Welt.* Munich, 1985.

——. *Zeichen. Einführung in einen Begriff und seine Geschichte.* Frankfurt am Main, 1977.

Eisermann, David. *Crèvecoeur; oder, Die Erfindung Amerikas. Ein literarischer Gründervater der Vereinigten Staaten.* Rheinbach-Merzbach, 1985.

Elder, Robert E. *The Information Machine: The United States Information Agency and American Foreign Policy.* Syracuse, N.Y., 1968.

Elliott, Andrew George. *Hell! I'm British: A Plain Man Looks at America, Americans, and Englishmen.* London, 1939.

Elliott, J. H. *The Old World and the New, 1492–1650.* Cambridge, 1970.

Ellwood, David. *Europe and America in Cultural Diplomacy.* London, 1973.

Engelbrecht, Helmut. *Lehrervereine im Kampf um Status und Einfluss. Zur Geschichte der Standesorganisation der Sekundarschullehrer in Österreich.* Vienna, 1978.

Enzensberger, Hans Magnus. *Einzelheiten.* Vol. 1, *Bewusstseins-Industrie.* Frankfurt am Main, 1962.

Ergert, Viktor. *Fünfzig Jahre Rundfunk in Österreich.* Vol. 2, *1945–1955.* Salzburg, 1975.

Espinosa, J. Manuel. *Inter-American Beginnings of United States Cultural Diplomacy.* Washington, D.C., 1977.

Eudes, Yves. *La conquête des esprits. L'appareil d'exportation culturelle américaine.* Paris, 1982.

Evans, John Martin. *America: The View from Europe.* New York, 1976.

Ewen, Stuart. *Captains of Consciousness.* New York, 1976.

Ewen, Stuart, and Elizabeth Ewen. *Channels of Desire.* New York, 1982.

Fabian, Bernhard. *Alexis de Tocquevilles Amerikabild.* Heidelberg, 1957.

Fabris, Hans H., and Kurt Luger, eds. *Medienkultur in Österreich.* Vienna, 1988.

Faenza, F. *Gli Americani in Italia.* Milan, 1976.

Fehring, Johannes, and Walter Heidrich. *Der neue Jazzstil: Moderne Phrasierung und deren richtiges Spiel.* Vienna, 1948.

Fellner, Fritz, ed. *Dichter und Gelehrter: Hermann Bahr und Josef Redlich in ihren Briefen 1896–1934.* Salzburg, 1980.

Ferro, Marc. *Analyse de film, analyse des sociétés. Une source nouvelle pour l'histoire.* Paris, 1975.
———. *Cinéma et histoire.* Paris, 1977.

The Film Centre / UNESCO, ed. *The Film Industry in Six European Countries.* Paris, 1950.

Fisch, Jörg. *Die europäische Expansion und das Völkerrecht.* Stuttgart, 1984.

Fischer, Ernst. *Die österreichische Kulturkrise.* Vienna, 1951.

Fischer, Heinz-Dietrich. *Reeducation und Pressepolitik unter britischem Besatzungsstatus. Die Zonenzeitung "Die Welt" 1946–1950. Konzeption, Artikulation und Rezeption.* Düsseldorf, 1978.

Fischer, Manfred S. *Nationale Images als Gegenstand vergleichender Literaturgeschichte: Untersuchungen zur Entstehung der komparatistischen Imagologie.* Bonn, 1981.

Fraenkel, Ernst, ed. *Amerika im Spiegel des deutschen politischen Denkens.* Cologne, 1959.

Frankel, Charles. *The Neglected Aspect of Foreign Affairs: American Educational and Cultural Policy Abroad.* Washington, D.C., 1966.

Frei, Norbert. *Amerikanische Lizenzpolitik und deutsche Pressetradition: Die Geschichte der Nachkriegszeitung Südost-Kurier.* Munich, 1986.

Frenz, Horst, and Hans-Joachim Lang, eds. *Nordamerikanische Literatur im deutschen Sprachraum seit 1945. Beiträge zu ihrer Rezeption.* Munich, 1973.

Freund, Gisèle. *Photographie und Gesellschaft.* Reinbek bei Hamburg, 1979.

Frith, Simon. *Jugendkultur und Rockmusik. Soziologie der englischen Musikszene.* Reinbek bei Hamburg, 1981.

Fritz, Walter. *Geschichte des österreichischen Films.* Vienna, 1969.
———, ed. *Kino in Österreich 1896–1930.* Vienna, 1981.

Fritz, Walter, et al. *Österreichische Film- und Fernsehchronik 1945–1955.* Filmkunst no. 44. Vienna, 1965.

Galantiére, Lewis, ed. *America in the Mind of Europe.* London, 1951.

Galinsky, Hans. *Amerikanisch-deutsche Sprach- und Literaturbeziehungen.* Frankfurt, 1972.

Garcilaso de la Vega, el Inca. *Royal Commentaries of the Incas*. 2 vols. Austin, Tex., 1966.

Gassman, Friedrich. *The Literary Evolution of the "Wild West" in Germany*. Los Angeles, 1966.

Gatzke, Hans W. *Germany and the United States: A Special Relationship?*. Cambridge, Mass., 1980.

Gauss, Karl-Markus, ed. *Ernst Fischer. Kultur, Literatur, Politik*. Frankfurt am Main, 1984.

Gehring, Hansjörg. *Amerikanische Literaturpolitik in Deutschland 1945–1953. Ein Aspekt des Re-Educationsprogramms*. Stuttgart, 1976.

Geiss, Imanuel. *Geschichte des Rassismus*. Frankfurt am Main, 1988.

Gewecke, Frauke. *Wie die neue Welt in die alte kam*. Stuttgart, 1986.

Ghega, Carl. *Über die Baltimore-Ohio-Eisenbahn in Nordamerika und die nordamerikanische Lokomotive*. Vienna, 1844.

Giese, Fritz. *Girlkultur: Vergleiche zwischen amerikanischem und europäischem Rhythmus und Lebensgefühl*. Munich, 1925.

Gillett, Charlie. *The Sound of the City*. London, 1971.

Gilmore, Richard. *France's Postwar Cultural Policies and Activities in Germany, 1945–1956*. Washington, D.C., 1973.

Gitler, Ira. *Jazz Masters of the '40s*. New York, 1984.

Goddard, Chris. *Jazz away from Home*. New York, 1979.

Godholt, Jim. *A History of Jazz in Britain, 1919–1950*. London, 1984.

Gorer, Geoffrey E. *Hot Strip Tease and Other Notes on American Culture*. London, 1937.

Götsch, Paul, ed. *Das amerikanische Drama*. Düsseldorf, 1974.

Gramsci, Antonio. *Philosophie der Praxis*. Frankfurt am Main, 1967.

Greene, Graham. *The Quiet American*. Harmondsworth, 1980.

Grenville, John A. S. *Film as History: The Nature of Film Evidence*. Birmingham, 1970.

Greuner, Reinhart. *Auftrag und Ende: Der Einfluss der anglo-amerikanischen Besatzungspolitik auf die Wiedererrichtung eines imperialistischen Pressewesens in Westdeutschland*. Berlin (GDR), 1962.

Grossberg, Mimi. *Österreichische literarische Emigration in den Vereinigten Staaten 1938*. Vienna, 1970.

*Grosstadtjugend und Kino. Eine Untersuchung der Arbeitsgemeinschaft Jugend und Film*. Vienna, 1959.

Grünwald, Oskar, and Ferdinand Lacina. *Auslandskapital in der österreichischen Wirtschaft*. Vienna, 1970.

Guback, Thomas H. *The International Film Industry: Western Europe and American Film since 1945*. Bloomington, Ind., 1969.

Guggisberg, Hans Rudolf. *Alte und neue Welt in historischer Perspektive*. Bern, 1973.

Guilbaut, Serge. *How New York Stole the Idea of Modern Art: Abstract Expressionism, Freedom, and the Cold War*. Chicago, 1983.

Haeusserman, Ernst. *Mein Freund Henry*. Vienna, 1983.

Halfeld, Adolf. *Amerika und der Amerikanismus*. Jena, 1928.

Hamm, Charles. *Music in the New World*. New York, 1982.

Hanke, Lewis. *Aristotle and the American Indians*. London, 1959.

Hansen, Allen C. *USIA: Public Diplomacy in the Computer Age*. New York, 1984.

Hansen, Karl Heinz. *Radio Free Europe*. Munich, 1972.

Hark, W. *America: Ideal and Reality. The United States of 1776 in Contemporary European Philosophy*. London, 1947.

Harley, J. E. *World-Wide Influence of the Cinema*. Los Angeles, 1940.

Haug, Wolfgang Fritz. *Kritik der Warenästhetik*. Frankfurt am Main, 1971.

Heald, Morrell, and Lawrence S. Kaplan. *Culture and Diplomacy: The American Experience*. Westport, Conn., 1977.

Hedin, Sven. *Amerika im Kampf der Kontinente*. Leipzig, 1942.

Heinemann, Manfred, ed. *Umerziehung und Wiederaufbau. Die Bildungspolitik der Besatzungsmächte in Deutschland und Österreich*. Stuttgart, 1981.

Henningsen, Manfred. *Der Fall Amerika. Zur Sozial- und Bewusstseinsgeschichte einer Verdrängung. Das Amerika der Europäer*. Munich, 1974.

Herm, Gerhard. *Amerika erobert Europa*. Düsseldorf, 1964.

Herskovits, M. J. *Les bases de l'anthropologie culturelle*. Paris, 1967.

Higham, Charles, and Joel Greenberg. *Hollywood in the Forties*. New York, 1970.

Hill, Patricia R. *The World Their Household: The American Women's Foreign Mission Movement and Cultural Transformation, 1870–1920*. Ann Arbor, Mich., 1984.

Hirsch, Fred, and Richard Fletcher. *The CIA and the Labour Movement*. Nottingham, 1977.

Hitchcock, H. Wiley, ed. *New Grove Dictionary of American Music*. 4 vols. New York, 1986.

Hobsbawm, E. J. *The Age of Capital, 1848–1875*. London, 1975.

Hoenisch, Michael, Klaus Kämpfe, and Karl Heinz Pütz. *Amerikanische Kulturpolitik in Deutschland, 1945–1949: Bibliographie, Materialien, Dokumente*. Berlin, 1981.

Hoffman, Raoul. *Zwischen Galaxis und Underground*. Munich, 1971.

Hollander, A. N. J., ed. *Contagious Conflict: The Impact of American Dissent on European Life*. Leiden, 1973.

Holt, Robert T. *Radio Free Europe*. Minneapolis, 1958.

Holthusen, Hans Egon. *Amerikaner und Deutsche: Dialog zweier Kulturen*. Munich, 1977.

Honour, Hugh. *The European Vision of America*. Kent, Ohio, 1976.

———. *The New Golden Land: European Images of America from the Discoveries to the Present Time*. New York, 1976.

Horton, Forest Woody, Jr., ed. *Understanding U.S. Information Policy*. 4 vols. Washington, D.C., 1982.

Hülsemann, Johann Georg. *Geschichte der Demokratie in den Vereinigten Staaten von Amerika*. Göttingen, 1823.

Humboldt, Alexander von. *Kosmos*. 5 vols. Berlin, 1845–62.

Huntley, James Robert, ed. *Teaching about the American Impact on Europe*. London, 1970.

Hurwitz, Harald. *Die Stunde Null in der deutschen Presse. Die amerikanische Pressepolitik in Deutschland 1945–1949*. Cologne, 1972.

———, ed. *Die Pressepolitik der Alliierten*. Frankfurt am Main, 1956.

Information Services Branch, ed. *Jazz erobert die Welt*. Vienna, 1948.

Isaac, Julius. *The Effect of European Migration on the Economy of Sending and Receiving Countries*. The Hague, 1953.

Italiaander, Rolf, ed. *Teenagers*. Hamburg, 1958.

*Ein Jahr Wiener Theater 1945–1946. Almanach über die erste Spielzeit der Wiener Bühnen nach der Befreiung Österreichs*. Vienna, 1946.

Jamieson, John. *Books for the Army: The Army Library Service in the Second World War*. New York, 1950.

Joesten, Joachim. *C.I.A.: Wie der amerikanische Geheimdienst arbeitet*. Munich, 1957.

Johnson, Walter, and Francis J. Colligan. *The Fulbright Program: A History*. Chicago, 1965.

Jonas, Manfred. *The United States and Germany*. Ithaca, N.Y., 1984.

Jones, George Frederick. *The Salzburger Saga: Religious Exiles and Other Germans along the Savannah*. Athens, Ga., 1984.

Jones, Howard Mumford. *O Strange New World*. New York, 1965.

Jones, LeRoi. *Blues People*. New York, 1963.

Joseph, Franz M., ed. *As Others See Us: The United States through Foreign Eyes*. Princeton, N.J., 1959.

Junker, Detlef. *Der unteilbare Weltmarkt. Das ökonomische Interesse in der Aussenpolitik der USA 1933–1941*. Stuttgart, 1975.

Kahle, Günter, et al. *Simón Bolívar in zeitgenössischen Berichten (1811–1831)*. Berlin, 1983.

Kähler, Hermann. *Der Kalte Krieg der Kritiker*. Berlin (GDR), 1974.

Kaminsky, Stuart M. *American Film Genres*. Dayton, Ohio, 1974.

Kammer für Arbeiter und Angestellte, ed. *Freizeitgestaltung der Arbeiter und Angestellten Wiens. Eine statistische Untersuchung im Jahre 1961*. Vienna, 1963.

Kandel, I. L. *United States Activities in International Cultural Relations*. American Council on Education. Washington, D.C., 1944.

Kellermann, Henry J. *Cultural Relations as an Instrument of U.S. Foreign Policy: The Educational Exchange Program between the United States and Germany, 1945–1954*. Washington, D.C., 1978.

Kelly, Terence. *A Competitive Cinema*. London, 1966.

Keyserling, Graf Hermann. *Amerika. Der Aufgang einer neuen Welt*. Stuttgart, 1930.

Keyserlingk, Robert H. *Austria in World War II: An Anglo-American Dilemma*. Kingston, Ont., 1988.

Kisch, Egon Erwin. *Beehrt sich darzubieten: Paradies Amerika*. Berlin, 1930.

Knapp, Manfred, et al. *Die USA und Deutschland 1918–1975: Deutsch-amerikanische Beziehungen zwischen Rivalität und Partnerschaft*. Munich, 1978.

Kohl, Karl-Heinz. *Entzauberter Blick. Das Bild vom Guten Wilden und die Erfahrung der Zivilisation*. Frankfurt am Main, 1986.

Kraushaar, Elmar. *Rote Lippen. Die ganze Welt des deutschen Schlagers*. Hamburg, 1983.

Kuisel, Richard. *Seducing the French: The Dilemma of Americanization*. Berkeley, Calif., 1993.

Kunert, Günter. *Der andere Planet: Ansichten von Amerika*. Munich, 1975.

Ladame, Paul A. *Le rôle des migrations dans le monde libre*. Geneva, 1958.

Lange, Horst. *Jazz in Deutschland. Die deutsche Jazz-Chronik, 1900–1960*. Berlin, 1966.

Langenbucher, Wolfgang. *Der aktuelle Unterhaltungsroman: Beiträge zu Geschichte und Theorie der massenhaft verbreiteten Literatur*. Bonn, 1964.

Lange-Quassowski, Jutta. *Neuordnung oder Restaurierung? Das Demokratiekonzept der amerikanischen Besatzungsmacht und die politische Sozialisation der Westdeutschen: Wirtschaftsordnung—Schulstruktur—Politische Bildung*. Opladen, 1979.

Laserson, M. M. *The American Impact on Russia, 1784–1817*. New York, 1962.

Lebel, J. P. *Cinéma et idéologie*. Paris, 1971.

Lee, John, ed. *The Diplomatic Persuaders: A New Role of the Mass Media in International Relations*. New York, 1969.

Lefebvre, Henri. *Kritik des Alltagslebens*. Kronberg, 1977.

Leitich, Ann Tizia. *Drei in Amerika*. Vienna, 1946.

Lenschau, Thomas. *Die amerikanische Gefahr*. Berlin, 1902.

Leonard, Neil. *Jazz and the White Americans: The Acceptance of a New Art Form*. Chicago, 1962.

Lethen, Helmut. *Neue Sachlichkeit 1924–1932*. Stuttgart, 1970.

Levi, Carlo. *Christus kam nur bis Eboli*. Munich, 1982.

Lingeman, Richard R. *Don't You Know There's a War On? The American Home Front, 1941–1945*. New York, 1970.

Loth, Wilfried. *Die Teilung der Welt*. Munich, 1982.

Lothar, Ernst. *Die Rückkehr*. Vienna, 1949.

Lüddecke, Theodor. *Amerikanisches Wirtschaftstempo als Bedrohung Europas*. Leipzig, 1925.

McCrum, Robert, William Cran, and Robert MacNeil. *The Story of English*. London, 1986.

MacDonald, J. Fred. *Television and the Red Menace: The Video Road to Vietnam*. New York, 1985.

McGrath, J. *Is American Democracy Exportable?*. London, 1968.

MacKenzie, John M. *Propaganda and Empire: The Manipulation of British Public Opinion, 1880–1960*. Manchester, 1984.

McLuhan, Marshall. *The Gutenberg Galaxy: The Making of a Typographic Man*. New York, 1961.

——. *Understanding Media: The Extensions of Man*. New York, 1964.

McMurray, Ruth, and Muna Lee. *The Cultural Approach*. Washington, D.C., 1947.

McPhail, Thomas L. *Electronic Colonialism: The Future of Broadcasting and Communication*. Beverly Hills, Calif., 1981.

Madariaga, Salvador de. *Americans*. London, 1930.

Maltby, Richard. *Harmless Entertainment: Hollywood and the Ideology of Consensus*. Metuchen, N.J., 1983.

Marchetti, Victor, and John D. Marks. *The CIA and the Cult of Intelligence*. New York, 1974.

Marcus, Greil. *Mystery Train: Der Traum von Amerika in Liedern der Rockmusik*. Reinbek bei Hamburg, 1981.

Marjasch, Sonja. *Der amerikanische Bestseller. Sein Wesen und seine Verbreitung unter besonderer Berücksichtigung der Schweiz*. Bern, 1946.

März, Eduard. *Österreichische Bankpolitik in der Zeit der grossen Wende 1913–1923. Am Beispiel der Creditanstalt für Handel und Gewerbe*. Vienna, 1981.

——. *Österreichs Wirtschaft zwischen Ost und West. Eine sozialistische Analyse*. Vienna, 1965.

Matthias, L. L. *Die Entdeckung Amerikas. Anno 1953*. Hamburg, 1953.

Matthiessen, F. O. *From the Heart of Europe*. New York, 1948.

Matz, Elisabeth. *Die Zeitungen der US-Armee für die deutsche Bevölkerung (1944–1946)*. Münster, 1969.

Mead, Margaret. *. . . und halte Dein Pulver trocken*. Vienna, 1947.

Mead, Robert O. *The Atlantic Legacy: Essays in American-European Cultural History*. New York, 1968.

Meissl, Sebastian, Klaus-Dieter Mulley, and Oliver Rathkolb, eds. *Verdrängte Schuld, Verfehlte Sühne. Entnazifizierung in Österreich 1945–1955*. Vienna, 1986.

Mellinger, Frederic. *Das Theater am Broadway*. Berlin, 1950.

Melly, George. *Revolt into Style: The Pop Arts in Britain*. Harmondsworth, 1970.

Mercillon, Henri. *Cinéma et monopoles*. Paris, 1953.

Merritt, Anna J., and Richard L. Merritt. *Public Opinion in Occupied Germany: The OMGUS Surveys, 1945–1949*. Urbana, Ill., 1970.

——. *Public Opinion in Semisovereign Germany: The HICOG Surveys, 1949–1955*. Urbana, Ill., 1980.

Metken, Günter. *Comics*. Frankfurt am Main, 1970.

Mettler-Meibom, Barbara. *Demokratisierung und Kalter Krieg: Zur amerikanischen Informations- und Rundfunkpolitik in Westdeutschland 1945–1949*. Berlin, 1975.

Metz, Christian. *Sprache und Film*. Frankfurt am Main, 1973.

Meyer, Hildegard. *Nord-Amerika im Urteil des deutschen Schrifttums bis zur Mitte des 19. Jahrhunderts*. Hamburg, 1929.

Meyerhoff, Arthur E. *The Strategy of Persuasion: The Use of Advertising Skills in Fighting the Cold War*. New York, 1965.

Mickelson, Sig. *America's Other Voice: The Story of Radio Free Europe and Radio Liberty*. New York, 1983.

Miller, Arthur. *Timebends*. London, 1987.

Minifie, James M. *Expatriate*. Toronto, 1976.

Mintz, Sydney W. *Sweetness and Power: The Place of Sugar in Modern History*. New York, 1985.

Mitchell, B. R. *European Historical Statistics, 1750–1970*. London, 1975.

Mitchell, J. M. *International Cultural Relations*. Winchester, Mass., 1986.

Mitterauer, Michael. *Sozialgeschichte der Jugend*. Frankfurt am Main, 1986.

Mohl, Gertrud. *Die Aufnahme amerikanischer Literatur in der deutschsprachigen Schweiz während der Jahre 1945–1950*. Zurich, 1961.

Moltmann, Günter. *Aufbruch nach Amerika: Friedrich List und die Auswanderung aus Baden und Württemberg 1816/17. Dokumentation einer sozialen Bewegung. Unter Mitarbeit von Ingrid Schöberl*. Tübingen, 1979.

Monaco, James. *How to Read a Film*. Oxford, 1978.

Mönning, R. *Amerika und England im deutschen, österreichischen und schweizerischen Schrifttum der Jahre 1945–1949. Eine Bibliographie*. Stuttgart, 1951.

Morse, Edward L. *Modernization and the Transformation of International Relations*. New York, 1976.

Mottram, E. N. W. *American Studies in Europe: Inaugural Lecture*. Groningen, 1955.

Münster, Ruth. *Geld in Nietenhosen: Jugendliche als Verbraucher*. Stuttgart, 1961.

Naury, Charles, ed. *American Music*. New Brunswick, N.J., 1972.

Neske, F., and I. Neske. *Wörterbuch englischer und amerikanischer Ausdrücke in der deutschen Sprache*. Munich, 1972.

*Eine Neue Welt für unsere Jugend*. Vienna, 1953.

Nevins, Allan, ed. *America through British Eyes*. New York, 1948.

Newton, Francis [E. J. Hobsbawm]. *The Jazz Scene*. London, 1959.

Ney, John. *Die europäische Kapitulation. Thesen und Prognosen zur Amerikanisierung Europas*. Luzern, 1971.

Ninkovich, Frank. *The Diplomacy of Ideas: U.S. Foreign Policy and Cultural Relations, 1938–1950*. Cambridge, 1981.

Norman, Albert. *Our German Policy: Propaganda and Culture*. New York, 1951.

Obergottsberger, Hugo, and Monika Berthold. *25 Jahre Fulbright-Programm in Österreich*. Vienna, 1975.

O'Connor, John E., and Martin A. Jackson, eds. *American History/American Film*. New York, 1979.

Oertel, Rudolf. *Macht und Magie des Films*. Vienna, 1959.

O'Gorman, Edmundo. *The Invention of America*. Bloomington, Ind., 1961.

Otruba, Gustav. *Österreichs Wirtschaft im 20. Jahrhundert*. Vienna, 1968.

Palm, Kurt. *Vom Boykott zur Anerkennung. Brecht und Österreich*. Vienna, 1983.

Palmer, Robert T. *The Age of Democratic Revolution: A Political History of Europe and America, 1760–1800*. Princeton, N.J., 1959.

Panfilov, Artzem F. *Broadcasting Pirates; or, Abuse of the Microphone*. Moscow, 1981.

Pattison, Robert. *The Triumph of Vulgarity: Rock Music in the Mirror of Romanticism*. New York, 1987.

Pearson, Homer. *The Pattern of Propaganda in Music*. Poughkeepsie, N.Y., 1944.

Peez, Alexander. *Die amerikanische Concurrenz*. Vienna, 1881.

Perry, Ralph Barton. *Amerikanische Ideale*. 2 vols. Vienna, 1949.

Petschar, Hans, and Georg Schmid. *Erinnerungen und Visionen: Die Legitimation Österreichs in Bildern*. Graz, 1990.

Pilgert, Henry P. *The History of the Development of Information Services through Information Centers and Documentary Film*. Historical Division, Office of the Executive Secretary, Office of the U.S. High Commission Germany. Frankfurt, 1951.

——. *Press, Radio, and Film in West Germany, 1945–1953*. Frankfurt am Main, 1953.

Pilgert, Henry, and Helga Dobbert. *Press, Radio, and Film in West Germany, 1945–1953*. Bad Godesberg, 1953.

Pinthus, Kurt, ed. *Das Kinobuch*. Zurich, 1963.

Pleasants, Henry. *Death of a Music? The Decline of the European Tradition and the Rise of Jazz*. London, 1961.

——. *Serious Music—and All That Jazz*. London, 1969.

Plischke, Hans. *Von Cooper bis Karl May*. Düsseldorf, 1951.

Pluch, Thomas. *Grosser Bruder Fernsehen. Die elektronische Kulturrevolution*. Vienna, 1984.

Pomaret, Charles. *L'Amérique et la conquête de l'Europe*. Paris, 1931.

Powers, Thomas. *CIA. Die Geschichte. Die Methoden. Die Komplotte. Ein Insider-Bericht*. Hamburg, 1980.

Preuss-Lausitz, Ulf, et al. *Kriegskinder, Krisenkinder, Konsumkinder. Zur Sozialisationsgeschichte seit dem Zweiten Weltkrieg.* Weinheim, 1983.

Price, James R. *Radio Free Europe: A Survey and Analysis.* Washington, D.C., 1972.

Price, Marsden. *The Reception of United States Literature in Germany.* Chapel Hill, N.C., 1966.

Prinz, Friedrich, ed. *Trümmerzeit—Kultur und Gesellschaft Münchens unter amerikanischer Besatzung 1945–1948/49.* Munich, 1983.

Proce, H., and Carl E. Schorske. *The Problem of Germany.* New York, 1947.

Puig, Jean Louis. *Etude de films américains reflectant le climat de la guerre froide 1950–1963.* Nanterre, Université de Paris 10, 1977.

Raeithel, Gerd. *"Go West": Ein psychohistorischer Versuch über die Amerikaner.* Frankfurt am Main, 1981.

Rauchensteiner, Manfried. *Der Sonderfall: Die Besatzungszeit in Österreich 1945 bis 1955.* Graz, 1979.

Ray, Robert B. *A Certain Tendency of the Hollywood Cinema, 1930–1980.* Princeton, N.J., 1985.

Reader, Keith. *Cultures on Celluloid.* London, 1981.

Reilly, Alayne P. *America in Contemporary Soviet Literature.* New York, 1971.

Riess, Curt. *Knaurs Weltgeschichte der Schallplatte.* Zurich, 1966.

Ritter, Alexander. *Deutschlands literarisches Amerikabild.* Hildesheim, 1977.

Robbins, Warren. *Report on the USIS Cultural Program in Germany.* Washington, D.C., 1960.

Rock, George. *The History of the American Field Service, 1920–1955.* New York, 1956.

Rosenberg, Emily S. *Spreading the American Dream: American Economic and Cultural Expansion, 1890–1945.* New York, 1982.

Rosenmayr, Leopold, Eva Köckeis, and Henrik Kreutz. *Kulturelle Interessen von Jugendlichen. Eine soziologische Untersuchung an jungen Arbeitern und höheren Schülern.* Vienna, 1966.

Rositzke, Harry. *The CIA's Secret Operations.* New York, 1977.

Rossi, Joseph. *The Image of America in Mazzini's Writings.* Madison, Wis., 1954.

Rosten, Leo C. *Hollywood: The Movie Colony.* New York, 1948.

Roth, Paul. *Cuius regio—eius informatio: Moskaus Modell für die Weltinformationsordnung.* Vienna, 1984.

Rowse, A. L. *The Elizabethans and America.* London, 1959.

Rubin, Ronald I. *The Objectives of the U.S. Information Agency: Controversies and Analysis.* New York, 1968.

Rudolf, H. E. *Amerikanisch in Abkürzungen. Eine Anlage zu jedem englisch-deutschen Wörterbuch.* Vienna, 1946.

Ruffié, Jacques, and Jean-Charles Sournia. *Die Seuchen in der Geschichte der Menschheit.* Stuttgart, 1987.

Ruland, Richard. *America in Modern European Literature: From Image to Metaphor.* New York, 1976.

Russet, Bruce Martin. *Community and Contention: Britain and America in the Twentieth Century.* Cambridge, Mass., 1963.

Sadoul, Georges. *Geschichte der Filmkunst.* Vienna, 1957.

Salaman, R. N. *The History and Social Influence of the Potato.* Cambridge, 1949.

Salzbacher, Joseph. *Meine Reise nach Nord-Amerika im Jahre 1842. Mit statistischen Bemerkungen über die Zustände der katholischen Kirche bis auf die neueste Zeit.* Vienna, 1845.

Salzinger, Helmut. *Swinging Benjamin.* Frankfurt am Main, 1973.

Sanford, C. L. *The Quest for Paradise: Europe and the American Moral Imagination.* Urbana, Ill., 1961.

Sayre, Nora. *Running Time: Films of the Cold War.* New York, 1982.

Scheel, Klaus. *Krieg über Ätherwellen.* Berlin (GDR), 1970.

Schiller, Dan. *Objectivity and the News: The Public and the Rise of Commercial Journalism.* Philadelphia, 1981.

Schiller, Herbert I. *Communication and Cultural Domination*. White Plains, N.Y., 1976.

——. *Culture, Inc.: The Corporate Takeover of Public Expression*. New York, 1989.

——. *Mass Communications and American Empire*. Boston, 1969.

Schlander, Otto. *Reeducation. Ein politisch-pädagogisches Prinzip im Widerstreit der Gruppen*. Bern, 1975.

Schlitter, Hanns. *Die Beziehungen Österreichs zu Amerika 1778 bis 1885*. Innsbruck, 1885.

Schmid, Georg. *Die Figuren des Kaleidoskops: Über Geschichte(n) im Film*. Salzburg, 1983.

Schmidt, Georg. *Der Film, wirtschaftlich, gesellschaftlich, künstlerisch*. Basel 1947.

Schmidt-Joos, Siegfried. *Geschäfte mit Schlagern*. Bremen, 1960.

Schmidt-Phiseldeck, Conrad Friedrich. *Europa und Amerika, oder die künftigen Verhältnisse der civilisierten Welt*. Copenhagen, 1820.

Scholz-Wancke, Katharina. *Pop-Import*. Hamburg, 1969.

Schrenck-Notzing, Caspar. *Charakterwäsche: Die amerikanische Besatzung in Deutschland und ihre Folgen*. Stuttgart, 1965.

Schüler, Andreas. *Erfindergeist und Technikkritik: Der Beitrag Amerikas zur Modernisierung und die Technikdebatte seit 1900*. Stuttgart, 1990.

Schulz, Hans-Jürgen. *Die geheime Internationale. Spitzelterror und Computer. Zur Geschichte und Funktion der Geheimdienste in der bürgerlichen Gesellschaft*. Frankfurt am Main, 1982.

Schürch, Ernst. *Aus der neuen Welt: Mit der schweizerischen Pressemission in Amerika*. Bern, 1919.

Schwegel, H. *Die Einwanderung in die Vereinigten Staaten von Amerika. Mit besonderer Berücksichtigung auf die österreichisch-ungarische Auswanderung*. Vienna, 1904.

Scott, Franklin D. *The American Experience of Swedish Students*. Minneapolis, 1956.

——. *The United States and Scandinavia*. Cambridge, Mass., 1950.

Seldes, Gilbert. *The Movies Come from America*. London, 1937.

Seliger, Helfried Werner. *Das Amerikabild Bertolt Brechts*. Bonn, 1974.

Servan-Schreiber, Jean-Jacques. *Die amerikanische Herausforderung*. Hamburg, 1968.

Shaw, Arnold. *Rock 'n' Roll. Die Stars, die Musik und die Mythen der 50er Jahre*. Reinbek bei Hamburg, 1978.

Shaw, George Bernard. *The Political Madhouse in America and Nearer Home*. London, 1933.

Short, K. R. M., ed. *Western Broadcasting over the Iron Curtain*. London, 1986.

Sidons, C. [Karl Postl]. *Die Vereinigten Staaten von Nord-Amerika nach ihren politischen, religiösen und gesellschaftlichen Verhältnissen betrachtet*. Stuttgart, 1827.

Signitzer, Benno. *Österreich im internationalen Mediensystem: Beziehungen und Abhängigkeiten*. Salzburg, 1980.

Silbermann, Alphons. *The Sociology of Music*. London, 1963.

Silberschmidt, Max. *The United States and Europe: Rivals and Partners*. London, 1972.

Sinclair, John, and Robert Levin. *Music and Politics*. New York, 1971.

Skard, Sigmund. *The American Myth and the European Mind: American Studies in Europe, 1776–1960*. Philadelphia, 1961.

——. *The United States in Norwegian History*. Westport, Conn., 1976.

Sklar, Robert. *Movie-Made America: A Cultural History of American Movies*. New York, 1975.

Smith, Adam. *The Wealth of Nations*. New York, 1985.

Smith, Carlton Sprague, and Eric Neff. *Bi- and Multi-National Cooperation in Germany*. Frankfurt am Main, 1952.

Smith, McCaul. *How Do You Do? Englisch in allen Lebenslagen*. Vienna, 1945.

Smith, Paul, ed. *The Historian and the Film*. London, 1976.

Snyder, Harold, and George E. Beauchamp. *An Experiment in International Cultural Relations: A Report of the Commission on the Occupied Areas*. Washington, D.C., 1951.

Sombart, Werner. *Warum gibt es keinen Sozialismus in den Vereinigten Staaten?*. Tübingen, 1906.

Sommer, Walter. *Die Weltmacht USA im Urteil der französischen Publizistik 1924–1939.* Tübingen, 1967.

Sorensen, Thomas C. *The Word War: The Story of American Propaganda.* New York, 1968.

Sorlin, Pierre. *The Film in History: Restaging the Past.* Oxford, 1980.

Soupault, Philippe. *The American Influence in France.* Seattle, Wash., 1930.

Southard, Frank A. *American Industry in Europe.* Boston, 1931.

Spaulding, E. Wilder. *The Quiet Invaders: The Story of the Austrian Impact upon America.* Vienna, 1968.

Spoerri, William T. *The Old World and the New: A Synopsis of Current European Views on American Civilization.* Zurich, 1937.

Spachinger, Othmar, et al. *Die österreichische Schule 1945–1957.* Vienna, 1975.

Stadler, Friedrich, ed. *Vertriebene Vernunft.* 2 vols. Vienna, 1987–1988.

Stammel, H. J., and Friedrich Gassman. *The Literary Evolution of the "Wild West" in Germany.* Los Angeles, 1966.

Stammler, Heinrich. *Amerika im Spiegel seiner Literatur.* Linz, 1949.

Stanley, Robert. *The Celluloid Empire: A History of the American Motion Picture Industry.* New York, 1978.

Starr, S. Frederick. *Red and Hot: The Fate of Jazz in the Soviet Union, 1917–1980.* New York, 1983.

Statistisches Zentralamt, ed. *Theater, Film, Rundfunk, Fernsehen.* Beiträge zur Statistik, 39. Vienna, 1959.

Stead, W. T. *The Americanization of the World; or, The Trend of the Twentieth Century.* London, 1901.

Stearns, Marshall. *The Story of Jazz.* New York, 1956.

Steinberg, Cobbett. *Reel Facts: The Movie Book of Records.* New York, 1978.

Stephens, Oren. *Facts to a Candid World: America's Overseas Information Program.* Stanford, 1955.

Stich, Sidra. *Made in USA: An Americanization in Modern Art. The Fifties and Sixties.* Berkeley, 1987.

Stiefel, Dieter. *Entnazifizierung in Österreich.* Vienna, 1981.

Stiewe, Willy. *Das Bild als Nachricht.* Berlin, 1933.

Stölting, Elke. *Deutsche Schlager und englische Popmusik in Deutschland. Ideologiekritische Untersuchung zweier Textstile während der Jahre 1960–1970.* Bonn, 1975.

Stott, William. *Documentary Expression and Thirties America.* Chicago, 1986.

Strauss, David. *Menace in the West: The Rise of French Anti-Americanism in Modern Times.* Westport, Conn., 1978.

Swann, Paul. *The Hollywood Feature Film in Postwar Britain.* London, 1987.

Sypher, Wylie. *Rococo to Cubism in Art and Literature.* New York, 1960.

Szanto, George H. *Theater and Propaganda.* Austin, Tex., 1978.

Szilassy, Baron J. von. *L'empire du travail. La vie aux Etats-Unis.* Plon, 1905.

Taylor, P. M. *The Projection of Britain.* Cambridge, 1981.

*Technological Frontiers and Foreign Relations.* Washington, D.C., 1985.

Tent, James F. *Mission on the Rhine: "Reeducation" and Denazification in American-Occupied Germany.* Chicago, 1982.

Theoharis, Athan. *Spying on Americans.* Philadelphia, 1978.

——, ed. *Beyond the Hiss Case: The FBI, Congress, and the Cold War.* Philadelphia, 1982.

Thompson, Kenneth, ed. *Institutions for Projecting American Values Abroad.* Vol. 3. Lanham, Md., 1983.

Thompson, Kristin. *Exporting Entertainment: America in the World Film Market, 1907–34.* London, 1985.

Thomson, Charles. *Overseas Information Service of the United States Government*. Washington, D.C., 1948.

Thomson, Charles A., and Walter Laves. *Cultural Relations and United States Foreign Policy*. Bloomington, Ind., 1963.

Tischler, Barbara L. *An American Music: The Search for an American Musical Identity*. New York, 1986.

Tocqueville, Alexis de. *Democracy in America*. New York, 1969.

Todorov, Tzvetan. *Die Eroberung Amerikas: Das Problem des Anderen*. Frankfurt am Main, 1985.

Trefousse, Hans L. *Germany and America*. New York, 1982.

Trimborn, Hermann. *Das alte Amerika*. Stuttgart, 1985.

Trollope, Frances. *Domestic Manners of the Americans*. London, 1839.

Tunstall, Jeremy. *The Media Are American: Anglo-American Media in the World*. New York, 1977.

Tyson, James L. *U.S. International Broadcasting and National Security*. New York, 1983.

Urzidil, Johannes. *Das Glück der Gegenwart: Goethes Amerikabild*. Zurich, 1958.

Vaillant, Jérôme. *La dénazification par les vainqueurs*. Lille, 1981.

Vian, Boris. *Der Kommissar und die Grüne Pantherin. Gesammelte Schriften*. Frankfurt am Main, 1984.

Viera, Joe. *Jazz in Europa*. Munich, 1965.

Viereck, W., ed. *Studien zum Einfluss der englischen Sprache auf das Deutsche*. Tübingen, 1980.

Voechting, Fritz. *Über den amerikanischen Frauenkult*. Jena, 1926.

Wagnleitner, Reinhold, ed. *Diplomatie zwischen Parteiproporz und Weltkonflikt. Briefe, Dokumente und Memoranden aus dem Nachlass Walter Wodaks 1945–1950*. Salzburg, 1980.

——. *Understanding Austria: The Political Reports and Analyses of Martin F. Herz, Political Officer of the U.S. Legation in Vienna, 1945–1948*. Salzburg, 1984.

Walcher, Jakob. *Ford oder Marx: Die praktische Lösung der sozialen Frage*. Berlin, 1925.

Walker, Alexander. *Hollywood, England: The British Film Industry in the Sixties*. London, 1974.

Wallerstein, Immanuel. *The Modern World System*. Vol. 2, *Mercantilism and the Consolidation of the European World Economy, 1600–1750*. New York, 1980.

Wallpach, Heinrich. *Die österreichische Filmindustrie (Filmproduktion). Daten und Fakten*. Vienna, 1979.

Watt, D. Cameron. *Succeeding John Bull: America in Britain's Place, 1900–1975*. Cambridge, 1984.

Weber, Paul C. *America in Imaginative German Literature in the First Half of the Nineteenth Century*. New York, 1926.

Wedge, Bryant. *Visitors to the United States and How They See Us*. Princeton, N.J., 1965.

Wehdeking, Volker C. *Der Nullpunkt: Über die Konstituierung der deutschen Nachkriegsliteratur (1945–1948) in den amerikanischen Kriegsgefangenenlagern*. Stuttgart, 1971.

Weiner, Robert. *Das Amerikabild von Karl Marx*. Bonn, 1982.

Wells, H. G. *The Future in America*. New York, 1906.

Welter, Ernst Günter. *Die Sprache der Teenager und Twens*. Frankfurt am Main, 1961.

*Welt im Film 1945–1950: A Microfiche Catalogue of the Imperial War Museum's Holding of Material from the Anglo-American Newsreel Screen in Occupied Germany, 1945–1950*. London, 1981.

White, Llewellyn, and Robert D. Leigh. *Peoples Speaking to Peoples: A Report on International Mass Communication from the Commission on Freedom of the Press*. Washington, D.C., 1946.

Whitehouse, J. Howard. *America and Our Schools*. London, 1939.

Whitton, John B., and Arthur Larson. *Propaganda: Towards Disarmament in the War of Words*. Dobbs Ferry, N.Y., 1964.

Willett, Ralph. *The Americanization of Germany, 1945–1949*. London, 1989.

Williams, Francis. *The American Invasion*. London, 1962.

Winkler, Allan M. *The Politics of Propaganda: The Office of War Information, 1942–1945*. New Haven, Conn., 1978.

Wirsing, Giselher. *Der masslose Kontinent: Roosevelts Kampf um die Weltherrschaft*. Jena, 1942.

Wood, Michael. *America in the Movies; or, "Santa Maria, It Had Slipped My Mind."* New York, 1975.

Woodruff, William. *America's Impact on the World: A Study of the Role of the United States in the World Economy, 1750–1970*. London, 1975.

Woodward, C. Vann. *The Old World's New World*. New York, 1991.

*Zehn Jahre Aufbau 1945–1955. Salzburg—Kleinod von Österreich*. Salzburg, 1955.

Zimmer, Jochen. *Popmusik—zur Theorie und Sozialgeschichte*. Dortmund, 1973.

Zwerin, Mike. *La Tristesse de Saint Louis: Jazz under the Nazis*. New York, 1986.

ARTICLES

Adler, Eduard. "The First Decade of Austrian American Relations, 1776–1786." In *Americana-Austriaca. Beiträge zur Amerikakunde*, vol. 4, pp. 1–13. Vienna, 1977.

Adler, Les K. "The Politics of Culture: Hollywood and the Cold War." In *The Specter*, edited by Robert Griffith and Athan Theoharis. New York, 1974.

Aigner, Karl. "Die Blicke im Zeitalter ihrer technischen (Re-)Produzierbarkeit. Zum photographischen Verhältnis von Vor-Bild und Ab-Bild." In *Die Zeichen der Historie. Beiträge zu einer semiologischen Geschichtswissenschaft*, edited by Georg Schmid, pp. 163–71. Vienna, 1986.

"American Books in Overseas Libraries." *Publisher's Weekly*, September 14, 1946, pp. 1850–53; October 28, 1950.

"Amerikawagen: USIS Library on Wheels." *US International Information Administration Newsletter*, May 1953.

Angermann, Erich. "Die Auseinandersetzungen mit der Moderne in Deutschland und den USA in den Goldenen 20er Jahren." In *Deutschland und die USA*. Braunschweig, 1968.

Aron, Raymond. "Transatlantische Beziehungen." In *Amerika und der europäische Geist*, edited by Lewis Galantiére, pp. 58–70. Vienna, 1951.

Ashliman, D. L. "The American Indian in German Travel Narratives and Literature." *Journal of Popular Culture* 10 (Spring 1977): 833–39.

———. "The American West in Twentieth-Century Germany." *Journal of Popular Culture* 2 (Summer 1968): 81–92.

———. "The Study of Popular Literature in Germany." *Journal of Popular Culture* 2 (1968): 332–38.

Barba, Preston A. "Cooper in Germany." *German American Annals* 12 (January/February 1914): 3–60.

Baritz, Loren. "The Idea of the West." *American Historical Review* 66 (April 1961): 618–40.

Barraclough, Geoffrey. "Europa, Amerika und Russland in Vorstellung und Denken des 19. Jahrhunderts." *Historische Zeitschrift* 203 (1966): 280–315.

Barrett, Edward. "Truth Is Our Weapon." In *Institutions for Projecting American Values Abroad*, vol. 3, edited by Kenneth W. Thompson, pp. 10-1–10-8. Lanham, Md., 1983.

Basler, Otto. "Amerikanismus: Geschichte des Schlagwortes." *Deutsche Rundschau* 224 (August 1930): 142–46.

Battle, Lucius D. "The Role of Music in Cultural Exchange." *U.S. Department of State Bulletin* 48 (June 10, 1963): 915–17.

Beer, Siegfried. "The Development of Teaching and Research on United States History in Austria." In *Guide to the Study of United States History outside the U.S., 1945–1980*, vol. 1, edited by Lewis Hanke, pp. 177–93. White Plains, N.Y., 1985.

Behn, Fritz. "Amerikanismus in Deutschland." *Süddeutsche Monatshefte* 27 (June 1929): 672–74.

Beloff, Max. "The Projection of America Abroad." *American Quarterly* 1 (1949): 23–29.

Benna, Anna. "Österreichs erste diplomatische Vertretung bei den Vereinigten Staaten von Amerika." *Mitteilungen des österreichischen Staatsarchivs* 29 (1976): 215–40.

Bergel, Egon. "Die Eigenart der österreichischen Einwanderung nach Amerika." In *Americana-Austriaca. Beiträge zur Amerikakunde*, vol. 2, pp. 93–130. Vienna, 1970.

Bergstraesser, Arnold. "Zum Problem der sogenannten Amerikanisierung Deutschlands." *Jahrbuch für Amerikastudien* 8 (1963).

Betts, Raymond F. "Immense Dimensions: The Impact of the American West on Late Nineteenth Century European Thought about Expansion." *Western Historical Quarterly*, April 1979, pp. 149–66.

Bitterli, Urs. "Begegnung, Beziehung und Zusammenstoss von Kulturen." *Zeitschrift für Kulturaustausch* 34 (1984): 231–40.

Blaukopf, Kurt. "Österreichs gefährdete Grossmacht. Musik." In *Bestandaufnahme Österreich 1945–1963*, edited by Jacques Hannak, pp. 392–415. Vienna, 1963.

Bonheim, Helmut. "American Books in Vienna." *Nation*, January 14, 1961, pp. 37–38.

Bornemann, Ernst. "The Jazz Cult." Part 1: "Intimate Memoirs of an Acolyte." *Harper's Magazine*, February 1947, pp. 141–47.

———. "The Jazz Cult." Part 2: "War among the Critics." *Harpers's Magazine*, March 1947, pp. 261–73.

Boyd-Barrett, Oliver. "Media Imperialism: Towards an International Framework for the Study of Media Systems." In *Mass Communication and Society*, edited by James Curran, Michael Gurevitch, and Janet Woollacott, pp. 116–35. London, 1977.

Broderson, Arvid. "Themes in the Interpretation of America by Prominent Visitors from Abroad." *Annals of the American Academy of Political and Social Science* 295 (September 1954): 21–32.

Bronner, Augusta V. "Eine amerikanische Philosophie." *Die Bastei* 1, no. 6 (1946/47): 29–30.

Brooks, George R. "The American Frontier in German Fiction." In *The Frontier Re-examined*, edited by John McDermott, pp. 156–57. Urbana, Ill., 1967.

Brooks, Paul. "Books Follow the Jeep." *Publisher's Weekly*, December 8, 1945, p. 2528.

Browne, Donald R. "RIAS Berlin: A Case Study of a Cold War Broadcast Operation." *Journal of Broadcasting* 10 (Spring 1966): 119–35.

Brüning, Eberhard. "Amerikanische Dramen an den Bühnen der Deutschen Demokratischen Republik und Berlins von 1945 bis 1955." *Zeitschrift für Anglistik und Amerikanistik* 7 (1959): 246–69.

Buchanan, William. "How Others See Us." *Annals of the American Academy of Political and Social Science* 295 (September 1954): 1–11.

Bungenstab, Karl-Ernst. "Entstehung, Bedeutungs- und Funktionswandel der Amerikahäuser." *Jahrbuch für Amerikastudien* 16 (1971): 191–203.

Bungert, Hans. "Zum Einfluss des Englischen auf die deutsche Sprache seit dem Ende des Zweiten Weltkrieges." *Journal of English and German Philology* 62 (1963): 703–17.

Carstensen, Broderson. "Amerikanische Einflüsse auf die deutsche Sprache." *Jahrbuch für Amerikastudien* 8 (1963): 34–55.

Clément, Alain. "Amerika als Herausforderung des Westens." *Sprache im technischen Zeitalter* 56 (1975): 325–30.

Coarse, R. H. "The Market for Goods and the Market for Ideas." *American Economic Review* 64 (1974): 384–91.

Cohen, Emanuel. "Film Is a Weapon." *Business Screen* 7 (1945): 43, 72, and 74.

Cook, Laurence R. "Magazines for Friendship." *Field Reporter*, May–June 1954, pp. 36–39.

Cooper, David S. "American Music in Europe." *Musical Courier* 155 (June 1957): 10–11.

Cooper, Martin. "Revolution in Musical Taste." In *The Impact of America on European Culture*, pp. 68–78. Boston, 1951.

Cracroft, Richard H. "The American West of Karl May." *American Quarterly* 19 (Summer 1967): 249–58.

Criscietello, John J. "The Role of American Books." In *Propaganda and the Cold War*, edited by John B. Whitton, pp. 106–12. Washington, D.C., 1963.

Culbert, David. "American Film Policy in the Re-Education of Germany after 1945." In *The Political Re-Education of Germany and Her Allies after World War II*, edited by Nicholas Pronay and Keith Wilson, pp. 173–202. Beckenham, Kent, 1985.

Cunliffe, Marcus. "American Studies in Europe." In *American Studies Abroad*, edited by Robert H. Walker, pp. 46–52. Westport, Conn., 1975.

Curti, Merle, and Kendall Birr. "The Immigrant and the American Image in Europe, 1860–1914." *Mississippi Valley Historical Review* 37 (September 1950): 203–30.

Damon, S. Foster. "American Influence on Modern French Music." *Dial*, August 15, 1918, pp. 93–95.

Déak, Ernö. "Die Auswanderung aus Österreich im 19. und 20. Jahrhundert." In *Siedlungs- und Bevölkerungsgeschichte Österreichs*, edited by the Institut für Österreichkunde, pp. 163–98. Vienna, 1974.

Decsey, Ernst. "Jazz in Vienna." *Living Age*, March 1, 1928, pp. 441–45.

Doss, Erika. "The Art of Cultural Politics: From Regionalism to Abstract Expressionism." In *Recasting America: Culture and Politics in the Age of Cold War*, edited by Lary May, pp. 195–220. Chicago, 1989.

Duckworth, D. "Der Einfluss des Englischen auf den deutschen Wortschatz seit 1945." *Zeitschrift für deutsche Sprache* 26 (1970): 9–31.

Durzak, Manfred. "Abrechnung mit einer Utopie? Zum Amerikabild im jüngsten deutschen Roman." *Basis* 4 (1974): 98–121.

——. "Perspektiven des Amerikabildes, historisch und gegenwärtig. Reisen in der Zeitmaschine." *Sprache im technischen Zeitalter* 56 (1975): 297–305.

Edwards, Herbert T. "Films in the U.S. Overseas Information Program: The World Sees America." *Educational Screen*, May 1949.

Eltis, David. "Free and Coerced Transatlantic Migrations: Some Comparisons." *American Historical Review* 88 (April 1983): 251–80.

Engelbrecht, Helmut. "Die Eingriffe der Alliierten in das österreichische Schul- und Erziehungswesen nach 1945." In *Umerziehung und Wiederaufbau*, edited by Manfred Heinemann, pp. 278–308. Stuttgart, 1981.

Evans, Luther H. "United States Libraries Abroad." *Record, Department of State*, May/June 1951, pp. 6–7.

Feather, Leonard. "Let Hot Jazz Melt Joe's Iron Curtain." *New York Journal American*, October 4, 1952.

——. "Music Is Combatting Communism: Voice of America Shows Bring Universal Harmony." *Down Beat*, October 8, 1952, pp. 1 and 19.

Fellner, Fritz. "Der Plan einer 'Vortragsmission Redlich-Apponyi' in den Vereinigten Staaten von Amerika. Ansätze und Vorschläge zum Aufbau einer österreichisch-ungarischen Propagandaaktion im neutralen Ausland während des Ersten Weltkrieges." In *Beiträge zur neueren Geschichte Österreichs*, edited by Heinrich Fichtenau and Erich Zöllner, pp. 469–88. Vienna, 1974.

Ferro, Marc. "Film as an Agent, Product, and Source of History." *Journal of Contemporary History* 18 (1983): 357–64.

Fichtner, Paula S. "Viennese Perspectives on the American War of Independence." In *East Central European Perspectives of Early America*, edited by Bella Kiraly et al., pp. 19–29. Lisse, 1977.

Fink, H. "Ein Starangebot: Englisches im Versandhauskatalog." *Muttersprache* 86 (1976): 368–82.

Freeman, Thomas. "The Cowboy and the Astronaut: The American Image in German Periodical Advertisements." *Journal of Popular Culture* 6 (Summer 1972): 83–103.

Frei, Norbert. "Amerikanische Pressepolitik im Nachkriegs-Deutschland." *Zeitschrift für Kulturaustausch* 37 (1987): 306–18.

———. "Die Presse." In *Die Bundesrepublik Deutschland. Geschichte in drei Bänden*, vol. 3, *Kultur*, edited by Wolfgang Benz, pp. 275–352. Frankfurt am Main, 1986.

Freienfels-Müller, Richard. " 'Amerikanismus' und europäische Kultur." *Der deutsche Gedanke* 4 (1927): 30–35.

Frenz, Horst. "Eugene O'Neill on the German Stage." *Theatre Annual* 11 (1953): 24–34.

Freymann, Richard. "The Eclipse of German Musical Hegemony." *Music and Letters*, April 1, 1942.

Freymond, Jacques. "America in European Eyes." *Annals of the American Academy of Political and Social Science* 295 (September 1954): 33–41.

Galinsky, Hans. "America's Image in German Literature." *Comparative Literary Studies* 13 (1976): 165–92.

Gans, Herbert J. "Hollywood Films on British Screens: An Analysis of the Functions of American Popular Culture Abroad." *Social Problems* 9 (1962): 324–28.

Gesek, Ludwig. "Zur Geschichte der Wochenschau in Österreich." In *Zeitgeschichte im Film- und Tondokument*, pp. 177–81. Göttingen, 1970.

———, ed. "Kleines Lexikon des österreichischen Films." In *Filmkunst*, nos. 22–30. Vienna, 1959.

Glanz, Christian. " 'Jazz' in Österreich 1918–1938: Personalstudie Charly Kaufmann." *Mitteilungen des Instituts für Wissenschaft und Kunst* 43 (1988): 46–48.

Gleason, Philip. "World War II and the Development of American Studies." *American Quarterly* 36 (1984): 343–58.

Goody, Brian R. "New Orleans to London: Twenty Years of the New Orleans Jazz Revival in Britain." *Journal of Popular Culture* 2 (Fall 1968): 173–94.

Gordon, Jay E. "Operation Celluloid." *Hollywood Quarterly* 2 (1947): 416–19.

Gottas, Friedrich. "A Hungarian Traveler's View of America in the First Half of the Nineteenth Century." In *The Mirror of History: Essays in Honor of Fritz Fellner*, edited by Solomon Wank et al., pp. 213–33. Santa Barbara, Calif., 1988.

Grünzweig, Walter. " 'Niemals verging sein deutsches Herz.' Charles Sealsfield in der Literaturkritik der NS-Zeit." *ÖGL* 30 (January / February 1986): 40–61.

Guback, Thomas H. "American Interests in the British Film Industry." *Quarterly Review of Economics and Business* 7 (1967): 7–21.

———. "Film as International Business." *Journal of Communication* 24 (1974): 90–101.

———. "Theatrical Film." In *Who Owns the Media?*, by Benjamin Compaign et al., pp. 199–298. White Plains, N.Y., 1982.

Haas, Hanns. "Die Vereinigten Staten von Amerika und die alliierte Lebensmittelversorgung Österreichs im Winter 1918 / 19." *MÖSTA* 32 (1979): 233–55.

Haines, Gerald K. "Under the Eagle's Wing: The Franklin Roosevelt Administration Forges an American Hemisphere." *Diplomatic History* 1 (Fall 1977): 373–88.

Hamm, Wolfgang, Wolfgang Kolneder, and Stefan Paul. "Popmusik—Profite für das Kapital." *Sozialistische Zeitschrift für Kunst und Gesellschaft*, no. 6 (1973): 3–75.

Hanisch, Ernst. "Historische Überhänge in der österreichischen politischen Kultur." *Österreichische Zeitschrift für Politikwissenschaft* 13 (1984): 15–19.

Hanke, Lewis. "Pope Paul III and the American Indians." *Harvard Theological Review* 30 (1937): 65–102.

Hansen, Harry L. "Hollywood and International Understanding." *Harvard Business Review* 25 (1946): 28–45.

Hausjell, Fritz. "Entnazifizierung der Presse in Österreich." In *Verdrängte Schuld—verfehlte Sühne*, edited by Sebastian Meissl, Klaus-Dieter Mulley, and Oliver Rathkolb. Vienna, 1986.

——. "Die gescheiterte Alternative. Das Modell der Sozialisierung der Betriebsgewinne einer Zeitung am Beispiel der 'Salzburger Nachrichten' (1945–1960)." *Medien und Zeit* 2 (1987): 17–30.

Helt, Richard C. "A German Bluegrass Festival: The 'Country-Boom' and Some Notes on the History of American Popular Music in West Germany." *Journal of Popular Culture* 10 (Spring 1977): 821–32.

Hillway, Tyrus. "American Studies in Austria." In *American Studies Abroad*, edited by Robert Walker, pp. 89–94. Westport, Conn., 1975.

Houtte, Hubert van. "Documents on Commercial Conditions and Negotiations with Austria, 1783–1786." *American Historical Review* 16 (1911): 567–78.

Howard, Grace H. "Letter from Austria." *Wilson Library Bulletin*, April 1948, pp. 615–17.

Hubert-Lacombe, Patricia. "L'accueil des films américains en France pendant la guerre froide (1946–1953)." *Revue d'histoire moderne et contemporaine* 31 (1986): 301–13.

Iriye, Akira. "Culture and Power: International Relations as Intercultural Relations." *Diplomatic History* 3 (1979): 115–28.

Iurlano, Giuliana. "La cultura liberale americana in Italia: 'Il Mulino' (1951–1969)." *Nuova rivista storica* 67 (1983): 671–706.

Jackson, John B. "Ich bin ein Cowboy aus Texas." *Southwest Review* 38 (Spring 1953): 158–63.

Jantz, Harold. "Amerika im Deutschen Dichten und Denken." In *Deutsche Philologie im Aufriss*, vol. 3, edited by Wolfgang Stammler, pp. 309–72. Berlin, 1962.

——. "The Myth about America: Origins and Extensions." *Jahrbuch für Amerikastudien* 7 (1962): 7–8.

Jerrentrup, Ansgar. "Aspekte der Entstehung übernationaler jugendlicher Alternativ- und Gegenkulturen und ihr Verhältnis zur Popularmusik." *Zeitschrift für Kulturaustausch* 36 (1986): 108–19.

Joesten, Joachim. "The German Film Industry, 1945–1948." *New Germany Reports* 3 (May 1948).

Johnstone, William C. "The Educational Program: An Integral Part of the Campaign of Truth." *Department of State Bulletin* 12 (1950): 20–24.

Jones, Dorothy B. "Hollywood's International Relations." *Quarterly of Film, Radio, and Television* 11 (1956 / 57): 362–74.

Kaindl, Kurt. "Das Tor zur weiten Welt: Illustrierte der fünfziger Jahre in Österreich." In *Die "wilden" fünfziger Jahre. Gesellschaft, Formen und Gefühle eines Jahrzehnts in Österreich*, edited by Gerhard Jagschitz and Klaus-Dieter Mulley, pp. 222–31. St. Pölten, 1985.

Kaminsky, Stuart M. "The Samurai Film and the Western." *Journal of Popular Film* 1 (1972): 312–24.

Kammel, Rudolf. "Die Situation der österreichischen Filmwirtschaft." *Filmkunst* 35 (1961): 11–12 and 50–52.

Kandl, Leo. "Pressefotografie und Fotojournalismus in Österreich bis 1960." In *Geschichte der Fotografie in Österreich*, 2 vols., pp. 311–24. Bad Ischl, 1983.

Kapp, Friedrich. "Zur deutschen wissenschaftlichen Literatur über die Vereinigten Staaten von Amerika." *Historische Zeitschrift* 31 (1874): 241–88.

Keller, Fritz, and Elisabeth Hirth. "Die CIA als Mäzen; oder, Wie autonom ist autonome Kunst?." *Zeitgeschichte* 13 (June / July 1986): 311–18.

Kemp, Wolfgang. "Nach '45—Anmerkungen zur Entwicklung der Nachkriegsfotografie." *Fotogeschichte* 6 (1981): 67–71.

Knoles, George H. " 'My American Impressions': English Criticisms of American Civilization since 1919." *American Quarterly* 5 (Summer 1953): 113–20.

Könenkamp, Wolf-Dieter. "Die Hosen des Siegers." *Zeitschrift für Kulturaustausch* 36 (1986): 12–22.

Koopes, Clayton R., and Gregory D. Black. "What to Show the World: The Office of War Information and Hollywood, 1942–1945." *Journal of American History* 64 (1977): 87–105.

Kotthorst, Erich. "Von der Umerziehung über den Geschichtsverlust zur Tendenzwende. Selbstverständnis und öffentliche Einschätzung des Geschichtsunterrichts in der Nachkriegszeit." In *Geschichte und Geschichtsbewusstsein*, edited by Oswald Hauser, pp. 126–49. Göttingen, 1981.

Kühnelt, Harro Heinz. "Die Aufnahme der nordamerikanischen Literatur in Österreich." In *Nordamerikanische Literatur im deutschen Sprachraum seit 1945*, edited by Horst Frenz and Hans-Joachim Lang. Munich, 1973.

Larsen, Cedric. "The Domestic Motion Picture Work of the Office of War Information." *Hollywood Quarterly* 3, no. 4 (1948): 434–43.

Lasch, Christopher. "The Cultural Cold War: A Short History of the Congress for Cultural Freedom." In *Towards a New Past: Dissenting Essays in American History*, edited by Barton Bernstein, pp. 322–59. New York, 1969.

Leab, Daniel J. "How Red Was My Valley: Hollywood, the Cold War Film, and I Married a Communist." *Journal of Contemporary History* 19 (1984): 59–88.

Lehmann, John. "The Lesson of the Pupil." In *The Impact of America on European Culture*, pp. 23–33. Boston, 1951.

Lerner, Daniel. "World Imagery and American Propaganda Strategy: An Essay toward Political Research." *Columbia Journal of International Affairs* 5 (Spring 1951): 13–26.

Lesch, Edgar. "Die amerikanische Rundfunkpolitik und der Aufbau der Rundfunkanstalten in der amerikanischen Besatzungszone." *Zeitschrift für Kulturaustausch* 37 (1987): 325–31.

Lesky, Erna. "American Medicine as Viewed by Viennese Physicians, 1893–1912." *Bulletin of the History of Medicine* 56 (1982): 368–76.

Loory, Stuart H. "The CIA's Use of the Press—a 'Mighty Wurlitzer.' " *Columbia Journalism Review* 13 (September / October 1974): 9–18.

Lowe, Herman. "Washington Discovers Hollywood." *American Mercury*, April 1945, pp. 407–14.

Lowry, Edward G. "Trade Follows the Film." *Saturday Evening Post* 128 (November 7, 1925): 12.

Ludlow, J. M. "The Growth of American Influence over England." *Atlantic Monthly*, November 1894, pp. 618–23.

Luebke, Frederick C. "Austrians." In *Harvard Encyclopedia of American Ethnic Groups*, edited by Stephan Thernstrom, pp. 164–71. Cambridge, Mass., 1980.

Luger, Kurt. " 'Es ist alles irgendwie so vorbeigezogen.' Erinnerungen an den Alltag, Medienereignisse und Bilder der Zweiten Republik." In *Medienkultur in Österreich*, edited by Hans H. Fabris and Kurt Luger, pp. 45–101. Vienna, 1988.

Lunzer, Heinz. "Der literarische Markt. 1945 bis 1955." In *Literatur der Nachkriegszeit und der fünfziger Jahre in Österreich*, edited by Friedbert Aspetsberger, Norbert Frei, and Hubert Lengauer, pp. 24–45. Vienna, 1984.

McClure, Arthur F. "Hollywood at War: The American Motion Picture and World War II, 1939–1945." *Journal of Popular Film* 1 (1972): 123–35.

MacDonald, J. Fred. "The Cold War as Entertainment in Fifties Television." *Journal of Popular Film and Television* 8 (1978): 3–31.

McNeil, Lowry W., and Gertrude S. Hooker. "The Role of the Arts and Humanities." In *Cultural Affairs and Foreign Relations*, edited by Paul J. Braisted, pp. 45–87. Washington, D.C., 1968.

Maier, Charles S. "Between Taylorism and Technocracy: European Ideologies and the Vision of Industrial Productivity in the 1920s." *Journal of Contemporary History* 5 (1970): 27–61.

——. "The Politics of Productivity: Foundations of American International Economic Policy after World War II." *International Organizations* 31 (Autumn 1977): 607–33.

Mandrillon, Joseph. "Philosophical Investigations on the Discoveries of America." In *Was America a Mistake?*, edited by Henry Steele Commager and Elmo Giordanetti. Columbia, S.C., 1967.

Mann, Klaus. "Karl May: Hitler's Literary Mentor." *Kenyon Review* 11 (1940): 391–400.

Marcus, H. "Zum Twen-Deutsch." *Zeitschrift für deutsche Wortforschung* 18 (1962): 151–60.

Marias, Julian. "From Spain." In *As Others See Us*, edited by Franz M. Joseph. Princeton, N.J., 1959.

Marwick, Arthur. "Der Film ist Realität." In *Die Zeichen der Historie. Beiträge zu einer semiologischen Geschichtswissenschaft*, edited by Georg Schmid, pp. 297–310. Vienna, 1986.

Marx, Karl, and Friedrich Engels. "Manifest der Kommunistischen Partei. Februar / März 1948 London." In *Karl Marx, Friedrich Engels*, vol. 4, edited by the Institute for Marxism-Leninism of the Central Committee of the SED. Berlin, 1964.

——. "Vorwort zur ersten Auflage des 'Kapitals.' " In *Karl Marx, Friedrich Engels*, vol. 23, edited by the Institute for Marxism-Leninism of the Central Committee of the SED. Berlin, 1962.

Matthews, Jane de Hart. "Art and Politics in Cold War America." *American Historical Review* 81 (October 1976): 762–87.

Mayer, Gerald M. "American Motion Pictures in World Trade." *Annals of the American Academy of Political and Social Sciences* 254 (1947): 31–36.

Mazrui, Ali A. "Uncle Sam's Hearing Aid." In *Estrangement: America and the World*, edited by Sanford J. Ungar. New York, 1985.

Meier, Ernst. "Die Lizenzpresse in der amerikanischen Besatzungszone Deutschlands 1945–1949." In *Monumentum Bambergense. Festgabe für Benedikt Kraft*, pp. 211–20. Munich, 1955.

Meier, Hugo A. "American Technology and the Nineteenth Century World." *American Quarterly* 10 (Summer 1958): 116–30.

Milo, Daniel. "La bourse mondiale de la traduction: Un barometre culturel?." *Annales* 39 (January / February 1984): 92–115.

Minifie, James M. "At an Alarming Rate." *Saturday Review of Literature*, October 19, 1946, pp. 9–11 and 37–41.

Monaco, Paul. "Movies and National Consciousness." In *Feature Films as History*, edited by K. R. M. Short, pp. 62–75. London, 1981.

Morpurgo, J. E. "Hollywood: America's Voice." In *The Impact of America on European Culture*, pp. 51–63. Boston, 1951.

Morris, Lawrence S. "U.S. Information Please!." *Record*, May–June 1951, pp. 1–5.

Mosser, A. "Concentration and the Finance of Austrian Industrial Combines, 1880–1914." In *International Business and Central Europe, 1918–1939*, edited by Alice Teichova and P. L. Cottrell, pp. 57–71. Leicester, 1983.

Murphy, Brian. "Monster Movies: They Came from beneath the Fifties." *Journal of Popular Film* 1 (1972): 31–44.

Nabokov, Nicolas. "Musiker und Komponisten." In *Der Einfluss Amerikas auf die europäische Kultur*, pp. 32–44. Berlin, 1952.

Nadeau, Maurice. "Que pensez-vous de la littérature américaine?." *La revue internationale* 3 (February 1947): 115–19.

Nenning, Günther. "Literatur und Kalter Krieg." *Forum* 27 (1980): 13–14.

Ninkovich, Frank. "Cultural Relations and American China Policy, 1942–1945." *Pacific Historical Review* 49 (August 1980): 471–98.

——. "The Currents of Cultural Diplomacy: Art and the State Department, 1938–1947." *Diplomatic History* 1 (Summer 1977): 215–37.

——. "The Rockefeller Foundation, China, and Cultural Change." *Journal of American History* 70 (March 1984): 799–820.

——. "The Trajectory of Cultural Internationalism." In *Educational Exchanges: Essays on the Sino-American Experience*, edited by Joyce K. Kallgren and Dennis Fred Simon. Berkeley, Calif., 1987.

North, C. J. "Our Foreign Trade in Motion Pictures." *Annals of the American Academy of Political and Social Science* 128 (1926): 100–108.

Oliver, Paul. "Blue-eyed Blues: The Impact of the Blues on European Popular Culture." In *Approaches to Popular Culture*, edited by C. E. W. Bigsby, pp. 227–39. Bowling Green, Ohio, 1976.

Otruba, Gustav. "Österreichische Jesuitenpadres des 17. und 18. Jahrhunderts in der Weltmission und als Erforscher der Erde." *Österreich in Geschichte und Literatur* 5 (1961): 29–36.

Pauer, Hans. "Bildkunde und Geschichtswissenschaft." *MIÖG* 71 (1963): 194–210.

Pearlin, Leonard T., and Morris Rosenberg. "Propaganda Techniques in Institutional Advertising." *Public Opinion Quarterly*, no. 16 (Spring 1952): 5–26.

Pearson, Homer. "Music at War." Typescript, Vassar College, 1943. In Library of Congress, Washington, D.C.

Pelt, Mark H. Van. "The Cold War on the Air." *Journal of Popular Culture* 18 (Fall 1984): 97–110.

Peters, H. F. "American Culture and the State Department." *American Scholar* 21 (Summer 1952): 265–74.

Peterson, Richard A., and David G. Berger. "Cycles in Symbol Production: The Case of Popular Music." *American Sociological Review* 40 (1975): 158–73.

Peukert, Detlev. "Edelweisspiraten, Meuten, Swing: Jugendsubkulturen im Dritten Reich." In *Sozialgeschichte der Freizeit*, edited by Gerhard Huck, pp. 307–27. Wuppertal, 1980.

Piaget, Jean, and Anne-Marie Weil. "The Development in Children of the Idea of the Homeland and of Relations with Other Countries." *International Social Science Bulletin* 3 (1951): 561–78.

Portelli, Alessandro. "The Paper Tiger and the Teddy Bear." In *Cultural Change and the United States since World War II*, edited by M. Gonnaud, S. Perosa, and C. W. E. Bigsby. Amsterdam, 1986.

Portes, Jacques. "Les origines de la légende noire des accords Blum-Byrnes sur le cinéma." *Revue d'histoire moderne et contemporaine* 33 (1986): 314–29.

Prader, Hans, and Michael Unterleitner. "Das 'Trade Union Recovery Program' der amerikanischen Gewerkschaften in Westeuropa und Österreich." *Österreichische Zeitschrift für Politikwissenschaft* 5 (1976): 89–106.

Prawy, Marcel. "Der Text macht die Musik. Anmerkungen zur Ankunft des Musicals in Europa." *Forum* 3 (March 1956): 110–13.

Pütz, Karl-Heinz. "Business or Propaganda? American Films in Germany, 1942–1946." *Englisch-Amerikanische Studien* 5 (September 1983): 394–415.

Raeithel, Gerd, et al. "Europäische Amerika-Urteile im 20. Jahrhundert." *Sprache im technischen Zeitalter* 56 (1975): 333–41.

Rathkolb, Oliver. "Bürokratie und Musikalltag am Beispiel der Wiener Staatsoper. Thesen zur musikalischen Zeitgeschichte zwischen den Kriegen." *Mitteilungen des Instituts für Wissenschaft und Kunst* 43 (1988): 26–29.

——. "Die Entwicklung der US-Besatzungspolitik zum Instrument des Kalten Krieges." In *Kontinuität und Bruch 1938–1945–1955. Beiträge zur österreichischen Kultur und Wissenschaftsgeschichte*, edited by Friedrich Stadler, pp. 35–50. Vienna, 1988.

——. "Der Kalte Krieg und die österreichische Buchproduktion 1948." *Medien und Zeit* 1 (1986): 49–57.

——. "U.S.-Medienpolitik in Österreich 1945–1950. Von antifaschistischer 'Reorientierung' zur ideologischen Westintegration." *Medien-Journal* 8 (1984): 2–9.

——. "U.S.-Medienpolitik und die neue österreichische Journalistenelite." *Medien und Zeit* 2 (1987): 3–16.

——. "Die 'Wien-Film'-Produktion am Rosenhügel. Österreichische Filmproduktion und Kalter Krieg." In *Medienkultur in Österreich*, edited by Hans H. Fabris and Kurt Luger, pp. 117–32. Vienna, 1988.

Ratzenböck, Veronika. "Arrivederci Hans, das war Dein letzter Tanz." *Aufrisse* 3 (1984): 13–16.

——. "Expeditionen in eine exotische Heimat. Schlager in den fünfziger Jahren." In *Die "wilden" fünfziger Jahre*, edited by Gerhard Jagschitz and Klaus Dieter Mulley, pp. 264–73. St. Pölten, 1985.

——. "Steig in das Traumboot der Liebe." In *Die ungeschriebene Geschichte*, edited by Wiener Historikerinnen, pp. 161–68. Vienna, 1984.

Ravault, René-Jean. "L'imperialisme boomerang." *Revue française d'études américaines* 24/25 (May 1985): 291–311.

Renner, Gerhard. "Der Anschluss der österreichischen Filmindustrie seit 1934." In *Die veruntreute Wahrheit. Hitlers Propaganda in Österreichs Medien*, edited by Oliver Rathkolb, Wolfgang Duchkowitsch, and Fritz Hausjell, pp. 1–34. Salzburg, 1988.

Reynolds, David. "Whitehall, Washington, and the Promotion of American Studies in Britain during World War II." *Journal of American Studies* 16 (August 1982): 165–88.

Rice, Howard C. "Seeing Ourselves as the French See Us." *French Review* 21 (May 1948): 432–41.

Rosten, Leo C. "Movies and Propaganda." *Annals of the American Academy of Political and Social Sciences* 254 (1947): 116–24.

Rudel, Julius. ". . . and Nobody Missed the Waltz." *Theatre Arts*, June 1956, pp. 78–80 and 92–93.

Russell, Bertrand. "The Impact of America on European Culture." In *America in the Mind of Europe*, edited by Lewis Galantiére. London, 1951.

Sadler, M. T. H. "The Meaning and Need of Cultural Propaganda." *New Europe* 7 (May 23, 1918): 121–25.

Sartre, Jean-Paul. "American Novelists in French Eyes." *Atlantic Monthly*, November 17, 1946, pp. 114–18.

Schlag, Wilhelm. "A Survey of Austrian Emigration to the United States." In *Österreich und die angelsächsische Welt: Kulturbegegnungen und Vergleiche*, edited by Otto Hietsch, pp. 139–96. Vienna, 1961.

Schlegelmilch, Wolfgang. "Zum Amerikabild von Haupt- und Realschülern." *Jahrbuch für Amerikastudien* 13 (1968): 158–73.

Schmid, Georg. "Die 'Falschen' Fuffziger: Kulturpolitische Tendenzen der fünfziger Jahre." In *Literatur der Nachkriegszeit und der fünfziger Jahre in Österreich*, edited by Friedbert Aspetsberger, Norbert Frei, and Hubert Lengauer, pp. 7–23. Vienna, 1984.

——. "Kinogeschichte der Zwischenkriegszeit." In *Österreich 1918–1938. Geschichte der Ersten Republik*, vol. 2, edited by Erika Weinzierl and Kurt Skalnik, pp. 705–14. Graz, 1983.

——. "Zur Geschichte asymmetrischer Kulturbeziehungen am Beispiel des französischen und österreichischen Films." *Zeitgeschichte* 15 (October 1987): 27–36.

Schmidt, Martha R. "Training for Democracy in the United States Information Centers." *Special Libraries*, July/August 1950, pp. 224–29.

Schmitt, Albert. "Neues zum deutschen Amerikabild von 1775–77." *Modern Language News* 91 (1976): 397–423.

Schwers, Paul. "Die Frankfurter Jass-Akademie im Spiegel der Kritik." *Allgemeine Musikzeitung*, December 2, 1927, pp. 1246–48.

Scrutineer. "Secret Blacklist: Untold Story of the U.S.I.A." *Nation*, October 30, 1954, pp. 376–79.

Shain, Russell E. "Cold War Films, 1948–1962: An Annotated Filmography." *Journal of Popular Films* 3 (1974): 365–72.

——. "Hollywood's Cold War." *Journal of Popular Film* 3 (1974): 334–50.

Shi, David E. "Transatlantic Visions: The Impact of the American Cinema upon the French Avant-Garde, 1918–1924." *Journal of Popular Culture* 14 (1981): 583–96.

Shippey, T. "The Cold War in Science Fiction, 1940–1960." In *Popular Culture: Past and Present*, edited by Bernard Waites, Tony Bennett, and Graham Martin, pp. 308–22. London, 1983.

Signitzer, Benno, and Hans Heinz Fabris. "Austria and the International Media System: Relations and Dependences. Theses and Materials for Discussion." In *Small States in Europe and Dependence*, edited by Otmar Höll, pp. 220–35. Vienna, 1983.

Sklar, Robert. "Empire to the West: Red River (1948)." In *American History/American Film: Interpreting the Hollywood Image*, edited by John E. O'Connor and Martin Jackson, pp. 167–81. New York, 1979.

Smith, Henry Nash. "The Salzburg Seminar." *American Quarterly* 1 (1949): 30–37.

Smither, Roger. "Welt im Film: Anglo-American Newsreel Policy." In *The Political Re-Education of Germany and Her Allies after World War II*, edited by Nicholas Pronay and Keith Wilson, pp. 151–72. Beckenham, Kent, 1985.

Sobchack, Vivian S. "Beyond Visual Aids: American Film as American Culture." *American Quarterly* 32 (1980): 280–300.

Sprunck, Alphons. "Zwei österreichische Forschungsreisende aus der Zeit Josephs II." *Mitteilungen des österreichischen Staatsarchivs* 12 (1959): 414–26.

Stave, Joachim. "Noch einmal: Die Halbstarken." *Muttersprache* 68 (1958): 189–93.

Steiner, E. A. "How Returning Emigrants Are Americanizing Europe." *American Review of History* 39 (June 1909): 701–3.

Stern, Simon. "Machinery and Liberty." *American Artisan and Patent Record* 1 (May 1865): 2.

Sterne, Margarete. "The Presidents of the United States in the Eyes of Austro-Hungarian Diplomats, 1901–1913." *Austrian History Yearbook* 2 (1966): 153–71.

Stewart, Ollie. "An American Opera Conquers Europe." *Theatre Arts* 39 (October 1955): 30–34 and 94.

Stiefel, Dieter. "The Reconstruction of the Credit-Anstalt." In *International Business and Central Europe, 1918–1939*, edited by Alice Teichova and P. L. Cottrell, pp. 415–30. Leicester, 1983.

Stourzh, Gerald. "Bibliographie der deutschsprachigen Emigration in den Vereinigten Staaten, 1933–1963. Geschichte und politische Wissenschaft." *Jahrbuch für Amerikastudien* 10 (1965): 232–66; 11 (1966): 260–317.

——. "Die deutschsprachige Emigration in den Vereinigten Staaten: Geschichtswissenschaft und politische Wissenschaft." *Jahrbuch für Amerikastudien* 10 (1965): 59–77.

Strack, Manfred. "Amerikanische Kulturbeziehungen zu (West-)Deutschland 1945–1955." *Zeitschrift für Kulturaustausch* 37 (1987): 283–300.

Straube, Harald. "Jazz und Schule." *jazzforschung/jazzresearch* 1 (1969): 181–87.

Straumann, H. "Amerikanische Literatur in Europa. Eine geschmacksgeschichtliche Überlegung." *Anglia* 76 (1977): 208–16.

Strauss, David. "The Rise of Anti-Americanism in France: French Intellectuals and the American Film Industry, 1927–1932." *Journal of Popular Culture* 10 (1977): 821–32.

Strout, Cushing. "Tocqueville's Duality: Describing America and Thinking of Europe." *American Quarterly* 21 (Spring 1969): 87–99.

Sturmberger, Hans. "Die Amerika-Auswanderung aus Oberösterreich zur Zeit des Neo-Absolutismus." *Mitteilungen des oberösterreichischen Landesarchivs* 7 (1960): 5–53.

Tacke, O. "Die Bedeutung der westlichen Fremdsprachen für den demokratischen Schulunterricht." *Zeitschrift für Anglistik und Amerikanistik* 1 (1953): 66–72.

Temperley, Howard. "Anglo-American Images." In *Contrast and Connection: Bicentennial Essays in Anglo-American Studies*, edited by H. C. Allen and Roger Thompson. London, 1976.

Thistlethwaite, Frank. "The Citadel and the Caravan: Anglo-American Relations in the Twentieth Century." *American Quarterly* 9 (Spring 1957): 22–33.

Tichy, Frank. "Ein fauler Hund." *Forum* 35 (October 11, 1988): 60–67.

Toinet, Marie-France. "Mots et concepts politiques: Impérialisme culturel?." *Revue français d'études américaines* 24 / 25 (1985): 279–90.

Tracy, M. E. "Radio and the Monroe Doctrine." *Current History* 49 (November 1938): 29–31.

Urbanová, Anna. "Zum Einfluss des amerikanischen Englisch auf die deutsche Gegenwartssprache." *Muttersprache* 76 (1966): 97–114.

Vance, Earl L. "Freedom of the Press for Whom?." *Virginia Quarterly Review* 21 (1945): 340–54.

Viereck, Karin, W. Viereck, and I. Winter. "Wie Englisch ist unsere Pressesprache?." *Grazer Linguistische Studien* 2 (1976): 205–26.

Vittorini, Elio. "American Influences on Contemporary Italian Literature." *American Quarterly* 1 (1949): 3–8.

Wagner, Josef, and Karl Stangl. "Die Filmwirtschaft in Österreich in ihrer historischen, rechtlichen und wirtschaftlichen Entwicklung." In *100 Jahre Handelsministerium*. Vienna, 1959.

Wagnleitner, Reinhold. "The Irony of American Culture Abroad: Austria and the Cold War." In *Recasting America: Culture and Politics in the Age of Cold War*, edited by Lary May, pp. 285–301. Chicago, 1989.

——. "Die Kinder von Schmal(t)z und Coca-Cola: Der kulturelle Einfluss der USA im Österreich der 50er Jahre." In *Die "wilden" fünfziger Jahre. Gesellschaft, Formen und Gefühle eines Jahrzehnts in Österreich*, edited by Gerhard Jagschitz and Klaus-Dieter Mulley, pp. 144–73. St. Pölten, 1985.

——. "Der kulturelle Einfluss der amerikanischen Besatzung in Salzburg." In *Salzburg und das Werden der Zweiten Republik*, edited by Eberhard Zwink, pp. 47–58. Salzburg, 1985.

——. "Die kulturelle Reorientierung Österreichs nach dem Zweiten Weltkrieg: Prolegomena zum Phänomen der symbolischen Penetration." *Zeitgeschichte* 11 (June / July 1984): 326–44.

——. "Propagating the American Dream: Cultural Policies as Means of Integration." *American Studies International* 24 (April 1986): 60–84.

Weinberg, Gerhard. "Hitler's Image of the United States." *American Historical Review* 69 (1964): 1006–21.

Wendelken, Peter. "Der Einfluss des Englischen auf das heutige Werbedeutsch." *Muttersprache* 77 (1967): 289–308.

Weiss, Walter. "Der Zusammenhang zwischen Amerika-Thematik und Erzählkunst bei Charles Sealsfield (Karl Postl)." *Literaturwissenschaftliches Jahrbuch der Görres-Gesellschaft* 8 (1967): 95–118.

Westermeier, Clifford P. "Buffalo Bill's Cowboys Abroad." *Colorado Magazine* 52 (Fall 1975): 277–98.

Williams, Stanley T. "Who Reads an American Book?." *Virginia Quarterly Review* 28 (Autumn 1952): 518–31.

Wilson, Elmo C., and Frank Bonilla. "Evaluating Exchange of Persons Programs." *Public Opinion Quarterly* 19 (1955 / 56): 20–30.

Wittke, Carl. "The American Theme in Continental European Literatures." *Mississippi Valley Historical Review* 28 (June 1941): 3–26.

Wolf, Gary K. "Dr. Strangelove, Red Alert, and Patterns of Paranoia in the 1950s." *Journal of Popular Film* 5 (1976): 57–67.

Woll, Allen L. "Hollywood's Good Neighbor Policy: The Latin Image in American Film, 1939–1946." *Journal of Popular Film* 3 (1974): 278–93.


*DISSERTATIONS AND THESES*

Acinapura, Joseph N. "The Cultural Presentations Program of the United States." Master's thesis, University of Colorado, 1970.

Adler, Kenneth P. "The Voice of America and Competing Foreign Broadcasts: Comparison and Evaluation." Master's thesis, University of Chicago, 1950.

Adlgasser, Franz. "Brot für Kinder und Erwachsene. Die American Relief Administration und Österreich 1919–1923." Diplomarbeit, University of Salzburg, 1989.

Alexander, Thomas Ley. "The Relationship between United States Foreign Policy Aims Respecting the Federal Republic of Germany and the Information Center Service (USIA) Support of These Objectives." Ph.D. diss., American University, Washington, D.C., 1964.

Ashliman, D. L. "The American West in Nineteenth-Century German Literature." Ph.D. diss., Rutgers University, 1969.

Babin, Gregory. "The Book Selection Policy of the United States Information Libraries." Master's thesis, University of Washington, 1950.

Ballenger, Sara E. "The Reception of the American Novel in German Periodicals, 1945–1957." Ph.D. diss., Indiana University, 1959.

Beijerinck, Frits Hendrik. "Die Entwicklung der Tonfilmindustrie. Ein Beitrag zur Weltelektrovertrustung." Ph.D. diss., University of Basel, 1933.

Berger, Gottfried. "Das Bild der Vereinigten Staaten von Nordamerika in der deutschen Reiseliteratur des 19. Jahrhunderts. Unter besonderer Berücksichtigung von Werk und Persönlichkeit des Österreichers Karl Postl." Ph.D. diss., University of Vienna, 1945.

Breen, Robert. "Das deutsch-amerikanische Austauschprogramm im Rahmen der Umorientierung Westdeutschlands." Ph.D. diss., University of Heidelberg, 1956.

Browne, Donald R. "The History and Programming Policies of RIAS." Ph.D. diss., University of Michigan, 1961.

Buckingham, Peter Henry. "Diplomatic and Economic Normalcy: America's Open Door Peace with the Former Central Powers, 1921–1929." Ph.D. diss., Washington State University, 1980.

Cürten, Ulrich. "Europäische Amerikanistik seit 1945. Ihr Bild vom Wandel des amerikanischen Weltverständnisses." Ph.D. diss., University of Freiburg, 1967.

Deckardt, Waltraud. "Die wissenschaftliche Arbeit Kinos und seiner Mitarbeiter im Rahmen des Sonora-California-Planes." Ph.D. diss., University of Vienna, 1973.

Deicke, Gertrud. "Das Amerikabild der deutschen öffentlichen Meinung von 1898–1914." Ph.D. diss., Hamburg, 1956.

Dittrich, Eva. "Tendenzen der Pop-Musik." Ph.D. diss., Vienna, 1977.

Eastment, Diana Jane. "The Policies and Position of the British Council from the Outbreak of War to 1950." Ph.D. diss., University of Leeds, 1982.

Efroymson, Clarence W. "Österreichs Beziehungen zu den Vereinigten Staaten von Amerika während des Vormärz." Ph.D. diss., University of Vienna, 1952.

Ehrenfreund, Norbert. "The Birth of a New German Press: The Story of Postwar German Newspapers in the American Occupation Area (1945–1949)." Master's thesis, Columbia University, 1950.

English, Gary Clyde. "United States Media-Diplomacy." Ph.D. diss., Emory University, 1968.

Fabritz, Eleonore. "Der amerikanische Bürgerkrieg im Spiegel zweier österreichischer Tageszeitungen: 'Das Vaterland' und 'Der Botschafter.'" Ph.D. diss., University of Vienna, 1963.

Felsenreich, Maria. "Der Einbruch der nordamerikanischen Dramatik in die deutschsprachigen Spielpläne." Ph.D. diss., University of Vienna, 1961.

Fett, Ronald R. "America's Role in International News Exchange: A Study of the AP, UPI, INS, and Voice of America since World War II." Ph.D. diss., University of Illinois, Urbana, 1949.

Fink, H. "Amerikanismen im Wortschatz der deutschen Tagespresse, dargestellt am Beispiel dreier überregionaler Zeitungen." Ph.D. diss., University of Mainz, 1968.

Frank, Erika Olga. "Modern American Language in the Service of Present Day Advertisement." Ph.D. diss., University of Vienna, 1947.

Friebel, Rudolf. "Österreich und die Vereinigten Staaten bis zum Gesandtenaustausch 1838." Ph.D. diss., University of Innsbruck, 1955.

Fritz, Walter. "Entwicklungsgeschichte des österreichischen Spielfilms." 4 vols. Ph.D. diss., University of Vienna, 1966.

Geis, G. L. "American Motion Pictures in Norway: A Study in International Mass Communication." Ph.D. diss., University of Wisconsin, 1953.

Gibson, Delbert L. "French Impressions of American Character and Culture, 1900–1930." Ph.D. diss., University of Wisconsin, 1930.

Glietenberg, Ilse. "Die Comics, Wesen und Wirkung." Ph.D. diss., University of Munich, 1956.

Götz, Rainer. "Der Wandel des Amerikabildes in der deutschsprachigen Literatur seit 1945: Mythos Amerika und Realität USA." Ph.D. diss., University of Graz, 1979.

Greaser, Constance U. "The Role of the Voice of America in the Hungarian Revolt of 1956." Master's thesis, University of Southern California, 1968.

Grünzweig, Walter. "Das demokratische Kanaan: Charles Sealsfields Amerika im Kontext amerikanischer Literatur und Ideologie." Ph.D. diss., University of Graz, 1983.

Haupt, Else. "Stil- und sprachkundliche Untersuchungen zum deutschen Schlager." Ph.D. diss., University of Munich, 1957.

Hauptfeld, Georg. "Österreich und die grossen europäischen Nachrichtenagenturen zwischen den beiden Weltkriegen." Ph.D. diss., University of Vienna, 1948.

Hausmann, Astrid. "Die amerikanische Aussenpolitik und die Entstehung der österreichischen Republik von 1917–1919." Ph.D. diss., University of Vienna, 1972.

Hiller, Alfred. "Amerikanische Medien- und Schulpolitik in Österreich 1945–1950." Ph.D. diss., University of Vienna, 1974.

Hörmann, Walter. "Der Film als Weltwirtschaftsfaktor." Ph.D. diss., University of Innsbruck, 1949.

Kim, Kyong-Kun. "Die 'Neue Zeitung' im Dienste der Reeducation für die deutsche Bevölkerung." Ph.D. diss., University of Munich, 1974.

Künewalder, Ingeborg. "Die historische Darstellung der amerikanischen Nachrichtenagenturen." Ph.D. diss., University of Vienna, 1950.

Lehr, Alfred Paul. "Die Finanzierung der Filmproduktion, ihre einzel- und gesamtwirtschaftlichen Voraussetzungen unter besonderer Berücksichtigung der Filmwirtschaft in Österreich." Ph.D. diss., University of Vienna, 1948.

Leidenfrost, Josef. "Die amerikanische Besatzungsmacht und der Wiederbeginn des politischen Lebens in Österreich 1944–1947." Ph.D. diss., University of Vienna, 1986.

Lettner, Lydia. "Die französische Österreichpolitik 1943 bis 1945." Ph.D. diss., University of Salzburg, 1980.

Levy, Alan Howard. "The Unintegrated Personality: American Music and the Muses of Europe, 1865–1930." Ph.D. diss., University of Wisconsin, Madison, 1979.

Link, Benjamin. "Die österreichische Emigrantenpresse in den Subkulturen von New York City 1942 bis 1948." Ph.D. diss., University of Salzburg, 1972.

Louthan, Shirley. "The McCarthy Sub-Committee and the American Overseas Libraries." Master's thesis, Western Reserve University, 1958.

Lympius, Ingeborg. "Die diplomatischen Beziehungen zwischen Österreich und den Vereinigten Staaten von Amerika während des amerikanischen Bürgerkrieges." Ph.D. diss., University of Vienna, 1966.

Mackay, LaMar Seal. "Domestic Operations of the Office of War Information in World War II." Ph.D. diss., University of Wisconsin, 1966.

Malamud, René. "Zur Psychologie des deutschen Schlagers." Ph.D. diss., University of Winterthur, 1946.

Mangelberger, Franz. "Die Verwendung der Photographie in österreichischen Zeitungen." Ph.D. diss., University of Salzburg, 1982.

Marshall, Carl Richter. "Der amerikanische Bürgerkrieg, von Österreich aus gesehen." Ph.D. diss., University of Vienna, 1956.

Martin, Donald Warren. "Österreichisch-ungarische Propagandatätigkeit in den Vereinigten Staaten von Nordamerika 1914–1917." Ph.D. diss., University of Vienna, 1958.

Massoud, Mahmoud Ahmed. "The United States Information Program in the Middle East and South Asia." Master's thesis, American University, Washington, D.C., 1963.

Meisels, Lucian Otto. "Die politischen Beziehungen zwischen den Vereinigten Staaten von Amerika und Österreich 1933–1938." Ph.D. diss., University of Vienna, 1961.

Meisels, Simone. "Die Beziehungen zwischen Österreich-Ungarn und den Vereinigten Staaten von Amerika 1917 bis November 1918, mit speziellem Augenmerk auf die Bemühungen um einen Sonderfrieden." Ph.D. diss., University of Vienna, 1961.

Mosberg, Paul Otto. "Die Lizenzpresse in der US-Zone 1945–1949. Eine Darstellung ihrer Entwicklung und ihrer politischen Aufgaben unter besonderer Berücksichtigung der Anordnungen der amerikanischen Besatzungsmacht." Ph.D. diss., University of Erlangen, 1952.

Müller, Henning. "Theater im Zeichen des Kalten Krieges: Untersuchungen zur Theater- und Kulturpolitik in den Westsektoren Berlins 1945–1953." Ph.D. diss., University of Berlin, 1976.

Norton, Sharon Lee Mueller. "The United States Department of State International Visitor Program: A Conceptual Framework for Evaluation." Ph.D. diss., Fletcher School of Law and Diplomacy, 1977.

Nussbaum, Ernst-Werner. "Der Anzeigenmarkt der österreichischen Tagespresse nach dem Zweiten Weltkrieg." Ph.D. diss., University of Vienna, 1949.

Ortner, Lorelies. "Untersuchungen zum Vokabular deutscher Popmusikzeitschriften." Ph.D. diss., University of Innsbruck, 1977.

Papen, Charlotte. "Die Rolle der Presse in der Konsularberichterstattung und ihre Verwendung zur Regelung der Auswanderung in Österreich-Ungarn 1860–1900." Ph.D. diss., University of Vienna, 1949.

Paulovsky, Louis Heinrich. "Das Eindringen und die Aufnahme von Amerikanismen in das britische Alltagsenglisch der Gegenwart." Ph.D. diss., University of Vienna, 1943.

Petricek, Walter. "William Saroyan als Dramatiker." Ph.D. diss., University of Vienna, 1949.

Pirsein, Robert William. "The Voice of America: A History of the International Broadcasting Activities of the U.S. Government, 1940–1962." Ph.D. diss., Northwestern University, 1970.

Portisch, Hugo. "Das Zeitungswesen und die öffentliche Meinung in den Vereinigten Staaten von Amerika vor und während des Bürgerkrieges 1861–65." Ph.D. diss., University of Vienna, 1951.

Rathkolb, Oliver. "Politische Propaganda der amerikanischen Besatzungsmacht in

Österreich 1945–1950. Ein Beitrag zur Geschichte des Kalten Krieges in der Presse-, Kultur- und Rundfunkpolitik." Ph.D. diss., University of Vienna, 1981.

Reichardt, Robert Heinrich. "Die Schallplatte als kulturelles und ökonomisches Phänomen. Ein Beitrag zum Problem der Kunstkommerzialisierung." Ph.D. diss., University of Basel, 1962.

Reininghaus, Alexandra. "Oskar Maurus Fontana. Das Profil eines österreichischen Journalisten." Ph.D. diss., University of Salzburg, 1983.

Rieger, Philip. "Änderungen in den Lebensverhältnissen und den Verbrauchsgewohnheiten von Wiener Arbeitnehmerhaushalten 1952/1957." Ph.D. diss., University of Vienna, 1960.

Riegl, Kurt. "Thornton Wilder." Ph.D. diss., University of Vienna, 1951.

Ruskin, Daniel F. "USIA Comes to Africa: A Case Study of U.S. Overseas Information, 1960–1965." Master's thesis, University of Wisconsin, 1967.

Sadofsky, Wilhelm. "Die Geschmacksbildung an den Wiener Theatern von 1945 bis 1949." Ph.D. diss., University of Vienna, 1950.

Schachner, Eva Maria. "Das Bild von den Vereinigten Staaten von Amerika im österreichischen Vormärz." Diplomarbeit, University of Salzburg, 1976.

Schmid, Eva. "Wenzel Philip Leopold von Mareschal, ein österreichischer Offizier und Diplomat, 1785–1851. Mit besonderer Berücksichtigung seiner diplomatischen Verwendung in Süd- und Nordamerika." Ph.D. diss., University of Vienna, 1975.

Schmid, Georg. "Amerikanische Österreichpolitik zur Zeit der Pariser Friedenskonferenz 1919." Ph.D. diss., University of Salzburg, 1968.

Schnürer, Monika. "Der österreichische Film der dreissiger Jahre—ein Produkt ökonomischer und politischer Abhängigkeiten." Diplomarbeit, University of Vienna, 1987.

Schönberg, Michael. "Amerikanische Informations- und Medienpolitik in Österreich 1945–1955." Ph.D. diss., University of Vienna, 1975.

Schulmann, Lawrence Daniel. "United States Government Educational, Literary, and Artistic Cultural Exchange Programs, 1948–1958, as a Technique of American Diplomacy." Ph.D. diss., New York University, 1967.

Schweikert, Ingeborg. "Dr. Johann Georg Ritter von Hülsemann." Ph.D. diss., University of Vienna, 1956.

Senzer, Heinz Peter. "Die Tagespresse in der amerikanischen Besatzungszone Deutschlands nach dem Zweiten Weltkrieg." 2 vols. Ph.D. diss., University of Vienna, 1951.

Sieder, Elfriede. "Die alliierten Zensurmassnahmen zwischen 1945–1955. Unter besonderer Berücksichtigung der Medienzensur." Ph.D. diss., University of Vienna, 1983.

Smekal, Walter. "Die Stellung der amerikanischen Presse- und Aussenpolitik zur internationalen Lage nach dem Zweiten Weltkrieg." Ph.D. diss., University of Vienna, 1950.

Smith, Kent W. "The United States and the Cultural Crusade in Mexico, 1938–1945." Ph.D. diss., University of California, Berkeley, 1972.

Soucek, Carol Boyce. "The Use of Theater Abroad in United States Government International Cultural Relations (1949–1975)." Ph.D. diss., University of Southern California, Los Angeles, 1975.

Stadler, Franz. "Der Heftroman. Formen und Inhalte, Geschichte, Produktion und Massenwirksamkeit dargestellt am Beispiel des Bastei-Verlages." Ph.D. diss., University of Salzburg, 1979.

Swigard, Beulah H. "The Americas as Revealed in the Encyclopédie." Ph.D. diss., University of Illinois, Urbana, 1939.

Thaller, Manfred. "Studien zum europäischen Amerikabild: Darstellung und Beurteilung der Politik und inneren Entwicklung der Vereinigten Staaten von Amerika in

Grossbritannien, Deutschland und Österreich im Vergleich zwischen 1840 und 1941." Ph.D. diss., University of Graz, 1975.

Thron, Hans-Joachim. "Schulreform im besiegten Deutschland. Die Bildungspolitik der amerikanischen Militärregierung nach dem Zweiten Weltkrieg." Ph.D. diss., University of Munich, 1972.

Trice, Cicil W. "America and Weimar Culture, 1919–1933." Ph.D. diss., University of Oklahoma, 1979.

Tschögl, Rudolf. "Tagespresse, Parteien und alliierte Besatzung. Grundzüge der Presseentwicklung in der unmittelbaren Nachkriegszeit 1945–1950." Ph.D. diss., University of Vienna, 1979.

Venus, Theodor. "Die Entstehung eines Massenmediums. Am Beispiel des Rundfunks in Österreich." Ph.D. diss., University of Vienna, 1982.

Viereck, Karin. "Englisches Wortgut, seine Häufigkeit und Integration in der österreichischen und bundesdeutschen Pressesprache." Ph.D. diss., University of Innsbruck, 1979.

Waldsburger, Jean. "Die Rationalisierung der Arbeit (mit besonderer Berücksichtigung des Taylorsystems)." Ph.D. diss., University of Bern, 1923.

Woess, Augustine. "Die Rezeption der Dramen Eugene O'Neills in Österreich." Ph.D. diss., University of Salzburg, 1977.

Wurtsbauer, Heinrich. "Lizenzzeitung und Heimatpresse in Bayern." Ph.D. diss., University of Munich, 1952.

Zäckel, Eugenie. "Der Einfluss James Fenimore Coopers und Washington Irvings auf die deutsche Literatur." Ph.D. diss., University of Vienna, 1940.

Zeltner, Renate. "Die Politik des Präsidenten Woodrow Wilson im Spiegel der österreichischen diplomatischen Berichte 1912–1917." Ph.D. diss., University of Vienna, 1961.

Zindler, H. "Anglizismen in der deutschen Presse nach 1945." Ph.D. diss., University of Kiel, 1959.

NEWSPAPERS AND MAGAZINES

Die amerikanische Rundschau
Die Bastei
Berichte und Informationen
British Film Year Book
Christian Science Monitor
Deine-4-H-Klub-Zeitung
Demokratisches Volksblatt
Erziehung
Film Daily
Film Daily Year Book
Forum
Funk und Film
Gewerkschaftliche Nachrichten aus den USA
Heute
International Motion Picture Almanac
International Motion Picture and Television Almanac
Index de la Cinématographie Française
Landwirtschaftliche Nachrichten aus den Vereinigten Staaten
Life
Linzer Volksblatt
Look
Medizinische Nachrichten aus den Vereinigten Staaten
Der Monat
Motion Picture Herald
Nation
Die neue Auslese
Neues Österreich
New Republic
Newsweek
New York Herald Tribune
New York Times
Oberösterreichische Nachrichten
Der Plan
Die Presse
Profil
Die Radiowoche
Salzburger Nachrichten

Saturday Evening Post
Saturday Review of Literature
Der Spiegel
Time
Das Tor
Der Turm

Variety
Verleger Informationen
Wiener Bildwoche
Wiener Illustrierte
Wiener Kurier

# Index

Motion Picture Export Association (MPEA), 70, 227, 229, 240, 243, 244, 248, 249, 250, 257, 260, 261, 262, 264, 265, 267, 269
Mutual Broadcasting Company, 56

National Cash Register, 23
National Security Agency, 63
Nationalism, 47, 58, 160, 163
Nestroy, Johann, 8
New York International Acceptance Bank, 41
News and Features Division, 98

*Oberösterreichische Nachrichten*, 71, 90; founding, 90; ownership, 91; reporting, 92
Office of Facts and Figures, 51, 53
Office of Foreign Relief and Rehabilitation Operation, 52
Office of Inter-American Affairs, 51, 52
Office of International Information and Cultural Affairs, 52
Office of Public Information, 52
Office of War Information, 51, 52, 53, 69, 110, 222, 257; Bureau of Motion Pictures, 222, 229, 238, 239
Open Door Policy, 65

Pan-Am, 23, 49
Paramount, 217, 231, 232, 234, 240, 296
Pasetti, Otto de, 168
Patton, George S., 10
Peez, Alexander, 36, 38
Photography, 78, 101, 102, 105, 131
Pinter, Margot, 167, 168
Pleasants, Virginia D., 168
Popular culture, x, xii, 52, 53, 54, 57, 59, 82, 94, 117
Prawy, Marcel, 70, 188, 192, 200, 267, 269
Presley, Elvis, xiv, 218, 219, 221, 289, 291
Private Council of Voluntary Aid, 52
Psychological Offensive, 77, 78, 79, 98, 111, 112, 113, 114, 130

Radio Corporation of America, 23, 49
Radio Free Europe, xi, 61, 64, 109, 117, 213, 276
Radio Liberty, 61, 64, 109, 117, 213, 276
Radio Moscow, 109
RAVAG (Austrian Radio Company), 76, 110, 111–13, 115, 118, 189, 205; broadcast time, 111

Reagan, Ronald, 57, 61, 279
Record Labels: ABC-Paramount, 217, 286; Capital, 286; Columbia, 217, 286, 296; Decca, 286; Deutsche Philips, 217; Ember, 216, 286; EMI (Electrola), 217, 296; EMI-Lindström, 286; Grammophon, 216, 286; Mercury, 286; Philips, 286; RCA, 23, 217, 286, 296; RCA-Victor, 286; Roulette and King, 217; Siemens-Elektro A.G.-Deutsche Grammophon, 286; Teldec, 217, 286
Reeducation, 66, 67, 77
Reinhardt, Max, 192
Reinhardt Seminar, 187
Reischek, Andreas, 111, 118
Relief Control Board, 52
Reorientation, 67, 69, 72, 74, 77, 79, 82, 84, 87, 151, 156
Reorientation Branch, U.S. Army, 83, 85, 86, 87, 89, 168, 169, 189
Reuters, 49, 100
RIAS-Berlin, 64, 109, 213
RKO Pictures, 253
Rockefeller, Nelson, 51
Rockefeller Foundation, 48, 78, 158
Roosevelt, Franklin D., 43, 54, 243, 246, 270
Rosenberg, Emily, 49, 54, 232
Rot-Weiss-Rot (Radio Red-White-Red), 70, 76, 78, 80, 81, 92, 109, 110, 112, 113, 114, 115, 117, 118, 119, 120, 143, 152, 187, 189, 195, 198, 213, 276; broadcast time, 111, 113; commercials, 116, 118; function, 117; influence, 110, 115; programming, 110, 111–14; programs, 78, 80, 90, 112, 113, 116, 119, 120; public opinion, 112, 115; reforms, 113, 114
Rousseau, Jean-Jacques, 19
Rudel, Julius, 200, 201

*Salzburger Nachrichten*, 71, 78, 84, 88, 89, 90, 91, 102, 132, 214; articles, 87, 215; founding, 87; ownership, 88, 90; reporting, 87, 88
Salzburg Festival, 167, 196, 220, 284, 293
Salzburg Seminar in American Studies, 164, 165, 210
Sascha-Filmfabrik, 252, 254, 255, 279
Savalle, Joseph, 110
Schiller, Friedrich, 187
Schönberg, Arnold, 196, 197
Sharin, Eugen, 257–60, 262, 263

CPSIA information can be obtained
at www.ICGtesting.com
Printed in the USA
LVHW020933011221
704952LV00006B/785